NEW PERSPECTIVES
IN CULTURAL
ANTHROPOLOGY

NEW PERSPECTIVES IN CULTURAL ANTHROPOLOGY

ROGER M. KEESING
University of California, Santa Cruz

FELIX M. KEESING

WITH ILLUSTRATIONS BY THE AUTHORS

HOLT, RINEHART AND WINSTON, INC.
New York   Chicago   San Francisco   Atlanta
Dallas   Montreal   Toronto   London   Sydney

Acknowledgments

From the book *Sorcerers of Dobu* by R. Fortune.
Copyright 1932 by E. P. Dutton & Co., Inc. Renewal ©,
1959, by Reo Franklin Fortune. Dutton Paperback edition.
Published by E. P. Dutton & Co., Inc., and reprinted with
their permission and Routledge & Kegan Paul Ltd.

From *Yąnomamö: The Fierce People*, by Napoleon A. Chagnon.
Copyright © 1968 by Holt, Rinehart and Winston, Inc.

Preface

IN MANY RESPECTS this is a new and different book from my father's. It was not meant to be when I agreed in 1965 to revise *Cultural Anthropology*. Then I envisioned an updating but not a drastic transformation—a plan that seemed fitting for a revision of a distinctive book that had inevitably become dated. But by the time completely rewritten sections began to outweigh sections retained from the original book, there seemed little reason to strive for preservation. My Freudian friends have watched all this with apprehension and awe, but I no longer doubt that it was a wise course. I can only hope that I steered it well.

To entitle a book *New Perspectives* . . . would seem to challenge the wrath of the gods. Even to write an introduction to cultural anthropology requires a goodly measure of *hubris* in a field now so diverse and specialized. But having turned a revision into a new book built on the original—and having done so to reflect not only a change in findings in the field but also an emerging new set of anthropological premises—I have used "New Perspectives" to express a double meaning: the perspectives are **in** cultural anthropology and **on** *Cultural Anthropology*.

Beginning as it did within the framework of the original book, the present version is more like the original in structure than it would be had I set out to write a new book (for example, starting anew I might well have abandoned the rather traditional chapter organization). But the present book differs from the original in a number of ways. Coverage has become narrower, but more intensive, focusing on the "core" concerns of social anthropology at the expense of topics like material culture, historical linguistics, folklore, and art. Coverage of physical anthropology and archaeology have been reduced in some respects. Such narrowing partly reflects the availability now of good introductory books in many of these fields. There seems a need for an introduction to social anthropology that can be used for a course concentrating in this field, or one that can be combined with a satisfactory text in physical anthropology or prehistory.

Comparison of this book with the original *Cultural Anthropology* will show that the section on language has been moved up to a key position more commensurate with its conceptual importance, and that the materials on the history of anthropology have been placed in a final "reference" section, where they can be used at the instructor's discretion.

The division of the chapters into consecutively numbered sections—the "problems" of the original—has been preserved. It makes cross-referencing easier and will assist the instructor in assigning sections or rearranging their order. Suggestions for further reading, given in the final "reference" portion of the book, are listed separately for each section.

As in the original, illustrative case materials are set off from the body of the text and scattered through it. Here they are consecutively numbered as "examples," for ease of cross-referencing. In the original and in most other texts, examples are introduced from various parts of the world, but few attempts are made to tie them together. To give the reader a greater sense of cultural richness and integration, and to lend a continuity to case materials, the Trobriand Islanders and several other peoples are used to illustrate a number of points.

An introductory book is written with one eye on the student reader and one eye on colleagues armed on all sides with the swords of specialized knowledge. I have tried to write for student, not colleague (hence, for instance, many assertions are not documented with references). And I have sought to challenge student readers by dealing with difficult problems, but not to mystify them. Too often an introductory book portrays a field as well known and fully explored; here I have sought to lead the student to the frontier, and to give him a feeling of how much lies beyond.

My intellectual debts are many and diverse. The reader may particularly note the influence of my teachers Clyde Kluckhohn and Gregory Bateson, and the writings of Noam Chomsky, C. O. Frake, Clifford Geertz, Ward Goodenough, E. R. Leach, Claude Lévi-Strauss, Harold Scheffler, and Victor Turner.

A marked influence on my thinking will be less apparent to anthropologists: my participation, with scholars from a number of fields, in a "Symposium on Structure" at MIT in May 1969, honoring Cyril Stanley Smith. We explored, with philosophical depth, the nature of structure and the formal design of phenomena too complex for our present models, across a wide range of fields. John R. Platt, Cyril Smith, and Paul Weiss have had a particularly strong influence on my thinking about anthropology.

For helpful suggestions on the task of revision, I am indebted to G. and L. Spindler, W. Elmendorf, and M. Salovesh; for helpful readings of all or part of the new manuscript, to W. Davenport, W. Elmendorf, J. Fritz, L. Grimes, D. Keesing, J. Middleton, F. Poole, R. Randolph, S. Schlegel, B. Scholte, E. Schusky, H. Selby, A. Smith, G. Spindler and A. Zihlman. Student assistants G. Hendren, W. Scherrer, and N. Smith assisted in many ways; and many typists in the Stenographic Pool at the University of California, Santa Cruz, struggled bravely with cryptical inscriptions and short deadlines. The staff at Holt, Rinehart and Winston, Inc., notably David Boynton, assisted in many ways and kept open with great patience and expense a tenuous communications channel to a remote Solomon Islands jungle; Marie Lonning and Ruth Stark helped greatly in editing and producing the book. George D. Spindler gave much encouragement as well as advice.

I am indebted to my wife and children for putting up bravely with even more tribulations, to make the book possible, than academic families must usually endure: vacant looks into space and a vacant chair at mealtimes; missed vacations and missing hands in the division of labor; imposed silence and my cloistered isolation.

Finally I owe a great debt to my students at the University of California, Santa Cruz, who have put up patiently with bad puns and Trobriand Islanders, and have tried very hard to teach me that wisdom is more important than skill.

R. M. K.

Contents

Case Examples

NEW PERSPECTIVES
IN CULTURAL
ANTHROPOLOGY

Part One

THE STUDY OF MAN
Variations on the Themes
of Human Life

WHAT IS cultural anthropology? What do anthropologists do? In what ways are their views of man distinctive? In Chapter I we will look at the nature of anthropology, particularly of cultural anthropology. We will look closely at "fieldwork," the anthropologist's journey into the life and world of another people.

In Chapter II we will look in preliminary fashion at some essential concepts of anthropology—particularly "culture" and "society"—that can serve as foundations for new ways of thinking about man and of perceiving ways of life very different from our own.

I *What Is Cultural Anthropology?*

THE JOURNEY into anthropology can well begin with a parable—one that happens to be true. A Bulgarian woman was serving dinner to a group of her American husband's friends, including an Asian student. After her guests had cleaned their plates, she asked if any would like a second helping: a Bulgarian hostess who let a guest go hungry would be disgraced. The Asian student accepted a second helping, and then a third—as the hostess anxiously prepared another batch in the kitchen. Finally, in the midst of his fourth helping, the Asian student slumped to the floor; but better that, in his country, than to insult his hostess by refusing food that had been offered.

In a world suddenly made small, this is too true a parable of the human condition. For man has spent the vast span of his time on earth separated into small groups, each with its own language, its own view of the world, its own body of customs, its own premises. Now these differences divide men, and generate suffering and conflict at a time when men need desperately to understand one another and to join in a common enterprise. Yet if these gulfs between ways of life keep peoples apart, they also illuminate the nature of man and the customs and beliefs we ourselves take for granted.

These patterns of assumption, perception, and custom that divide Egyptians and Chinese, that divide Americans from both, and each of us from Australian aborigines or African tribesmen, are the focus of cultural anthropology. By viewing men's customs comparatively, across the widest reaches of time and space, the anthropologist seeks to distinguish what derives from being human from what derives from being born into a particular group of humans in a particular time and place. Anthropology is a study of universalities and uniqueness; a study of startling contrast and surprising similarity; a study of meaning and logic in what seems bizarre. It is a study of ourselves, as reflected in the mirror of ways of life far different from our own.

Man is at once an animal and a transformed being. He builds on biological foundations a scaffolding of meanings and conventions that are his own creations, and that can vary enormously and be tinkered with endlessly. He does not discover his world; he creates it. He populates it with beings and forces he cannot see, and believes to be eternally true and right the rules, conventions, and meanings he himself creates and is constantly changing.

Man is, in short, a very peculiar beast. And we are prone to misunderstand his nature, because we confuse what it is to be human with what it is to be our particular kind of human, living in our world of custom and belief. We project that world onto other people's words, and inevitably we distort and misunderstand them. The best corrective we have—the best way of seeing other ways of life from the inside, of seeing ourselves from the outside, and of seeing man's humanity through it all—is to study ways of life as different from ours as possible. That has been the challenge to the cultural anthropologist. It has carried him to the remote jungles and deserts of the world, seeking new vantage points from which to view other peoples, ourselves, and Man.

In the chapters to follow, we will trace this quest and the light it has shed on the human condition. In this chapter and the next we will place anthropology in the context of the sciences and introduce some basic concepts. In Part Two (Chapters III–V) we will trace man's biological background, the gift of language, and the historical development of cultures. In Part Three (Chapters VI–XV) we will examine the ways of life of non-Western peoples—their kinship organization, legal systems, religious beliefs, and so on. Finally, in Part Four (Chapters XVI–XVII) we will examine the individual within his society, and the changes that are transforming human life in city and jungle.

1 · Anthropology as a Field of Knowledge

"Anthropology" derives from the Greek forms *anthrop-*, 'man,' and *logos*, often translated 'study.' Obviously anthropologists are not the only scholars concerned with "man-study." What, then, do anthropologists do and study that makes their approach to man distinctive? We can best begin to find an answer by setting out a series of broad propositions about the anthropological study of man:

1. It has stressed study of the *likenesses* and the *differences* among men: that is, a *comparative* viewpoint.
2. Where practically all other students of man concentrate upon "civilized" peoples, particularly of the modern West, study of the range of human differences has led anthropologists to focus on the "primitive" peoples scattered over remoter regions of the earth. Contemporary anthropologists,

however, are applying their theory and research methods increasingly to peasant peoples, modern towns and cities, and whole nations.

3. To understand likenesses and differences among modern men, research has been carried far back of written history to uncover, to the fullest extent possible, the *origins* and *development* of man and his customs.

4. Anthropologists examine both the *physical* (biological) and the *cultural* and *social* characteristics of man.

5. From this broad viewpoint, anthropologists seek generalizations about man and his behavior. Here they collaborate in numerous ways with scholars in other disciplines (biologists, psychologists, sociologists, economists, political scientists, historians, students of literature, and others) who study man in terms of their own special interests, and who have confined their research almost wholly to peoples in the literate traditions, especially Western societies. Anthropologists feed materials to such scholars, and in turn draw upon their knowledge. This comparative and holistic approach makes anthropology in some respects a synthesizing field of knowledge, and provides a total or composite view of man probably achieved in no other discipline.

The anthropologist W. L. Warner has, for example, studied and reported both on a tribe of Australian Aborigines, the Murngin, and on a midwestern American community, "Jonesville" (Rockford, Illinois). The Murngin live in tiny mobile camp groups of a few families, and forage after wild products in terrain where Jonesville people would soon die of starvation (Warner, 1937).[1] Jonesville people occupy a small city, the life of which would be almost wholly incomprehensible to the Murngin; it is not only the hub for surrounding farm people but also part of the vast national and international milieu of modern civilization which has reached the Murngin only recently (Warner *et al.*, 1949).

The Murngin minimize technological activities, having only light equipment that a man and woman can carry, and some caches of ceremonial objects at sacred spots. But they have elaborated their marriage and kinship systems to a point far more complex than those found in Jonesville. The Murngin religion, too, with its elaborate totemic and other interpretations of the world and of man, and its long-drawn cycles of initiation into adulthood and other rituals, would appear to an independent observer to be by and large much more complicated than the religious life in Jonesville. Yet both Murngin and Jonesville people have systems of child training. They have leaders, organize work, play games, enjoy music, laugh and talk, and otherwise share many elements of common "human nature." In opposite

---

[1] In the pages to follow, this anthropological method of showing references will be used. The cited works are listed in the Bibliography. Different works by the same author are listed separately, by year. When page references are given, they are preceded by a colon (for example, Smith, 1951: 31–33, cites a passage appearing on pages 31 to 33 in Smith's 1951 book).

Figure 1. An Australian Aborigine carries his worldly goods—spears, spear-thrower, and lighted fire-stick—as he leads his family on a change of their encampment. (After a photograph by Robert Tonkinson.) RMK

corners of the earth, both of these peoples have developed a rounded way of life and a view of the world which (at least until novelty intrudes) is valued as best and right. This can usefully forewarn us that being "primitive" in a technological sense does not imply being simple, unsophisticated, or childlike in custom and belief.

2 · *Cultural Anthropology*

Anthropologists are as motley a collection of scholars as one could find wearing any single academic hat. In a large anthropology department, it would not be strange to find a human biologist specializing in the fossil bones of early man; an archaeologist excavating ancient communities in the Middle East; a linguist analyzing the structure of West African languages; a folklorist studying Eskimo mythology; a specialist in kinship and marriage among Burmese tribesmen; and an expert on Mexican-American farm laborers in California. Each of them would probably have a Ph.D. in anthropology.

What do they all have in common? What unites so broad a field? What subfields within anthropology draw together specialists with common interests?

Surprisingly, the Eskimo myth expert could probably tell you a good deal about the teeth of fossil men, and the African language specialist could probably tell you a good deal about marriage systems in Burma. Broad graduate training continues to give anthropology a unity that might at first glance seem a myth.

Yet as the ranks of anthropologists increase and technical knowledge expands, the subfields of anthropology grow more specialized and of necessity more separate. A first and basic division separates the human biologist, a *physical anthropologist*, from his departmental colleagues. He and a still fairly small number of fellow specialists deal with man as a biological organism—his evolutionary development and primate relatives, his racial differentiation and evolutionary adaptation. Each of the others—the archaeologist, the linguist, and the folklorist, as well as the student of Burmese kinship or Mexican Americans—might well call himself a *cultural anthropologist*.

Within this broad area of cultural anthropology, *prehistoric archaeology* or *prehistory* is a major and specialized subfield. Popular stereotypes of the archaeologist digging in ancient ruins have some substance, but they are quite misleading. Unlike classical archaeologists, prehistorians study peoples without written records. Their attempts to reconstruct ancient ways of life take them through old rubbish heaps more often than temples, and they use atomic age scientific methods to find clues to the past. Moreover, increasingly their investigations have been linked theoretically with anthropolgical studies of living people.

The *anthropological linguist* may be particularly interested in the structural design of languages or in historical relationships between them. He usually has a special interest in unwritten languages and a special concern with the relation of language to other aspects of culture; but his strongest professional ties are likely to be with other linguists (who in different universities may occupy various niches).

The anthropological study of folklore and mythology is less clearly a special subfield, and we will not treat it as such. Again, however, our expert on Eskimo myths would have close common interests with his fellow anthropologists and also with folklorists in other disciplines.

Most often "cultural anthropology" is used to label a narrower field concerned with the study of men's customs: that is, the comparative study of cultures. We have seen that "comparative" in this sense implies a focus on ways of life that to other social scientists are exotic—on primitive peoples and others of the non-Western world.

But one can study cultural man in very different ways, exploring different sorts of relatedness between men's ways of life. For years anthro-

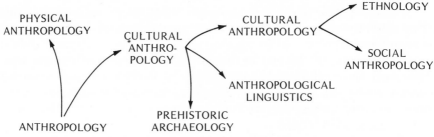

Figure 2. The Subfields of Anthropology.

pologists, originally attached more to museums than universities, looked mainly at the natural history of man, at the historical connections between peoples (an enterprise obviously closely linked to the prehistorians'). Such study of culture history is often called *ethnology*. (The latter term is often used in Europe in place of "cultural anthropology," where "anthropology" may mean the study of human biology).

A more modern focus, in the study of cultural man, has looked not for historical connections between peoples but for scientific generalizations about man's social behavior and cultures. In recent decades *social anthropology* has replaced ethnology as the "core" area of cultural anthropology. The social anthropologist continues the traditional focus on primitive and other non-Western peoples, though increasingly he may study modern complex settings as well. He is also allied with social scientists in other disciplines in seeking to throw scientific light on human social life.

The relationship between these subfields of anthropology is set out schematically in Figure 2. Note that "cultural anthropology" is used in both a wider and narrower sense.

What unites all these subfields? To say that anthropologists are all concerned with the "study of man" is true but hardly enough. So are specialists on Beethoven, Euripides, the Oedipus complex, and the Boer War—and almost all other members of humanities and social science faculties. Anthropologists wear a common disciplinary hat due more to the historical unfolding of academic tradition than to intellectual unity. On the cultural anthropology side, archaeology and ethnology have grown up together as complementary approaches to the natural history of man. And the focus on non-Western, especially primitive, peoples has been a common thread uniting the anthropological linguist, ethnologist, anthropological folklorist, and social anthropologist. The widest gulf is between physical and cultural anthropology. Yet even this gap has narrowed in recent years, as anthropologists have begun to study intensively the social life of man's close primate relatives. Whatever the historical roots of anthropology's unity, the result has been profoundly important. The anthropologist, commanding a great range of evidence on man's social behavior in the widest reaches of time and space, and his biological heritage, is uniquely equipped to generalize about human nature, human differences, and human possibilities.

The problems and findings of social anthropology will be our primary concern in the chapters to follow. In that sense, the book is mainly "about" cultural anthropology in its narrower sense, and predominantly "about" social anthropology. But looking first at man's biological heritage, his distant past, and his most precious gift, language, will enable us to explore with clearer vision the intricate designs of the thought-worlds of men and the complex mazes of their social life.

3 · Cultural Anthropology and Science

For modern Americans the "scientific" mode of approaching the world is treated with a special reverence and accorded great prestige. Science has taken us to the moon and will take us beyond; it has given man technological domination of his planet and insights into the nature of the universe and the biology of life.

The "social sciences" or "behavioral sciences"—psychology, political science, economics, sociology, social anthropology, and other allied disciplines —have felt a strong push from two directions. On the one hand, there is the prestige that derives from being a "science," and there is an array of methods and models that have been so powerful in exploring the natural world that they invite application to the study of human behavior and social life. On the other hand, as has been observed so many times as now to be trite, man's abilities to understand, control, and predict human behavior, and to grapple with problems of war, hostility, ignorance, and poverty, have been outstripped by his technology. We have the means to destroy human social life but lack the wisdom to direct its course.

Are the social sciences, and here specifically anthropology, entitled to wear that sacred mantle of "science"? That depends in part on how broadly or narrowly one defines the term. Some scholars treat it widely as a method of approach to experience; others more narrowly as a body of organized and demonstrated knowledge.

The scientific method is frequently referred to as a mood of objective observation and description. Man here asks primarily the factual questions "What?" "When?" "Where?" "How?" He leaves to other moods—those of the philosopher, the theologian, the artist, the humanitarian—such more evaluative questions as "Why?" (in the sense of ultimate meanings), "Which is best?" "How can it be helpful?" (Science does, of course, provide an expanding body of knowledge to enrich these other approaches.) This very broad view of science would include as "scientific" what has been called historical or descriptive science. The emphasis here is upon documenting unique data of experience in time and in space. History would be included, and even some phases of what are conventionally "humanistic" studies, for example, literary criticism, philology.

A narrower view of science, however, would admit only those types of study that are directed toward *significant problems* and *controlled observa-*

tion (including experiment) in which the concern is to uncover *generalizations* relating to regularities, or "laws," on which *predictions* can be based.

Philosophers, especially in Europe, have long debated whether the methods and models of the natural sciences can in fact be applied to human behavior. Those who argue that the behavior of living organisms, and of man in particular, is so complex and distinctive as to be impervious to the assaults of the "scientific method" have some strong points in their favor. By using controlled observation one can, of course, make a great many statements about what stickleback fish, gorillas, or drivers on Wilshire Boulevard will and will not do in particular circumstances. But one cannot anticipate very well the behavior of any particular driver (except to define some of the limiting conditions of what he will not do). This is what makes the croquet game in *Alice in Wonderland* so marvelous. For its mathematician-author populated the game with living organisms as pieces of equipment— flamingoes for mallets, hedgehogs for balls—and thus rendered unpredictable all the constants that make an orderly game possible.[2] Man, in particular, as transformed and intellectual animal, is separated from the rest of the world of nature by a gulf the methods of natural science may never bridge.

If this gap between the natural and the behavioral sciences has closed considerably, it is not so much because we are getting more "sciency" about studying behavior. Rather, with quantum mechanics the same indeterminacies have permeated every level of the natural world from the subatomic to the cosmic. Moreover, the same feature that gives the scientific approach its great power paradoxically exacts great costs of understanding as well—its sharp, controlled, selective focus. Biologists can zero in on cells, or macromolecules, or biochemical constituents, or organs: but whatever they focus on, they pull it out of the context of some wider system, losing sight of the lower-level elements that comprise it and the higher-level system in which it is a constituent. By asking narrow questions, we may leave big ones aside. We are only beginning to learn how to perceive complex wholes as well as carved-up pieces, how to retrieve the big questions and begin to examine them. Man may not be easier to grasp scientifically than many had thought: the natural world may be harder to study.

Even the sacrosanct "scientific method" is beginning to lose its sacredness. The great biologist Paul Weiss once remarked that "nobody who followed the scientific method ever discovered anything interesting." The role of insight and intuition, rather than rigorous induction from "the data," is increasingly clear. Thomas Kuhn's *The Structure of Scientific Revolutions* (1962) has exploded many misconceptions about science as a means to "ultimate truths" and has brought science much closer to other facets of human enterprise than its special niche in popular thought. A firmly established scientific Truth can be seen in the longer view as a temporary agreement to ask the questions in such a way that a particular set of answers fits.

---

[2] An illustration I have borrowed from Gregory Bateson.

Finally, new scientific modes of talking about complex systems—particularly those lumped together as "cybernetics"— have narrowed the gulf between human behavior and other phenomena of the world of nature. The "behavior" of an individual, a brain cell, a social group, or the trees, plants, animals, and microorganisms of a forest can be described in terms of complex webs of interconnection. Events are so interwoven that everything "causes" everything else, and balance and direction steer the total system. With such new ways of talking about the world, "behavior" no longer stands so far apart from the phenomena of nature.

If all this does not provide a simple answer to whether social anthropology is "scientific"—or can be, or should be—it throws useful light on the question itself. The anthropologist is trying to make sense of phenomena that, in scientific terms, are extraordinarily complicated. Like the astronomer, he cannot do very much to experiment with the things he is studying, because they are human beings and are in their own communities—not captives in psychology classes. The human brain is a natural system of fantastic and mystifying complexity. And the social behavior of human beings is the product of so many intertwined variables that the narrow crystal focus of science seems scarcely adequate to this challenge.

The social scientist faces other grave problems. As a human being observing human beings, he inevitably interprets the scene in terms of his own experience and concepts; and by the very process of observing a scene, he changes it. (These problems are far from negligible in the natural sciences.) The anthropologist faces special problems in that his world of experience, his perceptual screen, is so different from that of the people he is observing. But this has its advantages as well. It enables him to see that many of the devices whereby his social science colleagues in other disciplines produce data to be manipulated "scientifically"—tests, questionnaries, interviews, polls, experiments—depend on the observer having the same conceptual scheme as the observed. He sees too that these devices often render subtle and complex patterns spuriously objective, and misleadingly precise. Being "sciency" (and hence impersonal, objective, experimental, and number-minded) can in cultural terms be seen as a special and peculiar preoccupation of ours—a modern substitute for the mystical powers of magic.

The anthropologist has no similarly elaborate bag of methodological devices to depersonalize and objectify his encounter with other human beings. In a sense, he has only his common humanity. To see what he does, and can do, with it we must turn to a mode of exploration that is peculiarly anthropological.

4 · Fieldwork

"Fieldwork," the extended study of a community and its way of life, is in many ways the core experience of anthropology. First, of course, it is the source of the information and generalizations the anthropologist brings home. The articles and books he writes distill out the essentials of his knowledge and refer ultimately to particular experiences with particular people. "Bridewealth among the Agawaga is paid to the bride's father, who keeps the largest share and divides the rest among his close lineage kin," writes the anthropologist—and his reasons for saying so are the events surrounding the eight marriages that occurred in the Agawaga village where he lived, plus his questioning and his records of remembered past marriages. Such documentation of a way of life is called *ethnography*.

But fieldwork is more than that. For the anthropologist, fieldwork has been a kind of vision quest. By immersing himself in another way of life, he comes to view himself, his own way of life, and man, in a new perspective. It is a profound experience, uncomfortable and sometimes shattering, but richly rewarding as well.

What does fieldwork actually entail? That depends in part on where the anthropologist goes to study. In the 1920s and 1930s, when the colonial frontiers were teeming with "primitives" and the ranks of anthropologists were thin, fieldwork usually meant going into an isolated primitive tribe armed with notebooks, camera, and quinine, and setting up a residence in a native village for a year or longer. By the time an anthropologist arrived on the scene there were usually colonial administrators collecting taxes and imposing peace, and there were trade stores and missionaries. But after the pioneering style of Malinowski, the ethnographer set up housekeeping with the locals and did his or her best to ignore these intrusive influences. Since World War II, with new nations emerging on these frontiers and the rapid transformation of primitives into peasants, peddlers, and parliamentarians, fieldwork is increasingly done in less isolated and less primitive settings. An Anatolian or Mexican village, an African port town, a Haitian market town, or an American ghetto may be the setting for fieldwork; as the world changes, the pressures for direct relevance to human problems increase, and the ranks of anthropologists expand.

Whether the setting is city, town, village, or jungle hut, the mode of anthropological research is in many important respects the same. Most essentially, it entails a *deep immersion* into the life of a people. Instead of studying large samples of people, the anthropologist enters as fully as he can into the everyday life of a small group of people. For him, they are a microcosm of the whole. He learns their language and tries to learn their mode of life. He learns by "participant observation," by living as well as viewing the new patterns of life he finds. Successful fieldwork is seldom possible in a period much shorter than a year, especially where a new language and culture must be learned; ideally it is a good deal longer.

The ethnographer brings with him techniques of mapping and census taking, and skills of interviewing and observation. But his position is radically different from that of the political scientist or economist or sociologist studying events in his own society. His place, and his task, are in many ways more like those of an infant. Like an infant, he does not understand the noises, the visual images, the smells, that carry rich meanings for those around him. His learning must be of the same magnitude, and his involvement correspondingly deep. He can administer questionnaires to find out about the world he has entered little better than an infant can, and for many of the same reasons: he does not know what the questions are that have answers and would have no medium for asking them. Time, deep involvement, a lot of guessing, a lot of practice, and a lot of mistakes enable him to begin to make sense of the scenes and events of this new cultural world.

He is not an infant, of course. And that makes his task harder as well as easier. Unlike an infant, he can take care of himself (though not always very well, in a jungle or desert); and he can often use an interpreter to find out something about what is going on. The difficulty is that he—unlike the infant—already knows a native language and a set of patterns for thinking, perceiving, and acting. Instead of filling in an empty framework with the design of his people, as an infant does, he must organize his knowledge in terms of an existing design, and interpret new experiences in terms of familiar ones. This renders his learning slower and harder (consider how much harder it is for an *adult* to learn a new language); and it inevitably distorts his perceptions.

Through all this, the anthropologist goes through routines of "gathering data"—taking a census, recording genealogies, learning about the local cast of characters, and querying informants about matters of customs and belief. What goes into his notebooks comes mainly from such routines. As we will see, marked advances have been made in recent years in minimizing the distorting effect of the ethnographer's own conceptual scheme and in analyzing another way of life in terms of the categories and premises of the people being studied. But as we learn more about learning, it seems increasingly likely that much of what the ethnographer learns never goes into his notebooks: it is in that realm that for lack of a better term we can call the "unconscious"—a knowledge of scenes and people and sounds and smells that cannot be captured in the written word.

What informants can tell the ethnographer about their customs may be a similarly inaccurate and partial rendering of what they see, do, think, and feel. Sometimes it is distorted by the intent to deceive or by linguistic misunderstanding. In any case, what people tell the ethnographer about their way of life must be cross-checked and substantiated and filled out by detailed records of actual events and transactions. A modern anthropological study is a far cry from the older style where one simply said "descent is patrilineal" and left it at that. Detailed statistical tables, and often maps and genealogies, enable the author's colleagues to reconstruct the network of people and events from which generalization were worked out.

The anthropologist in the field, though he may be concerned with methodological rigor, is above all in an intensely human situation where all of his insight, intuition, and empathy must be brought to bear. Characteristically something of a stranger in his own cultural world, he is deeply caught up in the lives of the people whose experiences he is sharing.

As a vision quest, the anthropologist's path has different stages and different experiences for each fieldworker. "Culture shock"—the initial impact of radically different settings and customs—is common. So too are waves of despair where rejection, hostility, and incomprehensibility close in on all sides.

Consider the encounter from the other side. A people's life is interrupted by a strange foreigner, often with a family, who moves into the community, bringing all manner of new and strange things. This man seldom fits any of the "kinds" of foreigners they have learned to deal with—missionaries, traders, government officers, politicians, or whatever. He is insatiably curious about things private, sacred, and personal, for reasons and motives that are incomprehensible. He must be accorded a role of some sort; his clumsy efforts to speak properly, his bad manners, his intrusions into daily life, must be tolerated. All this attention may be flattering, but it may breed suspicion, hostility, and jealously. In a less isolated and more sophisticated community, "being studied" may smack of condescension and may offend pride, not arouse it.

On the anthropologist's side, ethical problems loom large. Should he try to protect the identity of his community and its people by disguising names and places? Can he intervene in matters of custom and health? Can he betray the confidence of his informants in some grave violation of the law?

And how deeply can he really penetrate into another way of life? Sitting in a Solomon Island mountain hamlet chewing betel with my friends, and bantering in their language, I feel a oneness with them, a bond of common humanity and shared experience. But can they feel that with me? Can I be more than a visiting curiosity and celebrity, a rich white man who will soon go back to his world?

Such are the challenges, the frustrations, the doubts, and the insights of the anthropologist in fieldwork. From this experience, this immersion in another cultural world, he may return to write a book and to impress his colleagues with learned jargon. But whatever the course of his vision quest, his world will never look the same.

The return to the simplicity of a tribal or peasant way of life, intensely personal and devoid of hardware, has a strong appeal. Anthropologists have usually championed a somewhat romanticized view of "their people" and have stalwartly defended the value and even the nobility of primitive life. The popularized return of the "noble savage" in American folk culture of the late 1960s—as an ideological counter to the alienation and impersonality and frenzy of modern life—has left anthropologists in a curious position. They find themselves pointing out that primitives can be nasty too, that the foibles of human nature and the arbitrariness and nonsensicality of cultural conventions know no geographical boundaries.

And primitive peoples often *are* nasty, if we are prepared to think a bit about what "nastiness" can mean in this context. When peoples whose cultural conventions are very different encounter one another, the deportment of one people can be wicked, noble, nasty, uncouth, violent, sullen, silly, hilarious, or immoral from the standpoint of the other people. Looking relativistically, we can hardly dismiss another people as "nasty"—only as different. Yet such an ethical relativism is ultimately hard to live with. Those who might be prepared to accept cannibalism on the Amazon as a wholesome and nutritious custom are unlikely to be so generous about genocide as a Nazi custom or *apartheid* as a South African one. And if we are prepared to seek panhuman standards of ethics and values, we will find societies where aggression or morbid suspicion has gotten out of reasonable control—where people fall further short of the highest aspirations of man in some respect than the rest of us. "Nastiness" is the wrong word here, but anthropologists sometimes encounter "noble savages" whom even they find it hard to like very much. Those who would romanticize fieldwork and primitive life can find in a recent account of fieldwork among the Yanomamö of South America a sobering note:

> We arrived at the village . . . and docked the boat along the muddy bank. . . . It was hot and muggy, and my clothing was soaked with perspiration. It clung uncomfortably to my body, as it did thereafter for the remainder of the work. The small biting gnats were out in astronomical numbers, for it was the beginning of the dry season. My face and hands were swollen from the venom of their numerous stings. In just a few moments I was to meet my first Yȧnomamö, my first primitive man. . . .
>
> The entrance to the village was covered over with brush and dry palm leaves. We pushed them aside to expose the low opening to the village. The excitement of meeting my first Indians was almost unbearable as I duck-waddled through the low passage into the village clearing.
> I looked up and gasped when I saw a dozen burly, naked, filthy, hideous men staring at us down the shaft of their drawn arrows! Immense wads of green tobacco were stuck between their lower teeth and lips making them look even more hideous, and strands of dark green slime dripped or hung from their noses. We arrived at the village while the men were blowing a hallucinogenic drug up their noses. One of the side effects of the drug is a runny nose. The mucus is always saturated with the green powder and the Indians usually let it run freely from their nostrils. My next discovery was that there were a dozen or so vicious, underfed dogs snapping at my legs, circling me as if I were going to be their next meal. I just stood there holding my notebook, helpless and pathetic. Then the stench of the decaying vegetation and filth struck me and I almost got sick. I was horrified. What sort of welcome was this for the person who came here to live with you and learn your way of life, to become friends with you? They put their weapons down when they recognized Barker [a missionary] and returned to their chanting, keeping a nervous eye on the village entrances.
> We had arrived just after a serious fight. Seven women had been abducted

the day before by a neighboring group, and the local men and their guests had just that morning recovered five of them in a brutal club fight that nearly ended in a shooting war. The abductors, angry because they lost five of the seven captives, vowed to raid the Bisaasi-teri. When we arrived and entered the village unexpectedly, the Indians feared that we were the raiders. On several occasions during the next two hours the men in the village jumped to their feet, armed themselves, and waited nervously for the noise outside the village to be identified. . . .

. . . I had not eaten all day, I was soaking wet from perspiration, the gnats were biting me, and I was covered with red pigment, the result of a dozen or so complete examinations I had been given by as many burly Indians. These examinations capped an otherwise grim day. The Indians would blow their noses into their hands, flick as much of the mucus off that would separate in a snap of the wrist, wipe the residue into their hair, and then carefully examine my face, arms, legs, hair and the contents of my pockets. . . .

So much for my discovery that primitive man is not the picture of nobility and sanitation I had conceived him to be. I soon discovered that it was an enormously time-consuming task to maintain my own body in the manner to which it had grown accustomed in the relatively antiseptic environment of the northern United States. Either I could be relatively well fed and relatively comfortable in a fresh change of clothes and do very little field-work, or I could do considerably more fieldwork and be less well fed and less comfortable.

Eating three meals a day was out of the question. I solved the problem by eating a single meal that could be prepared in a single container, or, at most, in two containers, washed my dishes only when there were no clean ones left, using cold river water, and wore each change of clothing at least a week to cut down on my laundry problem, a courageous under-taking in the tropics. I was also less concerned about sharing my provisions with the rats, insects, Indians, and the elements, thereby eliminating the need for my complicated storage process. I was able to last most of the day on *café con leche*, heavily sugared espresso coffee diluted about five to one with hot milk. I would prepare this in the evening and store it in a thermos. Frequently, my single meal was no more complicated than a can of sardines and a package of crackers. But at least two or three times a week I would do something sophisticated, like make oatmeal or boil rice and add a can of tuna fish or tomato paste to it. . . .

Meals were a problem in another way. Food sharing is important to the Yanomamö in the context of displaying friendship. "I am hungry," is almost a form of greeting with them. I could not possibly have brought enough food with me to feed the entire village, yet they seemed not to understand this. All they could see was that I did not share my food with them at each and every meal. . . .

Despite the fact that most of them knew I would not share my food with them at their request, some of them always showed up at my hut during mealtime. I gradually became accustomed to this and learned to ignore their persistent demands while I ate. Some of them would get angry because I failed to give in, but most of them accepted it as just a peculiarity of the subhuman foreigner. When I did give in, my hut quickly filled with Indians, each demanding a sample of the food that I had given one of them. If I did not give all a share, I was that much more despicable in their eyes. . . .

The thing that bothered me most was the incessant, impassioned, and aggressive demands the Indians made. It would become so unbearable that I would have to lock myself in my hut every once in a while just to escape from it: privacy is one of Western culture's greatest achievements. But I did not want privacy for its own sake; rather, I simply had to get away from the begging. Day and night for the entire time I lived with the Yanomamö I was plagued by such demands as: "Give me a knife, I am poor!"; "If you don't take me with you on your next trip to Widokaiya-teri I'll chop a hole in your canoe!". . . I was bombarded by such demands day after day, months on end, until I could not bear to see an Indian.

It was not as difficult to become calloused to the incessant begging as it was to ignore the sense of urgency, the impassioned tone of voice, or the intimidation and aggression with which the demands were made. It was likewise difficult to adjust to the fact that the Yanomamö refused to accept "no" for an answer until or unless it seethed with passion and intimidation —which it did after six months. Giving in to a demand always established a new threshold; the next demand would be a bigger item or favor, and the anger of the Indians even greater if the demand was not met. I soon learned that I had to become very much like the Yanomamö to be able to get along with them on their terms: sly, aggressive, and intimidating.

Had I failed to adjust in this fashion I would have lost six months of supplies to them in a single day or would have spent most of my time ferrying them around in my canoe or hunting for them. As it was, I did spend a considerable amount of time doing these things and did succumb to their outrageous demands for axes and matches, at least at first. More importantly, had I failed to demonstrate that I could not be pushed around beyond a certain point, I would have been the subject of far more ridicule, theft and practical jokes than was the actual case. In short, I had to acquire a certain proficiency in their kind of interpersonal politics and to learn how to imply subtly that certain potentially undesirable consequences might follow if they did such and such to me. They do this to each other in order to establish precisely the point at which they cannot goad an individual any further without precipitating retaliation. As soon as I caught on to this and realized that much of their aggression was stimulated by their desire to discover my flash point, I got along much better with them and regained some lost ground. It was sort of like a political game that everyone played, but one in which each individual sooner or later had to display some sign that his bluffs and implied threats could be backed up. I suspect that the frequency of wife beating is a component of this syndrome, since men can display their ferocity and show others that they are capable of violence. Beating a wife with a club is considered to be an acceptable way of displaying ferocity and one that does not expose the male to much danger. The important thing is that the man has displayed his potential for violence and the implication is that other men better treat him with respect and caution (Chagnon, 1968: 4–9).

"Primitive" man, as he is encountered by the field anthropologist and as we will see him in the chapters to follow, is neither noble nor debased, neither childlike savage nor elemental man unsullied by the ills of civilization: he is simply human. And that means that however limited his hardware, however unencumbered and unharried his mode of life, he lives enmeshed in a web of conventions that are his own creation; he strives and competes for absurd goals; he sets standards he cannot reach, devises rules he does not follow; he plays the roles his culture lays down, voices sentiments he does not feel. This creature of cultural convention is the Elemental Man.

II   *Culture and People:*
Some Basic Concepts

THE STUDENT of human social life faces a different conceptual problem than the physicist. The technical terms he uses are drawn mainly from the language of everyday life, yet he must give them a precision that makes communication more exact. In this chapter we will examine the conceptual foundations on which anthropologists build. In particular, we will explore the anthropological concept of "culture" and its relationship to "society."

Social scientists are far from agreed on what they mean by these terms. Any concise definition would raise controversy. Many have argued that the solution would be simply to impose a standard definition—by fiat or agreement—so that everyone would know what everyone else meant. But the problem is less simple than that. Scientists are human beings, equipped with that wondrous device, the human brain; and thus they have a remarkable ability to comprehend complex, overlapping, and contextually distinguished patterns of meaning of a single word. We have scarcely begun to understand how this process works. Until we do, trying to define complex and abstract concepts on paper is likely to be very indirectly related to the way people, including scientists, understand (or misunderstand) one another.

In laying a conceptual foundation for the chapters to follow, we will not simply define technical terms so that the definitions can be memorized. What they mean must be learned by looking at the complex patterns in the world for which they provide shorthand labels.

5 · The Anthropological Concept of "Culture"

The anthropological concept of "culture" has been one of the most important and influential ideas in twentieth-century thought. The usage of "culture" adopted by nineteenth-century anthropologists has spread to other fields of thought with profound impact; and it is now commonplace for humanists and other social scientists to speak, say, of "Japanese culture."

Yet, paradoxically, the notion of culture implied in such usages has proven too broad, and too blunt, for carving out the essential elements in human behavior. The reaction of some has been to abandon the term as a central conceptual tool; the response of others has been to sharpen and narrow the instrument to render it more precise.

"Culture," in the usage of anthropology, does not of course mean cultivation in the arts and social graces. It refers, rather, to the totality of man's learned, accumulated experience. "A culture"—say, "Japanese culture"—refers to those socially transmitted patterns for behavior characteristic of a particular social group.

Anthropologists have not been totally precise, or totally consistent, in their usages of this crucial concept. Some representative attempts at definition reveal different facets of "culture":

> That complex whole which includes knowledge, belief, art, morals, law, custom, and any other capabilities and habits acquired by man as a member of society.—Tylor (1871)

> The sum total of the knowledge, attitudes and habitual behavior patterns shared and transmitted by the members of a particular society.—Linton (1940)

> (All the) historically created designs for living, explicit and implicit, rational, irrational, and nonrational, which exist at any given time as potential guides for the behavior of men.—Kluckhohn and Kelly (1945)

> The mass of learned and transmitted motor reactions, habits, techniques, ideas, and values—and the behavior they induce.—Kroeber (1948)

> The man-made part of the environment.—Herskovits (1955)

> Patterns, explicit and implicit, of and for behavior acquired and transmitted by symbols, constituting the distinctive achievement of human groups, including their embodiments in artifacts.—Kroeber and Kluckhohn (1952)

Goodenough (1957, 1961) has recently argued that most such definitions and usages have blurred a crucial distinction between patterns *for* behavior and patterns *of* behavior. In fact, Goodenough says, anthropologists have been talking about two quite different orders of things when they have used the term "culture"—and too often they have moved back and forth between the two sorts of meaning. First, "culture" has been used to refer to the "pattern of life within a community—the regularly recurring activities and material and social arrangements" characteristic of a particular human group (Goodenough, 1961: 521). In this sense, "culture" has referred to the realm of observable phenomena, of things and events "out there" in the world. Second, "culture" has been used to refer to the organized system of knowledge and belief whereby a people structure their experience and perceptions, formulate acts, and choose between alternatives. This sense of "culture" refers to the realm of ideas.

Following Goodenough's lead, we will use "culture" to refer to systems of shared ideas, to the conceptual designs that underlie the ways in which a people live. Culture, so defined, refers to what men *learn*, not what they do and make. As Goodenough expresses it, this knowledge provides

> standards for deciding what is, . . . for deciding what can be, . . . for deciding how one feels about it, . . . for deciding what to do about it, and . . . for deciding how to go about doing it (1961: 522).

This ideational notion of culture is not a radically new one. Note that Kluckhohn and Kelly's 1945 definition of culture in terms of "designs for living" follows a similar course. Nor is it without philosophical problems. There are many who shrink from postulating such "mentalistic" entities. Yet there is a strong and powerful precedent, as we will see, from the study of language. Linguists have made impressive advances by distinguishing language, as a conceptual code, from speech, the overt behavior based on that code. As in any question of scientific conceptualization, the ultimate test of a definition or distinction lies in what you can do with it. It is too early to be sure that an ideational concept of culture will, in the long run, be a valuable and workable analytical tool; but at present it is clearing exciting new paths into little-charted territory.

An initial difficulty in the study of culture is that we are not in the habit of analyzing cultural patterns, and seldom are even aware of them. It is as though we—or the people of any other society—grow up perceiving the world through glasses with distorting lenses. The things, events, and relationships we assume to be "out there" are in fact filtered through this perceptual screen. The first reaction, inevitably, on encountering people who wear a different kind of glasses is to dismiss their behavior as strange or wrong. To view other peoples' ways of life in terms of our own cultural glasses is called *ethnocentrism*. Becoming conscious of, and analytical about, our own cultural glasses is a painful business. We do it best by learning about other people's glasses. Although we can never take our glasses off to find out what the world is "really like," or try looking through anyone else's without ours on as well, we can at least learn a good deal about our own prescription.

With some mental effort, we can begin to become conscious of the codes that normally lie hidden beneath our everyday behavior. Consider the problem that a single American girl continually encounters of where to place the width of her stern on the roughly forty inches of front seat of an American car when a male is driving. Does she sit in the middle? Close up? Against the door? Clearly there is a code here, and clearly it is based on communications and shared understandings about the girl's relationship to the driver. In long-standing American courtship ritual, she is supposed to begin somewhere in the middle; and as the relationship becomes more intimate, she acknowledges this by moving closer and closer to him. If she is angry, she moves against the door, expressing coolness and distantness. If the driver is ineligible for courtship, she sits in a neutral position; to move against the door would communicate the wrong thing. How soon the girl moves over, and how far, clearly expresses something about what kind of girl she is as well as what her relationship to the driver is. Such codes are learned but not written; and constantly tested and compared but seldom talked about. They are premises and rules and meanings we draw on to communicate and to understand one another, yet we are rarely conscious of them.

Consider another set of American codes in action. Smith, a junior executive, comes into the office of Jones, his senior boss. Smith, a young man on the way up, plays golf with Jones on Saturday. Outside the office, he had asked Jones's secretary if "Mr. Jones" was in; but once inside, he addresses Jones as "Ed"—thereby affirming that he is "in" in terms of a personal relationship. Then the secretary comes in, and addresses her boss as "Mr. Jones" (even if she enjoys martinis or more with him after work). Jones calls her "Miss Brown" or "Barbara." Smith may well shift to "Mr. Jones" while she is in the office, then back to "Ed" when she leaves. Now Roberts, another junior executive equivalent in rank to Smith, comes in. But he does not play golf with Jones or see him socially, and does not address him by his first name. At this point, with Roberts addressing the boss as "Mr. Jones," Smith may either shift to "Mr. Jones" or keep calling the boss "Ed." So intricate are these normally unconscious codes, yet so well understood by all, that Roberts, Jones, and Smith all know precisely what Smith is communicating by making either choice: either formality and equal status with Roberts (by "Mr. Jones") or competitive advantage and "one-upmanship" (by "Ed").

Project from these examples to the vast body of other shared understandings we need in order to eat in a restaurant, drive in traffic, or shop in a supermarket—and what the anthropologist means by "culture" will begin to come into view.

"Culture" consists not of things and events that we can observe, count, and measure: it consists of shared ideas. A Bulgarian hostess serving a second or third helping is not part of "Bulgarian culture"; but the conceptual principles that lie behind her acts, the patterns of meaning that make them intelligible, are. Bulgarian culture is something learned, something in the minds of Bulgarians, and thus it cannot be studied or observed directly. Nor could our Bulgarian woman tell us all the premises and principles on which her behavior is based. Many are as hidden from her perception as they are from ours.

When, then, should we worry about "culture" at all, if it leads us into a never-never land of unobservables and shadowy mentalistic formulations? Some would argue that we should focus on *behavior*, on things observable and measurable; and should leave "the mind" to the philosopher or meta-physician.

A number of major issues are at stake here, and philosophers of science are far from agreed on them. Some who are prepared to talk about "culture" in this mental or cognitive sense regard it simply as a hypothetical abstraction that makes sense of what people are observed to do and say. There is then no sense asking whether such a "construct" is "true" or "real"—only whether or not it works. If we are of another persuasion, cultural codes "really exist," and if we are clever and patient enough we can find out what they are like.

To clarify the issues, we must be clear what we mean by saying that a "culture"—say, Hopi Indian culture—is an *abstraction*. First of all, "a culture" is a *composite*. No single Hopi knows about all aspects of his people's way of life because each person participates in only some segments of the network that is Hopi society. Specialists in ritual or technology will know elements of their culture that others will not; even men and women will know different segments of their cultural code. The anthropological description of "Hopi culture" puts together into a composite these various segments of the code.

Second, "a culture" is a generalization. Since no two Hopi will have precisely the same version of the code, what we describe as common to all of them is in one sense a kind of common denominator, more general—and thus abstract—than the detailed variants of each Hopi. But this is not all—or we would be left with such a bare skeleton common denominator that it would not enable us to produce or account for the acts that Hopi themselves produce. An individual Hopi Indian must build his own theory of the code, and he can only tell that it is "correct" by seeing if it works. The anthropologist, like the Hopi, builds a version of the code that yields answers that work. In describing "Hopi culture," he is attempting to build a theory that accounts for the ability of Hopi to behave as they do. That is all he, or any young Hopi Indian, can do.

"Hopi culture"—or particularly the code of a large-scale society like "Japanese culture"—is an abstraction in a third sense. Some elements of the code will be shared by all or most Japanese, and enable farmers to interact with city dwellers and tradesmen to interact with executives. Other elements will be common to farmers, or to particular kinds of farmers, or to farmers in a particular community. Furthermore, a farmer and a business-man in that community will share some elements of the code that neither shares with his counterparts in neighboring communities. A view of "culture" as an ideational code enables the anthropologist to deal effectively with such variations, much as a linguist does in dealing with dialects. He can, where relevant, distinguish the "subcultures" of particular social strata, occupational groups, or localities. These naturally account in greater detail for events on this limited scale, just as a study of some regional dialect accounts in some detail for pronunciation, idioms, and vocabularly in this area. Where his concern is more general, he can speak of the common code of which these are variant versions—the Japanese language, or "Japanese culture." In each case, it is concern with some particular problem or phenomenon, on a particular scale, that determines which "level" of the code he describes.

Still, one might object, why do we have to talk about this shadowy hypothetical entity "culture," which by definition we can never observe or record? Why can one not simply study acts and events in a social system without invoking a metaphysical entity like "culture"? This, surely marks the way toward a precise science of human behavior. Or does it?

There are compelling reasons why we cannot understand human behavior without postulating an ideational code lying beneath it. These reasons have become clear mainly through the study of language, that symbolic code around which human social life is woven. We will examine them in Chapter IV. Meanwhile, equipped with an ideational conception of "culture," we must see how it relates to a second central concept in social science, "society."

6 · The Relation of "Culture" to "Society"

"Culture" ultimately refers to ideas "in people's heads." "Society" refers ultimately to the people themselves. "A society" is a collectivity of people sufficiently separated from those around them (usually because they share a common language and culture different from that of surrounding peoples) to constitute a distinct unit.

But just as "culture" is an abstraction, so too is "society." It refers to an enduring aggregate of people that remains despite the death and birth of individual members. In a more abstract sense one can conceive a society, or a social group, as a set of *positions* that individuals fill. An individual, then, is a "member of society," but not a "member of a culture." Rather, he shares or participates in a culture.

Moving in the direction of abstractions from human beings and their behavior—not the ideas we infer to lie behind that behavior—we reach concepts of "social structure" or "social organization."

As Geertz puts it, culture is "an ordered system of meaning and of symbols, in terms of which social interaction takes place"; and a social system is "the pattern of social interaction itself."

> On the [cultural] level there is the framework of beliefs, expressive symbols, and values in terms of which individuals define their world, express their feelings, and make their judgments; on the [social] level there is the ongoing process of interactive behavior, whose persistent form we call social structure. Culture is the fabric of meaning in terms of which human beings interpret their experience and guide their action; social structure is the form that action takes, the actually existing network of social

relations. Culture and social structure are then but different abstractions from the same phenomena (1957: 33–34).

"Social structure" (or, as some would call it, "social organization") is an abstraction from patterns of actual behaviors and events—a web of relationships; "culture" refers to patterns of ideas (but of course we can only infer these from the same behaviors and events). In Chapter VIII we will return to the relationship between social and cultural facets of human life.

Here an analogy may make the contrast more clear. Imagine that, as an experiment, we set eight chairs in a circle. Four chairs are black, four are white, and the chairs are numbered, as in Figure 3. We give each of eight participants an instruction that tells him what kind of chair to sit in and what to do while sitting in it.

A. WHITE EVEN-NUMBERED CHAIR: Try to impress the person two seats to your right with your knowledge of music, poetry, or art.

B. WHITE ODD-NUMBERED CHAIR: Disagree with everything the person on your left says.

C. BLACK EVEN-NUMBERED CHAIR: The person two seats to your left may not know what he is talking about, but flatter him along and agree with whatever he says.

D. BLACK ODD-NUMBERED CHAIR: Try to change the topic of conversation.

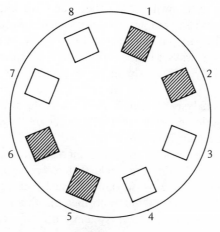

Figure 3.

When we turn our eight participants loose, the results can be at least roughly anticipated (hopefully the chairs will not be used as weapons). However, there are two quite different kinds of generalizations that we can make about the results of the experiment. First, we can look at the patterns of interaction that take place. It is immediately clear that the occupants of chairs 1 to 4 and 5 to 8 form two largely separate social systems (however small scale). Only the occupants of chairs 1 and 5 would intrude into both sides. (Had our instruction to them been to change the topic of conversation to their left, the two groups would have been fully separate.) The flow of interaction, of agreement and disagreement, would crystallize in particular patterns (even in repetitions of the same experiment), even though the actual conversations would vary widely. We could sort out *roles* and social positions; and abstracting from these patterns, we could describe the "social structure" of our experimental groups.

A second mode of description would simply be to say that the instructions specified the rules of the game; and that the patterns of interaction were simply expressions of a set of "rules" about what to do in what positions. The *instructions* would constitute the special "culture" of the group. Further, we could note that if we increased the number of chairs or shifted the arrangement of colors, while keeping the instructions the same, the social structure would change while the culture remained the same.

Neither mode of analysis is intrinsically better than the other. Each illuminates some facets of the same events. As long as the cultural "rules of the game" fit neatly the kinds of social arrangements and situations—as they did in the isolated tribal groups where anthropologists devised their conceptual tools—a description of cultural structure often makes more clear sense of what happens than a description of social structure. Sociologists, on the other hand, have emphasized descriptions of social structure: partly because in studying their own society they can take cultural principles for granted, partly because in complex modern societies ordered social life goes on despite great diversity in cultural codes. In fact, what we badly need, and are exploring, are ways to show both facets, and their interrelationship, at once. For especially in a world of rapid change, the cultural order and patterns of social organization slip far out of fit with one another. We will see in §63 Geertz' analysis of such a case, where he usefully underlines the inadequacies of describing either the social order or the cultural order without showing the interplay between them.

The notion of "a society" becomes increasingly blurred as what historically were separate units are melded into composite modern states. Sociologists and anthropologists working in such settings usually focus on segments of social networks: ethnic minorities, neighborhoods, social groups, or organizations. The term "social system" usefully covers such smaller segments as well as entire tribes or nations.

When he maps a people's culture, an anthropologist moves in his thinking from real human individuals to an abstract picture of the ideas they are supposed to share. When he maps the structure of a society, he begins with real people and moves to an abstract model of roles and networks.

Without such abstractions from the real world he cannot deal theoretically with relationships *between* people—with the way they communicate and the way they group together in ordered social life. But as with all simplifications, there is a cost. We screen out the uniqueness of each human individual and his or her world of experience. And we see parts and elements and aspects, but lose sight of wholes—missing the integration, the total patterning, of human thought and human action.

Concepts borrowed from psychology, notably "personality," aid us in thinking about individual uniqueness and psychological processes. But crucial insights and discoveries still elude explorers along these frontiers of science. What we need as a foundation for theories of culture and social structure is solid knowledge about a series of interfaces that remain largely hidden from view: the connections between neurophysiological processes and the world of thought; the relationship between genetic channeling and learning; the relationship between conscious and unconscious psychological processes; and the interplay between patterns of thinking and forces of motivation.

The shaky foundations on which social scientists now build leave their theoretical constructions provisional and vulnerable. Not simply the details, but the basic assumptions and frameworks, may have to be reformulated. Of all the things in the world too complicated to yield as yet to the assaults of science, the human brain and its opposite face, the mind, are the most complex. The anthropologist, struggling not only to make sense of the minds and behavior of human beings, but at the same time to cross the gulfs between his culture and another, faces an awesome task. Even if perhaps, in an ultimate sense, he cannot succeed, his attempt still can yield rich rewards in understanding.

Whatever analytical abstractions the social scientist uses to carve out formal patterns that he can manipulate with the tools of science—whether models of "culture" or "social structure" or whatever—the richness of every-day human experience and the uniqueness of real people remain essential sources of insight. That he himself is human may be the social scientist's best means of understanding man and his social life.

We will use the term "culture," in the chapters to follow, to refer to the ideational codes of a people with which they conceptualize their world and interact with one another. The complementary abstractions of "social system" and "social structure" bring into focus patterns of relationship between people. We will return to the articulation of cultural and social in Chapter VIII.

In the next three chapters, as we view man in evolutionary perspective—his biological heritage, his gift of language, and the development of his cultures—we will build on these foundations for conceptualizing culture. In Chapter III, we will examine the evolutionary emergence of human culture from its antecedents in the animal world. In Chapter IV, we will see in language a set of conceptual models for studying culture. In Chapter V, we will see the development of more and more complex modes of social and cultural organization. These conceptual foundations will be reinforced and tied together in Chapter VI, as we look in more detail at the structure of cultural systems.

Finally, our warning about the costs of such abstractions in showing elements and facets of human life at the expense of integrated wholes introduces a theme that will emerge often in the chapters that follow. Anthropologists, like other explorers of the natural and social world, have been better at dismantling the phenomena they study, to analyze the pieces separately, than at putting the pieces together to see how they interact and how they form wider systems.

Part Two

MAN IN EVOLUTIONARY PERSPECTIVE
Human Biology, Language, and the Growth of Culture

FOR SEVERAL million years, man and his immediate ancestors lived by hunting other animals and gathering wild foods. By about a million years ago, these manlike creatures had evolved into man. They had developed a larger and more complex brain, making possible that special gift which sets man apart from the rest of the animal world: language. With it, he could plan, communicate about the world, and pass on his knowledge across generations.

Yet that knowledge has been built up slowly. Only within the last 100,000 years has the imperceptibly turning snowball that was human culture begun to turn noticeably. In the last 10,000 it has begun to roll faster and to grow far beyond its original nucleus. Within the last 1000 years the snowball has rolled faster and faster; and in the last 100 it has spun and grown beyond all bounds as man has harnessed the atom and reached toward the planets.

In Chapter III we will look at human evolution and what man shares with his primate cousins. In Chapter IV we will look at language, the gift of tongues that makes man a very different kind of animal. The structure of language will give us crucial insights into the nature of culture. In Chapter V we will glimpse the growth of culture and will briefly view the peoples of Africa, the Americas, Asia, and the Pacific as they were when European explorers intruded on the scene.

III Culture and
Biological Heritage

MAN IS a peculiar kind of primate. Paradoxically, we can understand his peculiarity only in the light of his primateness. Scientists have known for more than a century that man is a product of biological evolution, a single strand in the web of nature. But students of his culture have stressed how man is different and unique, the way his abilities to cumulate experience and communicate symbolically enable him to transcend his animal past. Thus it was the task of the physical anthropologist to tell us how early ape became man; and the task of the cultural anthropologist to explore man as transformed being.

We now have important new evidence on the social life of living primates, on the human past, and on the biological roots of behavior. But more importantly, our perspectives have changed. We have come to stress continuities, not radical differences; and this has given us clearer insights into what is shared, how we became distinctive, and how we are distinctive. Here we will sketch, necessarily very briefly, man's evolutionary heritage, the relationships between human and animal behavior, and the biological bases of human variation.

7 · Man in Evolutionary Perspective

Since the work of Darwin, scientists have known that man has evolved as part of the world of nature, and that man is a primate—hence that his nearest living relatives are apes and monkeys. The detective work of tracing how, when, and where man evolved from primate ancestors is one of the most fascinating stories in science, and much remains to be done. Fortunately, excellent books are becoming available that focus directly on the course of human evolution and the studies that have brought it to light. Here we can only speed through several million years of development, glimpsing the elements most important to our study of cultural man.

Evolution, in its main outlines, is too sweeping a subject to explore here; and for many, this would be familiar ground. Evolution occurs through *adaptation* to ecological niches, to environmental possibilities. The genetic diversity in any biological population, produced by the mechanisms of genetic reproduction and mutation, is statistically channeled by *natural selection* (that is, by differential probabilities of reproduction). Through these processes, the niches afforded by environmental possibility are filled in by *adaptive radiation*. Forms become specialized to particular niches. As environments change, or more successful forms win out over old ones in the same niche, the forms of life undergo major changes over long time spans. Some organisms successfully survive major environmental changes because they are generalized rather than specialized; they can solve a range of problems, hence can adapt to a range of environments.

Man and his primate relatives represent cumulative products of these evolutionary processes over long time spans. With his closest cousins, chimpanzees and gorillas, man shares highly complex biochemical patterns such as blood groupings and susceptibilities to disease; with more distantly related primates such as Old World monkeys, he shares, for example, stereoscopic vision and an opposable thumb. He is connected by more distant common bonds to animal species throughout the web of nature.

In recent years, the evolutionary path leading to man has been dramatically revealed by a series of discoveries in Africa—at Olduvai Gorge and more recently at such sites as Omo and Lake Rudolph. What has been a fragmentary record with tiny scraps of evidence is becoming rich: at last we are learning about continuities, ranges of variation, and ecological settings. But before we glimpse briefly this emerging evolutionary picture, three cautions are in order.

First, any detailed summary would be out of date before it reached print, since major new discoveries are emerging every year. The days when a few skull fragments might be the major find of a decade are long past. Second, though we now know a great deal about the environments in which the ancestors of men lived and the ways they exploited them, there will inevitably be many things we do not know. Artists' fantasies to the contrary, we do not know if they were black, white, or well-camouflaged green, bald or hairy, smiling or dyspeptic—though we can narrow the possibilities a bit. Finally, for years finding fossils was like discovering new islands or continents with only natives on them—you *named* what you found as something new, exotic, and unique (naming it after your anatomy teacher or the hotel where you were staying). Thus older writings populate the ancient world with dozens of different "species," in violation of all principles of biosystematics. Reducing the number of labels has created new confusions for the unwary.

Our look at man's evolutionary past must begin somewhere. The best place for us to begin, because it sets the stage for the evolutionary drama to follow, is with a primate named *Ramapithecus*. He lived in the tropical forests of the Miocene geological period, some fourteen million years ago, in places at least as far apart as Africa and India. Though he was probably a generalized arboreal animal, his jaws and teeth—the only remains we have—point strongly in a human direction. At this stage, the record through the long Pliocene period goes almost completely blank—for some ten million years. It is in this period that many of the most crucial developments that led to man took place; and we can only speculate about why, how, and in what sequence.

When the path leading to man comes out into view again, at the beginning of the Pleistocene period, it is with the now-famous australopithecines. Latest finds move the datings of the earliest australopithecines further and further back, to perhaps four million years. From small, arboreal primates had evolved ground-living, upright-walking, tool-using *hominids* ("manlike animals").

Because new fossil finds are changing the details of the australopithecine picture so rapidly, we will paint it with very broad brushstrokes. We will then return to the problem of what happened in that Pliocene period where our evidence disappears from view.

The earliest australopithecines were small—about half the size of modern men. They stood fully upright, though they were better at running than at walking. With a brain size only about one-third that of modern man, they must have been limited in intelligence and the ability to communicate (though the relationship between absolute brain size and intelligence is indirect). How limited were these abilities remains in doubt.

Two different australopithecine forms emerge in the record, and this is proving increasingly important. The best guess is that the smaller one, *Australopithecus,* made tools, was an evolutionary successful hunter of the grasslands, and developed into man. The second, *Paranthropus* (the experts differ about labels, but this one avoids confusion), may not have used tools, and evolutionarily led to a dead end, though he survived well into the Pleistocene period where early men had begun to dominate the scene. *Paranthropus* was larger and heavier. Why two such hominids lived in the same general environment for hundreds of thousands of years is not yet clear. Biologically this suggests that they exploited different ecological niches. There is a good chance that *Paranthropus* was a vegetarian, though he may have hunted at times, as do modern chimpanzees.

Now let us go back to the Pliocene and speculate about how *Ramapithecus* or something like him might have evolved into australopithecine forms. From a primate pattern basically designed for upright posture, but not *bipedal* (hind legs) *locomotion*, our Miocene ancestor had developed into an upright walker. This is associated with a change from a life centered in trees to a life centered on open grasslands. In the same transformation sequence, intelligence had increased—though how much is not yet clear. Jaws and teeth had changed markedly in a human direction.

It is dangerous to argue about what caused what—not simply because we will never know, but because that is not the way evolutionary change takes place. Rather, a change in one respect makes another change adaptive, which reinforces the original change, and so on in complex circuits of interconnection. And when this pattern of what in cybernetics is called "positive feedback" leads to a strong adaptive advantage, it can rapidly transform one kind of animal into another.

We know that an ape did not simply "descend from the trees" and start things off. Rather, *Ramapithecus*-like animals living at the margins of grasslands doubtless made collecting forays on the ground. And gradually this environment presented a more and more challenging ecological niche to which some species, in the Pliocene, became increasingly well adapted.

A key piece in the puzzle, not yet solved, is whether tool-using by animals on the ground makes bipedal locomotion adaptive, or whether being bipedal frees the hands to use tools. A cybernetic model suggests the process may have gone in both directions. Use of tools, as well as the hunting they made increasingly possible, gives a strong adaptive value to increased intelligence—again, in complex networks of interconnection, not straight chains of cause and effect. Crude tools, in this view, would be far older than most anthropologists had thought.

One possibility that bears note as the behavioral similarities between men and chimpanzees mount up is that the separation of these evolutionary lines may be far more recent than the wildest speculations had suggested, possibly as recently as five million years. From a common ancestor adapted to both arboreal and terrestrial life may have emerged, in a rapid burst of evolutionary development, the bipedal australopithecines of the savannah found in the oldest layers at Omo, Lake Rudolph, and Olduvai Gorge. If so, *Ramapithecus* would be expelled from our ancestral closet; but so far the evidence is mainly indirect, biochemical, and uncertain.

At this stage we can return to the australopithecines, especially the larger and more advanced forms of *Australopithecus*, whose remains have been found in Africa from a period roughly two million to one million years ago. The magnificently rich stratigraphy of Olduvai Gorge allows us to identify as almost certainly the handiwork of these hominids a crude type of stone tool turned up in the early deposits. These crude tools, of a type technically called "Oldowan," are simply river pebbles with a few chips knocked off to form edges and points. If you found them in a stream bed, they would be indistinguishable from the products of natural forces; but hominids carried them to other places where they could only be crude tools.

Olduvai Gorge also gives a remarkable vista of man evolving out of *Australopithecus*. In the lowest levels of Bed II comes a form Leakey calls *Homo habilis*, which very probably lies on the evolutionary line from *Australopithecus* to that widespread form of early man that now will move to center stage, *Homo erectus*. *Homo habilis* apparently lived contemporaneously with his more dimwitted uncle, *Paranthropus*, who has left no descendants.

Homo erectus, coming to dominate the scene by the beginning of the Middle Pleistocene (perhaps as early as a million years ago), was a radical evolutionary advance. His bipedal locomotion was more effective, he was considerably larger, his skull, though massive, was beginning to change markedly in a manlike direction. That is partly because of his most important change—a dramatic increase in brain capacity. In terms of sheer bulk, his brain averaged almost three-fourths the size of modern man's. Whether *Homo erectus* had a form of language is not clear. There are strong indications that the increase in brain size was associated with the development of an at least rudimentary language and of more sophisticated and complicated toolmaking. (It has been suggested that the brain development and thinking operations used in language and toolmaking are closely linked; see, for example, Holloway, 1969). Intelligence, as reflected in communicating, problem solving, and toolmaking, would produce the complex of adaptive advantages required for rapid evolutionary development.

Homo erectus was widespread. His remains have been found in Africa, China, Java, and Europe. At some stage, he acquired the use of fire. Probably hunting and gathering wild foods in bands, he roved widely and followed seasonal patterns. The great Choukoutien Cave near Peking, where the most detailed evidence has been found, shows that he hunted a wide range of animals and cooked his meat in regular campsites. These advances are impressive, though they undoubtedly were built up slowly over thousands of years. Only armed with fire could these earliest men become "cavemen" and evict the other inhabitants. And regular camps permit a division of labor where women and children gather foods, and men can divide their hunting activities and regroup to share the kill. The Ambrona Valley sites in Spain where early men (apparently but not certainly *Homo erectus*) drove migrating animals into bogs in large-scale hunts show that smaller bands could join together in cooperative enterprises.

The stone tool industry *Homo erectus* developed, in which hand axes are a dominant feature, remained on the scene much longer than he did— until some 75,000 years ago. But no sign of *Homo erectus* himself appears after a period more than 300,000 years ago. *Homo sapiens*, in the form of "Neanderthal Man" in Europe and the Middle East, and his contemporaries in Africa ("Rhodesian Man") and Southeast Asia ("Solo Man"), does not appear on the scene until about 110,000 years ago. What lies between *Homo erectus* and the Neanderthal populations is glimpsed only from a few skull fragments found in Europe.

"Neanderthal Men" are the prototypical "cavemen" of popular stereotypes. Historically, the Neanderthaler has been maligned, his features brutalized, and his posture bent in exaggerated fashion. In fact, Neanderthalers were not only more successful evolutionarily than their predecessors (in

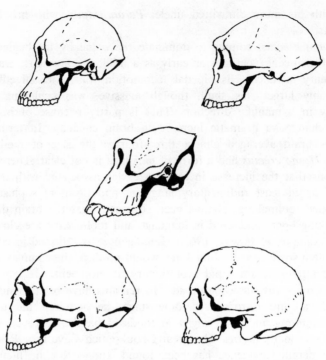

Figure 4. Evolution of the Human Skull. At the top left is the skull of a late australopithecine (reconstructed); at the top right is the skull of Homo erectus (reconstructed). Below, left, is a Neanderthal skull; and at bottom right is the skull of a modern European. In the center, to show points of contrast with modern apes, is the skull of an adult female gorilla. All skulls are drawn to the same scale. Any such sequence must be viewed with caution. Skulls are based on individual specimens, whether fully known or reconstructed; and any individual skull selected from a population cannot be viewed as a "type." (After Le Gros Clark.) RMK

terms of spread, numbers, and apparent performance), but they were in most important respects very similar to modern men. The Neanderthalers, found first, who gave rise to the misconceptions of their brutal features and primitive posture, were in fact a late and specialized variant that may have represented an evolutionary adaption to an increasingly hostile Northern European environment. The earlier European forms, and particularly those in the Middle East, are less extreme in their brutish countenance. And those in the Middle East have been found in physically diverse populations that represent a range all the way from the Classic Brute to forms much like modern man. From such diverse gene pools, modern man seems to have developed in a period around 35,000 years ago. Modern man did not evict the Neanderthals or bash them into extinction; it seems very probable that he simply evolved from them—though the newly evolving populations may then have spread into northern pockets of specialized Neanderthal population and replaced them by fair means or foul.

Though earlier writers stressed the size, robustness, prominent chin, and noble mien of "Cro-Magnon" man, who followed the Neanderthals in Europe, he seems to have been almost as much a figment of ideological fantasy as the brutish Neanderthaler. In any case, by this stage changes in culture had outstripped changes in human biology as means of adaptation. We will return briefly to these early populations of modern men in §9, and again in Chapter V.

We cannot linger here to look in more detail at the fossil record of man's past—though that record and the detective work of deciphering it are so fascinating that those who explore further will be well rewarded. In the next section we will look at primate social behavior and will ask in what ways man's culture is unique. What is important for us at this stage is to note, first, man's biological continuities with the past; the time span, perhaps ten or fifteen million years but possibly as short as five million, that separates him and his nearest primate cousins from a common ancestor; and the early development of bipedal locomotion and the later remarkable increase in brain size that mark most clearly man's biological distinctiveness.

8 · Animal Behavior and the Nature of Man

Until the 1960s, most cultural anthropologists dealt with man in biological perspective by stressing how different and unique he is, and how his ability to use language and cumulate custom set him apart from other animals. After a decade of rethinking, man looks no less remarkable, and in sum perhaps no less unique, in the animal kingdom; but we have come to look at him in a very different way.

Human behavior was contrasted, in the older studies, with the social life of insects, the instinctive behavior of animals (with their limited reliance on learning), and the behavior of trained animals like dogs and parrots as manipulated by man himself. What little we knew about behavior of other primates came mainly from zoos and laboratories.

Across the animal world our understanding of behavior patterns has been advanced dramatically. Ethologists like Lorenz and Tinbergen have documented the "innate releasing mechanisms" whereby birds, fishes, and other forms are programmed to respond to environmental stimuli; have explored new modes of protolearning such as "imprinting"; and have studied animal communication. Even classic interpretations like the "bee dance" for communicating about honey have been reevaluated. The evolution of behavior patterns as well as physical structures has become a central concern. As we begin to see how complicated genetic templates for behavior are and how they interact with environmental stimuli, simple distinctions between "instinct" and "learning" are no longer adequate.

With these new ways of looking at the world of nature have come new perspectives on man himself. We are looking for continuities with our animal past, not simply contrasts. Central in this enterprise has been systematic study of man's closest animal relatives in their natural habitats. Rich evidence is being built up on the social life of many primate species. Particularly fascinating are behavioral studies of chimpanzees and gorillas, man's closest animal kin; and studies of the baboons that, like early hominids, live on the ground in open grasslands—and whose ancestors shared these environments with australopithecines.

What can these studies tell us about the nature of man? Like cultural anthropology itself, primate behavior studies give no immediate, easy, and unequivocal answers about the extent and nature of human aggression, about how the incest taboo or language or the family originated, about how central sexuality is in human biology and psychology. But they allow us to say much more, and speculate much better, than we could without them.

Studying the range of variation in primate behavior enables us to reconstruct with fair confidence a number of things about the behavior of the ancient primates from which we and modern apes are descended. Examining man and the fossil record of his development in the light of that primate pattern, we can make fairly good guesses about how and why man changed in adapting to his mode of life as hunter and gatherer—a mode he maintained relatively unchanged for hundreds of thousands of years. We can also speculate about how man's biological heritage equipped him for those spectacular leaps of technology whereby human life has been transformed in the last 10,000 years; and we can ask how a biological and psychological nature adaptive to man the hunter serves him in a radically refashioned modern world.

Here we will briefly summarize the primate evidence on a series of aspects of behavior relevant to man's evolution, biological nature, and social life. Having done so, we can better reflect on continuities and contrasts with his animal past.

Sexuality

In the light of Freudian theory about the primacy of man's sexual drives (and the voyeurism we indulge in at zoos), we might expect sexuality to be fundamental in primate social groupings. Yet primate interest in sex varies tremendously and nowhere is it a preoccupation. In some species, sex is a major theme; yet in others, sexual behavior is infrequent or inconspicuous. Particularly among the apes, copulation is rarely observed. Schaller (1963), studying the mountain gorilla, observed copulation only twice in thirteen months. Chimpanzees are somewhat more active sexually, but in one study only four copulations in eight months were observed.

A crucial factor of primate sexuality is that females are (as with dogs) sexually receptive only during *estrus* periods. In most primate species, copulation takes place only during a small proportion of a female's total life span. Usually there is some seasonality of mating, so that within a group (not only for individual females) sex is far from a continuous element of social life.

There are of course elements of cyclical sexuality in humans. The menstrual cycle is the most obvious; but there are suggestions that with the cycle of ovulation go variations in female sexuality. One can even find hints, in the literature on some tribal societies where virtually no cultural restrictions are placed on the expression of sexuality among unmarried young people, that sexual intensity might conceivably run a seasonal cycle. The problem is that this, too, is more likely to be a cultural overlay. Human biological sexuality is so interwoven with cultural and symbolic elements that even with comparative study it is very difficult to separate these strands.

How the evidence on primate sexuality is to be interpreted is not yet fully clear. Whatever social groups are like among nonhuman primates, it cannot be primarily sexual drives that keep them together. Yet the human female is sexually responsive throughout the year in a way we can presume her distant primate forebears were not. The point has been overstressed by some writers, and the contrast too starkly drawn. But in no primate species other than man (and the gibbon, for different reasons) are male and female paired in a stable and continuous relationship. Evolutionarily this can hardly be a coincidence; and it is an important link between man's biophysical nature and his social life.

Dominance

Modern studies have shown that hierarchies of dominance (of which the barnyard "peck order" has been a classic example), and patterns of actual or threatened fighting within and between groups, pervade the animal world. Combat, actual or threatened, clearly has been highly adaptive—as a mode of dispersing populations across terrain, maintaining order within social groups, and maintaining viability of species through differential reproduction.

Nonhuman primates universally use fighting or physical threat within groups to establish hierarchies of dominance. In some primates, notably baboons, there is a clear ranking (of adult males or of females and males) that determines leadership and access to food, sex partners, desirable branches, a shady spot to sit, and so on. In other species, dominance is less clear-cut, is less enduring, and pervades fewer corners of life.

Baboons, partly because their safety as ground-living animals depends on tight organization, have particularly clear, rigid, and pervasive patterns of dominance. Yet even here the precedence of a dominant male in matters of food and sex may well have been overemphasized in early studies. In man's closest relatives, chimpanzees and gorillas, dominance is much less emphasized.

Within a primate group, actual fighting for dominance is rare, though there may be a good deal of pushing, jostling, or nipping to reinforce dominant status. It is worth remembering that the animals in a group know one another well—they are not dealing with strangers. Usually threats, "display" behaviors, or simply conventional acknowledgments of submission keep each animal in its place, maintaining internal order in the group.

Dominance is rewarded. Thus among baboons the most dominant male moves in the middle of the troop as its leader, sits in the shade while others sit in the sun, is groomed by his "followers," and tends to have precedence in matters of food and sex. Dominance is also its own reward: primates, like children and prime ministers, seek the satisfaction of being "king of the mountain."

Primate Groups in Space

The size, composition, and stability of primate groups vary a good deal. How big and how permanent groups are affects their relations with their neighbors. In chimpanzees, larger social groupings shift in membership. Changes of group are possible, and hostility against outsiders must be curtailed. In many species, membership is quite stable, and intergroup hostility serves to maintain "boundaries" and achieve spacing of animals in relation to resources.

Characteristically, there is remarkably little interaction between different species of animals in the wild, apart from the dramas of hunter and hunted. Modern studies show that different animal species in the wild mingle surprisingly freely. It is common around a water hole to see antelope, zebras, warthogs, baboons, giraffes, elephants and even lions intermingling, seemingly oblivious of one another. Animals spaced out and in flight are very often fleeing the hairless ground-dwelling bipedal primate who for more than half a million years has probably been the most dangerous predatory animal in Africa.

Most primate species occupy *home ranges*, but not *territories*. In animal behavior studies, a territory is a clearly bounded area an animal defends by force if necessary. Most primates have overlapping ranges in which they feed and move, but do not defend their perimeters.

The size of home ranges and territories occupied by primate groups varies considerably. Arboreal primates such as the gibbon and the howler monkey occupy quite small territories, much less than a square mile. Gorillas and baboons, spending most of their time on the ground, may rove across an area of up to fifteen square miles. In general, primates stay within an area much smaller than what they can see from the treetops or in their foraging. An important development in man has been a great expansion of spatial horizons. Studies of modern hunters suggest that early man had to hunt over much larger areas than were used by his primate ancestors; so that one step on the road to being human was an increase in mobility and an expansion of ranges.

Modern studies of primates in the wild increasingly show the flexibility and openness of the "boundaries" between home ranges. Any argument that violent defense of territorial boundaries is biologically old and basic in man must rest most unsteadily on the evidence of primate studies. Relations between primate groups seldom involve physical confrontation. More often the noise of a foraging band avoids a collision course; and if collision occurs, it would be more usual for primates to resolve it by ritual threat behavior than by fighting. The question of "aggression," of whether man is an "instinctive killer," inevitably arises, thanks to the popular books by Ardrey (1966) and Lorenz (1966). The reader interested in a careful critical appraisal of these works could usefully refer to a collection of excellent papers edited by Ashley Montagu (1968). Dominance, threat, and fighting are biologically old, though it is overly simple to lump them as "aggression." In our primate relatives, complex threat and display behavior (such as the bluff charge of the gorilla that misled early observers into thinking these gentle and peaceable animals were brutal, hostile, and dangerous) is common; and in the great apes and baboons it can ultimately be backed by great strength, powerful jaws, and massive canine teeth. Whether man may still have "aggressive" drives is, psychologically and biologically, a very complicated question. But if he has, massive brain development has added mechanisms of psychological control and cultural convention to restrain them. As these capacities for control were evolving through natural selection, and as bipedal locomotion freed man's hands for new tools of offense and defense, the massive jaws and teeth and many mechanisms of agressive display (such as erectile hair) were disappearing. Man has replaced them with a sharp tongue.

Learning and Infantile Dependence

A major trend in primate evolution has been a prolonged period of physical maturation. The young have become dependent for longer periods, and to greater degrees, on maternal care and the physical security provided by the group. This is associated with an increasing importance of social learning and may be an evolutionary adaption to it. A newborn ape or monkey becomes immediately and completely dependent on its mother for survival—beginning with a "clinging" response that has deep psychological as well as physical roots. How dependent it remains, for how long, increases progressively as we approach man. Close dependence of infant on mother lasts for at least a year in monkeys, and three or four years in chimpanzees and gorillas. Man's evolution has prolonged to extreme degrees this period of dependency of the young.

Though laboratory primates had long shown talents in learning, we are only now beginning to appreciate the importance of learning among non-human primates. Rhesus monkeys reared away from their kind, for example, do not know how to copulate properly (though it is peculiarly human to worry about being proper at such moments). And only through modern studies of primates in the wild are we coming to realize how centrally adaptive it is for an infant primate to grow up in a group setting where models of the behavior that must be learned are visible on all sides. For this means that groups can cumulate, and pass on through learning, patterns of foraging, knowledge of an environment, and modes of intergroup relations that are adaptive in the setting they inhabit but would not be somewhere else. Such plasticity was long thought to be peculiarly human, but we have simply carried it to a new plane with the advent of language.

One crucial point to note here about modern primates and our inferred ancestors is that the dependence of the young makes the mother-child bond evolutionarily old and central (in fact it is common to many other mammals as well). This pair, not a "family" with a regularly associated male, is the basic building block of primate social units. In speculating about the origin of the human family and its evolutionary correlates, we need to put together these mother-child bonds with the disappearance of the estrus cycle. The mother-child unit, once the mother became sexually receptive more or less continually, provided the conditions for permanent association of particular males with particular females and their offspring. In evolutionary terms, selection was pushing toward such groupings as adaptive to the mode of life of early hominids. Precisely how and why is open to speculation.

Tool-using

Is man the toolmaker of the animal kingdom? Toolmaking has often been underlined as separating men from their animal relatives. Yet even this sharp boundary has been increasingly challenged by modern studies of animal behavior.

Consider the following examples of tool-using from the animal world: an otter using a stone brought from the ocean bottom to crack open mollusc shells; a baboon using branches to pry rocks up and get larvae from underneath; a chimpanzee using twigs to fish termites from a nest; a gorilla using branches to frighten an anthropologist away.

Hall (1963: 131 ff.) emphasizes that tool-using as an adaptation for food getting, nest building, or the like, may not be a great evolutionary advance, but simply another way of doing a specialized job. Most animals that use tools do so only to obtain food. Furthermore, the use of branches or stones for aggressive displays (which occur mainly in apes, seldom in monkeys) is not necessarily a close approximation to man's use of clubs or stones as hunting or defensive weapons. But recent studies of chimpanzees show that their tool-using goes much further in a human direction than Hall had thought.

Figure 5. A wild chimpanzee uses a grass stem to fish termites from a nest. (After a photograph by Baron Hugo Von Lawick.) RMK

The Miocene apes from which man is descended probably used objects at hand, as chimpanzees and gorillas do, for a range of purposes. The evolutionary progression that brought the ancestors of man onto their hind legs on the hazardous savannah probably involved more frequent and more effective use of tools. As we have seen, crude pebble tools seem to have been used for as long as two million years before hand-axe cultures developed:

> Tool use per se does not indicate intelligence, as evidenced by man's history when for a long time his ancestors had small brains and yet used tools as part of their way of life. It was not until late in the Pleistocene that there were large-brained hominids and complex tool traditions, and it was at this time that the transition to skillful use of tools occurred (Jay, 1968: 499).

Here the evidence can be read in two ways. On the one hand, studies of the great apes—particularly Goodall's observations on chimpanzees in the wild—bring them dramatically into a province long thought to be exclusively man's. Chimpanzees *make* tools, albeit simple ones; their use must be *learned*; and their elaborations are by no means limited to the modes of food getting or threat that Hall had suggested. But on the other hand, the great development of the brain that made language possible to men also made possible more complex modes of toolmaking that may require quite similar mental operations (Holloway, 1969). Once more, the primate evidence both places us with our close relatives and separates us from them.

Group Size and Structure

Most nonhuman primates are organized in groups ("troops" or "bands") of between ten and fifty. Within a given species there may be a wide range of variation in the size of actual groups. There are also species where groups are either larger or smaller than this range. In some baboons, groups of well over one hundred are found. Among the gibbons, Southeast Asian apes who represent a quite specialized adaptation, an adult male and female and their offspring comprise the group. We will see that in our closest relatives, the gorilla and chimpanzee, social groups are less clear-cut and stable than those of most other primates.

One problem is to define what the "group" is. Among the hamadryas baboon, adapted to life in a desert setting, aggregations of as many as seven hundred sleep in the same cliffs. They break up in the morning into groups of regular baboon size; these, in turn, are composed of smaller and more stable groups consisting of one male and one or more females with their young.

Mountain gorillas have been observed most commonly in groups of five to thirty individuals, though groups as small as two have been observed. All groups contain at least one large, mature male and one or more females and their young. The larger groups contain other males, but they are usually peripheral and often drift out of the group; in any case, one male is dominant. Chimpanzee groups are less stable and much less clearly defined. The animals within a single area may join in different groups for different purposes. Sometimes adults and adolescents of both sexes travel together, minus all females with young (who travel in a separate band). Sometimes bands comprising adult males and females plus mother-young pairs are found; and sometimes adult males band together. Mothers with young move less than other adults, so that adult bands of two to six, as well as single individuals, commonly forage and travel. "Groups" are short-lived, and what stability they have seems to be based on the chimpanzee version of friendship.

Nothing closely resembling the human "nuclear family" of father, mother, and children is found in nonhuman primates. The gibbon pattern is a specialized convergence only superficially similar to that of humans. As we will see in Chapter IX, the most unusual human variations on the family pattern preserve the mother-child pair as a stable unit but associate adult men with them in some unusual way. What makes "the family" possible and central in man is a complex of much longer childhood dependence, continuous sexual receptivity by females, a taboo on matings within the nuclear group (the "incest taboo"; see §34), and a sexual division of labor based on sharing. Nonhuman primates, with only very limited and partial exceptions, do not share food. A coordination of work, a division of labor, and a sharing of food are necessary if the primate band is to evolve into the human band of hunters and gatherers.

If early hominid males cooperated in collective hunting using crude weapons (as they would have had to do, as slow bipeds in an environment of fast quadrupeds); if females provided for young and gathered wild leaves, roots, fruits, grubs, and small animals; and if they shared the results of these ventures, then a powerful mode of adaptation to the African grasslands would have been possible. Sharing must be viewed as a crucial protohuman innovation. In such a mode of life, selection seems to have favored stable association of a male, a female, and their young.

Little detailed evidence on the primate background of the "incest taboo" is available. But among the apes and some monkeys, there is suggestive evidence that mother-child bonds are preserved as special ties into adolescence and adulthood. In some species this bond seems to be incompatible with sexual relations. Sade's recent observations on the inhibition of mother-son mating in Rhesus monkeys (1968) are particularly interesting. Studying this question raises grave difficulties under the usual conditions of field studies. Animals are hard to identify, the time span of observation usually too short. Nonhuman primates refuse to supply the observer with genealogies. Man's incest taboo, prohibiting mating of father and daughter and brother and sister as well as mother and son, is a peculiarly human, yet fundamentally important, cultural convention. After decades of debate, specialists are far from agreed as to how it developed, but they agree that it was a crucial step toward human social life.

Intraspecies Variability

How similar is the behavior of a particular primate species in different environments? This is a crucial question, and one we could not begin to answer as long as the ranks of primatologists were thin and highest priority had to go to covering as many species as possible. But as studies have intensified, we are now getting comparative evidence on baboons, chimpanzees, and other primates living in a range of settings.

Why does it matter whether all chimpanzees live in groups of the same size and behave in the same way? Because if they do not, the behavior patterns would seem not to be genetically laid down—they would seem to be *learned*. And to the extent that primates adapt to different environments by learning specialized patterns of social grouping, territoriality, food getting, and the like, and by transmitting them across generations, the gulf between them and cultural man has been narrowed considerably.

Thus desert-dwelling hamadryas baboons, as we have seen, sleep in large cliff colonies and move in small groups with a single male—while savannah-dwelling baboons sleep in trees, move in larger bands of several males, and have different patterns of food getting and territoriality. Similar variations are turning up in some other species. Experts infer that few of these differences are genetically laid down.

That these variations represent ecological adaptations is increasingly clear. Where different species of primates (or other animals) share the same environment, the social organization of each species is likely to be transformed in a parallel way (that is, to show more dense or more dispersed population, greater fluidity or greater stability of groups, larger or smaller group size, and so on). This, of course, assumes that an environment rich in resources for one species is not poorer for another species.

It is tempting to assume too quickly that observed differences in behavior patterns and social grouping in different environments reflect variations in learned principles. Here the primatologists can well borrow insights from students of human social life, as they come close to the domain of human behavior. In a human society the same cultural conventions for making decisions about where to live after marriage or how to affiliate with a kinship group may have widely different outcomes in different settings. Members of a tribe who live in a mountain valley may live in scattered homesteads of one or two families, while members of the same tribe dwelling along a lakeshore are grouped into hamlets of a dozen or more families. Does that mean they have learned different patterns of culture? Probably not. These tribesmen may simply be applying the same principles and strategies to different situations, so that the cumulative results of their decisions are different. Variations in outcomes do not necessarily imply differences in codes, learned or innate.

To the extent that primate behavior patterns are genetically laid down, their actual expression in different settings could reflect similar variations. At least the case for local learning, when we find different behavior in the same species, is far from clear-cut. This is an area of great current interest, where the gap between primate and human social behavior might be narrowed considerably, but where premature speculation could well mislead us.

Play

Young primates play. So, of course, do puppies, kittens, otters, and other mammals. Yet play becomes particularly important among primates because so much depends on learning and because play is central in the learning process. The similarity of play of nonhuman primates to human play is striking—particularly with chimpanzees and gorillas. The following description from Schaller's field notebooks on the mountain gorilla will strike a familar note in a retired babysitter or playground-watcher:

> A juvenile and a 1¾-year-old infant sit about four feet apart. Suddenly the juvenile twists around and grabs for the infant, which rushes away hotly pursued by the juvenile. The juvenile catches the infant and covers it with his body, propped on elbows and knees. Twisting and turning, struggling and kicking, more and more of the infant emerges from beneath the juvenile.

Freedom gained, the infant grabs an herb stalk at one end and the juvenile snatches the other end. They pull in opposite directions; the juvenile yanks hard and the infant is jerked forward. They then sit facing each other, mouths open, and swing their arms at each other and grapple slowly. Another juvenile comes dashing up, and in passing swipes at the juvenile and all three disappear running into the undergrowth (Schaller, 1963).

Bateson has pointed out how important play is in the evolution of communication. If an animal is to distinguish when its attacker is serious and when it is "just playing," the physical message of attack must be *labeled*—that is, the animals must send *messages about messages*, telling how they should be interpreted. That ability to label messages opens the way toward the games, the art forms, the fiction and fantasy, of man's cultures (Bateson, 1955). The importance of play in humans, and the development of organized games, are underlined in recent research by John Roberts and his associates. Games, they argue, provide crucial models or "templates" for learning the serious business of being adults. Here, once more, we can see in primate social behavior the foundations on which man's cultural life is built.

Communication

Observers of chimpanzees in the wild have commented on the din they produce—crashing, screeching, making vocal noises amazing in volume and variety. They and other nonhuman primates communicate with a richness equaled in few if any other animals.

Students of primate communication have noted that we are prone to misunderstand the primates' modes of exchanging messages. We want to know what a particular sound or gesture "means." But actually primate communication seldom conveys information about "the world." Rather primates mainly communicate about their own internal emotional and physical states and about their relationships with one another. We will see that nonhuman primates do not have the brain structure needed to name things in or about the world.

Primates do not usually send signals one at a time, so that a particular noise denotes anger, a particular gesture denotes affection, and so on. Rather, the same signal or message is communicated in many modes simultaneously—by vocalization, gesture, touch, smell, and facial expression. The same vocal sound may carry quite different messages, depending on the other signals that accompany it and on the social and environmental context. We should remember that most communications take place within groups of animals that know one another well. Signalling *between* groups tends to be simpler and more direct, as when bands of foraging chimpanzees signal one another's approach with loud noise from afar to divert the other group from a collision course.

Much technical data have been gathered on primate communication which we cannot explore here. The interested reader could usefully consult Marler (1965), Altmann (1967), Reynolds (1968), and Lancaster (1968). Particularly intriguing are the similarities in gestural communication between man and his primate relatives—suggesting that many gestures we had thought to be arbitrary products of cultural learning may be deeply based in our evolutionary heritage. The chimpanzee evidence collected by Jane Van Lawick-Goodall is particularly striking:

> Much of our gestural repertoire has been inherited from our ancestors. Chimps embrace each other in greeting; they reassure by touching each other; they seek reassurance by stretching out the hands, palm up, waiting to be touched by the other's hand. . . . Chimps greet with a kiss, probably a ritualized form of offering food (summary by Eibl-Eibesfeldt, 1968: 484).

We will return in §10 to the relationship between human and animal communication. To go further, we need to look at the nature of the remarkable human capacity for language on which man's cultures are built.

Having scanned the evidence from primate social life, we should consider its impact on the long-held view that man's culture makes him unique in the animal kingdom. There is a conceptual problem that needs to be dealt with at the outset. In the process of biological evolution there can be, in a sense, no sharp and sudden break, no emergence in a single organism or a single generation of a radically new mode of organization. Evolutionary change is gradual and continuous. It reflects changes in statistical frequencies within populations, rather than sudden new patterns. Though individual mutations have an immediate and all-or-none character, the wider patterns of change they may contribute to are complex and gradual.

In that sense, the idea of an ape without culture giving birth to a man with culture, or of the transition taking place in one or a few generations, is biologically untenable. There must have been "protomen" with "protoculture" even if the end result of that evolutionary sequence was a radically new mode of organization. An argument that distant ancestors of whales and porpoises could not swim very well is irrelevant to the question of whether present marine mammals represent a radical evolutionary change.

The question must be whether, through infinitesimal cumulative changes, hominids evolved the capacity for a radically different mode of organization represented in man; and whether that new mode can usefully be characterized by the term "culture." So laid out, it is plain that the question could be argued forever without being resolved. That depends on how we define "radically different" and how we define "culture."

If we look carefully at the evidence, how we answer the question hardly matters. Man *does* have a new mode of organization, but it is no longer easy to dash off in a few words where that "newness" lies. Our friends the "chimps" have used their tools to knock down the material props of our distinctiveness, and their learning to undermine ours. Man's new mode of organizing and manipulating experience builds on and through language.

It is made possible by a vast increase in brain power. It makes possible what Holloway (1969) calls "the imposition of arbitrary form upon the environment": man creates, through symbols, a thought-world of his own. Yet this new mode of integration builds on evolutionarily old elements, and there is no reason to assume smugly that man represents its ultimate possible expression.

The path to that integration was gradual, leading through "protoculture" and "protolanguage." Chimpanzees are turning out to be farther along that path than we had long thought; but the path has led—as did life on land, or in the air, at earlier evolutionary stages—to whole new modes of existence. If the continuities along this path rule out overly simple generalizations about "culture," man still appears as a new and radically transformed primate. Insisting, on principle, that man was qualitatively different has been poor science and has deprived us of the insights of evolutionary biology. Man as transformed ape is more comprehensible and no less wondrous than he was as a disembodied creature of culture.

9 · Variation in Man: Race, Culture, and Individuality

How are constitutional differences such as those of race, bodily form, and sex, related to differences in cultural behavior?

Racial differences almost inevitably come first to mind. But human individuals differ not only in the high-visibility exterior trim that the layman associates with race, but also in very complicated genetic and biochemical patterns. These produce variations in bodily build, vision, susceptibility to disease, metabolic rates, capacities for kinesthetic imagery or abstract mathematical reasoning, and hundreds of other characteristics that remain genetic mysteries.

Modern studies of population genetics and microevolution, and increased understanding of the biochemical and hereditary bases of behavior, make older and simple views of human differences untenable. Let us return, in our sketch of human evolution, to that period when Neanderthal men were giving way to fully modern forms such as the Cro-Magnon population. There is no certain knowledge of what such early men were like other than what the bones tell. It could be hypothesized that, as in other animals, there were somewhat taller (or longer) and shorter individuals, bulkier and thinner ones, darker and lighter ones, and so on. Put technically, man, like other complex organisms, tends to be *polymorphic*, to assume a range of varying forms.

Without doubt, these early humans lived in small groups, perhaps of a few families, and kept moving in quest of the wild foods and game animals on which they subsisted. No large groupings could be assembled in any one area without starvation, so that, as numbers increased, members of the original groups "hived off" and moved to new areas. Individuals probably mated for the most part within their own group or with members of immediately neighboring groups. Each band, as with so many other animals, would tend to establish a territory, which it would defend if necessary to control resources. What biologists call the *breeding population* was very small and tended to be stable. Recent estimates of the size of breeding populations among some of the very remote hunting and gathering peoples of today show them as mating almost exclusively within groups of fifty to five hundred persons. If humans had not built up their cultures so as to foster increasing movement and interaction, some localized groups might have been well on their way to complete *reproductive isolation*: that is, they would have been differentiating toward the point where interbreeding could no longer occur, the process of *speciation*.

Such small groups, spreading out over the warmer land zones of Asia, Africa, and Europe, provided at first what geneticists and ecologists might consider approximately ideal conditions for genetic differentiation. Sometimes here, sometimes there, a *mutation*, or biochemical change in genetic potential, would occur in an individual. In a small inbreeding group such a mutant character had its best chance to become a continuing part of the local "gene pool," or store of hereditary materials. Not only had it to survive the first cross between the individual concerned and a "normal" mate, but it also had to become more or less established in the breeding line, which was most likely to happen through continued very close inbreeding. The whole range of known human variations, from giant to pygmy stature, from near-black pigmentation to albinism, from straight to frizzly hair, must trace back ultimately to mutation processes. Probably, too, almost all the physical characteristics distinguishing modern man from his ancestors trace back to mutants established here and there over the earth in times of early man. A complicating factor in trying to trace the history and geography of particular characteristics, as with the distribution of pygmy size or prominent noses, is that similar mutant variations may have occurred more than once in different places; moreover, the genetic basis of most such overt characteristics is very complex.

Other forces making for difference were also favored in small breeding populations. One is known as *genetic drift*, the chance statistical variation in gene materials from generation to generation. Two small groups branching from the small parent group, for example, would tend over passing generations to "drift" genetically along different lines, through selective "shuffling" of genes, even without mutation. They would, with passing time, have different *frequencies* of characteristics, through greater survival of some gene material and lessened survival of others.

Natural selection of genetic patterns that were adaptive in particular settings played a major part in shaping human populations. Thus, diseases, diets, solar radiation, temperatures, and other environmental factors gave selective advantage to some genetic characteristics and militated against others. Many of that small percentage of mutant genes that conferred selective advantage would become established. Skin color, stature, body form, and other variable physical features represent adaptations to different environmental pressures on man (Baker and Weiner, 1966). The pervasiveness of adaptation in the microevolution (small-scale differentiation) of man, and the speed with which natural selection can reshape a population when pressures are strong, are being increasingly realized.

Blood groups usefully illustrate our newer perspective. In the early 1950s it was hoped that the racial history of man could be traced accurately by recording the frequency of blood-group genes (not only A, B, and O but many other genetically determined blood groups). The assumption was that early human populations developed blood-group frequencies through genetic drift when breeding populations were small; and that as populations increased, frequencies were stabilized. The blood groups were assumed to be selectively neutral; they could thus serve almost as genetic "fingerprints" in the detective work of tracing past population movements. Modern studies have shown that blood-group frequencies are affected by natural selection, though how and why is not yet fully clear. In fact, whenever a population contains a range of genetic diversity in some feature, modern geneticists look for selective forces maintaining the alternative genes in a *balanced polymorphism* (see, for example, the discussion of the sickle cell and malaria in §27). In man, cultural conventions about mating, food, child care, fighting, and disease may impose additional selective pressures that lead to shifts in gene frequencies. Modern physical anthropology has become increasingly concerned with the complex interplay of biological and cultural sides of man.

It is at this point that the term "race" becomes relevant. Though in popular usage it is emotionally charged and imprecise, it has a straightforward and important meaning in evolutionary biology. A race is a geographically separated, hence genetically somewhat distinctive, population within a species. That distinctiveness is based on constellations and statistical frequencies of genetic characteristics. The invisible features of blood chemistry, with known genetic determinants, are more important to the geneticist of race than high-visibility characteristics such as skin color or eye form, which may be very complicated and obscure genetically.

To characterize major racial divisions of man in brief word pictures, we must describe external features, not gene frequencies. Populations in west Asia, Europe, and north Africa became marked by a high frequency of lighter pigmentation, of taller stature, of prominent noses and chins, and some of the other characteristics that we associate with the "Caucasoid" type. In east Asia, straight and rather heavy-textured hair, little body hair, broad faces, an overhanging fold of flesh (called an *epicanthic fold*) more or less covering the upper eyelid, and certain other characteristics associated with the "Mongoloid" type, gained high frequency. In the isolated Australian area, reached by small migrant groups who crossed the intervening water channels from the Asiatic continental shelf. Aborigines have carried forward into modern breeding lines what appear to be rather early developed characteristics of man in south Asia: the rugged-faced, heavily-haired "Australoid" type, and the dark-pigmented, frizzly-haired "Negritoid" type.

In this period when regionally diverse adaptations were taking shape, interbreeding between genetically diverse populations—*hybridization*—was also going on. Population movements and contacts resulted in a flow of genes, notably selectively adaptive mutant forms, from one population to another. Hybridization is a very old and very basic process in man.

Seen in genetic terms, the boundaries between races are not sharp. Rather, in the frequency of clusters of genes or of visible characteristics like stature or skin color, we find *gradients* or *clines*. Races do not change at the "border"; rather, statistical frequencies shift, usually gradually.

What has been happening to man biologically over the last few thousand years? We will see in the next chapter how—with agriculture and other food producing techniques, and the rise of urban states—certain populations took the lead in what was to be a vast population increase. The tiny groups initially affected by the food producing revolution in the Mesopotamian area, in Egypt, in the Indus Valley of India, and in the Yellow River Valley of China, entered upon what might be called a "swarming period." Their particular gene complexes went, so to speak, into mass production. These influences spread in turn to nearby areas, notably Europe. So today we find in these zones massive human populations dominated by the Caucasoid or the Mongoloid type of characteristics, but with many subtypes. By contrast, Negro African, north and central Asian, aboriginal American, and Pacific Island populations had more limited stimuli to population growth. Moreover, here and there in remote zones, there continued into modern times numbers of tiny groups still hunting and gathering wild foods and breeding mostly within their immediate local lines: Australian Aborigines, African Bushmen, Pygmies, and others.

As populations expanded, migration, contact, and interpenetration of hitherto separate groups became the rule, as witness familiar European history. The prospects of any human groups becoming inbred and specialized to the point of reproductive isolation, hence of separating *Homo sapiens* into distinct species, fell away. Mutations, though continuing to occur, had less likelihood of becoming established. Genetic drift became of less total significance. The range of selective forces widened, particularly those of cultural selection. Selection continues to assume new forms. With modern medical discoveries, for example, many individuals who would formerly have been eliminated now survive and reproduce. Industrialization and city life foster new marriage and family patterns. Hybridization operates on a worldwide scale, and is particularly characteristic of contact frontiers and urban centers. The continuing unity and generalized character of the human species and the development of culture thus go hand in hand.

Figure 6. Cultural Conventions Can Shape Human Biology. The practice of head flattening was formerly widespread among South American Indians; marriage regulations or dietary customs may shape constitution in more subtle ways. The frame at left was used in Argentina. (After Imbelloni.) On the right is a skull from Bolivia, in the U.S. National Museum. FMK

Let us sum up so far. In the many millenia when modern men were hunters and gatherers in relatively isolated small populations, drift and particularly selection produced distinctive constellations of genetic characteristics in different areas. The differences were minor in terms of the vast range of features common to all *Homo sapiens.* Moreover, each population contained a broad spectrum of genetic diversity.

The population explosions and massive population movements of the last few thousand years have radically changed the picture—with hybridization on all sides, and cultural buffers of technology created between men and environment. The process of genetic differentiation in man, which had in biological terms never gotten very far, has been thoroughly rearranged and muddled by the cultural revolutions we will glimpse in the next chapter.

In what ways is human social behavior shaped by biological factors? What is the relationship betwen human biology and culture?

Our attention to primate social behavior reflects a conviction that biology shapes cultural man to a greater degree than most anthropologists fifteen or twenty years ago were prepared to accept. Striking advances in bio-

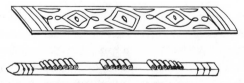

Figure 7. Human Biology Shapes Cultural Conventions. These mustache lifters are used by men among the Ainu of northern Japan—who characteristically have profuse mustaches and beards—when eating and drinking. The upper one is a common type; the lower one is for ceremonial use. FMK

chemistry, genetics, and neurophysiology have begun to reveal the incredible complexities of the biological mechanisms of heredity, learning, and thinking. The human infant is by no means as plastic, as subject to radically variable cultural shaping, as many had believed. What is learned and learnable, even language itself, is probably guided by genetic templates to greater extent than most cultural anthropologists had thought possible.

A recurrent theme in the chapters that follow is that the seemingly endless diversity in cultures has been overemphasized. Variations in cultures as ideational systems may be more shallow than deep, more a diversity of content than variation in form and structure. To the degree this turns out to be the case, the universals of form and structure presumably largely reflect constraints of biology.

These are debatable issues. Beyond rapidly changing frontiers of knowledge, our view is blurred and clouded. Yet with growing evidence of biochemical and genetic shaping of human behavior and limiting of cultural possibility, the conviction grows that what we share biologically, as humans, is vastly more important than what divides us, as individuals and groups.

With the great plasticity of the human infant as a premise of anthropology, the biological differences between male and female have probably been underestimated. Is it really the case, as Margaret Mead had argued in *Sex and Temperament in Three Primitive Societies* (1935), that the temperament of males and females is defined mainly by cultures, and not our biological nature? In the light of our primate ancestry, and the marked *sexual dimorphism* (difference between male and female) of most nonhuman primates, this would be surprising indeed. Male primates characteristically are specialized in size, strength, and temperament for dominance, defense, and combat. Females are specialized for bearing and nurturing young. The biological bases of human maleness and femaleness, in temperament and such biological patterns as tolerance for pain, probably run deep—a point explored in semipopular terms by Montagu (1968), and Tiger (1969).

But these explorations of the biological influences on human behavior cannot be understood unless the other side of the coin is viewed as well. For cultures *are* extraordinarily variable, and human infants *are* amazingly plastic. Through cultural learning an infant can become a Yanomamö tribesman, Zulu warrior, Hopi Indian farmer, Mexican peasant, or Manhattan apartment dweller. Biological "givens" like the drives of hunger, thirst, and sex are endlessly refashioned and rearranged by cultural conventions. Hunger will serve to illustrate. It can be "normal" in different societies to eat one meal a day, or two, or three, or more—and that determines when a person gets hungry. It also determines what he gets hungry for. Rotten grubs at four in the afternoon are no more and no less "natural" than ham and eggs in the morning. Even in the transformation of a genetic design laid down at the moment of conception into a living human being, through growth and maturation, cultural and environmental influences loom large. Thus children of Japanese immigrants to the United States are significantly taller than their parents; and the "overbite" in the mouths of most of today's readers is apparently an adaptation in the maturation process to eating soft foods. Culture fashions, from our genetically laid down potential, what we become. Only by knowing the vast range of ways cultures can fill in the openings left by nature can we see in perspective the possibility that the shape of the openings may be less flexible than we had thought.

There is no evidence that the contrasts between an aggressive Yąnomamö and the peaceful Hopi Indian, or their ways of life, reflect any genetic differences between the two populations. Because biological predispositions are channeled in such complex ways by cultural conventions, the possibility that genetically based differences in temperament or capacities underlie cultural differences would be exceedingly difficult to explore. In a world where racists seek to rationalize their hates and fears on scientific grounds, and anthropologists have fought running battles against them, it has been impossible to investigate such questions as dispassionately as sound science requires.

What racists are hoping is that science will provide rational grounds for discrimination and separatism, by showing that some other "race" is biologically inferior in intelligence or other capacities. Some have pointed to the "inferior" performances of nonwhites on I.Q. tests and other tests as reflecting inferiority in innate abilities. The problem, of course, is that white middle-class Americans have invented endless "tests" that in fact test how well people know white middle-class American culture; and are thus able to "prove" that children who have grown up in such environments know their cultures better than those who have not. College entrance examinations are unfortunately no exception. African Pygmies could doubtless devise tests that the children of suburbia would fail.

There are unfortunate ironies in all this. We know that within any population there is a wide range of variation in the genetic patterns underlying kinesthetic imagery, abstract mathematical reasoning, memory capacity, musical abilities, and so on. Races are statistically distinctive populations in terms of genetic frequency. Yet racism has often forced anthropologists into the biologically awkward position of denying that such genetic constellations could vary *between* populations as well as within them. They very well could, yet in the present social and political climate the question cannot be investigated as a purely biological issue. Any answers that emerged, in scientific terms, would probably not provide legitimate fuel for racist fires. They would not "prove" that one race is more intelligent or energetic or whatever: "intelligence" involves a number of very complex genetic systems, apparently, and each of the many elements of "intelligence" probably has its own patterns of statistical variation. Somehow people who begin with an idea that races are stratified in their biological capacities always assume that they belong to the top layer, and not the middle or the bottom.

The "superior civilization" that is supposed to show that Northern Europeans are genetically superior is mainly a cumulation of elements borrowed from "inferior" peoples—Middle Eastern, Chinese, African, and others. Moreover, the "superiority" supposed to be manifest in genetic patterns thousands of years old has somehow appeared only in the last few centuries: if we had observed the "races" in 1000 B.C. or A.D. 800, the "superior" Northern Europeans would have seemed a sorry and backward lot in comparison to their genetically underprivileged contemporaries in other parts of the world.

The racist conclusion for which scientific rationales are sought is that all human beings do not merit equal opportunities to express their genetic potentialities. Yet what is most striking about any human population is its resources of diversity. Every human population has its geniuses and its dolts. But virtually every member of every population has remarkable capacities to learn and use language and culture creatively. Given on the one hand these high common denominators of human ability and on the other the occurrence of both unusual talent and subnormality in every population, there can be no grounds for treating human populations as if they fell onto neatly graded shelves, with one's own group on the top shelf.

It is becoming increasingly clear that genetic and biochemical factors play a major part in shaping "temperament" or personality, and that every population contains a reservoir of great diversity in these genetic templates of personality. What this genetic raw material is shaped into, and how this diversity is utilized, are matters of cultural learning and social organization. We will return to these questions in §61. Here we will turn to that most unique of man's gifts, the one that enables him to transcend and mold his evolutionary heritage: Language.

IV *Language and Communication*

MAN'S UNIQUENESS in the animal kingdom, as we have seen, arises largely from his capacity to build and manipulate symbols. It is language, man's great symbolic code, that allows him to transcend so many of the limitations imposed by biology, to build cultural models of his world and transmit them across generations.

To learn about man and his nature, we must learn about language. This is not simply because language is what makes culture possible, and what makes man unique in nature. Language is also the keystone of culture itself: a largely unconscious but highly complex system of "rules" and designs whereby knowledge about the world and principles for action are coded. It is also the best explored and mapped segment of culture, and hence provides a set of crucial clues about how men think and perceive, and how what they know and believe is ordered.

In the sections to follow, both linguistic and nonlinguistic systems of communication will be placed in evolutionary perspective. We will glimpse in general outline the design of language structure that has been emerging in recent research. Then we will examine the articulation between language and other areas of culture, and the value and limitations of language as a model for the rest of culture. Finally, we will reconnoiter the path toward a broader understanding of communication, linguistic and nonlinguistic.

10 · Linguistic and Nonlinguistic Communication in Evolutionary Perspective

A social world where people communicated with one another only through language would be colorless and flat—like a place where people could only exchange typed messages with others they could not see. It is what we "say" to one another by physical appearance, expressions, gestures, tone of voice, and the way we arrange ourselves in space that adds rich dimensions to human social life. We not only send "linguistic messages" to one another, but we also exchange information about our internal states (what "mood" we are in), about our relationships to one another (are we hostile or friendly?), and about the way our linguistic messages or acts are to be interpreted (are we joking or serious, playing or fighting?). Such nonlinguistic communication is the very fabric of social life.

But it is language that makes us human. No other animal, as far as we know, has a code that enables it to "talk" about *things* in the world; no other has a code that *names* objects or events and makes propositions about them (Lancaster, 1968). Yet ethologists have discovered among many species communicational codes that convey information about the internal state of the animal, the relations between animals, or the way each other's "messages" are to be taken (how does a dog know whether another dog's biting is play or combat?). It is man's capacity to *name* things—to "symbol," as Leslie White puts it (1944)—that has made possible his great leap forward. Culture in all but the most rudimentary sense is impossible without the rich linguistic codes we used to build models of our world and to store and transmit across generations the cumulations of experience.

Many writers have speculated about the evolutionary development that led from a primate communications system to human language. Neurophysiological findings, summarized by Lancaster (1968), show that the ability to name and make propositions about things depends on brain structures found only in man. There seems little question that the enlargement of cortical areas of the brain in early hominids was associated with the development of language. Lancaster (1968) provocatively speculates that the early stage in language learning when a child uses a simple grammar of two "parts of speech" may replicate the earliest forms of protohuman language. The child uses a small set of key words that serve as grammatical operators, and an open class of labels for "things." Armed with such a simple grammar, Lancaster argues, early hominids would have been able to communicate about their environment in a way their predecessors could not, and would have been much more effectively adapted to a life as terrestrial hunters.

In language, unlike animal communications systems, the relationship between the sign and what it stands for is arbitrary. This relationship is not laid down in biological codes. Language, to use again Holloway's phrase (1969:395), entails "the imposition of arbitrary form upon the environment." Whether the word "cow" refers to four-legged beasts with hooves and udders, or to butterflies, houses, or celestial bodies, is a matter of arbitrary convention. There is no similarity between the beast and the sign. In the jargon of communications, most language signs are *non-iconic*: the sign is not modeled on the thing it stands for. Moreover, the message depends on whether features are present or absent, not on the degree or magnitude of some feature. Linguistically, a sentence is the same sentence whether it is whispered or shouted. It becomes a different sentence only when one or more relevant features are removed, added, or changed—as when a singular noun is pluralized.

The differences between language and other communications codes with evolutionarily old biological roots go beyond this ability to symbolize, to communicate about "things" with arbitrary, non-iconic signs. Only language rests squarely on social learning. Only language has a "duality of patterning" so that smaller building blocks (sounds) are combined into meaningful larger blocks (words) that can in turn be constructed into sentences. Men thus use *sequences of signs* in a way no animals do (though as this is written first reports have come in of chimpanzees learning to manipulate strings of signs). The duality of language patterning makes possible another crucial and distinguishing feature of human communication: its *productivity*. From a set of elements, speakers *create* messages, messages that may be new and unique, yet are implied in the code.

For each of these "design features" (Hockett, 1960) distinctive of human language, we can find fuzzy borderline cases or partial instances in the animal world. Moreover, as with every major evolutionary advance, the gap between language and nonlanguage must have been spanned by a gradation of transitional forms. Yet, despite these continuities, language as a total system is quite unlike the communications systems of other animals, and represents a major new evolutionary plateau.

But these evolutionary continuities should have made us more cautious in assuming that language, because it is evolutionarily new, has no genetically laid down roots. That infants must learn their language need not imply that they begin with blank slates. That symbols and linguistic rules are arbitrary does not rule out their being biologically limited and channeled. We will shortly see how these possibilities are being explored.

Recall the statement that a sentence is the same whether it is whispered or shouted. If this caused some discomfort for the reader, it was with good reason. For the total *message* we communicate to the listener by a whispered utterance is likely to be quite different from that communicated by the same sentence spoken or shouted. We, like chimpanzees, send a great amount of nonlinguistic information by means of vocalization—by volume, intonation, "tone of voice." A whispered sentence, and the spatial closeness of speaker and hearer that usually goes with it, communicate something about the relationship between speaker and hearer, and their relationship to others who are present. Recall that this is what animals communicate about most often: their relationships to one another and their emotional states.

And this is a crucial point. Two different mechanisms, and to some extent even different regions of the brain—one evolutionarily old and basic to animal communications, the other evolutionarily new and unique to human communications—are interwoven in the process of everyday message exchange between human beings. Language has not *replaced* older mechanisms; it has been added to them and interlinked with them. How this works remains a mystery. The evolutionary implications of these co-ordinate communications systems in man have been provocatively explored by Bateson:

> If . . . verbal language were in any sense an evolutionary replacement of [nonverbal] communication . . . we would expect the old, preponderantly iconic systems to have undergone conspicuous decay. Clearly they have not. . . . This separate burgeoning evolution [of nonverbal communication] alongside the evolution of verbal language indicates that our iconic communication serves functions totally different from those of language and . . . performs functions which verbal language is unsuited to perform. . . .
> It seems that the discourse of nonverbal communications is . . . concerned with matters of relationship—love, hate, respect, fear, dependency, etc.— . . . and that the nature of human society is such that falsification of this discourse rapidly becomes pathogenic. From an adaptive point of view, it is therefore important that this discourse be carried on by techniques which are relatively unconscious and only imperfectly subject to voluntary control (Bateson, 1968: 614–615).

Elsewhere, Bateson has explored more general implications of this iconic coding of cultural patterns. It now seems likely that many cultural patterns are coded and processed in evolutionarily old structures of the brain. These patterns are generally inaccessible to consciousness, and they may well turn out not to be describable in language, based as it is on a qualitatively different kind of coding. Bateson's explorations suggest that these deep and unconscious codings of culture deal not with things but with *relationships*, not with content but with pattern. Such codings of pattern and relationship not only underlie man's nonlinguistic communication; they may well also be reflected in many other facets of human behavior. Even the foundations of art—templates of symmetry and pattern, of rhythm and harmony, the bases of poetry and music and metaphor—may lie in these prelinguistic structures of the brain (Bateson, n.d.). We will return to this problem in §58.

Note that in man, as to some extent in other animals, these iconic modes of coding and processing are not concerned solely with information that is genetically laid down. In man, particularly, this coding is used to process information that is learned, and hence shaped by cultural convention. This is one reason why nonlinguistic communication in man is so difficult to study. The people being studied cannot talk about it well; neither can the observer, even if he grasps the patterns involved. Moreover, in this little understood interweaving of cultural learning and biological programming we are prone to overemphasize one or the other.

Thus ethologists like Eibl-Eibesfeldt (1970) look in man's expressions and gestures for evolutionarily old and biologically laid down patterns. But the evidence so far is meager, and there is a great temptation for a biologist to use it selectively. Anthropologists like Birdwhistell (1966) have probably gone too far in the other direction, in stressing culturally patterned variation in nonlinguistic communication. Certainly there are wide ranges of variation that no biological explanation could account for, but there is a growing probability that many gestures and expressions build on biological templates. Here the complex interplay of the old and the new, the biological and the cultural, will have to be unraveled in the years to come. Certainly there is no "natural" reason why a wave of the hand with palm forward is a gesture of farewell, a wave with palm backward is a gesture of beckoning: there is simply too much cultural variation. The person laughing in the back row at the movie while Hollywood Indians wave good-bye to one another is likely to be an anthropologist.

In evolutionary terms, language presents us with a paradox. Without it, developed culture and the elaborations and variability of human social life would be impossible. Yet if language were not augmented by the rich nonlinguistic communicational codes that in many ways resemble those of our animal cousins, our social lives would be drab and mechanical. At the same time, in man the arbitrariness of cultural convention has shaped our nonlinguistic codes as well.

The structure of language and the means for studying languages have provided modern cultural anthropology with crucial theoretical foundations and models. In the sections to follow, we will explore these theoretical foundations, the structure of languages, and the relations between language and other domains of culture. In §16, we will look more closely at non-linguistic communications and the possibilities of a broadened study of communication.

11 · Conceptual Problems for Studying Language

When we talk to one another, we accomplish a commonplace miracle: commonplace because we do it so effortlessly and so often; miraculous because *how* we do it remains largely a mystery, despite the frontal assaults of science.

Consider a few facets of what we do in speaking and understanding one another.

First, we do not simply produce and understand sentences we have heard before. We *create* sentences we have never heard, many of which have never been used by anyone before.

Second, deciphering the meaning of sentences we hear—something we accomplish almost instantly—is an immensely complex analytical feat. Consider the four English sentences below:

> They are buying glasses.
> They are drinking glasses.

> They are drinking beer.
> They are drinking companions.

Despite the outward similarities between the pairs, we can almost instantly perceive the radically different patterns of meaning they convey. Hearing "They are eating companions" (or "flying airplanes can be dangerous") we can perceive two possible underlying patterns of meaning.

Third, though the actual sounds of speech are unbroken continuous sequences, we hear them as strings of distinct "blocks" of sound. And though no two repetitions of the same word or sentence are acoustically the same, we perceive them as if they were.

Fourth, when we listen to speech sounds, we do not simply select from these sounds the elements and features that are relevant and discard the rest. We *create* the sentences we hear, out of imperfect sequences of sounds that are often incomplete or partly garbled. The listener reconstitutes the design of the sentence in his mind, even though he must fill in the missing pieces; and he can do that only by perceiving its structure.

Finally, a person's knowledge of his language, and the processes whereby he speaks and understands, are almost entirely hidden from his consciousness.

These facets of speaking and understanding profoundly shape the way linguists approach language. If linguists are to grasp and analyze how men achieve the commonplace miracle of speaking and understanding speech, they must probe beneath outward, observable behavior. They must postulate, for the speaker and listener, a *theory* of the language they share. Without postulating such an underlying cognitive (mental) code or theory in the minds of their subjects, linguists could analyze what speakers *did* say—but they could not account for what they *could* say. They could not account for the way a speaker *creates* sentences, many of which he has never heard; they could not account for our ability to decode complicated sentences so as to grasp their meaning; and they could not account for the way the listener creates a sentence design in his mind out of the muddled and often incomplete sounds he hears.

Every child learning his language must likewise use a limited and imperfect sample of speech by the adults he grows up with to arrive at a "theory" (hidden from his consciousness) of the code they are using. It is this theory, more or less shared by all speakers of a language, that linguists seek to describe. The contrast between actual speaking and underlying code was first clearly drawn by de Saussure (1916) in a distinction between *parole* ('speech') and *langue* ('language'): the first, actual speech behavior; the second, the code underlying it. More recently, Noam Chomsky has phrased this as a contrast between *performance* and *competence* (the underlying theory or code).

Competence is the knowledge of his language (which by definition the linguist can never observe directly) the speaker-hearer draws on to produce sentences and understand them. Performance is actual speech behavior—with its pauses, hemming and hawing, false starts, ungrammatical utterances, and endless variability. Here we will refer to this contrast as that between competence and performance; or, more generally, simply as the contrast between *language* (the conceptual code) and *speech* (its manifestation in actual behavior and sound).

Note at this stage that the distinction between language and speech parallels the one we drew in Chapter II between culture and behavior. Linguistic competence can be seen as one element of "cultural competence." To those who would argue (of speaking or other social behavior) that we should concentrate on observable behavior, and not postulate slippery and metaphysical-sounding mental codes as lying behind acts, the evidence from language is devastating (Chomsky, 1959).

Modern linguists have chosen as their primary goal the analysis of language, of linguistic competence. Speech behavior provides major evidence about linguistic competence, but so too do the intuitions of native speakers about the sentences of their language.

This does not mean that the linguist is uninterested in the behavior of speaking. One of the major current challenges to research is to incorporate a theory of linguistic competence *into* a wider theory of linguistic performance. Here the commonplace miracle of speaking poses unsolved mysteries: "At the present time, there are no theories of linguistic performance. Indeed, there is only the most fragmentary knowledge of the relevant parameters of such a theory . . ." (McNeill, 1970a: 1139; see also Bever, 1970, Hymes, n.d.).

How is the competence of speakers of a particular language to be described? The nature and design of a grammar have been heatedly debated for years. Linguistic journals are filled with controversy, often bitter, about basic principles and details. The anthropologist following these skirmishes and forays into new territory is hard-pressed to know which side to back. Yet it is clear that linguists have advanced—on a narrow front—much farther than anthropologists (partly because linguists have skirted around many of the hardest questions); and hence that anthropologists must continue to look to linguistics in search of models and methods for understanding man.

In the section to follow, our bets ride mainly on the presently dominant approach to language, transformational linguistics. But they are placed with the serious reservation that transformational linguistics is changing markedly and can best be viewed as a way station on the path to a more powerful and general theory (Hymes, n.d.). The mysteries of speaking—a miracle that most of us take for granted—loom large despite impressive progress. As we look in broad outline at language structure, a recent semiserious remark by a linguist exploring the frontier will give useful caution: "The life expectancy of a theory in linguistics is seventeen minutes, except late on Friday afternoons."

12 · *The Structure of Languages*

The transformational approach to linguistics burst upon the scene in 1957 with Noam Chomsky's book *Syntactic Structures*. For several decades linguists had been working inductively from the sound systems and grammatical arrangements of languages to try to discover their structure. Chomsky argued—and demonstrated mathematically—that currently accepted theories of language structure *could not* account for some of the major properties, processes, and constructions of languages. Chomsky, insisting that linguistic theories be formalized like mathematical systems (so that their powers and defects would come clearly into view), began to outline a more powerful approach to language structure.

In the years that have followed, Chomsky's first mapping of language structure has been redrawn and expanded many times. We can view the present state as a sort of third-generation transformational linguistics, one that is moving toward a fourth and fifth, whose design can only be guessed. Chomsky, his colleagues, and the younger transformational linguists who have followed and often challenged him are far from agreed on many issues.

They *are* basically agreed on the premises of their enterprise, on the fundamental questions and the strategies for attacking them. These can be briefly summed up:

1. The goal of a grammar is to describe formally the competence of a speaker (and hearer) of a language. By making all of the rules of language competence explicit, we can see precisely what the theory does and does not account for. The "speaker-hearer" whose competence is described is idealized, in the sense that he knows his language perfectly; hence his competence is a kind of ideal and hyperefficient composite of what actual speakers are inferred to know about their language.

2. Such a grammar must account for the creativity of language: for the sentences a speaker *could* use as well as those the linguist has actually recorded. Hence the native-speaker's intuitions about sentences proferred by the linguist, as tests of the grammar he is trying to devise, provide crucial evidence. (In fact transformational linguistics works best on the linguist's native language, so he is his own "informant.")

3. The rules of a grammar should link together the meaning (what we will call the "conceptual structure") expressed by a sentence and that sentence as a pattern of sounds. No links in the chain that connects conceptual structure to sound patterns should be left unspecified (a goal linguists are still far from attaining).

4. Any particular grammar should fall within a structural design common to all languages—a *universal grammar*. A primary goal of describing particular languages in terms of a universal grammatical model is to enrich our knowledge of language universals. We will return to this facet of transformational linguistics in §13.

The idea of a gulf between outer patterns of sound and inner patterns of meaning (or conceptual structure) is fundamental to modern transformational linguistics. Metaphorically, we can see a sentence as having an outer face and an inner face. The speaker begins with a conceptual structure and converts it to a pattern of sound; the hearer begins with a pattern of sound and must reconstitute the conceptual structure it expresses.

How meaning is assigned to sentences (the inner face) is the realm of *semantics*. How sentences are mapped into sounds (the outer face) is the realm of *phonology*. The rules that span the gulf between sentences in a form that can be interpreted semantically and the same sentences in a form that can be converted into sounds comprise the realm of *syntax*.

These syntactic rules are viewed by Chomsky (1965) as linking the "surface structure" of sentences with their underlying "deep structure." This can be illustrated by looking at two sentences:

John was eaten by cannibals.
John was drunk by midnight.

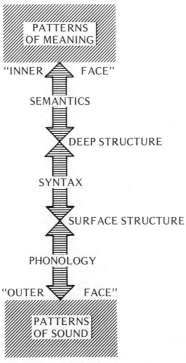

Figure 8. A Transformational Model of Language (schematic). The separation of semantic and phonological rules from the syntactic rules that connect them is not as clear-cut as the diagram might imply. Just how these interconnections are organized is not yet fully understood. RMK

In word order and apparent outward form the two sentences are very similar. Yet to interpret them correctly we must reconstruct the first sentence as expressing an underlying "Cannibals ate John," and analyze the second in a very different way. Syntactic rules specify formally the relationship between the deep structure and surface structure of sentences in a language. The realms of syntax, semantics, and phonology are schematically illustrated in Figure 8.

Syntactic structures were the focal point of Chomsky's attack on the linguistics of the 1950s. Thus the realm of syntax has been explored in considerable detail (though with far from complete success). In the last few years, phonology has been studied intensively as well, and the "outer face" of sentences is becoming fairly well understood. Semantics lags far behind, remaining in what a recent theorist described as a "hairy mess." That mess lies squarely in the anthropologist's path as he seeks to communicate across and about cultures. In the subsections to follow we will look first at syntax, then at phonology, and finally—very briefly—at semantics. We will then return to semantic problems, viewed from the anthropologist's side of the mess, in §14.

Syntax

In his original 1957 rethinking of linguistics, Chomsky thought of the rules of syntax in a special mathematical sense. They were to *generate* all the grammatical sentences of a language and none of the ungrammatical sentences. (This had nothing to do with whether the grammatical sentences had a sensible meaning: he proferred the now-famous sentence "Colorless green ideas sleep furiously.") Because of the creativity of language, these syntactic rules have to have a special property. Though the rules must be finite in number, they can "generate" an infinite number of possible sentences.

Those familiar with mathematics and the notion of "recursion" will understand what "generate" means here. An illustration of a kind of generative device is the Spirograph toy, which enables a child to draw a great variety of circular and oval designs by holding a pencil in a hole in a geared plastic disk and turning the disk around the gears of a second, larger, disk. In fact the disks and holes correspond to a set of mathematical ratios or formulas, which can be said to "generate" the designs.

Chomsky's formalization of syntactic rules begins with "S" for "sentence" and rewrites it as NP (noun phrase) plus Pred P (predicate phrase). Elements are then successively filled in as follows:

S → NP + Pred P
NP → Det + N
Pred P → Aux + VP

Such elements as "Det" (determiner), "Aux" (auxiliary), and VP (verb phrase) then are successively rewritten, as possible sentence designs are spun out like Spirograph patterns. (With the three rules given, one can already spin out the sentence pattern Det + N + Aux + VP.)

Here, Chomsky has been much misread. His *generative grammar*, in generating sentence designs, is not intended to represent the way a speaker produces sentences. (To Chomsky, that would deal with "performance," not "competence.") Obviously a speaker begins with something-to-say, not an "S" for "sentence." The linguist Lees has observed that transformational grammar is intended to generate the sentences in a language only in the sense that zoological theory is intended to generate all the kinds of animals that have existed. That is perhaps too extreme, but it usefully underlines the often misunderstood point that grammatical rules do not represent the way speakers produce sentences.

That said, we can look at the primary problem in syntax: how the underlying designs of sentences are linked to their outward form—that is, how "deep structure" and "surface structure" are systematically related. (Recall "John was eaten by cannibals" and "John was drunk by midnight.")

The kinds of rewrite rules (S → NP + Pred P) we have glimpsed produce the basic designs or "deep structure" of sentences. The abstract derivation of a sentence ("The boy pushed the ball.") can look like this:

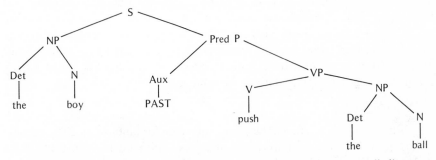

Though we have put actual words on the bottom of the "tree" diagram, one might better think of these deep levels of syntax as producing a large number of *designs* of sentences, rather than actual sentences. The same abstract skeleton or design may underlie a great many different sentences: "The cat ate the rat," "The plumber fixed the pipe," and so on. Moreover, these sentence designs are very different from actual sentences in word order, agreement, and so on, and contain many grammatical markers and complex symbols, like PAST for a past-tense marker.

These syntactic rules not only generate such sentence designs; they also link them together in complex constructions. By *conjoining* two sentence designs, one can produce the framework of a sentence like "The big boy chased the kite and the small boy pushed the ball." By *embedding* one within another, one can produce more complex designs, like that underlying "The boy whose father works with mine pushed the ball I found yesterday."

The deep structure representation of a sentence makes possible an interpretation of its meaning (though as we will see it is far from clear yet how this is achieved). But there remains a wide gap between the deep structure of a sentence and its surface representation. First of all, the special conventions of a language with regard to word order, agreement, and other features must be applied (so that for the sentence diagrammed on page 67, "PAST + push" must be converted to "pushed").

Second, a sentence ("The cannibals ate John," represented as The + cannibal + PL + PAST + eat + John) can be rearranged to express a passive ("John was eaten by cannibals"), a negative ("The cannibals did not eat John"), a question ("Did the cannibals eat John?"), and such complicated forms as "Hadn't John been eaten by cannibals?" Note that while the change to passive does not alter the deep structure, the negative and question forms modify the deep structure and hence the meaning.

The rules that rearrange and modify the strings of deep structure in these ways are called *transformational*. Transformational rules differ from regular rewrite rules in that they operate on whole strings and rearrange or modify them (whereas rules like Pred P → Aux + VP take a single element and expand it).

Some of the transformational rules of a language are mandatory (like the one that converts PAST + push). Others are optional (like the one that turns "The cannibals ate John" into a passive). Successively applied to the deep structure representation of sentences, they convert sentences into their surface form, which needs then to be translated into sound. Some of them (transformations for negatives, questions, and the like) also modify the deep structure representations of sentences.

Phonology

Phonology is a crucial facet of language for anthropologists because it has provided several important analogies and models—some of which anthropologists must now discard.

The best place to start, in understanding how sentence designs are cloaked with sound, is with the noise-producing equipment man can use to transmit linguistic signals. The mouth is a sound chamber. To differentiate signals, sounds of different acoustical frequencies must be produced. By moving the tongue and lips, causing the vocal cords to vibrate or not, opening or closing the nasal passages, and obstructing the flow of air through the chamber in different ways, a speaker can produce distinctive patterns of sound.

The vocal cords, which act as "resonators," are turned on in normal speaking and turned off when we whisper. But even in normal speaking they go on and off. They are vibrated for a "d" and are not vibrated for a "t" (which is otherwise formed in the same way). That is, "d" is *voiced* (as in "din") and "t" is *unvoiced* (as in "tin"). The same contrast is used to differentiate "goal" from "coal," "zoo" from "sue," "bin" from "pin," and "van" from "fan."

The nasal passage, which acts as an auxiliary resonating chamber, can be opened or closed, allowing us to distinguish "m" from "b" ("mat" versus "bat"), "n" from "d," and "ng" from "g" (as in "tang" versus "tag").

Vowels are produced by passing air through the vocal chamber. They are distinguished from one another by the movement of the tongue in two dimensions—up and down, and front and back. They can also be distinguished as "rounded" (with the lips rounded, as in "o" and "u") and "unrounded." Each form of articulation concentrates sound in a particular frequency range.

Consonants impede the flow of air by breaking it (stops, like "t" and "d") or impeding it so as to produce sounds through turbulence (fricatives, like "s" and "th"). These are technically defined by the point of articulation—bilabial (with the lips), or dental or alveolar (the palate, behind the teeth), or velar (the back of the palate, as in "k" and "g"), or some combination (such as labiodental, with lips and teeth, as with "f").

To understand how phonological systems work, we must keep foremost in mind that what matters most is not what sounds are used in a language. What matters are *contrasts between sounds*. For actual sounds vary continuously, blending imperceptibly into one another, and one instance of a word is never precisely like another. Yet we treat sounds as though they fell into neat, separate compartments. We apparently do so on the basis of *distinctive features*. Distinctive features are either-or contrasts: voiced or unvoiced, nasal or non-nasal, high or low, tense or lax, aspirated (with a puff of air, as with "p" in *pin*) or unaspirated, stop or fricative, and so on. Roman Jakobson, Morris Halle, and others have argued that distinctive features are always binary (either-or). By the intersection of a set of distinctive features, the "sound compartments" of a particular language are uniquely defined. Each contrast between "words" (except two words that are phonetically identical, like *pair* and *pear*) reflects at least one contrasting feature.

For years linguists have treated these separate compartments of sound, known as *phonemes*, as the elementary units of a language. They were, for any particular language, like a chemist's table of elements: from them were put together, according to that language's special rules of combination, the compounds that carried meaning. Linguists worked out "discovery procedures" for beginning on a new language (where one could never tell what contrasts between sounds would turn out to be distinctive) and finding out what phonemes were its basic elements. One began with a *phonetic* transcription that could distinguish all the contrasts in sound that *might* make a difference. Then one winnowed out all those contrasts that turned out not to matter, thus moving to a *phonemic* transcription.

If there was any solidly established linguistic principle, it was the central importance of phonemes. Anthropologists looked enviously at these units the linguists had found, as they rummaged through the messy data of cultures looking for equally neat, separate, compartments that expressed the uniqueness of a particular way of life. As we will see, American anthropologists have borrowed heavily in recent years from this mode of linguistic analysis—seeking ways to discover the unique structure of a culture and the features it treats as distinctive in carving up the world of experience (§14).

Yet modern transformational linguistics places the phoneme in jeopardy as a central unit of language. What had been treated as a separate (and primary) *level* of language is now seen as a stage in a process, connected to syntactic rules in complicated linkages.

Rather than treating phonemes as a separate level, one can regard the surface structure representation of sentences as containing packages of information about sound. This information apparently is coded in terms of distinctive features, but not strictly speaking in terms of phonemes. The phonological rules of a language fill in a great deal of the necessary information about the sound of words on the basis of regularities in sound patterns. Thus if the second sound in a word (say, "stack") is an unvoiced stop, the information that the first sound is also unvoiced is redundant in English; there is a quite regular rule in English that any fricative at the beginning of a word, followed by an unvoiced stop, must be unvoiced. A cycle of such rules fills in all predictable blanks.

Other phonological rules shift, delete, and rearrange patterns of sound, and assign stress patterns. Such rules deal with the syntactic structure of the string of words, not the individual words themselves. Thus the word "stack" is pronounced differently in "Put it on the stack behind the barn," and "Shall I put it on the stack?" This difference is determined by the syntactic design of the sentence: the intonation contours would be the same if we substituted "box" for "stack" in each sentence. Still other phonological rules assign sound patterns to grammatical markers like PAST and PLURAL. English phonological rules for pluralization, for example, must assign a voiced fricative to "bed*s*," an unvoiced fricative to "ship*s*," and a vowel and fricative to "horse*s*."

Precisely how phonological rules work is still a matter of exploration and controversy, spurred by Chomsky and Halle's major study of *The Sound Patterns of English* (1968). Here, as elsewhere in linguistics, what had in the 1950s been accepted as solidly established theory is open to reexploration, controversy, and rethinking.

Semantics

The most difficult link to analyze, in the chain between ideas and sounds, is that of "meanings": that inner face where the deep structure of a sentence must be mapped onto a conceptual structure—that is, assigned a meaning.

One of the elements of a speaker's linguistic knowledge must include a *lexicon,* in effect a kind of mental dictionary. Like a dictionary, this must include information about what each word "means," and also some information about its sound-shape (how it is pronounced). It also must include information about what "part of speech" the word is—that is, which slots in sentence designs it can fit into.

But how does a "mental dictionary" represent the meanings of words? This is an exceedingly difficult problem. The possibility that distinctive features are used to contrast *meanings,* as well as *sounds,* has been extensively explored. The multiple senses of a single word have suggested a kind of hierarchical, treatment in which semantic features appear at different levels, as with Katz and Postal's suggested scheme for "bachelor" in English (1964):

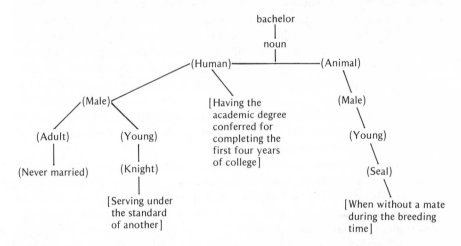

Others have struggled with the way different "senses" of a word like "bachelor" have different grammatical functions. (This is more clear for "table": you move a table and table a motion.) Some linguists have suggested that the problem can best be solved by treating each "sense" of the "same word" as a separate lexicon entry. Here linguists are facing a problem that pervades the study of language and of culture more generally. Our methods for analyzing structure are most efficient at dealing with phenomena in sequences of steps—at treating features, or rules, or processes, one at a time. Yet men's equipment for perceiving and thinking seems to operate in terms of the simultaneous *relationship between* features as patterns. An analogy may be useful. When a witness sees a bank robber, he perceives the robber's face and appearance as total patterns of features. Yet when a police artist tries to draw a composite picture of the robber, the witness must pick out nose, eyebrows, mouth, chin, and so on, one after another. Recognizing meanings probably depends partly on the same kinds of mental processes as recognizing faces; yet linguists and anthropologists are forced to pull features apart, as do the witness and police artist, and treat them one at a time. We will return to this problem in semantics in §14.

The same kind of problem may underlie many of the difficulties in formalizing a grammar in sequences of rules. The way we actually create and understand sentences may depend on perceiving total patterns, as well as performing sequences of analytical steps (Bever, 1970). This may partly account for a gulf between a transformational grammar of language competence and the psychological processes of speaking and understanding that is beginning to emerge in psycholinguistic research.

Such a contrast between psychological processes and our formal models may also underlie the difficulties on another side of the "hairy mess" of semantic theory: how the meanings of individual words are shaped and transformed by the syntactic design of the sentence in which they occur. For the meaning of a sentence is not simply the summing up of the meaning of the individual words in it—a problem those who have sought to devise ways of translating Russian and Chinese by machine are grimly aware of. How these meanings are joined and shaped by their place within a syntactic design is a question guiding much current research, but so far there are few clear answers.

The "third-generation" of transformational linguistics (being pioneered by scholars like Lakoff, Ross, and McCawley) has turned its focus toward the "inner face" of language—the face where meaning is assigned to sentences. Whether there is a separate "deep structure" representation of a sentence to which meaning can be assigned (as argued by Chomsky, 1965) has been thrown in serious doubt. Rather, semantic rules and syntactic rules may be woven together in ways much more complex than Chomsky's exploratory mappings had suggested.

This usefully underlines the provisional and rapidly changing character of modern grammatical descriptions. In a field where theories are obsolete by the time they reach print, the anthropologist may look in vain for solid foundations like the "good old phoneme" on which to erect his models and analogies. But the questions being asked are larger and more exciting than they used to be, and we will shortly see more clearly how important to the anthropologist the tentative answers may be.

13 · Linguistic Universals

How diverse are human languages? Does each have a unique design, or are they all variations on the same design? Are there linguistic features that predictably go together, so if a language has one it has the other?

Such questions remained in the background for many years. Scholars studying languages outside our own Indo-European family, especially American Indian languages, were struck by how different and diverse these languages were. These scholars showed how we distorted the structure of such languages by looking at them in the mold of Latin or English. Linguists uncovered patterns of sound, and ways of building "words" and ordering sentences, that were radically different from those familiar in European languages.

But in recent years the trend has moved in the other direction. Linguists have been asking different questions: Given the whole range of ways human beings *could* communicate by making noises, what portion do they actually use? How does a child, hearing a jumble of noises, devise a theory of his language? And what would he already have to "know" to be able to do it? In short, the emphasis has turned to a quest for *linguistic universals.*

We can begin by distinguishing two kinds of universals, "substantive" and "formal." A "substantive" universal would be a particular "thing" all languages have: a part of speech like a verb, a particular rule, a particular distinctive feature. A "formal" universal is some element of language design that each language fills in with a distinctive content. Thus a lexicon, transformational rules, and phonological rules would be formal universals according to transformational theory, as "phonemes" and "morphemes" would be in the older descriptive linguistics.

Evidence for substantive universals has come mainly from two directions. First, linguists like Greenberg (1963, 1966) have searched through many grammars looking for recurrent features and patterns. Greenberg has explored statistically the potential universality of such features as parts of speech, looking for combinations of features that predictably go together (so that if a language has feature X, it will have feature Y). He argues, for example that a mode of binary contrast where one feature is "marked" and the contrasting one is "unmarked" is used again and again in languages in semantics, phonology, and syntax. The notion here is that one of the contrasting pair (the unmarked one) is dominant; so that in some contexts the contrast is "neutralized" and the marked feature gives way to the unmarked. (An English example is "long" [unmarked] versus "short" [marked]— we ask "How long is it?"; not "How short is it?") The status of such universals is discussed in Greenberg (1963).

A second source of substantive universals has been the theory of distinctive features in phonology, particularly in the work of Jakobson and Halle. Recall their theory that there is a fairly limited set of possible distinctive features of contrast between sounds, out of which any particular language uses a particular subset. Though the theory is controversial, both in its emphasis on universals and its exclusive use of binary contrasts, it has been widely accepted. Further, it has led scholars like Chomsky to argue that there probably is a universal set of semantic distinctive features but that we have not yet found it.

Each major theory of language structure advances its own categories of formal universals. Transformationalists have made particularly clear their models of language design and have emphasized the universal structure that underlies the particularities of each language. Chomsky (1965, 1966) argues that the rules producing "deep structure" in every language are the same or very similar. There is, in short, a *universal grammar* underlying the distinctive patterns of each language. The appearance of diversity, he argues, is created by the transformational rules that convert deep structure into surface structure (and are different for every language), and by the varying phonological features and rules that flesh out the universal skeletons of language with very different shapes.

Chomsky then returns to a question that is of utmost importance in understanding man—his evolution, his nature, and his cultures (Chomsky, 1968). Is a human infant a "blank slate" who must build a theory of his language from the noises he hears? Or is he born with an abstract model of language "programmed" in his brain, so that learning his language requires him to fill in this design with the peculiarities of the speech he hears? The assumption that the infant begins with a more or less blank slate underlies most of twentieth-century linguistics. Furthermore, with regard to learning culture generally, anthropologists have almost all assumed a blank slate consisting of *capacities* (to manipulate and associate symbols) but no built-in design of cultural structure and content.

In arguing that man's capacity for language is genetically programmed, Chomsky has exploded a bombshell in social science—and it is too early to predict the outcome. But he has some very strong arguments on his side with regard to linguistic competence. He argues that from the sounds a child hears he would not be able to devise a theory with the right overall design unless he already "knew" what he was looking for. How is it that a small child is able to learn the complex structure of his language when linguists armed with mathematics and computers are just beginning to decipher these complexities? If it were merely a matter of going from noises to theory, surely the linguist would have an advantage over the child! Furthermore, if it were a matter of building a theory from scratch, some children would be able to do it well, others would have worse theories, and the less bright would not learn to talk at all. Yet all children of anywhere near normal intelligence acquire competence in the speaking patterns of their group almost automatically: which strongly suggests that they already *have* it, but simply need to learn about the particular language spoken around them (see McNeill, 1966). Chomsky argues, then, that at birth a child *knows language*— but he does not know *a* language. In childhood he can apply his general theory and learn several languages if he samples enough of each. Later, apparently, our general model of language becomes so fused with the particularities of our native language that learning French or German becomes a conscious struggle (and we are likely to end up with an English model of French, not a French one). Finally, if the structures of languages were *created* by men rather than biologically channeled, they would be far more diverse than they are. The outlines of a universal grammar, and many of its details, are coming clearly into view. There is little doubt that languages are far more similar in their basic structure than linguists had thought.

We have barely begun to explore the implications of an innately specified language design for genetics, neurophysiology, and evolution. Eric Lenneberg's pioneering work in this field has put together what little we know and what possibilities seem open (1967), but this frontier remains largely unmapped. At first glance the theory of innate specification may seem more radical in biological terms than in fact it is. For across the animal kingdom, organisms acquire the preponderance of their communicative codes not through learning but through genetic programming. To assume that the structure of languages is entirely a matter of cultural creation and must be learned anew by each infant, would in fact separate language from animal communications codes by a far wider gulf than would the Chomskyan "innatist" position.

The most recent research, at the time of writing, suggests that the outlines of the universal language design are indeed genetically programmed, but that an extreme "innatist" position that the *specific rules* of a universal grammar are genetically laid down may go too far. First of all, language learning is part of an overall unfolding of cognitive development. Many of the details of linguistic design may reflect innately laid down ways of discovering, organizing, and coding that a child uses to make sense of the phenomenal world—of which speech sounds are only one part—and to operate in it. What is genetically programmed, then, may be more general and abstract than the specific rules of "deep structure" uncovered by linguists seeking universals of grammar. That points toward the possibility of a universal *cultural* design, partly innately laid down—a possibility to which we will return in §22 and §60. Second, it suggests that linguistic competence (and more generally, cultural competence) can best be thought of as the result of an unfolding *process*—of an interaction between rules and patterns programmed in the mind and the world of experience to which they are applied. (Here Bever, 1970, and McNeill, 1970b, assess the possibilities; see also Moltz, 1965).

The answer probably lies somewhere in between the most extreme "learned" and "innate" positions, but much farther on the "innate" side than most students of man have for years even been prepared to speculate. Just where it lies is a major challenge to linguistics, psychology, neurophysiology, genetics, and evolutionary biology. The cultural anthropologist will find the emerging answers to these questions crucial in the years to come.

14 · *Language and Culture*

What is the relationship between language and culture? This old question acquires a new look in the light of modern cultural theory. For if language is the conceptual code underlying speech, and culture is the conceptual code underlying social behavior, language clearly is *part of* culture. One can now ask in what ways language is similar to, different from, or a source of clues about, the *rest* of culture.

When we talk about "a language" or "a culture," we confront the difficulty we can call *code variability*. Your theory for speaking English (as well as the way you actually speak, which is not the same thing) is different from everyone else's. Your theory for shaking hands—how, when, and with whom—is not the same as everyone else's. Furthermore, there are things you probably do not know about electrical wiring, pole vaulting, and nuclear physics that are part of our language and culture. How, then, can we speak of "the English language" or "American culture" as a common code? The same problem confronts us when we talk of Hopi Indian language or Hopi culture.

Linguists manage the problem by talking about *dialects* (of regions and social classes) and finally *idiolects*, the special versions of a language characteristic of each speaker. For most purposes, it has been useful to focus on the common features of the code that all speakers share, and to ignore dialect and idiolect variations. "English" (or "German") is thus an abstract model of what is common to its speakers (though it may not correspond to all versions). It is also a composite, since it includes the special vocabularies of electrician, pole vaulter, and physicist. In addition, the edges of "French" and "German" are not sharp: French blends into Italian, and German into Dutch, along country borders. But linguists have found it conceptually useful to ignore the "marginal speaker" most of the time.

For many purposes the cultural anthropologist can usefully follow the simplifying assumptions linguists make about code variability. He can speak of "Hopi culture," ignoring code variation and messy cultural borders, and lumping together the knowledge of Hopi wife, Hopi artisan, and Hopi priest. But there are problems lurking here, as we will shortly see.

An important approach to the borders between language and the rest of culture has come in recent years from American anthropologists much influenced by linguistics (notably Goodenough, Frake, and Conklin). The world of things and events, through the eyes of another people, is most clearly mirrored in the categories of their language. How a people class animals, birds, plants, or winds may be quite different from the way we do it. Thus the Kwaio of the Solomon Islands label fresh water as one substance, salt water as another; they place birds and bats in one category, in contrast to moths, butterflies, and the like; they class fish and marine mammals together; and they label with a single term most colors we could call blue and black. Are they bad primitive "scientists"? Not at all. Rather, just as a language can use different kinds of sound contrast (nasalized versus nonnasalized, rounded versus unrounded), so a culture can use different features to distinguish between categories. Our categories are not right, and theirs wrong—they simply use different contrasts to carve up the world of meaning. What looks like bad science may reflect failure of the Western observer to understand another people's underlying premises about classifying. Upon discovering in an ornithology book that the large green parrot and the large yellow-and-blue parrot which Kwaio label with different terms are in fact male and female of the same species, I confronted my Kwaio friends with this striking discovery. "Of course," they shrugged, wondering why I didn't know that all along.

Systems of folk classification are often highly complicated and elaborated. Conklin, for example, found that the Hanunóo of the Philippines have more than 1800 distinct "species" labels for the plants on their environment, while Western botanists class them into less than 1300 species (Conklin, 1962). Though people elaborate *folk taxonomies* in focal areas of cultural importance (so that Eskimos can make very fine distinctions about snow and snow conditions), they also classify endlessly phenomena that are of very little concern in their daily lives. Man, apparently, is an incurable and compulsive classifier (Lévi-Strauss, 1962; see §58).

Study of such folk conceptual systems has come to be called *ethnoscience*. The hope of such studies is that we can penetrate the conceptual world of a people through analysis of their linguistic categories. This has spurred greater interest in semantics.

An early hope was that lexical categories could be defined by the intersection of distinctive features, as in phonology. Thus *componential analysis* seeks to define a set of words that contrast with one another (a "contrast set") in terms of a set of intersecting features. Thus we might define "chair," "couch," "stool," and "bench" in terms of three dimensions—seating capacity, padding, and backrest.

A. *Seating capacity*
    A_1 single   "chair" A_1C_1
    A_2 multiple
B. *Padding*
    B_1 upholstered   "stool" A_1C_2
    B_2 bare   "couch" A_2B_1
C. *Backrest*
    C_1 present   "bench" A_2B_2
    C_2 absent

There are a number of problems in such an approach. First, the choice of dimensions is often quite arbitrary, so there are often dozens of possible solutions. Many English speakers probably use shape (round versus square) to distinguish stools from benches and chairs. Especially in dealing with another culture, there is little assurance that the analyst's distinctive features mean anything to the people he is studying. No convincing sets of universal semantic features (like those of phonology) have been advanced; and since there are a great many things in the world people could treat as distinctive, in contrast to the few ways they can make noises, we probably can expect none (except in the most physiologically restricted areas like color perception; Berlin and Kay, 1969).

Second, a distinctive-feature approach classes things by what they are not, paying most attention to semantic *boundaries*. Yet increasing evidence suggests that we class things by what they are, not simply by the outer boundaries of categories. It is impossible to produce an intuitively convincing distinctive-feature definition of a weed (in contrast to a flower), a dog, or a chair (in contrast to the other objects in a room). The intersection of features seems far too simple a model to deal with the human ability to *recognize patterns*. As suggested by our earlier analogy of the witness to a bank robbery, we instantly perceive the *relations between* a great many features as forming a coherent and recognizable pattern. Thus we perceive a pattern of "dogness," whether the dog is large or small, black or white, barks or does not, wags tail or has none, has four legs visible or none, and so on.

How pattern recognition works and what coding of knowledge and mental logic make it possible, are a mystery and a challenge. Communications engineers and neurophysiologists are struggling with it on both a theoretical and practical level. The commonplace human ability to read handwriting—most of the time—defies the efforts of science to design scanners so that written materials can be fed into computers (though with printed material the problem is partly manageable). We can recognize our friends from patterns of features when their backs are turned or they are partly obscured from view; but to "teach" a computer to do that, or even to recognize individuals (say, from videotape) when their features are in full front view, is extraordinarily difficult. It suggests that we are working with a logic different from that of the human mind—one which is too clumsy at expressing relationships. We will return to this problem shortly. But from a standpoint of semantics, it seems very likely that the way we associate patterns of sounds, in contexts, with "meanings" is at least partly based on the same capacities for pattern recognition that we use in visual perception. If so, it is no wonder that our attempts to define meanings formally fall short of the mark.

The most intriguing and influential formulation of how language and the rest of culture interrelate is the "Whorfian hypothesis." Benjamin Lee Whorf, an insurance executive for whom linguistics was an avocation, produced a series of papers based mainly on his research on the Hopi Indian language (published in Whorf, 1956). He argued that the European languages embody not only ways of speaking about the world; they embody a *model of* that world. Contrasting "Standard Average European" with Hopi, he sought to show how our ideas of "thingness" are shaped by the grammatical treatment of nouns, and how our model of time as past, present, and future—ticking past like an endless belt—reflects the tense system of our language. Hopi concepts of time and space, as built into their language structure, represent a different model of the universe—a model, Whorf argues, that should make the theory of relativity more intuitively meaningful to a Hopi than a European.

This powerful and plausible hypothesis has been pursued by other writers as well, notably Dorothy Lee. She drew on data from Wintu Indian and Trobriand (Melanesian) languages to distinguish between "lineal and non-lineal codifications of reality" and other linguistically structured contrasts in world view (see §58, especially Ex. 65 [1]).

The hypothesis has been tested extensively, yet the results have consistently been ambiguous. This is partly because, like a jellyfish, it is hard to get hold of—you grab it and it slithers somewhere else. Does Whorf mean that it is the grammatical framework that structures thought? How can you find out, because both are in that realm of ideas which is by definition unobservable? You can get at language structure only through speech and can get at thought only through speech (or introspection). This imposes both a circularity and a consistent impression that the "test" is missing Whorf's point. The hypothesis remains largely impregnable because it has been untestable.

The Whorfian hypothesis has been eroded more by the shifting tides of intellectual fashion and the waves of linguistic theory than by empirical disproof. The Whorfian thesis is a somewhat etheral expression of a conviction that languages and cultures are unique—that "the worlds in which different societies live are distinct worlds, not merely the same world with different labels attached" (Sapir, 1929). If our focus is on how different men are, how diverse their conceptual worlds and how variable their cultures, then the Whorfian thesis is both an expression and a partial explanation of that diversity.

Yet in recent years both anthropologists and linguists, having taken for granted a great variation in the content of custom and the details of language, have focused increasingly on how similar languages and cultures are. A quest for universals and similarities in basic design and underlying structure became in the 1960s both fashionable and theoretically necessary. Chomsky, as we have seen, argues that the deepest structures of syntax and the basic linguistic design are the same in all languages; and that the kind of linguistic features Whorf used to illustrate the contrasts between European and Hopi reflect differences in "surface structure." They imply differences not in thought but in ways of expressing the same thoughts. If this were not so, it would seem impossible to move between different linguistic codes the way some bilinguals can—as with the "simultaneous translation" used in the United Nations.

Further erosion has come from evidence and increasing conviction that thinking and manipulating language are not ultimately the same thing. To interpret Whorf as trying to find *correlations* between linguistic structures and modes of thinking is inevitably misleading; rather, he saw linguistic categories

---

[1] Examples, set off from the body of the text, begin in Chapter VI and are scattered throughout subsequent chapters. They are consecutively numbered, for ease of cross-referencing. A list of examples, giving the page number for each, follows the Table of Contents.

and classes as the units or vehicles of thinking itself. Since these linguistic elements are organized into grammatical systems, so the organization of thought must inevitably mirror this structure. Yet the basic assumption that the elements of perception and thought are the elements of language now seems tenuous and misleading at best. We should not reject Whorf's ideas out of hand. They are among the most powerful partial truths of the century, and they make us vividly aware of variability on a level where many do not expect it. But whether that level represents the depths of thought or simply linguistic conventions for expressing thought is much in doubt.

15 · Linguistic Models and Cultural Anthropology

These glimpses of language structure enable us to reinforce considerably the conceptual position set out in Chapter II. It is worth summing up at the outset some of the major insights about the study of culture we can draw from linguistics:

1. A distinction between ideational code and its enactment in behavior, such as we drew in defining "culture," finds strong support in linguistics. The linguists' distinction between language, as a conceptual code, and speech (*langue* versus *parole*, competence versus performance) has proven so powerful conceptually that we can make a similar one with considerable confidence.
2. We will need to study the cultural code (even though it cannot be directly observed), not simply the patterning of behavior, because
    a. Codes are finite, while behavior is creative and potentially infinite in variability. Without a code theory we cannot account for the creativity of behavior, for what may happen next as well as what has already happened.
    b. Codes have sharp edges and neat rules, while behavior has fuzzy edges and only statistical regularities. Without knowing the code we cannot tell which things, acts, and events a people treat as the same and which they treat as different. The psychological code imposes sharp edges and even creates perceptual patterns that do not exist "out there."
    c. Without knowing the code we cannot anticipate how people will react to new objects and situations.
3. The "rules" of cultural codes, like the rules of language, are mainly unconscious. At least we cannot expect people to be able to tell us what their "rules" are. The ideologies and rules of thumb men do talk about may or may not correspond to the rules they use to navigate in the world.
4. The overall design of all cultures, like the design of all languages, is likely to be similar. We know little so far about what that structure is like, but the design of the whole code may be somewhat similar to

the design of the segment linguists have explored. We can expect cultures to vary greatly in content and particular rules (though we might hope for such things as universal distinctive features).

5. If Chomsky is right about built-in language design and the acquisition of language, the general outlines of cultural design my be partly or largely "built-in."

6. We can use linguistic variability as a guide for studying code variability in cultures. At times we can assume "Hopi culture" is a single system, ignoring variation and fuzzy boundaries. At other times we can use the equivalent of dialect (*subculture*) and idiolect (*personal culture*) to talk about code variation.

7. The transformationalist emphasis on syntax, on how the elements of language structure are built into larger designs, can usefully point our attention toward the "syntactic" rules for constructing behavioral sequences. We continually produce behavior sequences, as well as sentences, that we have never experienced before, building new combinations of familiar elements. Where most attention in anthropology has been directed to the "phonology" of concepts and categories, we can now start exploring the "syntax" of action.

8. Finally, transformational linguistics has all but demolished the hope for systematic *discovery procedures*, ways of going from the observable "facts" (what people say and do) to a theory of the ideational code that underlies "facts" without making leaps of guesswork and intuition. The emphasis has shifted from how systematically we arrived at a theory to whether or not it *works*—and that has come to depend heavily on whether it accounts for the intuitions of the people under study.

Though language is unquestionably a crucial source of evidence about the rest of culture and how we can study it, some modern theorists have gone farther than seems justified in taking linguistic structure as a model for the rest of culture.

There are three main shortcomings in using linguistic analysis as a dominant model for studying culture. The first and most important set of problems comes not because language is different from the rest of culture, but because linguists have pushed aside many facets of language as outside their concern.

Most linguists have not analyzed *what* people will say in particular situations, only the set of rules that link meanings with sound patterns. Yet the anthropologist's problems center on the part the linguist takes as given— the system of knowledge, belief, assumption, and convention that produces particular ideas at particular times. He is concerned with social contexts, with a world of cultural meanings. He is concerned with "things to say" more than he is concerned with devices for turning them into sounds. This is not to say that the processes whereby we organize and formulate ideas are unrelated to the processes whereby we turn them into patterns of sound. But *how* they are related is a matter for exploration, not simple assumption.

Linguists have made other simplifying assumptions that the anthropologist can scarcely afford to follow. Chomsky, searching for a universal design of languages of which French, Chinese, and Hopi are all expressions, can well afford to ignore the differences between the grammars of two different Frenchmen. But many of the anthropologist's problems lie on precisely this level. Not only are there diverse versions of French or Hopi culture; we all have code *repertoires*, and we can move from one to another (colloquial to formal, for instance). This all means that code variability and what it communicates *are part of the code*. Finally, the linguistic competence of different people in the same society is clearly not the same, in terms of the wider social and cultural setting—as witness the child from an American ghetto whose dialect and limited code repertoire restrict his social opportunity. All this suggests that understanding of code variability, in linguistic and cultural terms, will be a major challenge in the years to come.

A second set of limitations of language as a model for the rest of culture reflects a problem we have already seen in discussing human communications in evolutionary perspective. For language carries only part of the rich communication on which human social life depends. Nonlinguistic communication is crucial, even in understanding the meanings of the sentences we exchange in language. "I feel just great" may mean what it "says" or just the opposite. We are able to interpret it correctly because the speaker labels it as sarcastic or "true." But this labeling is by expression, gesture, intonation, or red eyes; it is not part of the sentence. "You old son of a bitch" *may* be dire insult or friendly camaraderie among age-mates. The grammar of English does not tell us what it means.

Moreover, as we have seen in §10, much of our cultural knowledge may be coded and organized in ways quite different from the coding of language; and many segments of cultural knowledge may not be accessible to exploration and description through the medium of language.

This problem brings to light an important vulnerability of transformational linguistics that suggests anthropologists must be careful in using its models as windows on the human mind. Though some linguists are cautious in making the assumption that their formalizations reflect the way the mind actually works, their strategies of inference often seem based on this assumption. They seek, as it were, to find out how our knowledge would have to be organized in order for us to do what we do, by using models of logic and mathematics.

Yet, as we have suggested, the formal languages of logic and mathematics we now command seem too clumsy at expressing relationship and total patterns to account for the psychological processes of perceiving and thinking. The same inadequacy emerges in neurophysiological research which increasingly raises doubts that such logico-mathematical models could correspond to the actual operation of the human brain: ". . . The whole logical pattern of the nervous system seems to depart in many significant ways from the conventional procedures in mathematical logic. . . . It seems that the language of the brain is much 'simpler' than any we have been able to devise so far" (Singh, 1966: 183, 327). Rather than discovering the structure of language from mathematical formulations, we may end up having to invent mathematical systems to replicate our ways of thinking and perceiving: "Discovery of this primary logico-mathematical language actually used by the neural net, the living brain, is the next major advance that still awaits its Newton and Gauss" (Singh, 1966: 324).

16 · Communication: A Wider Perspective

The limitations of linguistic models as means for understanding culture and social behavior point up a need for a wider study of *communication*. How communication can best be studied, and what a science of communication might look like, are still far from clear. But some of the questions we will want to ask, and some tentative explorations of them, are beginning to emerge.

Studying communication would shift our attention to *messages*, not simply the sentences of language. Messages are conveyed not only by language but by gesture, expression, tone of voice, and arrangement in space. Much of our communication is not about "the world" but about our internal states and our relationships with one another—recall that these are the main areas where animal communications are elaborated. Many messages tell us how other messages are to be interpreted—whether they are "true," "serious," "joking," "threatening," and so on. A pioneer in this field, Gregory Bateson, calls these second-order messages-about-messages, "metacommunication." By metacommunication, we put "frames" around messages that tell us how they are to be interpreted (recall "you old son of a bitch" in the last section). Bateson has argued that such framing, evolutionarily at least as old as mammalian play, reaches new and important complexity in man (Bateson, 1955). Paradoxes in which the "framing" messages contradict the messages within the frame are basic to this process. Animals biting one another but at the same time framing or labeling it as "just play" show the simplest form of such contradiction: the bite is not what it seems to be. But in man, art, fantasy, symbolism, and ritual develop these paradoxes more fully. Consider the multiple frames of metacommunication in an Ingmar Bergman film. The events on the screen are not going on in the world, but are projected film images—a first-order fiction all movies share. But unlike the newsreel that may have preceded it, the Bergman film is "fictional" in a second-order sense. Yet the scenes portrayed in the film are not simply what they seem to be: the clock on which the camera lingered may be a metaphor of time, or of impending death. Several further layerings of symbolism, each involving new frames and further paradoxes, may exist. And finally, there is a framing so that trying to interpret the symbolism becomes a game between

Bergman and the viewer, a game that continues among the viewers when the lights go on and the other frames are dissolved.

Much of the richness of cultural structure lies in such framing of contexts. Our ability to participate in the events of our cultural world and understand what is going on depends not so much on knowing what will happen next—we often do not know that—as on knowing the right frames. The ethnographer living temporarily in a different cultural world has only gone half way when he understands a strange language and strange customs. The harder half is knowing when to laugh. And if he learns that and the other framings of the culture, you are not likely to read about them in his book. Like the wings of a butterfly, they yield better to poetry than to science.

The rich codes of nonlinguistic communication are much more difficult to study than those of language, but some progress is being made by such pioneers as Birdwhistell, Hall, and Bateson. Hall, in his study of the way cultures use physical space to communicate about social relationships, brings to consciousness many patterns we normally take for granted. Americans surround themselves with a kind of envelope of private space, a sort of invisible plastic bag. This space is normally inviolate in our everyday interaction. Try, for instance, in talking to people, to move gradually closer and closer to them; you will find them retreating to preserve their envelopes intact. Only in a few contexts, such as lovemaking and contact sports, do we invade one another's envelopes. Even in a crowded bus or subway, when our envelopes get all squished together, we go to considerable lengths to affirm to one another that we are not really invading private space; we depersonalize the close physical encounters by staring into space, reading tabloid newspapers, and so on.

Birdwhistell has made remarkable observations about the use of body movement and gesture in different cultures (1966). If common biological templates underlie human codes for gesture and expression, they are radically modified by cultural conventions. In a remarkable film taken in zoos around the world, for instance, Birdwhistell recorded dramatic similarities in the way Frenchmen "communicate" with a particular kind of animal in contrast to Chinese or other zoo-goers. Here cultures not only pattern the nonverbal "languages" used in everyday communication, but even shape their extension to as unfamiliar a situation as relating to animals.

A science of human communication will have to deal with messages, not simply the sentences of language; and it will have to explore rich and subtle nonlinguistic codes as well as those of language. But is a concentration on *codes*, on the cognitive "theories" that underlie behavior, enough? Hymes (n.d.) in particular has argued that it is not. If we want to understand how humans *select* and *create* messages—not simply how they encode them—we need to look at contexts and social relationships as well.

Not only are the messages we exchange by speech and gesture dependent on the social situation; the very code, or version of the code, we use may depend on social factors. Three examples will illustrate. To use the Javanese language in a particular situation, a speaker must choose one of three levels or styles of speech—a "lowest" (and most rough and informal), a "highest" (or most formal and elegant), or a middle level. There are also ways to make the lowest style even lower and the highest even higher. What levels a speaker of Javanese knows will depend on his social class, but each speaker will have some repertoire to choose from. His choice depends not only on his status but also on that of the person spoken to, the relationship between them, and the situation. A single sentence illustrated by Geertz (1960)—"Are you going to eat rice and cassava now?"—is so completely transformed when spoken on different levels in Javanese that only one word—the one for cassava—is the same on both the highest and lowest levels. Even more radical code switching occurs in Paraguay. Guarani, an Indian language, has remained the dominant language of the people. Yet Spanish is the official language and is used in government, schools, and commerce; and more than half of the Paraguayans are bilingual in Spanish and Guarani. They use Spanish in formal social relationships, official business, and to express respect; and they use Guarani with friends and relatives, in making love, and in talking with status inferiors (Rubin, 1968). The assumption that one language code corresponds to one culture, and one cultural code corresponds to one social system, has been a convenient simplification. But Sorensen's study of multiple codes among Indians in the Northern Amazon shows even more dramatically that it is an assumption we will have to abandon. Here more than twenty-five "tribes" speak distinct languages, though many aspects of culture are uniform through the area. However, since a man "belongs to" his father's tribe but must take a wife from a different tribe, his mother and his father come from tribes speaking different languages. An individual normally knows both his father's code and his mother's code, and most individuals learn two or three other languages as well. The social organization is based on assumptions of code diversity (Sorensen, 1967).

To say that alternative codes or repertoires are still part of "cultural competence" will hardly suffice. For in these societies—or in any complex society—individuals have widely divergent cultural codes or versions of codes. The *distribution* of code versions and the social organization in which they are distributed become crucial.

An emerging science of human communication must thus widen its frame beyond the concerns of grammatical theory. It will have to be a study of messages, not simply sentences; of nonlinguistic as will as linguistic communications; and of contexts and networks as well as codes. Moreover, the largely iconic communication of expression, gesture, and intonation in man can only be understood in terms of the similarly iconic codes of animal communication; and that means, in turn, that a science of human communication will have to be placed within a wider evolutionary perspective.

This underlines the emergence, across the frontiers of science, of new modes of describing complex systems in the language of communications— in terms of *messages, redundancy, information, feedback, circuits,* and so on. Here cybernetics and general systems theory are beginning to provide a unifying language of science and the foundations for a general theory of communication or *semiotics.* Such a general theory had first been envisioned by de Saussure in 1916; but it now seems that a general science of communication could unite the study of biological and social systems in a way de Saussure could scarcely have imagined:

> . . . It is amply clear even now that the genetic code must be regarded as the most fundamental of all semiotic networks and therefore as the prototype for all other signalling systems used by animals, including man. From this point of view, molecules that are quantum systems, acting as stable physical information carriers, zoosemiotic [animal communications] systems, and, finally, cultural systems, comprehending language, constitute a natural sequel of stages of ever more complex energy levels in a single universal evolution. It is possible, therefore, to describe language as well as living systems from a unified cybernetic standpoint. While this is perhaps no more than a useful analogy at present, hopefully providing insight if not yet new information, a mutual appreciation of genetics, animal communication studies, and linguistics may lead to a full understanding of the dynamics of semiosis, and this may, in the last analysis, turn out to be no less than the definition of life (Sebeok, 1968: 12).

Here we have wandered beyond the frontiers of the known. As we examine the social systems and ideational worlds of men in comparative perspective in later chapters, we will stay within the frontiers most of the time; to do otherwise would obscure the many insights the findings of anthropology can reveal. But we will venture to the frontiers when it is important to do so—when to stay within the bounds of present knowledge would disguise the fact that what anthropologists know and understand about man shrinks in comparison to what they do not know.

Looking at language takes us a long step forward in understanding the nature of man and human social life. We see what is evolutionarily a new mode of organizing experience and communicating about it; and we see more clearly the nature of the ideational codes that pattern human behavior—what we call "culture." Nonlinguistic codes, growing from old evolutionary roots, are revealing as well, but they suggest how much more remains hidden.

Here, we return to the past—the distant past. We will see in the archaeological record of early men and the emergence of modern life the way language enabled man to cumulate very slowly a new kind of knowledge, and new modes of organization.

V   The Growth of
Culture

MAN'S LONG time span on earth—perhaps a million years since *Homo erectus* first evolved—has seen an infinitesimally slow development of culture slowly accelerating, then speeding, and finally in the last century expanding at a runaway pace. In this long record, students of the human past seek both to unravel specific strands of connection and development in regional settings, and to step back to view the sweep of human development in more general perspective.

Though man's fascination with origins and with the development and spread of customs is old, his ability to learn about his past with a measure of control and precision is new—and still rapidly developing. Sweeping attempts to understand how man's customs evolved, which occupied armchair theorists in the latter nineteenth century (§67), and later efforts to reconstruct world history from the present distribution of customs (§69), have given way to prehistoric *archaeology* as a means to understand the human past.

In the sections to follow, we will note the kinds of evidence archaeologists can use to shed light on the past; we will very briefly examine the main sequences and stages of cultural development; and we will glimpse in preliminary fashion the peoples of the Americas, Africa, Asia, and the Pacific in the "ethnographic present," the time when Europeans first intruded on the scene.

17 · Available Evidence on the Distant Past

The archaeologist who seeks to reconstruct a way of life long vanished faces a formidable task of detective work. The clues are likely to be meager: the objects people made from materials durable enough to survive; fishbones or shells that reveal what they ate; postholes or hearths that, with their arrangements in space, may yield clues to settlement patterns; special materials whose outside origin can be traced; and perhaps the smooth patina on a cutting edge that yields clues about what it was used for.

Fortunately the modern archaeologist has at his disposal some powerful scientific tools. Without them his clues would be too sparse to narrow the range of possibility much. Radioactivity of organic matter permits radiocarbon datings; analyses of pollen or soil or rocks may yield clues about datings, spatial relationships, and the climate and physical environment. Specialists in other fields identify animal bones, use infrared photography, analyze substances chemically or spectrographically, and apply all the power of physical science to make the most of these sparse clues to the past.

By building up from these clues and the technical evidence they make possible, an archaeologist can often go amazingly far toward reconstructing a way of life far in the past. But is it enough to start from the clues and work up? Recently archaeologists have begun to perceive the potential added power of beginning with a theory and working "down." Instead of discovering an old living site and analyzing the clues found there to reconstruct the mode of life of its inhabitants, we might better begin with an overall environment (or "ecosystem"—see Chapter VII). Beginning with theories about how men adapt to an environment and how it shapes their social lives, we could infer where key settlements would have been and what sorts of evidence might illuminate past life in this setting. By using theory to guide the search for evidence, we can test the theories; and the sites studied become, by their nature, pieces in a wider puzzle.

The theory-minded archaeologist is predisposed by the evidence he has to work with to focus on the material rather than the ideational side of human life. The side of culture he can best reconstruct is a mode of adaptation to the physical environment—tools, settlement patterns, subsistence economy. Of the rich ideational dimensions of human life he can at best find a few leavings in the form of pottery decorations, carvings, rock paintings, or the like. Consider the possibility that Australian Aborigines had died out (perhaps due to new diseases spreading from Asia) several centuries before Europeans arrived there. Apart from a few cave paintings and other art forms, our only record of these peoples would have been a meager collection of stone tools, temporary campsites, and an occasional record of long occupation. We could have made useful inferences about settlement patterns. We could find evidence of a pattern of gleaning wild foods and hunting kangaroos and other animals; but even wooden boomerangs and spear-throwers would probably have disintegrated beyond recognition, along with sacred objects and bark paintings.

Yet because Europeans found living Aborigines, and because some in the Central Desert and remote Arnhem Land survived the first onslaught of "civilization," we know that their way of life was anything but simple. Australians devised systems of kinship and marriage so intricate and elaborate that modern scientists armed with high-powered mathematics and computers have not been able to decipher all of them—no matter how diligently these Stone Age puzzle-builders tried to diagram them in the sand. And their cosmological and mythological systems are so rich, complicated, and symbolically sophisticated that years of study have not fully penetrated them. These riches the Australians carried in their heads, not their hardware; we know about them only because we could do ethnography of the living. But even here, theoretically minded archaeologists are looking for new ways to glimpse men's social arrangements and ideational worlds in the leavings of the past.

Whether we should give theoretical primacy to man's ideational worlds and social conventions, or to the way he evolves ways of life adaptive to his environment and technology, is an important, old, and still unresolved question in cultural anthropology. We will encounter it at a number of points in the chapters to follow, especially in §28. An archaeologist's evidence leaves him little choice: if his theories focused on the ideational side of human life, he would be a very frustrated detective.

At this stage we can briefly sketch the long and infinitesimally slow development of culture and its acceleration in the last few thousand years. Here we will make no effort to go into detail. There are now many books that explore the intricacies of prehistory. Rather, our aim will be to place the range of cultural variations that anthropologists have studied among modern non-Western peoples in a wider perspective of cultural development, and to sketch the processes of cultural change over long time spans.

18 · *Man as Hunter and Gatherer*

For perhaps as long as a million years, early men used crude tools to enable them to compete with, and hunt successfully, the animals that shared their environments. The stone that provided their cutting and chopping tools was also highly durable and has survived over great time spans to provide crucial evidence on early technology.

The vast period when tools were chipped from stone, lasting until roughly the last ten thousand years, is called Paleolithic—"Old Stone Age." Note the possible confusion with "Pleistocene," which refers to a geological period—a confusion enhanced by division of each into "Lower," "Middle," and "Upper." Here we will try to minimize this potential confusion.

If we return now to the australopithecines, we can begin to see the tremendous conservatism in human technology over vast time spans. Crude Oldowan choppers and flakes like those made by the dimwitted australopithecines some two million years ago were still used well over a million years later by *Homo erectus* in the Choukoutien caves—though probably augmented by more sophisticated tools of bone and wood. Not until some half a million years ago had *Homo erectus* in Europe developed a markedly more sophisticated stone technology.

In other respects, as we saw in Chapter III, *Homo erectus* was a more advanced creature in his cultural organization than the australopithecines. In the Choukoutien caves he left evidence of fire and of hunts for large animals that required more organization and intelligence than the australopithecines could have mustered. His prey included elephants, bison, horses, camels, wild boars, rhinos, saber-toothed tigers, and cave bears, along with the deer that were his most frequent victims. The organizational side of hunting these large animals is crucial here and must have imposed considerable selective pressure for higher intelligence. *Homo erectus* doubtless armed himself with wooden spears, and did not subdue saber-toothed tigers with his bare hands; but the choppers that were his primary stone tools were useful mainly in skinning and carving animals, not killing them. With such dramatic hunting, we should not overlook the collecting of wild

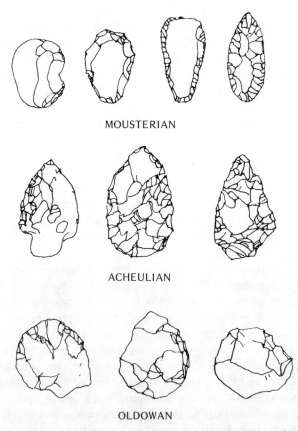

MOUSTERIAN

ACHEULIAN

OLDOWAN

Figure 9. Paleolithic Tool Kits. From bottom to top, these three sets of tools illustrate major stages in the early refinement of stoneworking techniques. RMK

fruits and berries, grubs, and other unspectacular foods that probably were essential in his diet.

By half a million years ago, *Homo erectus* had, at least in Europe, replaced the crude choppers with more sophisticated tools. These included flake tools and, most characteristically, hand axes formed by striking flakes off a core, which is given a crude but effective cutting edge and shaped sides. These hand-axe-dominated stone tool traditions, steadily but very slowly refined, have been classified in great detail; they are the main evidence we have of the men who lived in Europe over the long time span of some 200,000 years or more between the last fossil finds of *Homo erectus* and the Neanderthals. That these stone (and bone and presumably wood) technologies were "simple" and tremendously conservative does not mean that they required little skill. Making stone tools is a difficult and delicate art at which only a few modern men—mostly prehistorians—have become proficient. But the process of experimentation and innovation seems to have been very, very slow.

The later hand axes, of an industry technically called "Acheulian," show the beginnings of greater sophistication and presumably of increasing brainpower applied to technological problems. By 150,000 years ago or before, early men had acquired a technique of creating long, straight, sharp edges on a flint core. This was done by tapping off small flakes according to a planned pattern. Increasingly, from this point onward, we find diversity in the human tool kit. And we see evidence of men perceiving in an unworked piece of stone a finished tool into which it could be systematically transformed. Unfortunately, we know as yet almost nothing else about the men who made them, except by interpolating between what we know of *Homo erectus* and what we know of the Neanderthal men that next come on the scene.

The earliest Neanderthal populations in Europe have been dated back as far as 110,000 years. In this early period, their tools continued the earlier hand-axe industries. By about 75,000 years ago, however, Neanderthal populations had developed a more sophisticated complex of hardware. Central here was a stone industry called "Mousterian." Here more specialized core and flake tools appear in abundance—sometimes in puzzling "tool kits" where one level will be dominated by scrapers, another with borers and knives, and another with saw-edged and notching tools. One of the advances in stoneworking here was the manufacture of prepared cores from which a series of flake tools of the desired shape could be struck—an important first step in the direction of Henry Ford's assembly line.

What is more important, we begin to get a more vivid picture of how these early men lived. Neanderthals in Europe, first of all, mastered a range of environmental conditions from a mild interglacial climate to a late period of glaciation when perpetual winter closed in. In the mild early period, we see Neanderthal man using core and flake stone tools, bone points, and sharpened animal ribs to hunt a wide range of large and small game, especially horses and deer. He presumably also relied extensively on gathering wild foods. As the weather got colder, he moved into caves and relied heavily on fire, which by now was well under human control. Reindeer, ibex, and chamois became increasingly important, and presumably fewer wild vegetable foods could be gleaned. There is evidence that he could build fairly elaborate dwellings when that was feasible.

There are important signs of religious rites and esthetic concern in Neanderthal sites. Burials show evidence of ritual treatment of the dead, and other possible signs of religious cults come from arrays of cave bear skulls. Finally, there are a few objects from Neanderthal sites that most probably served esthetic, not utilitarian, ends. Clearly, by this time early human cultural horizons had expanded greatly.

The diversity of Neanderthal populations in their hardware and ecological adaptation emerges more and more strikingly from the record. We see by now a creature much more numerous than his forebears, much better able to use his technology to adapt to the challenge of a new environment than *Homo erectus*—who presumably to a large extent had to move to follow the game animals and flora on which his subsistence depended. From the earliest tools of a hunting australopithecine, hominids had used objects as extensions of their physical equipment—so too do chimpanzees, in a limited way. But in the Neanderthal population, we first glimpse dramatically how cultural traditions mediate betwen man and environment and begin to give him a new control over his world.

Some 35,000 to 40,000 years ago, hunters armed with a more complex technology, and fully modern biologically, took the stage. New techniques of working stone are immediately apparent and serve to define the "Upper Paleolithic." Instead of knocking off flakes by percussion, man developed a much more controlled method for removing chips, even down to tiny size: *pressure flaking*. A bone or hardwood tool, pressed with skill against the stone matrix, will flake out even delicate and intricately shaped artifacts, as with arrowheads or Solutrean leaf points and long flat blades. Near the end of this period a *pecking and grinding* technique was developed by which stone which does not fracture well could be shaped out, even if the surface was left more or less roughly pitted. The tool kit often became greatly elaborated.

The Upper Paleolithic is also marked by great elaboration of bonework, especially in the late European technology called "Magdalenian." Among bone artifacts were borers and projectile points, including an important new invention, the harpoon, with a detachable head, often barbed; spear-throwers to add force to projectiles; needles and toggles (for buttoning), indicative of clothing; carved figurines; necklaces and other bodily ornaments; and a perforated "baton" of unknown use. Many ethnologists hypothesize that these bone industries of the European Upper Paleolithic are reflected in the circumpolar traditions of bonework still so important to groups scattered along northernmost Asia, and on into the Eskimo zones of North America.

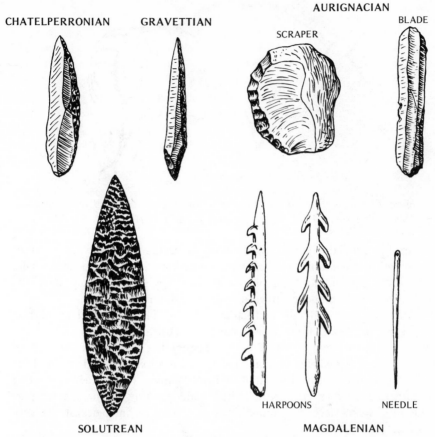

Figure 10. Typical Artifacts of the Upper Paleolithic. Chatelperronian and Gravettian points; Aurignacian pressure flaking and blade; Solutrean laurel-leaf point; Magdalenian bonework. FMK

Animal remains in their refuse dumps indicate the great reliance of these people upon larger cold-weather mammals: among them the reindeer, the wooly mammoth, the European bison, the wild horse. Here there was considerable regional variation. Fishing was also a source of food. The food quest is also the main theme of the well-known "cave art" traditions so much publicized since the first "galleries" came to light in southern France and northern Spain in the 1860s. From early and mostly crude gravings in outline on objects and on cave walls, these visual representations became elaborated in the later Upper Paleolithic into often realistic sculptures and cave paintings. Judged by our art standards (we know nothing except by inference of the standards of these early peoples), these traditions represent a first great efflorescence of esthetic creativity. Representations of animals, and the much less frequent and cruder representations of men, probably reflect religious beliefs, especially hunting and fertility magic. It must be noted that

Figure 11. Bison Pierced by Weapons. Niaux cave in the Pyrenees, a Magdalenian site. (After Cartailhac and Breuil.) FMK

such art has limited regional distribution. It occurs selectively in parts of Europe and in some form (for example, bone carving) through north Asia. Most Upper Paleolithic traditions—and they are found widely over the world—show little tendency toward artistic elaboration.

Man has been a hunter and gatherer for by far the largest proportion of his span on earth. Even if we leave the australopithecines out of the picture, less than one percent of human history has involved knowledge of agriculture. Our knowledge of man's social organization and mode of life over this period is necessarily inferential and speculative. Even modern hunting and gathering peoples give us a limited understanding of the greater part of this time span, since they represent accelerating technologies at the very end of the Paleolithic:

> In the last few thousand years before agriculture, both hunting and gathering became much more complex. This final adaptation, including the use of products of river and sea and the grinding and cooking of otherwise inedible seeds and nuts, was worldwide, laid the basis for the discovery of agriculture, and was much more effective and diversified than the previously existing hunting and gathering adaptations (Washburn and Lancaster, 1968: 295).

We can infer from modern hunting and gathering societies, archaeological remains, and the necessities of collective hunting of large animals that the basic social unit at this level of technology was the *band*. At times, when game animals were particularly abundant, larger and more complex social groupings may have emerged. Just how bands were organized in terms of size, composition, marriage patterns, and the like, over the longer spans of time, remains a matter of guesswork. We will see in Chapter VII how modern bands are organized, and will glimpse some of the ways they are adaptive to ecological pressures.

At this stage, let us return to the chronological record to see the accelerating pace of technological advance.

Figure 12. Engraving of a Mammoth. One of fourteen in the Grotte des Combarelles, a Magdalenian site. (After Capitan and Breuil.) FMK

19 · Man as Food Producer

With the slow retreat of the cold belt northward and the resulting migration of the large mammals adjusted to such a habitat, regional ways of life appear to have become considerably diversified. In the European area, what has been classified as the "Mesolithic" is marked by a number of cultural traditions to which special names are given, such as the Maglemosian in northern Europe, the Tardenoisian in middle Europe, and the Azilian in southwest France.

Childe and other archaeologists have described in great detail the Maglemosian hunters and fisherfolk. In the wake of the ice, much of northern Europe and Asia became a great forested and lake-flooded zone in which these new adaptations were worked out. A heavy, picklike tool suggests the importance of wild root plants in their subsistence. Shore and lake areas provided fishing. In waterlogged zones of western Europe, built-up mounds apparently make the most satisfactory living sites, judging from their numbers. With a favorable conjunction of fish or game and seasonal wild plants, a permanent village might be built up.

Similar diversity in subsistence economy developed in the Middle East, as the decline of the last glacial brought a warmer and drier climate. It was in Middle Eastern communities with economies of mixed hunting and gathering that the basic innovations leading to agriculture and domesticated animals were worked out.

As early evidence about the origin of agriculture began to come in, anthropologists spoke of the "food producing revolution" that brought man into a new mode of life. This implied a sharp break in technology, a burst of innovations and discoveries leading to radical change. More modern perspectives show the origin of food producing to have been less sudden revolution than very slow evolution. Processes that had begun during the Upper Paleolithic enabled "Mesolithic" communities to cumulate over many centuries the innovations that in the end led to agriculture and domestication of animals.

One important development late in the Upper Paleolithic was *specialized hunting*—a concentration on particular species of game animals. The reindeer seems to have been particularly amenable to being used, as one writer puts it, as a "walking larder." In the Middle East, Natufian populations of the Levant (what is now Israel) specialized in hunting gazelles; and in the Zagros Mountains of Iraq and Iran, goats were the target of specialized hunting (though in both places vegetable foods were crucial in subsistence). In such hunting patterns lay keys to later domestication of animals.

Another crucial development was the gathering in the "hilly flanks" of the Middle East of wild grains such as barley and einkorn. Here is where the approaches to agriculture turn up vividly in early sites. At Shanidar Cave, for instance, by the ninth millenium B.C. weapons for hunting herds of wild goats are augmented by slotted reaping-knives for wild grains. The Natufians, dated at around 8000 B.C., harvested wild grains, as we can infer from sickles with sheen still on the edges, and pestles and mortars for grinding. They worked stone by pecking and grinding, and used bone harpoons, awls, needles, and beads. They had the bow and arrow, as indicated by stone points. The dog, apparently domesticated, was already an associate of man. Natural rainfall enabled the grain crops to grow in quantity, so that hamlets or villages could be permanent. The sickles of such grain users were sometimes arcs of stone with a pressure-flaked inner edge. Alternatively, a wood or bone handle might have set in it a row of sharp, toothlike flakes of stone. Such small flakes, called *microliths*, were used in arrows, in sickles and knives, and probably in other implements, including a razor.

The transition to agriculture came with no earth-shaking overnight discoveries or radical shift in style of life. Rather, at about the same time in the Levant, the Zagros Mountains, and Anatolia, this diversified mode of life was modified by shadings of degree until wild cereals were sown and improved by breeding. At Jarmo, in what is now northern Iraq, an early mode of agricultural life has been dated at about 6750 B.C. Besides sickles and other indications of grain cultivation, this site yielded houses of substantial construction made of sun-dried mud; bones of apparently domesticated cattle, sheep, goats and pigs; pottery; and stone "spindle whorls" indicative of weaving. In the Levant, early communities have been excavated, including Jericho, where in the period 7000 B.C. to 6000 B.C. wild grains had probably been domesticated and had begun to make possible sedentary modes of life. Several of these food producing communities lie on top of

Natufian sites, making clear the continuity in these ways of life—not dramatic "revolution." Some archaeologists have suggested that early Jericho and some other permanent communities of this early period may in fact still have depended on gathering abundant wild grains.

By 6000 B.C., pottery had come on the scene and was being used for containers and cooking vessels. The settled communities, clusters of houses made from sun-dried brick, still depended on stone tools and on many things made with them. Pottery developed rapidly, and local patterns of manufacture and decoration flourished and spread. To illustrate, by around 6000 B.C. at Catal Hüyük in Southern Anatolia, a settlement some 32 acres in area reveals a large and stable population. Cultivated cereals included barley, einkorn, emmer, and bread wheat (early versions of modern cereal crops). Sheep, goats, and dogs were domesticated. Yet wild ox, wild pig, and red deer were hunted to augment the diet. The inhabitants lived in rectangular houses separated by courtyards. Houses were rebuilt many times over long periods. Access to houses was through openings in the roofs. Flint, greenstone, and obsidian polished tools were used, in addition to those of antler and bone. The polished obsidian mirrors found at Catal Hüyük were presumably an early reflection of female vanity. Woolen textiles were used for clothing, and apparently for wall hangings. Reliefs and paintings richly decorated some rooms, suggesting family shrines. Carved figures of bulls, rams, and leopards suggest elaborate symbolic systems.

The technological level of these early food producing communities is called "Neolithic" (New Stone Age). This reflects the use of ground or polished stone tools. While that is an important advance in toolmaking, it is obviously a far less crucial transformation than food producing. Moreover, the development of metallurgy in the Middle East followed fairly closely on the heels of agriculture and permitted further refinements in hardware.

But the development of culture is not principally a matter of hardware, but of patterns of resource exploitation and the transformations of social organization they make possible. If in the Paleolithic archaeologists seem morbidly interested in stone tools, it is largely because they have so few other clues to what they would really like to know about: population sizes, spatial distribution and mobility, the division of labor, subsistence patterns, and so on. By the time man reaches the "Neolithic," the label is still a convenient shorthand but archaeologists need no longer focus on hardware, especially on stone.

At this point, it is worth backtracking to consider developments in the New World. American Indians unquestionably came from Asia across the Bering Straits, though precisely when and why remains unclear. Those who argue for an early date—15,000 to 40,000 years ago—have produced no unequivocal evidence, and arguments on this score have gone on for years.

We know that in the period around 10,000 B.C., big game hunters with a technological complex related to Siberian peoples of the same period were occupying the plateau area of northwest North America and the High Plains east of the Rockies. We do not know whether an earlier population had already been in the Americas, having come through the northern route during a temporary period of warmer climate. If so, they left just enough clues lying about to titillate the imagination and so far to frustrate all attempts at solid proof.

In any case, the Americas north and south were occupied in the following several thousand years, with local adaptations to new environments and changing climates. Thus, for instance, a desert culture developed in the arid Great Basin west of the Rockies, with an emphasis on hunting small animals and gathering wild vegetables foods. In the wooded area of eastern North America, hunting of large animals became augmented by gathering plant foods and shellfish. The archaic culture of the east resembles in many ways the Mesolithic development of Northern Europe, which was undergoing similar environmental changes. Dogs were domesticated, antler and bone were used for tools, polished stone came into use, and local copper was used for weapons. Trade was widespread, as in the European Mesolithic.

Agriculture apparently developed in Mesoamerica independently of its Old World origin. Though evidence of possible later contact crops up, the whole series of parallel developments in the Old and New Worlds—agriculture, urbanization, and their consequences—pose a continuing challenge to theoretical interpretation by prehistorians. For even the high civilizations of Mesoamerica were constrained by the absence of innovations that would probably have spread from the Old World had contacts been profound: the plough, the wheel, and systems of writing (though there are limited American innovations that provide partial equivalents to writing). Moreover, the cultivated plants on which the Mesoamerican development was based are all native to the New World, not the Old.

As in the Middle East, domestication of plants was a gradual process, not a sudden revolution; it did not occur in only one place; and it did not involve only a single plant species. By far the most important in a complex that also included squash and beans was maize ('corn'). The study of the domestication and development of maize is a triumph of detective work. Geneticists and ethnobotanists, notably Paul Mangelsdorf of Harvard, have worked to reconstruct the genetics of wild precursors of maize, even though such forms have been replaced by domesticated forms. Archaeologists, working in the valleys of Mexico, have worked back through successive stratigraphic levels finding smaller and earlier carbonized maize heads, enabling morphological comparison and radiocarbon dating.

In the Techuacan Valley of Central Mexico, wild maize was being gathered systematically by at least 5200 B.C. By 3400 B.C. the first signs of domestication had appeared. Maize was only one of several domesticates, along with beans and squash. There is some evidence for their domestication earlier than maize, perhaps as early as 7000–6000 B.C. Productivity of the cultivated forms was low, and the inhabitants still lived in caves and open camps and relied heavily on hunting and gathering wild plants. Eventually plant breeding gave rise to more productive varieties, and settled life became possible. By the second millenium B.C., village communities were well established, and pottery began to be made. This pattern, which spread into the American Southwest and probably Southeast, gave rise to the civilizations of Mesoamerica and to elaborated ways of life in parts of North America. It is probable that in a second and tropical area root crops— notably manioc—were domesticated. The sweet potato, also an American domesticate, was spread by Spanish and Portuguese into South Asia and Africa and probably spread by direct contacts into Polynesia.

Another sequence of Neolithic development, for which our evidence is much less complete, occurred in South Asia. Until very recently, pre-historians knew that a separate complex of plants and animals had been domesticated in Asia; but because of the late appearance of food producing in China, it was assumed that the seminal ideas came from the West. But if the first datings from recently excavated sites in Thailand hold up, this view will have to be radically changed. In one cave site, seeds of peas, beans, water chestnuts and cucumbers have been found, along with stone tools; and the first datings suggest they may be as old as 9700 B.C. Datings for bronze and the domestication of rice are also being pushed back by the Thailand finds. The world's first farmers may well have lived in Southeast Asia.

In any case, the full development of the Southeast Asia Neolithic produced a complex of crops (rice, taro, and yams, a starchy tuber un-related to the sweet potato) and domesticated animals (pigs and chickens) that was to be crucial in the spread of the Neolithic into tropical regions of the Old World. The possibility remains open that Africa may also have been a center in the domestication of tropical root crops.

Let us step back now and look in worldwide perspective. The critical innovations of Neolithic technology in the Middle East, Southeast Asia, and Mesoamerica had established the foundations for the development of civilization. In these "heartland" areas, environmental conditions provided a maximum range of flexibility in subsistence and maximum possibilities for innovation. As this new complex diffused into other areas, only a few innovations could provide successful new modes of adaptation. In tropical rain forests of Africa, Asia, South America and the Pacific, agriculture could become crucially important. The trick was to use decaying vegetable matter and ashes from cleared forest to create fertile land for a single crop, then to let it revert to jungle (see §27). Domesticated animals could augment subsistence, but not provide it, in these tropical settings. In deserts, grassy steppes, or arctic tundra, agriculture was of little use. But domestication and herding of animals could become even more important than in the early Middle Eastern communities, and specialized to these environments (§27).

So the Neolithic complex gave a strong upwards push toward civilization in the "heartland" areas, but also a strong sideways push out into the Paleolithic world. Most of the Americas, much of Africa, most of the Pacific, and many pockets in Asia and areas of the far north remained essentially Neolithic in technology (despite the spread of metalworking into Africa and Southeast Asia). They remained correspondingly "tribal" in their modes of social organization, until Europeans intruded upon the scene. At the remotest margins, and in the most hostile environments, hunters and gatherers with Paleolithic technologies and band forms of social organization survived into modern times.

In §20 we will examine the path toward "civilization" and complex state societies. Then, in §21, we will return to view the primitive world in the "Ethnographic Present," the time of European discovery.

20 · The Path to Urban Society

In both the Middle East and Mesoamerica, the momentum generated by the innovations of the Neolithic gave rise to new and profound transformations of society. The rise of urban societies in these two areas, apparently independently, has challenged explanation. When we add the civilizations of Egypt, the Indus Valley, North China, and Peru, we can see a major shift taking place in the nature and dimensions of human societies.

Though a series of leading theorists have picked up the challenge, it is still far from clear just what was cause and what was effect, what was primary and what secondary. Partly this is because the evidence is tantalizingly incomplete and fragmentary—so there is leeway for alternative interpretations, and much need for guesswork.

Whereas the key Neolithic innovations in the Middle East took place on and around the "hilly flanks," the spotlight now shifts to the river valleys. The valleys of Mesopotamia were not rich in natural resources. Yet they had abundant water, and when that water could be harnessed, agriculture on increased scale could support the social changes that were to come.

The record becomes intricate and detailed at this stage of human history. Rather than trying to keep a focus on Mesopotamia, Mesoamerica, Egypt, Peru, India, and China at once, we will find it more useful to summarize the major transformations in society in the course of urbanization, drawing particularly on the evidence from Mesopotamia and Mesoamerica.

1. Populations were considerably increased, due to greater agricultural productivity.

2. Populations clustered into towns that became focal points of commerce, government, religion, and defense.

3. Kinship-based and egalitarian social groupings were superseded in importance by emerging *classes*, as power and wealth became concentrated

in fewer hands. Social stratification increased in depth, inequality, and rigidity.

4. Centralized political authorities emerged. Just how and why must be examined for each area, and the process is not clearly understood. Control of waterworks, redistribution of specialized resources, military operations—all were important in giving rise to central political power, but their balance is not clear.

5. Increased specialization in the division of labor, and the rise of full-time craftsmen, created a greater economic interdependence of populations.

6. The urban centers became hubs for radiating systems of political and economic integration. Thus, for instance, specialized resources from different regions could pass into the center and be redistributed.

7. The development of temples and priesthoods separated the religious sphere increasingly from the secular sphere.

8. From theocratic patterns of political organization, the movement (at least in Mesopotamia and Mesoamerica) was toward militarism and the conquest of neighboring areas.

Just what, in these developments, was cause and what was effect is a difficult question on which experts are far from agreed. Perhaps we can best visualize the sequences not as a row of dominoes falling over in chains of cause and effect, but rather as a network of interconnection where economic, social, and ideational factors interacted on one another. First in Mesopotamia, then in Egypt, and later in Asia and the New World, this transformation pattern unfolded that was to change irrevocably the nature of human life.

The comparability of the Middle Eastern and Mesoamerican sequences has challenged scholars to use them as a test of theory. A major interpretation of the two sequences by Adams (1966) attempts to sort out from the tangled variables which changes in the emergence of urban society were most basic, and which changes were secondary consequences. Having shown striking similarities in the two sequences, he argues that ecological and economic forces were not the prime movers—that reorganizations on the social plane played a major part in reshaping them.

In looking at the Mesoamerican sequence, Sanders and Price (1968) lay a greater weight on ecological factors, and particularly on population growth, as a prime mover. Their interpretation makes clear the complexity of interplay between technology, its demographic consequences, and their social ramifications. Clearly, any sharp separation between social and ecological factors, and any simple "domino" theory of change, will not be adequate. As with the process of biological evolution (recall the complex interrelatedness of bipedal locomotion, tool-use, increased intelligence, and skull form), a much more complex "cybernetic" model is needed here. The challenge will not be to find what causes what, but to trace the complex circuits of interconnection through which changing patterns of ecological and social events generate changes in the system of social life.

The unfolding of early urban states and empires in Mesopotamia, Mesoamerica, India, and China becomes exceedingly complex. We will not try to trace it here, except to sketch some recurrent patterns that will be important in relating these urban centers to the comparative picture of man that will emerge in succeeding chapters.

An important point is that the focus of Western historians on the early empires of Mesopotamia and Egypt, and then on the emergence of Greece

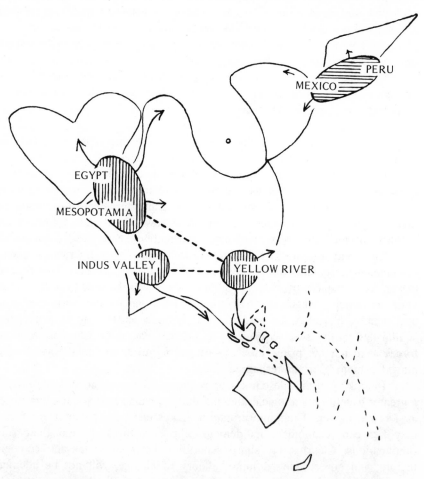

Figure 13. Early Centers of Civilization. This simplified map is based on a north-polar projection—a more revealing way of grouping the world's major land masses, in terms of the processes of prehistory, than the more familiar Mercator projection. FMK

and Rome, gives us a very distorted view of world history. Overlooked are the great Bronze Age cities of the Indus Valley in India, Mohenjo-Daro and Harappa, around 5000 years ago. By 3500 years ago, urban centers were emerging in the great bend of the Yellow River in China. In Mesoamerica urban centers emerged later, but they ran a spectacular course parallel in many ways to that in Mesopotamia. The scale of the great cities in the Valley of Mexico and the Andes, even in comparison to those of Medieval Europe, is impressive. Apparently Teotihuacan in Mexico was the largest city in the world around the middle of the first millenium A.D. We will shortly see how our Europe-centered perspective distorts our vision of the "age of discovery" and of more recent history. It is an interesting exercise to rethink the history of the world if we look at it with China, not Europe, as the center. Europeans could then be regarded as clever barbarians from a distant tip of the Asian land mass who for several centuries overran China, as other barbarians had several times before, and then were repulsed. It is a sobering thought as the latter twentieth century unfolds.

Three processes that were going on around the margins of these urban centers will be important in the chapters to follow. The first was the relation between urban civilizations and the mobile peoples of the grasslands beyond the tilled fields. No matter how high and solid their walls, cities were for several thousand years vulnerable to the attacks of the "horsemen of the steppes." Scythians, Huns, and Mongols struck into settled areas of the Middle East and Europe. Aryan-speaking herders moved through the passes into India; Hsiung-Hus and others raided into China, undeterred even when the Great Wall was built. Along the borders of cultivation and herding in Asia and Africa, this basic struggle has carried on into modern times. Attacking herders were at times able to lay waste to or even permanently destroy agricultural city-states. Sometimes, however, they moved into conquered centers and established ruling dynasties, as in China and India. Egypt had its herder rulers, the Hyksos. The dramatic confrontations between pastoral and settled peoples hide the way they have depended on one another's existence. We will see in §27 how populations have moved in and out of the "camps" of farmers and nomads as conditions changed.

A second process that will be important in the chapters to follow was going on within the urban states—but it was going on in the countryside. *Peasants* were emerging: village peoples who continued to farm for their own subsistence, but whose agricultural surpluses—in the form of trade or tribute—went to the urban centers to feed rulers and specialists. Peasants comprise a large and important slice of the world population in the twentieth century, and they have been on the human scene since the rise of urban centers. As we will see (§41), the study of peasants has become a major theme of modern anthropology.

A third and related process has taken the great urban traditions, with their sophisticated religions and literatures, and implanted them in local village settings—both within the area where they developed and far away. Thus in India the Sanskritic tradition has penetrated village settings (see Ex. 35 Chapter XI); and Buddhism has taken root in Ceylon, China, and elsewhere. Hindu and later Islamic civilizations profoundly affected local patterns of life in what is now Indonesia (see Ex. 68, Chapter XVII). This interplay between indigenous models of the cosmos and social world, with old Neolithic roots, and the great tradition of civilization, has been another important theme in modern anthropology (see §42).

Rather than trace developments farther into the domain of the historian, we will examine briefly those peoples on whom much of the book will focus: the "primitive" tribesmen who remained beyond the reaches of early empires until European expansion swept across the non-Western world.

21 · Non-Western Peoples in the "Ethnographic Present"

As Europeans during the "age of discovery" ventured into the New World, Africa, and Asia, they encountered complex and diverse patterns of social life. To map out in any detail which peoples were living where and doing what would take volumes. Here we will only sketch in broadest outline the main culture areas of the primitive world.

Before we do, it is worth pausing to reflect how silly it is to conceive of Columbus, Magellan, and Marco Polo as "discovering" anything. Our hopelessly smug and provincial Europe-centered view of world history assumes that strange creatures and places were out there waiting to be "discovered" by us civilized folks. The Scandinavians and Italians argue about who really found America first, without considering that Paleo-Indians might have a claim. Arab and Chinese trading ships plied the Far East, Africa, and India long before Europeans "discovered" them; and world travelers like the Arab Ibn Battuta journeyed to the far reaches of a world Europeans were not to visit for several centuries. Perhaps the absurdity of a Europe-centered notion of "discovering the world" can best be perceived by quoting from the reports of an urbane and sophisticated Arab from the great city of Baghdad who "discovered" Europeans (in what is now Russia) in A.D. 922:

> They (the Rus) are the dirtiest creatures of God. They have no shame in voiding their bowels and bladder nor do they wash themselves when polluted by emission of semen nor do they lave their hands after eating. They are, then, like asses who have gone astray. They come from their own country, moor their barks on the strand of the Atil . . . and build on its bank great houses out of wood. In a house like this ten or twenty people . . . live together. Each of them has a resting bench whereon he sits and with them are the fair maidens (slave girls) who are destined for sale to the merchants and they have intercourse with their maidens while their comrades look on. At times a crowd of them come together and do such things . . .

As a matter of duty they wash daily their faces and heads in a manner so dirty and so unclean as could possibly be imagined . . . The girl brings each morning a large vessel with water and gives the vessel to her master and he washes in it his hands and face and the hair of his head; he washes it and combs it with a comb into the bucket, then blows his nose and spits into the bucket. He holds nothing impure back but rather lets it go into the water. After he has done what is needful, the girl takes the same vessel to the one who is nearest and he does just as his neighbor had done. She carries the vessel from one to another until all in the house have had a turn at it and each of them has blown his nose, spat into, and washed his face and hair, in the vessel (translated in Blake and Frye, 1950).

Hopefully somewhat chastened about the "age of discovery," we can take a quick Cook's Tour of the primitive world.

Africa can serve as a starting point. Almost four times the size of the United States (about 11 million square miles), it is dominantly tropical. Its major geographic features, somewhat simplified, comprise a northern strip with a "Mediterranean" climate; vast desert and scrublands across the north and to the southwest (Sahara, Kalahari, and so on); tropical rain forests and savannas especially in west-central zones; and wooded and grassy (veldt) plateaus particularly in east-central and southern zones. River systems, including the narrow Nile "tube," provide major lines of communication away from the open veldt lands.

Two very specialized and isolated groups, formerly much more widespread than now, have remained food gatherers. The south African *Bushmen* of the Kalahari are primarily desert hunters and gatherers of wild foods. The central African Pygmies inhabit the deeper rain forests and are primarily gleaners of roots and fruits, though also taking game as opportunity offers. Both these peoples live in small mobile bands. They trade with neighboring food producers, but neither their habitat nor their cultural values have favored abandonment of a food gathering way of life.

Elsewhere (for example, among the Negro peoples of central and south Africa) the numerous ways of life fall into two great types, one based on agriculture, the other on herding. Generally to the west, agriculture is emphasized, with domesticated and wild animals having a supplemental role. Numerous groups, particularly in the coastal rain forests and in higher country, practice shifting cultivation, utilizing the natural rainfall without irrigation. Clearing and burning new patches of land as the soil becomes exhausted after a growing season or two, they tend to be mobile and rarely aggregate in communities larger than what might be called a "hamlet" of a few families. Other groups, particularly in the Nile and Niger valleys, along the southern edge of the Sudan, and on the Ethiopian highlands, practice more settled and diversified agriculture. They use more or less extensive irrigation, the plow and hoe, and fertilization for soil maintenance. Larger villages, and even towns and small city-states, could be established. The highly organized Negro "kingdoms" of west Africa, such as Ashanti,

Figure 14. Culture Areas of Africa. Simplified to show the six major types of habitat utilization. FMK

Dahomey, Yoruba, and Benin, with their notable political and artistic traditions, rest on such an economic and social base. Ashanti, for example, encompasses about a half million people. Important crops usually include yams, millet, sorghum, and bananas; and nowadays maize, peanuts, and manioc (tapicoa).

The herders fall broadly into two groups. Mainly to the east and south are cattle herders. These peoples have, so to speak, grazed their way outward over the generally rich natural pasturelands to cover much of Africa, reaching the extreme south perhaps some four centuries ago. Cattle are the only kind of domestic animal sedentary enough, and yielding enough food, to enable a pastoral people to base themselves in permanent villages.

Villagers have often maintained kin and political ties as they "hived off." Their tribes and kingdoms are frequently large. Usually having strong warrior traditions, cattle herders tended to dominate adjacent cultivators, and this relation sometimes results in an organized herding-pastoral society in which the herders are the dominant and aristocratic element. In the south a people called the *Hottentots*, products of hybridization between Bushmen and incoming Negro groups, have adopted cattle herding.

Northern Africa, generally lacking rich grasslands, can rarely support cattle, and agriculture becomes impossible in the dry zones—at least in terms of the indigenous technology. Here herding is the characteristic activity, with sheep, goats, horses, and (in desert areas) camels, variously the animals central to the economy. Pasturage conditions combine with the habits of these animals to make life typically mobile. Sheep and goats move slowly, but the camel herds here and in Asia may travel great distances seasonally between summer and winter pastures. The tent-living kin group, ranging a territory, is usually the basic spatial unit. Where intensive cultivation is possible in north Africa, as along the Mediterranean coast and up the Nile "tube," wheat is the most valued crop. Here villages, towns, and city centers were developed. The donkey or ass becomes an important animal for transport.

Africa, though remaining tribal in many areas, had greater access to the innovations of the last few thousand years than many parts of the primitive world. Like southeast Asia it has been an area into which elements from centers of early civilization have filtered; and itself showed some early flowerings of civilization. The use of metals, particularly ironsmithing, had by historic times spread almost universally in Africa; possibly only certain Bushmen groups and a people called *Bube* on the island of Fernando Po remained to historic times in the "Stone Age." The institutions of centralized political organization, including "kingship," had spread not only to adjacent Nilotic and Ethiopian groups but also to some of the west African and the cattle-herding peoples. In the process they assumed many variant and complex local forms. The plow, writing, trade in gold, ivory, and slaves, and other relatively late cultural elements have their own southward and westward pathways and distributions. Since the seventh century the Islamic religion has diffused over large zones of north and west Africa, just as somewhat earlier Coptic Christianity had spread into limited areas, as in Ethiopia.

Africa, with its great population and linguistic and cultural diversity, its range of ecological adaptations and social and political systems, has been a crucial area of anthropological concentration. With local variations on common cultural themes, Africa provides a laboratory for intensive comparative analysis; with great contrasts it enables us to see wide ranges of human possibility. The great complexity of tribal Africa, its regional patterns, and its culture history can be explored by the interested reader in Murdock's encyclopedic compilation on the peoples of Africa (1959).

Europeans in "darkest Africa" have been prone to view the peoples they encountered as having lived in those ways in those places "since time immemorial." It is worth a brief excursion back in time, in Africa, to consider the peoples speaking the great family of Bantu languages who now inhabit most of the southern half of Africa. For the evidence now indicates that Bantu-speaking peoples have exploded across southern Africa within the last 2000 years, from a probable point of origin in the Cameroon Highlands of the West Coast. This expansion was possible when plants, probably domesticated in the Southeast Asian Neolithic (and adapted to rain forest environments), opened up these environments in West Africa to shifting cultivation. Over longer time periods, Africa emerges as a swirling, moving scene with populations shifting, splitting, conquering, and mixing. Cultural intrusion and domination are old, not new, in Africa; in the southern half of Africa, Europeans are but the most recent intruders to invade.

This glimpse at the pre-European cultures of Africa illustrates basic principles of distribution and of regional and local adaptation that will hold for other zones as well. The Paleolithic understratum of food gathering shows through in isolated and marginal areas. The cultures of Bushmen and Pygmy peoples have selectively changed and developed over the generations to modern times; yet they hint at some of the ways of living that enabled early man to occupy much of the continent. With Neolithic innovations, cultural alternatives were widened; ecological pressures then shaped the choices between cultivating and herding that provide the broadest marks of difference in traditional African ways of life. Finally, the picture is not simply one of local populations adapting over very long periods to particular environments; here, as elsewhere in the tribal world, peoples had been meeting, moving, displacing, borrowing, and changing long before Europeans intruded on the scene.

We can now turn to the vast island-dotted zone of the Pacific. Three different zones can usefully be examined: Malaysia, Australia, and Oceania. Each has had a distinct history and pattern of settlement.

During periods of Pleistocene glacial advance, sea levels were lowered and early man could get out into Java (reached by *Homo erectus* and Solo populations). Apparently early *Homo sapiens* populations got into the now partly submerged continental platform that includes Australia and New Guinea, judging by recent datings in Australia. By the last glacial, *Homo sapiens* populations were apparently widely spread in this area and the Malaysian zone (what is now Indonesia, Malaysia, and the Philippines). As in Africa, food-gathering groups survive from this Paleolithic understratum. The pygmy *Negritos* and other short-statured collectors, or gleaners, of the rain forests from the Andaman Islands through Malaya and the Philippines have nomadic ways of life. Their bands, made up of a few families, move over considerable territories after roots, fruits, and game. In more open and often desert Australia, and in Tasmania, the main subsist-

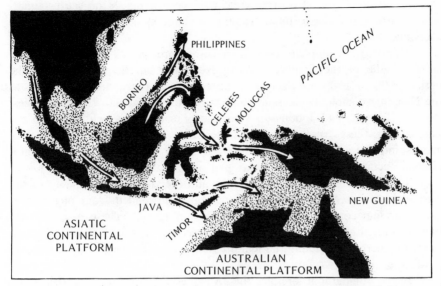

Figure 15. Early Migrations in the Southwest Pacific. Hypothetical movements into Australia and New Guinea during the last glacial. Dotted areas, now shallow seas, were more or less dry land, and present channels were narrower. FMK

ence was derived from hunting. The so-called *Aborigines* accumulated few material goods other than what a man could carry and yet range after game, and what a woman could carry and still gather roots and tote children. But, as seen earlier, they developed elaborate forms of social structure and religion. As with the Bushmen of Africa, their specialized adjustment to restrictive desert environments is, to Western eyes, a marvel of survival.

In Malaysia, the Negrito peoples have taken over a few selected elements from later-coming groups, including iron tools. Later peoples also introduced some goods and ideas into northern Australia in pre-European times: for example, the polishing of stone. But, in general, the Neolithic complex spread in coastal and river valley areas in Malaysia, carried by the brown-skinned peoples who became dominant in southeast Asia.

Shifting cultivation of rain forest, where new gardens are cleared each year and old ones are allowed to return to jungle growth, appears to have been the major innovation. It is practiced throughout the Malaysian zone from the southeast Asian uplands through to New Guinea and nearby island chains. Irrigated agriculture, especially with the plow and the water buffalo as a draft animal, is limited in Malaysia to lowland zones, and here and there to terraced slopes. No peoples are herders as such, though families and individuals may occasionally become occupationally specialized in handling the domestic animals characteristic of the area: water buffalo, pigs, and chickens. Among coastal peoples great reliance was placed on sea products, so that fishing became a major tradition and for some groups the essential economic base.

The very incomplete archaeological record points toward Thailand as the cradle of the Southeast Asian Neolithic; but South China, in the period 3000 to 1500 B.C., seems to have been a crucial diffusion point, as the Neolithic complex took shape and began to spread into the Philippines, Borneo, Taiwan, and Indonesia. One line of early movement out into the Pacific took these Neolithic peoples, probably speaking Austronesian languages, into the western fringes of Micronesia, probably from the Philippines. Human occupancy of the Marianas had apparently begun by 1500 B.C.

Toward the south, in New Guinea and the islands immediately to the west and east, were dark-skinned populations descended from migrants to the Australian continental platform in the last glacial. These peoples were hunters and gatherers of the interiors of these large islands, though Neolithic elements (perhaps including agriculture) may have reached New Guinea in advance of migrant groups.

In the ethnographc present, the "Melanesian" peoples of the Bismarck Archipelago, Solomons, New Hebrides, New Caledonia, and Fiji have presented a puzzle. They physically resemble African Negroes (though modern genetic studies show very different patterns of blood chemistry and suggest a parallel course of adaptation rather than any close connection). Their social organization and ways of life are amazingly diverse despite a similar technology and scale of social life. Their cultures have seemed to observers to have an unmistakable "primitive" stamp in contrast to the peoples to the west and east—the lighter-skinned, straight-haired Malaysians and Polynesians. Yet most Melanesians east of New Guinea speak Austronesian languages historically related to those of the Malaysian area and Polynesia. Culture historians have expended boundless energy and imagination trying to account for the dark-skinned Melanesians with their cannibal predilections, in between Polynesians and their Malaysian cousins but speaking uncomfortably similar languages.

One way of playing the checker game was to jump the Polynesians around to the north of the Melanesians, through the tiny islands of Micronesia, whose peoples also speak Austronesian languages and are physically akin to Malaysians and Polynesians. By this route, the historian could also bring in influences from the Asian high civilizations to account for things the Polynesians did that looked especially sophisticated. Since Eastern Polynesians had elaborate conceptions of rank and theology their Western cousins lacked, one needed only to jump some checkers farther across.

Another way was to move Polynesians through the middle of Melanesia. They could then be seen as civilizing the resident savages of the Solomons and New Hebrides and enlightening them with some Pidgin Austronesian, before moving on to their destiny in Polynesia. These checker games were all the more fun because there was no archaeological evidence to limit the theories. More fancifully, Polynesia was populated by the Lost Ten Tribes of Israel, refugees from the Lost Continent of Mu, and American Indians, in what Douglas Oliver has called "the great oceanic regatta." Such theories ignore the fact that the affinities of Polynesian culture are overwhelmingly with East Asia.

Archaeological evidence is still limited, but it suggests that most of the Melanesian islands east of New Guinea and the adjacent New Britain and New Ireland were not inhabited until, beginning around 1500 B.C., early Austronesian-speaking peoples settled the area, coming from somewhere in the Malaysian zone (either along the coastal islands of New Guinea or through western Micronesia). They brought with them pottery making, yams, taro, pigs, chickens, dogs, bark-cloth manufacture, and other elements of the Southeast Asian Neolithic; and their orientation to the sea made them mobile and ideally suited to be "Vikings of the Pacific." Only after these ancestors of modern Polynesians had settled this largely uninhabited Melanesian zone, and some groups had moved from Fiji into what is now Polynesia, did large-scale movements of dark-skinned peoples into Melanesia probably begin. Presumably they were from New Guinea, where for some millenia they had been hunters and gatherers. Only with the spread of Neolithic technology into the area would populations have expanded rapidly. Whereas only a few large islands near New Guinea had supported hunters and gatherers (as fauna thin out to the eastward), now these expanded populations could find viable ecological settings in Melanesia. Highly complex movements, interbreeding, and borrowings would have occurred in the Melanesian area. Archaeology suggests that these darker-skinned populations did not get out as far as Fiji until after A.D. 1000.

Modern Melanesia, if this reading of the early evidence stands up, is thus indeed a composite—but the early culture historians, by assuming that the "archaic" layer was on the bottom, got the layer cake upside down. But any such analogy greatly oversimplifies the highly complex history of local populations. As Kroeber early suggested, malaria—which occurs in Melanesia but not Polynesia—may have helped to shape the physical contrasts between their modern inhabitants.

In the "ethnographic present," then, Pacific islanders represent variations on the Southeast Asian Neolithic complex, adapted to tiny coral atolls and large islands covered with rain forest, oriented toward sea or mountains. Where Polynesia is an area of relative cultural uniformity, with great elaborations in some places of systems of rank and theology, Melanesia is an area of great local diversity. Probably this is in part because most of its dark-skinned immigrants were oriented inward toward the "bush" rather than outward toward the sea and in part because their cultures and populations incorporate elements that reflect several thousand years of diversification as hunters and gatherers. Given an earlier Austronesian-speaking population in the area, and the same new technology superimposed on ancient diversity, it is no wonder that Melanesians are a baffling combination of contrasts and uniformities. Micronesians show great similarities to Polynesians in some respects, important differences in others (the former, for instance, stress descent in the female line; most of the latter stress descent in the male line). Micronesia has apparently been a meeting place of early Austronesian-speakers from the Central Pacific and populations and influences out of Southeast Asia, notably the Philippines.

A great division here shows between the grain-growing area, marked above all by rice, which covers roughly Malaysia, and the root- and fruit-growing area of Oceania to the east. Roots and fruits such as the yam, taro, banana, and breadfruit are comparatively low-yield crops, though mostly easy to cultivate, calling merely for simple digging-stick gardening. Even irrigated cultivation, which developed in some places, did not permit local settlement size to rise above that of a large village of, perhaps, five hundred persons at the maximum. Rice, by contrast, is a very high-yield crop when given efficient irrigated cultivation. In the most favorable zones, such as the volcanic soils of Java, rice cultivation with the plow and water buffalo opened the way for very large villages, overcapped by towns and even city centers when combined with trade, commercial fishing, and other elements of the lowland economic complex of Asia. In areas poorly suited to irrigated rice, the roots and fruits which were carried by migrants into Oceania may also serve as staples. "Dry rice," grown widely in upland areas of Southeast Asia, is cultivated on the same shifting pattern as yams and taro.

Only the Australian Aborigines, who as we have seen were cut off from the Southeast Asian Neolithic by their continental isolation, and a few other scattered peoples, remained hunters and gatherers into the ethnographic present. Some, like the Andaman Islanders of the Indian Ocean, were cut off by isolation (and in this case a ferocity that discouraged Neolithic tourists). Others, like the "Negritos" of Malaya and northern Luzon, remained as isolated pockets as Neolithic peoples filled in surrounding areas.

The rise of great civilizations in Asia profoundly influenced tribal peoples long before we got around to "discovering" these areas. Thus there was a diffusion into the more accessible parts of Malaysia of the great religions which took form in Asia. When, around 200 B.C., the older Brahman faith in India was threatened by the rise of Buddhism, refugee monks appear to have settled in southeast Asian centers, which were then developing on the basis of trade in spices, gold, and other goods. In turn, several centuries later the renascence of Brahmanism in India made Buddhism a refugee faith which was to gain its longer-term hold in outer places such as southeast Asia, China, and Tibet. By the seventh century A.D., records show local city-states in Sumatra and Java, as well as on the adjacent Asian mainland, with rulers and aristocracies variously Brahman or Buddhist—or combining elements of the two traditions.

Space does not permit telling the story of subsequent Malaysian states and empires, rarely described in history books. Modern Indonesians, Annamese, Burmese, and others look back on what appear as "Golden Ages," marked in their countries by great architectural ruins, and by dramatic and religious traditions. Offshore Malaysia was largely protected from the dynamic conquests and pressures of thirteenth-century Mongol expansions. By the fifteenth century, however, Islamic expansionism overwhelmed the Javanese and other Brahman- and Buddhist-oriented centers. The so-called Madjapahit empire of Java was overthrown in or about A.D. 1475. Its aristocratic survivors appear to have joined with the Balinese to the east, and dominantly Brahman Bali has remained impervious to Islamic penetration up to the present. Islamic assimiliation and settlement had moved as far as the southern Philippines, and was beginning in the north, when in 1565 Legaspi started conquest and Christianization in that archipelago. The Spanish, after centuries of holding back the Islamic tide from across the Mediterranean, found themselves holding the line again halfway around the world: no wonder they called the Moslem Filipino a "Moor" or *Moro*.

India has of course been a cradle of Eastern civilization for millenia. Yet even here there is a patchwork of local cultural variations with roots in the tribal past. And in marginal regions, tribal pockets remain—as with the Nagas, who ignore and occasionally defy the central government, and peoples of Assam who have become anthropologically crucial because of their systems of marital alliance (§34).

There is simply too much history, in this heartland-Asian area of ferment and change over thousands of years, to carve up and classify peoples in regional terms. Only at the margins of Asian civilization where tribal peoples remained in relative isolation, as in the island Pacific, can we begin to describe "culture areas."

In central Asia, pastoralists have adapted Neolithic herding innovations in many specialized ways. Their geographic position around the major trade routes between East and West has given them a key place in world history. In §27, we will briefly examine herding as a mode of ecological adaptation.

North America has long been the testing ground for culture-area and trait-distribution studies. One problem in dealing with the area is that the distribution of language families does not match at all neatly the major zones of ecological adaptation. Thus Athapaskan-speaking groups range from the Tanaina of coastal Alaska to the Navaho and Apache of the arid Southwest. In the Northwest Coast and other areas, there are peoples living next to one another in very similar manner who speak unrelated languages.

How many "culture areas" there are in North America depends in part simply on how far back you stand, what degree of detail you use to lump or split. It also depends on whether some attempt is made to take differences in language or social organization into account, rather than simply patterns of adaptation to the physical environment.

Driver (1961), drawing on extensive distributional studies, arrives at thirteen areas plus four in Mesoamerica and the Caribbean. By lumping two Arctic and three sub-Arctic areas marked by lesser variations, Driver's North American areas are reduced to ten:

Arctic. Here we find the familiar Eskimo peoples, marked by only limited regional variation, with an economy based on hunting and fishing.

Sub-Arctic. Scattered and mobile Indian bands in this zone concentrated on hunting, with caribou as the main source of food.

Northwest Coast. Along this narrow coast and island strip, preservation and storage of salmon from the seasonal runs enabled its Indian occupants to adopt a sedentary village life. A notable accumulation of heavy goods, and an extremely competitive status system associated with ceremonial wealth, developed in this highly specialized setting.

Plateau. In the area drained by the Columbia River, a combination of elements from Northwest Coast, Plains, and Great Basin provides ways of life adaptive to this area, based mainly on salmon fishing.

Plains. The horse, acquired around 1600, enabled the full development of familiar Plains culture, based heavily on buffalo hunting; but this efflorescence built on older nomadic patterns of hunting.

Prairies. In what is now the Middle West, mixed economic modes involved hunting and farming, and bases in permanent villages.

East. In woodland settings, farming predominated and political organization attained considerable complexity among Iroquoian peoples and in the Southeast. Food producing, based on a dry-gardening economy emphasizing maize, squash, and beans, was practiced with increasing intensity from the north (where hunting was likely to be a major occupation) to the south. Community life tended to become correspondingly more sedentary, with larger villages sometimes reaching nearly town size.

California. In this area of great cultural diversity, storage of seasonal seeds and acorns, notably in basketry containers, enabled the population groups to occupy sedentary villages or hamlets if they so elected. This was especially possible when dependable marine foods such as shellfish were added to the diet along with the universally hunted wild game.

Great Basin. In these arid and harsh environments, ways of life based on gleaning wild foods and hunting small animals that were worked out very early in the area persisted into the ethnographic present.

Oasis. Here desert environments are marked by oasislike streams and springs where settled life and agriculture are possible. In this setting, patterns of cultural adaptation could emphasize maize cultivation and dense, stable population, in the Pueblos. Or alternatively, descendants of food gathering peoples could work out in sheep herding the distinctive and highly adaptive pattern of the modern Navaho.

Variations of these adaptations to dry environments occur in Baja California and Northern Mexico. To the south, Mesoamerica shows the overlays of developed civilizations on underlying earlier patterns. At the time of Spanish conquest, irrigated agriculture had supported large urban populations and the great political developments of Aztec civilization. The Mayans had achieved impressive sophistication, building on the foundations of shifting cultivation of maize; but perhaps in part because of this precarious ecological foundation, as well as Aztec expansionism, Mayan civilization had fallen into decline by the time of Spanish conquest. The complex Mesoamerican scene is now splendidly documented in the *Handbook of Middle American Indians* (Wauchope, 1964–1967).

South American cultures are more difficult to group, because the evidence for the vast area is less complete. The great Inca empire, with its intensive cropping of maize, sweet potatoes and other plants, its waterworks, and its complex social and political organization, is a first and most spectacular "culture area." Beyond this the lines are more difficult to draw, but the following very broad picture can be sketched.

The Circum-Caribbean or Antilles Area. Here the characteristic economy practiced among the surviving aboriginal groups is one of tropical dry gardening and fishing, which enabled the peoples to live in settled communities.

The Chibcha and Amazon Areas. The South American tropical forest area shows a cultural continuity with the circum-Caribbean. The many economic variations here include different reliances on garden products (especially manioc), hunting, and fishing. As with the rugged and forested New Guinea terrain, conditions have favored great cultural variability. The area is well known for the elaborate use of drugs, including poisons; it is also the region from which the hammock comes.

The Guanaco Area. The guanaco is the wild llama of the pampas, a great grassland zone in which the peoples had a hunting way of life much like that of the buffalo hunters of the North American plains. The aboriginal cultures, now almost extinct, also received a temporarily extended mobility with the coming of the horse.

The Fuegian Area. The cold and rugged zone around the Strait of Magellan was sparsely populated with fishing and hunting peoples, notably the *Yahgan* and *Ona*. Their marked dependence on sea mammals, their elaboration of bone technology, and their migratory patterns of settlement are in some respects reminiscent of the Eskimo. It may be noted that the *Handbook of South American Indians* (Steward, 1946–1950) links the Guanaco and Fuegian areas and the remoter tropical forest tribal zones into a "marginal" category.

Recent studies increasingly suggest that many South American Indian groups living in marginal rain forest areas of Brazil, Bolivia, and elsewhere may have once had much more complex social and political systems, and more solid economic bases, than in modern times. When the Inca empire disintegrated, many peoples at the far margins of that system, who had been tied into it, may have returned to simpler patterns of life. These are based in some cases primarily on hunting and gathering. This would help to explain patterns of social organization seemingly more elaborate than their present ecological base, as among the Siriono of Bolivia.

In these sketches of the major world areas in the ethnographic present, the limiting and shaping role of the physical environment—given the technology with which men face it—has been an underlying theme. We will return in Chapter VII to consider man-in-environment, and in what ways and by what mechanisms adaptation shapes patterns of human life.

Clearly, whether men are hunters and gatherers, limited by small populations and the need for mobility, or have acquired the complex of Neolithic technology that permits larger populations and settled residence, or live in centralized states, affects almost every corner of their lives, from art to zoological classification. Given a particular "stage" or "level" of technology, the range of possible social and political institutions is greatly narrowed.

One way to look at human societies in comparative perspective is to take these "levels" one at a time and examine the whole complex of social and cultural forms characteristic of each. Thus we might look first at the *band* societies of hunters and gatherers, some of whose cultural patterns reach far into the human past and some of which derive from the late stages of the Paleolithic. We would then turn to *tribes*, societies with Neolithic technologies, building on kinship as a dominant organizing principle and lacking centralized political organization. Then centralized *chiefdoms*, and finally complex *states*, where elements of the urban revolution have become central, would be examined. At each level, recurrent solutions to organizational problems turn up in different parts of the world. This approach is broadly *evolutionary* in its assumptions, and it has been widely followed in recent years (see, for example, Service, 1962).

An alternative approach is to look in turn at the main institutions of human society—economic organization, political system, religion, and so on. In Chapters VII to XV, we will follow this approach and build on its advantages. We are able to see in this way the range of variation possible for man in each of these domains of life, and hence to attain valuable insights about ourselves and about human possibility. But at the same time, we can see how that range of possibility is limited by the scale and technological complexity of a society.

Part Three

THE ORGANIZATION
OF SOCIETIES
AND THE STRUCTURE
OF CULTURES

AUSTRALIAN ABORIGINES, roaming desert territories in search of food, live in a different world than Indian villagers or African pastoralists. Yet they face many of the same problems of organizing groups, allocating scarce resources, preserving order, maintaining continuity across generations, and understanding a world where life is fragile and human effort is often overturned.

In the chapters to follow we will explore how societies in different parts of the world, differing in levels of technology and size, deal with these problems. Sometimes it will be most revealing to look at a particular problem—say, the mode of political organization—as it is handled by hunting and gathering peoples, then as it is handled by tribesmen with Neolithic technology, then as it is handled in larger and more complex societies. At other times it will be most revealing to juxtapose the widest variations found in different parts of the world to illuminate the full range of human possibilities.

But our aim will never simply be to reveal curiosities. We will explore how customs and beliefs fit together and make sense in terms of a people's premises and logic; we will see common themes emerge in human life everywhere; and by this broad comparative view we will seek to throw our own way of life, and the nature of man, into sharper relief.

VI The Structure of Cultures

CULTURAL ANTHROPOLOGY is a study of human differences, seen against a background of what is shared. But how different are men in different times and places, how diverse are their ways of life? The paradox that modern anthropology presents us with is this: Each culture, as an ideational system, is a unique set of concepts, categories, and rules. Yet at the same time, a common design underlying that uniqueness is beginning to emerge. Moreover, similarities in social arrangements and customs in widely separated parts of the tribal world lead specialists to hope that regularities and even "laws"—similar sequences of cause and effect—will emerge from this seeming diversity.

Anthropology, then, is a study of uniqueness and regularity. Here, as we introduce a series of chapters on kinship, economics, politics, religion, and other aspects of primitive societies, we will focus on the nature of cultural uniqueness, touching on its moral implications, will glimpse the quest for a common underlying design, and will examine the search for "cross-cultural" regularities.

22 · Cultural Uniqueness and the Search for Universals

In what ways are cultures unique? Is each culture a distinct universe of categories and meanings and values that must be understood only in its own terms? Or is there some common design that underlies the apparent diversity?

Such questions have been muddled by the tendency Goodenough underlined (see §5) to confuse culture as an ideational system with culture in the sense of the "pattern of life within a community." Clearly it is quite a different matter to ask whether a people's conceptual structure is unique and must be understood in terms of its own categories and inner logic than it is to ask whether the way a people organize social groups or gain their livelihood is unique.

Here we will continue to treat cultures as ideational systems. In asking about the uniqueness of cultures, we are thus asking about the way knowledge is organized by different peoples, about the structure of their models of the world and their recipes for action. In §24 we will examine the search for regularities in modes of social groupings and processes, economic activities, and other facets of the "patterns of life" worked out in different times and places.

The questions, though different, are not unrelated. Ideational systems must of course be compatible with the needs of subsistence and must produce workable social arrangements if they are to endure.

The position that the conceptual world of each people is unique and can only be understood in its own terms has been a dominant force in recent American anthropology. This position derives largely from the theoretical foundations of American linguistics. Each language was viewed as a separate universe of categories and principles of arrangement. Thus the "parts of speech" and grammatical principles of each language had to be worked out afresh. Central here was the notion that the phonemes of a language (§12) represented its unique way of carving up distinctive blocks of sound. In fact the label introduced by the linguist Pike (1967) for analysis of an ideational code in terms of its own distinctions and categories is *emic*—from "phon*emic*," analysis in terms of the phonemes distinctive of a particular language.

Ironically, at the same time in the latter 1950s when these ideas about language were diffusing into American cultural anthropology, the transformationalist revolution was gathering momentum in linguistics. And as we saw in Chapter IV, it has cast aside the dogma that each language is a unique conceptual universe. Its quest is for a general and universal design of which each language is a variant form. Each language must be described in terms of the theory of that design (though by studying different languages we will enrich our general theory). At the deeper levels of structure, languages are very much alike. Their differences are relatively superficial, differences of content but not structure, of details but not general principles. Furthermore, transformationalists argue that the outlines of this design must be innately laid down.

The transformationalist argument for a universal language design is far from overwhelming, though it is powerful. The great bulk of transformationalist analysis has so far dealt with English, and secondarily with Russian—both Indo-European languages. But at least linguistics can no longer be considered a solid foundation for anthropological assertions of cultural uniqueness.

But here as in §13 it is worth sorting out two types of universals—*formal* and *substantive*. In linguistics a formal universal is some class of features, like transformational rules, that occur in every language (though just what the rules are may vary widely from language to language). That is, a formal universal is a principle or mode of *organization*. In contrast, a substantive universal is some feature of the *content*, rather than the organization, of an ideational code—for instance, a particular part of speech or type of semantic category.

The case for a universal linguistic design rests most strongly on formal universals—on the general organizing principles of linguistic competence. Just how similar languages are in grammatical categories and rules, semantic systems, and the like is at the moment an open question. It is quite possible, for other areas of culture, that great diversity (and hence, in some sense, "uniqueness") of *content* fills in an organizational framework that is universal. Hence both the contentions of uniqueness and of universal design for cultures might, in different senses, be valid.

Those who have argued that cultures must be analyzed in terms of their own internal order have pointed most directly to the content, not overall structure, of cultural codes. Two such studies will serve to illustrate:

Example 1:　Hanunóo Color Terms

In his study of the way the Hanunóo of the Philippines conceptualize and deal with the plant world, Harold Conklin was led to explore the way they classified colors (1955). Other investigators using standard color chips had found considerable differences in the way the color spectrum is divided up; but what Conklin found was more interesting. For the whole system for classification turned out to be quite unlike ours; and moreover the "domain" that was being classified seemed rather different from our notion of "color." For instance, one distinction crucial in classifying Hanunóo "colors" turned out to be whether the object was wet and lush, or dry.

Such studies seemed to show not only that peoples vary in the particular categories and features they use to classify their universe, but that the "domains," or large segments, into which they divide the world of experience might well not be the same as ours. It was not simply that their categories for classifying birds or plants, or directions, or supernaturals, were different from ours. How could we even be sure that the very concept of "bird" or "direction" (or "color") was part of their ideational world as well as ours?

Example 2:　Trukese Residence Rules

Two different anthropologists, doing a census of the same tiny island several years apart, classified the same households very differently in terms of an anthropological scheme for recording "postmarital residence" (where husband and wife reside after marriage). How could this be so? One of them, Ward Goodenough, concluded that in fact the Trukese perceive a set of alternatives for choosing a place of residence quite different from those in the anthropological scheme. To understand their choices, one had to under-

stand how they conceived the alternatives, and which choices they perceived as different, and the same. Otherwise, the anthropological scheme was wedging the distinctively shaped pegs of Trukese culture into a standard set of round and square holes (Goodenough, 1956).

Such substantive diversity, uniqueness of content, is by this time well documented. At the same time, the range of variation is turning out to be a good deal less wide than we thought it might be. The same domains are turning up in different cultures, and the diversity in semantic categories in at least some domains is turning out to be a good deal less extreme than one might have expected.

Anthropologists may have exaggerated diversity because of the methods they have been using. Recall our illustrative attempt to define "chair," "stool," and "bench" by the intersection of distinctive features (§14). By this method, any object one sits on either is a chair or is not: there can be no degrees of "chairness." If we applied this method to the Kwaio of the Solomon Islands, who use a single term for fishes and porpoises, we would have to say that their conceptual scheme is quite unlike ours, and treats different features as distinctive. If the *boundaries* of categories are unique in each culture, the conceptual worlds are unique.

But are they? If we instead conceive of a word as having one or more partly overlapping "cores" of meaning from which concentric circles of extended meaning, metaphor, and doubtful application extend outward, we see a different possibility. The cores may be much more similar in different cultures (at least in some domains) than the way they extend out toward the boundaries. Occasionally, the Kwaio contrast "real fish" with porpoises, which have "warm blood like us," or contrast "real birds" with bats, which are classed by the same term. The possibility that such cores of meaning are more similar than comparison of category boundaries would suggest has not yet been systematically explored, but this now appears to be the case with ways of classifying colors (Berlin and Kay, 1969) and kinds of relatives (Lounsbury, 1964).

Formal universals are a different matter. (Even those who have argued most strongly for uniqueness, for example, have seen in *taxonomies* a universal mode of classifying things in the world.) The problem here is that we do not yet know enough about the brain, about thinking, about the organization of knowledge, about perception, to draw the outlines of a universal design. An ideational approach to culture is badly in need of what is beginning to emerge in linguistics—a general theory. We are still in the stage of examining fragments, and classifying bits and pieces. We do not yet have a framework to fit them into. We do know a good deal about what men sharing a cultural code are able to *do* in communicating. And that implies that cultures include at least the following:

1. Principles for assigning patterns in the perceptual world—things, people, events, processes, and contexts—to *categories*. (There is growing evidence that these categories of thinking are not all labeled in language).

2. Basic premises about interrelatedness of things and events: ideas of causality, rules of logic and inference, concepts of time and space, and so on; and basic "cosmological" and "ontological" premises about what orders of existence or categories of being there are, what kind of a universe this is, and so on.

3. Sets of propositions about the interrelations of particular things and events, based on these premises: propositions that parallel our sciences of botany, zoology, astronomy, and so on.

4. Sets of propositions about desirable goals or end-states, including standards for choosing among alternatives, and ideal general standards against which specific alternative courses of action are judged.

5. Techniques for dealing with the environment, physical and social, in such a way as to maximize these goal-states.

6. A very broad category of norms that tell us how to act appropriately in particular situations: who should do what, when, and how. (These include standards for responding to breaches of the normative code by others).

7. Rules for encoding and decoding linguistic and nonlingustic messages.

But the essence of the problem is the *formal structure* of these segments of knowledge—how they are put together and how they are processed in human thought. Our list tells nothing about this structure.

It seems probable that there are different levels of arrangement: from the deepest levels of unconscious premises and abstract relational principles that could not be verbalized, to the normative principles we do not habitually verbalize but can often conjure to consciousness, to our ideologies. These ideologies may have little relation to the implicit codes whereby man lives, but it is characteristic of this strange animal that he will fight and die for them.

A crucial question here is the extent to which the design of cultures is programmed genetically. As our sketch of language (Chapter IV) suggests, this specification may go much further than most anthropologists have been prepared to speculate. Here the frontiers of linguistics, genetics, and neurophysiology will bear close watching.

Whatever the overall framework of cultural knowledge and thinking and however channeled by genetic programming, men fill in this framework with an extraordinary range of concepts, beliefs, and rules. The French anthropologist Claude Lévi-Strauss has shown with particular vividness how the human mind operates on the raw materials of experience to produce endlessly elaborated conceptual schemes (§58).

But despite this diversity, men's cultures and "patterns of life" have more in common than a universal organizing blueprint. They have more in common partly because humans live in a world that has many common features, whether men are in snow or desert or rain forest, in the mountainous interior of a continent or on a tiny oceanic atoll—day and night, stars, a lunar cycle, shadows, wind and rain, birth, death, and regeneration; partly because their constitution and biological drives are the same; partly because the constants of mating, birth, infancy, growth, and eventual death provide the framework for life everywhere; and partly because all men live in a universe where life is fragile and most events are beyond human control. All these things make the *contents* of cultural codes far more similar than they might be. Cultures represent varying ways of doing, and thinking about, the same things.

Further limitations on variation in cultural codes come from the exigencies of life in organized societies. Many of the forms of social arrangement or custom that man *could* think of simply would not work. Many he has devised have not survived—not necessarily because the tribe died out in a struggle for existence, but because the system changed into something more viable.

To what degree there are "substantive universals" in culture and patterns of social life, and what they might be, are old anthropological questions. Those who have sought to find a set of categories or compartments that every culture fills in have been hoping to be able to convert tens of thousands of pages about disparate customs into a framework for comparison. They have also hoped to reveal more clearly what the limits of human variability are and what organizational and operational challenges confront every society.

Some scholars have sifted carefully through masses of data looking for features all societies share. Others have worked from the top down, seeking to find a series of problems that every society faces—some resulting from man's biological nature; some from his psychological, intellectual, and perceptual processes; some from constants in the life cycle; and some from organizational problems of perpetuating the group, socializing its young, controlling internal conflict, and the like.

A classic study of "common denominators" of culture was made by George Peter Murdock (1945), for years a leading pioneer of American comparative anthropology. He observes that there are "exceedingly numerous" resemblances between all cultures; for example, the category of "funeral rites" always includes expressions of grief, means of disposing of the corpse, and rituals to define the relations of the dead with the living. These universal similarities, however, do not carry down at any point to specific detail of cultural behavior. Even such a universal category as "incest" is subject to wide variations as to which particular kinsmen are forbidden to mate. Murdock concludes that the true universals of culture are not identities in behavioral habits, but rather "similarities of classification." While actual behaviors such as acquiring a spouse, teaching a child, or treating a sick person vary enormously, few competent observers, according to Murdock, would hesitate to group these divergent acts under the unifying categories of marriage, education, and medicine. It is in such uniformities of classification that cultural universals lie.

Some studies of "cultural universals" have emphasized biological and psychological "needs" (Malinowski, 1944). Others have emphasized the "functional prerequisites" of ordered social life (Aberle et al., 1950). Clyde Kluckhohn, in an important evaluation of the question of universals (1953), gives balanced emphasis to the biological, ecological, and sociological pressures that limit human variability.

Less theoretically ambitious are schemes of classification that produce the chapter titles of anthropology books (including this one): "economics," "religion," "material culture," and so on. Such ethnographic "tables of contents" are represented in the handbook *Notes and Queries in Anthropology*, produced by British anthropologists as a guide for the professional ethnographer and amateur student of custom.

One difficulty of any such scheme is that it looks at a way of life from the outside in. To illustrate, let us take "religion" (a good standard chapter title). What in a particular tribe fits into this category? Our scheme might say that religion has to do with the supernatural. But "natural" and "supernatural" are our categories, not necessarily those of the tribe. Even if they have similar concepts, what is "natural" to them may not be to us. As we have seen, the way they carve up that universe, their world of ideas and meanings, may be organized in ways quite different from our classifying scheme.

Another problem in analyzing a tribal society in the conventional Western framework—economics, politics, law, religion, and so on—is that these different "aspects" of society get all muddled up with one another. A single transaction, a single social relationship, may at the same time be "economic," "political," "legal," "religious," and what not. But to look at it this way, to say that these separate elements are confounded in primitive societies, is a bit ethnocentric to say the least. In the longer sweep of human history, men have in the main treated rights vis-à-vis people, rights vis-à-vis things, transactions with humans and transactions with "supernaturals," as part and parcel of the same system.

What has happened in the last few thousand years is an increasing complexity and differentiation of states and empires so that the distribution and flow of scarce material goods is governed by money and markets; the distribution and flow of rights over people has been concentrated in governments; legal rights and duties are managed in courts; and relations with supernaturals are managed by priests and a church. The theoretical structures of academic disciplines like economics and political science are predicated on this separation into fairly neat compartments. Even anthropologists slip into the pattern of viewing tribal societies as though they too should be composed of separate compartments.

We will use such headings, for chapters and sections, as a convenient way of arranging for comparative study the way different societies deal with the same challenges. But as we proceed, we must be aware that such schemes cannot capture the richness, integration, and variability of cultures as ideational systems. We must also be aware that things, acts, and events cannot be labeled solely as "economic," "political," or "religious." When a Trobriand Islander of Melanesia presents most of his yearly yam harvest to his sister's husband (see Ex. 19), his act is at once an expression of kinship, an economic transaction, and a political statement. Each is a facet of the same event, and each is illuminated when we look from a different direction. Having looked at these different facets of human social life in comparative perspective, we will return in §58 to the way these elements are organized in a particular culture, and to the nature of cultural integration.

23 · *Cultural Diversity and Cultural Relativism*

The diversity of men's modes of thought and belief, and the variety of custom and world view, have led to a troubling realization. What according to our values and moral standards may be evil or wrong or unthinkable may be treated by another people as valuable and right. Thus a South American people may practice cannibalism or raid their neighbors to collect their heads; or they may kill infants to limit population or placate their ancestors. On what moral grounds can we condemn their acts? How can we impose our standards on their world? For if they had our technological power, they might with equal validity condemn and suppress those customs and beliefs of ours that violated their standards.

The concept of "cultural relativism," and particularly of "ethical relativism"—a position that each way of life can be evaluated only according to its own standards of right and wrong—has profoundly affected American anthropology. Its most articulate spokesman was Melville Herskovits, who referred to cultural relativism as a "tough-minded philosophy." He argued that it underlined the "dignity inherent in every body of custom," and met a "need for tolerance of conventions" different from our own (1951, 1955).

Critics have risen against this position, both in philosophy and anthropology. Some have argued that ultimate values and general ethical commitments are very similar in different cultures, and have sought a kind of universal common denominator of ethical codes.

The extent to which this is true is open to considerable debate. But does this matter? Let us step back and look at humanity in global perspective, seeing man as able to imagine a better world than he has managed to create, to conceive lofty and noble standards he can reach for but seldom attain. Is it really necessary that a vision of the desirable has been glimpsed and sought in every pocket of the tribal world for it to be a worthwhile and philosophically defensible goal for mankind? Are the wisdom of sages, prophets, and philosophers, and man's highest aspirations and greatest insights, to be thus canceled out in favor of common denominators?

Moreover, cultural relativism leads us into moral impotence in a world where few are prepared to foresake the right to judge. Genocide, racism, and wars of oppression have been and are the "custom" of millions of people, yet even the advocate of cultural relativism in the abstract is unlikely to withhold his judgment about them.

But here then lies a dilemma. For much of the conflict and injustice in the modern world has been caused precisely by the powerful seeking to impose their values and ideologies on one another and on the weak—to spread their particular vision of the millenium. How, then, can we transcend ethical relativism without committing the obverse, ethical imperialism?

There is no simple answer. Many anthropologists would urge that cultural relativism is not a position one can ultimately live with—but that it is a position we need to pass through in search of a clearer vision. By wandering in a desert of relativism, one can sort the profound from the trivial, examine one's motives and conscience, customs and beliefs. Like all vision quests it can be lonely and dangerous; but it can lead to heightened perceptions of ourselves, of what it is to be human, and of what man could be if he would. In a world where people foist their political dogmas and religious faiths on one another, where modern ideological inquisitions save souls by dispatching them with flame and lead, we sorely need such wisdom.

A major step in this direction is to understand how *different* peoples are, and in what ways. In the chapters to follow, we will glimpse the branching paths of human possibility that have been explored by peoples in different times and places. The reader should then be able to reflect on these troubling moral issues with greater insight.

24 · *Methods of Cross-Cultural Study*

Scholars have sought for many years to discover regularities across the range of cultures in what-goes-with-what. Many have hoped to read, from such patterns of association or covariation, sequences of development or chains of cause-and-effect.

In a classic 1889 paper, Sir Edward Tylor proposed that by examining correlations between forms of descent or kinship and forms of marriage, one could discover complexes of custom that fit together and could infer sequences in the development of social institutions. Though here, as so often, Tylor showed visionary brilliance, those who sought to follow his lead ran into difficulty. As reports on primitive custom came in from all over the world and began to pile up, the task of pulling related observations from the library and rendering them comparable became almost insurmountable for any single scholar.

A major assault on this problem came from the Yale Institute of Human Relations, beginning in 1937. G. P. Murdock and his associates worked out a system whereby materials from a great many world cultures could be reproduced verbatim and organized according to a standard indexing code. This enterprise, now known as the "Human Relations Area File," is now shared by a number of American universities that now have full sets of the data.

Between 1937 and 1943 the outline was used to build up comprehensive files on nearly 150 cultures. The latter have been in turn put to use for "cross-cultural" reference by various scholars, as with studies of social structure by Murdock (1949) and of sex and reproduction by Ford (1945).

A typical user of the file arrives at a hypothesis (on some theoretical grounds) that cultures with characteristic A will tend to have custom X, while cultures without A will not have X. If A and X are related in some obvious way (if A is square-shaped houses and X is square-shaped roofs) their association will be uninteresting. If A is a way of disciplining children and X is a type of magic, a kind of art style, or a legal system, a demonstration that they are associated lends support to the theory that led to the prediction.

The user goes to the file and rates all societies, or a sample of them, in which A and X or their absence are relevant features—or ideally he has several other people rate the cultures, so as to minimize the chance he will read the evidence his way. He then builds a matrix table that shows the distribution of A and X (where $\bar{A}$ is "not $\bar{A}$" and $\bar{X}$ is "not X").

$$. \ X \ . \ \bar{X} \ .$$

A	14	7
$\bar{A}$	7	21

That is, of 49 societies in his sample, 21 had characteristic A and 28 did not; 14 of those with A also had custom X, while 7 did not. On the other hand, most of those societies without A did not have X. This seems a convincing indication that A and X go together, but just *how* convincing? We need a way of knowing how often patterns like this would appear purely by chance, even if A and X were completely unrelated. This is partly a matter of the sample size. An identical proportion would be represented if the table read $\dfrac{2 \mid 1}{1 \mid 3}$, yet this could happen very easily if the first seven were pulled randomly out of a hat. If the sample were ten times as large, $\dfrac{140 \mid 70}{70 \mid 210}$, it would be all the more convincing. Statistical measures are used to give a *significance level* for such a pattern—telling us how convincing the association is by showing how improbable the purely chance occurrence of such a pattern would be if the variables were unrelated.

This method has been used in recent years to study a bewildering variety of hypotheses—about the relation between child-rearing techniques and religious beliefs, love magic, witchcraft, menstrual taboos, initiation rites, and a host of other things; about the relation of social structure to religious beliefs, art styles, childhood games, and the like; the relation of subsistence economy to everything from sleeping arrangements to stature and mythology. Leaders in such studies have been J. W. M. Whiting and his former students from Harvard, but they have come from other directions as well.

Useful as the Human Relations Area Files (HRAF) have been, it takes time, resources, and human judgment to use them; and they so far include only a limited sample of world societies. To broaden the sample and take advantage of developing electronic data processing systems, Professor Murdock published (1957) a "World Ethnographic Sample." In it, 565 societies were scored according to fifteen criteria (dealing with mode of subsistence, forms of kinship grouping, and so on). The results, tabulated in columns, could be analyzed by computers, by factor analysis (a means of clustering together a set of variables correlated with one another), or other means.

In his journal *Ethnology*, Murdock has expanded this sample and refined his coding system, so that by 1967 the societies in his published *Ethnographic Atlas* totaled almost 1200. The coding categories cover such items as subsistence economy, kinship groups, high gods, games, division of labor, social stratification, and house types. The coding is designed for punch cards, so the variables can be easily processed by computers.

The many recent comparative studies using these larger coded samples include two massive attempts to "correlate everything with everything," and find out what variables were associated to a statistically significant degree. Thus Coult and Habenstein (1965) used a computer to test all possible correlations between Murdock's variables and mark those that were statistically significant. Textor (1967), in an even more massive summary, built by computer all the fourfold tables possible in cross-correlation of 526 variables, for 400 societies, and weeded out by hand and computer the statistically insignificant and spurious associations. What remains is a massive source of hypotheses to be tested by more intensive means.

Further attempts to reduce or analyze the complexities and obscurities of such "random search" statistical summaries have come from factor analyses by such scholars as Driver and Schuessler and methodological assessments like that of Köbben (1967). Driver and Schuessler (1967) reveal strikingly how seeming worldwide correlations may hold well on some continents and slightly if at all on others. Murdock's expanded new sample should yield valuable new insights on this and other comparative problems.

The cross-cultural method is fraught with difficulty. First of all there is what has come to be known as "Galton's Problem"—that some cases included in a sample may not in fact be independent, but may reflect a common historical origin for the pattern in question. Various sophisticated techniques have been proposed for circumventing this danger. But the whole problem of what is an independent observation and what is a representative sample clouds the application and validity of simple statistical methods.

Second, correlations do not show cause and effect, yet most scholars are trying to read such "directionality" into their findings. If A and X tend to go together, it may be because A "causes" X or because X "causes" A. But it can be because a third and undiscovered factor "causes" both A and X. Actually it can be argued that our very notions of linear causality are biases of our own culture, and that in nature things do not happen that way. We should expect to encounter complex cybernetic systems, where "causality" connects elements in intricate networks—so that a change affects the whole system.

Third, because of the uniqueness of cultures, coding them in terms of standard categories inevitably distorts their structure. Classifying residence patterns or kin groups in a society is easy if the ethnographer simply says "residence is patrilocal" or "there are six patrilineal clans." If the ethnographer gives pages and pages of statistics and cultural detail, it is often apparent that none of the coding categories really fits. The more we know, the harder it may be to reduce rich cultural detail into holes in punch cards.

All anthropologists admit that errors and distortions are introduced in such coding. But those who "believe in" cross-cultural methods feel that the errors will cancel out and that, if anything, empirically valid patterns will be disguised, not magnified, by them (Köbben, 1967). Many of those who do not believe think that the errors are cumulative and that the whole notion of cultures "having" or "not having" a standard set of features like a catalogue of spare parts is fundamentally wrong. They believe that revealing cross-cultural comparison will come from study in depth of a few well-chosen cases, not massive but superficial statistical studies. Yet even most critics of large-scale statistical comparisons regard them as useful sources of hypotheses for more intensive study.

At this point we begin a journey through the cultural worlds of other peoples as they have been explored by anthropologists. The journey must be brief and selective, pausing occasionally to take a closer look at case materials. But it will suggest the vistas that lie beyond and will open the way for the reader to explore further.

In a sense one could begin the journey in any area from kinship to cosmology. But it will be most useful to look first at ecology and the adaptation of peoples to their physical environment. Having "anchored" these peoples in the physical world that shapes their lives, we can then explore the social and conceptual worlds they fashion themselves.

VII Man and Environment: Technology and Cultural Ecology

In Chapter V we sketched the major stages in man's development from scattered hunter and gatherer to technologically sophisticated urban dweller. On this path, man's relations to his environment—and the environment itself—have been radically transformed.

One of the most useful ways to look at the range of societies anthropologists have studied is "ecologically." Ecology has been defined as "the science of the interrelation between living organisms and their environment, including both the physical and biotic environments, and emphasizing inter-species as well as intraspecies relations" (Allee et al., 1949: 1). Each species within an environment is thus seen as part of a complex web of interconnection, an *ecosystem*. A decrease in rainfall may force many species to use a few water holes, which makes food more readily available to lions but reduces their range, which affects the population and distribution of antelopes, which affects the grasslands, which affects other species, and so on—not in linear chains of cause-and-effect but in networks where every change affects many parts of the system.

When we look at man in ecological terms we see him as one component in complex webs of interrelationship with his physical environment and other organisms. The nature of this ecosystem will of course depend on the environment; we have glimpsed men living in a range of settings from desert to arctic tundra to steaming jungle. But what kind of animal man is, within an ecosystem, will also depend on his technology—on the tools and skills with which he faces a physical setting.

In anthropology, ecological perspectives have been limited and partial. When man looks at himself as part of an ecosystem, he views himself as star, and other species as the supporting cast. When the observer is an anthropologist, he is centrally concerned with *culture* as mediating man's relations with environment. He concentrates on the way adaptation to an ecosystem shapes a culture, and on the way a culture shapes an ecosystem and man's place in it. The recent emphasis on cultures as ideational systems further predisposes us to look at the way a people themselves conceptualize an environment and their relations to it (as in "ethnoscience"; see §14). Yet a primitive horticulturist may be as unaware as a twentieth-century pesticide-using farmer of his place in his ecosystem and his often disruptive effects on it.

The cost of such a perspective is that it focuses on the special and transformed kind of animal man is. The power of an ecological approach, as it has developed in recent general systems theory in biology, comes precisely from not doing this—from stepping back far enough to see the general pattern of interconnections between organisms rather than taking a grasshopper's eye, or lion's eye, view. On this level, a cultural convention that married sons garden with their father is not different in kind from a biological "convention" that lions hunt in pairs. Both may have profound effects on an ecosystem.

Man's specialness, in ecological terms, lies in this: What a lion does in any environment will be broadly the same. He is not likely to eat berries or fly south for the winter. He can survive in only a limited range of settings. Yet man's culture, particularly his technology, can radically alter what kind of an animal he is. Ecologically, the early American Indian hunter was not the same sort of beast as the modern American farmer who, in the same spot, radically transforms his environment with chemical fertilizers and farm machinery.

In looking at these relationships, we will be touching on crucial questions about the nature of man. Men must wrest a living from their environment, armed with whatever tools and skills they possess. They also spin intricate webs of custom, complex patterns of ritual and cosmology. On which side lies man's essential nature? Is he basically a pragmatist, building cultures to fit the pressures of the environment? Or is he basically a spinner of webs, his designs limited but not shaped by the demands of mundane existence?

25 · Technology and Levels of Social Integration

In Chapter V, we skimmed quickly over those developments along the path to modern urban societies that gave men more control over their environments and made possible social life on a larger and more complex scale.

In looking comparatively at men's ways of life, it is useful for some purposes to group together societies that represent roughly equivalent "levels" of technology and social and political integration. Just how this grouping can best be arranged is a matter of some debate among specialists; and, as we will see, anthropologists are far from agreed on how cultural development can best be interpreted and on what part technology has played in it.

Peoples in the ethnographic present whose subsistence economies are based on hunting and gathering—Eskimos, Australian Aborigines, Andaman Islanders, African Bushmen and others—have usually been grouped together. They are not, of course, any "earlier" than other peoples encountered by Europeans in the primitive world (though they sometimes have been exterminated faster). But because they were for various reasons cut off from the spread of the Neolithic food producing complex, they provide our best living evidence on what human societies were like before the Neolithic. We have noted, however, that the hunters and gatherers of the ethnographic present have many technological skills acquired by man only in the few thousand years before the Neolithic; they do not represent "survivals" from the depths of the Paleolithic.

Hunting and gathering peoples of modern times show some broad similarities in the nature and scale of social groupings and political integration. They are often spoken of as representing a *band* form of social and political organization. In §26, we will look briefly at the technology of modern hunters and gatherers, at the ways they shaped and were shaped by ecosystems, and at their characteristic modes of social organization.

The many peoples of Africa, the Americas, Asia, and the Pacific whose ways of life rested on an essentially Neolithic technology have often been grouped together as another "level" in the development of culture and society. Horticulture and the raising of domestic animals—still augmented in many places by hunting, fishing, and gathering of vegetable foods—provide the major subsistence bases for such peoples. Here once more one cannot usefully view primitive horticulturists as relics of the early Neolithic. For as we have seen, the Neolithic hardly represents a stage in a chronological sense; and these peoples of the ethnographic present represent developments *from*, rather than survivals *of*, the early food producing complexes. Many peoples in Africa and Southeast Asia whose subsistence economies are built on food plants of the early Neolithic complexes—yams, millet, taro, dry rice—were using iron tools when Europeans arrived on the scene.

In §27, looking at shifting cultivation and pastoralism, we will glimpse these technologies that developed from the early Neolithic; and we will see how they shaped the lives, and environments, of these peoples who were on hand to greet (or eat) the first Europeans in so many corners of the globe. A frequent label for societies of this scale is *tribal*. The basis for such a lumping of societies is a mode of political organization that has been called a *tribe*. In a narrowed technical sense, a tribe is a population unified by common language and shared customs but without any overarching government or centralized political organization. Instead, local groups characteristically based on kinship are the major political units. They are bound together by ties of intermarriage and hence networks of kinship; and by overarching social categories (such as traditional descent from the same distant ancestor) that provide a rationale for temporary political alliances between groups.

Though "tribal" is often a useful term for people with Neolithic technologies who lack central political organization, it has been used by some writers (in preference to "primitive," with its condescending connotations) to refer to modern hunters and gatherers as well as horticulturists and pastoralists, and to societies with central chiefs as well as those without them.

Writers who stress the way technology shapes social and political institutions have often distinguished further stages along the path toward the stratification and political integration of the urban state. Thus the tribe, lacking any overarching political organization, can be distinguished from the *chiefdom*, where political offices unite kinship groupings and provide some centralized authority and control. Finally, in the *state*, we find in varying degrees the social stratification, economic specialization and complexity, and political centralization we saw emerging in the early Middle East. (See particularly Service, 1962).

In this chapter, our focus will be on technology and ecology among "primitive" peoples—hunters and gatherers and tribesmen. In the chapters to follow, particularly XI, XII, and XIII, we will examine complex societies and the new modes of organization they entail. At the end of this chapter, we will look at some of the interpretations of this sweep of human development, and of the nature and importance of these "levels" of technological advance and social integration.

26 · *The Ecology of Hunters and Gatherers*

If we look across the vista of man's time on earth, we see him—for almost the entire span—as collector of food from his environment. His technologies were limited, if often ingenious; and they often equipped him less well to compete in an ecosystem than many of the hunting and plant-eating animals that shared it with him. Yet man could plan, organize, build rules, communicate, and cumulate his knowledge and innovations. The flexibility and adaptability of his technology and mode of life enabled him to survive in a great range of settings.

Our view of man as food collector is inevitably partial and selective. Few hunters and gatherers survived into modern times, and those that did were in forbidding environments or remote margins where the transformations of technology and the expansions of civilization had not yet penetrated. It is too easy to take as our image of the hunter and gatherer an Australian Aborigine or Bushman in parched desert, or an Eskimo on ice; and to forget that aboriginal Australians lived for millenia around temperate Sydney harbor as well as the desert (they were just exterminated faster).

Our evidence, though partial, gives us valuable insights on the two sides of man as food collector in ecosystems: on the way he affected these systems and on the way they shaped his mode of life.

Characteristically, hunters and gatherers live in *bands*, each exploiting a territory. They face environments in loosely knit clusters of families, able

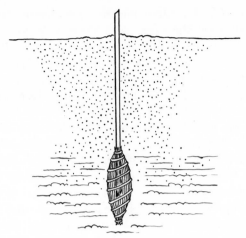

Figure 16. Bushman Filter Pump. Water is drawn from underground sources through a hollow reed with a grass filter at the lower end. (After Passarge.) FMK

to organize into sizable groups for some economic and ritual activities, yet able to disperse into smaller family groups or forage individually. Such flexibility is crucial in facing seasonal changes in environment and adapting to the different demands of hunting large animals and foraging for wild foods or hunting small game (Lee and DeVore, 1968).

Figure 17. A Bushman of Africa's Kalahari Desert tests his sinew bowstring in preparation for a hunt. With these arrows, poisoned with the juice of crushed beetles, Bushmen kill kudu, springbok, wildebeests, and other large game. (After a photograph by the Marshall Expedition.) RMK

The technologies of modern hunters and gatherers are highly limited in terms of the control they give men over their environments and the efficiency with which investments of energy yield a return. They are also highly ingenious. At this technological level, man adjusts to an environment, changing his patterns of living to follow the cycles of an ecosystem. He has a oneness with the world of nature that modern men, and even Neolithic peoples, have lost.

Australian Aborigines or African Bushmen living in parched deserts can glean a living by using a range of grubs, plants, and sources of water that would not even be noticed by a European traveler. Material possessions are minimal. An Australian Aborigine may travel with no more than a digging stick, hunting weapon, and bundle of sacred objects, with no fixed home base. Temporary camps may be made with no shelters or with crude lean-tos that are abandoned as the band moves on. Hunting weapons for large animals may include bows and arrows, spears, snares, pit traps, and such specialized inventions as blowguns, boomerangs, bola (a rope with weights to entangle an animal's legs), and spear-throwers.

Fire is produced by friction in various ways: the fire drill, operated by hand or with a bow to turn the drill; the fire-plow, or stick pushed in a groove; or the fire saw, a stick drawn back and forth across a piece of wood. Yet apparently in at least one isolated pocket, the Andaman Islands, hunting and gathering man had lost the ability to produce fire. Survival depended on keeping the home fires burning, which can be a problem if home is where you happen to hang your dilly bag. Without pottery or metal, men relied on such vessels and containers as bamboo tubes, animal skins, and even empty ostrich eggshells.

Modern studies of Australians, Bushmen, and Pygmies have revealed how central in their survival is the undramatic collecting of vegetable foods by women. Hunting—dramatic, collective, ritually central, and, when successful, punctuating the daily routine—is easily overemphasized. But modern evidence reveals that roots, fruits, nuts, and other vegetable foods collected by women provide the staple base needed for survival (as in Lee's study of the Bushmen, 1968 and 1969). Game, to be sure, provides the times of plenty and contributes crucially to the diet; but man as hunter, bereft of great speed or keen sense of smell and dependent on limited weapons, is hard-pressed in what for any carnivore is a difficult game of chance.

Such a mode of subsistence imposes mobility on man and limits the scale and nature of his political and social organization. Certain forms of organization are particularly adaptive and have been found among widely separated hunting and gathering societies. *Patrilocal band* organization is simple yet flexible, and highly adaptive to scarce, dispersed resources. The basic principle of organization is that a man must marry a girl from a different band and she comes to live with his band. Thus any band consists of a cluster of mobile families whose men are related by birth to one another and their territory, and whose women are outsiders. This gives any individual links of kinship with other bands (his mother's, his mother's mother's, his father's mother's) while preserving the unity of the men who hunt on the territory. Furthermore, hunters can use the knowledge of local animals and terrain they acquired as boys (as they could not, if they went to live with the wife's band).

However, recent field studies of hunters and gatherers suggest that the "patrilocal band" is an idealization; and that partly due to ecological pressures affiliation is more flexible, and mobility more possible, than the "patrilocal band" would imply. Seasonal cycles may lead groups to gather and then scatter, with shifts of membership. Where resources are richer and more concentrated, larger, composite, social groupings may occur. Even in small and scattered bands, there may be great variety in the composition of local groups. The !Kung Bushmen, for instance, require that a young husband join his bride's band and contribute to its hunt for a number of years. The internal composition of bands is thus highly variable and shifting (Marshall, 1960). When resources are highly fragmented, as among the Shoshoni of the American Great Basin, nuclear families may be the only enduring social units (Steward, 1955).

Lee and DeVore (1968) usefully summarize the social and political implications of ecological pressures among hunters and gatherers. The relationship of men to resources is fragile and largely beyond direct human control. On the one hand, fluctuations in the food supply make fixed and exclusive access to resources unfeasible. On the other hand, demographic fluctuations in groups preclude strictly fixed group membership. By outmarriage, by fairly flexible rules of affiliation, by fission of bands that grow too large, and by reciprocal rights to hunt and gather on one another's territories, a flexible and adaptive balance between people and resources is preserved. Fixed and formal assignment to groups according to ideologies of descent and kinship is rare. We will see in Chapter VIII that even among Neolithic tribesmen, ecological pressures continue to demand a flexibility in social organization likely to be hidden beneath ideologies of descent.

Among hunters and gatherers, such ecological constraints on the dispersal, population, and mode of organization of man are fairly direct. More subtle constraints and influences take place in the realm of belief, ritual, and world view as well. Man perceives his oneness with nature immediately and directly (Lévi-Strauss, 1968). Colin Turnbull's picture of the world view of the African Pygmies of the Ituri Forest in *The Forest People* (1961) shows man *in nature*—not against nature—with striking vividness. Hunters and gatherers may see their environment as controlled by indwelling spirits, or they may symbolically express unity with plants and animals in *totemism*. This is a belief that a particular social group has a special relationship with a particular type of animal or plant, expressed in ritual, myth, rules against eating the "totem" species, and the like. The effects of ecological adaptation on the ideational realm may be even less direct: religious practices may serve adaptive ends of which their participants are unaware. Thus it has been suggested that divination by scapulimancy (cracks on animal shoulder blades) among some North American hunters may have served as a kind of primitive randomizing device for finding game, and that sexual license at rituals among Baja California Indians may have served to articulate a cycle of human reproduction with seasonal variations in food supply.

What about the other side, man's effect on ecosystems? At this technological level, it was much less dramatic than it became with the advent of agriculture. Man's role as hunter and gatherer was much more that of another species within the system, locked in a complex network of interdependence. Populations were small and scattered. Man's modes of life, his numbers and distribution, were geared to the animal and plant species on which he lived. He doubtless in the short run produced many ecological "runaways" by hunting out particular animals or changing migration patterns. But the imbalances he created in the long run limited and controlled him, creating new equilibrium. As hunter (and prey) among hunters, gatherer competing with herbivores for wild foods, man was inextricably bound in a web of nature. When technology transformed him into a new and far more numerous kind of being, his influence on ecosystems became profound and disruptive.

27 · *The Ecology of Tribal Food Producers*

In §19 we glimpsed the nature and timetable of the technological revolution whereby man became a food producer. We have seen in barest outline the range of tribal peoples in Africa, the Americas, Asia, and Oceania who— when Europeans arrived on the scene—had filled in most of the habitable world with a mosaic of variation.

Across this range one can scarcely generalize about men-in-ecosystems without leaving out all that is interesting. Clearly with increased food supplies, man became a much more common animal. He radically transformed his environments and his relations with them. The complexity of this process is usefully illustrated by a classic study by Livingstone (1958) concerning the relationships of man and malaria in Africa. Apparently the hold of malaria in West Africa was established when, with the advent of Neolithic technology, primary rain forests were cut into a patchwork of cultivation and secondary forest—changing the balance of sunlight and rainfall and providing in man an abundant host for malarial parasites. Malaria has since held man in its grip, keeping populations down, shaping their distribution and in many respects their social patterns. Livingstone shows this web of biological interconnectedness in the operation of an abnormal hemoglobin in human blood, the "sickle cell," common in these areas of West Africa. A person inheriting the gene from both father and mother suffers a fatal anemia; a person inheriting one sickling gene and one normal gene acquires a resistance to malaria—and so the frequency of the abnormal gene is kept in dynamic balance. Not only does this illustrate the subtle interconnections between human settlement patterns and subsistence and biological components of the environment, but also it usefully reminds us that crucial components of men's ecosystems include disease-producing microorganisms as well as plants and animals.

Two major modes of ecological adaptation, among the great range of variations, are particularly striking and common: "shifting cultivation" and pastoralism.

We will look first at shifting cultivation. Early agriculture on and around the fertile hilly flanks of the Middle East, and later in rich river lands, had involved an artificial extension of the environments where the plants had grown in the wild. When men in the tropical rain forests of Africa, Meso-america, Southeast Asia, and the Pacific developed modes of cultivation, their challenge was much more difficult. Though plants suited to tropical climates were domesticated, especially in Southeast Asia, the task of creating an environment where these plants could grow was by no means easy.

We think of a tropical rain forest as a lush and fertile place. But this is seldom true, except where volcanic soil creates a rich environment. More commonly, tropical soils are infertile. Under the towering forest canopy, primary rain forest is by no means the lush tangle of vegetation of Holly-wood's stereotype. Not enough sunlight penetrates to support thick under-growth, except where rivers or other openings break the canopy. What fertility there is comes from the thick layer of decaying vegetation fallen from above. When the giant forest trees are cleared—an immense task with polished stone adzes and fire—the ground is opened for planting yams, taro, maize, dry rice, or manioc. Burning the leaves and branches accumu-lated in clearing the area temporarily enriches the soil. But then the problems set in. Torrential rains and hot sun leach out the nutrients quickly, and can laterize the soil into infertile crusts. By the time a crop has been harvested, the soil is often exhausted. After a second crop, if it is possible at all, the soil is likely to be useless for cultivation. (Meanwhile, hungry insects and birds from the surrounding forest have done their best to harvest the crops ahead of the men who planted them).

The solution worked out by Neolithic man in the tropics was a sys-tem known as "shifting" or "swidden" cultivation. Any family or kin group must have considerably more land than is needed for gardens at any time. As a crop is harvested in one garden, a new garden is cleared and planted. The old garden is allowed to lie fallow, and secondary growth of grasses, bushes, and then forest covers the old garden. At some optimum point— often ten or twenty years if land is sufficient—a balance is struck between renewed fertility of the land and the difficulty of clearing it again for a new garden. One of the little understood problems of such systems is how popula-

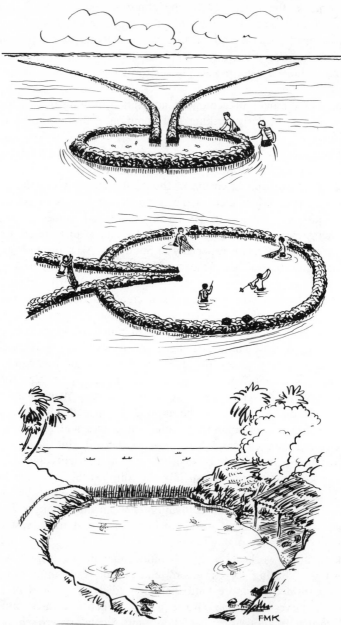

Figure 18. Neolithic technology opened new marine resources to man. Here, in the Pacific, are a Micronesian fish pond built of rock in a shallow lagoon (above); and a turtle pond in the Lau Islands, Fiji (below). These can be used for live storage, and hence represent a kind of marine "farming." FMK

tions remain in balance with land resources. Here complex interrelationships between nutrition, human fertility, longevity, and diseases such as malaria probably came into play; and we do not yet understand them. Shifting cultivation has often been condemned as wasteful. Yet careful modern studies have shown that—given the limitations of technology—swidden cultivation is often an exceedingly effective adaptive system.

Usually the ground is worked only by simple digging sticks, often improvised and at best hardened by fire. Technically, such cultivation without the use of the plow is called "horticulture" rather than "agriculture." Polished stone axes and adzes, the original cutting and felling tools of Neolithic man, were supplanted by iron in some areas, making it more feasible to fell virgin forest where it was available.

Usually the starchy yams, taro, manioc, and sweet potato, and the more nutritious and high-yield rice and maize (in the Americas), provide the bulk of subsistence food. (The true yam is a quite different plant from the sweet potato). Pigs and other domestic animals may be central in the prestige economy. In coastal areas new and more efficient modes of food gathering were developed, as Neolithic canoe and fishing technology brought rich marine resources within reach. At times fishing even approached a kind of farming.

Furthermore, men armed with Neolithic technology—and the more sedentary mode of life it made possible—could build more elaborate and permanent houses and acquire physical property on a scale impossible for mobile hunters. Neolithic man has moved well along the progression to Western Man, trapped by his own hardware so that moving to a new house becomes a traumatic experience.

Shifting cultivation poses many constraints on the social order. Very large populations cannot concentrate in permanent villages. Rather, smaller villages, dispersed hamlets, or shifting homesteads scatter the population through the terrain. In the tribal world, large and permanent communities usually occur either where intensive cultivation has been possible (as with the rice-terracing peoples of Northern Luzon in the Philippines) or where some rich local resource makes food gathering on a large scale possible (as with the salmon-fishing Indians of the American Northwest Coast or the sago palm gathering tribesmen of New Guinea swamplands).

Two examples of the complicated interconnections between cultural forms and ecosystems among shifting horticulturists will be useful.

Example 3: Kwaio Residence Patterns and Ecology

The Kwaio of the Solomon Islands live in scattered clusters of homesteads, dotted through rugged mountains and moved every few years. At first glance, one would expect these moves to follow the annual shifting of gardens. But there turns out to be only a very indirect relationship between where people live and where they make their gardens, which are far enough away to minimize depredation by domestic pigs. Kwaio say they move when their ancestors get angry about violations of taboos, and make people or pigs sick. Observation confirms that they move when some grave violation occurs or when it is discovered through divination that they have defiled the settlement. Yet stepping outside to view this as an ecosystem, this pattern of moves minimizes and isolates diseases and distributes the population in relation to resources—and hence is highly adaptive.

Example 4:   Ritual Cycles and Ecology among the Maring

The Maring of the New Guinea Highlands sacrifice pigs to cement relations with ancestral spirits. Periodically, great numbers of pigs are killed ceremonially. It has been argued vividly that these cycles of rituals not only keep Maring ancestors in order; they serve to maintain a delicate ecological balance between men and environment, and help to regulate fighting and maintain networks of trade and alliances (Rappaport, 1967).

This raises the question of how customs can be subject to a selective weeding out, so that those customs survive and are elaborated which are adaptive sociologically and ecologically (even if the people themselves do not know why). We will return to this important question in §28 and §40.

Pastoralism is a second classic mode of food producing adaptation. The herding of cattle—or camels, reindeer, sheep, and other animals—takes many forms, yet a general contrast with agriculture emerges. Neolithic cultivation creates miniature environments in which domesticated plants can thrive. But the technology of tribal man enabled him to exert little control over the environments needed by large domestic animals. Patterns of rainfall and vegetation and the mobility and requirements of the animals largely structure men's modes of pastoralism. Pastoralists are in some places fully nomadic, moving continually to follow resources; in others, they migrate seasonally to fit into an ecological cycle. They may have fixed territories and permanent bases or they may have free access to grazing lands.

The mode of life of a pastoral people is not *determined* by ecological factors, however strongly it may be shaped by them. How cultural and ecological factors are intertwined here comes out clearly in a study of two pastoral peoples of East Africa.

Example 5:   The Jie and the Turkana

The Jie and Turkana are two of a cluster of tribes very closely related culturally and linguistically. The Turkana split off and migrated several centuries ago into a larger but much more arid and barren region. Gulliver (1965) documents the close similarities between Jie and Turkana in the cultural principles governing property rights, livestock, and family structure.

In their more densely populated, more fertile setting, Jie maintain permanent settlements and aggregate into fairly stable large groups. Though there are no formal property restrictions on where one's cattle can graze, mobility is limited and the population is fairly stable. Among the Turkana, living in a marginal desert environment, camels and goats play a major part as well as cattle. Settlements are constantly moved, there are no permanent points of reference, families act as isolated units, and alliances are temporary. Here an ecological setting limits and shapes the way a cultural pattern can unfold. On the one hand, social organization has undergone major changes in this adaptation to a new environment. On the other, had Turkana entered this new environment with different concepts of rights over animals and territory and different principles of kinship, their adaptations to the new setting would have taken different forms.

Historically, pastoralism represents an offshoot from the mixed agriculture and herding complexes of the Middle Eastern Neolithic—an offshoot in the opposite direction from the complex of tropical shifting cultivation, in adaptation to dry grasslands.

The fully nomadic peoples like the Mongols ironically represent not an independence from settled agricultural communities but a kind of symbiotic interdependence with them. The horsemen who were the scourge of Egypt (the Hyksos), of Medieval Europe, of China, depended on settled communities for many of the products they needed to survive; and in turn the herds of the nomads contributed centrally to the economy of settled groups during the periods of peace. Nomadic life offered an escape from poverty for peoples on the margins; yet in times of drought the settled communities provided a refuge for nomads.

Neolithic man transforms his environment, often drastically. Partly this reflects a more powerful technology; and partly a tremendous expansion in population it made possible. (We have seen how, in West Africa, Neolithic farmers changed virgin rain forest into a patchwork of cultivation; and how, with permanent settlements and the clearing of forest cover, malaria became established). He was often more disruptive; modern man is not the first polluter and despoiler of his environment. Shifting cultivation can get out of hand ecologically, turning old gardens into useless scrub grasslands rather than secondary forest. Large areas of New Guinea have been permanently deforested. Massive erosion can result from overcultivation or overgrazing. Even with his limited technology, Neolithic man was a dominant and disruptive force on the ecological scene. Manhattan may have been ruined by the time the Indians sold it.

28 · *Ecology, Evolution, and Adaptation*

In these relationships between man and environment, between culture and ecosystem, and between technology and social organization, common themes and patterns emerge. Urbanized states are larger and more complex than tribal groups, and clearly this is geared to increased technological mastery. The social organization of pastoral nomads is obviously adaptive to their mode of life. Moreover, similar sequences and adaptive patterns turn up in different times and places.

How are these regularities and sequences to be interpreted? This has been a dominant question in twentieth-century anthropology. A number of major theoretical positions have been articulated, and we will glance at the most important.

Models of evolutionary progress in culture had been prominent in nineteenth-century anthropology (§67). The proposed evolutionary schemes had been scathingly criticized early in the twentieth century by scholars concerned with detailed facts and sound evidence, and "cultural evolution" fell into general disrepute.

A lone dissenting voice for many years was Leslie White. One of the remarkable figures of anthropology, White stuck to his guns against assults from many sides. Since the mid-1940s, he has propounded and elaborated a modern approach to cultural evolution that in recent years has profoundly affected anthropological thinking (see for example, Sahlins and Service, 1960; Dole and Carneiro, 1960).

The premises of White's evolutionary theory can be fairly simply stated:

1. Cultures as symbolic systems have emergent properties, and hence must be studied in their own terms—not in terms of biology, individuals, or environments. White thus called for a science of "culturology," a study as it were of how cultures behave, not how individuals behave.

2. The "behavior" of cultures is directly geared to their technological control over environments. The laws of a science of culture will deal largely with the way technology-in-environment generates cultural forms (social and political organization, and even to a large degree religion and philosophy). Much of White's work explicates the seeming paradox whereby cultures are emergent symbolic systems to be studied in their own right, yet patterns of ideas and custom are generated by technology and economy.

3. Man's technology has progressed through the harnessing and conversion of energy more and more efficiently. Technological advance can be defined in terms of thermodynamic efficiency.

4. Cultural systems have evolved into higher forms in response to these technological advances (which we have glimpsed in Chapter V). This evolution is reflected in higher levels of integration, from the *band*, to agricultural or pastoral *tribes*, to *chiefdoms*, and finally *states*, each embodying greater spans of integration and control, greater internal differentiation, and so on. Evolutionarily higher forms have greater adaptability and hence replace evolutionarily lower forms (as in the spread of Western technology to the tribal world).

Julian Steward (1955) has attempted to bridge between the sweeping scale of White's evolutionism and the particularism of "anti-evolutionists."

White, he argues, has moved beyond the nineteenth-century position that all cultures have passed through similar stages. But the cost has been to deal with evolutionary levels in such general terms that the power of the evolutionary model is lost: one has reduced multiple sequences to their common denominator, and hence canceled out the most crucial variations. Instead, Steward argues for a focus on "multilinear evolution"—a search for similar sequences of development in different times and places. Thus the agricultural developments leading to urbanization in Mesopotamia and Central America, and their social and political consequences, reflect parallel processes.

Sahlins (1960) has clarified the issues by distinguishing between two distinct ways we can look at cultural evolution. "Specific evolution" involves the diversification of cultures to adapt to a range of environments. It stresses variability, divergence, and convergence (where the same kinds of influences and processes can have widely different outcomes in different settings, and similar pressures may produce similarities between ways of life that had been quite different). "General evolution" takes a more distant and generalizing perspective. It examines directions of progress, in the control of energy and in levels of cultural integration and complexity. On the first level, we should not look for progress or speak of evolutionary stages, but should examine modes of differentiation and adaptation. On the second level, we should not seek to account for details and variations.

Sahlins' distinction is useful,. and it foreshadows a decreasing emphasis on the great sweep of evolutionary progress—which, once noted, does not account for the sort of variation anthropologists usually deal with. Adaptation, not evolution, is the key concept; and it is here that a view of man as part of an ecosystem is most useful. Many scholars who are dubious about vast evolutionary models share a common ground with followers of White in their concern with cultural adaptation to ecosystems.

Steward had pioneered such studies in a series of classic papers (some collected in Steward, 1955) that examined the adaptation of hunters and gatherers (of whom the Basin Shoshoni Indians were his prime example) and other peoples. The "core" areas of a culture were those centering around the subsistence economy—settlement pattern, the size of groups, and so on. They in turn shaped other areas of culture. But given an environment and technology, a range of alternative modes or organization was possible.

Subsequent studies have explored the sorts of relationships between man and ecosystem we have illustrated—studies of mountain peoples of northern Pakistan, of African cattle herders, New Guinea pig breeders, and so on.

A major theoretical question underlying these ecological studies is the extent to which sets of ideas and customs arise, or are changed, in response to pressures from the environment. The conservative position for many years has been that an environment poses problems and restricts alternatives, but that cultural forms are not *determined by* ecological adaptation.

Kroeber, writing in the 1920s, summed up the discussions of his time by saying that the directly "determining" factors of cultural phenomena are "not nature which gives or withholds materials," but "the general state of knowledge and technological advancement of the group; in short, historical or cultural influences" (1923: 182). Early food gatherers in Europe roved unnoticing over fertile cultivable soil and mineral fields, and California Indians ground their acorns over oil pools that were later to be marked by forests of derricks. The geographer-anthropologist Forde cautiously observes that between the physical environment and human activity there is always "a middle term, a collection of specific objectives and values, a body of knowledge and belief: in other words, a cultural pattern" (1934: 463–464).

Extreme arguments on both sides have been advanced. Some, like White, have stressed the way technology shapes other areas of culture. Others, like Lévi-Strauss, view technology as limiting feasibility, but not as shaping the cultural products of the human mind (§58). A more productive middle position is to view the relationship between cultural creativity and ecological channeling not simply as a limiting of possibility but as a two-way pattern of interaction. Human beings have a remarkable capacity to prefer as their staple food the one that happens to grow best or be easiest to catch in their environment; but they also will take a useless plant and invest it with rich symbolic significance that "adaptation" can scarcely account for. The problem is to keep both sides of man in view—to see him both as pragmatist, choosing adaptive paths, and as symbol manipulator, elaborating complex, rich, and variable codes. We will face this problem again.

We are touching here a basic question about man—about what he is and can be. The complex many-sidedness of man seems distorted by the very act of looking at him, since we can see only one side clearly at a time. If we focus on his intellect, we hide his emotions partly from view. If we analyze the formal order of linguistic and cultural codes, we miss more subtle patterns that yield to art and intuition but not to science. If we focus on man as follower of custom, we lose sight of him as creator and shaper of custom. If we focus on technological and pragmatic man, we disguise the richness of ideational worlds and religious experience. There seems to be no perspective for seeing all sides of man at once. And so, as we proceed, we must focus on facets one at a time, only glimpsing how they fit into a total design.

In the three chapters that follow, we will explore a broad area central in anthropology for many decades—the organization and structure of social groups in primitive societies, especially groupings based on *kinship*. This will lead us past esoteric Inner Mysteries around which large cults of anthropologists gather. It will also provide a framework of the social groupings of tribal societies that we will need in subsequent chapters to understand economic, political, and legal processes.

VIII Social Organization in Tribal Societies: Kinship and Descent

A STARTING POINT in understanding and mapping another way of life is to find out about the cast of characters—what kinds of people there are and how they are organized into social groups and networks. Exploring *social organization* in non-Western societies has been a major challenge to social anthropology.

The most complicated, fascinating, and important modes of social grouping in primitive societies are based on kinship. Thus for decades the anthropological study of social organization has been above all the study of systems of kinship and marriage. Yet other modes of social grouping, based on community, age, sex, and inequality, are woven into the designs of social life in jungle as well as city; and in modern complex societies they come increasingly to the fore.

In the next three chapters, which are closely tied together and complementary, we will look at the social organization of tribal societies. We will glimpse continuities as well—back to the social organization of hunting and gathering peoples, and forward to complex modern societies. We will begin by setting out some useful guides for thinking about man's social life, building on foundations laid in Chapter II. Then, in this chapter, we will look briefly at the way kinship and descent structure tribal social life. In the next chapter our exploration of tribal social organization moves on to marriage and family structure. In Chapter X, we will examine the way such factors as age, sex, and inequality are used to organize social groupings, especially in tribal settings. Finally, at the end of this third chapter on tribal social organization, we will look at some theories and interpretations of why a particular society comes to be organized in a particular way.

29 · *Social Organization: Some First Principles*

Anthropologists, when they talk about "social organization" or "social structure," often mean by that a set of problems centering around kinship in a broad sense. Biological facts of sex, infantile dependence, and the life cycle impose broad constraints on human life in all times and places. On this biological framework, human societies have worked out principles of mating, family structure, and relatedness by birth, descent, and marriage that are far less varied than they might be. Study of these principles has been a central theme in anthropology since the latter nineteenth century; and the puzzles they pose have by no means yet been solved. Social organization is, as we have noted, not simply a matter of kinship—but, rather, of all the modes of organizing social groupings that bind men together and make ordered social life possible.

Fortunately, some basic ways of thinking about people and groups are as useful when we focus on American suburbia as when we look at the complicated kinship groupings and age-grades of a Brazilian Indian tribe. A key here is to distinguish, as we did in §6, between two facets of human social life, the cultural and the social.

To study social organization, it is often said, one begins with *social relationships*. But what *is* a social relationship? If we take two people, A and B, we can see two sides or facets to their "relationship." First there are the ways they interact, the things they do and say in their dealings with one another. But there are also their *ideas about* their relationship, their conceptions of one another, the understandings and strategies and expectations that guide their behavior.

Both patterns of behavior and conceptual systems have "structure," in the sense that they are not helter-skelter or random. But they are different *kinds* of structure. Imagine an intersection governed by traffic lights. If we observed it for a while, we could record the "behavior" of the cars in terms of the density of traffic in various directions at various times; and the number of cars that stop, go through, and slow down, according to sequences of changing lights. From these records would crystallize patterns of regularity, the "social structure" of the intersection. We would probably find the social structure of an American intersection quite different from a Latin American counterpart. But alternatively, we could describe the principles for making decisions about what the driver should do in the intersection—not only the laws that are written down, but the unwritten "rules" about honking horns and going through while the lights are changing. These "rules" also have a structure; but it is quite different from the patterns of traffic flow.

In tribal settings before European intrusion, the situations a person encountered in life usually corresponded fairly neatly to the guides for action his culture laid down—though as we will see some lack of "fit" is basic to human life. In times of rapid social change, these gulfs between the way the world is and the cultural guides for living in it become increasingly wide. Thus driving "rules" in a Latin American country can lead to chaos if the number of cars is quadrupled and freeways and cloverleafs are introduced. And the Brazilian Indian from the savannas of Matto Grosso would hardly be equipped to cope with downtown Sao Paolo. We need to perceive and study the structure of both social and cultural orders if we are to understand process and change, and to see how individuals, finding paths through the maze of life, are fitted together into wider networks.

In the next three chapters, and those that follow, this distinction between the cultural (ideas, categories, and "rules") and the social (people, acts, events, and groups) will be centrally important. It enables us to see, first of all, the familiar social science concept of *roles* in a new light. If we distinguish the realm of people and events from the realm of ideas, roles clearly fall into the latter. They are not, as many would treat them, *positions* strung out in imaginary social networks. Rather, they are sets of conventions and expectations, cultural guides to appropriate behavior. It is as though the people in a society were message-exchanging devices in a communications network. Each device can send and receive in a number of different *modes*, and in each mode a somewhat different set of code rules for constructing and sending messages is used. *Roles*, these different modes and the special rules that go with them, are part of the *code system*. They are in a quite different realm from people (the message-exchanging devices) and their interaction (the messages).

The distinction between social and cultural also enables us to see a contrast between *cultural categories* and *social groups*. A cultural category is a set of entities in the world (people, things, events, supernaturals) that are classed as similar for some purposes, because they have in common one or more culturally relevant attributes. Thus trees, weeds, bachelors, and left-handed baseball pitchers are categories in our culture. As categories, they exist in people's conceptual worlds: the category "cow" does not eat grass. Note also that not all of them have one-word labels in our language. Nor are they sets of entities we keep in separate "chunks" in our conceptual world. Rather, they are sets we *draw mental lines around* in particular contexts. Ladies who wear size seven dresses comprise a relevant category in only a very few contexts (mainly for people who make or sell dresses, while they happen to be at work). Thus any single entity can be classed, in varying contexts, as belonging to dozens of different cultural categories. A category of human beings, grouped conceptually because of some socially relevant features they share in common (like "men" or "warriors" or "descendants of ancestor X"), we can call a *social category*.

A *social group*, on the other hand, consists of actual warm-blooded human beings who recurrently interact in an interconnected set of roles. Thus groups can be distinguished from forms of aggregation, such as crowds or gatherings, whose interaction is temporary and limited. Members of a social group need not all interact face-to-face, though such *primary groups* are common in the small-scale communities anthropologists usually study. What defines a group is its internal organization, the connection of its members in a set of interconnected roles. Thus the stockholders of a Western corporation comprise a *secondary group*. Although most of its members do not interact with one another, they are bound into a group through their relationships with the management.

Who belongs to a group is seldom neatly defined by some cultural principle like being descended from the same ancestor or being the right age or social class. Such membership in a social category usually defines *eligibility* to be a member of a group. Whether an eligible person actually takes part in a group is likely to depend on the circumstances of life history, on economic interests and resources, on personal choice.

To illustrate some basic points about categories and groups, we will look at a hypothetical example from our own society—one that parallels closely the kinship-based categories and groups of tribal societies.

Imagine that three generations ago, in a New England community, ten men organized and founded a music festival which has gone on ever since. Priority for tickets to the festival now goes to the Patrons of the festival, who comprise all those descendants of the ten founders who take part in meetings and maintain an active interest. Many of the descendants *eligible* to be Patrons have, of course, moved away and lost touch. But if they ever moved back, they could become active again, and if they happened to visit on the day of a performance a good seat would always be found for them. At any performance, there will also be persons in the audience who come as guests of Patrons or who are simply filling in the remaining seats.

What sorts of social units have we here? First, all descendants of the founders, whether Patrons or those who have moved away or lost interest, form a *social category*. Their descent status makes them eligible to activate a set of rights if they can and wish. Second, those descendants who are Patrons comprise a *corporate group*, which ultimately controls the activities of the festival (and whose members enjoy the attendant privileges, though they may well not turn up at a particular performance). Finally, the audience actually attending a performance comprises a *gathering*. But if they gathered in some more organized fashion to perform a common task (to erect a new stage, for example), we could call the mixed bunch who actually came an *action group* or *task group*. The anthropological literature is full of confusions about "clans" and "lineages" and "kindreds" where these distinctions between groups and categories, corporations and action groups, have been blurred or overlooked.

30 · Kinship in Tribal Societies

A most striking feature of tribal societies—whether in African jungle, tiny Oceanic atoll, Near Eastern desert, or Arctic tundra—is the pervasive importance of kinship in social life. Our own lives have increasingly been shaped by urbanization, machine-age technology, a vast world economy, and mass communication. We find it hard to understand a way of life where relationships with people are preeminently relationships with relatives. In many societies, all members of the tribe or community trace relationships of blood or marriage with one another; in some places, a person is either your relative or your enemy. And such systems have probably prevailed through most of man's years on earth.

Study of the forms of social arrangement built around kinship has been a dominant theme in anthropology for almost a century. Almost all the leading figures in anthropological theory have participated at one time or another in debates about kinship, and a very extensive body of technical literature continues to expand. Even those who are not specialists in this area must lead their readers through the intricacies of kinship—in a jargon incomprehensible to the uninitiated—in describing the life of a primitive people. We will not attempt here to cover all the technical concepts and controversies, though the reader who makes his way through the pages that follow will be well on his way toward understanding more technical works in the field.

Before we begin, it will be rewarding to ask why anthropologists have worried so much for so long about the intricacies of kinship.

Kinship as the Basic Idiom of Social Relations

In the societies anthropologists usually study, one has to make sense of kinship to make sense of anything else. Even where people in a non-literate society are competing for economic advantage or political power, they are likely to talk about what they are doing in terms of kinship. Moreover, kinship ties serve as models or templates for relationships to non-relatives and often to deities. Relationships of "fictive kinship"—such as our "godparents" and the much more important *compadrazgo* or ritual co-parenthood of Latin America—are modeled on blood ties. In many places supernaturals are metaphorically treated like fathers (or maternal uncles—a reminder that our notions about paternal authority are by no means universal).

The anthropologist who enters a primitive community can anticipate that people do not always live up to the ideal standards of behavior between relatives, and that they act toward one another in many roles other than those based on blood relationship. Yet his first challenge is to sort out the cast of characters, and he has usually found it useful to begin with complex webs of connection by blood and marriage. Having done so, he can proceed to decipher the complex social processes carried out in this idiom and perceive how kinship serves as a basic model for relating to one's fellow men. The anthropologist often finds that until he himself has been assigned a place, albeit fictional, in this scheme of kinship, he cannot take part in the life of the community.

Kinship as a Focal Point of Values

Obligations between relatives are viewed as morally binding, and their fulfillment ranks high among the paramount virtues of a tribal people. If we think back to man's primate ancestry, and the transformations of social organization that opened the path to the ways of Neolithic and modern man, the reasons for this begin to emerge.

What three major transformations made human social life possible? First, the continuing association of a male—"the father"—with the primate nuclear group of mother and offspring. Second, the prohibition of mating within this enlarged nuclear group—the "incest taboo." And, finally, the systematic *sharing* of food and other scarce resources, both within and between these nuclear groups.

Kinship systems build on the complex of relationships between father and mother, between parents and children, and between siblings, and extend them out to and beyond members of a local band. The obligations of kinship have a central symbolic significance we can understand in the light of these three transformations. They symbolize, for man as hunter or tribesman, the collective as opposed to the individual, social obligation rather than self-gratification; and they symbolize the cultural in contrast to the biological. As we will see, the rule that one must marry someone outside one's own band creates and symbolically underlines interdependence between groups, making possible the organization of a wider society. In the light of our primate ancestry, it is not surprising that until the urban revolution has created new forms of social and political order, kinship has been central in the thought-worlds of man, as expression and symbol of what makes him human.

Limited Variation in Kinship Systems

A third and major reason for our attention to kinship, especially in comparative studies, is this. Many areas of culture have an extremely wide variation in different societies: house shapes, art forms, methods for disposing of the dead, modes of dress, and so on. The variations are as wide as physical and environmental possibility, and human imagination, permit. (Though we will see in §57 and §58 how even here the human mind imposes its own constraints on cultural possibility). Yet far less variation occurs in the realm of kinship. We find over and over again variations on the same themes, different combinations of familiar elements. This should not surprise us. Even human imagination can devise only so many ways of assigning parentage, tracing descent, classifying relatives, transmitting rights across generations, forming groups, and regulating mating. Given the common elements of human biology we sketched in Chapter III, the range of possibility is distinctly limited.

It is good intellectual exercise, and a rewarding challenge, to try to devise ways men could have solved these biological problems without assigning parentage to childen, without using some form of marriage to make these assignments (thereby creating family units), and without building from such parent-child-marriage links a network of kinship connections. Yet although in some ways societies have approached these limits, all known societies have some form of marriage and attribute some importance to kinship. Once these commitments have been made, the range of possibilities is greatly narrowed.

It is worth looking briefly at some of the outer limits of variation at this point. By approaching the subject of kinship with some classic natural experiments in the possibilities of human life, we will get a first glimpse of the fascination of kinship systems, and a reminder that we can understand them only by breaking out of our assumptions about what is "natural" and viewing them in terms of their own logic.

Example 6: Banaro Social Structure

The Banaro of New Guinea live in villages that are divided into two "halves"; and everyone belongs to one side or the other. A child belongs to the side of his father; but this is also the side of his mother, because a man must marry a girl from his own side. But if each side is self-contained, how are the two sides bound up together into a single society? Because every man has an "opposite number" on the other side, and to pass through the various stages of life he is dependent on this opposite number. If we look at a man we will call A, and his opposite number B (who is not related by blood or marriage since all A's kinsmen are on his own side), we see this dependence most clearly when A's son marries. It is B, not the groom, who sexually initiates the bride—on an altar and disguised as a "goblin." B then has regular sexual relations with the bride until she has her first child; and only then is A's son permitted to live with her. The first child is the "child of goblin" and has a special (but not kinship) relation to B's side (Thurnwald, 1916).

Example 7: Nayar *Taravad* and Marriage

Among the Nayar castes of South India, the basic social group, the taravad, *was composed of men and women descended in the female line from a common ancestress. Children became members of their mother's* taravad, *not their father's. In fact the only "marriage" in anything like our* sense was a religious ritual before the "bride" reached puberty. After that a woman had many lovers, who simply visited her; the presumed father of a child had only the most minimal ritual attachment to the child (Gough, in Schneider and Gough, 1961).

Example 8:   Nuer "Ghost Marriage"

Two unusual forms of marriage among the Nuer, pastoralists of the Sudan, will illustrate other possibilities. A widow ideally marries the brother or another close relative of her dead husband; or she may simply take lovers. The socially defined father of any children she bears is the dead first husband (what has been called "ghost marriage"). In another form, an old and important woman may "marry" a girl. The woman finances marriage transactions as if she were a man. The girl then bears children by lovers, and the old woman is treated (for purposes of inheritance and the like) as their "father" (Evans-Pritchard, 1951).

Example 9:   Toda "Fatherhood"

Another possible system for marriage and assigning parenthood is found among the Toda of India. One woman ideally had several husbands (in many cases brothers). How, then, to decide which one is the father for social purposes? By a ritual "presenting of the bow," which determines the father of this and subsequent children until it is another husband's "turn." If the man who has last gone through this ritual dies, and until another husband does so, any children born are considered those of the dead man (Rivers, 1906).

Example 10:   Father and Mother in Mota

Another possibility, from Mota in the South Pacific Banks Islands, is the validation of fatherhood by the payment of an expensive midwife's fee. If the father is unable to make this payment, another man can do so; and this man then assumes the role of father to the child. In such a case, the woman who bore the child no longer raises it; the wife of the man who paid the midwifery fee assumes this role (Codrington, 1891).

Mota provides another interesting variant as well: a man is expected to marry the widow of his maternal uncle.

Example 11:   The *Ghotul* of the Muria

The Muria of India have worked out an intriguing way of handling the problems of sex and marriage. Boys and girls spend their adolescence living together in coeducational "dormitories" called ghotul. The aim is free sexual *relations between all dormitory-mates, and any regular pairing off is discouraged. In some dormitories no couple is allowed to sleep together for more than two nights in succession. Yet the marriage rules specify that a boy must marry a girl from a different dormitory (Elwin, 1968).*

These variations, though revealing and intriguing, still remain within fairly narrow limits. Other social experiments, consciously constructed in some Utopian spirit, have gone farther in transcending the limits of kinship, marriage, and the family—as with Israeli *kibbutzim* or modern American "communes." Like the "natural experiments" that are primitive societies, they should be viewed not as curiosities but as systematic expressions of premises, ideologies, and logics that may differ from our own. The challenge is not to view a system as bizarre, but to discover the set of cultural meanings according to which it makes sense.

Despite the range of variation we have glimpsed, remarkably similar modes of kinship organization turn up across the ethnographic world. Thus the same mode of classifying relatives or organizing groups through common descent may turn up in Africa, the South Pacific, and aboriginal North

Figure 19. A Muria girl combs the hair of a dormitory mate. These two are the senior boy and girl in their ghotul, *and they decide who will sleep with whom on a particular night. (After Elwin.) RMK*

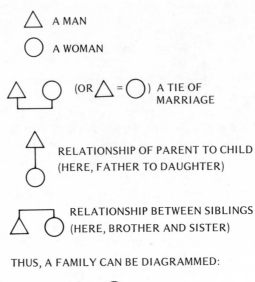

Figure 20. Anthropological Conventions for Diagramming Kinship Relations.

America—without historical connection. One of the challenges in the study of kinship is to seek out the way elements of kinship organization interlock as systems, so that the same clusters of elements may develop in different times and places. This entails a search for recurrent chains of cause-and-effect, such as those proposed by scholars like Steward and White (§28) and Murdock (§24). We will return to this search in §40.

Kinship, like chess, provides endless fascination for the specialist and an aura of mystery, unintelligibility, and triviality to the outsider. Yet there is a practical urgency to understanding at least the outlines of non-Western modes of kinship organization. In a world where more and more people are seeking to operate in, and change, societies quite different from their own, ignorance of these outlines can be disastrous. We must perceive forms of kinship, descent, and marriage quite different from our own in terms of their own structure and inner logic. "Common sense," being cultural sense, can be a poor guide indeed in another cultural world. Those who have condemned "bride-price" as degrading to women; those who have forced "natural" laws of inheritance on peoples who pass property to their sisters' children and not their own; those who are bewildered or morally outraged by marriage customs or forms of the family very different from their own—

all face frustration in trying to change what they do not understand, and cause disruption, bewilderment, and even disaster for the people whose ways of life they seek to transform.

31 · *What Is Kinship?*

"Kinship," to us, intuitively refers to "blood relationships." Our relatives are those connected to us by bonds of "blood." Our in-laws, to be sure, are related by marriage and not blood—and so are some of our aunts and uncles. But it is successive links between parents and children that are the essential strands of kinship.

But is this true in other societies? Consider the Toda or Nuer, where the child's socially recognized father may be a dead man—or, with the Nuer, a woman. And how can we talk about "blood" relationship between father and child, or mother and child, in cultures that have quite different theories or metaphors about the connection between parent and child? In some, the mother is thought to contribute no substance to the child, but only to provide a container for its growth. The Lakher of Burma, for instance, believe that two children with the same mother and different fathers are not relatives at all.

Moreover, the Trobriand Islanders of Melanesia and some tribes of Australian Aborigines staunchly deny that copulation between father and mother is the cause of pregnancy—hence seemingly denying the father a physical connection to the child. One of several theories of procreation advanced by the Trobrianders is that women are impregnated by ancestors while wading in the lagoon—which apparently leaves their spirits undampened. There has been much debate for years about this "ignorance" of paternity: whether it is a matter of theological dogma, like Christian virgin birth, whether it reflects a radically different theory of "causality," and so on.

But, at least, such variations must lead us at the outset to be wary of assuming that kinship is simply a matter of "blood relationship." It is safest to broaden our scope considerably and to say that relations of kinship are connections *modeled on* those conceived to exist between a father and child and between a mother and child. In a particular culture these connections may be viewed as the same for father and mother (as with our "blood" relations) or as different—based on metaphors of seed and soil, of bone and flesh, of substance and container, or whatever. Moreover, "modeled on" leaves room for those cases like Mota, Nuer, and Toda where a socially defined parent is known not to have actually fathered or borne the child. (Adoptive parenthood in our society and many others would similarly be modeled on "natural" parenthood).

In all known societies, a person traces kinship in this broad sense to relatives through both father and mother. A great many societies class some relatives by marriage, notably spouses of uncles or aunts, as if they were *consanguineal* relatives (relatives by birth). We do this ourselves. Usually a separate class of *affines*, relatives by marriage (like our "in-laws"), is distinguished.

The great importance of these networks of kinship ties in tribal societies has been underlined already. But the ways tribal peoples use networks of kinship very often parallel the ways we use them. Our ties with relatives appear most clearly on special occasions like Christmas or birthdays, when presents or cards are given or exchanged, and especially on the major events in our lives—our christening or Bar Mitzvah, our wedding, our funeral.

So too in tribal societies the ties of kinship between individuals come out most dramatically in the focal points of a person's life—his birth, initiation, feasts, marriage, death. In many societies, a person's relatives, or his close relatives, comprise an important social category, which is then called a *kindred*. From kindreds are crystallized the action groups that cluster around a person at the time of major events in his life. Note, however, that kindreds are not separate and enduring social groups, though action groups are recruited from them, any one person is included in the kindreds of many different people. Your Uncle Harry is someone else's father and another person's cousin—and if all three of you got married on the same day, Harry would be hard-pressed to be in all three places at once.

Kinship ties in a tribal society play a part in many spheres of life where they are no longer important to most of us. The people who live in a community, the people who work together, the people who compete and quarrel are, as we will see, mainly relatives. Before we can understand how kinship shapes social groups in tribal societies, and before we can look at an old preoccupation of social anthropologists, the way kinds of relatives are classified with "kinship terms," we must look at some organizational problems in tribal societies and ways in which kinship is used to solve them.

32 · Descent and the Organization of Tribal Societies

Organizational Problems of Tribal Societies

Consider the problems of organizing a society with, first, a Neolithic technology (say, shifting horticulture in a tropical or semitropical setting); second, a population in the thousands or tens of thousands speaking the same language and having generally similar customs; and third, no central government or formal political organization embracing the entire tribe or major sections of it.

In such a society a set of major organizational challenges is faced:

1. How will localized groupings with some kind of stable political order be formed?

2. How will the relationship of people to land resources be defined? (This technology is incompatible with a fixed relationship between individuals

and small partitioned tracts of land. Shifting cultivation, or pastoralism, imposes a need for mobility and flexibility in the relation of people to the resources of their environment).

3. How will the rights of individuals and groups be maintained across generations, and how can they be adjusted to the demographic fluctuations whereby some groups proliferate and others dwindle?

4. How will individuals have freedom of movement, and allies, in groups other than their own?

5. How will political relations between groups be maintained without any overarching governmental structure? And once war or feuding breaks out between groups, how can it be stopped?

The basic elements of kinship organization apparently were part of man's cultural heritage built up during millenia as hunter and gatherer. First and most basic was the tracing of kinship networks between individuals. Second, there was a system of *band* organization in which mobile local groups exploited territories. Third, there was the *incest taboo* (about which more shortly) prohibiting marriage with close kin; and probably, in at least many cases, its extension into a rule that a mate had to be found in a different band. The latter meant that a wide range of any person's relatives, through his mother, his grandmothers, and others, were in other bands— and that helped to bind bands together in peaceful political relations.

These heritages from their long past as hunters and gatherers provided the ingredients for solving the organizational problems of Neolithic tribesmen. While some of these solutions may well have been worked out long before the Neolithic, the tribesmen of the "ethnographic present" have elaborated a bewildering variety of specialized adaptations, only a few of which we can cover here. But the essential principles on which they build are simple enough.

Descent as an Organizing Principle

The key principle for solving these problems is *descent*. If we define rights over a territory with reference to an ancestor three or five or ten generations back—who founded or owned or conquered the territory—then we can neatly relate the people descended from that ancestor to the territory. But organizationally, this by itself will not suffice. From the standpoint of any particular ancestor, he has too many descendants. From the standpoint of any living individual, he has too many ancestors—eight great grandparents, sixteen great-great grandparents, and so on. If he had rights over the territories of each, the result would be an unworkable organization in which practically everyone had rights practically everywhere.

A further principle is needed, a principle that limits and excludes. The simplest way is to define only a few of the descendants of a founding ancestor as having rights over the territory and to exclude the rest. The

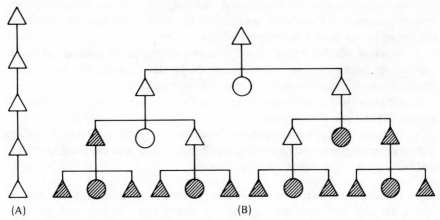

Figure 21. Patrilineal Descent. Figure 21A shows how descent is traced through a line of men. Figure 21B shows a descent category formed by patrilineal descent. It is simplified in that, in the real world, families are not all composed of two brothers and a sister. Living members of the descent category are indicated by hatching.

most common principle of descent is *patrilineal* or *agnatic*. Using a set of diagrammatic conventions used in kinship studies, Figure 21A shows how descent is traced patrilineally through a line of men. Figure 21B shows an idealized and simplified patrilineal descent category. Note that women, as well as men, are members of a patrilineal descent category; but that only men transmit this membership to their children.

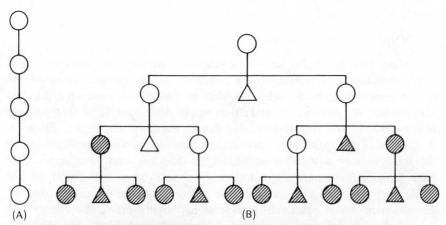

Figure 22. Matrilineal Descent. Figure 22A shows how descent is traced through a line of women. Figure 22B shows a descent category formed by matrilineal descent. Living members of the descent category are indicated by hatching.

An apparent mirror image is *matrilineal* or *uterine* descent, where descent is traced through a line of women (Figures 22A and 22B). As we will see, organizationally matrilineal descent is by no means the neat mirror image of patrilineal descent it appears to be on the diagrams.

These rules of descent permit neat solutions to the organizational problems of tribal societies set out in the last section. Consider a rule of patrilineal descent, combined (as it usually is) with a rule of *exogamy*, that male members of a descent group must marry girls from other groups. The patrilineal descendants of the founder of a territory can be organized as a *corporation* sharing rights to the territory. This means that problem (1), membership in local groups, is solved. Problem (2), the relation of men to territories, is solved. Problem (3), how rights are transferred and maintained across generations, is solved by the perpetual corporation and the rule of descent. Problem (4), how individuals can have ties to other groups and territories, is solved by the rule of exogamy—for a person will have outside allies in his mother's group, his father's mother's group, and so on. Problem (5), how political relations between groups can be maintained, can be at least partly solved by using these ties of intermarriage, and common descent from more distant ancestors, as bases for alliances.

But the overall solution is not that simple, as we will see. Moreover, some cautions are needed at the outset. First of all, patrilineal descent or matrilineal descent from the founding ancestor does not usually make a person a member of a descent corporation, an actual social group. In most societies using these organizational principles, being descended in the correct line *entitles* a person to be a member of a descent corporation. That is, patrilineal or matrilineal descent defines a category of persons entitled to be members. Whether they actually *are* members depends on the circumstances of life history and often on individual strategy and choice. In this respect, "descent groups" are like the corporation controlling our New England music festival: not all those eligible to be members actually are members. Moreover, in many such societies many people actually act as members of descent corporations even though they do not have the proper descent "credentials." This gap between descent entitlement and corporation membership—between being in a cultural category and being in a social group —is often important in making such forms of organization flexible and adaptive.

Second, once we perceive this gulf between descent entitlement and corporation membership we can understand another mode of forming descent corporations. This is to say that *all* descendants of a founding ancestor, through any combination of male or female links, comprise a descent category. Such a nonexclusive mode of tracing descent is called *cognatic descent*. As we noted earlier, an individual then belongs to many cognatic descent categories. The organizational problem is then to use patterns of residential history, strategy, and choice to narrow any particular individual's corporation membership down to a single group, despite his eligibility and secondary interests in the other groups and territories from whose founders he can trace cognatic descent.

Third, chains of descent often serve to define rules and rights other than corporation membership. Thus, succession to a position or office might be determined by descent in the male line; or individually owned property might be inherited in the female line. Some anthropologists would not want to call this "descent." But in any case, descent *categories*—patrilineal, matrilineal, or cognatic—may be accorded cultural relevance even where no corporate groups are involved.

Finally, this enables us to understand how, in a single society, different modes of tracing descent may be used for different purposes. Thus we must be wary of talking about a *society* as "patrilineal" or "matrilineal," as many anthropologists used to do.

Example 12:   The Tallensi of Ghana

The Tallensi, farming tribesmen of Ghana, have a complicated social and ritual organization in which patrilineal descent is central (Fortes, 1945, 1949). Thus corporate groups of Tallensi society are composed of persons patrilineally descended from a common ancestor. The Tallensi so emphasize patrilineal descent that they have often been cited as a classic example of a "patrilineal society."

Yet Tallensi individuals are bound together by complex webs of kinship on the maternal as well as paternal side. A man sacrifices to the spirits of his mother and close maternal relatives, as well as those on his father's side.

Furthermore, a Tallensi individual does not only have an interest in his father's corporate descent group; he also has secondary interests in his mother's group, his father's mother's group, and others to which he is more distantly related through a female link. When members of a patrilineal descent group sacrifice to their ancestors, any descendant through female as well as male links is entitled to partake of the sacrificial meal. Moreover, not only are members of a patrilineal descent group forbidden to marry one another, as in many such systems; but any man and woman who are descended from the same ancestor by any chain of male or female links are forbidden to marry. Such patterns, it has recently been argued, show that the Tallensi conceptualize their relatedness in terms of cognatic descent, as well as patrilineal descent and bilateral kinship (Keesing, 1970).

Finally, the Tallensi also attribute importance to relationship in the female line. Thus two persons who are descended, even distantly, through a chain of female links from a pair of sisters are conceived to have special and close ties; and witchcraft powers are specifically believed to be passed through such lines of matrilineal descent.

Here, then, in a single society seemingly dominated by patrilineal descent, we find—used in different ways for different purposes—the three major modes of conceptualizing descent, as well as widespread webs of bilateral kinship.

Patrilineal Descent as an Organizing Principle

What a typical patrilineal descent system is like can perhaps best be visualized by describing one in terms familiar to Americans. Imagine a town of some ten or twenty thousand people, composed of six districts. Each district is made up of some five or ten small neighborhoods. All of the people in the town have one of a dozen names—Smith, Jones, Brown, and so on. Children, as in our society, have the same last name as their father; and the rule of marriage is that no two people with the same last name can marry.

In a particular *neighborhood*, the houses and land on a particular street are all owned by people with one name. Let us narrow our focus to the Smiths living on Elm Street. All of them are descended from Sam Smith, the grandfather of the oldest men now living. The land on Elm Street they live on is owned by them collectively. Each Smith has a separate household for his family, though families assist one another in their work.

John Smith, one of the older men, acts as spokesman for these Elm Street Smiths in business and property matters, and leads them at religious services in the shrine at his house. One of the peculiarities of the legal system is that should one of the Elm Street Smiths get married, injure someone, or commit a crime, all of the Elm Street Smiths join together to bear the costs, or are all held accountable. To an outsider, one Elm Street Smith is as good as another. Note that it is only the Smith men, their wives (who are not Smiths), and their unmarried children who live on Elm Street. The married daughters of Smiths have gone to live with their husbands.

On the next street lives a group of Joneses, and on the other side a group of Browns. But within this neighborhood, there are six other streets of Smiths. All of these Smiths are descended from a common great-great-grandfather, and they recognize this at a neighborhood Smith church (where the founding Smith is buried) where they occasionally gather for collective rites. The neighborhood Joneses, Browns, and others also have their own churches. The people with a common name and a common church own only church property collectively, and although they do a few nonreligious activities together, they are not a tight little group like the Elm Street Smiths.

All of the Smiths within the district seldom see one another, except at a yearly religious outing, but they have a general feeling of unity based on the common descent they trace from a Smith ancestor seven generations ago.

Finally all Smiths in the *town* believe that they are descended from a founding Smith, though they do not know how they are related. They have a few common religious symbols, but have no further social unity.

In everyday circumstances the Smiths on Elm Street are a separate corporation, and deal with other Smiths (even those in the same neighborhood church) as they would with anyone else. But if the Elm Street Smiths quarrel with Browns on a nearby street, or another neighborhood, matters can escalate so that the Smiths are joined by some or all Smiths of the neighborhood and the Browns are backed by other Browns. But such alliances, which may sometimes unite Smiths of the same *district* (but different neighborhoods), are temporary and limited to the particular dispute at hand. When things are settled—and this often comes from the arbitration of Smiths whose mothers are Browns and Browns whose mothers are Smiths—these alliances dissolve.

There are many variations on this pattern in the tribal world, and we will glimpse a few of them. First, some important features of patrilineal descent systems can be illustrated in terms of the Smiths and Joneses, and some needed technical terms defined.

First of all, note that the Elm Street Smiths are related by common descent; but so too are all the Smiths in the neighborhood, all the Smiths in the district, and—according to tradition—all the Smiths in town. That is, descent categories can be formed at higher and higher levels, with more and more remote ancestors serving as the point of reference. But note that the Elm Street Smiths form a *descent group*, while all the Smiths in town form only a descent category. The Smiths on Elm Street form a solid little local corporation, or "corporate group," with collective property, collective legal responsibility, and so on. The Smiths in the neighborhood form a group too, but the things they do and own as a group are much less important. The more inclusive descent categories serve to define the limits of *exogamy* or "out-marriage," and provide the bases for political alliances. We will look more closely at the latter in Chapter XIII.

Such descent groups and categories, based on descent from more and more remote ancestors, are called *segmentary*. To see why, and to understand how they form and change, we have to think of them in terms of processes in time. Consider the Elm Street Smiths, a group based on common descent from grandfather Sam Smith. If we visited Elm Street three generations later, Sam Smith would be a great-great grandfather, and far too many Smiths would be descended from him to live on Elm Street. So how can the system work?

It works because what looks at any single point in time as though it were a stable and permanent arrangement of people, territories, and genealogical connections is in fact only a temporary crystallization. Over longer periods new groups are forming, old ones are dying out. When we look three generations later, John Smith (who was *leader* of the Smiths before) may now be treated as the *founder* of the Elm Street Smiths, who now will include his descendants but not those of the other men who lived with John Smith on Elm Street. Some of John Smith's brothers and cousins may by this time have no living descendants; others may have had only daughters, or granddaughters, who married and left. The descendants of others may have proliferated, but moved elsewhere to found new corporations, often due to internal quarrels or feuding. After the span of three generations, what had been a Jones street may now be a Smith street. All the Browns in the whole neighborhood may now have disappeared.

If we looked over a longer time span, descent groups would be seen as proliferating, dwindling, hiving off, disappearing, and by conquest or succession or shifts of affiliation, constantly changing their relationship to the lands. Nor do these rearrangements of peoples and lands always follow the neat genealogical lines our first view had suggested. Anthropologists have found that more often it is the genealogical "charters" that are edited and rearranged to fit the realities of group structure and political relations at a given time. A segment of people who show up on the genealogies as

Figure 23. Smiths, African Style. Here the segmentary patrilineal organization of the Tallensi of Ghana (Ex. 12) is ritually expressed. These men are the religious leaders of Tallensi maximal lineages, each roughly equivalent to a neighborhood of Smiths in our example (and composed of local corporations like the Elm Street Smiths). Their lineages are united by traditions of common patrilineal descent to form a clan (roughly equivalent to a whole district of Smiths). When the religious leader of one of the maximal lineages dies, each of the other maximal lineages must send a representative to the funeral. Here, they ritually "sow a field" for the dead leader. (After a photograph by Fortes.) RMK

Smiths may in fact be remnants of some other group allied with or protected by Smiths; and distantly "related" groups may not unite in feuding because they are Smiths, but may be "Smiths" because they unite in feuding.

Another important feature of such a system of patrilineal descent groupings is that for any particular corporation and territory—say the Elm Street Smiths—there are actually two partly overlapping categories of membership. First, there are all those men, women, and children whose fathers were Elm Street Smiths, and hence are members of the corporation by birth. But not all of them live there. The adult Elm Street Smith women have mainly left to live with their husbands, and hence are scattered around other streets and neighborhoods. Second, there is the group of persons actually living on Elm Street: Smith men, their wives (who are not Smiths), and their children. The *descent group*, which is only partly localized, and the *local group*, which is only partly based on descent, are usually both important in different contexts—and it is dangerously easy to confuse them.

Finally, two technical terms are needed. A *lineage* is a descent group consisting of people patrilineally or matrilineally descended from a known ancestor through a series of links they can trace. When descent is in the male line (as with Smiths and Joneses), we can call these "patrilineages." When descent is in the female line, we speak of "matrilineages." A larger descent category like all the Smiths in the town, who believe they are descended from a common ancestor but do not know the actual connections, is called a *clan*.

The tribal world contains many fascinating variations on the "typical" system of segmentary patrilineages illustrated by the Smiths and Joneses.

Example 13:   Segmentary Lineages among the Tiv

Among the Tiv of Nigeria the whole population of some 800,000 traces descent by traditional genealogical links from a single founding ancestor. Moreover each level of the segmentary hierarchy corresponds to a separate territorial segment. It is as though instead of Smith lineages being scattered around a neighborhood also occupied by Joneses and Browns and others, a whole neighborhood was made up of Smiths, and a whole district was made up of Smiths, Browns, and Joneses, all of whom traced common descent from the same distant ancestor, and so on. Figure 24 illustrates this mode of segmentary organization among the Tiv.

In this and other real segmentary patrilineage systems, the people do not of course live in a town, but are scattered over large areas. The tribal equivalent of "Elm Street" occupied by a corporate patrilineage is likely to be a territory of several square miles, with the people clustered in villages or hamlets or scattered homesteads.

How big these local corporations are is another important axis of

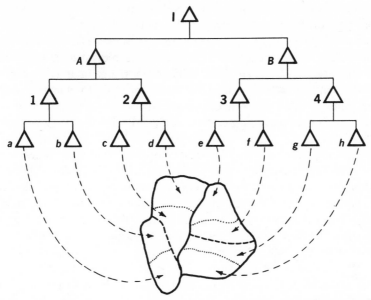

Figure 24. Segmentary Organization among the Tiv. Note here how the geographical distribution of lineages corresponds to their genealogical relationships. (From P. Bohannan, 1954, by permission of the International African Institute.)

variation: they may consist of twenty or thirty individuals or several hundred. Systems also vary in the depth of segmentary hierarchies. The Tiv, all tracing descent from a single ancestor, illustrate one extreme. At the other extreme, local lineages like the Elm Street Smiths may trace no higher-level connections of common descent with one another.

The relative importance of descent groups (including out-marrying sisters) and descent-based local groups (excluding sisters and including wives) also varies. At one extreme are systems where the wife loses all legal interests in her patrilineage-of-birth and acquires full interests in the corporation into which she marries. Among the early Romans, a girl when she married was ritually removed from her lineage and was ritually introduced into her husband's lineage—even acquiring a new set of ancestors, those of her husband. The husband's legal rights over her then replaced those of her father (Fustel de Coulanges, 1864). In some other systems ties to the husband are very weak, marriage is fragile, and the wife retains full legal interests in the lineage of her birth. The logical extreme of this (though there descent is matrilineal) is the Nayar system, where marriage scarcely exists at all and the residential groups comprise brothers and sisters. Usually there is some balance struck between the strength of a woman's ties to her brother and lineage of birth and her ties to her husband and his group.

Even if we look only at male members, not the in- and out-marrying women, the correspondence between membership in a descent category and membership in a local group is sometimes far less neat than our example of Smiths and Joneses suggests. This is where our distinction between categories and groups—between those *entitled* to rights in a corporation and those who actually exercise them—is badly needed. In many "patrilineal" systems, notably those in the highlands of New Guinea, a very large proportion of men (sometimes more than half) are not living in the territory to which they have rights through patrilineal descent. Instead they are scattered around, some living in their mothers' territories, others in their fathers' mothers' territories, and so on. Some of a person's legal rights and ritual relationships may be based squarely on patrilineal descent, so that a person retains them no matter where he lives—but these then have no direct correspondence with local groupings. The same lack of neat correspondence between local groupings and the scheme of patrilineal descent emphasized in the "official charter" occurs in some African societies, like the Nuer, who seem on the surface to be very much like the Smiths and Joneses, and who conceive their political relationships in terms of patrilineal descent (see Ex. 42).

Our quick look at patrilineal modes of solving the organizational problems of tribal societies can well end on this note of disorder, this lack of neat correspondence between the formal model of descent and the realities of who actually lives where and does what with whom. Recall how patrilineal descent seemed a beautiful formal solution to the five organizational problems laid out at the beginning of this section. But there were hidden difficulties. One was at the end of challenge (3): ". . . how can they be adjusted to the demographic fluctuations whereby some groups proliferate and others dwindle?" A second was hidden in (5): "how will political relations between groups be maintained . . .?" Because without a central government, the system must adjust to the shifting tides of warfare, power, and feuding.

These problems prevent any unilineal descent system from being as neat and stable as its formal blueprint. There *must* be flexibility to accommodate demographic shifts, adapt human groupings to the resources and pressures of an ecosystem, follow the tides of politics, and allow room for the strivings and foibles of human individuals. The question is not, as some have posed it, whether a society is "neat" or "messy"—for all social life is a layer cake of order and disorder. It is, rather, by what mechanisms are flexibility and adaptibility maintained and how are they justified, ignored, rationalized, or disguised ideologically?

Matrilineal Descent as an Organizing Principle

Matrilineal descent, the tracing of descent ties from an ancestress through a line of daughters, is much less commonly used than patrilineal descent in solving the organizational problems of tribal societies.

The prevalence of patrilineal descent groupings makes intuitive good sense to Americans—at least American males. But this is partly for the wrong reasons. We tend to think of a system based on descent through women in terms of a matriarchy—a mirror image of a patrilineal system where the women wear the pants (loincloths?). In fact matrilineal descent organization does present some structural problems, but ironically it is not because women wear the pants, but because men do. The "board of directors" in a matrilineal descent corporation is normally made up of men. In fact in some ways it is better to think of the line of descent in such societies as running not from mother to daughter but from a man to his sister's son.

Our first look at matrilineal descent groupings will be an actual example from the tribal world, the Trobriand Islanders of Melanesia. We have already touched on their interesting notions of procreation. They are one of the most fascinating and best known peoples of the tribal world, and we will encounter them many times in the chapters to follow.

Example 14: Matrilineal Descent in the Trobriand Islands

In Chapter XII we will look more closely at where and how the Trobriand Islanders live. For the moment it suffices to know that they are a Melanesian people living near New Guinea, practicing shifting horticulture and living in villages scattered through rich garden lands of their large island. Here their system of matrilineally organized descent groups will be outlined. In the chapters to follow, the picture given here in somewhat simplified form will be filled in in greater detail as we look at Trobriand villages, economics, and political processes.

The garden lands are divided into territories. Each territory contains sacred places from which, mythologically, its ancestress is supposed to have emerged. From her are descended, in the female line, the members of a dala. *Since the precise genealogical links are not known but the groups are strongly corporate,* dala *are known in the Trobriand literature as "sub-clans." A Trobriand sub-clan is a matrilineal descent group consisting of*

(1) men related through their mothers, their mothers' mothers, their mothers' mothers' mothers, and so on;

(2) the sisters of these men, and other women similarly related in the female line; and

(3) the children of these women (but not the children of the men).

The genealogical structure of such a group is similar to that diagrammed in Figure 22b.

Given a sub-clan, associated with the territory it owns by these traditions of emergence, let us see who lives there. Such a sub-clan is centered in a village, in its territory. Since the sub-clans are exogamous, husbands and wives do not belong to the same sub-clan. Who, then, stays in the sub-clan's village? Is it the women, who provide the continuity of descent and whose children provide the next generation of corporation members? Or is it the men, who control the "board of directors," and one of whom is its leader? Either the women or the men must marry out.

In the Trobriands, it is the women of the sub-clan who go away to live with their husbands. How, then, do their sons end up in their own sub-clan villages and lands, instead of their fathers'? The answer is that during adolescence, a time when boys are freely drifting in and out of sexual liaisons and are relatively independent, a boy moves away from his parents' household and goes to the village of his own sub-clan. His sister remains attached to her father's household until she marries. Note that ideally, as a man's own sons leave him, his sisters' sons are moving in to join him.

The village, in this simplest case, thus consists of

(1) adult men and young men of the sub-clan;

(2) their wives, who belong to different sub-clans; and

(3) the young children and unmarried daughters of men of the sub-clan.

A sub-clan is, as we will see in Chapter XIII, ranked as either "chiefly" or "commoner." Within these "ranks" the actual prestige and power of sub-clans varies considerably. But whatever its status, the Trobriand sub-clan is a strong and enduring landowning corporation, with strict rules of exogamy.

Each sub-clan is said to belong to one of four "clans." The importance of these "clans" is obscure, but it is clear that they are vaguely defined social categories of sub-clans traditionally associated by matrilineal descent and having symbolic connections with certain bird and animal species. They are not corporate groups, and a single clan may include some of the highest-ranking and lowest-ranking sub-clans. The rule of sub-clan exogamy is extended in theory to all members of the same clan, but some marriages to "clan members" from other sub-clans do in fact take place, and sex relations with them are regarded as naughty but not outrageous.

The system as it has been outlined is simple and stable: one sub-clan owning one territory with one village in it, where male members and their families live. That relationship, validated by the myths of origin, implies great stability and permanence. In fact the Trobriand dogma of procreation, that denies a role to the father, asserts that the children born of the sub-clan are a sort of reincarnation of its ancestors, thus underlining the continuity of the social order.

But as we saw in dealing with patrilineal descent groupings, the real social world of real people is always less neat and stable than that. Descent corporations do not stay the same size: proliferation, dwindling, and extinction of lineages require mechanisms for groups hiving off, collapsing, and taking over one another's lands. At any time, the interests, strategies, and alliances of individuals and groups, and the variations of demography, require that residence and affiliation be more flexible and variable than the dogma would have it.

In reality, if we could look at the Trobriand social scene over a period of a century or two (before the introduction of transistor radios), the identity and arrangement of sub-clans and their territories would almost certainly shift drastically over that time span. One mechanism whereby this occurs is the branching off of a segment of a proliferating (and usually, an im-

portant) sub-clan so that it attaches to the village and territory of another sub-clan. This can take place when a girl from sub-clan B marries an important man from sub-clan A, who then—to bolster his strength and prestige —gives his sons a foothold in the A village. The sisters' children and matrilineal descendants of these sons-who-stayed-put then establish a branch of sub-clan B in the village of sub-clan A (see Fig. 26, page 192).

By this mechanism, many local segments of sub-clans are living in different territories from those where their ancestors are supposed to have emerged. Moreover, many villages are composed of two or three or more sub-clan segments. Sometimes the attached "immigrant" sub-clan segments outrank and politically dominate the original "owners." This upsets our neat earlier equation: 1 village $=$ 1 sub-clan. For one village can contain its original sub-clan plus segments of one or two other sub-clans. And conversely, segments of a single sub-clan may be attached in several different territories, so that the sub-clan segment, not the whole sub-clan, is the locally based corporate group. We will see in Chapter X (Ex. 25) that in many respects the village (when composed of two or more sub-clan segments) is as important as the sub-clan in Trobriand life.

A second adjustment of the Trobriand descent system to ecological pressures and the shifting complexities of social life concerns residence. On close examination, it turns out that a surprisingly large percentage of Trobriand men are not living in the village where their own sub-clan segment is based. Many are living in their fathers', fathers' mothers', or other villages. This does not mean that sub-clans as corporations are all messed up—only that a man can be an active member of his corporation even if he happens to be living somewhere else (Powell, 1960, 1969a, 1969b).

Finally, the whims of demography are subject to human rearrangement, since a great many children are adopted into households other than those of their birth. This does not affect their sub-clan membership, but it shifts them into different households (often those of sub-clans other than father's or mother's) during their childhood.

Thus, as with patrilineal descent among the Smiths and Joneses, matrilineal descent in the Trobriands shapes strong corporate groups that solve many of the organizational problems of tribal life in this setting. By allowing flexibility, choice, and readjustment of living arrangements, it also permits effective adaptation to the changing pressures of an environment and the shifting tides of social life.

Another way to organize localized matrilineal corporations is to have the women stay put on their land and to have the male members go out to live in their wives' places.

Example 15:   The Hopi Indians

The pueblo-dwelling Hopi Indians have a highly intricate social and ceremonial organization. The major descent groupings are exogamous matrilineal clans, each tracing relationship to a particular animal, plant, or natural phenomenon. These clans are landowning corporations. They are also central in the elaborate ceremonial cycles, in which each has a special part to play and a special set of ritual paraphernalia.

These clans are segmented into unnamed matrilineages, localized in sections of the pueblo. The "core" of these local groupings is a line of matrilineally related women. A Hopi man joins his wife's household—and as we will later see she can send him packing any time she pleases. A typical household consists of an older woman (and her husband if she still has one); her daughters and their husbands and children; and her unmarried sons. Note that the husbands are outsiders, and that the senior woman's grown sons have married and moved elsewhere. Thus, while the lineage retains effective control over its women and their children, the adult men are scattered as outsiders in their wives' households.

The system hangs together partly because of a complicated series of crosscutting memberships and ritual obligations in other kinds of groups not based on descent. But it also works because men, by marrying girls of the same community where they and their fellow clan-members live (which they can do because a number of clans are represented in a pueblo), manage to remain near their "real home" and to participate collectively in their clan's ceremonial activities and corporate affairs. Thus the male "board of directors" of a matrilineal corporation functions in important situations even though the men are scattered around the pueblo in their wives' households.

We will consider at the end of Chapter X what processes and pressures may foster the development of patrilineal descent groups or matrilineal descent groups. Either, as we have seen, can be a workable and adaptive corporation, though the matrilineal descent pattern entails some special organizational problems.

Other Forms of Descent Organization

It is worth emphasizing that it is not a *society* that is matrilineally or patrilineally organized. Recall that two or more modes of descent may be relevant in different contexts in the same society. *Double descent*, where corporate patrilineal descent groups and corporate matrilineal descent groups occur in the same society, provides the most dramatic illustration.

Example 16: Double Descent among the Yakö

The Yakö of Nigeria, living in large towns of as many as 11,000 people, are organized in a way very similar, at first glance, to our patrilineal Smiths and Joneses. A small patrilineage group, like the Elm Street Smiths, resides together in a compound. But whereas Smith streets were scattered in among Jones and Brown streets, Yakö compounds are grouped together into a cluster, a large local patrilineage that corporately owns land. Finally, a series of patrilineage clusters are grouped together into a clan, occupying a single "district" of the town. This correspondence between territories and segmentary levels recalls the Tiv (Ex. 13). The clans are exogamous, so a Yakö man's wives (he often has several) come from other districts.

Yet at the same time, the Yakö trace matrilineal descent; and any Yakö belongs to his mother's matrilineal clan. Whereas the patrilineages are concerned with real estate and ritual involving lands and first fruits, the corporate matrilineal clans are concerned with movable property, with legal responsibility for their members and rights to payments for their death, and with ritual involving fertility spirits. Any man belongs, of course, to his father's patrilineage and to his mother's matrilineage.

Thus two different modes of corporate group organization, through patrilineal and matrilineal descent, fulfill complementary functions in different spheres of Yakö life. Since only full siblings normally belong to both the same patrilineage and the same matrilineal clan, people opposed in one situation may well be allies in another—hence helping to bind together the large Yakö communities (Forde, 1950).

Anthropologists have realized rather recently that *cognatic descent*, where any series of male or female links to the founding ancestor establishes descent entitlement, can also produce workable descent corporations. The problem is to narrow down, from the many groups where a person *could be* a member, the one where he actually *is* a member. Here a number of mechanisms are possible. One is to specify that a couple can live with either the husband's or the wife's group; but whichever they choose, their children belong to that group. Another is to give privileged status, among those persons eligible for membership, to those who trace descent in the male line. Thus other things being equal, a chain of affiliations with the father's group will be made, though some people in each generation will affiliate with their mother's group due to economic strategies or the circumstances of life history. A person seldom has as much freedom to choose or change his membership as the formal rules seem to imply. In practice, cognatic descent can produce corporations similar to those based on unilineal descent and just as efficient organizationally. In a sense the difference is that cognatic descent builds into the rules a great range of flexibility and then uses only a portion of that range, while unilineal descent gives little flexibility in the rules yet allows it, as needed, in some disguised form.

Example 17: Cognatic Descent among the Kwaio

The Kwaio of the Solomon Islands (Ex. 3) divide their mountainous terrain into dozens of small territories. Each is believed to have been founded by known ancestors some nine to twelve generations ago. All cognatic descendants of the founding ancestor of a territory have rights to live there and use the land, and most of them raise pigs for sacrifice to the ancestors associated with that territory.

Yet a person obviously cannot live in, and have equally strong rights to, the many territories (often a dozen or more) to which he is related by cognatic descent. Usually he has a strongest affiliation to only one territory and to a descent group based there. Those who are affiliated with the descent group form the nucleus of the landowning corporation; they are, so to speak, voting members with full rights. The other cognatic descendants, affiliated somewhere else, have secondary rights and lesser ritual interests.

How, then, does a person come to have a primary affiliation out of the large number of potential ones through his father and mother? In practice, he seldom affiliates with a descent group other than that of his father or mother. But which? First of all, a person who is patrilineally descended from the founding ancestor of a territory is considered to have the strongest rights in the corporation and the greatest say in its ritual affairs. Second, a woman normally resides in her husband's territory, and a person usually affiliates with the group with which he grew up as a child. All of these factors combine so that most people affiliate with their fathers' descent groups, and, cumulatively, most descent groups are made up mostly of patrilineal descendants of the founding ancestor. Cognatic descendants then have a secondary interest in the corporation. Yet in every generation, due to the circumstances of life history, some people grow up with their maternal relatives and affiliate with the mother's descent group. As long as they maintain an active participation in the corporation, they are treated as full members.

However, many men do not live in the territory where they have primary interests. In fact, Kwaio residence is quite fluid (Ex. 3), and many men live in four or five territories or more in the course of their lives. They take an active, though secondary, interest in the ritual and secular affairs of several different descent groups. Depending on the context of the moment, a member of group A and a member of group B may both be participating in the ritual affairs or feast of group C, in which both have secondary interests based on cognatic descent.

Here the interplay of cognatic descent and patrilineal descent, and the strategies of feasting and gardening and the circumstances of life history, produce solidly corporate yet flexible and adaptive descent groups (Keesing, 1970).

Descent-based corporations provide effective solutions to the organizational problems of tribal societies. Hunting and gathering peoples may conceive the relatedness of band members to their territory as based on descent (as with many Australian aboriginal peoples), but the pressures toward corporate control of resources mainly arise with the advent of food production. With the urban revolution and advanced technologies, nonkinship forms of social grouping come to the fore, as we will see in Chapter XI. However, anthropologists working in peasant communities or even in urban settings often encounter important social groupings based on descent.

Corporate groups based on descent turn out to be far from universal in the tribal world. There are other, equally adaptive, solutions to the same problems. Many swidden horticulturists of Southeast Asia, in particular, and some pastoralists such as the Lapps, use bilateral kinship as the major principle of social organization. Thus in many parts of the Philippines, Borneo, and Indonesia, property is owned by family groups, and social structure is built up out of local groupings—families, settlements, and neighborhoods. Here, bilateral kinship assumes much of the "functional load" that is carried in other places by descent groups. Local groups are made up of consanguineal and affinal kin, and action groups are crystallized temporarily out of personal kindreds. Such systems are perfectly "workable," and we have at last begun to pay attention to how they work.

Example 18:   The Subanun of the Philippines

The Subanun are swidden horticulturists scattered through the mountains of Mindanao. They lack any formal political structure, and are organized in no enduring communities larger than households and no enduring kinship groups larger than the family. Yet they maintain complex networks of kinship relations and legal rights that weave families together. A family, consisting of parents and unmarried children, forms an independent corporation—owning property, sharing legal accountability, and producing and consuming its own subsistence crops.

Two families arrange a marriage between their children, through prolonged legal negotiations. Until an agreed bridewealth payment is completed, the married couple must contribute labor to the bride's parents, but in marrying they leave the parental families and found a new and independent corporation. The family corporation formed by a marriage, like a legal partnership, is dissolved by the death of either partner (or by divorce), and its property is divided. Surviving members or divorced partners—even a widow or widower with no unmarried children—form a new corporation, however fragmentary, economically self-reliant and legally independent. Only remarriage or adoption can incorporate survivors of a dissolved family into a new one. Once married, a Subanun can never return to his natal household. However, the contractual obligations between parental families that sponsored the marriage is strong and enduring: if one spouse dies, his or her household is legally obligated to supply another one if they can.

Marriage between close kin, even first cousins, is common. Given the independence of every family and the absence of larger corporate groupings, marriage of close kin entails few problems; every marriage is by its nature an "out-marriage." Each household lives in a separate clearing, as far from others as the arrangement of gardens permits. Though three to twelve neighbhoring households comprise a dispersed "settlement," these alignments are only temporary. Any family is the center of a unique cluster of neighbors and kinsmen, bound first to the two families that sponsored its formation and later to the families with which it is contractually linked through marriage sponsorship. As Frake, their ethnographer, observes,

> *Despite [the] network of formal and informal social ties among families, there have emerged no large, stable, discrete socio-political units . . . The Subanun family [is] . . . largely a "sovereign nation." But . . . the Subanun*

family is not a descent group. Its corporate unity endures only as long as does the marriage tie of its founders. The continuity of Subanun society must be sought in the continuous process of corporate group formation and dissolution rather than in the permanency of the groups themselves (Frake, 1960: 63).

It is well to end this brief look at descent systems with a cautionary note. Descent groupings are obvious and easily recorded, and they lend themselves neatly to comparative schemes. Yet anthropologists may often have overestimated the importance of descent at the expense of more subtle principles of social grouping, which might emerge if they only looked for them. Focusing on descent categories, they have used great ingenuity to explain why people who are not patrilineally related to a place happen to be living there. But this may be to confuse figure and ground. We might do better to focus on local groups rather than descent categories, on the strategies of gardening, friendship, property interests, and the like that lead people to live where they do. A people may talk about the cumulative outcomes of individual choices in terms of ideologies of descent even though "descent rules" actually have little to do with who decides to live where and do what. Descent may be, in some societies, more a way of thinking about local groups than of forming them.

33 · Kinship Terminology

The epitome of all that seems arcane and obscure in kinship studies, to the uninitiated, is the long preoccupation with kinship terminologies: the way people classify kinds of relatives.

Kinship terminologies are highly systematic, and invite algebraic fun and games. They also invite comparison, since the same complex patterns are found on different continents. And for decades, they have promised to provide some kind of Rosetta Stone for understanding social organization, since they clearly represent some kind of mapping of the social world of a people. But we are not yet sure how to read them.

Our way of classifying kin as "uncles," cousins," and so on, is not an immutable fact about the world. It is an arbitary set of cultural conventions, and in fact a quite unusual one. It may seem obvious that a people should have words for "brother" and "sister" (different words, to be sure, like the French *frère* and *soeur*). Yet such categories do not occur in more than eighty percent of the world's languages.

First of all, a great many peoples place at least some of what we call "cousins" in the same categories as siblings. Thus, as we will see, a person's father's brother's children may be classed with his own children. But even ignoring these wider ranges of terms for siblings, we find seven major ways of classifying siblings, of which ours is but one. The most common form uses *relative sex* (whether the relative classified is the same sex as the speaker or the opposite sex) as the crucial criterion. This form is particularly common in Melanesia. In the Pidgin English of New Guinea, these Melanesian categories have been labeled with the borrowed English words "brother" and 'sister." An English-speaker is unruffled when a New Guinean man talks about "brother belong me" and "sister belong me." But a New Guinean woman refers to her sister as "brother belong me" and her brother as "sister belong me"—which raises an occasional colonialist eyebrow.

We need not delve here into the many forms of kinship classification and the long debates about how they map the social universe. But a very brief look at two Trobriand kinship terms will serve to illustrate the puzzle-like nature of kinship terminologies, the ways those of tribal peoples differ from ours, and two sharply opposed ways of interpreting them now on the forefront of social anthropology debate.

Recall that even in societies with strong corporate descent groups, bilateral networks of kinship connect individuals in different corporations, as well as within them. After nearly a century of serious study, it is not yet clear whether kinship terms in tribal societies are

1. basically ways of classifying relatives on the basis of *kinds of genealogical connections* between them and "ego," the person doing the classifying (as in our society); or
2. basically ways of dividing up a person's social universe into major *"kinds" of people*—"kinds" that may well be based not on genealogical connections but on membership in corporate groups or local groups, or even broad categories like "marriageable woman."

Let us turn to the Trobriand kinship terms to illustrate. What we know about the meaning of these Trobriand words comes mainly from the man who first studied them in detail, Malinowski (see §71). He gives us these meanings by listing the closest genealogical positions covered by each term. We will have to do the same. But the proponents of the second position above object from the outset—for that presupposes that these words are used to classify genealogical connections, not "kinds" of people in the Trobriand social universe.

TERM A: *tama*

Malinowski tells us that *tama* include a person's father, his father's brother (FB, for short), his father's sister's son (FZS for short, using Z for "sister" to distinguish it from "son"), and all of the members of father's matrilineal clan in his own generation or lower generations. We look at two possible interpretations of the meaning of *tama*, based on positions (1) and (2) above.

Interpretation 1

Tama means, most centrally, 'father.' However, its meaning extends out to include other persons whose relationship is culturally similar to that of the father. These extensions are based on two principles that reflect equivalence or substitutability.

The first principle, very, very common in the tribal world, is that two siblings of the same sex are treated as equivalent in the reckoning of kinship. Thus, in Trobriand and hundreds of other tribal societies, FB = F, MZ = M, FFBS = F, and so on. The way the latter equivalence works will illustrate how distant collaterals (who would be cousins in our system) are classed with parents, siblings, or children. Note the logic of the following chain: FFB = FF, thus FFBS = FFS, which = FB, which = F. By the same principle, a man classes his brother's children with his own, and a woman classes her sister's children with her own.

The second rule of extension whereby *tama* are classed together occurs much less frequently, almost always in societies organized along matrilineal lines like the Trobriand Islanders. By this rule, a person's FZ is classed with FM in the reckoning of kinship. And when that is so, then the same equivalence looked at the other way around means that a woman's brother's child is classed with her son's child in the reckoning of kinship. Note that in a system of matrilineal corporations, a woman's brother and her son are members of her group, but their children are born into different groups. This rule is one variant of a principle of kinship classification known as "Crow" (after the Crow Indians).

This Crow principle leads to an equivalence between FZS = FMS = FB = F (which is why FZS is *tama*). As we will see, such chains of equivalences also class FZDS and other men in the father's sub-clan as *tama*.

Interpretation 2

All that is nonsense. The notion of "extension" from one's "real" father to other fathers simply superimposes our genealogical biases (and our feeling that father is different from uncles) on the Trobrianders. All *tama* are "real *tama*." In fact, what the word *tama* means is 'domiciled man of my father's sub-clan hamlet.' Father is one of them, so is father's brother; but so too are a range of others whose genealogical relations to ego vary widely. This is not to say that a Trobriander does not or cannot distinguish his mother's husband from other *tama*—simply that for purposes of this carving up of his social universe, they are the same "kind" of person.

Term B: *tabu*

The category *tabu* is "self-reciprocal," like our "cousin" (if you are my cousin, I am your cousin). It includes, first, both grandfathers and both grandmothers; FZ, FZD, FZDD; any man or woman of the grandparents' generation; any ancestor or ancestress; any woman of the father's, father's father's, or mother's father's clans. Reciprocally, it includes all grandchildren; a women's MBC (C is "children"), her MMBC, descendants, and so on.

Interpretation 1

The basic meaning of *tabu* is 'grandparent' (and, reciprocally, 'grandchild'). Extension to other men and women of the grandparents' generation, and to ancestors and descendants, reflects a general cultural equivalence based on their removal by age and generation from "ego."

The other equivalences, of FZ, FZD, FZDD, and—reciprocally—of a woman's BC, MBC, and MMBC, reflect the "Crow" rule we have already encountered. That is, FZ is equivalent to FM, hence is a *tabu*; and by applying this rule repeatedly, FZDD = FMDD = FZD = FMD = FZ = FM (hence *tabu*). (The classing of FZDS as *tama* reflects a similar chain, for a man).

Interpretation 2

The Trobrianders are not concerned with long chains of genealogical connection, which they often do not know anyway; rather, they are concerned with kinds of people who play some similar part in their lives. *Tabu* are in fact classed together not because of some positive feature they share in common, but because, as ego passes through the various stages of the life cycle, they are distant and marginal to him—and in some respects dangerous. It is from this category of persons marginal to his life that he must find a wife, since girls in other categories are ruled out by the rules of exogamy.

Both sorts of interpretation have strong adherents at present. Position 1 was first advanced in the early 1960s by Floyd Lounsbury, though it builds on some quite old principles of kinship analysis (Lounsbury, 1964, 1965). It has attracted widespread support. Position 2 has been argued for some years by British social anthropologists, notably Edmund Leach and Rodney Needham (Leach, 1959; Needham, 1971).

The strength of position 2 lies in an intuitive fit to the society involved. Each society's set of "kinship categories" is viewed as a unique conceptual universe, and it is explored and mapped in terms of the social groupings, categories, and distinctive customs of the people under study. (In the Trobriand case, however, recent evidence on the variability of residence patterns makes the "fit" less convincing).

The strength of position 1 lies at the opposite pole, in its generality of application. Consider the Trobriand categories. Not only the two we explored, but the whole range of others, are almost precisely matched on the other side of the earth among the Cow Creek Seminole Indians of Florida. Yet Seminole social organization has almost none of the special features used by proponents of position 2 to account for the Trobriand categories. Using Lounsbury's equivalence rules, we find that many kinship terminologies from different continents fall into place as subvarieties of the same family, though there is no historical connection between them. On the debit side, some of the equivalences the rules specify do not really make much intuitive sense. To many, the whole operation looks uncomfortably like Lounsbury's first oral description of it—"a trick that works."

The long-standing motivation behind studies of kinship terminologies has been that if we could find how they map the social universe of a people, we could acquire a key to comparative analysis. More recently the formal symmetry and algebraic possibilities of kinship terminologies have made them a focal concern in ethnographic semantics or "ethnoscience" (§14). Formal analysis of kin terms has become, for many, an end in itself. Attempts to use *componential analysis* in semantics have mainly dealt with kinship terms. (Recall the attempt in §14 to define "chair," "stool," and "bench" in terms of the intersection of distinctive features). When componential analysis is used to define the meaning of a kinship term, such criteria as generation, sex, or relative age are used as distinctive features. Thus a kinship term Lounsbury would treat as having a primary meaning of 'father' (with extensions to FB and more distant kin) might be componentially defined as "male + first-ascending-generation + father's-side." FB and FFMBDS thus fit the definition as neatly as father himself. The difficulties in formal semantic analysis of kinship terms again confront anthropologists with our continuing inability to describe or understand semantic competence. The pattern recognition and contextual sorting we use thousands of times a day remain a mystery.

In looking at kinship terminologies we have deviated slightly from the main course—to glimpse an area anthropologists have explored with fascination for decades. Our primary goal has been to see how kinship and descent intertwine in forming the fabric of social order in tribal societies. We are now prepared to trace out, in the next chapter, the bonds of marriage and family structure that stitch the fabric together.

IX Social Organization in Tribal Societies: Marriage and Family Structure

HERE WE will continue to explore the structure of tribal societies, looking first at marriage in comparative perspective and then at the family. As we see how descent corporations shape marriage and family organization, it will be clear why we have to approach the latter through this indirect route. This chapter, like the last, deals with phenomena anthropologists lump broadly together as "kinship."

34 · Marriage in Comparative Perspective

Does marriage occur in all societies? Anthropologists trying to compare customs are always caught in a dilemma: how far to stretch the meaning of a term like "marriage" so that it covers customs quite different from ours without losing its shape altogether.

Recall the Nayar (Ex. 7), where a kind of formal rite in childhood that has nothing to do with the later sexual liaisons leading to pregnancy is the closest thing to "marriage." Recall also the Nuer, with an old woman "marrying" a young girl (Ex. 8). Moreover, in some societies there are several different kinds of union between a man and woman, some more formal and some less so.

What matters for us is that the perspective our culture gives us toward marriage is quite misleading when we look at the tribal world. Whatever kind of bond a society uses to associate men with mates and offspring, we are prone to misunderstand it for some fairly simple reasons:

1. Marriage is characteristically a *relationship between groups* (often corporate descent groups), not simply a relationship between individuals. The logic of a marriage system that otherwise seems bizarre may become clear if we shift our view and examine it as an enduring contract between two corporations.

2. Marriage entails a *transfer or flow of rights*. The exact set of rights passing from the wife's group to the husband's (or vice versa)—work services, sexual rights, rights over children, property, and so on—varies widely. But if we ask what rights are transferred, and assume that something tangible or intangible passes back in the other direction to balance the transaction, we are well on our way to understanding many otherwise peculiar looking marriage systems.

3. Marriage is seldom primarily a sexual relationship. First of all, in a great many societies a husband and/or wife are permitted sexual access to persons other than the spouse (for example, in Murdock's large 1949 sample, 63 percent of societies permitted sexual relations between a man and his wife's sister). Furthermore, marriage may be primarily a contract creating an economic corporation, may be primarily a formal means of legitimatizing children, may be a mode of political alliance between groups, and so on.

4. Strict monogamy is the exception, not the rule. Again in Murdock's sample, monogamy was the sole permitted marital arrangement in only about one out of four societies.

5. The rights transferred in marriage and the contractual relationship between husband's group and wife's group do not necessarily terminate with the death of one or both partners. This again is a reflection of marriage as a contract between groups.

If we keep these perspectives in mind as we approach varying forms of marriage—particularly if we are prepared to view marriage as a long-term contract between corporations entailing reciprocal transfer of rights and valuables—we avoid the worst pitfalls of ethnocentrism.

Incest and Exogamy

An essential element in the analysis of marriage, and later of the family, is the universality of the *incest taboo*. All known societies prohibit mating or marriage between parent and child and between siblings. One of the key questions of social anthropology is why this should be. There are, to be sure, very special cases where brother and sister were *expected* to marry. But such cases, as in the royal families of ancient Egypt and ancient Hawaii, represent not an ignoring of incest taboos but an overriding, due to the extreme sacredness of the royal family, of the taboos that applied to others. If the royal family approached the status of the gods, they could not marry mere mortals—and hence a brother and sister married to preserve and enhance the sacredness and purity of the royal line.

Though incest taboos are universal, those to whom they apply vary widely from society to society. Even in America and Europe, incest laws are far from standardized; and in tribal societies, the boundaries are far more variable. Sexual relations may be forbidden between members of the same lineage or clan, between all fourth cousins and closer relatives, and so on. Thus, though the "core" of prohibited relatives—parents and children —is the same, the extension of the taboo to wider categories of relatives takes many shapes. Even this universal core is reduced in one or two cases to exclude one set of half-siblings. Thus half-siblings with the same mother can apparently have sexual relations among the Lakher of Burma.

Many theories—psychological, sociological, evolutionary—have been advanced to explain the universality of the incest taboo. For some theories there is no positive evidence and there are strong reasons for complete rejection. Thus modern scholars no longer take seriously the claim that there is an "instinctive horror" of incest. The theory that humans raised together since infancy have less sexual attraction for one another may contain grains of truth but have major defects. In this case, what are we to do about the Oedipus and Electra complexes posited by the psychoanalysts? And why, if there is no desire, is it necessary to have such an emotionally charged rule? A number of early writers saw the incest taboo as a primitive device to prevent inbreeding. With the development of population genetics this theory was abandoned—then revived again in more sophisticated form by a distinguished group of anthropologists (Aberle et al., 1963). The genetic foundations of this rethinking of the incest taboo have recently been challenged by Livingstone (1969).

A number of theorists have sought ecological or demographic explanations of the incest taboo. One views protohuman "families" as unlikely to contain mates of appropriate age—hence the need to mate outside the group. But, again, why an emotionally charged rule to validate what people are doing anyway? More recently it has been suggested that it would be ecologically adaptive to protoman as hunter to bring in a new adult member from outside the group. The possibility that inhibiting of mother-son matings may be a primate foundation for the human incest taboo is difficult to study in the wild because of the time span involved: Sade's recent observation of such inhibition among rhesus monkeys (1968) underlines this possibility.

Other interpretations of the incest taboo have focused on its social consequences. Malinowski contended that the conflicts, jealousies, and tensions that would result if sexual relations were permitted within the nuclear family would lead to disruption of society. The roles of parents and children are incompatible socially and psychologically with the roles of sexual partners. This, too, is a partial but inadequate theory. Other sociologically based theories have viewed incest taboos (the prohibition of sexual relations within the group) as reflecting a rule of exogamy (the prohibition of marriage within the group). In a characteristically brilliant early insight, Tylor suggested the social significance of exogamy:

> Exogamy, enabling a growing tribe to keep itself compact by constant unions between its spreading clans, enables it to overmatch any number of small

intermarrying groups, isolated and helpless. Again and again in the world's history, savage tribes must have had plainly before their minds the simple practical alternative between marrying out and being killed out.   (1889: 267)

This theory, that exogamy creates an alliance and interdependence between groups, was refined by later scholars like Fortune (1932b).

This leads usefully to a clarification of "exogamy" and "endogamy," and their relationship to the incest taboo. Many scholars have viewed exogamy (out-marriage) or endogamy (in-marriage) as traits that some tribes have and some do not. But in a more general sense, all societies are exogamous in that closest relatives are nonmarriageable (through the incest taboo) and endogamous in that one is supposed to marry someone from the same tribe or (at the very least) a member of the same species and opposite sex. Looking at marriage this way, we see that there is always some starting point of nearness and stopping point of distantness for permitted marriage; the problem is to find the boundaries.

A difficulty in the view that exogamy is universally implied in the incest taboo is that many societies prohibit marriage within ego's lineage or clan, but treat *incest* as a quite different and more serious matter (involving prohibited sexual relationships, not prohibited marriage). We fall more easily than we should into the trap of equating permitted marriage with permitted sex (with that traditional American interest in girls who are fine to sleep with but not to marry). The same "trap" exists with endogamy. In the American South, where racial endogamy has been legally enforced, Negro females have been fair game. Recall also the English gentleman constrained by class endogamy but encouraged and entitled to wench about.

In a sense it is foolhardy to try to build a theory of how the incest taboo evolved, because we will never know—it will inevitably be something of a "just so story." But on the other hand, incest is a crucial meeting ground of man's biological nature with the arbitrary conventions that govern his social life. To "explain" the incest taboo requires a theory of how biological, ecological, psychological, sociological, and cultural factors combine to shape human behavior. We have not yet succeeded in such syntheses— hence our theories of incest, like most of our theories of man's social behavior, are one-sided and partial.

A final theory of incest, advanced by the French anthropologist Claude Lévi-Strauss, views the incest taboo as the crucial transition between nature and culture—and hence the bridge between nonman and man (1949). Lévi-Strauss combines the insights of Tylor and Fortune with those of the French sociologist Marcel Mauss, in his explorations of exchange and reciprocity in human societies (see §47). Lévi-Strauss argues that protomen, living in bands within which they mated and raised their young, were self-sufficient. There was no basis for union of the bands into a wider society.

The crucial step toward culture (and hence wider social integration) would have been a renunciation by the males of a band of their own females, so as to obtain as mates the females of other bands. Lévi-Strauss views this as a great social gamble which, once it paid off and established bonds of exchange between bands, was the essential step toward human society. The incest taboo became The Rule symbolic of culture itself and the transition from natural to cultural order. It acquires a central fascination in the ideational and emotional world of men. Note that Lévi-Strauss's theory, like Tylor's, accounts for rules of exogamy, but not necessarily for incest taboos.

Alliance Systems

On his theory of exogamy and exchange, Lévi-Strauss has built a widely influential theory of marriage. Where most anthropologists had focused on descent and kinship, Lévi-Strauss focused on the exchange of women by groups of men as the essential element in social structure. Such systems of exchange are solutions to the "primal" problem of how to get women back from other groups in place of one's own, whom The Rule prohibits as mates. Kinship and descent systems, in Lévi-Strauss's view, are *primarily* devices for defining and regulating the nature of this exchange.

Lévi-Strauss argues that we are misled by the fact that for us there is a seemingly endless number of young ladies from which we can find a mate. For us the gamble imposed by The Rule is a statistical one—we renounce our sisters and get a splendid selection in return. This is not necessarily the simplest or safest solution to guarantee the return of a spouse, particularly in the tiny societies characteristic of most of man's history.

What is simpler and safer, in a society of tiny scale, is to specify a rule for the *exchange of women with other groups*. Lévi-Strauss calls systems that specify a rule for the exchange of women among groups *elementary systems* of kinship. A society that simply specifies a range of prohibited spouses is a *complex system*.

He argues that though elementary systems are rare, they occur at the primitive margins of the tribal world and, in vestigial form, in the ancient systems of China and India. Thus they may once have been far more widespread, perhaps the characteristic forms of society until the last several thousand years. The simplest system for exchanging women is one where the whole tribe is divided into two exogamous descent categories (our side and their side—with one's side determined by either patrilineal or matrilineal descent). Such categories are called *moieties*. They represent the simplest form of what Lévi-Strauss calls *direct exchange* (échange restreint): men of each side give their sisters to the other side and get wives in return. More complicated forms of direct exchange are found in Australia. Australian Aborigines (perhaps partly because they were unencumbered by a complex technology) worked out extraordinarily complicated systems to conceptualize their universe and social relationships. Not only was complexity an end in itself among these Stone Age mathematicians; they borrowed whole elaborations from their neighbors to keep up with the Joneses, and superimposed them on their own systems, where they often fit quite badly. Thus you cannot try to decipher an Australian system with strong faith that there *is* an answer that works—Aborigines were quite adept at cheating when they found themselves checkmated (and hence unmated) by the rules of their own game.

Fortunately we can avoid the intricacies of Australian kinship. The basic principle is something like pie cutting. A moiety system cuts the tribal pie in half. If some other principle is used to cut in the other direction (for example, alternate, generations or matrilineal descent), each half of the pie is subdivided, and there are four sections. A man must then marry a girl not only in the other half but in a particular section (the other section from that of his mother); and his children belong to the other section of his own half. More complex Australian systems subdivide each section to make eight, and a man must marry a girl in only one. When slicings are more complicated, when pieces of one people's pie are grafted into another's, and when dirty old men form the upper crust, Australian pies are almost impossible to digest anthropologically.

Such exchange systems, however complex, are still "direct" in Lévi-Strauss's sense. He showed how an alternate form is possible, under a rule that your group gives its women to one set of groups and receives women from a different set of groups. Such a system of *indirect exchange* (échange géneralisé), Lévi-Strauss argues, risks more in the gamble of renouncing one's own women—but the rewards in terms of social integration are greater. No pair of groups can achieve self-sufficiency and hence social isolation—and this interdependence of social units makes possible a "global integration."

The societies practicing indirect exchange lie mainly in Southeast Asia—Assam, Burma, and a few parts of Indonesia. Ideologically they conceive their systems as "marrying in a circle," and phrase their marriage rule in terms of a kinship category, including mother's brother's daughter and many more distantly related girls, from which a man must select a wife. Both the "circles" and "mother's brother's daughter marriage" have led to endless confusion and controversy among the scholars who, following Lévi-Strauss's lead, have pored over the meager evidence on these groups.

The picture that has emerged is of systems far more complex and dynamic than "marrying in a circle" would suggest. These societies are usually composed of many small localized patrilineages. It is these lineages that serve as "alliance groups" in the marriage system. These lineages may be ranked, and markedly unequal in status, as with the Kachin of Burma (Leach, 1954). Or they may be unranked, as among the Purum of Assam (Needham, 1962). In either case, marriage becomes an instrument of political negotiation and status. A few marriages in each generation may serve to maintain the political status of lineages. Other marriages are less important and in some societies need not necessarily conform to the marriage rule.

From the standpoint of any single lineage, some girls may be nonmarriageable because their lineages share common descent at a higher segmentary level. Some lineages may simply be too far away for marriage to be likely. But there remain two other crucial categories of lineages. There are lineages whose girls have married men of one's own lineage (they are "wife-givers") and lineages to which one's own has given women (they are "wife-takers.") The basic marriage rule is that no other lineage can be *both* wife-giver and wife-taker. While actual patterns of marriage may deviate from the ideal model, most "wrong marriages" (at least those that are politically consequential) are treated *as if* they were right ones, and hence simply readjust the shifting network of alliances. Such an alliance system is usually prominently reflected in the cosmological scheme of a people. The contrast between wife-givers and wife-takers is mirrored in cosmological dualisms (right-left, sun-moon) and in ritual symbolism. This "global" and encompassing structure has led Needham (1962) to make a sharp distinction between such societies, which "prescribe" marriage into a particular category, and others which merely specify "preferred" marriages. This distinction has led to great controversy and eventually to repudiation by Lévi-Strauss himself.

The endless debates about "prescriptive marriage" systems have seemed to outsiders the height of trivial and sterile formalism in kinship studies. But beneath the technical argument has lain a central problem we encountered with Smiths and Joneses. There is a profound gulf between the ideal conceptual models and ideologies central in a people's thought-world and real people competing, choosing, and manipulating. Real people live in a world of ecological pressures, economic and political strivings, individual variability, and the whims of life history. A way of life consists, in a sense, of accommodations and adjustments between a lived-in world and a thought-of world. The debates about "prescriptive marriage" basically reflect the different perspectives we get if we focus on the pragmatic, complex, and muddled patterns of living (in which case the neat formal design of a "marriage system" dissolves away), or on the crystalline models of thinking (so that the design comes into sharp and clear focus). Anthropologists are still looking for a way to keep both perspectives centrally in view at once.

Transactions in Marriage

Far more common than the "elementary" systems are those that are "complex" in Lévi-Strauss's sense—where by renouncing one's own women one acquires access to a range of women from other groups. But our understanding of such systems in tribal societies still runs afoul of our tendency to view marriage as a relationship between individuals, not groups, and hence to overlook or misunderstand the transactions and contracts involved.

Extremely common is the payment of *bridewealth* by the husband's descent group or relatives to the wife's people. This may involve cows, money, ceremonial valuables, and the like. What looks like "buying a wife" (and hence "treating women as chattels") is in fact a delicate contract between corporations involving a transfer of rights.

The "payment" of dozens of cattle, or handsome valuables, is immediately visible and spectacular. If we assume that the transaction is balanced, we are led to search for the hidden and intangible "scarce goods" which are transferred in the other direction to balance the exchange. The most important usually turn out to be rights over the bride's children (so that some anthropologists have urged that "bride-price" be called "progeny-price"). If the parties to the contract are patrilineages, what the husband's lineage is "buying" is not so much the wife as her future children, as lineage members. But this is too simple, because bridewealth usually involves a transfer of other rights—to the wife's sexuality, to her work, and more generally to her presence, where her own relatives are compensated for losing her.

In some societies "bride service" is an alternative form to bridewealth. Here the groom or suitor resides with the girl's people and works for them for some specified period. This is often a way for a man of little means, who cannot afford bridewealth payments, to acquire a wife. An equivalent or alternative means of acquiring a wife "free," in some societies where bridewealth is usual, is permanent residence with the bride's kin. Here the children may even affiliate with their mother's people, not their father's.

Note that in terms of Lévi-Strauss's theory, bridewealth may be a sort of transitional form between a system where wives are exchanged (directly or indirectly) and a system such as our own. For the cattle or valuables serve in a sense as *tokens* that guarantee a return of women. Often a people conceptualize bridewealth this way: The cattle you get in exchange for your sister are the symbolic equivalent of a wife, because they are the means to your own marriage.

Bridewealth is less commonly paid where descent is traced matrilineally. Here, the husband's lineage does not acquire rights over children. Such payment usually occurs where the husband's lineage compensates the wife's lineage for loss of her work services (and hence occurs when wives go to live with their husbands' people).

Why, then, the payment of *dowry* in Europe and many parts of Asia? This turns out to be not "payment for a husband." Rather, it usually is a payoff to the out-marrying wife and her children for her share in the family estate, in societies where women and men share rights in property but women marry out and leave their estate. However, dowry can become entangled with concepts of rank, so that important families pair off in strategic alliances of property, and dowry becomes a demonstration of wealth to secure prestige. Bridewealth, dowry, and other marriage transactions not only are common in prescriptive alliance systems as well, but may reach great complexity there—as where there is a flow of "male" and "female" goods symbolically expressing alliance relationships.

The nature, centrality, and complexity of the affinal relationships between kin groups are vividly illustrated by the Trobriand Islanders, whose matrilineal descent system and kinship terminology we have already encountered:

Example 19: Affinal Relations in the Trobriands

The most dramatic, and best known, custom that binds affines together is called urigubu. *The Trobrianders grow tremendous quantities of yams, root vegetables that can be stored for long periods after harvest. In fact they grow far more than they need. Yet the husband and wife who produce the yams keep much less than half of their crop, the less desirable tubers, for their own use. The rest they give away in formal presentations.*

But to whom? Ideally, the bulk goes from the producer to his sister's husband. Figure 25 illustrates this presentation. In one sense the presentation is from the man X to his sister Y and her children, who are members of his sub-clan (vertical hatching). However, recent evidence makes it clear that Trobrianders think of this primarily as an obligation of X to his sister's husband, Z, who is the head of Household 1. A man also makes urigubu *yam presentations to his mother and father (after he has left their household and gone to form one of his own in a different place).*

Though these are the most common forms of urigubu, *we know from new evidence that these obligations fall upon the sub-clan as a corporation, not just on individual households. It is the responsibility of men of the corporation to muster and assign resources so that proper amounts of* urigubu *yams go to the households of all of the sub-clan's married females.*

The logic of this custom seemed to be well deciphered. The adult men

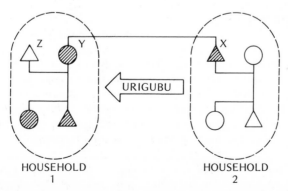

HOUSEHOLD
1

HOUSEHOLD
2

Figure 25. Urigubu *Presentation of Yams in the Trobriands. This shows the most basic form of* urigubu. *However, X may also present* urigubu *yams to his mother and father, or to other women of his sub-clan and their husbands. Hatching indicates membership in the same sub-clan.*

lived on the corporation's property; the women through whom descent was traced never lived there (recall that they live with their fathers until marriage). Urigubu seemed to be, like dowry, a payoff to the out-marrying women in produce from the lands of their corporation. This interpretation is now less satisfying. New evidence more clearly shows urigubu as a relationship between male affines (brothers-in-law), not between brothers and sisters It also shows that because of deviations in the ideal patterns of residence " . . . most of the adult males who garden for [women of the sub-clan] do not reside in their sub-clans' villages, so that the urigubu they provide is not the produce of the land of their, and their sisters', own sub-clans" (Powell, 1969b).

But with this new evidence has come a realization that though the Trobrianders do not have a prescriptive marriage system, sub-clans are linked together in complex webs of affinal alliance. A marriage is a political act, establishing a formal bond and contractual relationship between corporate sub-clans that lasts as long as the marriage; and the urigubu presentation annually reaffirms it.

Symbolically, the urigubu underlines both the unity of the men of the corporation in meeting their obligations to affines, and the unity of its male and female members. Moreover, there is an element of subordination implied in the urigubu presentations. Symbolically, they imply the dominance of the husband's sub-clan—hence, as we will see in Chapter XIII, their easy conversion into a more formal tribute to the high-ranking sub-clan of the husband.

The large scale and dramatic presentations of yams in the annual urigubu are countered by periodic reciprocation of valuables (youlo). But these represent only one element of the complex webs of transactions and obligations that bind together the sub-clans and individuals in a Trobriand marriage. To understand what happens when, and after, a Trobriand girl marries we have to think in terms of two different marriages and two affinal relations between sub-clans. Marriage 1 is her parents' marriage, which affinally links her mother's sub-clan, A, with her father's sub-clan, B. Then there is marriage 2, her own marriage to a man from sub-clan C, which affinally links her sub-clan A with sub-clan C. At the time of marriage 2, there are eight different presentations of food and valuables to and from the bride's kin. But curiously, most of them are between the C's and the B's; the A's stay mainly on the sidelines. The B's again play a central part when the daughter becomes pregnant. It is the women of the B's who make a pregnancy cloak, the B's who perform magic, the B's who are directly involved in the events of birth of the children, though these children are A's. If marriage 1 is ended by the death of the husband, his wife's relatives, the A's, must prepare the body and conduct mourning rituals; the dead man's sub-clansmen, the B's, must abstain from direct contact. If marriage 1 is ended by the wife's death, the A's must abstain and the affinally related B's take the lead. At the final mortuary rite, the dead spouse's sub-clan makes large presentations to the survivor's sub-clan, and the affinal relationship ends.

Why the B's should play such a central part in the marriage of the A daughter to a C man, and in the death of an A wife, will have to remain a *mystery for the moment. We need more pieces for this puzzle before we can solve it and see a new side to* uriguba *presentations, in Ex. 61.*

Looking at marriage as a contractual relationship between groups helps to free us from our preoccupation with husband and wife. It is useful to ask, in this light, how far marriage in tribal societies is based on free choice by the marrying pair, and how far it is constrained by rules or senior kin.

Here we find great variation. First of all, even in societies that do not require marriage to a girl in a particular kinship category, some types of marriage may be strongly preferred or socially desirable. Thus, marriage with MBD or FZD or some other relative may be the ideal form, with other arrangements permitted but less favored. Where this occurs, the preferred form may be a way of consolidating property or "getting around" the rule of descent or inheritance. When people say it is "best" for a person to marry a particular kind of relative, we can only understand them by asking " 'Best' for whom, when, and why?" Again the Trobrianders give a good example.

Example 20:   Father's Sister's Daughter Marriage in the Trobriands

Trobrianders sometimes told their ethnographers that the "best" person for a man to marry was his FZD. But only a few Trobrianders actually do. Why?

Think back to the process we noted whereby a higher-ranking sub-clan gets a foothold in the village and territory of another (Ex. 14). This is diagrammed in Figure 26. Number 1, the leader of the "owning" sub-clan, A, contracts a marriage with a girl, 2, from a high-ranking and powerful sub-clan, B. We can now see a good reason why he would contract such a marital alliance: the powerful B's must provide him uriguba *yams, and are placed in something like a tribute-paying relationship to him. Moreover, the B's become obligated to help him politically and economically.*

It is another good short-term gambit politically for the A leader to keep his oldest son, 3, in his own village, rather than his returning to the B village. But in the longer run, the A's run the danger of giving a foothold to the B's in their A village (recall that this is how new sub-clan segments get established in other villages). Moreover, the son's status in the A village is precarious. The A's can evict him if they wish, and he and his children have no secure rights there—unless he manages to create a little branch of the B's. How can the leader of the A's achieve security for the son and his children without giving the B's a foot in the door and running afoul of his own A supporters? If the son were to marry an A girl (his FZD or the daughter of some other close aunt in his sub-clan—they are both classed as his tabu) *what would happen? The son's land rights would be legitimized, since he and his A wife could garden on her land. Their children would be A's, so they would be "owners." That means that the B's are likely to gain no foothold in the A village. This is diagrammed in Figure 27. Thus by this marriage, arranged usually by childhood betrothal, the father achieves the short-term benefits of a politically advantageous marriage without its potential long-term costs. What looks at face value like a simple statement of marriage preference in fact describes a subtle political ploy in the power struggles of sub-clans and leaders that we will see in greater detail in Chapter XIII.*

An important preferential form occurs among the Bedouin, other Middle Eastern Arabs, and some other Islamic peoples. This is "parallel cousin marriage," where a man has rights to marry his *bint 'amm*, ideally his father's brother's daughter. The structural causes and consequences of this peculiar form have been much debated. Marriage with father's brother's daughter implies lineage *endogamy*. That is, given a system of patrilineal descent, a man is expected to marry a girl in his own group. With generations of such in-marriage, the skeins of genealogical connection become

STEP 1: The A leader 1 marries a girl 2 from sub-clan B.

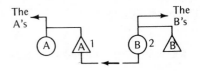

STEP 2: The daughter of 1 and 2 marries out. Her brother 3 stays in the A village and establishes a precarious foothold.

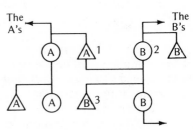

STEP 3: As 1 and 2 die or become elderly, the children of their daughter who married out may be encouraged by the B's to return to their maternal uncle 3 instead of to the B's village. They and their descendants establish a new branch of the B's.

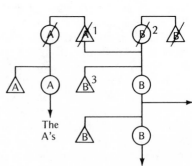

The New B Segment

Figure 26. The Establishment of a New Trobriand Sub-Clan Segment.
RMK

highly complicated, and any two people can usually trace relationship through many pathways. Given a rule that patrilineal connections should be traced where possible, some have argued that many people would end up marrying the "right" kind of girl even without that as a special preference. But this overlooks the *right* to marry FBD, and focuses on the marrying pair rather than their fathers. In a sense, FBD marriage is like direct exchange (but combined with lineage endogamy, not exogamy): brothers directly exchange their sons and daughters. In some of these societies, both men and women have property rights, and it has been argued that FBD marriage is a way of keeping property consolidated among close lineage members. The marriage preference also clearly reflects ideas about the ritual impurity of women, so that the relationship between and through two men contrasts with a relationship between or through a brother and a sister.

STEP 1: The A leader 1 marries a girl 2 from sub-clan B.

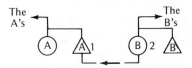

STEP 2: The father 1 arranges his son's marriage with his sister's daughter (the son's FZD).

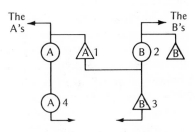

STEP 3: The children of 3 and 4 are A's, so 3's main interests lie with the A's with whom he has grown up. 3's sister's children are likely to return to the B village, where their interests are secure.

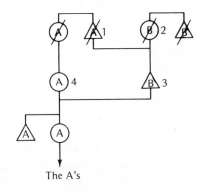

Figure 27. Father's Sister's Daughter Marriage as a Political Stratagem. RMK

The many systems where marriage is "arranged" between a boy and girl who may never have met seem designed to appall Americans. What we read or write about such systems usually involves young lovers thwarted by arranged marriage to someone else, or an anguished bride going to a stranger in marriage. But if we can refrain from projecting our notions about romantic love on people who do not share them, such systems are far from oppressive: they simply treat marriage as a contractual relation between kin groups. The evidence is overwhelming that most of us "fall in love" because we expect ourselves to, and have been taught how to do it and what the symptoms are. (It is worth observing as well, however, that occasional impassioned lovers crop up in every society and if necessary defy or disrupt "the system.") Marriage as an instrument of political and economic alliance is so well known from European history that we should hardly be surprised by it in tribal settings.

Moreover, there are many tribal societies where marriage is the result of free "dating" or casual liaisons, and based squarely on personal choice. Here once more, human societies cover a great range of possibility in the modes of acquiring a mate.

Our whole time perspective on a marriage is likely to mislead us when we look at non-Western societies. A *marriage* takes place, in the form of a wedding or civil service; and then a *state* is established that continues until husband or wife dies or they are divorced.

In primitive societies, marriage is a long drawn-out *process* that involves several transactions or stages. The relationships established in the marriage transaction may continue long after death of one or both parties. Thus among the Kwaio of the Solomon Islands (Ex. 17), marriage entails an opening "down payment"; then a major feast, that may take place several months later, at which bridewealth is paid; and finally a third small feast where the bride's mother presents her with a married woman's pubic apron: only then is the marriage physically consummated. And in some societies marriage may become legally binding only after the first child has been conceived or born (compare the Banaro, Ex. 6).

The contract between husband's lineage and wife's lineage may endure even though either he or she dies. If he dies, rights over her sexuality and future children may remain with his lineage, so that the dead husband's brother or some other close kinsman replaces him as husband. This is known as "the *levirate*." This is what is happening in Nuer "ghost marriage" (Ex. 8), except that the dead first husband is still classed as father of the children. If the wife dies, her lineage may be contractually obligated to ship over a replacement—her sister, her brother's daughter, or some other close relative. This is known as "the *sororate*."

Even where a widow remarries a man in a different lineage (usually implying an initial marital contract where her own relatives retained ultimate legal control over her), her dead husband's lineage may have some "residual rights" and interests in her activities. Among the Kwaio of Melanesia, for instance, part of the bridewealth paid for a widow goes to her first husband's relatives.

The preference for a man to marry the widow of his maternal uncle in Mota (Ex. 10) is also worth mentioning, because it again illustrates our tendency to misunderstand other people's marital customs. Rather than being a bizarre custom, as felt by early observers, this is a quite sensible expression of a man's succession to the status and property rights of his MB (in a system, like the Trobriands, with matrilineal descent and Crow kinship terminology). In stepping into his uncle's shoes, he assumes the responsibility to take care of the uncle's widow (he also marries a younger girl who bears his own children).

Even after both husband and wife have died, the complex of obligations established in the marriage may endure. Among the Kwaio, the kinsmen who helped to finance a man's bridewealth payment are entitled to a major share of bridewealth when, years later, the daughters of the marriage they helped finance are married.

Marriage Stability and Divorce

The stability of marriage—how frequent divorce is and how it affects the transactions and other relations between husband's and wife's groups—is an important variable. In some societies marriage is very fragile, and divorces are common. In other societies, most marriages are permanent. Americans are concerned about mounting divorce rates, and we are likely to seek in such variations some "secret" for reversing this trend. But since divorce in non-Western societies so often involves a contract between corporations, it is hard to understand through Western eyes.

An early line of exploration showed that when bridewealth is high (in terms of the economy in question), marriage tends to be stable; but when bridewealth is lower, divorce is common. But that leads to what looks like a chicken-or-egg question: Is marriage stable *because* of the high bridewealth costs, or can a society afford to have high bridewealth only if it has a stable form of marriage?

One line of approach is to look at the rule of descent. Because the husband-wife and brother-sister ties are in more direct opposition with matrilineal descent, it has been argued that marital instability is a concomitant of corporate matrilineal descent groups. A "strong patrilineal descent system," it was argued, would be associated with stable marriage. But as we have already seen, what is really important is the relative strength of the brother-sister and husband-wife ties. When a girl's tie to her natal (birth) group is severed or greatly weakened when she marries, divorce is uncommon. When her affiliation to her natal group remains strong, she may enter into several successive marriages. This still does not fully "explain" differential marriage stability in patrilineal descent systems since it only pushes the question one step farther back. But it correctly underlines the importance of looking carefully at the relative importance of those two overlapping groupings in a unilineal descent system—the lineage, composed of unilineally related brothers and sisters, and the local group composed of unilineally related men (or more rarely women) and their *spouses*.

The causes of divorce in non-Western societies run the gamut from quarreling and failure to live up to expected roles (a lazy wife, an improvident husband) to infertility or adultery. Divorce may be highly formalized, or it may be just a matter of one partner ordering the other out or giving public notice that the union is over—a Hopi wife merely puts her husband's things outside her house door. More interesting to the social anthropologist is what happens to bridewealth payments, if any, and what becomes of the contract between kin groups (in terms of rights over children, kinship relations, and so on). Sometimes all or some bridewealth must be returned (though this may depend on the cause of divorce, whether the woman has borne children, and so on).

This underlies the importance of tracing out how rights are distributed and transferred in a society. It is no accident that some of the great early amateur ethnographers were specialists in jurisprudence who set about to study patterns of rights while most anthropologists were still studying patterns of basket weaving.

Plural Marriage

The frequence of plural marriage (polygamy) in tribal societies has already been noted. The more common form is *polygyny*, or marriage of a man to two or more women. In some areas, polygyny is the normal marriage pattern—as in most of tribal Africa.

We will see in discussing family structure that polygynous families pose some difficult structural problems. We tend to misunderstand the workings, and the problems, of such systems by placing ourselves in the shoes of co-wife or husband—and hence imputing sexual jealously and other notions of ours to them. Polygyny may be degrading to women in the eyes of a lady missionary—but what matters is whether it is degrading to the women who practice it. When a new wife means another worker to share the hard tasks of farming, a woman may encourage her husband to acquire one and may even take the lead in wife shopping.

Co-wives may be from different lineages, or they may be sisters (in what is called *sororal* polygyny). The latter, at least as a preferred form, avoids some of the conflicts that can disrupt polygynous families.

Polygyny may be practiced only by men of wealth or high rank, or it may be practiced by most men in the society. If the latter seems to imply an unbalanced sex ratio, recall that the same end might be achieved by having girls marry at fifteen and men at thirty-five—which is roughly

what happens in many polygynous societies. It may also result from differential mortality rates, as when some men are killed in warfare.

Conflicting interests of co-wives in the children each bears by a
single father provide a major source of division, both within households
and within patrilineages. The relations between half-siblings and the distribution of rights to each (in relation to their common father and different mothers) are always important in such systems. Lineage segmentation
in a patrilineal system often takes place between half brothers, with ties
through the different mothers (and their lineages or ancestors) reflecting
and symbolizing the contrast between segments.

In a good many societies two or more men may share sexual access
to one woman. These arrangements have been called *polyandry*. But it is a
delicate problem of definition whether they involve plural *marriage*, or simply
the extension of sexual rights by the husband to other men (for various
reasons in different societies). Only where fatherhood is assigned to two or
more husbands (as among the Toda, Ex. 9), or is in some sense collective,
does this actually involve plural marriage, rather than extension of rights of
sexual access. A common form of such plural mating involves a group of
brothers (what has been called *fraternal* polyandry). Polyandry is often
associated with population imbalance, produced in some places by female
infanticide. It is *not* characteristically associated with matrilineal descent or
an unusually high status of women.

The early evolutionary stage of "group marriage" or primitive promiscuity envisioned by earlier writers is a figment of Victorian imagination. The
rare cases where two or more men cohabit with two or more women are
extensions of plural mating—and they are complicated arrangements, not
simple and free collective ventures.

Example 21:   The Marquesans

*The Polynesians of the Marquesas emphasize rights of a firstborn son
and his aspirations to power and prestige. He often marries a woman of high
rank, and, in order to recruit male followers, adds some of her lovers (younger
brothers and men of lesser rank) as* retainers (pekio) *in his entourage. An
important man may take a secondary wife as* pekio, *and she may add her
lovers to the collection. That multiplies the ranks—and looks only secondarily
like the "group marriage" imagined by early ethnologists.*

We have seen how, to understand marriage customs that seem strange
or exotic at first glance, we must go beyond our own ethnocentric assumptions and search out their underlying logic. We ourselves, in narrowing
marriage down to an intense personal relationship between husband and
wife on which the rearing of children and so much else depends, have placed

a tremendous burden that human frailty very often cannot support. A return to the broader contractual relationships of tribal peoples would hardly be possible for us. But as the pressures of modern life rend more and more families apart, it is ironic to hear still about the "curious customs of the natives."

35 · The Family in Comparative Perspective

The family seems to us the most fundamental social group, the core of a social system. Why, then, not choose this as a starting place for the study of social organization? Why wait until we have dealt with kinship, descent, and marriage? The answer is that the structure of the family, in comparative perspective, is so intricately related to principles of descent and marriage that these principles form a necessary background to our understanding of the family.

As usual there are some messy problem of definition. Is "the family" universal? If so, in what sense? Some analysts have emphasized the universality of the nuclear family and its crucial functions in all societies of child rearing and the management of sex. Others argue that this confuses the biological universality of the nuclear family with its social relevance—and point to cases like the Nayar (Ex. 7) where the "nuclear family" is not a residential unit, an economic corporation, or in fact socially important at all.

It is useful to distinguish between the *family* and the *household* (or domestic group). The family is a cluster of positions to and through which an individual traces crucial kinship relations—so that the roles of father, mother, and siblings within this cluster are universally recognized and important. But the family may not comprise a separate social *group*, spatially or economically. *Households* are residential units and characteristically small corporations. They usually own property and produce and consume food collectively, in addition to providing the stable base for caring for and educating children.

A crucial key to the structure of households and their aggregation into larger communities is a society's system of *residence rules*. Most crucial are rules for postmarital residence. If the wife normally goes to live with her husband's people ("virilocal residence") or the husband goes to live with his wife's people ("uxorilocal residence"), this has a cumulative effect on who lives where and how they are related to one another. But this distinction still does not neatly classify all residence possibilities. Both postmarital residence among the Smiths and Joneses, and postmarital residence in the Trobriands (Ex. 14; recall that a young man moves back before marriage to the territory of his matrilineage and hence his mother's brothers), are "virilocal." To distinguish them the first has been called "viripatrilocal" and the second "viriavunculocal ("man's mother's brother's place).

By further ingenuity in naming, we can come up with a fairly comprehensive scheme.

The problem is to make such classifications meaningful in terms of the culture under study. What does "-local" mean? Is a couple residing across the street from the husband's parents and two doors down from the wife's parents living "virilocally," "uxorilocally," or "neolocally"? And how can this be compared with a society where husband's father lives in the same tent and wife's father lives across a hundred miles of desert? What does one do about variation, where some people follow one pattern and others another? As Goodenough has shown (Ex. 2), classifying residence can best be done in terms of the categories of the people under study. What do *they* conceive as the alternative forms of residence and how do they decide among them? We run grave risks of classifying as separate "types" two cases they view as equivalent, and classifying as instances of the same "type" choices they regard as different. Talking about "residence rules" cross-culturally can be a useful shorthand, but it disguises many hazards for the unwary. Gone are the days when we talked with confidence of a tribe where "residence is matrilocal"—things are always less simple than that.

We can now survey some of the possible forms of households, while bearing in mind that different forms often occur in the same society. We will see how the forms that seem strange or complicated are a logical expression of the forms of descent, marriage, and residence we have already examined.

Nuclear Family Households

Where nuclear families stand alone, they can best be understood in terms of the *absence* of factors that produce more complex forms. They occur where descent does not link unilineally-related men or women together (father and two married sons, married sisters) into larger households; and where plural marriage does not produce partial replication (as with three wives and their children, with a common father).

Thus nuclear families, by themselves, tend to occur where descent groups are absent or of lesser importance. In such societies, emphasizing bilateral kinship, nuclear families carry a very heavy "functional load"—as in our own society and among the Eskimo. It is not by chance that our examples come from each end of the continuum of societal scale and complexity. It is in the middle, in tribal societies, that proliferations of more complex households are concentrated.

In bilaterally organized societies, the nuclear family serves as the center of a child's social universe—in it he is reared, is cared for, grows up, and learns his culture. Sexual relations and hence reproduction and the continuity of the society are focused in the family. It serves as an economic corporation, owning property and producing (or acquiring) and consuming food. Linkages between nuclear families produce the larger social and political units—bands, villages, and neighborhoods—of a society. However, in other societies nuclear families may be culturally distinguished and socially important, yet be components of larger local groupings that we can also call "households" at a higher level, as we will see shortly.

Complex Households Based on Multiple Marriage

Since polygyny is so common (and is the dominant mode of marriage in tribal Africa and some other areas), polygynous household groupings represent a major form of local grouping. Organizationally the problems in such systems lie in the relationship between co-wives. If we forget about the problems of sharing the same sex partner, and use our intuitions about wives sharing the same kitchen, using the same checkbook, and agreeing on whose children get what, we perceive vividly the difficulties of polygynous households.

The best solution—though it seldom works perfectly—is for each wife to have her own household. The husband plays a secondary role in each; and where, as is common, a wife is sexually taboo for a long period after childbirth, the isolation of "matricentric families" is increased. The households are seldom fully independent economically, since a principal motive for polygyny is to create a joint work force and pool the productive efforts (as well as the reproductive efforts) of several women. But the "sub-households" are in many respects separate social units. This does not solve all tensions in polygynous households, and the roles of co-wives are always a delicate matter: there is, for example, a correlation between polygyny and witchcraft accusations. And if we know from American folk culture what it would be like to be henpecked, we can visualize the possibility (that haunts or afflicts many Africans) of being henyard-pecked.

When co-wives share a single household and hearth, the problems can be multiplied. Some African societies establish separate households for co-wives except when they are sisters (sororal polygyny)—on the assumption that sisters can manage, as they did in childhood, to coexist in the same household.

Example 22:   Polygynous Households among the Tallensi

The Tallensi polygynous family well illustrates both this mode of domestic organization and the way it can provide building blocks for larger domestic groupings. Most younger Tallensi men have only a single wife. Their domestic family, centered in a small courtyard and a mud-walled sleeping room, with kitchen and granary, may live in a single homestead, enclosed within mud walls. Sometimes the husband's mother would live with them, and as senior woman would have a separate courtyard and living quarters. More often, in this society where local groups are shallow patri-

lineages, the man with only one wife will occupy an "apartment" within the homestead of a father or an older brother.

By the time he is middle-aged, a man of substance will have acquired two or more wives. He probably will be living in his own homestead. Each wife will have her own little courtyard, her own sleeping room, her own kitchen. The senior wife (or the husband's mother) is a kind of leader in the women's realm, but for each wife her apartment is the center of life, a place where she is in charge and where only her own children and her husband have free access.

The male head of the homestead group controls the granary which supplies the component dug, *the units of mothers and their children. The importance of the* dug *unit in Tallensi social structure is profound. The lines of lineage segmentation normally do not cut across* dug *units, but divide half brothers with the same father, and their descendants.*

Though relations between co-wives are usually fairly amicable due to the separation of their spheres of influence, quarrels over shares of grain, rights of children, and other matters are common. The arrangement of "apartments" of co-wives reflects their social relationships: "Wives who are clan sisters will usually have adjoining quarters; wives who get on badly will be put in well-separated rooms. . . . If a woman has a quarrelsome disposition . . . her quarters will be separated from those of the next-door wife by a low party wall. . . ." (Fortes, 1949: 58).

In the case of polyandry, men and their children cannot build separate households in a mirror image of the polygynous form: men are not mirror images of women (and are flatly unable to nurse babies). And in any case, a woman cohabiting with several men cannot produce a child by each of them at once. Co-husbands then share a single household. Because they are so often brothers, the problems are minimized in some respects, but structurally these are still unusual forms.

Complex Households Based on Common Descent

Patrilineal or matrilineal descent and a pattern of residence that aligns a core of lineally related men or women together in a local group, combine to produce many complex family structures. "Extended" or "joint" families are produced when, with patrilineal descent, a father and his married sons form a household or two brothers form a household. Often this is a second-order grouping, where the component nuclear families act separately for some purposes and act together for others. Extended family households are also possible with matrilineal descent, as among the Zuni and Hopi (Ex. 15).

The line between households and larger local groupings becomes somewhat arbitrary once we start in this direction. That is, in a segmentary lineage system there will be at each level be a group of lineally related kin and their spouses: a man and his wife; a man, his wife, and his sons and their wives; patrilineal first and second cousins and their wives; and so on. For most societies it probably is sensible to use "household" to refer to groups that use a single dwelling and eat meals together (a "hearth group"). But here again it is impossible to build definitions that make sense of a particular culture under study yet work equally well for all other cultures. "Extended family households" take many forms, and can be based on parent-child or sibling-sibling links.

Example 23:   Patrilineal Extended Families among the Tiv

Among the Tiv of Nigeria, whose segmentary patrilineage system has been glimpsed in Ex. 13, the domestic unit of production is the compound group. The Tiv compound is an oval or circular arrangement of huts and granaries, with a central open space that is the "center of Tiv family life" (Bohannan and Bohannan, 1968: 15). The nucleus of the compound group is a senior man, the oldest in the group, who acts as its head. He arbitrates disputes, controls magical forces, and supervises production.

He has several wives, each of whom would normally have a separate hut in the compound. The compound group typically includes the head's minor children and unmarried daughters, and his married sons and their wives and children. To this extended family core may be added a younger brother of the head and his wives and children, or a nephew of the head. These may also be outsiders—friends or age-mates of the men at the compound—who live there. The membership of the compound group, especially

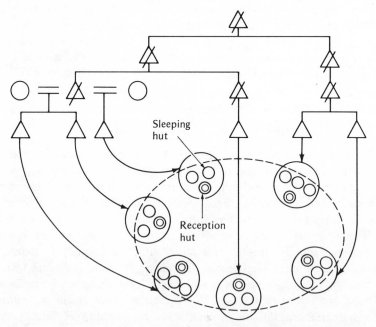

Figure 28. Map and Genealogy of a Tiv Compound. (After a diagram in P. Bohannan, Tiv Farm and Settlement [Colonial Research Study No. 15, 1954], *by permission of the Controller of Her Britannic Majesty's Stationery Office.)*

these others attached to the extended family core, may shift considerably over time. The genealogical composition and spatial arrangement of one Tiv compound are diagrammed in Figure 28.

While in a sense each wife who has a separate hut and her children constitute a separate domestic unit, the larger compound group—a patrilineal extended family augmented by outsiders—is the central domestic unit of everyday Tiv life and of collective economic enterprise (Bohannan and Bohannan, 1968).

A "rule of residence" can produce unilineally related groupings of kin even where no ideology of descent is emphasized. Thus in a *patrilocal band* (Chapter VII), where the sons of band members stay put and their wives come in from outside, most male members will come to be related through male links. Moreover, in a tribal society a rule of unilineal descent may be combined with just the opposite rule of residence. Descent groups may be formed by matrilineal descent though a woman goes to live with her husband's paternal kin. In such societies, other factors may keep the men of a matrilineage clustered closely enough that they can still act as an effective corporation. We now have a well-documented case of just the opposite relationship of descent and residence rules: where descent is patrilineal but postmarital residence is with the wife's kin.

Example 24: Shavante Households

The Shavante Indians of central Brazil are organized in corporate partrilineages. Like many of the Gê speaking peoples, they live in large circular villages that express spatially the schemes of their cosmology (Lévi-Strauss, 1963). Yet unlike their close cultural relatives, they cannot assign a sector of the circle to each lineage—because patrilineally related men are scattered around the circle in their wives' parents' households.

At marriage, a Shavante man goes to live with his wife's parents. A household consists, at one stage in its cycle, of a couple and their children. The children belong to their father's patrilineage—yet their father had come at first as an outsider into the hostile setting of his in-laws' house. Now, as he himself is established, his sons marry and must leave the security of their household. The daughters stay, marrying before puberty, bringing in their young husbands as insecure outsiders.

Ideally men marry more than one wife—posing obvious problems. The best solution is to marry two sisters. In fact young men of the same patrilineage can help to stay together, despite marriage, if they marry girls who live next to one another. Strategic marriage of a cluster of patrilineally related men to a local cluster of closely related girls is an ideal solution that helps to keep the lineage together (Maybury-Lewis, 1967).

It should also be remembered that even where the "rule of descent" and "rule of residence" correspond, they may not produce neat unilineal groups actually living together. We have seen how, where patrilineal descent is strongly emphasized in ideology (as with the Nuer of Africa), local groups still may include an assortment of bilateral kin and affines as well as patrilineally related men.

And this leads to the observation that the gulf between an ideal form ("nuclear family," "extended family household," "polygynous household") and the composition of actual households is often very wide. Households are always breaking up due to parental death, divorce, and the like— with widows, orphans, old people, and others attaching to existing households. In some societies, adoption (the jural assignment of a child to new parents, which may or may not entail breaking ties with the old ones) and fosterage are very common. In part of Polynesia, adoption is so frequent as to be almost the "normal" form. Here it serves among other things as a way of evening out population imbalance between property-owning groups, on islands where land is very scarce.

If we try to classify the households we actually encounter, we run the risk of defining almost as many "types" as there are households. A major step in the right direction came from Meyer Fortes, who showed that many different household "types" represent the same kind of family at different stages in a *developmental cycle* (1959). A household group characteristically passes through a "phase of expansion" where children are born, a "phase of dispersion" (that may overlap the first) where children marry, and a "phase of replacement" ending with the death of the original couple. The composition of a household (and hence what "type" it is according to older theories) depends on what stage of the cycle it happens to be in when we observe it.

We can go even further than this. A single set of cultural principles for making decisions about household membership, descent group membership, and the like may have extremely variable social outcomes when the principles are applied to the ever-changing circumstances of actual cases. Some families have all daughters, others all sons, and so on. We know a lot about how boys behave toward their mothers' brothers in many societies, but much less about what they do when mother has no brothers.

An emphasis on cultural principles for making decisions in the varying circumstances of social life promises to help to close the gap between the ideal conceptual world of a people and the muddled patterns of actual living.

Thus among the Kwaio of the Solomon Islands (Ex. 3 and 17), where the tiny settlements normally consist of one or several nuclear family households, I encountered one settlement consisting of fourteen people in five households. Yet none of these households included a married couple, nor were there any units of parent and child. The whole settlement consisted of adult bachelors and spinsters and the children of deceased relatives they were fostering. Yet this strange collection of motley households, a classifier's nightmare, was the cumulative result of a series of culturally appropriate decisions made in the face of adversity. If we look more carefully at the cultural principles for deciding among the alternative paths that life opens, rather than simply looking at, classifying, and counting the social groupings that result, we can make sense of the most complex patterns we find.

Such a quick survey of the complexities of kinship in tribal societies cannot provide a guide for all the forms of kinship grouping, marriage, and family structure the reader might encounter in the non-Western world. Nor will it enable him to pick up any technical journal article on kinship and read it with full understanding (though the reader who has worked carefully through these pages might, if he tried it, be pleasantly surprised). But the survey has tried to bring out some of the big questions underlying the small ones, and to give guidelines for thinking about the organization of tribal societies that could help an American to find the logic of a system quite different from his own. These guidelines will also serve us well in the chapters to follow.

X *Social Organization*
in Tribal Societies:
Beyond Kinship

KINSHIP, as we have seen, is a dominant organizing principle in tribal societies. But every society uses crosscutting principles of organization as well, and for good reason; for people who have in common their close genealogical relatedness are also divided by many things they do not have in common. Some kinsmen are old, some are young; some live close together, others live far apart. And each of the principles that separates people who are close kinsmen unites people who are not.

These crosscutting principles of age, sex, community, and rank are crucial in tribal societies in tying groups together. Moreover, as societies have increased in scale, complexity, and centralization these other principles— especially community—have largely supplanted kinship as dominant organizing principles.

In the sections to follow, we will examine the role of principles other than kinship in structuring men's social life. Our focus will continue to be on tribal societies. But the transition to more complex forms will be suggested at a number of stages; and in the next chapter we will consider more squarely the organization of complex societies and ways anthropologists have sought to study them.

36 · Community as a Principle of Social Organization

We have already touched on "local groupings" at several points. In discussing cultural ecology, we saw how the emergence of sedentary communities—and their size and permanence—are quite closely tied to subsistence technology and environment. In discussing kinship and descent, we saw how kin groups can be "localized," and in taking a comparative look at the family, we glimpsed the forms that these smallest local groups can take. Later we will look at the politics of territorial units, and hence at larger spatial blocks. But it is worth dealing more closely, though briefly, with local groupings in the midrange—*communities.* Communities emerge as important mainly where agriculture makes possible sedentary residence. Given the recency of the agricultural revolution (in comparison to man's whole stay on earth), stable and settled communities are a rather late development (recall Chapter V). In tribal societies they characteristically are interlocked with kinship organization. Yet as technological knowledge, market economies, and the like have increased the scale and density of settlement, localization has become more important and kinship less so. With the rise of cities, or movement to cities in developing countries, kinship recedes into the background.

Communities can be roughly classified according to scale. In some agricultural societies, especially those practicing shifting horticulture, homesteads or homestead clusters may be scattered around the landscape, and may often be moved to follow gardening cycles. On a slightly larger scale, *hamlets* range from a handful of households to a score of them, or more. *Villages* contain hundreds or even thousands of people. The development of *towns* has been comparatively late, the culmination of technological and economic changes we have glimpsed in Chapter V.

In tribal and peasant societies, it is useful to ask the following questions about the structure of a community.

1. Is it composed of smaller units that are spatially separate and similar to one another in structure?

A village or hamlet may be composed simply of separate households, or it may be some kind of composite. That is, it can be something like an orange in structure—composed of distinguishable segments. Such segments may be clearly visible to an outsider, or simply invisible cultural lines between the "pieces." One recurrent pattern is a separation into sub-hamlets, a cluster of which comprise a village. Another common pattern divides a community into residential areas, with some social and political separation, which we can call *wards* (the term *barrio* is also common, due to its prevalence in such Spanish-influenced areas as Mexico, the Philippines, and Puerto Rico).

2. Are communities or segments associated with descent groups or other kinship units? And if so, is each segment associated with one group or several?

The community may be located in a group's territory and contain its men and their wives. But alternately, the community may be composed of members of several groups. Whether kin groups are spatially segregated into segments (so that each ward or sub-hamlet corresponds to a descent group) is structurally critical. Even where the segments themselves contain more than one descent group, it is crucial whether at the level of individual households there is separation according to kin group or whether households are "mixed together." If the latter, the arrangement can usually be interpreted as an expression of the precedence of community over kinship. This has been the trend in societies of increased scale and complexity. In *cities*, particularly in colonial areas or developing countries, in the residential areas to which people flock from the countryside there is often a separation according to dialect, district, or village of origin. This provides in the large and impersonal scale of a city close social ties modeled on those of kinship.

3. Are the communities socially independent?

Do most marriages take place *within* the community? In tribal societies one often finds community exogamy, where each settlement (or cluster of settlements) is associated with an exogamous descent group. Here inter-marriage provides a linkage between settlements, and no settlement is in the long run socially self-sufficient. Other communities, especially where they are larger and composed of segments, are largely self-contained. That is, most marriages take place within the village, so that in terms of kinship and other social ties the system is a more closed one. Such relatively self-contained communities are particularly characteristic of peasant societies, so that a single village becomes a useful unit for study (§41). Economically the closure and self-sufficiency of communities is likely to be much less pronounced. Even in the tribal world, networks of trade and economic specialization are likely to bind communities into wider systems. We will see a vivid example of such a system in Chapter XII in looking at Trobriand economics. Economic ties beyond the community become even more im-portant in peasant societies. As we will see in the next two chapters, one of the difficulties in studying peasants is the contrast between the relative closure of the village socially and its openness as part of wider economic and political systems.

The Trobriand Islanders, whom we met in the last two chapters and will encounter again in the chapters to follow, usefully illustrate the struc-ture of local communities in a tribal society and the way this can articulate with the social and cosmological order of a people.

Example 25:   The Trobriand Village

Recall that the Trobrianders are organized in corporate matrilineal sub-clans, each of which is associated with a territory by traditions of ancestral emergence. In the simplest case, the Trobriand village is the "head-quarters" of a single sub-clan. This means that all or most of its male mem-bers, and their wives, live there; while the women of the sub-clan live elsewhere with their husbands.

As we noted in Ex. 14, however, a great many Trobriand villages con-tain segments of two or more sub-clans. In these villages, where sub-clan and village do not coincide, we can see that in many ways the whole village—

not the sub-clan—is the most important social unit. "The whole village is the context of family life" (Powell, 1969a: 188), not simply a person's own sub-clan segment.

Through processes glimpsed in Examples 14 and 20, the village may have one "owning" sub-clan and other sub-clan segments that are attached to it. (Some Trobriand villages are in fact "compound," in that there are two "owning" sub-clans, each of which may have sub-clan segments attached to it—a complexity we can ignore.) The importance of the village, as well as the individual corporate sub-clans based in it, comes to the fore in gardening: ". . . The village . . . is the effective unit of economic activities. . . . In the making of gardens, whole villages . . . operate as organized corporate bodies under the direction of sub-clan leaders and garden magicians" (Powell, 1969b: 581).

The spatial arrangement of the Trobriand village reflects both its unity and the partial separation of the sub-clan segments that make it up. Figure 29 shows the plan of a large and internally complex Trobriand village with a very high ranking "chief" (see Ex. 44). The arrangement is roughly circular, consisting of a central plaza with dancing ground and burial ground, and

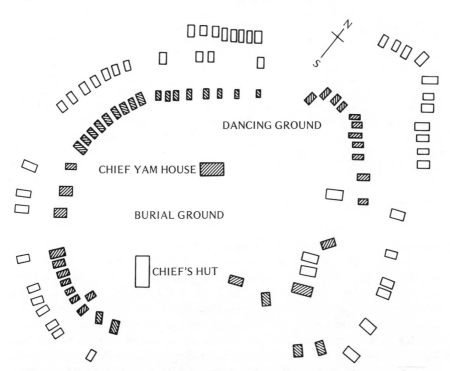

Figure 29. Plan of a Trobriand Village. This village, Omarakana, is the center of the most prosperous district and the seat of the most powerful "chief." (After Malinowski.)

two concentric rings of buildings with a "street" between them. The outer ring of buildings consists of domestic dwelling houses. The inner ring consists of yam storehouses and the bachelor houses in which the amorous adventuring of the young is centered.

In this particular village the presence of the very important "chief" shapes the distribution of residents around the outer circle. As we will see, "chiefs" are entitled to polygynous marriage, and this one had many wives, as well as outsiders resident as his "retainers." In a more typical village, each sub-clan segment based there would be associated with a sector of the circle. Thus the outer circle of buildings served to emphasize the partial separation of the segments, while the inner plaza symbolized the unity of the village.

Such a circular arrangement of the village is not an arbitrary custom. As Levi-Strauss (1963) has shown, the circular villages of Indians in central Brazil and other peoples represent a mapping out of basic cosmological principles. For the Trobriands he suggests that the concentric rings reflect a series of symbolic polarities in Trobriand culture.

> A circular street runs around the storehouses, with the huts of the married couples built at the outer edge. This Malinowski called the "profane" part of the village. Not only are there oppositions between central and peripheral and between sacred and profane. There are other aspects too. In the storehouses of the inner ring raw food is stored and cooking is not allowed. . . . Food can be cooked and consumed only in or around the family dwellings of the outer ring. The yam-houses are more elaborately constructed and decorated than the dwellings. Only bachelors may live in the inner ring, while married couples must live on the periphery. And finally, the two concentric rings . . . are opposed with respect to sex: "Without over-labouring the point, the central place might be called the male portion of the village and the street that of the women" (Malinowski, 1929: 10).
>
> In the Trobriands we see, therefore, a complex system of oppositions between sacred and profane, raw and cooked, celibacy and marriage, male and female, central and peripheral (Levi-Strauss, 1963: 137).

One of the most interesting patterns of community organization is that in which the larger communities are modeled on the structure of segmentary lineages. Fustel de Coulanges, in a classic early study of social structure (1864), showed that in ancient Greece and Rome the patrilineal extended family household centering around a sacred hearth fire and shrine provided a model that was replicated not only at higher levels of lineage structure (with lineage shrines and sacred fires), but also in the city-states. Thus an ancient city-state had its sacred fire and shrine symbolizing its unity, as though it were a descent group. A strikingly similar pattern has been described by Vogt (1965) among the modern highland Maya of Southern Mexico; and he suggests that this capacity to replicate a social and ritual pattern at successively higher levels may have enabled the pre-Columbian Maya to create the great temple centers for which they are famous.

37 · Sex, Age, and the Life Cycle as Organizing Principles

We have looked, in Chapter III, at the biological foundations of sexuality and sexual dimorphism on which cultures build. Given *la différence*, which is universally appreciated, every people must work out a way to express sexuality in a relatively orderly fashion and to establish templates for the relationship of men to women, men to men, and women to women.

One element here is a division of labor according to sex (§45). Another is the whole series of balances that we can sum up as the "status of women." What positions or roles are open only to men, and what ones are open to both men and women? Among the Australian Aborigines, for instance, females are excluded from religious spheres (rituals, secret societies, and the like), but among the Great Lakes American Indians, male and female shamans participate without distinction in the medicine lodge. Among the Isneg non-Christians of the northern Philippines, religious and magical matters are largely handled by female priestesses or seers. In our society males and females eat together, but in some societies they eat apart.

The "place of women" in a society is a matter on which Westerners are particularly prone to ethnocentric judgments. What they see as degrading—bridewealth payments, veil wearing, arduous physical labors, exclusion from all that seems exciting or valued—may appear quite different from within the other people's own world of values. (Kwaio women of the Solomon Islands were sometimes solicitous about the author's "lazy" wife who did not plant taro or sweet potatoes. "But what can you expect when you got her for nothing?")

American women may be more "emancipated" than most—and in recent years, having glimpsed equal treatment, many are now vehemently seeking to get it. Yet if in most societies the rights and duties of men and women, and their spheres of life, are not the same, close study has shown over and over again strong influence or control by women in the domestic realm and their frequent strong hand in what publicly are male affairs.

The position of men and women is closely bound up with the cosmological and symbolic order of a people. One of the fascinating complexes that turns up in tribal societies in widely separated corners of the tribal world, and even in the great civilizations—in Africa, Melanesia, the Near East, India—is a belief in pollution through the ritual impurity of women. The ideology of pollution varies to some extent from one area to another, but a common theme is contamination by menstrual blood—suggesting that the roots of these ideologies could be probed through psychoanalytic theory. Whatever their origin, beliefs in ritual pollution can be elaborated into bewildering complexities, as in India. In tribal societies they tend to reflect particularly vividly a people's model of their world. (Douglas, 1966).

Example 26:   Sacredness and Pollution among the Kwaio

The Kwaio of the Solomon Islands, like many Pacific peoples, have a concept of tapu *(from which our word "taboo" derives) that implies not only sacredness but also that which is dangerous and forbidden. Ancestral spirits, and the shrines and men's houses where the living communicate with them, are the focal points of sacredness. But the opposite pole is that of pollution. Just as sacredness centers in the world of men, so pollution centers in the world—and bodies—of women. Menstruation is highly polluting; women's urination and defecation only slightly less so; and childbirth is the most polluting of all. The sacred and the polluted both contrast with the mundane sphere is which men and women interact freely.*

This symbolic model is mapped, as in the Trobriand village, onto the layout of a tiny Kwaio settlement (Figure 30). At the upper margin of the clearing is the men's house where men sleep and eat, and which is sacred and off limits to women. At the lower margin is the menstrual hut, polluted and off limits to men. In the central clearing, which is mundane, is the dwelling house in which men and women mix freely. A man may move freely between dwelling house and men's house, and a woman between dwelling house and menstrual hut; but if he is sacred through sacrifice or she is polluted by menstruation, rites of desacralization or purification must be performed before the mundane realm can be entered. This cosmological and social mirror-imaging of sacredness and pollution is even more dramatically apparent in the most sacred of men's activities and the most

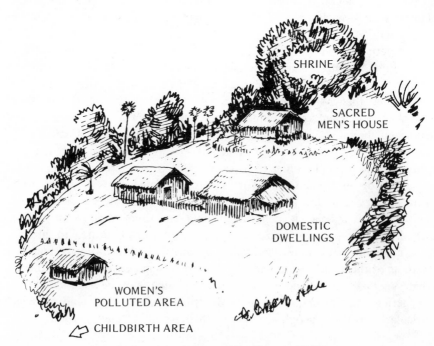

Figure 30. A Kwaio Settlement. RMK

polluting of women's: a high sacrifice by cremating a pig, and childbirth. The woman giving birth retires into a hut in the forest below the polluted menstrual area, out of all contact with men, and is attended by a young girl. The priest who sacrifices retires to the men's house near the shrine, out of all contact with women, and takes to his bed, where he is attended by a young boy.[1] We will return to such cosmological and symbolic orderings again in §57 and §58.

The life cycle and its biological sequence of maturation provide a set of organizational problems with which all societies must contend; and the solutions intermesh with a people's use of sex as an organizing principle. All societies must provide for children during their long period of dependence, and assign roles to people according to their stage in the life cycle. Men cannot build workable systems in which political decisions are made by newborn infants or mating begins at the age of ninety.

A society characteristically is divided into compartments or categories defined by age and sex. Just how this is done can vary within quite broad limits. All cultures have compartments for adult men and adult women. But there is great variation in the age when adulthood is deemed to begin for each sex (and, as we will see, by what sequence it is reached). More important at this stage is how high and wide the barrier is between the adult men's and adult women's compartments—that is, how radically different men and women are conceived to be, how sharply their cultural roles in the division of labor and ritual activity are contrasted, and how separate are their spheres of interest and activity. As we have seen, men may live in a sacred realm of men's houses, societies, cults, and so on—or in a world of warfare or high finance and social advancement—while women's place is in the home, performing the tasks of child support and everyday subsistence. We have noted how, in other societies, men's and women's roles are much less sharply contrasted, and their spheres of life largely overlap.

In the latter societies, getting girls to be women and boys to be men requires no drastic transitions. However, when the adult sex compartments are separate and thickly walled, getting young people into them requires major shifts. For girls, in such societies, there is seldom a sharp transition. But young boys are not men; and to make men of them is the major problem. One way this can be managed is to begin introducing young boys into the men's sphere of life early but sporadically, so that the transition to manhood is long and gradual. Many Polynesian societies (and some in Melanesia, like the Kwaio) use this solution. Here males learn early that they are men and that this makes a difference, with that difference becoming fully important as they mature physically and socially.

A more drastic solution is to leave young boys basically in the women's

---

[1] Here I have drawn on an analysis of a parallel symbolic system in a neighboring group by Elli and Pierre Maranda (1970).

sphere of life through childhood. Then, at some point that need not closely match physiological puberty, they are dramatically removed from daily life, subjected to some physical or ritual ordeal (often circumcision), and then incorporated into the adult men's compartment. Less commonly, in such societies, girls undergo a similar ritual transition from girlhood to womanhood. Such initiation rites have recently been a matter of much controversy. Involved here have been basic questions of cultural explanation that we will view again at the end of this chapter. Why do some societies drastically contrast men and women? If they do, and place their young boys in the women's category, certain entailments for child rearing and childhood experience follow; that is, the boys will have lived in a world of women, and it is then necessary to do something drastic to make men of them. But is it the early experiences and child-rearing techniques that cause the social organization to be what it is? Or the social organization that causes child rearing to be what it is? Anthropology involves a number of chicken-or-egg problems of this type, and the answers—if there are any—are still far from clear.

Rites marking the transition from one social category to another have been made famous by Van Gennep (1908) as *rites of passage*. The transition is ritually expressed, first, by removing the subject from the old category; placing him in an external, suspended state, cut off from regular contact; and, finally, ritually reincorporating him in a new category. Since others must establish a new set of relations with him, this is enhanced by the sequence of disappearance-reappearance—a kind of rebirth in the new state. This sequence in American culture comes to mind in initiations into fraternities, sororities, and secret orders. Viewed from the standpoint of families and friends, the seclusion of newlyweds on a honeymoon rather neatly follows Van Gennep's pattern.

Rites of passage can be seen dramatically in the life cycle, but they are also important in other situations. Where a society distinguishes sacred and mundane, or polluted, spheres of life, movement from sacredness or pollution back to ordinary life is likely to require rites of desacralization or purification. Attention to the symbolic aspects of rites of passage has increased in recent years, especially with realization of how important are "liminal" or halfway states and categories—"betwixt and between" the normally separate spheres of existence (V. Turner, 1964). Thus the Kwaio priest who conducted the high sacrifice is symbolically dead and with the ancestors in his period of seclusion (Ex. 26). We will return to the analysis of ritual symbolism in Chapter XV. Here we turn again to the life cycle.

Birth of a child does not necessarily introduce it directly into human society. This is a process, often a series of stages. It is likely to begin with a rite of some sort, sometimes connected with the mother's return from seclusion, sometimes with bestowal of a name. Anthropologists may have difficulty recording data on infant mortality simply because a newborn child is not yet a person, and hence, in death, is not accorded the recognition of a person who has died.

Childhood may be treated as a continuous phase of development, largely within the family, or may be marked by sharp transitions or discontinuities. Whatever the way childhood is managed in a culture—whether prolonged or foreshortened, continuous or broken into stages—physiological puberty and maturation change its character. Until this time, childhood is a period of more or less neutral sexuality and dependence. Full adulthood is usually attained only at marriage, when a new family is established and new economic responsibilities are assumed. The time between prepubertal childhood and full adulthood is a period that has been culturally treated in a number of ways.

We should be clear here that transitions between age categories need not correspond to stages of physical maturation. In any case, only the onset of menstruation for girls takes place at a precise time: the development of secondary sexual characteristics of puberty is spread over a period of years. Those societies that pass members through age categories individually are more likely to gear transitions to physical development (though external factors like the first successful hunt may define the transition points). Societies that initiate young people collectively in a large and elaborate production may do so at intervals of several years, producing a wide age-spread among initiates.

"Adolescence" may be treated as a separate compartment, differentiated into separate sections for boys and girls, or regarded as simply a kind of transition period between compartments. It may terminate with early marriage, pass into another category of young adulthood, or continue on until full adulthood is reached (in some societies well into the thirties or beyond). Reaching adulthood may be defined in terms of a set of stages, with ritual adulthood established at initiation, economic adulthood at marriage, and so on. In modern Western society adolescence is interpreted as a kind of social weaning from the family home setting, with an expectation of religious maturity coming early ("confirmation"), political capacity much later ("voting age"), and legal responsibility (no longer being a "minor") variously in between.

Cultures vary widely in their handling of sexuality in adolescence and before marriage. Americans, either those troubled by sexual "hangups" or those conceiving themselves to be liberated from them, have tended to think of primitive societies as free of sexual repression. Here Margaret Mead's early popular book on Samoan adolescence (1927) has been widely influential. In fact the management of premarital sexuality covers a wide spectrum. Many do, of course, regard sex as one of the good things of life, to be enjoyed freely (at least before marriage) when the mood strikes but not taken too seriously. The Trobrianders go rather further in this direction than most.

Example 27:   Premarital Sex in the Trobriands

Young people in the Trobriands are encouraged to indulge in sexual play in childhood and to begin sexual intercourse when that seems the thing to do. For girls that is very soon indeed—when they are six to eight years old, according to Malinowski (1929: 57). For boys intercourse begins, he says, at age ten to twelve. In earliest adolescence sexuality is free but very casual. In mid-teens Trobriand couples begin to pair off and to form more serious liaisons. Eventually one of these continues into a serious and permanent tie leading to marriage. Adolescents organize outings and trips that widen their range of sexual adventurings and add spice to sexual affairs close to home. Interestingly, periods of intense sexuality are geared to the seasonal gardening cycle. In the harvest season Trobrianders make hay while the moon shines.

Yet drastic repression of premarital sexuality occurs as well in the non-Western world. Thus virginity, and rites of defloration supposed to test it, are a recurrent theme. Ideas of purity and pollution among such peoples as the Bedouin are intertwined with enjoinment of chastity for girls. (Men usually, though not always, define *someone* as fair game). Even in the Pacific, where moonlight over the coconut palms has stirred many a Western fantasy of sexual freedom, there are many places where premarital chastity is enjoined.

Example 28:   Sexual Repression in Kwaio, Solomon Islands

Among the Kwaio, premarital chastity was enjoined for girls—and, since there were no permitted sexual partners, for men as well. Though premarital intercourse sometimes occurred, both partners were killed unless they could get off together safely to get married. That entailed getting the girl away from her own relatives, and to people who would intercede and finance the marriage. Since about one out of four adults of each sex never married, lifelong chastity was expected of many. Even affairs between older bachelor and spinster, or widow and widower, were serious offenses requiring compensation, though not usually a killing.

Since European contact, Kwaio men have enjoyed the favors of hospitable girls from areas to which they go for plantation work (work is what they say they go for; the wives of some disagree). Moreover, since killings have been prohibited, more than half of modern marriages follow a sexual affair. Affairs that do not lead to marriage require expensive compensation for lost virtue and diminished marriageability, yet are quite common.

In this area, as in many others, tribal societies provide crucial evidence on the possibilities open to us, and on the nature of man. The designers of utopias have not always used this evidence in exploring the realm of human possibility. Our primate relatives provide some important clues, but tribal man yields more direct evidence. Those who, in modern social experiments, would seek to ensure free sexual sharing between members of a commune and to rule out exclusive pairings might well ponder the comparative evidence about human mating more carefully than most probably have. Anthropologists command no supreme wisdom about human nature. But they have amassed a rich range of evidence about old human experiments in which ideologies have been tempered by a harsh world and man's animal nature, and have survived the test of time.

Cultural treatment of adulthood and its progression into old age shows considerable variability. Old age may be a culmination of adulthood, with respect and authority vested in wise elders; but in some societies, elders drift out of the picture, with younger men gaining power and prestige. However, in a kinship-oriented society the role of the elderly almost never entails the insecurity and alienation from family that have developed in our own society as a result of shrinking kinship ties, economic pressures, the isolation and mobility of nuclear families, and the "population explosion" in the ranks of the elderly due to medical advances. Another more subtle element here is the way our world view has changed—where time now stretches into the future, where progress and directional change move us inexorably away from the past. What we experience are *new* events, not the same patterns coming up again. In thinking of movement in straight lines, we have lost track of circles and cycles. Tribal man, living in a world of continuities with the past, a world of repeated cyclings rather than of progressive change, usually perceives old age in a very different way than we do. The son who cares for his aged and helpless parent is simply following a cycle where those who cared for him in helpless infancy are becoming helpless themselves—a cycle he himself will later follow.

Biologically, death may end the life cycle abruptly with finality. But in many societies death does not remove actors from the social scene—it moves them into a new role. Even though the notion of an afterlife is familiar, such cultural patterns as *suttee*, where an Indian wife goes to her death on her husband's funeral pyre, or the funeral feast where the Fijian elder takes place as guest of honor and submits to ritual strangling, do not "make sense" in our scheme of things. In §56, we will examine Hertz's classic study of seemingly bizarre mortuary practices in Borneo, which makes good cultural sense when one views the afterlife as a new social status and the funeral as a rite of passage.

The nature of ancestors and the way in which they enter human life will be touched upon in Chapter XV. Here we need to keep in mind that a people's social world need not include only the actors we can see and hear. A whole range of "religious customs" like sacrifice may be puzzling if we think of "the supernatural" as radically separate from "the natural," but quite intelligible if we see these events as communications and transactions with classes of social actors that are beyond our field of view.

Let us return now to the ways in which age is used in organizing social life. First, age is embodied in the notions of *generation* in kinship systems. Two warnings are needed here, however. Generation as a cultural construct may depart from generation in our genealogical sense—as witness the Trobriand kinship terminology. Also, though we think of parents' and grandparents' generations in terms of age stratification, we know that some of our aunts and uncles can be our own age or younger. Genealogical age and chronological age get far out of adjustment, and the implications of this for kinship studies have seldom been well thought through. But with these reservations, we can say with some cross-cultural confidence that relations between members of adjacent generations (parent and child) characteristically involve authority and hence are somewhat strained or ambivalent; while relations between alternate generations (grandparent and grandchild) are more free and indulgent.

Seniority or order of birth is a biological constant on which cultures build in various ways. Many societies take meticulous note of seniority. With some, *primogeniture* (being firstborn) has been of key importance in defining rank, succession, inheritance, and other social rights and responsibilities, as with European aristocracies. In such a society the status of the eldest child in the kin group would be very different from that of a younger child. Rarely is the youngest son the family heir, as among the Kachin of Burma (Leach, 1954), in what is called *ultimogeniture*. (In such a society advocates of birth control might make great headway distributing contraceptives through little boys).

A more dramatic use of age in the organization of societies is the formation of *age-grades* and *age-sets*. Age-grades are a formulation in cultural categories of the stages of the life cycle—so that (perhaps only for men) there is a set of age categories *through which people pass*, in terms of which their status is formally defined. Thus there may be a "young men" age stratum that fights, a "middle-aged men" stratum that conducts politics and feasting, and an "old man" category that conducts ritual affairs. The distinguishing feature of age-grades is some formal elaboration of what is almost universal—a set of age compartments that "stays put" while individuals pass from one to the other. Where such elaborations take place, they usually (but not always) involve initiation from one category to another, and collective, not individual, transitions between compartments.

More striking are systems of *age-sets*. Here age-mates are put together so as to form a group (with a name and corporate identity); and as they get older, they stay in the same named group. Thus what was a group of young men is thirty years later a group of middle-aged men; and by that time there may be two new age-sets of younger men. These systems often are very complicated, particularly in East Africa where they are most common. A distinction has been made between *cyclical* age-set systems, where the same age-set appears again every several generations like a duck in a shooting gallery; and *progressive* age-set systems, where a named age-set appears only once. The distinction is particularly interesting because cyclical and progressive age-set systems tend to be mirrored in corresponding contrasts in time reckoning, and in the cosmology and world view of a people.

Example 29: Nyakyusa Age-Villages

Among the Nyakyusa of Tanzania, a dozen or so youths of an age-set hive off to found a new sub-village on the periphery of their parental village and reside there for the early years of their marriage and child rearing. This is correlated with a strong avoidance rule between young married women and their parents-in-law. By the time they have raised children, younger age-sets will have hived off afresh (Wilson, 1951).

The social functions of age-sets vary widely. They may fight together, live together, and so on. In view of the preponderant anthropological attention to kinship, it is interesting that age-sets sometimes counterbalance kin groups in providing for collective security in blood-feuding and protecting age-mates' rights vis-à-vis their own kinsmen. The function of age-sets as complementary to, or a substitute for, kinship ties has been emphasized by Eisenstadt (1956) in the major study of age as an organizing principle.

Figure 31. A Nyakyusa Age-Village. Here a group of young men have built their huts at the edge of the parental village. (After a photograph by Monica Wilson.) RMK

38 · *Voluntary, or Interest, Associations*

For smaller societies kinship, age, sex, and community have been the dominant or central factors in social organization. Most statuses have thus been *ascribed*, not *achieved*. Yet apparently room has also existed in all societies for voluntary associations, groupings based on elective choice. One of the most striking developments of modern civilization has been the loosening of kin ties other than those of the nuclear family, and a vast increase in interaction based on such voluntary associations, both highly institutionalized and on casual and personal levels. We will see in the next chapter how the networks of personal ties into which individuals are bound pose a major challenge.in the anthropological study of complex societies.

By and large anthropologists have been remiss in paying attention to relations of friendship, alliance, and voluntary association that crosscut kinship lines, except where they are formalized or dramatized to unusual degree. Thus we know a good deal about the spectacular or dramatic secret societies like the Dukduk and Tamate societies of Melanesia, secret fraternal orders in Africa like the homicidal leopards, Plains Indian "military societies," and formal trade partnerships in New Guinea. We know far too little about the way friendship and less formal associations—subtle partnerships in gardening, trade, or other enterprises—crosscut kinship organization to weave the fabric of everyday social life. One of the side dividends from an increasing anthropological concern with the organization of complex societies is that in them one *must* pay attention to the ways individual bonds of friendship, economic strategy, and political alliance operate. In tribal societies anthropologists have tended to ignore them as "outside the system" of descent groups and kinship relations. In modern complex societies one must face the fact that they *are* the system—and that can give new insights into the forces that shape actual behavior in tribal societies.

The more formal voluntary organizations serve a wide range of functions in tribal societies. Consider the "functions" of an American college fraternity house as a dormitory, center of friendship, athletic team, sponsor of entertainment, closed ritual order, sowing circle for wild oats, and link to social groups in other areas—and part of the span of voluntary associations across the range of culture will have been covered. Tiger's study of *Men in Groups* (1969), in which he seeks to demonstrate the evolutionary roots and cross-cultural importance of male organizations, has aroused some of the ire reserved by the profession for those who popularize their theories; but it usefully attracts attention to forms of grouping that have long been slighted.

Example 30: Melanesian Secret Societies

The Dukduk secret society of the Bismark Archipelago in Melanesia takes into its lower grades of membership virtually all male members of the communities in which it is established. Parents wish their sons to belong for the prestige and privileges membership gives. A man who stays outside would almost certainly fall afoul sooner or later of one of its secret rules, and so be subject to fines amounting to more than the "fees" which entrance called for. The higher grades of the society, however, with their closer relation to the "great mystery," are reserved for important men. Entrance and passage through these grades become progressively more difficult and expensive, especially in terms of ceremonial wealth distribution. The innermost circle comprises the most important leaders in the area. The Dukduk conducts elaborate private and public rituals, notable for their masked figures. The Dukduk society serves subtle political functions by linking together with common rules and rites communities that have no ties other than the periodic arrival of the masked Dukduk figures.

In the Banks and Torres Islands of Melanesia, a number of men's secret societies or tamate are found on each island. A few major societies occur throughout the area. The clubhouses of these societies are set apart and forbidden to women and uninitiated boys. To become a member, a candidate must meet initiatory expenses, which vary according to the prestige and dignity of the society; and he must undergo fasting and seclusion. Once a member, he uses the clubhouse as a center of leisure-time activity, though as novice he must help to prepare meals. The ceremonial activities of the tamate involve festive dancing, but also periods of plundering and license when members in elaborate masks and costumes (Figure 32) impersonate ghosts and chase women and children. Each society has certain mysteries such as devices that produce the noises of "ghosts."

Figure 32. A Masked Tamate Masquerader (Banks Islands). (After a drawing by Codrington.) RMK

The tamate *apparently are politically important, as is the Dukduk society. To join a prestigious society or rise to prominence and power in it, a man has to expend great wealth, thus reinforcing his political power as a "Big Man" (§ 49). The occurrence of a few prominent* tamate *societies throughout the Banks Islands probably provides an avenue for political relationships and rivalries between communities.*

39 · *Inequality as a Principle of Social Organization*

Americans are the least likely social scientists in the world to have been able to understand and study intelligently the role inequality plays in the organization of other societies. As Dumont observes (1966), the ideology of equality—the premise that all human beings are fundamentally alike and are all entitled to equal access to rights, rewards, and avenues of life—is, in comparative terms, peculiar and recent. The diametrically opposed ideology of "hierarchical man" divides humans into different "species"—fixed by birth, placed one above another in rights and worth, yet each having its own contribution to make to the social whole. It reaches full cultural expression only in India (Dumont, 1966). Yet often in the tribal world, and over and over again in more complex societies, premises of drastic inequality underlie the social order.

Before the anthropologist or sociologist condemns as a human being, he must understand as a scientist. And those who have been able to explore matrilineal descent systems with dispassionate understanding have often not been able to do the same with social systems predicated on inequality. Too often institutions—such as caste in India and the treatment of black Americans—that have little in common beyond the way they violate our ideologies of equality have been arrayed together. Such a comparison seems hardly intelligible at all to an Indian social scientist (Sinha, 1967). Forewarned that we are predisposed by our ideologies to focus on inequality and hence to pull elements that share this feature out of their cultural context, we can very quickly survey systems of ranking and class in the tribal world. We will glimpse as well lines of continuity to the complex civilizations where premises of inequality are more fully expressed. We will trace some of them in the next chapter.

"Class" systems, as we will see, accord higher or lower status to *categories* of people. When it is actual *social groups* that are ranked, quite different forms of organization emerge. One set of possibilities emerges in the ranking of descent groups. Trobriand subclans are ranked (Ex. 44), though not to an extreme degree. In many parts of Polynesia a more complex and profound separation by rank organizes descent groups into a larger scheme. Lineages are ranked according to genealogical closeness to a line of direct descent from the gods, with corresponding chiefly ranks or titles.

Beyond the tribal world, in the extraordinarily complicated cultural melange of the Indian subcontinent, inequality between castes—as small-scale, economically interdependent, local, endogamous corporations—is worked out to an extreme degree. We will touch on caste in India in the next chapter. Many systems to which the term "caste" has been applied in comparative study, ranging from the tribal Nupe of Africa to Guatemala, Japan, and modern South Africa, turn out to be based either on inequality or social *categories*, not groups, or on the exclusion of a *pariah* class.

When a society is divided into different *kinds* of people, the categories may be called "classes." The term is most often used where the different kinds of people are stratified, in terms of legal rights, privileges, or prestige. The term "social class" covers a wide range. Every society distinguishes its members according to certain criteria—wealth, occupation, or the like—and hence has "classes" in a minimal sense. It is perhaps best to think of a continuum of "classness." Where social categories are clearly distinguished and ranked according to legal rights, and there are correspondingly sharp contrasts in dress, mode of life, and the like—then these are social classes in a full sense. Where there are only differences in privilege, opportunity, and power, as the break lines between categories become matters of degree, and as movement between categories becomes more possible—then there is less "classness."

At the first end of the scale lie the European feudal system, the Aztec state, some African states with hereditary aristocracies, and the like. Here, categories of royalty, nobility, and commoners—or some ranked order of two, three, four, five, or more levels—sharply divide a society in terms of rights, occupation, and way of life. In such societies, one's lot in life is largely fixed by the circumstances of one's birth.

Example 31: Natchez Social Classes

The Natchez Indians of Southeastern America had a complex social and ceremonial organization indirectly influenced by Mesoamerican civilizations. The Natchez were divided into two main classes, a graded nobility and commoners, referred to as Stinkards by the nobility. The nobility was composed of three classes: The highest Suns, from whom the ruling Great Sun came; the Nobles; and the Honored. The Great Sun was the oldest son of the highest ranking Sun woman, White Woman, in this basically matrilineal system. The perquisites of high rank were great: members of higher classes, and especially the Great Sun, had to be treated with deference and honorifics. There was a curious and asymmetrical rule of marriage: a member of the nobility, man or woman, had to marry a Stinkard. The Stinkard husband of a Sun woman did not eat with her, but stood like a servant. She could indulge freely in love affairs, but he could not; and when she died he was killed to accompany her. Their children, following the matrilineal principle of affiliation, became Suns. But just what happened to the children of male

Suns, Nobles, and Honoreds is not quite clear. If, as reported, the children of male members of the nobility dropped one class, rather than all becoming Stinkards (their mother's class), it would seem that there would soon be an excess of Nobles and Honoreds and not enough Stinkards to provide spouses for the nobility. In addition, some people could apparently rise one class by meritorious deeds. Unfortunately how the system worked is not clear—partly because the rules are in doubt, partly because we do not know how many were in each class. Apparently the nobility constituted a distinct minority. (Natchez society is summarized in Spencer, et al., 1965; possible solutions to the "Natchez Paradox" are analyzed by Fischer, 1964).

At the other end of the "class" continuum stand societies where there is no sharp differentiation into ranked social categories—as in a great many tribal societies. Even the so-called chief may enjoy whatever powers and rights he has only within his own group, not in the society as a whole. In the midrange are societies like ours, where family background, wealth, education, and occupation produce different styles of behavior—and where prestige, power, and opportunity vary according to one's "class." The boundaries are seldom clear, and they are impenetrable largely to the degree that one's style of life is learned in childhood and limited by opportunity and resources. In what sense there is an "upper class" in America becomes muddled by emotional and terminological issues; but in any case, the American "classes" are quite different from those toward the upper end of the "class" continuum.

In societies at the top end, class membership may be a rigid condition for occupying a whole set of interlinked positions (so that, for instance, only a member of the nobility can own land, give feasts, have retainers, practice polygyny, and join the priesthood). Such clusters of positions are ranked, so a person who is high-ranking or low-ranking in one position is similarly ranked in most other positions and situations. This leads to an articulation between the ranking of positions and the ranking of social categories. Here we can say that an *individual* has a certain rank.

Another variant is the ranking of formal individual titles, so that a person with the title enjoys rights and privileges in a whole range of situations (something that would be true, in miniature, of the officers in a small isolated military outpost).

Example 32:   Rank and Title among Northwest Coast Indians

Early accounts described the Indian tribes of the Northwest Coast of North America as organized into ranked social classes, or even "castes." Yet Drucker (1939) argues convincingly that apart from a basic division between freemen and socially inconsequential slaves, there were no social classes at all. Though there were many regional variations among such tribes as Kwakiutl, Nootka, Tlingit and Haida, common themes emerge. Everywhere it was individuals *who had distinctive rank and status, vis-à-vis others in the group. Everywhere, wealth bestowed and validated rank. "Each person's status had its own attributes which were not quite like those of anyone else" (216), even though the extent to which they were inherited varied a good deal. In a sense these ranks were like individual* titles, *a point particularly clear where a person's traditional name served as a kind of summation of his unique status. "So firmly rooted was this association of name and rank that the process of assuming a particular status, social, political, or ritual, consisted in taking (or having bestowed on one) a certain name. The Kwakiutl, among whom the system of naming reached its most profuse elaboration, had separate names for feasts, for potlatches, and for their secret society performances. A personal name was thus a key to its bearer's status and embodied all the rights, economic and ceremonial, to which he was entitled" (Drucker, 1939: 219).*

Whether or not there is a caste system—or even formally ranked classes —there may be a category of persons set aside from the rest of society. They may be excluded because of ritual impurity—as with the Indian untouchables or *eta* of Japan—and may perform essential but polluting economic services. They may be excluded on grounds of race (as with South Africa's blacks under *apartheid*) or religion (as with European Jews for centuries).

What distinguishes *pariah* or outcast groups is their enforced separation from the social structure of the dominant society. They are included—or exploited—economically, usually because of some special contribution in the division of labor. But for most social purposes, their existence is virtually denied. They are accorded a social niche because they do something: European Jews occupied a niche as financiers because they were free to collect interest; Indian untouchables occupied a niche as scavengers because they were free to collect filth; both the interest and the filth were symbolically polluting. Pariahs are not slaves. As we will see, slavery is quite different. But the American Negro was turned from a slave into a pariah, and his struggle to break through the barriers has shaken our society to its foundations.

Slavery is another phenomenon Americans are prone to misunderstand. We are likely to think of slaves as the lowest class of a society and to view them as economically exploited. Yet neither their low rank nor their exploitation for labor serves to define the position of slaves in all societies where they are found. Nor is slavery confined to large and complex societies. Nearly half of the primitive societies in Murdock's sample, including over two-thirds of those in Africa, have some form of slavery.

Slavery is a legal relationship of servitude not governed by a contractual or kinship obligation. The slave hovers in a kind of legal limbo where his master has all the rights (except that, as Malinowski observed, "You can't have your slave and eat him too"). He has no kinsmen beyond the nuclear family (if that—the master characteristically has no legal duty to keep slave families together).

But the everyday life of slaves is not necessarily lowly or degrading, and they are not necessarily economically exploited chattels. Slaves, not having economic or social interests in conflict or competition with their masters, may acquire great power and responsibility within a family or a court—even though slaves as a category in the wider society are set apart by inequality. Nor was the domestic or court slave usually exploited in the physical and economic ways that a plantation slave was. The "professors" of antiquity were often slaves in the households or courts where they tutored— and presumably exploited young princes with term-paper assignments. But we should not forget, in contrast, the dismal lot of the ancient galley slave, thwarted at every turn. At best his life was a two-sided monotony of either-oar alternatives.

In primitive societies, warfare is the most common source of slaves. How to move slaves outside the boundaries of social group membership, kinship, and legal independence is a problem, and the easiest solution is to capture people who are already outside. Alternatives are enslavement to pay off a debt (so that a child might be sold or "pawned"), or to punish a criminal.

40 · *Determinants of Social Organization*

Why do social structures "fit together" the way they do? Why does a particular combination occur in a particular place?

It is partly the hope of finding solutions to these puzzles that has led so many theorists into the study of kinship, descent, marriage, and other elements of social structure. Only a quick look is possible here at the volumes of theorizing in this field. To illustrate the different approaches, we will use a favorite laboratory for social anthropology—the South Pacific. Because of the fairly short time span of human occupation, the variations but small-scale of island environments, and the relative isolation of individual islands, this provides an ideal place to test theories of variation and change.

Recall from Chapter V the cultural laboratory the South Pacific offers: island Melanesia, with its rich diversity of social structure despite remarkable uniformity in the scale and settings of social life; and Polynesia, where basically similar ancestral cultures have taken root in a wide range of ecological niches and grown in very different ways.

An early approach to cultural variation in the Pacific viewed this as a marginal area into which successive waves of people migrated. Thus Graebner postulated six migrations, each bringing an inventory of things, customs, and social forms (for example, yams, fire saws, lunar mythology, secret societies, and matrilineal moieties). One simply mixed ingredients like cake batter to produce the recipe found on a particular island. Fortunately, we have learned at least that social structures are not like cake recipes—two parts matrilineal clans and one part cross-cousin marriage do not just mix together, despite the stirring reconstructions of these older writers.

Rivers (1918) postulated a similarly complicated sequence of migrations but attributed forms of social structure to the interaction (not simple mixture) of ingredients. "The dual organization" (with matrilineal descent and sexual communism, but with the power and the pretty girls in the hands of lecherous old men) served as the starting point for his theory of diversification of Melanesian societies. But "the dual organization" was itself a fusion of primitive aborigines and an immigrant population, who buried their dead in a sitting position and were far from upstanding even when they were alive (Rivers assumed that their morals had degenerated during their travels, like those of Englishmen in Paris or Cairo; Rivers, 1918, II: 566).

Modern theorists almost all reject such an emphasis on migration, mixture, and "diffusion" (§69) in shaping social organization. Some elements are borrowed, but they are reshaped to fit into existing patterns. Forms of social organization in two places often do have a common historical origin, but as they become different each continues to form an interlocking structure; and they change systematically, so that two societies with a common origin may come to be radically different, while two societies historically unrelated to one another may become structurally very similar.

But what are the "prime movers" or determinants in such sequences, and what are only secondary consequences? We are trying to reconstruct *processes* from observed differences. Scholars of different persuasions have had much leeway to argue about what determines what.

We have already looked, in Chapter VII, at modern theories of cultural evolution. Recall Sahlins' distinction (1960) between *general* and *specific* evolution. In general evolutionary terms, one can view the "tribal" societies of Melanesia and Polynesia—with horticulture, fishing, and polished stone technology—as representing a single evolutionary level. Polynesians on larger islands achieved a scale of political organization that approached evolutionarily higher forms; but Pacific Islanders were in general limited by their technology and environment to a single evolutionary level.

But how, then, to explain why some Polynesians have elaborate systems of social stratification, or ranking of lineages, and others do not? How to explain why some Melanesians trace descent matrilineally, others patrilineally, and others cognatically? These are questions of *specific* evolution.

Cultural evolutionists find the main answers in patterns of ecological adaptation. The interaction of technology and environment leads to patterns of production and redistribution of scarce goods for which particular forms of descent, social grouping, and political organization are adaptive. Sociological and ideological forms are then an adjustment to patterns of resource utilization.

Sahlins' argument for Polynesia (1958) will illustrate. He distinguishes two main types of social organization in Polynesia, "ramage" and "descent line." In the first, the whole society is ordered on a genealogical tree, with local lineages ranked according to seniority relative to the main descent line.

The high chief is the direct descendant of the gods through the most senior descent line. These ramifying genealogical lines and the differences in rank that go with them are used to redistribute surplus resources—food and other scarce materials. In a descent-line system, according to Sahlins, small and independent local lineages that do not trace descent links with one another are the main resources-exploiting groups. Rank is less emphasized and does not follow genealogical lines. Sahlins hypothesizes that ramage systems are adaptive on an island where resource zones are varied—people in some areas can produce one thing, people in another area produce a surplus of something else, and they redistribute these resources on the basis of their genealogical ties. Descent-line systems are adaptive, Sahlins concludes, where resource zones are uniform and each group has a "slice" of everything. Sahlins' theory has been much criticized on factual and methodological grounds, and he himself would no longer support it in this simple form.

The diversity of social organization in Melanesia has been attributed by another cultural evolutionist (Raulet, 1960) to a contrast in primary subsistence crops. Yam cultivation, with a regular seasonal food production cycle, gives an adaptive value to unilineal descent. The Trobriand Islanders plant huge yam gardens that are organized undertakings of entire sub-clans and villages; the yams are all harvested at the same time and can be stored for many months. Raulet would argue that for such planned collective ventures matrilineal (or patrilineal) descent groups are effective organizational units. Societies where taro gardens are planted irregularly throughout the year by temporary clusters of kin are more likely to be organized along flexible cognatic lines. Clusters of kin, not lineages, are likely to be the effective units in gardening and feasting. Thus Raulet would view the cognatic descent system of the Kwaio of the Solomons (Ex. 17) as an effective adaptation to the requirements of taro cultivation.

Though Raulet's interpretation seems too simple, some such ecological shaping of social structure could explain why, in the Solomon Islands, the Kwaio and the peoples of Choiseul Island (Scheffler, 1965) have very similar descent systems though they speak virtually unrelated languages; while peoples closely related to the Kwaio on neighboring islands have matrilineal descent systems.

Adaptation to the physical environment has been accorded a major role by most American social anthropologists even when they do not subscribe to general evolutionary theories. Murdock (1949), in the largest-scale attempt in decades at a theory of change in social structures, viewed the subsistence economy and the division of labor most suited to it as prime movers in changes of social structure. These then lead to shifts in postmarital residence—so that if women's role in subsistence becomes primary, more married couples will live with the wife's people, leading to a rule of uxorilocal residence. The coresidence of a group of related women and their husbands will lead to a rule of matrilineal descent and corporate matrilineages. Shifts in subsistence economy may then encourage a new residence pattern, as in the Trobriands, where men move from their parents' households back to their own sub-clan villages, with their maternal uncles; or to residence with the husband's father's kin, leading to an eventual break-down of matrilineal descent. For the Pacific, Murdock inferred an original simple form of social organization emphasizing bilateral kinship that evolved into unilineal forms under varying environmental conditions or remained cognatic or bilateral in emphasis in some places.

This view has been challenged from two directions. Lane (1961) has argued that to evolve complicated systems from simple ones is doing things the hard way. He argues that the ancestral systems were unilineal, and that the complex unilineal systems of Melanesia, like those of the Trobriands, represent variations of the ancestral form. Both the simpler cognatic social systems and more complex political organizations of Polynesia derive from the same ancestral cultures as the Melanesian systems, he argues, but they are adaptations to atoll environments and the organizational problems of spreading across the open Pacific.

Goodenough (1955) has accepted much of Murdock's argument, but in his pioneer studies of cognatic *descent* has added an important new twist. He suggests an ancestral system of cognatic descent where actual membership in either mother's or father's descent group was determined by residence. If a couple lived with the husband's people, their children affiliated there; if they lived with the wife's people, affiliation was with them. This then could easily shift into either patrilineal or matrilineal descent in an environment that favored a pattern of residence exclusively with either husband's or wife's kin. He suggested that where cognatic descent still occurred, it would provide a way of balancing out the ratio of people to land in environments where land was scarce. If a person's mother's descent group had dwindled, and father's had proliferated, he would be likely to join his mother's group in order to get more land. In the long run, Goodenough suggested, this should result in an even balance between people and land.

New evidence on this question has come from New Guinea, where great emphasis is placed on patrilineal descent but where many people actually live with their mother's or father's mother's groups. Here it seems that as land becomes more scarce, descent group members are less willing to let cognatic kin share their land—and hence land scarcity makes the system "more patrilineal," rather than "more cognatic" as Goodenough had sug-gested for smaller Pacific islands (Brookfield and Brown, 1963; Meggitt, 1965).

This evidence usefully illustrates how in a unilineal descent system the fluctuations of demography pose a serious problem. Some unilineal seg-ments proliferate (as when there are five brothers and between them they have twenty sons); and others dwindle (as when there is one son and three daughters, and the son's children are all girls). If resources are fixed and scarce, a means must exist to prevent some people from starving while other territories are unused. All unilineal systems with fixed and limited resources have some way of coping with these fluctuations—whether warfare, secondary patterns of cognatic affiliation or succession to land title, separation of descent status and active residence, segmentation and reallocation of land title, adoption, and so on. This is a major reason why, even where patrilineal descent is strongly emphasized, a quarter, a third, or even half of the men may not live on their patrilineage land. The difference between a "patrilineal descent system" and a "cognatic descent system" may lie more in the realm of ideology than practice (just as an economy in one country supposed to be based on "free enterprise" and an economy in another supposed to be "socialist" may be two ways of talking about the same thing).

The divergences between Murdock, Lane, Goodenough, and Goodenough's critics indicate that accepting ecological adaptation as a major determinant in social organization does not necessarily produce agreement on what goes with what. It is possible to "read" a body of evidence in many ways, depending on what one's position is on the details and conceptualization of social structure. But differences on these seemingly trivial questions tend to spring from fundamental disagreements about human social behavior and its study—whether one should focus on ideologies or actual events, whether social forms can be explained on psychological grounds, whether it is better to study one or a few cases in great depth or to survey a large sample statistically, and so on.

A rather different approach to social organization is represented in the writings of John Whiting and his students, who combine a basically psychoanalytic theory of culture with cross-cultural methods for seeking correlations between institutions. Early childhood experience (and hence the child-rearing practices of a society) are here seen as basic in laying down a more or less standardized personality; and many aspects of culture, including religious beliefs and rituals, are projections of the personality conflicts and problems produced by these early experiences. Whiting has paid special attention to *cross-sex identification*, where the desired and envied sex roles for a child are those of the opposite sex.

In §37 we discussed initiation ceremonies that remove boys from the women-and-children compartment and place them dramatically in the men's compartment. Whiting examines cross-cultural data and finds a complex of child-rearing patterns (for instance, a young boy sleeping with his mother and not with his father) that would lead boys to identify with females; and he interprets male initiation as a way of breaking this psychological pattern.

What leads to the standardized patterns of childhood experience in a society? Whiting views them as in large measure a by-product of subsistence economy—and in this respect he too invokes ecological adaptation as a major determinant of social structure, or at least of its most basic elements.

The complex of associated customs he finds worldwide could be applied to parts of the Pacific, especially New Guinea—mother-child sleeping arrangements, polygyny, a long taboo on sexual relations after childbirth, and male initiation. But others (like Young, 1965) have pointed out that if you begin with a sociological premise that men and women are radically different, then both the child-rearing practices and initiation ceremonies to get boys over the high wall from the women's to the men's compartment are likely to follow from it. Allen (1967) has looked with painstaking care at the Melanesian evidence and concluded that a radical contrast between male and female is found where unilineal descent and a corresponding rule of unilocal residence align group members of one sex together. This radical separation between men and women may lead to initiation rituals or secret societies and cult groups, or may be expressed in antagonism in everyday life. That depends on factors such as the status of women and the hostility or friendliness of intermarrying groups. Allen is quite prepared to admit that rituals of sexual antagonism or initiation may help people blow off steam psychologically, but his main argument is sociological: and it accounts much better than Whiting's for the variations on the same themes that occur in different Melanesian societies. Note that one still must account for rules of descent and residence, the status of women, patterns of marriage, and other aspects of social structure.

These present theories on the development of social organization requires some major acts of faith among believers. For example, almost all theorists would attribute the development of matrilineal descent to a pattern of uxorilocal residence, yet the great majority of recorded matrilineal systems now do not have this residence pattern—in fact, it is quite rare. Moreover, most of them make a major assumption far too lightly. They assume that a statistical pattern "automatically" produces a cultural rule—so that if most people reside in a certain way, a cultural norm will be produced so as to rationalize or validate what people are doing anyway. This assumption also underlies most theories of the incest taboo. Lévi-Strauss (1949, 1962) has rejected this passive view of man and has given ideational systems a greater weight. He views the building of arbitrary rules as the essence of being human and sees man as endlessly manipulating his environment intellectually (§58). Though social structures are limited and to some degree shaped by the pragmatic necessities of subsistence, man's intellect generates complex social forms—like those of Australia or central Brazil—just as it generates complex myths, rituals, cosmologies, and classifications of the environment. The requirements of marital exchange limit the possibilities of kinship systems, but they leave wide leeway for elaboration. Inventing rules becomes more than simply validating what people are doing; rules shape and change what people will do.

We need a theory of change in social structure that takes into account both the clear importance of ecological adaptation and the importance of man as creator and manipulator of rules. A promising approach (fore-shadowed in the Pacific in the work of Bateson, 1958, Meggitt, 1964, Scheffler, 1965, and Allen, 1967) would view a society as containing a set of "battle lines" that are always being fought or negotiated:

1. The relative status of men versus women—as represented in the division of labor, residence rules, property rights, lines of descent, ritual participation, rules of sexual conduct, and so on. (For a vivid recent description of action on this battle line in an African society, see Netting, 1969).

2. The relative importance of the tie between husband and wife and the tie between brother and sister; or, viewed another way, the competing rights over a woman of her husband and her brother.

3. The relative importance of collective rights and individual rights—as in the unity of brothers in corporate action versus their rivalry and separation, and the unity of lineages versus kinship ties between members of different lineages.

4. The opposition and conflict of descent or territorial groups over access to resources (land, women, property, prestige) versus their unity for common goals (peace, collective security, joint enterprise).

5. The unity of age-mates in different kin groups versus the ties of kin group membership that separate them.

6. One generation versus the adjacent ones, in terms of authority, rights, and access to resources (the last two may result in some contexts in alignment of old against young for access to power, females, and the like; and in others, to alliance of alternate generations).

Such boundaries of rights, duties, and authority are in this view continually open to negotiation—with rules being created, broken, redefined, and elaborated. Shifts in the ecological balance may enhance the bargaining power of men or women, increase the self-sufficiency of spouse-pairs, and so on; and it is cumulative individual deviations from a rule or norm that make possible the assertion of a new one. But changes in the rules are not simply *produced by* changes in ecology or in the statistical patterns of individual action. Rules are at once statements and metaphors about the state of the battle lines, challenges against previous rules, and targets for renegotiation. And violations and deviations from public norms are also, in a sense, assertions of new ones. Perhaps we need as well a Lévi-Straussian corollary to Parkinson's Law:[2] that the human mind expands and elaborates cultural detail to fill whatever "space" is available. This space may be produced by a freedom from ecological pressure (as on the Northwest Coast of North America), a freedom from material encumbrances (as in Australia), a seasonal cycle that provides a time of plenty and communal action, and so on. Or it may result from shifts in the "battle lines," where men acquire great

---

[2] "Work expands to fill the time available for its completion" (Parkinson, 1957).

strength vis-à-vis women, age-mates attain power vis-à-vis kin groups, and so on.

If this view is correct, the relationship between social structure and environment is indirect, mediated by ideologies and the dynamics of "negotiation"—so our search for perfect correlations of what-goes-with-what-under-what-conditions may be doomed to failure. But it enables us to break away from "equilibrium models" and views of social structures as "frozen" that hamper our understanding of change, and it connects the abstract formal structure of "the system" with the dynamics of social process and of individual psychology.

XI   *The Organization*
of Complex Societies

THOUGH ANTHROPOLOGY developed its concepts and methods by studying primitive peoples, a large and growing percentage of anthropologists do not direct their research at isolated tribal groups. Modern anthropology has increasingly become a study of peasant villagers, not of primitive tribesmen; and now it is reaching more and more into urban settings as well.

There is a large literature on peasant peoples, and many anthropologists have sought to interpret the emergence of the preindustrial cities and complex states that have given rise to peasantry in many parts of the world. To explore these rich fields in detail would require a volume in itself—and there are already good ones. It would also divert us to some extent from viewing, in the widest variations of tribal societies, the realm of human possibility. But we need to look briefly at peasants, and at the study of complex societies and men in urban settings, to understand the changing concerns of modern anthropology and its relevance to the problems of modern man. We can well do so at this stage because in the course of urbanization and in peasant life, men have built on and extended the non-kinship principles of social organization we have just examined.

41 · Peasants

Anthropologists have belatedly realized that a vast segment of the world's peoples have a distinctive mode of life that contrasts with that of the primitive tribesman and of the full participant in modern civilization: they are peasants. "The peasant is an immemorial figure on the world social landscape, but anthropology noticed him only recently" (Geertz, 1962: 1). In the 1950s and 1960s, he has been very much noticed: he has come to center stage in anthropology, to take his place with the tribesman—who increasingly is himself donning peasant garb.

What is a peasant? Most writers agree that an agricultural mode of life, with an emphasis on subsistence farming but a dependence on the products and markets of the wider society, is a dominant feature of peasant life everywhere. The peasant lives at once in a world of his own and a wider one. The center of that wider world on whose margins the peasant lives is the city.

But are these really the essential elements in defining the peasant condition? Wolf (1966a) argues that the peasant is a cultivator with a special kind of relationship to the world outside: "peasants are rural cultivators whose surpluses are transferred to a dominant group of rulers that uses the surpluses both to underwrite its own standard of living and to distribute the remainder to groups . . . that . . . must be fed for their specific goods and services . . ." (1966a: 3–4). It is the existence of peasants within a *state*, where they are subject to "the demands and interests of power holders" outside their social stratum—usually but not always centered in cities—that defines their status.

Peasants have been part of the human scene since the emergence of civilization in the Middle East and Mesoamerica. Our detailed knowledge of their economic life, social organization, and world view has of course been built up mainly through field studies of modern communities. The picture of peasant life that is emerging reveals men struggling to maintain life, continuity, and a measure of dignity while trapped on a kind of treadmill. It is, compared to the lot of tribal man—in the center of his own conceptual universe—an almost pathological existence; but man, with characteristic resilience, makes the best of it. Here we can very briefly sketch the economic, organizational, and ideational facets of peasant life.

Peasant Economies

In the next chaper we will look at peasant marketing within the context of economic anthropology. Here it is useful to see the peasant as leading a two-sided existence economically. First, he is a subsistence cultivator. He and his family subsist primarily on the fruits of their own labor. His technology and limited resources characteristically force him to scrape by from year to year, vulnerable to crop failure and demands from the ruling elite. Second, he contributes to an outside economy in the form of agricultural surpluses, or specialized products. Through markets and other networks of transactions his products go to maintain outside "power holders" and the specialists that provide services for them. But his performance within the outside economy is limited and channeled by the social organization and pressures of his own community, which guide his economic decisions.

Example 33: Pottery Production in Amatenango

In the Guatemalan peasant community of Amatenango (Nash, 1961), households engage in agricultural pursuits both for subsistence and for trade with neighboring communities. There is a lively trade of foodstuffs between communities, with each one partly specialized in its agricultural output. But Amatenango is more notable within the region for another specialized form of production: pottery making. Within an area nearly 40 miles long by 30 across, it is the only center for pottery production. People in every surrounding village must acquire and use Amatenango pottery. Thus pottery production is economically crucial to the households of Amatenango.

Practically every one of the 280 households in Amatenango makes pottery, through a combination of effort by men and women. The raw materials are freely available, the tools are minimal, and the needed skills are learned in childhood. Yet there is wide variation in the pottery output of the various households. Moreover, although pots are sold for money in markets, no household appears to produce nearly as many pots as it could. Why?

Manning Nash kept detailed records of pottery production in several households. He found that there is a seasonal rhythm in pottery making. Production reaches a peak just before a fiesta in Amatenango or a neighboring community. First, this is because that is when the household most needs cash; second, though the prices are not highest at these times, there is a convenient influx of potential buyers, so marketing is easy. Nash found also that there is a negative association between pottery production and wealth in land. The family with wealth in land can provide more of its own food, hence needs cash less; and more of its productive effort is likely to be devoted to agriculture.

But doesn't a household, like a firm, seek to maximize its gain (whether by pottery or agricultural production)? And if so, why is production limited and its peaks seasonal? Because as a unit in a complex system of kinship, local grouping, and religious organization, the Amatenango household is severely constrained by leveling mechanisms. "Getting ahead" of other households is in general neither feasible nor desirable. Household economic gains would in any case be short-lived: movable wealth is quickly consumed, and wealth in land is fractionated by inheritance in each generation. The leveling devices are rather subtle. First of all, what wealth a family has is drained by the costs of one of the many civil and religious offices in which a man must serve during his adult life. A wealthy household is particularly subject to the financial drain of ritual office. One office, the alferez (for which four men are selected each year), is particularly expensive and costs a tremendous amount; a family may take years to recoup. Finally, the household that outdid its neighbors in a quest for wealth would become highly vulnerable to witchcraft or accusations of witchcraft. Thus, the performance of a pottery-producing Amatenango household in the outside market economy is controlled by a series of social forces and mechanisms within the community. Despite the economic advantages on paper, it is not to a family's long-term social advantage to maximize its income by producing as much pottery as it could.

Markets, as we will see in §47, are elaborated into complex networks linking primary producers to urban centers. The flow of goods and services in peasant societies can take other forms as well. The *jajmani* system of India illustrates an important variant.

Example 34:   The *Jajmani* System in Rampur

The jajmani *system, a mode of reciprocal service and caste interdependence widespread in traditional village India, is well illustrated by its workings in the village of Rampur, near Delhi (Lewis and Barnouw, 1956). In Rampur, the Jat caste dominates the scene, with its control of land and agriculture; even the local Brahmans are its subservient tenants. The remaining ten castes include such occupational specialists as leatherworkers, sweepers, potters, washermen, and barbers.*

The jajman *is a kind of patron who provides grain, or reciprocal services, to his* kamin *('worker') in exchange for the traditional services of his caste. The Jats, controlling the land and its output of grain, are the dominant* jajman *in Rampur; the other castes provide them services, and receive grain, money, and sometimes supplies, clothing, or other benefits.*

The jajmani *relationship between a particular Jat family or group of families and a particular* kamin *is hereditary, so that such linkages were quite stable through time. The duties of a potter to his* jajman *are to supply earthenware vessels and to render certain services at weddings; in return he receives grain commensurate in value with the vessels, and additional grain when his children marry. A carpenter, in exchange for repairing agricultural tools, receives a fixed ration of grain each year; a barber, in exchange for shaving and cutting hair, can take as much grain at harvesttime as he can carry. Some* jajmani *linkages between caste specialists may occur, so that a barber may give shaves and haircuts to a potter and his family and receive earthenware vessels in return. However, in Rampur as in many other parts of India the* jajmani *system is undergoing change and breakdown as new jobs become available in urban centers, technological changes affect the traditional division of labor, and cash becomes more centrally important (Lewis and Barnouw, 1956).*

Economically, the lot of the peasant is far from bright:

Peasants live in a social world in which they are economically and politically disadvantaged. They have neither sufficient capital nor power to make an impression on the urban society. But they have no illusions about their position. Indeed, often they have no notion at all of that imaginary world which offers social mobility, entrepreneurs . . . , and the possibility of economic growth, rather than a stability fluctuating on the edge of disaster (Diaz, 1967: 56).

Peasant Social Organization

The social organization of peasant communities characteristically reflects elements of the tribal social systems from which they grew. Unilineal descent groupings may remain important. Thus patrilineages play significant roles in peasant social life in corners of the world as widely separated as Mexico, the Balkans, and China.

Networks of bilateral kinship and affinity help to weave the peasant community together. Moreover, modes of "fictive kinship," where social bonds are modeled on parental or fraternal roles, are often central elements in peasant social organization. Best known is *compadrazgo* or co-parenthood of Mesoamerica, primarily derived through Catholicism from Southern European customs but with roots in Mexican Indian cultures as well. Comparable but historically unrelated systems of fictive kinship have turned up as far away as Japan and Nepal.

Despite wider ties of actual and fictive kinship, the peasant community characteristically differs from its tribal counterpart in the independence of household groups. These may be nuclear families or extended families of various sorts. It also differs in the extent to which the whole village, not some kinship segment of it, is usually the focus of loyalty and identification. Considerable variation in the structure of communities has been documented (as would hardly be surprising when one is talking about India and Europe, China and Mexico). But here, as with many aspects of peasant societies, strikingly similar patterns turn up in different parts of the world. One of the most important is what Wolf (1957) calls "closed corporate communities"—where the community communally controls land, restricts its own membership, has its own religious system, and imposes barriers between its members and the outside world.

Foster (1961) has underlined the emphasis of *dyadic* relations in peasant life—that is, the way pairs of individuals are, in many different spheres of life, bound into relationships almost similar to contracts, though they are not enforced in law. Ties outside the family are, at least in the Mexican village of Tzintzuntzan, primarily between individuals rather than groups. They persist partly because they are never precisely balanced, and hence call for continuing reciprocity. Some dyadic ties are between persons of equal status; others are with *patrons* of superior status (including deities as well as people), who exploit and are "exploited" by the lower-status *clients* for mutual benefit.

Ties to powerful patrons outside the community help to link its residents into wider social networks. So do systems of markets, and "middlemen" who live in the community but have lines of communication to the sources of power. The social life of a peasant community, like its economic system, thus faces both inward and outward. It is the special dilemma of the anthropologist studying peasants that he must "capture" both the closed and self-contained nature of the community he studies and its articulation with a much larger social system that impinges on it in many ways.

The Peasant World View

The morality and value system of peasants, and their view of the world and their place in it, show vividly the "pathological" side of peasant life. Peasants are locked into a world that has passed them by. It has condemned them to poverty in comparison to urban elites. Their status is demeaned on all sides, and their self-conception is eroded. Pride and achievement, as well as money and the material things it buys, can easily become scarce "goods." Attempts to characterize "the peasant world view" in such ways can easily overgeneralize and can imply to be true of all peasants a pattern seen in one village or one country. Without implying that they are true of peasants in all times and places, we can glimpse some themes that have emerged in the recent literature.

Foster, drawing on his work in a Mexican village, sees the peasant world view as characterized by the "Image of Limited Good." That is, the peasant sees his social, economic, and natural universe "as one in which all of the desired things in life such as land, wealth, health, friendship and love, manliness and honor, respect and status, power and influence, security and safety, *exist in finite quantity* and *are always in short supply*" (Foster, 1965). From this follow the emphases many have noted in peasant societies: families competing independently against one another, with each seeking to conceal its advances and to guard against loss of relative position to others; competition for friendship and love, within families and outside them; preoccupation with health and illness; and an emphasis on manliness and honor (as with Mexican *machismo*). The peasant, in this view, can become almost paranoid about the possibility that others may be getting ahead or that, by his success, others will suspect he is getting ahead—leaving him open to gossip or to more dangerous sanctions of witchcraft or violence.

The religious ceremonials and ritual offices of Latin American peasants can be seen in part as leveling devices, as in Amatenango. Ritual office requires the outlay of money in exchange for a prestige that is soon dissipated. By going to the top of the religious ladder, a man slides back down the economic ladder to join his fellows. In peasant societies, the moral order is predicated on everyone trying to do everyone else in—at least beyond the close bonds of the family. This "us against the world" morality has been described in terms such as "atomism" and "amoral familism."

The study of peasants has been primarily a study of village communities. Economic networks and links to other communities have been traced out as they radiate from this village that is the center of study; and the world outside has been viewed through the eyes of the peasant on whose life it impinges. Other anthropologists have sought to conceptualize the wider systems of which peasants are a part. We will glimpse these studies of wider patterns in complex societies.

42 · The Study of Complex Societies

Can anthropology illuminate the development and structure of the vast and complex societies that have arisen through and since the urban revolution? There is a paradox here. An anthropology that refined its methods and theories by studying small primitive societies is perhaps less suited to the vast scale and complexity of civilized states than is history, sociology, or political science. Yet anthropology, if it is to be genuinely comparative and not "culture-bound" in reverse, cannot simply stop when social systems get too complicated. Moreover, the anthropologist's sensitivity toward cultural patterns and the close and human perspective he gets from living in and studying local communities, often make generalizations about complex states by his colleagues in other disciplines seem badly inadequate.

But can he do better? The attempts are interesting, but so far have been fraught with difficulty. A leading pioneer here was Robert Redfield, who went from a simple contrast betwen "folk" and "urban" to more sophisticated conceptions of the variety and workings of complex states. This development can be traced in a posthumous collection of Redfield's papers (M. P. Redfield, 1962). Thus Redfield came to distinguish, for example, between "primary civilizations" and "secondary civilizations." The former have developed from an indigenous folk tradition, as in India, China, Mesopotamia, and Egypt; the latter result from the superimposition of an outside civilized tradition on indigenous ones. Another approach has been to study the processes of urbanization in Old and New World. Thus, as we noted in Chapter V, Adams (1966) has emphasized social and political factors in the emergence of urban states, while Sanders and Price (1968) emphasize ecological and technological factors in the evolution of Mesoamerican civilizations.

But apart from such vast-scale classifications and developmental sequences, anthropologists are far from being able to conceptualize the complex ongoing processes and cultural richness of modern states. The problems and results can be illustrated by looking briefly at studies of India.

The phenomena of caste illustrate a first set of problems. Castes in India express an ancient Hindu ideology regarding human differences, hierarchically ordered. Thus local castes (*jāti*) are conceived in terms of the idealized fourfold divisions of society, or *varna*. These are the priestly *Brahman*, the *Kshatriya* as rulers and warriors, the *Vaishya* as landholders and merchants, and the lowest-ranking *Sudra* as cultivators and menials. According to Hindu cosmology and models of purity and pollution, castes are endogamous; socially separated, with eating and sexual contacts with members of lower castes viewed as polluting; ranked in a strict and unchanging hierarchy; fixed according to a person's birth; and associated with traditional occupations.

Yet anthropological studies of castes in village settings in India (see, for example, Marriott, 1955b; Leach, 1960; and Singer and Cohn, 1968) are giving quite a different view that makes the drawing of any total picture of Indian society incredibly difficult. Castes as local corporate groups are clustered in patterns that vary almost endlessly in local areas. A local caste hierarchy may correspond only very indirectly to the *varna* divisions of Hindu ideology. Thus a dominant group of cultivators may claim Kshatriya status, or may dominate Brahmans, as in Rampur (Ex. 34). There may simply be no agreed fit to the ideal categories. Individual castes may jockey for higher caste ranking, and even their closed endogamous membership may in some areas be permeable. Where separation of castes is stressed in ideology, their interdependence in wider systems is a dominant feature in village social life, as in the *jajmani* system. Castes do things for one another, in a complex division of labor: how they are *related into systems*, not separated, becomes the key question. Here, then, the student of Indian society faces on a village level a tremendous ange of variation in caste organization and a complex interplay between the religious and social ideology of the "Great Tradition" and a particular local "Little Tradition." As Marriott (1955a) puts it, "The intricacies of the Hindu system of caste ranking cannot be imagined as existing in any but small packages"; but from such small, diverse, yet mutually relevant packages, how can one depict that vast and complicated bundle that is India?

Study of caste points to a second problem. Caste in India and Indian-influenced areas such as Ceylon reveals a dramatic use of inequality as an organizing principles. Can caste in India then frutifully be compared with systems of structured inequality in the American South, Japan, or elsewhere? As we saw in §39, the experts are far from agreed about whether to view caste as primarily a cultural phenomenon or a social phenomenon. Students of the broad sweep of human civilization and the structure of complex societies continually battle with this problem of comparison: are they dealing with apples and oranges, or with apples that grow somewhat differently in each setting and hence can be usefully compared?

Religious beliefs and rites in village India illustrate another side of the interplay between "Great" and "Little" traditions that makes studies of total societies particularly difficult. Here, religion in an Indian village in Uttar Pradesh will usefully illustrate.

Example 35: Religion in Kishan Garhi

The village of Kishan Garhi is ancient and centrally located in the area of primary and early Aryan influence. Hence the influence of Sanskritic religion and the Hindu Great Tradition could be expected to be old and deep. It is. But that does not mean that religion in Kishan Garhi is simply an enactment of the rites, and a building on the beliefs, of the Great Tradition.

Fifteen of nineteen religious festivals in Kishan Garhi are sanctioned in universal Sanskrit texts; eight of them were probably universally observed in traditional India, and many others have wide regional distributions. But four festivals in Kishan Garhi have no Sanskritic rationales. Many of the festivals widespread in India are not represented. Moreover there are considerable diversity and disagreement about the connections to the Great Tradition of many of the rites in Kishan Garhi, and there are many elements of ritual procedure within Sanskrit-based festivals that have no apparent connection to the ancient epics that provide their rationale. If the combination of old and "new" (that is, ancient Sanskritic) elements gives an index of how far the rise of a Great Tradition has transformed religion in this village setting, then "we must conclude that spread and Sanskritization in Kishan Garhi have scarcely begun, despite their having continued there for some 3000 years" (Marriott, 1955a: 196).

By what processes does a Great Tradition develop from and diffuse into local Little Traditions? Marriott sees both an upward and a downward spread of cultural patterns. Through universalization, *local customs and patterns are incorporated into a developing religious literature and hence are spread through the Great Tradition to much wider areas (where they may compete with and restructure existing patterns). Through* parochialization, *the religious patterns that are elaborated by a sophisticated and educated priestly elite are filtered down to local levels. In both directions, upward and downward, these religious elements are transformed. "Seen through its festivals and deities, the religion of the village of Kishan Garhi may be conceived as resulting from continuous processes of communication between a little, local tradition and greater traditions which have their places partly inside and partly outside the village . . . A focus upon the small half-world of the village and a perspective upon the universe of Indian Civilization thus remain mutually indispensable for whole understanding, whether of Hinduism or of the traditional forms of India's social structure" (1955a).*

This split vision of the whole and its parts is what gives the anthropolgist his great advantage in understanding a complex civilization; but it gives him headaches as well, as he finds himself increasingly unable to describe the wider view without distorting the smaller.

As the anthropologist begins to develop models to relate traditional local communities to Great Traditions, he faces the further conceptual problems of dealing with rapid and vast-scale social change. His picture of modern India must deal with the intricacies of national and regional politics, with the workings of caste in urban settings as well as villages, with nuclear power plants as well as ancient modes of agriculture.

Anthropologists in India and other complex societies have increasingly found participant observation and fieldwork in depth only partially adequate research methods. The broader sweep of sociological survey techniques, as modified to fit non-Western settings, has proven necessary as well. Moreover, in extending his vision above a village level or directing it into urban settings, the anthropologist finds that it is not enough to look at what men do within organized groups. Any given individual—say, a market trader—lives in a world on which many different individuals impinge: his family and kin, of course, but now more often as individuals than as members of his group; also his trading associates, sources of financial assistance, suppliers, buyers, and so on. He moves in a wider range of settings than did the anthropologist's primitive tribesman, and he deals individually with different kinds of people in each of them. To describe such patterns of social life, anthropologists have increasingly explored models of "networks" linking individuals, or "action sets" (or "quasi-groups") of people who temporarily join in collective action. Such studies reveal pattern and process in small parts of large systems. If they give no clear total view of these wider systems, they help to balance and correct older ways of looking at societies as stable arrangements of groups. The newer models may also turn out to be very useful in understanding the more subtle facets of social life in isolated tribal societies: too often anthropologists have talked about clans and lineages and not about the mixed and temporary clusters of friends and neighbors who get jobs done together.

Hence the frustrations and rewards of studying complex civilizations anthropologically. The description of India or China or Japan by a political scientist or historian often seems starkly oversimplified to the anthropologist who knows life there from the ground up—from living with real people in local communities, rural or urban. It is clear that the anthropologist, in trying to do better, can breathe life into generalizations and can show how relations between kinsmen, friends, or patron and client go on in between the "cracks" of the formal social and political structure (Wolf, 1966b). It is also clear that, in the attempt, he can help to create better ways of viewing social process that he and his colleagues will be wise to try out in jungle or desert as well. But whether he can reconstitute from his knowledge of the parts, of people and processes, a clearer picture of the whole—of how a society works and how its culture is distinctive—remains in doubt.

43 · Men in Urban Settings

Anthropological studies of urban settings, though not new, have only recently aroused marked interest. Careful studies of kinship in modern cities, notably by Raymond Firth and his students and colleagues in London (1956), have shown that networks of kinship ties beyond the nuclear family play a much more important part in modern urban life than most social scientists had thought. And some anthropologists in Africa, India, and Latin America have followed up with serious study what becomes of tribal or peasant peoples when they come into cities. Notable here have been studies of voluntary associations and other urban patterns in West African cities by Little (1965), Lloyd (1966), and Plotnicov (1967).

Example 36: The Dancing *Compins* of Freetown

In the city of Freetown, Sierra Leone, Temne peoples have formed voluntary associations of a sort common in West Africa (Banton, 1957; Little, 1967). These are known as "dancing compins." Their ostensible function is to perform "plays" of traditional music and dancing. Performances are given for the weddings of members (both men and women), for special occasions such as visits by important people, and to raise funds.

Each compin is tightly organized, with officials, committees, and treasuries to which members contribute weekly and at the death of a fellow member. They maintain close discipline over members and compete for a good reputation for conduct as well as for performances. Fines are levied on members for breaches of rules. Great stress is laid on mutual aid in times of need.

Most members of a dancing compin *are migrants from rural towns and villages, and there is a strong local and regional bias in their member-ship. In many respects they function as an urban counterpart to the kinship-based corporations of traditional Temne society. They also serve to socialize new arrivals to the city in the ways of the world, and provide a closely knit group that contributes to their security in this new and otherwise often hostile setting.*

The origin of the dancing compins *reveals another side of their im-portance and appeal. The Temne were long regarded as the "hillbillies" of Sierra Leone by other peoples from less conservative groups. For young Temne, establishment of the first* compin *by a somewhat revolutionary Temne schoolmaster provided a rallying point around which they could build a new urban identity. As* compins *became established and acquired prestige, their combination of what was sophisticated and new with what was received from valued traditional elements of Temne culture gave them added influence. Some younger men used them as springboards to political leadership in tribal matters. "Thus, by founding voluntary associations individual Temne raised their prestige and rose in the social scale. These organizations pro-vided new leadership roles . . . By resuscitating certain aspects of the traditional culture and adapting it to urban needs these young men were able to further their modernist ambitions" (Little, 1967: 160).*

An anthropology of man in urban settings has come more dramatically to attention with Oscar Lewis' widely influential books on "the culture of poverty" as represented in Mexico (1961) and Puerto Rico (1966); and with a belated anthropological interest in America's minority groups (other than the Indians researchers have been annoying for decades).

Lewis's hypothesis that there is an international culture of poverty, with many broad similarities that transcend regional and national variations, has been highly controversial. Lewis suggests, and seeks to document with his selected life history materials, that the poor (at least in Western societies) pattern their lives partly on, but are largely excluded from, the major institutions of the larger society. Their social and economic lives and psycho-logical adaptations are shaped by exclusion and deprivation. Socially, the result is a lack of stable marriages and solid family life, with lovers drifting in and out, children leaving home early in search of an adventure that masks their economic frustration, and so on. Psychologically, "a strong feeling of marginality, of helplessness, of dependence and of inferiority" prevails (Lewis, 1966: xlvii).

The "culture of poverty" theory has been widely debated. Many feel that in his stress on pathological aspects in the life of the poor and on the negative at the expense of positive and creative cultural adaptations to a slum existence, Lewis has distorted the social problems of poverty and the paths to solution. Valentine, in particular, has offered an alternative interpretation and a set of research strategies for testing it (1968).

Here anthropological attention has begun to focus on urban minorities in America, particularly Negroes. With all of the economic, sociological, and psychological examinations of the black ghettos, we still know far too little about the subcultures that give ghetto life form and meaning. Do ghetto blacks lead a pathological existence, with broken families, social and economic and psychological frustrations, and a thwarted effort to emulate white middle-class values? Is the solution to open the economic doors so they can join that middle class? Valentine (1968) and others argue that this is not only too simple, but socially insidious. Some have seen the distinctive black subculture as rich in its own meanings and values; and have argued that ending social and economic repression can better be aimed at a positive transformation of that subculture than at eliminating it as a pathological state from which Negroes are to be lifted into the middle-class mainstream of American life.

How can such urban subcultures be studied in a way that is distinctively anthropological? Elliot Liebow (1967) has explored one possibility in *Tally's Corner*. He studied a small and shifting collection of Negro men in Washington, D.C., whose lives carried them to and clustered them around a particular street corner; and he traced their lives outward from it into short-lived jobs, sexual and marital relationships, and webs of friendship. It is a warm and human document, though it makes no claim to being systematic or to showing in miniature the overall patterns and problems of urban society. Another approach, by Keil (1966), is to document what is distinctive of black American culture by studying black jazz music as an expression of it—with the entertainers as bearers and shapers of that culture. The possibility that a mode of mass entertainment in a city can provide a window on cultural values and meanings has also been explored in Indonesia by James Peacock (1968).

An anthropology of urban settings has, despite such pioneering efforts, barely begun. Whether urban man will be illuminated in a way that is distinctively anthropological remains to be seen. It seems likely that more and more anthropological studies will be focused on urban man, both in non-Western cities and in those closer to home. This is a challenge of the future to which we will return briefly in §75.

Now, having looked beyond the structure of tribal societies to the ways anthropologists study more complex societies, we will return to a series of chapters that array the ways of man in comparative perspective. We turn first to a look at the economic side of tribal and peasant life.

XII *Economic Systems*

A SOLOMON ISLANDS TRIBESMAN, Batalamo, examines secretively the fiber bag of strung shell beads he has hidden away. He inspects the five valuables, made of multiple strings, he has been saving for his mortuary feast. He needs only two more, and he will have enough to present at his feast (see Ex. 43). That would be a respectable feast—but if he could get three or four more, instead of only two, his feast would be widely praised. He smiles, thinking of the reaction of his rivals.

But what about troublesome ancestor Kwateta, who has been making Batalamo's gardens grow badly? A small pig consecrated to Kwateta would straighten that out. But he has no extra piglets now, so that would mean getting one from someone else. He could buy one from Geleniu, but to do that he would have to break up one of his carefully saved valuables. Or he might borrow a piglet from his wife's brother Basuka and return one when his sow bore her litter. Brothers-in-law should help one another, and Basuka owed him a few favors. On the other hand Fuikwai might give him a pig in exchange for being taught that curing magic he had been asking about.

But how, Batalamo wonders, will he contribute to his relative Mae's bridewealth payment next week without using one of his largest saved valuables? If he does not contribute generously, Mae's powerful father will not contribute to Batalamo's feast, and that would mean less prestige.

Batalamo is allocating his resources strategically so as to maximize his goals. The models of the economist deal with just such patterns of choice and strategy, their statistical outcomes and complex interaction. Batalamo, like the stock-market investor, is "Economic Man" in action. But the economist deals with these processes in a very different setting. In a vast and impersonal market economy, money as a common thread of value ties decisions and transactions together into complex and systematic webs. The economist's models have traced these webs of interconnection with great precision and sophistication.

How can we deal with man as "economic" strategist, with the complexities of economic interconnection, in a setting as different as the Solomon Islands? Here the resources Batalamo commands include his magical knowledge and past favors as well as his shell valuables, his pigs, and his labor; and the knowledge, favors, and labor cannot normally be exchanged for, or valued in, shell beads. The goals he seeks to maximize include shell valuables—but note that he wants more of them so that he can give them away in exchange for *prestige*, not material advantage. He must also maximize his relations with ancestors, since without their help his family may sicken and die, and his gardens and feasts may fail.

The economic anthropologist, studying the whole range of men's social settings and customs, can begin with few of the assumptions and "givens" that make the economist's success possible. He must take each case as it comes. But in recent years, detailed studies have greatly enriched our knowledge of economic systems in tribal and peasant societies. Moreover, the gap between the subject matter of economics and economic anthropology is narrowing, as the societies anthropologists study become caught up in wider money economies and as economists turn to the study of developing nations.

Meanwhile, anthropologists have hotly debated wider theoretical issues. Are the basic postulates of Western economics culture-bound and applicable only to market economies? Or do they also apply to the behavior of Batalamo and Mexican peasant? Should economic anthropology study the allocation of scarce resources (like Batalamo's magic) among alternative goals (like keeping ancestors happy)? Or is this just circular double-talk? Should economic anthropologists simply study instead the different ways in which societies produce and distribute the material goods they need to satisfy their physical and social wants?

In the sections to follow, we will glimpse the range of settings in which anthropologists have seen "economic man" in action, and the range of economic processes they have documented. Fortunately, we need take sides only minimally in lofty flights of theoretical controversy.

44 · What Is "Economic"?

Robbins' classic view of economics as "the science which studies human behavior as a relationship between ends and scarce means which have alternative uses" (1935: 16) has been widely quoted in defining the proper scope for economic anthropology. If we take this view of man as maximizing values, as choosing between desired goals and allocating scarce resources, we face a frustrating conceptual problem. For we cannot then say that any particular spheres of life, or any particular behavior or institutions, are economic. Rather, all purposive behavior has an economic (that is, goal-maximizing) aspect. All behavior involves choices, and almost by definition every choice maximizes *something*, however vague.

Our conceptual problem, then, is how to use and build on the notion of maximizing, yet narrow our focus of attention to those patterns of acts and choices bound together into *economic systems*. And here we must broaden Western notions of "economic" so they fit Batalamo's system and others, yet retain their general shape.

Two complementary approaches can help us narrow our focus. Monetary transactions are one form of a more general phenomenon: *exchange*. Exchange systems take many forms, yet they all serve to link individual economic acts into wider networks, and entail shared standards of valuation. Focusing on exchange systems will illuminate economic processes in the full range of settings, from desert camp or jungle village to stock exchange.

But this by itself narrows our focus too much. For in primitive and peasant societies, many of the goods people consume have not been passed through networks of redistribution. The food a family eats, the clothes they wear, the house they live in, may all have been produced by the family itself. "Economics" in comparative perspective must focus not only upon exchange, but on the wider systems whereby material goods are produced, distributed, and consumed.

With such a dual perspective we can analyze the economic system within which our Solomon Islander Batalamo is operating, or any other. In the sections to follow, we will look at systems of production, examine modes of exchange and redistribution, and glimpse how they are organized into intricate economic systems.

45 · Systems of Production

We have already viewed in general terms the way subsistence technology can shape and limit a people's culture and social organization. Shortly, we will look more closely at production in the Trobriand Islands, particularly the agricultural system. Once more the Trobrianders will serve well to illustrate crucial contrasts with our society in the organization of work and modes of production.

A most crucial side of the organization of any society is the *division of labor*. Every society, however primitive its technology, assigns different tasks to men and women. These roles are shaped, though not determined, by biological differences. So too are the tasks assigned to the young and the aged.

Where subsistence is based on hunting and gathering or horticulture, household groups are likely to perform many of the subsistence tasks independently. Some subsistence activities (netting fish, hunting large game, felling rain forest trees) may require larger work groups; some specialized goods like tools or pots, and some specialized services like magic, may have to be obtained from the outside. But the division of labor is simple enough that the bulk of subsistence goods can be produced by members of the household group that consumes them.

The path to more complex and large-scale social systems leads through increasing specialization in the division of labor. The modern urban American, perhaps furthest in this direction of any human, can produce few if any of the material goods he consumes. As plumber, salesman, or teacher he makes a small and specialized contribution, for which he is paid; and through the medium of money he partakes of the cumulative products of the specialized services of thousands of people he will never see.

In tribal societies, full-time specialists among able-bodied adults are rare, though many command special skills or knowledge—as priest, artist, potter, canoe carver, or curer—that provide essential services to the community.

The organization of productive effort is closely tied to the structure of social groups. The unit of production in horticulture or fishing or herding may well be an extended family household or a shallow lineage. Yet we may assume too casually that they are descent groupings or other formal kinship units. If we look carefully, we sometimes discover that the units of production are informally organized groups of kin and neighbors that crosscut more formal groupings.

By looking closely at systems of production in the Trobriand Islands, we can see how complicated and intricate they are. We can also perceive how misleading are stereotypes of primitive man that have been unfortunately prevalent in popular thought. One can too easily imagine a society where people produce only enough to meet their physical needs and where each family produces what it needs—and a tropical island where food grows on trees would provide an idyllic setting for such a way of life.

Example 37: Trobriand Systems of Production

The Trobriand Islands consist of a flat coral island about 30 miles long, and several smaller surrounding islands (Figure 33). Trobriand villages are scattered along the west coast, with its shallow lagoons, and in the interior. No single village has access to all the material goods its people need; and nowhere in the Trobriands can one obtain some crucial materials. These include the green stone needed for blades of adzes and axes (which comes from Murua Island to the east); rattan for lashing, and bamboo, which come from Fergusson Island to the south; and clay for pottery, most of which is made in the Amphlett Islands to the south.

Furthermore, there are broad regions of specialization on the main island of the Trobriands. Along the western coast, circling the lagoon, are villages that specialize in fishing. The northern section of the island is a rich agricultural area, with villages scattered through the interior. Furthermore, some villages specialize in some special craft: one in polishing stone tools, another in woodcarving, another in decorating lime pots—all for export. Yet less handsome, everyday, articles of almost all kinds can be produced within any Trobriand village—dependent at most on the import of raw materials (Malinowski, 1935, I: 21–22).

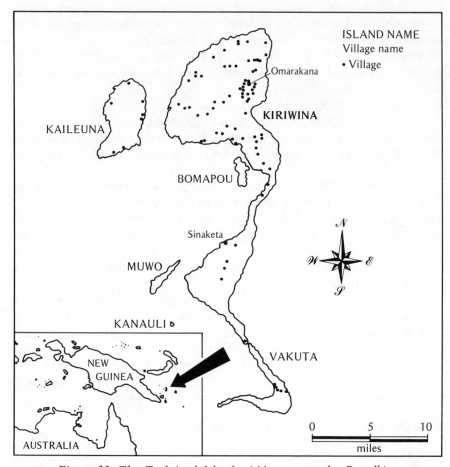

Figure 33. The Trobriand Islands. (After a map by Powell.)

Agriculture is by far the most important mode of production in the Trobriands. Our best information comes from the richest and most prosperous (and politically powerful) district in the north. The major crop is the yam, though taro is an important secondary subsistence food.

Because yams can be stored, a regular seasonal cycle of planting and harvest is possible, based on the cycle of winds and rainfall. This annual cycling of the yam season structures many aspects of Trobriand life: trading expeditions, warfare, ceremonies, and even sexual life.

Let us begin the cycle when an area is chosen for the year's cultivation, in this system of swidden horticulture. Here we can begin to sort out social units of production. The gardening team that will work the large area chosen for gardens usually consists of all residents of a village, even if the men belong to two sub-clans (see Ex. 25). In a large village with several sub-clans, there may be two separate gardening teams.

Even in the simplest case, where the gardening team includes men of only one sub-clan, it will also include other categories of people—due to the residence pattern where boys grow up in their father's household, then move to their sub-clan "headquarters." Married women on the gardening team will be in their husbands' places—not their fathers' (where they grew up) or their own (to which their brothers have moved.)

The gardening team does much of its work collectively, under the direction of a garden magician who is also its technical expert. The whole garden is divided into smaller squares. Each man has several squares within the large garden, which his household group cultivates. Tasks and rituals which call for large-scale cooperation are done by the whole gardening team for the whole garden; daily tasks are done separately by each family.

All adults in the Trobriands take a full part in agricultural production. Apart from the special services of the garden magician (who may be the leader of the village or his designated close relative), the division of labor is mainly by sex and age. Men cut the scrub; men and women clear ground and prepare for planting; men plant, and women weed; men train yam

Figure 34. Trobriand Horticulture. Here a man uses a simple digging stick to prepare the ground for the yams he will plant. The planting materials are saved from the previous year's crop. (After a photograph by Malinowski.) RMK

vines and thin roots; and both sexes take part in the harvest. Tools are simple: sharpened poles for digging and weeding, and stone axes and adzes for tree felling.

Each household group produces yams individually on its plots. Two factors of this production are crucial here. First, probably the most important sphere of life to a Trobriander is his garden production. Vast piles of accumulated yams, far above what he needs to feed his household, are his pride and joy—the more the better. He works enormously hard to produce great and "useless" quantities of food in an environment where man could wrest a livelihood with far more limited efforts.

Second, about half of the yams produced by a household go to the households of the husband's sister and other close female kin, in urigubu (Ex. 19). The yams the household gives away, to other households and to the leader of the sub-clan, are the best and largest it produces. The more and better the yams one presents, the greater is one's prestige. There even are spectacular "giveaway" contests of yams that are duels for prestige between sub-clans and villages. The symbolic side of Trobriand yam production comes out clearly if we note that many of the yams most highly prized and conspicuously displayed are not used as domestic food at all, and may simply rot. Furthermore, the high-value yams, displayed in storehouses (especially by leaders of high rank), become symbols of prestige and power.

So much, then, for our "noble savage," free from our crass ambitions and content to meet his needs in pristine self-sufficiency so as to save his time for more sensible pursuits. Though systems of production in other societies may be quite different and are often less dramatic, the Trobriand case usefully illustrates a number of important points.

First, the organization of production can be understood only against the background of social structure. Production may, in different contexts or with different scarce goods, take place in a whole range of social groupings of a society.

Second, a notion that production in a primitive society is concerned largely with meeting the subsistence needs of men is clearly too simple. To understand production—its motives and outcomes—we need to explore the value system of a society. Whether people "work hard" by our standards, or for things we think they should work for, depends on the conceptions of the desirable laid down in their culture. Trobriand Islanders, recruited to dive in their lagoon for pearls by white men, confounded their employers: they would exchange fine pearls only for traditional ceremonial trade goods, not money; they would refuse to dive for pearls when the gardens were in full swing; and they would fish rather than dive for pearls, even when the payment for pearls was ten or twenty times as great in exchange value as the fish they would barter (Malinowski, 1935, I: 20). Assertions in popular literature that native peoples are "lazy" and unmotivated should by now be perceived by the reader as implying not a lack of motivation but a pursuit of goals and values different from ours.

Before we examine the modes of exchange whereby scarce goods produced in a society pass through networks of distribution, it will be useful to look briefly at concepts of *property* in comparative perspective.

46 · *Property Concepts*

"Property" does not consist of *things*. It is more useful to view property in terms of *relations between people and "things*," where the "things" may be as intangible as knowledge of magic. In a non-Western setting, the crucial question is not "Who owns it?" but "Who has what *rights* over it?"

Reflection will show that when an American "owns" a piece of land, he is by no means the only one with rights over it. The city, the state, the country have rights over it, as he would discover if he tried to raise chickens in a suburban neighborhood or to deed his land to the government of China.

When land in a tribe is described as "communally owned," that may mean that a range of people (perhaps members of a lineage) have rights to live or garden there. But rights to sell any particular piece of land, or to claim first fruits, may be vested in individuals or smaller groups. Similarly, when land is described as "owned by the chief," that may only mean that he represents a symbolic figurehead. Lineages, households, or individuals may have the major rights over actual tracts of land. Since different rights apply at different levels, generalizations about who owns what are almost always misleading. The European colonial magistrate or administrator's usual first question, "Who owns it?", is often disastrous. The anthropologist must find out who has what rights over what 'things" in what contexts—and the answers are seldom simple.

The ways people classify kinds of property—land or livestock, tools, specialized knowledge, and so on—obviously vary according to their mode of subsistence. But the same distinctions appear over and over again: between *partible* (that is, divisible) and nonpartible property (rabbit farmers' heirs don't split hares); between movable ("real") and immovable property; between personal and collective property (can more than one person use it?); between material and immaterial, and so on.

The ways rights over property are transmitted across generations similarly vary within fairly narrow limits. A recurrent question presented by kinship ties is whether individually held rights over property pass successively down a line of brothers, or pass from father to son. *Seniority* is often used to pass rights from oldest son to oldest son (primogeniture), or to assign primary responsibility over property collectively held by a set of siblings. Whether men and women both receive rights over major property is obviously a crucial question, related to ideologies of descent and the symbolic significance of men and women.

Two important observations here relate back to our discussion of kinship and marriage. First, the corporate descent group effectively solves important practical problems in managing the relationships between people and scarce goods over long time spans. It keeps property intact while distributing rights (instead of, say, carving land into smaller and smaller pieces); and it maintains the continuity of rights across generations.

Second, anthropologists might do well to look more closely than they have at property rights and inheritance in comparative perspective. Leach has suggested, for instance, that looking at those societies where both men and women inherit similar property rights enables one to see a range of seemingly unrelated phenomena (dowry, fraternal polyandry, Bedouin parallel-cousin marriage) as solutions to the same problem—how to maintain the rights and interests of women without dispersing the estate. If anthropologists tried grouping societies on the basis of inheritance rules, not kinship or descent systems, they might stumble on a Rosetta Stone for the comparative study of social structure.

47 · *Modes of Exchange and Redistribution*

We have suggested that market transactions in complex societies are one manifestation of the more general principles of *exchange*. Study of a society's modes and mechanisms of exchange leads into the redistribution system whereby scarce goods pass through networks to people who did not produce them. Exchanging implies shared standards of value, and links individual acts of "maximization" into a wider system.

If we are to understand exchange systems in Africa or the Pacific, we will need to broaden our ideas about economic transactions. Many of our usual assumptions about transactions involving goods and services reflect the particular mode of exchange that dominates our economy; they may not fit other systems.

A major set of insights came from the French sociologist Marcel Mauss (1925). Mauss examined evidence on gift-giving in primitive societies, and argued that we were likely to misunderstand its essential nature. For "The Gift" in a tribal setting does not simply transfer title of an object from one person to another. Rather, the gift expresses and cements a social relationship: *A gift is a statement about the relationship between giver and receiver.* The thing given is a symbol of that relationship, and hence has value and meaning beyond its material worth. Furthermore, the relationship established or continued by the gift implies *reciprocity*. The relationship between giver and receiver may be symmetrical, as between feast-giving leaders or clans (so that an obligation is created to return in kind). Or the relationship may be asymmetrical: the giver may be dominant (so that he asserts his superior status and the receiver is obligated to reciprocate with tribute or services) or subordinate.

Above all, gift giving expresses and symbolizes human social interdependence. Thus it is enmeshed in systems of kinship and social stratification, and reinforces their structure. We have seen how Lévi-Strauss built upon Mauss's insights a model of kinship systems as modes of exchange, with women as the ultimate scarce good (§34).

This usefully warns us that the impersonality of transactions in a market economy, the focus on the goods exchanged rather than the relationship of the exchanging parties, can mislead us in looking at non-Western societies. At times, in fact, we label transactions and relationships "economic" precisely because they *are* impersonal and formal, in contrast to our relations with friends with whom we exchange Christmas cards and presents and wedding gifts. "Business and friendship don't mix" because they rest on different premises about social relations and obligations. In the tribal world, business and kinship and friendship are intertwined.

Karl Polanyi (1957, 1959), an economic historian of heretical bent, has given us further insights about how our Western economic institutions are likely to mislead us. He argues that there are three major modes of exchange in human societies: *reciprocity, redistribution,* and *market exchange.* Market exchange is the exchange of goods at prices based on supply and demand. Redistribution is the movement of goods up to an administrative center, and their reallotment downward to consumers. Reciprocity is the exchange of goods that takes place neither through markets nor through administrative hierarchies.

Polanyi sharply contrasts these modes of exchange as reflecting fundamentally different social means to distribute the material goods of a society. Though Polanyi argued at times as though any society could be characterized by the predominance of one of these three modes, his followers in economic anthropology have recognized that all three modes can occur in the same society. Reciprocity and redistribution may well be universal. Still, they argue, one mode is likely to be dominant, while others are peripheral.

Polanyi and Dalton (1961) have proceeded to argue that the basic models of economics, and notions like "scarcity," "economizing," "allocation," and "maximizing," properly apply only to systems of market exchange. To talk in such terms about tribal economics is to superimpose notions based on the market onto social institutions that differ in *kind*, not merely in degree and the nature of scarce goods. They argue for a comparative economics based on different modes of organization and exchange of the means of material subsistence. This has come to be known as the *substantivist* position.

So-called *formalists* have countered that studying maximization and allocation, and building on the insights and models of economics, can illuminate the workings of tribal and peasant societies. In fact, as evidence accumulates on how exchange systems are organized and interrelated in such societies, we are moving toward a middle position. Exchange systems that differ widely from ours *do* yield to modes of systematic analysis that draw on many concepts, methods, and models used by economists. In the absence of money, many scarce goods are hard to measure or count, and this poses serious problems. Yet at many points in complex networks it is possible to get data that bring standards of value and equivalence into view; and computer analysis permits us to discern patterns of connection that would otherwise be hidden.

What matters, then, are not great arguments about principles or what would or would not work. The challenge is to borrow or invent models that *will* work for the data at hand, and to work in a middle range where theories and ethnographic evidence both stay in view. Salisbury (1968) usefully sums up the issues and prospects on this frontier.

What is essential is that we not see "primitive man" as simply characterized by a single mode of exchange or economic transaction. Once more the Trobrianders will stand us in good stead, in showing us a spectrum of forms of exchange. Though most would be classified by Polanyi as based on reciprocity, there are strong elements of redistribution and market exchange involved as well. It is important to remember here that the same people and often the same goods are involved in different exchange patterns, so that they fit together into a wider system (Malinowski does not show precisely how—that is what we are beginning to learn to do now).

Example 38:   Trobriand Exchange

Here we will summarize the major modes and categories of Trobriand exchange, showing how they fit into a wider comparative perspective. We will begin with the kula, *one of the most remarkable and fascinating institutions of the tribal world (Malinowski, 1922; Uberoi, 1962).*

KULA

The Trobriand Islands form part of the d'Entrecasteaux Archipelago (Figure 35) lying off the southeastern end of New Guinea. Though the cultures of these islands form a related family, the customs and languages of each group are quite different. Yet they are united into a giant ring of ceremonial exchange several hundred miles across, so that each tribal group is a unit within the whole circle.

What they exchange around the ring are two kinds of intrinsically useless ceremonial objects collectively called vaygu'a. *Each kind is exchanged around the ring of islands in a different direction. Soulava, long necklaces of shell disks, move clockwise around the circle. Mwali, white armshells (Figure 36), travel counterclockwise. But what does "travel" mean? Who gets the objects? How are they exchanged?*

Let us look from the viewpoint of the Trobrianders—only one link in this chain, but the one we know best and are most concerned with here. The essential rule is that I ceremonially and publicly present you, my partner, with a Necklace. You are obligated to give me, some time later, an equally valuable Armshell. Our relationship, as partners, is lifelong, maintained by our periodic exchange of vaygu'a. *From any point in the Trobriands, a man receives Necklaces from partners to the south and receives Armshells from partners to the north and east.*

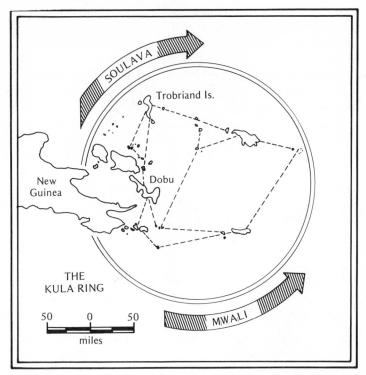

Figure 35. The Kula Ring. Necklaces (soulava) *are exchanged clockwise from island group to island group around the ring; armshells* (mwali) *are exchanged for them, in a counterclockwise direction. (Map by Gilbert Hendren.)*

An average man has a number of kula *partners, at home and over-seas. His partners at home are mainly friends and in-laws; and their exchange of* vaygu'a *is part of a relationship entailing different forms of exchange and assistance. He will also* kula *(that is, exchange* vaygu'a*) with one or two important leaders of high rank. These leaders, as we will see, acquire and validate prestige by the number of their* kula *partnerships and the importance of the valuables that pass through their hands.*

Kula *partnerships within a single district (like the Trobriands) constitute the "inland* kula*." Exchanges in the inland* kula *are smaller-scale, individual, and treated with less ceremonial formality than the overseas* kula*, which involves large-scale voyages and great complexes of magic and ceremony.*

The strategies and principles of overseas kula *transactions, as seen from the perspective of the important coastal Trobriand village of Sinaketa, are well summed up by Malinowski:*

> *Let us suppose that I, a Sinaketa man, am in possession of a pair of big armshells. An overseas expedition from Dobu, in the d'Entrecasteaux Archipelago, arrives at my village. Blowing a conch shell, I take my armshell pair and I offer it to my overseas partner, with some such words, "This is a*

Figure 36. Kula Valuables. The armshells (left) are made from the spiral trochus shell. The necklaces are made primarily of pink spondylus shell disks strung on fiber. FMK

vaga *(initial gift)—in due time, thou returnest to me a big* soulava *(neck-lace) for it!"* Next year, when I visit my partner's village, he either is in possession of an *equivalent* necklace, and this he gives to me as yotile *(restoration gift),* or he has not a necklace good enough to repay my last gift. In this case he will give me a smaller necklace—avowedly not equivalent to my gift—and will give it to me as basi *(intermediary gift).* This means that the main gift has to be repaid on a future occasion and the basi *is given in token of good faith—but it, in turn, must be repaid by me in the meantime by a gift of small armshells. The final gift, which will be given to me to clinch the whole transaction, would be then called* kudu *(equivalent gift) in contrast to* basi. . . .

If I . . . *happen to be in possession of a pair of armshells more than usually good, the fame of it spreads. It must be noted that each one of the first-class armshells and necklaces has a personal name and history of its own, and as they all circulate around the big ring of the* kula, *they are all well-known, and their appearance in a given district always creates a sensa-tion. Now all my partners—whether from overseas or from within the dis-trict—compete for the favour of receiving this particular article of mine, and those who are specially keen try to obtain it by giving me* pokala *(offerings) and* kaributu *(solicitory gifts). (Malinowski, 1922: 99–100)*

A man tries to maintain a reputation as a generous kula partner. The more important and numerous the valuables that pass through his hands (for he cannot keep them long or do much with them), the greater his prestige. This requires him both to give generously and to obtain strategically: he clearly cannot do one without the other. But the Melanesian prestige strategist, like Western capitalist, sometimes cuts a few corners. Here is how a Dobuan explained his strategies:

Suppose I, Kisian of Tewara, go to the Trobriands and secure an arm-shell named Monitor Lizard. I then go to Sanaroa and in four different places secure four different shell necklaces, promising each man who gives me a shell necklace, Monitor Lizard in return later. I, Kisian, do not have to be very specific in my promise. It will be conveyed by implication and assumption for the most part. Later, when four men appear in my home at Tewara each expecting Monitor Lizard, only one will get it. The other three are not defrauded permanently, however. They are furious it is true, and their exchange is blocked for the year. Next year, when I, Kisian, go again to the Trobriands I shall represent that I have four necklaces at home waiting for those who will give me four armshells. I obtain more armshells than I obtained previously, and pay my debts a year late. The three men who did not get Monitor Lizard are at a disadvantage in my place, Tewara. Later when they return to their homes they are too far off to be dangerous to me. They are likely to attempt to kill their successful rival, who did get the armshell, Monitor Lizard, by the black art. That is true enough. But that is their own business. I have become a great man by enlarging my exchanges at the expense of blocking theirs for a year. I cannot afford to block their exchange for too long, or my exchanges will never be trusted by anyone again. I am honest in the final issue (Fortune, 1932a: 217).

GIMWALI

Gimwali comprises Trobriand forms of barter—nonmoney transactions according to market principles. Here haggling and publicly acknowledged efforts to get the better of the other man prevail. Within or between Trobriand villages, it entails irregular barter of fish for vegetables or of newly manufactured items of various sorts.

Gimwali also takes place, on a large scale, on kula *expeditions. It is by this means that raw materials and manufactured goods from some segments of the* kula *ring are exchanged through the system to places that lack these objects and resources. Trobrianders thus get pottery, rattan, bamboo, green stones, and other items through the* gimwali *that accompanies the* kula.

While kula *partners are going through their dramatic interchanges, barter is going on around them. The rule is that no* kula *partners can barter (that would mix haggling with ceremonial); but everyone can barter with everyone else's partner.*

It has been argued that among other things the kula *constitutes a kind of regional peace pact under which otherwise hostile peoples can carry out this trade essential in their ecological setting.*

LAGA

Laga is a transaction type we know little about, but it is conceptually important. This entails the ceremonial transfer of title to a piece of important property (a garden plot or a large pig) in exchange for vaygu'a. *That is, the ceremonial valuables of the* kula *can be used for commercial transactions, though this is rare and lends a ceremonial character and importance to the exchange.*

Figure 37. Barter (gimwali) *in the Trobriand Islands. Here a fisherman, with his canoe pulled onto the beach, barters his catch for a bundle of yams. The items exchanged, and the standards of equivalence, are the same as in* wasi. *This form of* gimwali *exchange differs from* wasi *in that the items are directly exchanged on the spot, and that no particular partnerships are involved. (After a photograph by the Australian News and Information Bureau.) RMK*

WASI

A formalized exchange between coastal villages that specialize in fishing and inland villages producing yam surpluses is called wasi. *Here there are traditional alliances between villages; and within them, there are "partnerships" between a particular fisherman and a particular gardener. After the harvest, the gardeners will take a bunch of taro or yams to their coastal opposite-numbers. As soon afterwards as possible, the lagoon dwellers will stage a large fishing expedition. The haul of fish is taken directly to the inland village, where fish bundles are presented in exchange for the earlier yam presentation, according to fixed standards of equivalence.*

POKALA

The term pokala *covers a range of conceptually related transactions. First, it covers the presentation of gifts and services from junior members of a sub-clan or clan to senior members in exchange for anticipated material benefits and status advantage. Thus* pokala *gifts are a means of securing future political advantage, validating rights to matrilineal inheritance, or rendering tribute to one's ranking leader. It thus implies giving by one of lower status to one of higher status in exchange for obligations—obligations of protection, future status, future material advantage, and so on.*

Pokala in a different sense is used to denote tribute to a district chief or some other notable. The term is also used for a gift in the kula *to solicit favor in a future exchange. The essentials of* pokala *are (1) that it implies status asymmetry, with the giver below the receiver (in the* kula *this is apparently a form of flattery); and (2) that it creates a diffuse or specific obligation, so the giver improves his position vis-à-vis his rivals (even when the "giver" is a village sending tribute).*

URIGUBU

We know already that urigubu *is the presentation of yams by members of a sub-clan to the husbands of its female members who have married out (particularly by a man's household to his sister's household). This is a major focus of the production of great surpluses of important yams. These* urigubu *presentations are periodically countered by* youlo, *presentations of valuables from a man to his wife's kin.*

SAGALI

A sagali *is a distribution of food in connection with some ceremonial or special occasion—a mortuary feast, a commemorative feast, a competitive enterprise, or the like. Prestige in the system is achieved, expressed, and validated by being able to give away large quantities of food—to sponsor a feast, a war, a work project. Thus an important leader of a village or district gives away in* sagali *much of what he receives through* pokala *and* urigubu. *Thus,* sagali *functions as a mechanism of redistribution in Polanyi's sense, as well as a means of reciprocity for tribute and services rendered.*

The Trobrianders have other, less formal, patterns of gift exchange and reciprocal obligation between friends and among kin. This suffices, however, to show the range of intricate transactions whereby scarce goods in the Trobriands are exchanged and distributed.

Here, then, we have a range of modes of exchange. Some are ceremonial and transacted at set standards of equivalence with an implication of direct return. Others entail much less specific return obligations, such as *pokala*, or entail the supply-and-demand adjustments of the market (*gimwali*). For some, the return may simply be prestige (some forms of *sagali*).

There is nothing we would want to call "money" in the Trobriands, and the market principle is quite secondary or peripheral in the whole system of production and distribution. In some other Melanesian societies, we might be tempted to call the media of exchange "money."

Example 39:   Kapauku "Money"

Pospisil (1963a; 1963b) argues that cowrie shells among the Kapauku of New Guinea constitute true "money." Standard denominations of shells provide a common medium of exchange and a common measure of value. For shells one can buy food, pigs, crops, land, artifacts, labor, and medical and magical services; one can pay fines; one can finance one's marriage, and gain prestige and authority. Though there are common standards of "price" for many goods, these are subject to negotiation; and many prices are directly determined by supply and demand.

A system similar in many ways, though less completely developed, occurs among the Kwaio of the Solomon Islands, who use strung shell beads somewhat similar to Trobriand *soulava*. The largest "denominations" have special ceremonial value; but they can be built from, or dismantled into, shorter lengths or even individual beads (ten of which will purchase an areca nut for betel chewing).

Dalton (1965) argues that such valuables are not money, because they operate within markets that are peripheral to the main systems for production and distribution of goods. In the Kapauku case, this seems to be stretching matters. Clearly some tribal economies have developed standards of exchange-value that do many of the things money does in a Western economy.

Market principles are much more prominent in the societies of West Africa. Here we must distinguish between the marketplace, which may be colorful and prominent, and the abstract principles economists call *the market*. These principles are based on supply and demand and hence reflect statistical patterns of decision by buyer and seller. West African marketplaces fulfill many important functions of communication, security, and sociability; they also are focal points for the trade of specialized goods and surpluses. From the substantivist point of view, as markets they are still "peripheral," since the bulk of production for subsistence does not pass through the market. As tribal peoples have become increasingly urbanized and villagers have become tied more and more into money economies, these African markets have assumed a more central position.

Markets become crucial economically in peasant societies, where the local community is tied into a wider economic and administrative system radiating around an urban center. The peasant is at the margins of a complex network of market transactions, as we saw in §41. He may still produce much of what he consumes; but the wider system shapes his life and economic operations in many ways.

Example 40: Markets in Haiti

There are some 65,000 market traders in Haiti—about one person out of fifty in the total population. Fifty thousand are women, and in addition most of the peasants who buy and sell in markets are women. A woman brings her crop to the marketplace, selling some export items like coffee to licensed buyers and selling the rest to revendeuses, market traders (Mintz, 1959).

There are large market centers in the towns, connected by bus routes to numerous, less permanent rural marketplaces. Within a rural area, alternate marketplaces operate on different days, forming a "market ring" similar to those found in West Africa and Mexico.

Revendeuses can move and manipulate goods between marketplaces so as to buy and sell according to advantageous shifts in supply and demand. Many operate within a narrow geographical range on modest capital.

But larger-scale "operators" may move goods from one region to another or from urban center to countryside. Even larger-scale operators may buy manufactured or other goods in the main port and wholesale them to local market traders. Such "operators" obviously need more capital and maneuver financially on a larger scale than local market traders.

Such market operations have not eliminated the interpersonal relations of alliance and obligation as encountered in the Trobriands. For Haitians try to establish a favored trade relationship they call pratik, whereby particular partners transact recurrent business according to price or credit concessions (Mintz, 1961). Thus there is a personal, not impersonal, relationship, and a sense of mutual obligation. A revendeuse tries to establish pratik connections, as many as possible, on both ends of her trading, to render supply and sale more secure.

Transactions are based on cash currency according to fluctuating supply and demand. The Haitian system works efficiently because small quantities are traded, crops are diversified (so risks are minimized), capital is minimal, and goods are mobile. The revendeuse needs to make little profit, and by having stocks of commodities she can move from market to market, is able to come out ahead.

We now have a number of good studies of peasant marketing in Central America and Mexico. In most Mesoamerican markets the producer himself seeks out the most advantageous selling conditions, rather than working through a trader as middleman. Furthermore, the division between Spanish-speaking *ladinos* and rural Indians creates a crosscutting factor that affects peasant marketing in many areas. Many factors inhibit accumulation of wealth in rural communities. Among the Indian peasants in Mayan communities in Southern Mexico and Guatemala, much local wealth is channeled into financing access to religious and civil offices, as in Amatenango (Ex. 33). This acts as a leveling device, as do pressures of jealously and potential accusations of witchcraft.

Other studies of peasantry in Southeast Asia have shown variations on the same themes. In this literature, the nature of peasant marketing and the way it connects both with local social structure and with religion and subsistence consumption are coming vividly to light.

Here the theories and models of the economist, broadened to comprehend value systems of non-Western cultures and the articulation between markets and subsistence production, are proving to be more effective than the arguments of Polanyi and Dalton would lead us to expect. Increasingly, economists themselves are turning to studies of developing nations. And this has led them into the intricacies of production, distribution, and consumption in systems far different from our own. Economics, in the last decade, has of practical necessity become less culture-specific and more flexible in its models. As anthropologists expand their horizons, and as the societies they study are increasingly caught up in money economies, a productive collaboration is opening ahead that will leave behind the lofty theoretical controversies of the 1960s.

48 · *The Integration of Economic Systems*

We have glimpsed a range of modes of exchange, and how within a single society a number of interlinked modes may operate. A major challenge, for non-Western economies, is to see how the various sectors and networks of a society are interlinked. How, for Batalamo, are the demands of subsistence, ancestral support, and feast-giving prestige interconnected? How, for a Trobriand Islander, are the lure of pearl diving or *kula* manipulations balanced against the obligations to reciprocate *wasi* yams with fish or to help an in-law in his garden? How can we map the flow of yams, valuables, prestige, and obligation through the networks of exchange that pervade Trobriand life? How can we tie together what the Haitian peasant or *revendeuse* does in the market with what she does in her kitchen?

For these analytical tasks we are still inventing and sharpening our tools. The models of economics enable us to show relationships *within* an economic subsystem better than to show linkages between different subsystems—particularly in these societies where money provides no standard measure of value. The hardest challenges to economic anthropology lie in this middle range, studying interconnection between subsystems.

Here, a few general observations and an example from Africa must suffice. First, a society cannot be characterized by a single dominant mode of exchange without distorting how its economy works. A range of modes and networks of exchange—often entailing reciprocity, redistribution, and market exchange—are interlinked. Furthermore, some of the scarce goods used in subsistence are, in almost all societies, produced by those who consume them. Hence they pass through no networks of distribution outside the producing unit. *An empirical economy consists of interlinked subsystems.*

Second, maximizing values entails choosing between, as well as choosing within, these subsystems of the economy. Social change often involves no drastic shift in the economic institutions of a society (that is, in its modes of exchange and the social groupings and settings where it takes place). Social change may reflect a shift in statistical patterns of *allocating resources between them.* Time spent in the marketplace rather than the field, money spent on an outboard engine instead of pigs for the ancestors, cumulatively affect the whole nature of the economy and can produce rapid change or new equilibrium.

Third, in the absence of a pervasive money economy, these allocations involve standards of value and scarce goods that are exceedingly hard to study. To measure prestige, or the satisfaction a Trobriander gets by fishing for *wasi* instead of diving for pearls (and being paid ten or twenty times what the fish are worth in barter), is a sticky business. Where it is possible at all, it must usually be done by indirection—by studying patterns of choice or by documenting exchanges between things that can be directly evaluated or measured and things that cannot.

We can be partly encouraged by the fact that young Trobrianders manage to learn the values, procedures, and strategies that will enable them to play the games of Trobriand life—to make intelligent and intelligible economic decisions. The anthropologist deeply immersed in such a way of life can hope to make progress in the same direction. That is not to say that Trobrianders or other peoples necessarily understand their *economic systems.* An observer armed with sufficient data and a computer might well be able to understand the workings of the *kula* as a system better than a Trobriander in Sinaketa village.

Fourth, as the economic development and the monetization of the non-Western world accelerate, traditional anthropological assumptions that a tribe or community can be studied in isolation, that it is neatly integrated and relatively stable, become less and less realistic and useful. We glimpsed this problem in the last chapter and will return to it in the next. In studies of peasant and developing national economies, anthropologists are looking for ways to analyze how communities fit into wider systems and networks. Here they seek to map that range in between their own rich but narrowly focused knowledge of people, values, customs and meanings in a particular community, and the elegant but abstract global view of the economist. Exploration of the territory between can enrich both disciplines.

The integration of subsystems in a non-Western economy and the nature of economic change are well illustrated by the Tiv of Nigeria.

Example 41:   Integration and Change in the Tiv Economy

Tiv society, as we glimpsed it in Ex. 13 and Ex. 23, is structured in terms of segmentary patrilineages, with a patrilineal "compound" group as the core unit of production and consumption. Traditionally, Tiv conceived of three categories of exchangeable items. The first category of subsistence *items consisted primarily of garden foodstuffs (yams, corn, locust-bean, etc.), chickens and goats, and domestic utensils and tools.* The second category of valuables *consisted of slaves, cattle, a type of large white cloth, and brass rods. The third category consisted solely of rights over persons, especially of rights over* women *exchanged in marriage.*

Within the first (subsistence) category, barter in the spirit of a "market" prevailed: Tiv sought to secure an advantageous exchange. Valuables could likewise be exchanged for other valuables, though one would do so not for pragmatic value but for advantage in the quest for prestige. Exchanges of women were carried out through a highly intricate system of wards and women-exchanging groups.

The three categories of exchangeables are ranked in moral values, with subsistence at the lower end and women at the higher. Exchange within a category is morally neutral, though advantageous exchanges are sought. What the Tiv seeks to achieve is conversion *from a lower category to a higher category: to parlay food into brass rods or cattle, or to parlay the latter into a wife. Such conversions are the main strategic goals of the Tiv, as means to prestige, influence, and dependents. Downward conversion, as from brass to foodstuffs, constitutes a setback, to be avoided where possible. Accumulation within a category, without upward conversion, shows a failure or inability to play the game properly.*

Into this system came British administrators, missionaries, traders, money, and the tentacles of a wider economic system (P. Bohannan, 1955, 1959). About 1910, slave dealing was abolished. The administration, regarding the brass rods largely as a form of money, has over the years replaced them with British currency. This largely emptied the "valuables" category. Moreover, in 1927 a well-intending administration prohibited exchange marriages and substituted a system of bridewealth, paid in money, as the legal form—thus essentially eliminating the third and highest category, though modern Tiv marriage retains modes of exchange in covert form.

Meanwhile, many new material items that had no place in the old category system were introduced, and cash began to pervade the Tiv economy. This process was speeded by the imposition of a head tax in British money that forced cash-cropping on the Tiv before 1920. Moreover, the agricultural produce of Tivland flows into market channels that bring foodstuffs to urban areas. The Tiv as primary producers are part of a larger system over which they can exert little control. With pacification and transportation, Tiv men have themselves taken to trading subsistence goods over large distances.

How have such far-reaching changes been conceptualized in Tiv culture? Tiv have tried to fit money, and the new hardware one buys with money, into a fourth and lowest category. But money will not stay within these conceptual bounds. Most exchanges in and between categories now take place through the medium of money. Women's subsistence trade for money leads to a draining out of foodstuffs and makes it possible to build up cash through which prestige items can be bought. Their prestige value is eroded correspondingly.

Moreover, the bridewealth payment in cash forces the girl's guardian to trade down—to exchange a woman for money. Since the number of women is limited and monetary wealth rises with the export of food, bridewealth has become inflated. "As Tiv attempt to become more and more wealthy in people, they are merely selling more and more of their foodstuffs and subsistence goods, leaving less and less for their own consumption" (P. Bohannan, 1955).

The Bohannans' analyses of the Tiv economy in terms of the categories, values, and social groupings of the Tiv themselves (P. Bohannan, 1955, 1959; P. and L. Bohannan, 1968) are landmarks in the study of tribal economic systems in their own terms. Whether by taking a more abstract formalist approach to an economy like the Tiv, one could link wider subsystems together—including ones Tiv consign to other "noneconomic" realms —is a main challenge of the frontier. As Bohannan acknowledges, though no prestige goods ever entered Tiv *market* exchanges, "it might be possible for an economist to find the principle of supply and demand at work" within the prestige goods category. In Tiv marriage, again, "economists might find supply and demand principles at work, but Tiv adamantly separate marriage and market" (1959). But would it be possible and productive to look for a wider system of allocating scarce resources and maximizing goals, one that includes not only these Tiv spheres of exchange but penetrates those of land, lineage, and politics? (See H. K. Schneider, 1969.)

Economic anthropologists' battles to close the gap between elegant models, there to be borrowed, and the complicated realities of life in a small-scale society make this a lively, noisy, but productive line of anthropological advance. That advance depends on going beyond study of institutional frameworks and looking at processes, at patterns of strategy and choice. In this respect it parallels and at times links with another frontier of anthropological advance, the study of politics in non-Western settings.

XIII Political

Organization

IN EVERY COMMUNITY anthropologists have studied, "political man" has been at work. Decisions, organizing, the acquisition and use of power—they seem to be in the nature of the beast. Yet paradoxically, if you seek to define what is "political" or to delinate "the political system" in a small-scale society, you face endless frustration.

Looking at nonliterate societies as stable, isolated systems, we can see certain problems to be solved, by whatever institutional means, that we solve by formal political organization: maintaining territorial rights, maintaining internal order, allocating power to make decisions regarding group action. We can say that the "political organization" of a society comprises whatever rules and roles are used to manage these problems—whether or not there is any formal kind of governmental organization. This refinement of the "take me to your leader" approach has worked fairly well for some purposes. It enables us, for instance, to compare the way these problems are managed across a range of societies from the hunting-and-gathering band to the centralized state.

But the field anthropologist has increasingly confronted "political man," not in the pristine isolation of a primitive society; but manipulating a colonial administration, fomenting revolution, organizing a faction, uniting ethnic minorities, or running for a position in a government that did not exist five years earlier. Classifying and comparing kinds of "political systems" has increasingly given way to studies of political process at a local level (Swartz et al., 1966; Swartz, 1968). Here we will look both at the range of solutions to "political" problems at different levels and at political processes in changing societies. But underlying such a sketch will be more important questions about the nature of man. Do men everywhere seek and manipulate power? Are wars and conflict basic in the human condition, or are they problems generated by the complexities of modern life? The ideological return of the "noble savage" makes it urgent for us to ask whether "Establishments" and the political processes they reflect are products of Western civilization or are basic in the nature of man and human social life.

49 · Political Organization from Band to Empire

The non-Western political unit may not have such familiar trappings as a seat of government, policemen, code books of law, a flag, and other recognizable symbols. A Columbus could easily plant his country's flag on newly "discovered" soil with no idea that it might be covered by pre-existing rights of eminent domain. Yet the organization developed to hold together the thousand or so Polynesian Islanders of Tikopia is "almost as complicated as that which rules a city like London" (Gluckman, in Evans-Pritchard, 1954).

A comparative view of the ways men have solved problems of political organization will once more give us needed perspective. As in Chapter VII, it is useful to look at political organization initially in terms of levels of societal complexity. Service's (1962) "levels of sociocultural integration"—bands, tribes, chiefdoms, primitive states, and empires—provide a convenient way of organizing comparative materials. As Service himself now admits (1968), this does not mean that the distinctions between "levels" are neat or that they represent a simple evolutionary progression. We will use them as pegs on which to hang, for quick inspection, systems that are roughly comparable in scale and complexity.

In *band* societies, the primary problems usually center around territories, the distribution of resources, and relations between bands. Even mobile food gatherers such as the Eskimos, the Australian Aborigines, and the Andaman Islanders occupy a defined territory or locality. Each band has its customary range or "sovereign" area, to which it is linked by practical economic considerations, by history and sentiment, and usually by mythological and religious associations. The use of the region and its resources by members is subject to well-defined rules. So, too, are the relations of the group to neighboring units, including in some instances certain limited rights of hunting or otherwise using one another's territories and resources. The ecological adaptiveness of such flexibility has been underlined by Lee and DeVore (1968).

What constituted a band territory varied widely in different ecological settings. In the forested Andaman Islands each little band of forty to fifty persons occupied an area of roughly 16 square miles. On more barren sections of Australia the territory of a band was necessarily much larger, perhaps as much as 100 square miles for twenty people, but was also carefully defined. Among Eskimos the seasonal rhythms are important in shaping the travel, the settlement localities, and the periodic scattering out and coming together of groups within their wide territories. Those peoples depending on migratory wild herds like the buffalo and caribou have been most mobile and least fixed territorially, since hunting required them to move with game over a usually rather indefinite range.

The organization of decision making and the allocation of power in band societies are generally egalitarian (Service, 1966). That is, there is little stratification of rights and powers, and the leadership roles tend to be less formal and based more on personal powers than in larger and more complex societies. Demonstrated powers or abilities in the critical enterprises of band life—the hunt, relations with supernaturals, arbitration, or the like—distinguish the leader from his fellows.

Among Negritos of the Malay Peninsula, each camp had an acknowledged headman who took the lead in matters of common concern. Among the Eskimo of the Bering Strait region, men of superior courage and ability were likely to attract to them a group of adherents whose social, economic, and ritual life they regulated. The Yukaghir of northeast Siberia had a somewhat more specialized system of delegating authority. Camp affairs were directed by an "old man," who was the senior member of the dominant clan; by a shaman or practitioner in things supernatural, also of the clan; by a "strong man," who with his warriors conducted the tasks of war and did not need to be a member of the clan; and by a "first hunter," who with his companion hunters provided food and skins, also chosen for skill rather than clan membership. Usually, in band societies, general discussions and informal interchange gave an opportunity for the opinions of all participating individuals to be taken into account in political decision making.

Among *tribal* peoples the spectrum of solutions to political problems is much broader than in band societies. The problems themselves are broader, because populations are much larger, more closely aggregated, more complex and differentiated in their social organization.

A characteristic mode of political ordering in tribal societies, as we have seen, is the *segmentary lineage system*, such as we illustrated in §32 with the Smiths and Joneses. Here, in the absence of any central political organization, the Elm Street Smiths—normally an independent corporation—may enter into temporary alliances with neighborhood or district Smiths, depending on who the opponents are and what the conflict is about. The classic study of such a system is Evans-Pritchard's book on the Nuer of the Sudan, which set the framework for twenty-five years of intensive study of "tribes without rulers" in Africa.

Example 42:   Nuer Segmentary Organization

Some 200,000 Nuer live scattered across the swamplands and savanna of the Sudan. Though there is no overarching government, the Nuer maintain a measure of unity and orderly political relations between the territorial division Evans-Pritchard calls "tribes," and between segments of them.

A Nuer "tribe" is the largest group whose members are duty bound to combine in raiding and defense. Each tribe has a territory, a name, and

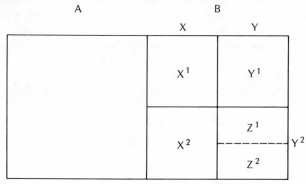

Figure 38. Nuer Political Organization. A and B are the major segments of a Nuer "tribe" (Evans-Pritchard, 1940). X and Y are the major branches of B, and they are in turn divided by segmentation. (From Evans-Pritchard, 1940, by permission of Oxford University Press.)

bonds of common sentiment. Within a tribe, feuds are supposed to be controlled by arbitration.

A tribe is divided into tribal segments. The relationship between segments is conceived in terms of hierarchies of patrilineal descent, as with the Smiths and Joneses—even though the actual correspondence between descent and the composition of territorial groups is quite messy. The basic principle is contextual opposition and alliance: "We fight against the Rengyan, but when either of us is fighting with a third party we combine with them" (1940: 143). On Figure 38, "when segment Z^1 fights Z^2, no other section is involved. When Z^1 fights Y^1, Z^1 and Z^2 unite as Y^2. When Y^1 fights X^1, Y^1 and Y^2 unite, and so do X^1 and X^2. When X^1 fights A, X^1, X^2, Y^1, and Y^2 all unite as B. When A raids the Dinka [the neighboring people] A and B may unite" (Evans-Pritchard, 1940: 143–144).

Disputes begin over many grievances—cattle, damage to property, adultery, rights over resources, to name a few. The Nuer are prone to fighting, and many disputes lead to bloodshed. Within the same village, Nuer fight with clubs or without weapons. Fights between members of different villages can lead to use of spears and to bloody war between men of each village. When a man has been killed, the dead man's close patrilineal kin will try to kill the slayer or one of his close patrilineal kin. The slayer goes to a "leopard skin chief" for sanctuary; the latter seeks to mediate and to get the aggrieved lineage to accept "blood-cattle" and thus prevent a blood feud. A killing involving members of low-level segments who thus have close social relationships, like Z^1 and Z^2 or even Z^1 and Y^1, is likely to be settled without blood vengeance. The more distantly related are the groups involved, the greater the probability of large-scale fighting between temporary alliances like the X's versus the Y's.

But what about the "leopard skin chief" who arbitrates disputes and provides sanctuary? Does this not mean some overarching political organization? Such a "chief" has ritual powers and a role as mediator and negotiator; but he has no secular authority, no special privileges. His performance in *peacemaking is possible because he* stands outside *the lineage and tribal system, not because he is central in it. He serves an important function which in other segmentary societies must usually be served by persons with conflicting obligations due to cognatic kinship ties that crosscut lineages. His presence enables Nuer to carry the posturing of hostility and threat further than they otherwise could, because he stands in the way of the actual killings most Nuer hope to avoid (Evans-Pritchard, 1940).*

Sahlins (1961) has argued that the Nuer and Tiv (Ex. 13) represent a specialized form of lineage system where each segment corresponds to a territorial bloc, and the arrangement of territories in space corresponds to the genealogical closeness of segments. Such an organization, he suggests, is particularly adaptive when a tribe is expanding into the territory of another people; effective alliances for aggressive "predatory expansion" would emerge at the right time.

Conflicts and feuds within a segmentary system in one sense upset the social order. But as Max Gluckman and his students have argued, they also maintain and renew it. Beyond the local descent group segment (like the Elm Street Smiths in §32), tribesmen seldom unite *for* anything; they unite *against*. Without feuds and conflict, social groupings would be much more atomistic and isolated from one another than they are. Moreover, the process whereby groups and alliances of groups settle feuds reaffirms their unity within a wider social system and moral order. It is Elm Street Smiths whose mothers were Browns who mediate in a feud between Smiths and Browns; and the resolution of feuds thus underlines the webs of kinship that bind groups together rather than the lines of descent that separate them.

Within a descent group like the Elm Street Smiths, political power and authority may be formally defined and assigned, or may be flexible and based on personal attainment. A spectrum of possibility in the political organization of Neolithic societies can be illustrated from the Pacific. Here two polar types of leaders are characteristic: "big man" and "chief" (Sahlins, 1963). The "big man," characteristic of Melanesia, leans in the direction of the leader in a hunting-and-gathering society; and the "chief," characteristic of Polynesia, leans in the direction of the head of a centralized state. In the middle of this spectrum lie the by-now familiar Trobriand Islanders. The line between a tribal mode of political order and a *chiefdom* is not always easy to draw, as the Trobriand case will illustrate.

Example 43: The Kwaio "Big Man"

The Kwaio of Melanesia (Ex. 17) are fragmented into dozens of local descent groups. Each of them owns a territory, and there is no central government or political office uniting these small groups politically. Influence, authority, and leadership in secular affairs come from success in mobilizing and manipulating wealth. A "big man" in a descent group is a more suc-

cessful capitalist than his fellows—the visible "capital" being strung shell beads and pigs, and the invisible capital being prestige. To acquire renown and be respected, a group must give large mortuary feasts honoring its important dead. If a man from group A dies, the dead man's relative from rival group B may be one of several emissaries allowed to bury him. The "big man" of group A will take the lead in a great mobilization of wealth by his group. The "pallbearers," including the one from group B, will be rewarded with large quantities of valuables. But all this must be reciprocated. When months or years later an equivalent member of B dies, an A relative has the right to bury him and the B's must give as large a presentation to him as was made in the first feast. What looks like an act of kinship obligation is in fact a duel for prestige between "big men," on behalf of their groups. A "big man" becomes big by manipulating wealth successfully. To attain great success, he must be an oldest son and he must have a fairly large group of close kin and fellow descent group members to mobilize. His strategy is to make people obligated to him, by contributing to their feasts, financing marriages, and otherwise investing his resources.

A "big man" has no formal authority or powers, no clear-cut position. He is simply a man who leads because people follow, who decides because others defer to him. A "big man" takes the lead in advancing claims or demands against other descent groups, and in settling feuds. He maintains internal stability and direction, Kwaio say, like the steersman of a canoe. A "big man's" oldest son may have some slight advantage in the quest for prestige and power. But there is no hereditary succession and no position to succeed to. "Bigness" is a matter of degree, in a society where every man gives some feasts and plays some part in the game of investment, and many descent groups have no clear-cut "big man."

The Melanesian big man has become one of the almost stereotyped figures in modern political anthropology, and the nature of his power can be neatly contrasted with that of his Central African counterpart, the village headman (Gluckman et al., 1949). The big man's powers are *personal*. Unlike the village headman, he occupies no office, his powers are achieved, and they are contingent on his continuing leadership as an entrepreneur. Whereas the village headman has authority over people, the big man commands resources (Epstein, 1968).

The Melanesian Trobriand Islanders combine some elements of the big man pattern with a system of chiefly rank, creating a political organization hard to pigeonhole in a classification scheme.

Example 44: Trobriand Political Organization

Recall the central elements in Trobriand social organization: the matrilineal sub-clans, the rule of residence after marriage that brings married men back to their sub-clan village, and the urigubu *presentations of yams from these sub-clan members to the husbands of their out-married female members.*

Figure 39. The Big Man as Patron. Here, a ceremonial image from the Melanesian Island of New Ireland. Big Men in New Ireland hire professional craftsmen to construct these dramatic three-dimensional pieces, with intricate fretwork and vivid colors. Such a figure is then displayed at a feast that expresses the Big Man's wealth and largesse. Such figures, characteristically flimsily constructed, are often then destroyed as a further expression of wealth. (From a specimen in the British Museum.) FMK

As we have seen, each matrilineal sub-clan has a village on its land; and some villages also contain a branch of a second sub-clan. A number of villages in the same area, related by intermarriage and traditional alliance, form a cluster (Powell, 1960).

Each village has a leader whose role is in many ways similar to that of the Kwaio "big man." But there are some crucial differences, for the Trobrianders have a pervasive concept of rank. It is not people who are ranked, but sub-clans. Basically, there are two ranks, "chiefly" (guyau) and commoner. Any village will thus be controlled by a sub-clan that is either of high or low rank. But the high-ranking sub-clans are themselves in a long-term competitive struggle for prestige and power; and hence there is a publicly known, if not official or clear-cut, ranking of guyau sub-clans.

Now, the leader of a commoner village, attaining his position by manipulating power and wealth and exercising wise leadership, is very much like the Kwaio "big man"—except that he and his group are pieces in a *wider design. The leader of a* guyau *village, however, has an important prerogative: he can take more than one wife. If you were a Trobriand man with six wives, imagine what would happen at harvesttime. You would get* urigubu *yams from six different sub-clans. And* urigubu *yams means prestige. This is precisely how the system works.* Urigubu *presentations become a form of political tribute. The more powerful a sub-clan, the more sub-clans in the same cluster and other clusters are placed in a politically subordinate position to it by strategic and manipulated marriage alliances. Sending a wife is, as it were, the first act of a tribute relationship. Commoners must also show formal physical deference to the leaders of the highest-ranking sub-clans, whose rank is symbolized by the high platforms on which they sit. The leader of a village of high rank symbolizes the status and prestige of his sub-clan while at the same time steering its decisions and policy and publicly representing it. He may have to mobilize his allies in warfare to maintain or improve its position relative to other important groups. Important leaders take the most prominent roles in* kula *exchanges, so that each flow of armshells and necklaces through the Trobriands validates or adjusts the balance of power and prestige of sub-clans and clusters.*

The leader of the highest-ranking and most powerful sub-clan in a cluster, by manipulating marriage alliances and effectively distributing wealth, comes to act as leader of that cluster. His role is similar to that of leader within a guyau *village, but on a larger scale. Once more his authority and powers are far from absolute. They are accorded to him as a representative of the will of the sub-clans in the cluster and because so many people are obligated to support him, or to defer to him, through his manipulations of wealth.*

Figure 40. Ceremonial Display of Yams in the Trobriands. This is the yam storehouse of a high-ranking leader. The yams have been presented to him as urigubu *by the sub-clans of his wives. Such displays symbolize the power and prestige of the leader's sub-clan and village. FMK*

There are two sides to this. A leader's rank reflects the rank of his sub-clan, his authority is that accorded to him by his group, and he contracts his marriages and receives his wealth as an expression of his group's power and prestige. Yet there is no regular hereditary succession to these positions of leadership, the network of strategic marriages must be established afresh by the aspiring leader, and the balance of power is constantly shifting (Powell, 1960). We have here a balance between the competitive openness of the Kwaio "big man" system and the formal crystallization of chiefly rank of the Polynesian systems.

In a *chiefdom*, ranked descent groups are linked into a wider pattern, with a hierarchy of authorities controlling economic, social, and religious activities. The pattern that links groups together creates an interdependence between them. Both the centralized authority and the linkage of groups into wider systems are well illustrated in Polynesia by the Hawaiians.

Example 45:   The Hawaiian Political System

The Polynesians of the Hawaiian Islands had an exceedingly complex and, in terms of the Neolithic world, sophisticated political system based on hereditary rank and classes, and theocracy and divine right; yet at the same time it was flexible and constantly shifting in terms of actual political alignments.

Hawaiian society was based on three major hereditary social classes— commoners, nobles, and inferiors. The commoners, by far the most numerous, were agriculturists, fishermen, and artisans—for the most part self-sufficient, but always living and working in the shadow of nobles to whom their very lives could be forfeit at any time, and supplying them with tribute. The nobles were ranked in sacredness and occupationally specialized as warriors, priests, and political officials. The hereditary ranking of nobles was based on descent from the gods, genealogically traced; rank of individuals and segments was traced in terms of birth order, with highest rank traced through firstborn child (male or female) of the firstborn child, down genealogical trees. The highest-ranking nobles were so sacred that elaborate and extreme deference—for example, prostration—was owed them by lower ranks, under penalty of death.

The islands were divided into chiefdoms, each ruled by a paramount chief whose powers over his subjects were seemingly absolute and were validated by divine right conveyed by his high god. The paramount chief's rule was administered and maintained through a cluster of high-ranking nobles who served as priests, counselors, and military leaders. The districts of his chiefdom were in turn ruled by local chiefs of high rank who exacted tribute and channeled much of it to the paramount chief to support the elaborate religious rites and secular life of the ruling elite. The nobles were supported almost entirely by tribute exacted from commoners in local areas, which in turn were administered by chosen chiefs and overseers of lower rank. The whole system was formally hierarchical, even feudal, in many respects, culminating in the rights of life and death, and dispossession, the paramount chief exercised over his subjects. Being of the highest rank and sacredness himself, this chief approached the status of the god who conveyed on him these divine rights. Secular political powers and ritual relations with the gods were united in his person. Seemingly this almost feudal system was fixed, stable, and immutable.

But in fact it was highly flexible and unstable. The territory of a chiefdom was established and maintained by conquest, and the political fortunes of paramount chiefs waxed and waned with their success or failure in battle and their success in holding their chiefdoms together in the face of insurrection and intrigue. The sacred mandate to rule had continually to be validated by secular success: if a chief lost in battle or a rival successfully challenged him by usurping the paramount chief's sole right to human sacrifice, it showed that he had lost his god's favor or that another's was more powerful. Even if a chief held his chiefdom together or extended its boundaries by conquest, his chosen successor—if any—immediately became the focal point of new rivalry and intrigue. Whole islands were added to chiefdoms, or lost; the political map, as well as its ruling cast of characters, was constantly changing. And with each new paramount chief or territorial conquest, the previous ruling elite lost their jobs—and very often their lives, in sacrifice to the new ruler's god. From the highest to the lowest levels of chiefly rule, office and privilege were conferred by a paramount chief and contingent on his political power. Only rarely, when the paramount chiefdom passed through an orderly dynastic succession, was there continuity of power at the lower administrative levels. As in the Trobriand system, the tides of political fortune were always shifting; gaining and preserving power required skilled direction and manipulation of physical and human resources—and a goodly measure of luck (Davenport, 1969).

Africa provides not only classic examples of segmentary lineage systems with no overarching political structure, but also a range of societies all the way to enormously sophisticated *states*. The way such central "governments" can build out of localized descent units is revealed vividly among the Bantu-speaking cattle herders of east and south Africa. A widely flung group of *kraals* (local settlements) may be organized in a hierarchy of importance, with the heads of senior family lines pyramiding up to the highest chief or king, who rules from the ancestral center. Sometimes larger political unities have grown out of marriages between neighboring groups, or the needs of common defense, or as a product of conquest.

Example 46: Zulu Political Organization

In the Zulu kingdom the armed power of the king maintained overall authority. Yet the king did not exercise this authority through a single structure of administration. All subjects had a direct loyalty to him, but through three lines of linkages: through provincial chiefs, through royal princes, and through age-regimental commanders (Gluckman, 1940). Differing groups of men were banded together in these differing links with the king. Their

Figure 41. Polynesian Aristocrats. Here a high-ranking chief among the Maori of New Zealand stands beside his wife. He holds a ceremonial weapon symbolizing his rank; she wears a cloak of kiwi feathers expressing hers. Such rank is based on seniority in lines of descent, hence is hereditary. (After a photograph by Lyndon Rose.) RMK

various leaders engaged in intrigue and tried to win adherents and control power; princes even struggled for the kingship itself. Struggles and rebellions may actually in this way have confirmed the overall unity of the Zulus and the authority of the king. Gluckman (1955) suggests that possibly a periodic civil war was a necessity for preserving national political unity and the royal power.

How states and empires have developed out of smaller-scale, less centralized, political groupings has been a subject of continuing debate among specialists. We have glimpsed some facets of this development in §20. Here, two centralized *empires* that developed in the Americas will serve to illustrate how far this progression carried in a few parts of the "primitive" world.

Example 47: The Inca Empire of Peru

The foundations of the Inca Empire of Peru comprised various tribes and petty states which, between A.D. 1100 and 1400, became consolidated under a dynasty of warrior-administrators. At its height somewhat before the first Europeans arrived, the empire covered an area of about 380,000 square miles, or more than the combined areas of France, Italy, Switzerland, Holland, and Belgium. The pyramid of Inca authority led from heads of households up *through a hierarchy of increasingly important officials said to have been in charge of approximately every ten, fifty, hundred, five hundred, thousand, and ten thousand households; thence to provincial officials, called "they-who-see-all," supervising jurisdictions containing forty thousand households; and so up to four great "viceroys," each in charge of one quarter of the empire and forming a kind of imperial council. Finally, at the peak of the system, was the supreme and godlike Inca. The internal ordering of this "monolithic" empire, as Vaillant calls it (1941), forms a fascinating story of political experimentation that contrasts at many points with our own.*

Example 48: The Aztec Empire

The Aztecs of Mexico showed an extreme version of what some political scientists have called the "garrison state." They drew much of their inspiration from the earlier civilization of the Mayas and Toltecs, and had a strongly theocratic system of government. The Aztecs, characterized as a "brusque and warlike people," established their capital at the present Mexico City soon after the middle of the fourteenth century A.D. All the men except for a few of the priests were soldiers, and they are said to have been arranged in ranks and given honors according to their war record. The people as a whole were divided into "great houses," somewhat equivalent to the wards of a modern city, though their exact nature has been much debated. Chiefs were elected from the most distinguished warriors for an indefinite term, and a council of chiefs conducted the general government. Chiefs could be removed if they did not measure up to requirements, but there was a tendency for the positions to become vested in certain powerful families which formed a military aristocracy. At the head of the empire was the supreme war chief or ruler, whose position had become hereditary by the time whites arrived to tumble the structure.

With full-time occupational specialization, class stratification, commerce and tribute, and military expansionism, political systems thus became highly complicated and elaborately structured. In the Old World they developed into the systems we must leave to the historian; in the New World, they were overturned by the intrusion of Spaniards riding the crest of a new wave of technological power.

We have glimpsed the spectrum of solutions to the "political" problems of maintaining internal and external order, and can perceive how the magnitude of the problems and the nature and range of possible solutions depend on population size and density, technology, and the internal complexity of the society. But does such a comparative view tell us all that anthropology is capable of telling us about political man in action?

50 · *Political Processes in Changing Societies*

Such a comparative view builds on simplifying assumptions that anthropologists, with their tradition of studying isolated primitive peoples and small communities, have usually been prepared to make:

1. The tribe or community being studied is relatively closed and self-contained, and can be looked at in isolation from its wider setting.

2. The society is relatively unchanging. It has an internal organization which is in *equilibrium*, so that when it is disturbed it will return to its normal state.

3. The culture under study is highly *integrated*, so that religion, kinship system, economic system, and other spheres of life fit together neatly and are mutually reinforcing.

4. The patterns of social life—the cast of characters, the roles they play, and the ways they perform—closely follow the scripts and staging instructions of the culture. Individual variations and deviations in culture and performance remain within a fairly narrow range, and thus perpetuate "The System" rather than markedly altering it.

In the preceding chapters we have been able to make these assumptions most of the time. Yet as we saw in Chapter XI, the modern field anthropologist increasingly finds himself in situations where these assumptions crumble in the face of his daily experience. Change is going on before his eyes, as tribal peoples are caught up in Westernization and become elements in emerging nations. Old cultural rules no longer apply to changed situations; new roles emerge and new social alignments are created; and the boundaries of tribal isolation are disintegrating.

In these settings the anthropologist concerned with political behavior can hardly be satisfied with trying to reconstruct how the "political system" worked before white men arrived. "The System" is changing before his eyes, and he sees political action shaping and responding to these changes.

Modern anthropological studies of politics have thus turned increasingly away from these assumptions about isolation, equilibrium, and integration. Defining "political" in terms of the organized systems for the maintenance of internal and external order simply will not do. We must view politics in terms of *processes*. These processes, according to a recent attempt at definition, are those "involved in the determination and implementation of public goals and for the differential distribution and use of power . . ." (Swartz, 1968).

What matters are not definitions, but some feeling for the way "political" processes are being looked at. This is a rapidly moving front in anthropology, not because of *what* is being studied but because on this frontier anthropologists are seeking ways to escape the bonds of the traditional assumptions about closed, stable, integrated societies.

First of all, they are now looking at "fields" of political events that cross the traditional boundaries of societies. We are learning belatedly about the way laws, bureaucracies, and political parties impinge on tribal or village peoples; and about the "political middlemen" who bridge the gulf between the outside world and their own people.

Second, they are making no assumptions about stability or equilibrium. Political processes produce new roles, new groups, new conflicts, and new integration. They do not simply keep the system going. Third, and related, one need not view the acts of individuals as submerged within "the system." Making no assumption that all participants share the same cultural rules, or that roles and groups are stable, we can see individuals as shaping and manipulating patterns of social life, not simply following them.

Fourth, we can see more clearly how cultural principles and social processes diverge, so that traditional codes no longer fit changed situations (Geertz, 1957). Here local-level political leaders may play decisive parts in redefining rules and manipulating situations. In a world where last year's chief may be next year's prime minister, such processes are crucial.

Studies of conflict and factionalism have dominated the recent literature (partly because conflict is by its nature more dramatic than harmony). Yet the "public goals" of political action may be to avoid conflict or to preserve unity. The leader quietly maintaining his control by building up loyalty and confidence is engaging in political action just as is the fiery orator fomenting revolution.

One example, from the diverse studies of political processes in modern societies, must serve to illustrate the newer approaches.

Example 49: Factionalism and Change in a Taiwanese Village

The Taiwanese village of Hsin Hsing has a population of about six hundred Chinese. Their traditional social structure has been built around several patrilineages (tsu), of which two have been most influential. The households of each tsu are centered in a small neighborhood or compound in the village. Though there are no marked concentrations of wealth or gulfs of social inequality, important families within the leading tsu have steered village politics and controlled alliances with neighboring villages through intermarriage and kinship.

When elections were introduced by the Chinese Nationalist government, elected offices of the village and the district of which it is a part were controlled by these leading families. The outcome of elections was, in effect, arranged so as to follow the traditional power of tsu and leading families in them, and to maintain the consensus and outward unanimity of action within tsu and village. The "mayor" of the district was chosen by the council of village representatives, again following lines of kinship and traditional influence. The elected officials were members of the gentry— men of education and standing.

But in the latter 1950s, opportunistic men outside the Village Establishment began to compete with these "respectable" leaders, using vote buying and other manipulations to get elected, and hence gain money and power. The high cost of getting elected, and its unsavory side, led traditional leaders to stay increasingly out of these contests.

Moreover, in 1959 and 1961, the government made election of the *district mayor a matter of popular vote, and redistricted voting for the dis-trict council so that villages no longer each had one representative. At the same time, the country's ruling Kuomintang party intruded increasingly on the local political scene.*

The result has been the emergence of political factions *crosscutting* tsu *and village lines. Consensus and harmony have been lost in favor of shifting factions, involving the poor and uneducated as well as the gentry, as active forces. Thus in the village of Hsin Hsing, a Farmers' Association and a Public Office faction organized at* district *level have competed for allegiance and control; and have divided* tsu *and family alliances. In the competition for votes, one candidate for village mayor chartered a bus to bring back from the city of Taipei thirty-six eligible voters. The district leadership of a faction enters local politics to provide patronage and avert the defection of supporters—playing on* tsu *unity, or seeking to disrupt it, as suits their cause. The traditional system has not been destroyed, but it has been radically transformed (Gallin, 1968).*

Here, with the disruption of traditional equilibrium and political order, the widening of the political arena beyond the local community, the emphasis on change and conflict rather than continuity and control, on process rather than structure, we see in miniature the focal points of the newer political anthropology.

Those who have wondered, through Trobriand examples, whether things in that Melanesian island setting are still as they were in 1914–1918, when Malinowski studied there, can be assured that change has reached those shores as well. In many respects the Trobrianders are conservative, still carrying out many patterns of the traditional culture we have described. Yet there is an airstrip at Omarakana village (the one mapped in Figure 29), one of many jarring notes in the modern Trobriand landscape. But it is the educated young Trobrianders who most strikingly exemplify the changes. The most articulate student spokesman of the New Left at the University of Papua-New Guinea in 1970 is a gifted young Trobriander. But in his challenges to established order, he has not lost sight of his cultural heritage: a member of a *guyau* sub-clan, he created a stir at a public debate by arriving adorned with kula valuables and awaiting his turn to speak by chewing betel in traditional fashion and sitting cross-legged on a table in the style of his mother's brother.

In their studies of political processes in changing societies, anthro-pologists are groping for new ways to conceptualize the cultural and the social, the enduring and the changing, the individual and the collective, the usual and the unusual. They are exploring ways to transcend the too simple, traditional assumptions about equilibrium and integration. One side of the challenge is vividly described by Victor Turner, writing about Mukanda, a ritual of the Ndembu of Zambia:

> A simile that occurred to me likened the cultural structure of Mukanda to a musical score, and its performers to an orchestra. I wanted to find some

way of expressing and analyzing the dynamic interdependence of score and orchestra manifested in the unique performance. Furthermore, I wanted to find a theoretical framework which would have enabled me to understand why it was that certain persons and sections of the orchestra were obviously out of sympathy with the conductor or with one another, though all were obviously skilled musicians, and well rehearsed in the details of the score. Neither the properties of the orchestra qua social group, nor the properties of the score, taken in isolation from one another seemed able to account fully for the observed behavior, the hesitancies in certain passages, the lapses in rapport between conductor and strings, or the exchanged grimaces and sympathetic smiles between performers (Turner, 1968a, 135–136).

The other side of the challenge, to build on Turner's analogy, is that in many societies—including our own—the musicians in ritual and secular performances no longer all have the same musical scores or the same notions of how they should be played. Some simply improvise. How, then, in a cacophany of discordant sound, can collective performances continue and be understood by performer or observer?

51 · War, Politics, and the Nature of Man

Must men fight? Is conflict inevitable? Are wars generated by man's social and biological nature? Or are they generated by imperfect social conditions that could be changed?

If we seek to gain in wisdom and vision from looking at the widest range of human societies, we are led to ask such sweeping questions. The evidence, we will see, is far from clear. As with most major questions about the nature of life or of man, the evidence can be read in different ways and used to "prove" different theses. One can use ethological, physical anthropological, and ethnographic evidence to "prove" that aggression and fighting over territory are deeply embedded in human biology (Ardrey, 1961; Lorenz, 1966). Or one can "prove" that men's basic nature is to cooperate, to share. Any such sweeping interpretation must be suspect. Yet some sifting of the evidence will give us useful perspectives.

An important first question is whether all men fight wars. We can usefully ask why men fight, in what different ways, and what social ends are served. Here we can begin to read the evidence in different ways. Some have argued, using a broad definition of "war," that it occurs in all human societies. Others respond by defining "war" more narrowly and showing that Eskimo or California Indian groups have no tradition of intergroup war in the sense of community or mass action (though individual feuding and vengeance killings might occur).

Quibbling over definitions is usually a waste of time. It is clear from the evidence that "warfare" takes widely varying forms in different societies. Unless we sort these variations out, we are likely to compare apples with oranges and pears and end with analytical fruit salad. A good deal of sorting out is possible if once more we look at societies in terms of levels of scale, technology, and complexity. Primitive bands do not all fight in the same way for the same reasons; but they have more in common than each would have with Mongol hordes, English Crusaders, or German Panzer divisions.

Among band societies, our data are unfortunately thin. Some bands clearly fought a good deal, for access to special resources, for vengeance, and so on. Thus Warner writes of the Murngin of Australia, "Warfare is one of the most important social activities of the Murngin and surrounding tribes. Without it, Murngin society as it is now constituted could not exist" (1937: 155). Yet when peoples of this technological level did fight, combat was sporadic, often minimally planned, individualistic, relatively disorganized, and lacking elaborate weaponry and tactics. In many band societies, group fighting was rare, and in some, probably nonexistent (here again we face sticky definitions and poor evidence). The headman of a Bushmen band summed up a typical point of view about the danger of fighting: "Someone might get killed."

In tribal societies, warfare was very often a vicious and deadly business, where neighboring kin groups or tribes were in constant danger. The frequency and scale of fighting, for many societies, is hard to assess. Very often our evidence comes from a period, just before Europeans imposed a peace, when traditional balances had been upset by new weapons and other outside influences. In the Solomon Islands of Melanesia, early records describe how predatory headhunters from Roviana decimated the populations of surrounding islands, with victims numbering many thousands. Yet not only did friendly European captains tow the headhunters into position for an occasional surprise attack in return for economic and political advantage; but also the whole ecological balance had been upset by introduction of steel tools. The gardening force had been freed from drudgery to carry on continuously what had been an occasional luxury for a few, and an armada of war canoes could now be produced to take them on headhunting expeditions.

Tribal warfare very often had two facets, and writers have had difficulty keeping both in view. The first side involves elaborate posturing and even pageantry, "productions" in the male realm that involved a great deal of action with very few casualties. Ritualized forms of combat and carefully followed "rules of play" often command attention: a tribal war often looked more like a football game than a ruthless struggle for territory or principle. Robert Gardner's classic anthropological film *Dead Birds* shows vividly this side of tribal warfare in New Guinea, though the other emerges as well.

This appearance of formal posturing in tribal warfare has often obscured its more serious and vicious side (Fried et al., 1968). Warfare to gain territory and hence adjust ecological balances has emerged as far more important among shifting horticulturists than earlier writers had thought (Vayda, 1961). Recent studies, especially in New Guinea, give a picture not of stability and equilibrium but of a constantly shifting scene where peoples are driven out and scattered and territories expand and contract. The impression Europeans got of a primitive world with groups and tribes that had been there "since time immemorial" was an illusion; the stability they found they often had created by their own intrusion.

Ritualized combat on the traditional "battlefield" gives a vivid picture of tribal warfare. But probably more often, aggression against the neighbors took the form of ambushes, of surprise attacks on undefended hamlets or people working in the gardens, and often killing of women and children.

One who set out to demonstrate through tribal warfare that aggression and cruelty run biologically deep in man could make a persuasive case: torture of captives and other bloody doings seem to bring out deep satisfactions in men. There is also an organizational side to this. In the tribal world of "we" versus 'they," the people over the next hill are likely to be enemies, and the people beyond that to be scarcely human. In such a world, "our" ancestors can easily develop an insatiable demand for "their" heads; or becoming a man may require homicidal raiding of the neighbors. Without governments to prevent or halt hostilities, tribal groups may live in constant danger.

In more complex societies with centralized political systems, the fragmented group-versus-group pattern of tribal warfare gave way to new forms. War as an instrument of the state, with conquest, trade, or tribute as its aims, was on a very different scale than tribal warfare. If there are deep biological roots to human aggression, their expression is probably more immediate and dramatic for the hunter or warrior than for the mercenary or merchant; the latter enjoyed his violence at the colosseum or the public execution or sacrifice.

And that provides a partial answer to those who surmise from the evidence of ethology and early man that killing and aggression are the nature of the beast. Given our new emphases on continuities with the animal past and our knowledge of men and protomen subsisting as hunters for hundreds of thousands of years, it would be surprising if man was by biological nature a docile animal. But with the development of culture, man created a world of symbolic goals and meanings and satisfactions, an imagined as well as a sensed world. "Aggression" (which, as we saw in Chapter III, is far too vague and inclusive a term anyway) can be displaced, channeled, aimed symbolically rather than physically. Culturally created organization can limit and direct its expression, channeling "human nature" into a wide range of social forms (Montagu, ed., 1968).

To despair that human life on global scale could be stable and peaceful —on grounds that "human nature" inevitably produces conflict and war—is too simple and pessimistic. To anticipate a golden age when reason and goodness will prevail and men will stop killing one another because it is madness is too simple and optimistic.

In a world where pushing a red button could kill millions and turn the planet into a burned-out wasteland, man cannot depend on suppressing his hostile feelings, hoping that all men will love all other men all of the time. They will not, and many of them at any moment will be wanting to kill one another. The solutions, if there are any, must lie in man's capacities to build new symbolic systems and to create new and more encompassing organizational forms. The progression from band and tribe to vast state partly has been a matter of expanding the scale of the "we." The "they" against whom men focus their hostility and aggression has shifted from the village across the mountain to the country across the sea. The *conceptual model* has not changed radically; it is the social systems that have been transformed. We have reached a critical point where higher levels of social and political organization that would unite peoples in common human enterprise cannot be achieved without a radical reorganization of our conceptual model. We have run out of human "theys" we can afford to hate and kill. Can man do without them? Science gives no answer; but men have no choice but to try.

XIV Social Control

A CULTURE CONSISTS of more or less shared rules for play-
ing the game of ordered social life. Yet these accepted standards of social
life are continually at odds with the drives and goals of individuals; and
because of this gap between collective standards and private interests, rules
are violated, or individuals play by their own rules. So the social scientist
sees two sides of the same problem. He must explain and understand *why
people follow rules* that thwart their private goals; and he must understand
how social order is maintained when the rules of the game are ignored or
broken.

Here, first, we will look more closely at those forces that promote
conformity to cultural codes. Then we will examine the mechanisms and
processes of "primitive law," the way men in non-Western cultural settings
control conflict and respond to breaches of social rules.

52 · The Forces of Social Conformity

Conformity and deviance are like a layer cake, and most social scientists
have concentrated on the icing and the top layers. Writings on "deviance
and conformity," especially in sociology, usually begin with a narrow conception of a "norm," as something people say should or should not be done.
You violate a norm if you steal, cheat, marry two women at once, go nude
in church, drive through a stoplight, or (if you are a man) wear lipstick—
whether or not you break a formal law. You conform when you follow
such norms; you deviate if you violate them.

Some norms are indeed public and are consciously followed or broken.
The anthropologist's knowledge about language codes reveals to him more
subtle "rules," akin to those of syntax or phonology. These "rules" are
implicit in our behavior, deeply ingrained in habit and unconscious mental
processes. Yet our following them lies at the heart of ordered social life.

The man who robs a bank is, in sociological terms, criminally deviant. But the anthropologist can perceive him as a routine-bound conformist as well. He comes to the bank appropriately clothed, walking rather than crawling, on the sidewalk rather than the roof or the gutter. He utters or writes his demands in hopelessly conventional English, and he makes his getaway on the right side of the street. One must conform unconsciously to a myriad of cultural rules and conventions to commit a "grammatical" bank robbery—which is, in fact, a complex act of communication. A Trobriand Islander would be hard-pressed to rob an American bank.

The rules we break, or would like to break, lie toward the surface of that complex and intricate system of shared knowledge we call "culture." To communicate, we are and must be rule followers. We will, for ease of explication, call those standards of behavior we talk and consciously think about as "public norms." Our unconscious rule-following on lower, hidden, levels does not explain why we follow public norms as often as we do, but it gives a different perspective on them. Another source of new perspectives on conformity and deviance is our growing understanding of man's biological heritage. Since the writings of Freud, a conflict between men's biological drives and the rules of ordered social life has usually been taken for granted. We are, biologically, animals—and to behave like men exacts a cost of frustration and repression.

Our views of man's biosocial life have changed dramatically with modern animal behavior studies. Freud was imagining the individual animal, driven by its aggressive nature and sexuality and free to express these natural drives. But we have seen animals in *groups*. That primates are "programmed" with drives for dominance, aggression, and sexuality does not imply their free expression: the young male baboon may be as thwarted as a Viennese psychiatric patient. Social organization—whether animal or human—requires that individual organisms pursuing their goals mesh together into ordered patterns of communication, acknowledged rights and powers, and collective action.

Moreover, the very notion of biological drives in man being "blocked" seems unrealistic at this stage. In looking at men's social organization and political and economic behavior in the preceding chapters, we have not been seeing a thwarting of the biological nature we glimpsed in Chapter III. Rather, we have seen *channeling* and, at times, *deflection* of these primate biological patterns. Culture reshapes and redefines and directs biological goal seeking. It defines for men in a particular time and place what *dominating* is, what a *territory* is, which females are desirable (and even what to do if you catch one). That is, a cultural code defines the goal-states toward which people should strive, building on but reshaping the templates laid down biologically. If we think of these goal-states in terms of a game, culture does not prevent people from playing a biologically satisfying game. It lays out the strategies for play and lays down the rules.

Anthropological questions about conformity and deviance mainly ask why, in these games of life, men cheat as seldom as they do. Or they ask why men play them at all. We will look quickly at some of the pressures that guide men into these cultural games and keep their play within accepted bounds.

First of all, childhood learning gives a person his conception of what kind of world this is and what he should be trying to do in and about it. It further underlines—by precept, example, folktale, game, myth, and so on—the moral virtues of his people and the costs of wrongdoing. Anthropologists have observed that ways of life differ in the degree to which they depend on the "internalization" of moral standards to guide behavior. Some peoples rely more heavily on *external* forces of social approval and disapproval. The contrast has been drawn, perhaps too sharply, in terms of "guilt sanctions" and "shame sanctions" (Mead, 1940; Hsu, 1953). Later a dramatic instruction in the moral order of one's people may come in an initiation ceremonial. We have seen that the initiates, before their symbolic rebirth, are frequently placed in seclusion. In such periods, intensive indoctrination in the moral virtues of one's people is common.

The pressures for conformity to the ways of one's group are familiar to all of us. The peer-group subcultures of American young people provide vivid examples. Even "nonconformity" is likely to be highly conformist and stereotyped: beards and bare feet can be a "uniform" just as much as Brooks Brothers suits and basic black with pearls.

Nor does the seeming conformity to custom in primitive societies necessarily imply great conservatism and lack of change (as earlier writers had often thought). American teen-age subcultures or dress fashions should immediately show us the flaws in the supposed equation, conformity = lack of change. As we will see in Chapter XVII, diversity of behavior occurs in the most small-scale societies, and change and innovation are constant.

Probably the most compelling pressures to conform come from enlightened self-interest. The games of social life call for coalitions, collective strategies, and mutual assistance. To play only for one's self most often does not get you to the goal fastest; usually it does not get you there at all. As in a game like chess or Monopoly, the best way to win is to use the rules, not break them.

The cynic who sees man as motivated only by self-interest and the idealist who sees man's destiny in selfless giving and sharing are seeing the grays of social life in black or white. Men have constructed the mazes of social life—because they have had to—so that the paths through them to individual goals are opened only by cooperation, by sharing, and by rule-following.

Sometimes the rewards of playing the game together and of helping one's fellows are immediate and direct. Sometimes they are long-range, as when a young person willingly serves titled leaders and elders in the expectation that later he will attain such status. Our society is rapidly losing a cycling kind of giving and return that is shaped by the life cycle and often axiomatic in the moral system of a tribal people: parents who care for their children when they are young and helpless will be cared for by them when they are old and helpless. Sometimes the rewards are diffuse, as with family cooperation or the satisfactions of friendship, security, or popularity.

We have seen (§30) the peculiar moral force of *kinship*. Fulfilling obligations to one's relatives would seem to run counter to self-interest. But if kinsmen do not always live up to ideal standards, they meet obligations well enough that kinship seems to have an extraordinary moral force. Why? On closer inspection, following kinship obligations turns out to advance, not conflict with, self-interest.

Example 50:   Kwaio Kinship and Self-Interest

Kwaio (Exs. 17 and 43) can get married, or advance their position in the game of prestige, only by amassing large quantities of shell valuables and ceremonially presenting them to other people. Yet as a Kwaio man tries to accumulate his capital for such a presentation, he constantly has to give away the valuables he is saving—to help finance a feast, marriage, or fine on behalf of a relative. Having spent months acquiring two or three large strings of shell, he may give them away to help someone else acquire prestige or get married. Why? Because of moral obligations of kinship? Closer examination brings two crucial facts to light. First, to get married or give a feast large enough to bring prestige, a man has to mobilize more valuables at a single time than he would be able to accumulate in a decade or a lifetime. Great numbers of his kinsmen must contribute to his mobilization of wealth (just as he has contributed to his relatives'). Some do so because they are obligated to reciprocate his help to them. Others are making him obligated to help them at some future time. Second, by helping kinsmen one is in fact investing. *A man who saved his capital rather than investing it would not only lose prestige by being stingy; he would be unable to amass enough valuables to acquire prestige through feasting. The trick, as in playing the stock market, is to come out ahead. Only a genius at financial manipulations can acquire great prestige as a feast-giving "big man" (Ex. 43).*

Though following or manipulating the rules is very often the best way to advance self-interests, men encounter over and over again situations where a shortcut across the boundaries of permissibility would get them to the goal faster. Rule-following does generate a measure of tension, frustration, and temptation.

One way to relieve these stresses is to suspend the rules at some special occasion or in some special context. A good orgy every now and then can be useful as well as enjoyable—and in many societies the neighbors approve. Sexual license in a limited situation, or overt hostility against the rules of the

Establishment, can be an effective way of "blowing off steam." Privileged sexual access outside of marriage, as betwen a man and his wife's sister, can relieve potential conflict and tension. *Joking relationships* involving joking and often sexual license between certain classes of relatives have been a classic focus of attention in social anthropology. So, too, have been the opposite side of the same coin, *avoidance relationships*, where strict rules of decorum or even of complete avoidance restrict interaction between a man and his mother-in-law, his sister-in-law, his sister, or some such relative or class of relatives.

Example 51: Familiarity and Avoidance in the Trobriands

Trobrianders illustrate both privileged familiarity and avoidance, though neither is in as extreme a form as found in some tribal areas. These customs will prove important in the next chapter. Though Trobriand brother and sister have common concerns in the sub-clan, and her sons are his heirs, the gulf of her sexuality separates them. From childhood onward, their relations are marked by distance and avoidance of any close contacts. As the sister begins her amorous adventuring, her brother must refrain from any knowledge of it. Even when she marries, matters surrounding her reproductive life are forbidden territory to him. The tabooed relationship between brother and sister is the most emotionally charged and morally fundamental rule in Trobriand culture.

But a man's father's sister has a very different relationship with him. "Her presence always carries with it the suggestion of license, of indecent jokes and improper stories" (Malinowski, 1929: 535). She is a kind of proto-typical sexual object for him—usually considerably older and hence seldom an actual sexual partner (though that is quite permissible), but treated with sexual familiarity and openness. A man cannot mingle with both paternal aunt and sister at the same time: the rules for each contrast too sharply.

Both joking and avoidance rules provide ways of controlling, chan-neling, and relieving pressures at the stress points of a social system, hence are subtle but important forces of social control.

The threat of actual punishment—by one's fellowmen or by "the gods"—has often been overemphasized by popular writers. In reaction, anthropologists have sometimes underestimated the importance of such negative sanctions. We will examine the *legal* consequences of rule-breaking and conflict in the next section. Other negative sanctions merit a quick inspection here.

Supernaturals often, though not always, keep a close watch on the moral conduct of the living. Moreover, customary rules and procedures are very often given a stamp of divine origin that validates them and gives them an aura of being ultimate, absolute, and sacred. To break the rules of social life is very often to break the laws that govern the universe.

A powerful force of social control in many societies is *witchcraft*. An extensive literature on witchcraft—in what societies it occurs and how often, what events trigger witchcraft accusations, and against whom they are directed—has been built up in recent years. Even in the outwardly peaceful and restrained social setting of pueblo Indians in Zuni or Hopi, violence may erupt with the driving of a witch into the desert. In many societies in Africa, North America, and elsewhere, the deviant who failed to meet the norms of kinship or play by the rules—or simply was more successful than everyone else—would be likely to be singled out as a witch and killed or exiled. Witchcraft accusations, which may in some societies assign responsibility for every death that occurs, give a splendid means to get rid of those who cheat, deviate, or succeed too much; and a splendid incentive to be an upstanding citizen. Moreover, fear that witchcraft will be directed against one makes conformity to the norms of social life strategically wise.

Example 52:   Kaguru Witchcraft and Social Control

The Kaguru of Tanzania believe that many of their fellows, male and female, possess uhai, *supernatural powers of witchcraft. Beliefs in witchcraft are conceptually quite separate from Kaguru religious beliefs, which center around propitiation of ancestors.*

Kaguru believe that most misfortunes, from death and illness to crop failure, loss of articles, and bad luck in hunting, result from witchcraft. Witches represent an inversion of the moral and symbolic values of the Kaguru, with their evil and antisocial intents and, in the most feared forms of witchcraft, their clan incest, cannibalism, and nakedness.

A Kaguru who suspects he is a victim of witchcraft will often suspect who the witch is; but he may go to a diviner to find or confirm the witch's identity. In the past, an accused suspect would be tried by the local community, usually with an ordeal. If found guilty, he or she would be clubbed to death. If innocent, the accuser would pay a large fine. Now public witchcraft accusations are illegal, but the suspected witch may learn of the charge in gossip or through some sign; or his garden may be damaged or his house burned. A man against whom such accusations are directed several times would probably move somewhere else.

Who is accused? Members of your own matrilineal clan are not supposed to be apt to direct witchcraft at you, but many accusations occur even within the closer bounds of a matrilineage. Although anyone might be a witch, the following are particularly suspect: (1) economically successful persons; (2) powerful chiefs and headmen; (3) nonconformists; (4) a wife her husband cannot easily control; (5) a woman envious of her co-wives; (6) people who refuse to meet important obligations to their kin (Beidelman, 1963: 74).

How does witchcraft serve as a force of social control? Beidelman (1963) notes that the powerful man may in fact encourage beliefs in his powers of witchcraft so as to increase his influence and control. A powerful man might be feared as a witch, but it would take corresponding power to accuse him. It is not clear how successfully, and by what means, witch-

craft accusations could be used in olden times to eliminate the strong man who went too far in wealth or power. Certainly political rivalries and disputed succession bring witchcraft accusations and suspicions to the fore. For the man of more limited means and powers, the threat of witchcraft accusation was a strong force for conformity and approved social behavior. "For most Kaguru, accusations or threats of witchcraft enforce conformity. This is done through fear of accusation against nonconformists and through fear of nonconformity being punished by the witchcraft of others" (Beidelman, 1963: 96–97).

Blood feuding may serve the same ends. Thus among the Kwaio of the Solomon Islands, a man would put up a bounty to avenge the killing of his close relative. Any member of the killer's descent group, or one of his close bilateral relatives, would be a suitable blood victim (and whoever killed one could claim the bounty). Often the killer's group would themselves provide a victim or even do the deed themselves to claim the bounty. The offered victim would be a girl thought wanton or quarrelsome or lazy, a boy or man who had sworn, or some other "undesirable." Bad boys and girls had considerably shorter life expectancy than good ones. (Modern Kwaio pagans, discouraged by the British administration from this mode of getting rid of undesirables, send them to become Christians.)

Conformity to the rules that govern social life is not a harsh burden of culture, a thwarting of men's drives. First of all, the goals of men are socially shaped and conventional. Second, to pursue them requires conformity to many implicit codes for communication—whether or not one plays according to the "rules." Third, the apparent conflicts between self-interest and socially acceptable behavior are misleading. Individuals striving for personal goals are players in a game that requires shared conventions, coalitions, and cooperation in a common enterprise. Staying within the boundaries—which are never that narrow—becomes a means of advancing one's position. In the long run, self-interest is social interest. With the wrath of supernaturals or the scorn or jealousy of one's fellow players, one seldom can win the games of social life. One often cannot play at all.

53 · *Law: A Comparative View*

Rules are broken, expectations are flouted, order is disrupted. However small-scale and closely integrated a society is, some people try to beat the system or operate outside the bounds of custom and the restraint of rules. Moreover, even though people may agree in principle about matters of custom, conflicts arise about who has what rights over particular people or pieces of property.

Societies respond in widely varying ways to breaches of social standards

or conflicts over rights. A killing or theft may set into motion a formal procedure of courts and punishments; or the offended party and his kin may
simply retaliate in kind if they can. Between these extremes lie a great
range of procedures and institutions that in some ways resemble Western
legal process and in other ways are quite different.

So the anthropologist is left in his usual conceptual dilemma. Should
he turn the concept of "law" into a very flexible but shapeless piece of
elastic and put it around anything that does in some society what law does
in ours? Or shall he extend the Western concept of law but retain its shape,
and then try it on primitive societies to see where it fits and where it does
not? Add to this conceptual dilemma the compulsive nit-picking to which the
legally minded are prone and you can understand the endless debates about
what is or is not "law" in non-Western societies.

Not being jurists or headhunters, we will avoid splitting hairs. What
matters is that we glimpse the range of ways in which societies manage
breaches of the rules; and by seeing "law" in comparative perspective, escape
ethnocentric views of other peoples and attain a clearer view of ourselves.

It will be useful to look first at a modern analysis of a "legal" system
more like ours than many in the primitive world (so that we can use the
word "law" without violating our intuitions), yet reflecting a way of life
quite different from ours.

Example 53:   Zuni Indian Law

*Zuni law, according to Smith and Roberts (1954), falls into a middle
range between societies without formal legal institutions or explicit legal
code, and those with well-elaborated legal systems. The legal system as
it works today among this group of some 2500 people, living in one large
pueblo, combines traditional elements and borrowings from American law.
The materials analyzed include 97 legal cases occurring between about
1870 to 1952, identified through court records and oral memories. The cases
were handled in traditional fashion by authorized members of the Zuni
priesthood and by the modernized Tribal Council. Cases fell into the following principal categories: witchcraft (18 cases cited in all); offenses against
the person, including murder (2 cases, both before 1900 and then handled
by the Tribal Council), rape (4 cases), fighting (5 cases), slander (6 cases);
offenses against the community, including drunkenness and drunken driving
(12 cases), breach of peace (1 case); offenses against property, including
theft (16 cases), but otherwise minor in terms of the elaborateness of
property law; property settlements after death or divorce (22 cases); domestic
relations (almost no cases except for divorce settlements).*

*Zuni legal procedure, though largely implicit, is "surprisingly well
developed." Regularities show in pretrial investigation, the conduct of trials,
the summoning of parties, testimony of witnesses, rules of evidence, the
use of precedents, and posttrial procedures. A distinctive Zuni practice is
to require a "fourfold affirmation"; that is, key questions may be repeated*

Figure 42. Status, Ritual, and Social Control in Zuni. Membership in numerous fraternities and other status groupings, and participation in an elaborate ritual life, are important forces in securing conformity to the established way of life. Shown here is a dance of the arrow order of the Great Fire Fraternity. (After Stevenson.) FMK

four times, with the rationale that the parties should be permitted to think and decide before being committed to an answer. "There is nothing at Zuni corresponding to the relationship of lawyer and client." A party usually pleads his own case, but others may speak in his behalf. The penalties for civil offenses, as in the Western legal practice, consist mainly of damages which compensate for injury, with the occasional addition of punitive damages in aggravated cases. Criminal cases have been similarly met with damages. The amounts are fixed by the "judge," and compensations or fines may take such forms as jewelry, clothing, livestock, or, nowadays, money. Imprisonment is a modern institution, and corporal punishment has been resorted to for witchcraft and revealing religious secrets.

In a final review of Zuni values as expressed in law, the authors note that the prestige or reputation of judges, plaintiffs, and defendants is deeply at stake in any trial. Generally speaking, it is "not desirable for any Zuni to be involved in public controversy or to be found guilty of an offense." Other deeply involved factors are kinship, sex in the context of reproduction, health, environment (as related to water, animals, and the like), and "beauty" (sensory and dramatic patterns). In each of these value categories, a distinction is drawn between "religious-legal" cases comparable with modern "canon law" and tried by religious authorities (for example, witchcraft, theft of ceremonial property) and "secular-legal" cases tried by secular authorities (fighting, rape, and others). Because Zuni culture is focused on religion, which is the area of greatest behavioral elaboration and interest, the "religious-legal" body of law tends to be the more elaborated field of social control. "Not only are the Zunis personally interested in their legal system," the authors conclude, "but they consider it of great importance to the community."

The range of variation from this relatively formal legal system, different as it is from ours, helps to reveal what is basic and what is secondary and specialized in legal systems. First of all, if we start out to find *the* legal system in a society, our quest may be misguided from the outset. There may be several "legal systems" in the same society. Different people may make decisions in different kinds of groups, or cases, or settings, with reference to different sets of standards. The different legal "subsystems" in a society may involve different spheres of life (as with religious and secular law in Zuni). They may involve different kinds of violations. Thus our distinction between civil and criminal offenses may be mirrored in a non-Western society, with what Radcliffe-Brown (1933) labeled more generally as a contrast between "private delicts" and "public delicts." Or they may involve different groups. Thus cases involving members of a lineage may activate one set of legal mechanisms, cases involving members of a larger community another, and cases involving members of different communities a third.

But how do we know a legal system, or a legal process, when we find one? Is it because there is a clear and codified (if not written) set of "laws"? No, says Pospisil (1968), a leading specialist. He argues that such abstract rules are rare and specialized in human societies (mainly limited to Western societies since the codification of Roman Law). Legal principles are more often implicit, flexible, and constantly changing. Increasingly, the legal processes and legal principles of a society have come to light by looking at *cases*, at specific instances where conflicts of rights or breaches of rules are socially resolved. The legal principles of a society emerge from the study of *decisions* in these cases.

Who makes these decisions? In what settings and by what processes? And if there is no formal code of laws, what guidelines or principles or precedents are used to make them? How are they enforced? Each of these questions, if followed out, would show a wide range of variation. Here we can afford only a quick glimpse at each.

Who makes legal decisions? Where the social organization is simple, as in band societies, they are likely to be made by the leader of the band. What legal powers he exercises may be contingent on his success in leading the hunt, dealing with supernaturals, or maintaining internal or external peace. So, too, the "big man" of Melanesia has power to make legal decisions only to the extent people defer to his skill and wisdom and his success and power as an entrepreneur.

In a tribal society, even where the leader of a descent group or community has formal rights based on his *position*, not simply his personal power, these are likely to be binding only to members of his own group. In a segmentary lineage system (as with the Elm Street Smiths of §32), who has the right to make decisions may depend on who the contending sides are and what the case is about. Offenses involving members of different corporations may lead to blood feuding or warfare; or they may be settled accord-ing to "legal" principles to avoid or end armed confrontation.

This usefully shows that—except in more complex societies where formal courts and legal specialists have developed—legal action is intertwined with politics. The power to make binding decisions in cases of conflict is, in less complex societies, political power. But for us to try to draw, or erase, a line between legal and political would be a waste of time. It is better to think of the political and legal as two ways of looking at events, sometimes the same events: each point of view illuminates a different facet.

In what settings do legal processes take place? In a society without formal legal institutions, the setting for litigation may be a feast, a spontaneous or arranged gathering, or some more organized council of those who make and influence decisions in a community. In some parts of the primitive world, particularly Africa, formal legal systems involving courts, trials, judges, appeals, and so on, are highly elaborated. Those who make legal decisions in them may be legal specialists; or they may be those who exercise political or religious leadership in other settings.

Example 54: The Tswana Court System

Schapera (1955) describes the court system of the Tswana, a series of tribes in south-central Africa. Before the intrusion of Western govern-mental authority, every local division of a tribe from the "ward" (a patri-lineal kinship group forming a settlement or group of settlements) upward had its own court, with the headman as judge, and these are still operating with limited powers. The "lower" courts of the ward and village had full jurisdiction in "civil" matters, that is, private rights of people regarding status, property, and contracts. But if the judge found any case too difficult he would refer it to a "higher" court. A "criminal" case (for example, in-volving bloodshed or sorcery), even if reviewed at lower levels, had to go to the tribal chief's court. Courts met when cases popped up. All those concerned gathered early in the morning at the judge's council place. The judge and his advisers sat facing the parties directly involved; behind the latter were the interested spectators. After the judge had briefly introduced the case, he called for statements by the plaintiff and then by the defendant. Anyone present could serve as a witness or ask questions. The judge's ad-visers then debated, one by one, the merits of the case, after which the judge made a final summary of the evidence and delivered the verdict.

Even in a society with elaborated courts, informal litigation may often be used to settle cases out of court. This underlines the need to look for more subtle and undramatic legal processes side by side with formal ones.

The actual procedures used in non-Western law vary so widely that we can glimpse only two of many forms far removed from the formal legal procedures of a court.

Example 55:   Eskimo Song Duels

Among Eskimo groups, with no formal mechanisms of government or courts, disputes are resolved within a "court" of public opinion, the small-scale Eskimo community. With no formal or codified set of rules, the Eskimo are free to treat each dispute over wife stealing, homicide, or the like as a unique constellation of people and circumstances (Hoebel, 1954).

For disputes less serious than homicide, most Eskimo groups have an unusual and effective way of blowing off the steam of hostility while resolving the legal issue: the song duel. Here each party to the dispute composes songs that ridicule his adversary and set out in exaggerated fashion his grievance or his version of the disputed events. Ribald satire, taunts, innuendo, distortion, and buffoonery bring mirth from the onlookers as the songs go back and forth. By the time the "case" has been made by each party, the litigants have blown off steam and public opinion has swung toward a decision that will redress valid grievances or dismiss weak ones. A perhaps more important function than legal decision making is that by their song duel the disputing pair have had their say in public and can resume their normal relationship—stung only temporarily by the "little, sharp words, like . . . wooden splinters" (Rasmussen, 1922: 236).

Example 56:   Ordeals among the Ifugao

Barton (1919), in his notable study of law among the non-Christian Ifugao people of the northern Philippine mountains, gives a careful account of use of the ordeal. Ordeals are resorted to in criminal cases in which the accused persistently denies his guilt, and sometimes when disputes cannot be otherwise resolved. The challenge to an ordeal may come from either the accuser or the accused, and refusal to accept a challenge means a loss of the case. The ordeal itself may consist of getting a pebble without haste from boiling water, taking hold of a hot knife, a duel with eggs, grass stalks, or spears, or a wrestling bout. If the accused comes unscathed from the ordeal he has the right to collect from his accuser a fine for false accusation. An ordeal is conducted in a juridical as well as a ceremonial atmosphere, and the gods are invoked to assure that justice will prevail.

What standards are used to make legal decisions, if there is no formal legal code? The conception of culture adopted here enables us to see this clearly. For men to operate in the world—for them to garden or build houses or conduct religious rituals—they need an implicit set of "rules" for acting, doing, and deciding. These need not be completely shared or consistent or neat; they are constantly being changed and adapted. Learning them and using them is easy for human beings. Verbalizing them, or writing them down in ways that correspond to implicit codes, is difficult and—generations of jurists and ethnographers notwithstanding—perhaps impossible. One of the central elements in the mystery that is man is how conceptual codes are linked to the ever shifting and complicated situations, the unique crystallizations of circumstance, we encounter in the world. Writing down a legal code takes one side of this miraculous and flexible linkage and hardens it into rigid laws. We then need enormous human wisdom and skill to reintroduce this flexibility into a system of courts—to follow the "spirit" of the law rather than the "letter," to recognize and cope with the uniqueness of each case. That, in a sense, is what the art of jurisprudence is all about. Tribal "jurists," unburdened by the letter of the law and able to treat each pattern of circumstances afresh, are doing what humans do very well. Those who argue cases, or decide them, can cite general principles and precedents to support their contentions: it is the essence of law, primitive or modern, that it be "legitimate." But the implicit codes whereby ideal principles and rules of thumb are translated into actual decisions and plans may remain largely hidden to those who use them.

How are legal decisions enforced? If they are without any effective sanctions and can be violated with impunity, we would hardly want to call them "legal." The "teeth" in the law may include physical punishment, forfeiture or destruction of property, banishment, and so on. The pressures to settle matters according to legal procedures and to accept legal decisions may be more subtle than the threat of direct punishment. The alternatives to legal settlement may be warfare or bloody vengeance outside legal channels.

We tend to think of law in terms of social control—and indeed a useful way to make a first exploration of legal processes in a non-Western society is to see what rules a people consider binding and what happens when they are broken. Yet the mechanisms and processes that are set into action when such rules are broken may not serve only as means of social control. Taking a person to court or claiming compensation for a grievance may be a matter of economic strategy, political rivalry, descent group segmentation, or religious principle. The affairs of life in the tribal world—or even of ours—refuse to stay in the tidy pigeonholes of the social scientist. Legal action is social action, in all its manifold complexity. Frake's vivid picture of litigation among a Subanun (Ex. 18) group in the Philippines will help to leave us with a view of law as a facet of social life, not a separate compartment:

> Litigation in Lipay . . . cannot be fully understood if we regard it only as a means of maintaining social control. A large share, if not the majority, of legal cases deal with offenses so minor that only the fertile imagination of a Subanun legal authority can magnify them into a serious threat to some person or to society in general. . . . A festivity without litigation is almost as unthinkable as one without drink.
>
> In some respects a Lipay trial is more comparable to an American poker game than to our legal proceedings. It is a contest of skill, in this case of verbal skill, accompanied by social merry-making, in which the loser pays a forfeit. He pays for much the same reason we pay a poker debt: so he can play the game again. . . .
>
> Litigation nevertheless has far greater significance in Lipay than this

poker-game analogy implies. For it is more than recreation. Litigation, together with the rights and duties it generates, so pervades Lipay life that one could not consistently refuse to pay fines and remain a functioning member of society. Along with drinking, feasting, and ceremonializing, litigation provides patterned means of interaction linking the independent nuclear families of Lipay into a social unit, even though there are no formal group ties of comparable extent. The importance of litigation as a social activity makes understandable its prevalence among the peaceful and, by our standards, "law-abiding" residents of Lipay. (Frake, 1963: 221).

XV *World View:*
Knowledge and Belief

MAN NOT ONLY weaves intricate webs of custom that regulate and order his social life, he also spins out wider designs of the universe, the forces that govern it, and his place in it. Religious beliefs and rituals are basic in these designs. So, too, are fundamental premises about the way things and events are interrelated, the nature of time and space, the way the world is and should be.

The religion and world view of a people are less immediately apparent, less readily studied, than their agriculture or their kinship system. Anthropologists have tended to look at them obliquely, as reflections or projections of social life, rather than as intellectual systems in their own right. But in recent years, major new insights have emerged as the thought-worlds of non-Western peoples have been more systematically explored and mapped. In this chapter, we will examine "primitive religion" and world view, emphasizing the new perspectives and models and necessarily sampling only briefly the rich variety of tribal religions.

54 · Religion in Comparative Perspective

What is religion? What is the difference between religion and magic? What is myth? Ritual? Such questions catch the anthropologist in his usual dilemma—trying on the one hand to render faithfully the shape and distinctiveness of a particular culture, and on the other hand to compare similar institutions in a range of societies. As particularist, he can show that any set of comparative classifications distorts the culture he studies; as generalist, he keeps trying to devise better ones.

Numerous scholars have sought to find a common denominator for all forms of religion. Recently, many have moved back toward Tylor's classic definition of religion as a "belief in spiritual beings." Thus, Goody (1961), Horton (1960), and Spiro (1966) have seen the extension of "social" relations to superhuman beings or forces as the feature common to all religions. Others, following Durkheim, have sought to find some special mood of "sacredness" that demarcates the religious from the secular.

The religions of men vary enormously in the powers and agencies they posit in the universe and the ways men relate to them. There may be a range of deities, a single deity, or none—simply spirits or even impersonal and diffuse powers. These agencies may intervene constantly in the affairs of men, or be uninvolved and distant; they may be punitive or benevolent. In dealing with them, men may feel awe and reverence, or fear; but they may also bargain with supernaturals or seek to outwit them. Religions may govern the moral conduct of men or be unconcerned with morality.

In describing the varieties of religious customs, older theorists tried to label and pigeonhole the various "types" of religions. Thus, a religion was "animistic," "theistic," based on "ancestor worship," or the like. Modern detailed studies of tribal religions have revealed their internal complexity, so that any one will turn out to contain elements of several "types."

It is perhaps futile to try to define "religion" precisely or to seek a common denominator amidst this variability. Malinowski and others have usefully asked not what religions *are*, but what they *do* in human life.

Religion has, first of all, *explanatory* functions. For all societies it answers overall "Why?" questions. The need to ask and seek to answer these "Why?" questions seems to lie in the higher brain development of man.

Second, it has *validating* functions. It supports with powerful sanctions the basic institutions, values, and goals of a society. As such, religion does not stand at one side of culture as a specialized compartment. It tends to interpenetrate all important and valued behavior. The strong ties between religion and economics, for example, range from the old emperors of China ceremonially tilling the symbolic field at the Temple of Heaven in Peking to ensure supernatural support for good crops to the Iowa farmer's "Give us . . . our daily bread." On the political side, statecraft and religion are functionally interrelated in numerous ways, as in prayers for the leader and for the state.

Third, it has psychologically *reinforcing* functions. Religion comes into especially sharp focus at points that are crucial in group and individual experience, especially where these involve anxiety, uncertainty, danger, lack of knowledgeable control, a sense of the "supernatural." Every people has to grapple with suffering, with "luck," with problems of good and evil. Their most universal and poignant focus comes in the crisis of death, which in all cultures is surrounded and cushioned with beliefs, rites, and procedures relating to sickness, the passing of "life," the handling of the body, the fate of the lost member, and the closing of ranks behind him. Religious rites and beliefs are often elaborated around other focal points of individual and group experience—pregnancy, birth, puberty, initiation to adulthood, marriage, succession to political leadership, or warfare. For an agricultural people the growing cycle of cultivated plants is likely to have high points that call for religious rites: planting, transplanting, ripening, harvest. The weather, safety of craft, and size of catch rally religious effort for fishermen. So, too, for herders there are the birth season, pasture conditions, and other points of crisis. Some high points of anxiety may be cyclical, and hence met with systematic preparations. Others may be irregular, as with death or the stampeding of a herd. Kluckhohn (1942) emphasizes this facet of religion. Its basic function, he states, is to provide a sense of security in a world which, "seen in naturalistic terms, appears to be full of the unpredictable, the capricious, the accidentally tragic." By giving "consistency and reality" to experience, the religious system carries man over areas of life "beyond control of ordinary techniques and the rational understanding which works well in ordinary affairs." Benedict (1938) correspondingly speaks of it as "the social life at those points at which it is felt most intensely."

Fourth, religion has *integrative* functions. It weaves together many segments of the customs and beliefs of a people into an overall design. It establishes and validates basic premises about the world and man's place in it; and it relates the strivings and emotions of men to them.

Clifford Geertz, in one of the most important essays on religion in decades, formulates a definition of religions in terms of what they do, and amplifies his definition brilliantly. "A religion is a system of symbols which acts to establish powerful, pervasive, and long-lasting moods and motivations in men by formulating conceptions of a general order of existence and clothing these conceptions with such an aura of factuality that the moods and motivations seem uniquely realistic" (1966: 4). Religion, in other words, bridges between the way the world is and the outlook men have on it, so that both the nature of the world and the emotions and motives of men are confirmed and reinforced. It is this double-sidedness, this creation through religions of both "models of" and "models for," that makes them so central in human experience.

55 · *Magic, Science, and Religion*

What is the difference betwen religion and magic? What is the relationship between magic and science?

Bronislaw Malinowski, in a classic essay (1925) sought to sort out the three. In this triangle, the difference between religion and science seemed clear enough from their separation in our own culture. But magic, he felt, had been much misunderstood—and hence its relationship to primitive "science" had been distorted. He turned, as usual—and as we have often turned in the preceding chapters—to his own experiences in the Trobriand Islands.

Example 57: Trobriand Magic

Trobrianders use their Neolithic technology with great skill, in wresting an abundant living from their island environment. Yet the efforts of men— in gardening, in the kula, *in fighting, in love—are not enough to produce success. Crops fail, exchanges are blocked, canoes are lost, villages are defeated, and lovers are spurned. In all of the enterprises central in Trobriand life, Trobrianders add to their best human efforts the powers of magic. Magic, when combined with human skill and diligence, will yield success—unless sorcery, stronger magic, error or other forces intervene. By knowing the magical spell, a man controls a form of power conferred on his people by ancestors who emerged from beneath the earth. At every step of communal gardening the magician for the group must perform magical rites without which the garden would not thrive, in the face of unpredictable weather, insects, and other threats. At every step in making and launching an overseas canoe, the magic that will ensure its safety and success is added to human skill.*

Does this mean that, for the Trobrianders, there is a muddled and naive way of dealing with the world? Is there a great gulf between pre-logical thinking of the native and the sophistication of the scientist? No, says Malinowski. The Trobriander possesses a rich store of empirical and rational knowledge about his environment and how he can use it. Without being a superb "scientist," within these technological limits, he could not have carved out this niche and exploited it as well as he has.

Why, then, does he use magic? Where and how is a boundary drawn between magic and primitive "science"? Malinowski tells us that the Trobrianders keep magic conceptually apart from empirical knowledge and action. Magic adds ancestrally-derived power to human effort at those places where that effort alone often is not enough. The crops do fail, disaster strikes men at sea, love is thwarted. Magic defends against anxiety where the gap between human effort and its fruition is wide. There is magic for dangerous fishing in open sea, but none for safe and sure lagoon fishing; there is magic for the kula *but not for everyday exchange and barter. "Thus magic . . . serves to bridge over the dangerous gaps in every important pursuit or critical situation. . . . The function of magic is to ritualize man's optimism, to enhance his faith in the victory of hope over fear" (Malinowski, 1925).*

More recent studies of tribal belief systems suggest a subtle ethnocentrism in generalizing from the way Trobrianders seem to put magic in a separate conceptual category, contrasting with their "science." For "magic" is more often our category than primitive man's. "Magical thinking" reflects a model of the universe that is far more deterministic than ours, a universe where things do not "just happen" by chance or accident. If a snake bites a man, it is the venom that directly causes his death. But what caused the snake and that particular man to intersect at a particular moment on a particular path? If a man sickens and dies, why was it he and not another? Most of us do not ask these questions. Most tribal peoples demand answers to them.

In such a universe, death, illness, and crop failure call for explanation. And such a far-reaching determinism invites men to try to manipulate the course of events in socially approved or socially disapproved ways. A sorcerer who uses fingernail parings of his intended victim, or a magician

Figure 43. An Australian Aborigine "Points the Bone." In this most feared form of aboriginal black magic, the sorcerer points a bone toward his intended victim and sings the prescribed words. Here, the sorcerer must point away from the sun, or his magical "missile" would turn on him. In the logic of magic, the bone is a kind of spear that can invisibly travel long distances with unerring accuracy. (After a photograph by A. P. Elkin.) RMK

who draws animals to ensure the abundance of game, is building on a logic quite different from ours—a logic where influences are spread by "contagion" and where like produces like. Such an all-embracing determinism and "magical" pattern of thinking dominate the tribal world.

Malinowski's sharp line between "magic" and "primitive science" can be hard and arbitrary to draw in such a deterministic universe. Consider a Melanesian curer putting a bundle of leaves on a patient's infected leg, after reciting a spell over them. Unlike his American physician counterpart, the Melanesian curer is trying to deal with why some illnesses and wounds get better when you treat them and some do not—hence he knows that both the spell and the leaves are necessary, and each depends on the other. Is it "magic" or "science"? If we sent the leaves to a pharmacological laboratory *we* might be able to decide, but the question would be meaningless to the curer. (If we tried to sort things out this way we might find last year's magic turning out to be next year's antibiotic).

"Magic," then, represents man's attempts to manipulate chains of cause-and-effect between events that to *us* are unrelated, in ways that to *us* are irrational. Magic—like prayer—"works" in the eye of the believer because the system of belief contains an explanation for both success and failure: the magician's beliefs are confirmed whether the garden grows well or dies. Paradoxically, the advance of Western science comes not from explaining more things, but from explaining fewer things, more systematically.

The gulf in our culture between scientific and religious modes of looking at the world has been greatly emphasized; and a similar gulf has often been sought or inferred in primitive cultures. Very often, a primitive people sets apart a segment of experience and custom as "sacred," and in this religious sphere a special mode of thought, action, and emotion prevails. The mundane, secular, and practical are thus separated from the sacred and religious—and one can distinguish between "folk science" and religion.

But there are sharp similarities between Western science and religious systems, as well—as anthropologists are beginning to realize as they drift back toward Tylor's early emphasis on the intellectual and explanatory functions of religion.

Example 58:   The World View of the Kalabari

The Kalabari, a fishing people who live in the swampy delta of the Niger River in Nigeria, have a highly complicated system of cosmological beliefs—a system which would seem to exemplify the "mystical" or "magical" mode of thinking many writers have attributed to primitive man. The contrast with a modern scientific view of the universe would seem profound.

Three orders of existence are postulated by the Kalabari as lying behind "the place of people"—the observable world of human beings and things. The first level is the world of "spirits." It is with the beings of this level that the living are most concerned, and with which their relations are mediated by ritual. The spirit world is populated by beings of various sorts. All of them are normally invisible and are manifest—like the wind—in different places.

First of all, every object or living thing has a spirit that steers or animates its behavior; when a person dies, or a pot breaks, spirit and physical form have become separated. But more important to the daily lives of men are three categories of "free" spirits. First, there are ancestral spirits, dead members of the Kalabari lineages which watch over every member, rewarding them when kinship norms are observed and punishing them when they are violated. Second, there are "village heroes." These formerly lived with men, but came from other places bringing new customs. Whereas ancestors are concerned with lineages, village heroes are concerned with the whole village—composed of several lineages—and its unity and community enterprises. The effectiveness of the village head depends on the support of village heroes.

A final category of spirits is the "water people," who are manifest as men and also as pythons, or rainbows. They are identified not with human groups, but with the creeks and swamps that are central to Kalabari subsistence. Water people control weather and fishing, and are responsible for deviant human behavior, whether positive (innovation or acquisition of unusual wealth) or negative (violation of norms or mental abnormality).

This triangle of spirit forces, interacting with one another as well as with men, shape and guide human life. Ritual cycles alternately reinforce relations with ancestors, village heroes, and water people.

But beyond the spirit world, and more abstract and remote from human life, are other orders of existence. A personal creator, shaping each individual's destiny from before birth, lays the design of his life. A pattern of power or of failure is preordained for any individual, and the events of his life are simply its unfolding. Even the time and manner of his death are laid down before birth. Even the destiny of a lineage, or a village, is viewed as laid down though it has no creator as such.

Finally, on a still more remote and abstract level, Kalabari conceive the entire world and all of its beings as created by a "Great Creator," and all the events of the world as the immutable unfolding of an ultimate pattern of destiny. Although offerings are made to one's personal creator, the spirit is one of resignation rather than manipulation: "The creator never loses a case," say Kalabari. The Great Creator is in most respects remote from human life.

Does this elaborate and, in scientific terms, fanciful scheme reflect a mystical mode of thought remote from modern science? In one sense, like all religious systems, it does, says the anthropological interpreter, Robin Horton (1962). That is, rather than keeping systematic control of the relationship between "the theory" and the evidence of observation, Kalabari allow a complex pattern of secondary and contingent explanation. When sacrifice attains the desired result this reinforces belief; when it does not, some other explanation—a competing spirit, a ritual mistake, or the like—is invoked. The belief is not called into question. The same, of course, is true of Christian prayer.

But is the contrast between Kalabari religious explanation and Western science really that profound? Horton argues that this reflects illusions about science, overemphasizing its objectivity and precision and misconstruing the relationship between data and theoretical model.

The world of the spirits is, in one sense, modeled on the everyday world of Kalabari life; but to make the events of that life intelligible, the spirit world represents a transformation that sorts out the component forces and spheres of human life. Thus, for example, village heroes appropriately represent the ties of community that transcend the separate loyalties of kinship and lineage. They came from outside places, not Kalabari lineages; they contributed innovations that distinguish the customs of each particular village; they simply disappeared, they did not die; and they left no descendants. They were creatures of community, without any of the ties of human kinship. Similarly, Horton argues, a model in science very often represents a transformation of the phenomena in the world of observables that gave rise to it. Thus the physicist's models of atomic structure are "hybridized" transformations of the revolutions of planets that served as a prototype for them.

Moreover, there is for the scientist no single level of reality, and no single model to represent it. Rather, the same pattern can be described in terms of subatomic particles or macromolecules. The nature of the explanatory or predictive task determines the appropriate model. Thus the models of time and space that suffice for a highway engineering project must be modified in sending a rocket to the moon, and must be modified again to deal with theoretical problems of astrophysics. A chemical manufacturer making caustic soda out of salt can use a simple chemical model, while a much more complex second-order model is required for dealing with a related theoretical problem in physics.

Similarly, the orders of existence postulated by the Kalabari are invoked in different contents to explain different orders of phenomena, to answer different orders of question. A temporary success or failure is intelligible in terms of the vicissitudes of relations with spirits; a series of catastrophes or failures is seen as the unfolding of destiny.

Furthermore, seeming contradictions between levels of explanatory models are as basic to the conceptualizations of science as the cosmology of the Kalabari—yet the levels complement and augment one another. Just as the successively higher levels of Kalabari existence are more and more abstract, less and less related to immediate experience and mundane existence, so too are the increasingly abstract models of physics. By eliminating features relevant at lower levels, each more abstract level unifies a greater range of phenomena with less and less specification of content. ". . . As tools of understanding, successive levels of Kalabari reality are committed to explaining more and more in terms of less and less" (Horton, 1962). And this is as true of the models of modern atomic physics, with its hypothetical particles and statistical models, as of the Kalabari conception of Great Creator and cosmic destiny.

The profound sophistication and complexity of tribal religions as intellectual systems have also emerged clearly in studies of myth, ritual, and cosmology among those classic "primitives" the Australian Aborigines (especially in the work of W.E.H. Stanner), and a number of African peoples, notably the Nuer (Evans-Pritchard, 1956), the Dogon (Griaule and Dieterlen, 1960), and the Ndembu (V. Turner, 1967, 1968b). We will see shortly how the French anthropologist Claude Lévi-Strauss has gone further still, in viewing primitive man as intellectual manipulator of his world of experience, whose sortings and arrangements pervade all corners of his life—from classification of plants to arrangement of villages and decoration of faces.

56 · Religion and the Social Order

Anthropologists have long perceived that a people's religious beliefs and their social organization are closely interrelated. It is clear that the supernatural order is to some extent modeled on men's social relationships. Conversely, religious beliefs validate and regulate their social relations. By legitimizing and rendering sacred the nature of authority and tradition, religion supports the social order and acts as a force for conservatism. In Chapter XVII, we will see how religious movements can also be a driving force of change.

One way to interpret the close relationship between religious and social is to view religion as a sort of distortion and projection of the world of man. Thus, one can find relationships between the kind of supernaturals posited by a people and the scale of their political organization. People with fragmented clans often have a cult of ancestral spirits for each clan; and people with a centralized state are more likely to have a high god or centralized pantheon. Sacrifice, which has fascinated Western scholars (partly because of Biblical and other early Semitic sacrifice) takes on a new light if we look at it this way. If we view relations with supernaturals as modeled on relations between the living, we see "sacrifice" as a spurious category that lumps together a wide range of quite different transactions between subordinate humans and superordinate supernaturals. The transactions among the living on which various forms of "sacrifice" are modeled range from tribute to bribery, manipulation to receive special advantage, obeisance, or expiation. Because the supernatural world is immaterial, what is given is converted to ethereal "substance" (while the sacrificers usually eat the material remains). What the supernaturals give in return is similarly intangible.

Similarly, ancestral spirits who punish the living for their violations of taboos or ritual procedures can be seen as a projection of the authority system of the living—the lineage elders elevated to a supernatural plane. Studies have correlated the nature of authority and the way it is transferred across generations with the nature of religious belief and ritual.

The classic study in this genre is Durkheim's analysis (1912) of Australian Aborigine religion. In worshiping the "totem" animals that symbolized each group, the Aborigines were in fact worshiping the units of society itself. Particularly in the seasonal *intichiuma* rite, the temporary social and emotional bonds that pulled together diverse groups were projected upon the cosmos: religion was society writ large.

Another classic is Hertz's study (1907) of double funerals in Borneo. At a first funeral, the dead man was buried and surviving relatives went into a ritual seclusion from social contact. Then the purified skull was exhumed, and a second funeral was staged which sent the spirit to the afterlife and freed the mourners to rejoin normal social life. Hertz interprets this as a treatment of death as a rite of passage to a new status (as with initiation ceremonies). The afterlife is invented so as to avoid treating death as final, and the second funeral reincorporates the living into their world and sends the spirit into his new one.

Intensive study of African societies has shown how beliefs in sorcery and witchcraft are related to social organization. The kinds of stresses and strains generated within lineage and family system are expressed in witchcraft. Sociological variables enable the anthropologist to account for the direction in which witchcraft accusations are pointed: whether to close or distinct kin, whether in one's own corporate group or a different one, whether at men or women, and so on.

Such interpretations have been highly revealing, but they also introduce a characteristic distortion. Man's social world is his only vantage point on life. It is inevitable and obvious that his models of the cosmos be drawn from that world. But one cannot legitimately argue from the resulting parallels and resemblances that religion is "nothing more" than a projection of social life. Why project at all? And as Geertz (1966a) cogently suggests, one could profitably focus on the way the world of the living is *transformed* in creating a model of the cosmos. Increasingly, we are perceiving that religions must be viewed as ideational systems, and their overall structure mapped. A focus on the parallels between religious and social has predisposed us to look at those segments of religious experience where the closest parallels occur, at the expense of the rest.

57 · Myth and Ritual

The sacred and formalized enactment of religious rituals, and the complex webs of myth regarding the origins and nature of man, his customs, and the world, have long fascinated anthropologists. But here they have been in a logjam in seeking to get closer to an understanding; and here again the logjam is beginning to break up as we look at religions as ideational systems with their own intricate structures of meaning, not as reflections of something more tangible and real.

In the realm of myth, new vistas are opening as we look at myths as designs having structure and meaning in their own right, rather than as reflections and projections of the social order. Malinowski (1926) and others since had insisted that the myths of a people be analyzed in their social context. To treat the myths of a tribe without looking at their social context—as, say, a psychoanalyst might—would be to distort their meanings and functions.

Example 59: Trobriand Origin Myths

In any Trobriand village, an essential element of life is the recounting of what we would call "myths." Members of a Trobriand sub-clan know, mark, and recount the history of the "hole" from which its ancestress and her brother emerged from the underworld. In that underworld, in the days before life on the earth, men lived as they do now. The ancestral brother and sister brought up with them the sacred objects and knowledge, the skills and crafts, and the magic that distinguish this group from others. Is this an attempt at primitive "explanation"? Is it an expression of the deep surgings of the unconscious—of incestuous desire or whatever? Or is it some disguised encapsulation of actual history? No, says Malinowski. It can only be understood in the rich context of Trobriand life and cultural meaning. Brother and sister emerged because they represent the two essential elements of the sub-clan; a husband did not emerge because he is, in terms of the sub-clan, an irrelevant outsider. The ancestral pair lived in separate houses because the relationship of brother to sister is marked by sharp taboos. But why recite the myth at all? Because it validates the rights of the sub-clan to the territory and encapsulates the magic and skills that make them sociologically and ritually unique. The myth of local emergence is the property of the local sub-clan; it does not float in limbo to be examined by a psychoanalyst, and it can be understood only in terms of how, when, and with whom it is used.

Other origin myths known by all Trobrianders relate the emergence of the four clans, legitimizing their food taboos but more particularly matters of rank and precedence. Finally, other local myths deal with the relative rank and position and dispersion of high-ranking sub-clans beyond their point of original emergence. Such myths, Malinowski says, validate the political structure and provide a mythological charter to justify and reinforce present social relations. Pulling Trobriand myths out of this social context, we could not understand them.

Not so, argues the French anthropologist Claude Lévi-Strauss. As we will see, Lévi-Strauss is seeking to explicate the universal workings of the human mind by looking at varied cultural forms as its artifacts. The realm of myth is crucial in this enterprise because here human thought has its widest freedom. Not every imaginable form of marriage, house style, or residence pattern is actually found—there are too many constraints, too many possibilities that are unworkable for ecological, technological, or purely physical reasons. But man can *think* all of these possibilities, and in myth his thoughts have freest reign.

What does man use this realm of myth for? Lévi-Strauss argues that men everywhere are plagued intellectually by the contradictions of existence— by death; by man's dual character, as part of nature yet transformed by culture; by dichotomies of spirit and body; by the contradictions of descent from a first man (where did a nonincestuous first mate come from?); and so on. The realm of myth is used above all to tinker endlessly with these contradictions, by transposing them symbolically. Thus the gulf between life and death can be symbolically mediated by rephrasing the contrast mythically as between an antelope (herbivore) and a lion (carnivore). By introducing a hyena, which eats animals it does not kill, one then in effect denies the contradiction.

Lévi-Strauss's original insistence that a myth, such as the story of Oedipus or of Asdiwal in Northwest Coast mythology, could be understood by itself has been modified considerably in his monumental four-volume *Mythologiques*. In *The Raw and the Cooked* (1969), the first volume, he examines a whole complex of myths among Indian tribes of Central Brazil, and draws heavily on cultural evidence in his interpretation. His exceedingly complicated and involuted decipherment of their "myth-o-logic" is an analytical tour de force.

But whether his interpretations will stand, and whether they can serve as guides for others to follow, remains in doubt. Terence Turner (n.d.), basing his interpretation on rich field evidence from one of the tribes involved, argues that Lévi-Strauss misinterpreted a crucial myth; more contextual evidence had been needed. One of the grave problems in this whole mode of analysis is to introduce more controls on a method that can discover—or create—structure in any cultural material. Whether Lévi-Strauss's interpretations endure, there is little doubt that myths have a logic, structure, and richness we had not suspected—and that most of the work of deciphering them still lies ahead.

Anthropological study of *ritual* has also undergone major transformations in recent years. Rites have been viewed by Durkheim (§70) and Radcliffe-Brown (§71) as reinforcing collective sentiment and social integration. The *content* of rites—whether the priest zigged or zagged, held a stick in his left hand or a leaf in his right—was a secondary and seldom manageable problem.

As the content of cultural systems has been shown to be increasingly systematic, with the bits and pieces seeming less and less arbitrary in relation to one another, such questions now seem crucial. The nature of ritual

Figure 44. An Ainu Bear Ceremony. Here, among these people of northern Japan, the major religious ritual is climaxed by the killing of a bear, raised from a cub for the purpose. Such a collective rite clearly reinforces the social order and the religious values that sustain it. Modern scholars would explore as well the world of symbolic meanings that lie beneath the outward acts. (From a Japanese print.) FMK

symbols has been revealed dramatically in the work of Victor Turner. Exploring the rituals of the East African Ndembu, he has mapped an extraordinarily rich structure of symbolism (1967).

Example 60: Ndembu Ritual Symbols

The key to this structure is a set of major symbolic objects and qualities that recur in many ritual settings: colors, especially red, white, and black; certain trees and plants; and other "things" accorded central importance in the Ndembu environment. Let us take, for instance, a certain tree, mudyi, *which exudes a milky sap when cut. The tree is used in several rituals, and we can ask what it "stands for." The answer is that it "stands for" a wide range of things: a broad fan of conceptually related meanings, from the basic and physiological (breast milk, nursing) to the social (mother-child relations, matrilineal descent) and abstract (dependency, purity). An actual ritual procedure involves not one symbolic object but a series of them in sequence. What, then, does the ritual "mean," if each object could have such a wide spectrum of possible meanings? A sequence of acts involving these objects, like a musical score or a sequence of words, has a* syntax; *and the possible meaning of each is limited and shaped by their combination and arrangement to form a message. But here again the message is not simple and unambiguous, because it is stated on many levels. A rite may at the same time be a statement about mothers and children, men and their matrilineages, and dependency of the living on their ancestors. Moreover, these multiple levels of meaning relate what is abstract and social with the gut-feelings and emotions of individuals related to their primary experience.*

Here, then, are the beginnings of a theory of symbolism that transcends the Freudian and the crudely sociological: the royal sceptre is neither simply a phallic symbol nor a symbol of the unity of the state—it is both.

Explorations of ritual symbolism by Turner and such scholars as Beidelman, Douglas, and Yalman show the need to view other realms of culture as intricate symbolic designs. A series of fundamental questions arises in such exploration: Can we really speak of cultural elements as "arbitrary"? Are there universal patterns of symbolism? Do people "know" what symbols "mean" in their culture?

It will be useful to ask these questions in terms of something more familiar in our cultural experience than African circumcision rites: the wearing of long hair and beards by young Americans (the "beatniks" of late 1950s and the "hippies" of late 1960s and beyond).

It has often been said that cultural conventions and symbols are *arbitrary.* Such a hair style, or a mode of dress, a house design, a ritual object or ritual procedure, could vary freely; a rule or fashion, or the relation betwen a symbol and what it symbolizes, is a matter of cultural convention. This arbitrariness of cultural symbols distinguishes them from the biological blueprints for animal behavior.

Is the wearing of long hair really "arbitrary"? Does the length of hair, like the width of neckties, fluctuate according to cycles of fashion? Or does long hair *mean* something? A Freudian psychologist, Berg, has argued that hair is universally a symbol of the genitals. Cutting it, or shaving, is thus a symbolic expression of castration. Letting it grow long expresses unrestrained sexuality. He cited much evidence from primitive societies to demonstrate the universality of hair as a symbolic expression of sexuality. When a Trobriand widow and her relatives shave their hair, for example, they are expressing their loss in terms of symbolic castration.

Edmund Leach critically examines this interpretation in his paper "Magical Hair" (1958). Leach notes that Berg's understanding of the evidence is often faulty: the Trobrianders are symbolically expressing not their grief but their innocence of having killed their affine by sorcery. Yet in looking at evidence from India and Southeast Asia, Leach finds impressive support for the symbolic association of hair with sexuality (if not necessarily with the genitals and castration).

Are long hair and beards then really arbitrary fashions? Or are they saying something for which long hair is an *appropriate symbol*? Strong evidence points to the latter, as Leach's paper impressively documents. What then is the symbolic message? Is it unrestrained sexuality, an expression of the sexual revolution? Clearly it is that, but is it only that? Leach argues that Freudians are mistaken in viewing sex as the ultimate referent of symbols. For if Indians were giving symbolic expression to their repressed sexuality, why should their art be pervaded by realistic sexual scenes and phallic monuments? And why should sexually liberated "hippies" express their sexual drives by cryptic symbolic means?

Leach argues that sex itself *can be a symbol of other things*. In India, sexuality (literally or indirectly portrayed) serves as a symbol of the great creative forces of the universe. In modern American protest movements unrestrained sexuality serves as an appropriate and powerful symbol of protest and defiance against a traditional morality and value system. The traditional system is in turn symbolized by rules of premarital chastity (and by shaven chin and short hair—as well as tennis racket and white shoes, to form the composite image of the "All American Boy": Berg might ask if it is coincidental that such a lad is "clean cut").

This leads to a final question examined by Leach. If long hair symbolizes sexuality (and more abstract social or cosmological patterns), then does the man on the street (or the path) correctly "read" the symbolic messages? Leach argues that these levels of cultural symbolism are indeed understood by most, if not all, participants in the social scene. They may not be conscious of the more subtle symbolism; and that may well be why it "works." Perhaps when a school board or a principal forces students to cut their hair, it is because they "know" full well what the hair symbolizes— even if they are not conscious of it. And the "dirt" of "unwashed" protestors may well be more symbolic than physical—a hypothesis that our usage of "dirty" in a sexual sense and studies of symbolic dirt and pollu-tion cross-culturally (Douglas, 1966) would suggest. As an experiment, I had two students, a boy and a girl, wear the same shoulder-length wig (each in a different shopping center), while a third observer asked passersby to describe their appearance. Virtually every adult interviewed described the boy's hair as "dirty" (though the wig was immaculate); none described the girl's hair as dirty. Is the "dirt" symbolic or physical?

Essential to such an interpretation is the way such symbols quickly become conventional—so that wearing long hair or a beard is a public and conventionally unconventional message about the social order, not necessarily a reflection of individual psychology. Whether the Trobriand widow is glad to be rid of her lazy and unfaithful husband is irrelevant to her performance of mourning ritual.

A culture, as we bring its patterning to light, is fantastically intricate, a web of interlinked symbols and meanings on many levels. An element—whether it is a design for house entrances, a ritual procedure, or a dress style—is limited not only by physical possibilities, but also by the "rules" of symbolic ordering in the culture. If it is "arbitrary" in the sense that it is not biologically laid down, it is far from arbitrary in the sense that any ele-ment could equally well be fitted into a cultural design. When a people conceive the cosmos dualistically in terms of male and female, right and left, and up and down, then what men's costumes can be like, and how the right sides of houses can be designed, must fit this symbolic pattern. Finally, for reasons that are still far from clear, there are universal themes and patterns in symbolism. The symbolic linkages RIGHT-SIDE-MALE-UP-SUN and their opposites (LEFT-FEMALE . . .) are found over and over again on different continents. Hair symbolism illustrates another recurrent theme, as do the phallic symbols familiar to students of Freud. An anthropology that has moved beyond cultural relativism and an insistence on uniqueness can begin to ask these questions openly and well. In the next section we will turn to them again.

58 · Cultural Integration, World View, and the Quest for Unique Design

The American anthropologist Robert Lowie, in a passage where he sought to emphasize how modern ways of life represent accumulations of borrowed elements, once referred to civilization as a "thing of shreds and patches." Critics were quick to point out the defects in the analogy. For the "shreds and patches" are not simply a random collection, randomly arranged. Rather, a culture forms an *integrated design*. Elements are borrowed only if they fit into the design or can be recut or recolored to fit. The various elements are systematically related.

Thus in a particular tribe, patterns tattooed on the face, the floor plan of a house, and the movements of a dance may all express a single cosmological scheme; and a people's taboo on talking to mothers-in-law, their mode of inheriting property, the sleeping arrangements in the house, their kinship categories, and their theory of procreation may be elements of an integrated system of logic and custom.

But these underlying designs distinctive of a culture are abstract and subtle. The people cannot usually talk about them. They lie hidden beneath the details of custom, and do not yield to any mode of direct exploration. For many years, anthropologists have groped for ways of uncovering and describing these underlying patterns of order and integration that constitute each culture's unique view of the world.

Our evidence on the Trobrianders has many gaps, but it will serve to illustrate some forms of cultural integration and some approaches to the underlying premises and symbolic order of a culture.

Example 61:   The Integration of Trobriand Culture

We can glimpse an important level of cultural integration by pulling together some elements of Trobriand social organization, custom, and belief. We can then see how elements that seem peculiar by themselves become intelligible in terms of a wider design. Many of these items have been introduced in the preceding chapters. Here we will set out schematically a series of "strange" customs and belief.

1. The doctrine of sub-clan perpetuity
   a. A brother and sister emerged together from the underworld and founded the sub-clan.
   b. The spirits of the dead descendants of this ancestral pair continue to be "members" of the sub-clan, along with the living. Though as baloma, *'spirits,' they have moved to a new plane of existence centered in Tuma, the island of the dead, their association with their sub-clan continues. (We will soon examine the* milamila *festival at which they annually return to visit living members of the sub-clan.)*
   c. New children born into the sub-clan are reincarnations of sub-clan spirits whose period as baloma *has come to an end. The sub-clan existed of old when men lived underground; and it has always been, and will always be, the same.*
2. The Trobriand theory of conception
   a. Copulation by the father does not "cause" the birth of a child—which is the reincarnation of a spirit of the mother's sub-clan. (There is an enormous literature and controversy about what Trobrianders "really mean" here.)
   b. The child's "blood" comes from the mother and her siblings.
   c. The child physically resembles the father, not the mother, because his repeated intercourse with the mother "molds" the child.
3. The avoidance relationship between brother and sister
   a. Brother and sister must avoid close social contact or any intimacy.

  b. *The brother must avoid all knowledge of his sister's sexual affairs.*
  c. *When she marries, he must avoid any direct involvement in her reproductive life.*

4. The rule of residence
  a. *A Trobriand girl and her brother grow up in their father's household, usually in a different village from her sub-clan's.*
  b. *Whereas the brother returns to his sub-clan village in adolescence, the daughter remains with her father until she marries.*
  c. *She then goes to live with her husband; thus at no stage in her life cycle does she normally live with her male sub-clan relatives in their territory.*

5. Rules of exogamy
  a. *A Trobriander is forbidden to marry, or have intercourse with, a girl in his sub-clan.*
  b. *Though marriage with them is regarded as wrong, sexual affairs with girls in different sub-clans of one's own clan are regarded as naughty and dangerous (and hence add spice to life).*

6. The relationship of a father to his children
  a. *The father is said to be a "relative by marriage" to his children.*
  b. *Half-siblings with the same mother and different father are treated as similar to full siblings. Yet half-siblings with the same father and different mothers are treated as nonrelatives. If they are boy and girl, it is regarded as all right for them to have sexual relations. Trobrianders say that the reason they cannot marry is that this would snarl up the* urigubu *yam presentations.*
  c. *A daughter belongs to her mother's corporate sub-clan, which is dependent on her and its other girls for their members in the next generation. Yet when she marries, it is her father and his sub-clan— not her own—with whom her husband's people exchange valuables.*
  d. *When the married daughter wants to become pregnant, her father asks his sub-clan ancestors to ask the ancestors of his wife's and daughter's sub-clan to send a spirit child.*

7. The relationship of children to their paternal aunt
  a. *For a boy, the aunt is the prototype of a sexually eligible woman, with whom he can joke freely or have sexual intercourse.*
  b. *Her daughter is said by Trobrianders to be the ideal wife for him (though as we saw in Ex. 20, arranged marriage with her is usually a political ploy).*
  c. *It is a girl's paternal aunt who takes the lead in events surrounding her pregnancy and childbirth; her aunt, not her mother, makes her a pregnancy cloak, for example.*

8. Urigubu and relations between affines
  a. Urigubu *yam presentations, in the ideal form, go from a man to his sister's husband.*
  b. *A second form of* urigubu *yam presentation is from a married son to his father.*
  c. Urigubu *is more widely a relationship between a corporate sub-clan and its female members' husbands and their sub-clans.*
  d. *When a spouse dies, his or her own sub-clan members cannot have*

any contact with the body, or outwardly mourn; these things are done by the kin of the surviving spouse, who then receive valuables from the dead spouse's sub-clan at the mortuary feast.

We could keep widening the circle of customs and show how they fitted together; but at this stage enough elements show to indicate that they are not simply "shreds and patches." Simply in setting these customs and beliefs out this way, their connectedness begins to emerge. We can see it more clearly if we penetrate deeper to find a symbolic structure underlying them.

We view our connectedness to our father and mother in terms of "blood relationship," which extends through them to uncles, grandmothers, cousins, and so forth. The Trobrianders view the connection between sub-clan members, and most vividly between brother, sister, and the sister's child, in terms of "blood." Blood implies perpetuity and continuity, as in 1 and 2b of the above.

Yet if the blood and the immaterial continuity with the spirits give perpetuity and unity to the sub-clan—as the dogma of conception insists— they cannot make the sub-clan independent and self-perpetuating. In the brother and sister taboo and rule against sub-clan incest, "blood" and sexual relations are inimical and sharply separate. We can think in symbolic terms of the rule BLOOD ⊃ NO SEX ("if blood, then no sex"). In the denial of physiological paternity we can see its mirror image, SEX ⊃ NO BLOOD.

The dogma of sub-clan perpetuity and conception symbolically asserts that the sub-clan is self-contained and self-sustaining. But Trobriand ideol- ogists come to terms with ecological, physical, and political necessity, and recognize the dependence of the sub-clan for a complex of services they themselves cannot provide. In the separation of blood and sex, this need for bonds outside the sub-clan is symbolically expressed.

But Trobriand ideology can define those bonds outside the sub-clan as radically different from those of "blood." They are bonds of influence, but not of substance—as expressed most directly in the father's "molding" of the child (Leach, 1961). The bonds outside the sub-clan are created by marriage, and most of them terminate when the marriage ends. We can view these ties as "affinal," and understand the Trobrianders now when they tell the ethnographer that the father is a "relative by marriage" (6a)— that is, connected by bonds of influence but not substance. We can see why they say paternal half-siblings share no common "blood" (6b).

Because the child's sub-clan is linked by an "affinal" and hence sexual bond to the father's sub-clan, father's sister is the prototypical sexual object, with whom a son can joke or have sexual relations (7a). Because the mother and her brother are separated by the gulf of taboo (3c), he and other men of her own sub-clan must avoid involvement in matters connected with her sexuality and reproductive life. Hence it is their "affines," the father's sub- clan, who receive marriage presentations (6c), who assist in her becoming pregnant (6d), and who provide magical and ritual services connected with her pregnancy and childbirth (7c) (Robinson, 1962). When a Trobriander is mourned and buried by his or her spouse's relatives, not fellow members of his or her own sub-clan (8d), it is because the evil "mist" emanating *from the dead could spread to those of common "blood"; but it cannot pass across the bonds of affinity, where no common substance provides a connection. When the affines have been rewarded for this final service at the mortuary rites, the affinal relation between the two sub-clans comes to an end (though the children continue to trace relationships of bilateral kinship, based on influence but not "blood," through a dead father; Sider, 1967).*

Thus the men of a sub-clan must send their sisters out for the sexuality, "molding," and childbearing they themselves can take no part in; and then must get back the sisters' sons who will be their successors. This sending away in a symbolic sense is reflected in the physical pattern of residence (4). A sub-clan's dependence on its affines for the services and influences its own members cannot provide is first of all expressed in the relationship of a man to his sister's husband, and in the next generation, in the relation of these two brothers-in-law toward children of the marriage (where the father and his sisters provide services the mother's brother cannot). Because a son is a member of his maternal uncle's sub-clan, his relation to his father structurally resembles and continues his uncle's "brother-in-law" relation to his father.

This comes out in urigubu *transactions (8).* Urigubu *transfers of yams can be viewed in part as a contractual obligation whereby a corporate sub-clan rewards its affines for the services they have provided. That a father can receive* urigubu *from his married son as well as or in succession from his brother-in-law (8b) makes sense if we see the young man as stepping into his maternal uncle's shoes. Here it is worth remembering back also to the Crow equivalence rule posited to account for Trobriand kinship terms: A woman's* brother *is equivalent to her* son *in the reckoning of kinship.*

Such webs of logic and interconnection can be traced throughout a culture. They show well the flaws in the "shreds and patches" analogy and the way seemingly strange customs fall into place when we see them as elements of a wider design. We will see shortly how even more elements fall into place if we penetrate to a deeper level in the symbolic structure of a culture.

Another way to map the unique design of a culture is "ethnoscience" (§14). This modern and influential approach to cultural structure builds on the assumption that the things and events in a people's conceptual world will be mirrored in the semantic categories of their language (Tyler, 1969). By finding out what "things" there are in a people's world, and what features of that world they treat as distinctive in assigning meanings, one could avoid superimposing our preconceptions and cultural biases on their conceptual system. Moreover, by using systematic eliciting methods modeled on those in linguistics, one could hopefully achieve greater rigor than the usual style of fieldwork permits.

Thus Frake has explored and mapped with great rigor the way the Subanun of the Philippines diagnose skin diseases (1961). He has since sought to extend this method to Subanun social interaction ("how to ask for a drink in Subanun" [1964b]); to social organization and ecology (the principles governing their shifting of settlements and gardens [1962a]); and to relations with supernaturals (1964a).

Frake and other students of "ethnoscience" are attempting not only to map the structure of small subsystems of folk classification with increased sophistication and rigor; they also hope to transcend the artificiality of a "chapter title" approach to a people's culture. "Economics" and "political structure" and so on are misleading but convenient organizing devices in a comparative survey like ours. But if we hope to describe the structure of a people's own conceptual world, they are worse than misleading. We want to find out what realms people divide their world into, not force it into our predevised compartments. Their systems might turn out to correspond in some respects to "chapter title" comparative frameworks. But that is something we would have to *discover* about another people's conceptual world; we cannot use a method that *assumes* it.

Example 62:   Subanun "Religious Behavior"

In Subanun culture, regular "meals" are on some occasions replaced by a "festive meal," where several families eat together and normal food is augmented by meat and rice wine. The events in the course of such a "festive meal" constitute a festivity.

One type of festivity differs from others in that some of the participants are not "mortals" but are invisible "supernaturals." The latter receive food from the mortals. Such presentations of food are called kanu, 'offerings.' *These offerings distinguish one type of festivity, a* ceremony, *from other types such as "labor-recruiting feasts" and "hospitality feasts." Note that there is no Subanun word for "ceremony"; yet it can be identified as a relevant segment of the Subanun world of experience by the way culturally distinctive acts and things are used.*

Planning and staging these offerings, and the ceremonies built around them, is a central theme of Subanun life. Offerings involve elaborate plans and organization and are deemed crucial to successful living. This sphere of Subanun life can be conveniently labeled as "religious behavior." But, insists Frake, that is not because it fits some general definition of "religion." From a standpoint of the Subanun thought-world, that is irrelevant. What matters is that this and other domains of Subanun culture, as they are described by the ethnographer, follow distinctions and categories relevant to the Subanun themselves (Frake, 1964a).

Using such an approach to explore the structure of Trobriand culture would be dangerous and difficult. Though Malinowski gives extensive linguistic materials, the full sets and contextual materials we would need to reconstruct semantic structure are rare. But Trobriand folk classification can usefully illustrate one point often missed in the ethnoscience procedure of looking at domains one at a time in isolation—at the classification of plants, or kinsmen, or birds, or firewood, or supernaturals. The logic of one sub-system may be intelligible only in terms of another, and the same symbolic principles may be used to order different domains.

Example 63:   Trobriand "Animal" Categories

The fauna of the Trobriands are sparse—reptiles, birds, bats, crabs, and insects. We do not know from Malinowski's writings how the Trobrianders classify different kinds of birds or snakes or what-not (though it is a good guess that like many Pacific Islanders they class birds and bats in the same category). But what concern us here are two higher-level categories that embrace all of these land creatures: "things of the below" and "things of the above." The former include snakes, crabs, iguanas, and lizards. The latter include birds, bats, and insects.

Analyzing these categories in ethnoscience fashion we might see the distinction between them in terms of terrestrial versus flying creatures—the "below" and "above" suggest that. Apparently insects that do not fly are still in the "above" category, which is puzzling. Digging deeper one might discover that "things of the below" are classed together because they come out of holes in the ground, and particularly because they all change their skin. But what kind of categorization is that? Looking only at this domain, we would probably remain mystified.

Students of symbolism like Leach (§57) would insist that the anthropologist's job is to go further than just *describing* the semantics of folk classification in the manner of ethnoscience. These are *cultural creations*, and we want to understand the logic of their creation—to know "why" as well as "what." Leach (1965) would have us look very closely at those strange animals that are neither fish nor fowl, that fall in the middle in a scheme of classification. He would have us look carefully at "odd" distinctions like shedding of skin, and would have us note that on the rare occasions when evil spirits take visible form, it is as reptiles. And he might have us note that when women who are witches change their form and become invisible flying *mulukuausi* that prey on men at night and at sea, their presence can be recognized by the smell of decaying flesh—what may be a symbolic transition between life and death. But why are these changes of form and state important? Snakeskins, witches, night, sea—is it all a giant puzzle? And why "creatures of the *below*"? If there is a structure in all this, it is deeper and more subtle.

Example 64:   The Structure of Trobriand Culture

To try to lay bare the whole structure of Trobriand culture would be far beyond our scope—if indeed it is possible using spotty library evidence, or possible for anthropology at all. But some of the possibilities can at least be glimpsed.

We can begin with some basics of Trobriand cosmology. Recall that the ancestors long ago lived underground—and then emerged through the sub-clan holes into the world. The baloma, spirits of the dead, live underground as well—though the details are vague (Malinowski, 1916: 170–171). We can draw these dualistic contrasts:

BELOW : ABOVE
SPIRITS : MEN
NONLIFE : LIFE
IMMATERIAL : MATERIAL
INVISIBLE : VISIBLE

To these, further analysis would add such contrasts as

DARKNESS : LIGHT
IMMORTAL : MORTAL
DEATH : LIFE

In such a scheme of symbolic dualisms it is worth looking always at mediating states and beings. Thus in dreams and visions the living can communicate with the spirits. The sub-clan holes—and holes in general—are avenues between above and below. So, symbolically, is the sea—on which spirit children come from Tuma, the land of the dead. Invisible witches, at night and at sea, may begin to make sense. But why evil spirits manifest as reptiles, why changing skins, why "creatures of the below"?

In their earlier existence men were immortal—and underground. When they aged, they sloughed their skins and grew new ones—as the baloma still do. Shortly after emerging from the sub-clan holes to the world above, men lost their immortality in a seemingly trivial incident. But the snakes and crabs and lizards that emerge from holes and still change their skins are mediators to the underworld, and retain the vestiges of immortality; in contrast to men and to birds, bats, and insects, they are creatures of the BELOW. It is as a creature of the BELOW, a snake or iguana, that an evil spirit becomes visible to men. Crabs, which brought sorcery to men from the spirit world, are slow to die for they too are medial creatures of the BELOW.

Elsewhere in Trobriand culture we could discern further symbolic contrasts that partly mesh with the preceding dualisms:

MOON : SUN
FEMALE : MALE
LOW : HIGH
COMMONER : "CHIEF"
AFFINITY : BLOOD

Moreover, there are the symbolic polarities to which Lévi-Strauss called out attention in his glimpse of the Trobriand village (Ex. 25):

PERIPHERAL : CENTRAL
COOKED : RAW

MARRIAGE   :   NONMARRIAGE
PROFANE   :   SACRED

A careful look at these arrays of dualisms shows that they do not simply line up in two columns such that everything in the right column or left column goes together in all contexts. Items in opposite columns may be contextually united—so that SPIRITS and SACRED clearly are not contrasted, and continuity of BLOOD passes through the FEMALE line.

Symbolic oppositions and mediations between them may be important elements in the structure of a culture. But they do not simply hang on pegs in a fixed array—they are used; and there is a "grammar" for using them in different contexts. How the symbolic system of a culture is used can be illustrated if we speculate about the highpoint of the Trobriand year, the milamila.

The milamila *is, in outward appearance, a harvest festival—a period of dancing, feasting, ceremonial visiting, exchanges of food and valuables, and heightened sexual activity. The* milamila *activities begin after the yams have been harvested, displayed, distributed in* urigubu, *and ceremoniously stored in yam houses. At this point, marking the annual break in the gardening and work cycle, a food distribution (*sagali*) and pageantry lead up to the first playing of slit drums and commencement of dancing. The* milamila *takes place through the first half of a lunar month and ends at the full moon. As the moon waxes, activities become more intense, with dancing going on through the night, organized visits by girls or boys of a village to a neighboring village to enjoy its sexual hospitality, and even organized visits by the whole population of a village to a neighboring village, with accompanying political maneuvering, mock threat, and exchange of ceremonial valuables.*

But there are a number of curious features that suggest a more subtle symbolic theme. They suggest that this is a context (or "frame"—see page 83) where symbolic polarities are joined or reversed. Female and male, the spirits and the living, the periphery and the center, the below and the above, are united or reversed. Unmarried sexuality emerges in Trobriand life as a mediation between polarities. Recall, for example, that the bachelor houses of the center of the village, the male domain, provide the focal points of premarital sex. The heightening of premarital sex in milamila, *and its emphasis in linking villages together, suggests its importance in bridging the polarities of Trobriand life, between MALE and FEMALE realms, between WE and THEY (note that married sex similarly links a sub-clan to its affines).*

Given the polarities between MOON : SUN and DARK : LIGHT, the way the milamila *reaches its climax at full moon may well reflect their symbolic union. Apparently the dancing in the village center, which attracts men and women around the slit drums—one symbolically male, another symbolically female—serves as a medium for the union of dualities. Men wear their festive ornaments emphasizing maleness in the day, during* milamila, *then take them off at night; and in some of the dances the male dancers put on women's grass skirts. Cooked food, symbolic of the women's and domestic realm, is normally taboo within the central plaza. But in the opening feast of* milamila, *cooked food is set out and distributed there.*

But the most dramatic union of symbolic oppositions in milamila *is the return of the* baloma *spirits to their village. Through the* milamila *period the spirits are present and are given food offerings and ceremonial valuables (the "spirit" of which they take). The element of symbolic reversal comes out vividly in the high platforms made for* baloma *of high rank—placing them ABOVE rather than BELOW. Moreover the* baloma *enforce the suspension of the normal rules of life. If they are not satisfied with people's conduct, as well as presentations of food and valuables, they can spoil weather or even the next gardening cycle. "Everybody had to be bound on pleasure, dancing, and sexual license, in order to please the* baloma" *(1916: 185). The* milamila *ends at full moon when the* baloma *are ritually sent back to their spirit home. The web of Trobriand symbolic structure only partly emerges from Malinowski's descriptions. But fascinating hints about the use of color, of direction and space, are glimpsed in his vivid pictures of the scenes of Trobriand life. They suggest that on a deeper level than Malinowski perceived, there are pattern, design, and a grammar of symbolic meaning beneath the diverse elements of Trobriand custom.*

As we move to these deeper levels of structure, more elements of a culture fall into place. But the solid foundations of ethnoscience, where interpretation builds directly from clear evidence, have dissolved into something more ethereal. How do we know Trobrianders think in terms of these dualisms, or use them in ordering their culture? If we had begun with the assumption that triadic structures were more basic than dualisms in human thought (V. Turner, 1966), could we have "found" them? These uncertainties mount as we go deeper; and many anthropologists would be unwilling to follow this far.

Can one penetrate more deeply still? Are there even more basic premises and principles that give a culture its unique shape? One avenue of approach is through the structure of the language. As we noted in §14, Whorf saw language not simply as expressing thought, but as channeling and shaping it. A people's language lays down and expresses their model of time, space, and relationships. Could we find more basic designs of the Trobrianders' world in the structure of their language? Dorothy Lee's own fieldwork with the Wintu Indians, and Whorf's explorations of Hopi language and world view, had convinced Lee that this was possible. Though she never met a Trobriander or heard one speak, she "lived" her way into their language by immersing herself in Malinowski's rich linguistic texts. A first attempt to draw the Trobriand world view (1940) contrasted it with that of an English speaker. But she had misgivings whether one could faithfully render the Trobriand world view in terms of what it was *not*, in terms of contrasts. In a second paper, she tried to draw the Trobriand world in its own terms— an immensely difficult challenge when one must write in English.

Example 65:   The Trobriand World View as Structured in Language

Among the Trobriand Islanders, as with other peoples, "language . . . incorporates the premises of the culture, and codifies reality in such a way that it presents it as absolute" to its speakers. The speakers of Trobriand (or Kiriwinan) "are concerned with being, and being alone. Change and becoming are foreign to their thinking. An object or event is grasped and evaluated in terms of itself alone." It is not defined, which implies contrast with other things—but is conceived in terms of what it is. *"Each event is grasped timelessly," seen in relation to other things only in that it is part of an "ordained pattern."*

> *If I were to go with a Trobriander to a garden where the* taytu, *a species of yam, had just been harvested, I would come back and tell you: "There are good* taytu *there; just the right degree of ripeness, large and perfectly shaped; not a blight to be seen, not one rotten spot . . ." The Trobriander would come back and say "Taytu"; and he would have said all that I did and more (Lee, 1949: 402). . . .*
>
> *History and mythical reality are not "the past" to the Trobriander. They are forever present, participating in all current being, giving meaning to all his activities and all existence" (403). . . .*
>
> *To be good [an object] must be the same always. . . . Trobriand being never came into existence; it has always been, exactly as now . . . (405).*
>
> *To the Trobriander, events do not fall of themselves into a pattern of causal relationships . . . the magician does not* cause *certain things to be; he* does *them (400–407).*
>
> *The Trobriander performs acts because of the activity itself, not for its effects; . . . he values objects because they are good, not good for . . . (408).*

Yet "being has no independent existence. It is itself only as part of an established pattern . . . Being is seen . . . as a fixed point in a single, changeless whole" (409).

> *For members of our culture, value lies ideally in change, in moving away from the established pattern . . . The Trobriander, on the contrary, expects and wants next year to be the same as this year and as the year before his culture emerged from underground (413).*

Finally, she speculates on the level and relevance of such linguistically structured contrasts in world view:

> *Do we who base our behavior on relationships read these relationships into reality, or are they given? Which codification is true to reality? I would say that the two . . . represent different facets of reality . . . Our peculiar codification makes us blind to other aspects of reality, or makes these meaningless when presented. But one codification does not exhaust reality . . . The Trobrianders, according to our view of life, should be bored automatons. Actually they act as they want to act, poised and sure, in activities which hold meaning and satisfaction (415).*

There are methodological problems in all this. Did Lee adequately grasp the structure of a language she had never heard a Trobriander speak?

Do other peoples in the area whose languages are closely related in most of the respects Lee cites really have the same world view? Moreover, there are now grave doubts whether the contrasts between Trobriand and English languages actually reflect profoundly different patterns of linguistic structure. Chomsky's work (§13) suggests that the contrasts reflect different "surface structure" rules for giving underlying sentence designs—which would be quite similar in the two languages—their outward trimmings. We will return shortly to this problem of uniqueness.

Other scholars have taken the whole range of customs and behavior as sources of clues about the deepest levels of "world view" or cultural integration. Many American anthropologists have considered a culture to be something like a geometry in its internal order. That is, there are a great many specific theorems, corollaries, principles, and relationships; but they are elaborations and implications of a smaller set of more general principles. Finally, underlying the whole system are a few general axioms, the "givens" of the system, cultural equivalents of "a straight line is the shortest distance between two points." House styles, kinship taboos, and ritual routines are viewed as like the specific theorems and rules of geometry. The anthropologist must search beneath them to find the underlying "givens" of the system.

A major attempt of this sort was Clyde Kluckhohn's exploration of the basic "givens" of Navaho Indian culture, based on years of intimate experience with Navaho life and analysis of Navaho custom and belief. From evidence as diverse as sandpainting designs, curing ceremonies, kinship arrangements, political action, and fears of witchcraft, Kluckhohn inferred a set of basic premises about the universe in terms of which these details make sense. The following premises are illustrative:

The universe is orderly: all events are caused and interrelated.
    a. Knowledge is power.
    b. The basic quest is for harmony.
    c. Harmony can be restored by orderly procedures.
    d. One price of disorder, in human terms, is illness.
The universe tends to be personalized.
The universe is full of dangers.
Evil and good are complementary, and both are ever present.
Morality is conceived in traditionalistic and situational terms rather than in terms of abstract absolutes.
Human relations are premised upon familistic individualism (1949).

Similarly deep involvement in the thought-world of another Indian people, the Ojibwa, led A. I. Hallowell to explore the categories, assumptions, and logic in terms of which Ojibwa order experience. These studies bring out particularly clearly how some of the distinctions we take most for granted—animate versus inanimate, natural versus supernatural—are by no means universal in human experience. Hallowell's most important writings are collected in *Culture and Experience* (1955).

These deepest "givens" of a culture have been variously conceptualized as "premises," "themes," "values." The search for them was a major goal in American anthropology in the 1940s and 1950s (§72), though in recent years most anthropologists have focused attention on narrower but more manageable problems.

The anthropological assumptions that underlie these searches for cultural integration and uniqueness, not simply the methods used in the search, are being increasingly questioned.

Can we still view a culture as a highly integrated whole, as a "seamless web" whose elements fit into a systematic design? Clifford Geertz, in a study of concepts of time and "person" in Javanese culture, expresses grave doubts.

> . . . Cultural integration [can] no longer be taken to be locked away from the common life of man in a logical world of its own. Perhaps even more important, however, it [cannot be] taken to be . . . all-embracing, completely pervasive, unbounded. . . . In the first place, . . . patterns counteractive to the primary ones exist as subdominant but nonetheless important themes. . . .
>
> But beyond this sort of natural counterpoint there are also simple, unbridged discontinuities between certain major themes themselves. Not everything is connected to everything else with equal directness, not everything plays immediately into or against everything else.
>
> . . . The problem of cultural analysis is as much a matter of determining independencies as interconnections, gulfs as well as bridges. The appropriate image, if one must have images, of cultural organization, is neither the spider web nor the pile of sand. It is rather more the octopus, whose tentacles are in large part separately integrated, neurally quite poorly connected with one another and with what in the octopus passes for a brain, and yet who nonetheless manages to get around and to preserve himself, for a while anyway, as a viable, if somewhat ungainly entity (1966*b*: 65–67).

The extent to which a culture, as an ideational system, fits together into total systems and neatly integrated wholes—even in the most stable and isolated tribal society—is now a problem to be investigated. The Trobriand illustrations show how cultures do make sense, and fit together, in a way a newcomer to anthropology might well not suspect. But as Geertz suggests, if we assumed that Trobriand culture should be totally integrated and self-consistent, it would be easy to create just as striking a picture of discontinuities and logical contradictions, showing how badly integrated Trobriand culture is. One of the remarkable things about the human animal is his ability to tolerate and operate with inconsistent and contradictory beliefs and customs: the world is filled with soldiers fighting for peace, adulterous Christians, rich Communists, and quarreling kinsmen.

The model of culture as resembling a geometry, with the complex details building on and expressing sets of underlying "givens," implies that these deeper levels are accessible to study. If we learn how to trace down through the layers of a culture, we can discover these "givens"—and describe them.

Whether these deeper levels are accessible to our probing, and describable in language if we could uncover them, has recently been questioned from another direction. This is a bold theoretical exploration of art, culture, and the human mind by Gregory Bateson (n.d.). The areas of human life where men spin out rational plans, formulate rules, and organize and classify, may represent only the uppermost layers of mental process. Like an iceberg, the human mind is a deep structure that reveals only its surface conformations to consciousness and outward inspection. The deep realms of unconscious thought deal not with *things*, but with *relationships* and *patterns*. (Note that as outlined in §10, these modes of coding may be largely prelinguistic.) Bateson argues that man's consciousness inevitably deals with bits and pieces, with segments carved out of wholes: the very process of conscious thought distorts and disrupts. So, too, does the attempt to describe these deep patterns in the channels of language.

In art, man attempts to reconstitute whole patterns, to recapture lost integration. The painter or musician or sculptor is saying something in his medium about total patterns, about the way elements fit together into wholes, about the relationship between levels. The esthetic "Gestalt" or perceptual vision of total pattern reconstitutes in the mind the fragmented pieces of experience. So, perhaps, does ritual. Recall the *mudyi* tree used in Ndembu ritual, the milk-exuding wood that symbolizes breast milk, motherhood, and matrilineal descent. These multiple levels of meaning, the restatement of the same pattern of relationship in terms of different "things," may similarly recapture a perceptual integration, a vision of how things fit together, that men lose in their everyday life.

One cannot do justice to Bateson's provocative speculations in so brief a summary. In fact, if his position is sound it is inevitable that language is inadequate to express these ideas. Like the words of a Zen Master, Bateson's paper rewards several readings and considerable reflection. It has many implications for the problems we have dealt with in these chapters. One is that the effort to lay out the design of culture, to produce a list of the basic premises on which a "cultural geometry" rests, may be impossible. A much more complex model of the mind and its circuits, and of the codes in which men organize knowledge of their world, may be needed. And these patterns of coding and their integration may reveal themselves—if at all—only to modes of analyzing and describing we have hardly begun to explore.

Can the premise that the design of each culture is unique still be held? There is unquestionably a wide range in the ways people conceive the universe to be ordered, in man's view of himself, of time, of change. Yet these increasingly seem to be variations *within* a common design, a design imposed by the structure of man's brain and perceptual equipment and the common elements of his biological endowment and social life.

Anthropologists came to assume that the design of each culture was unique partly because linguists insisted that each language was unique. As we have seen (§13), linguists now are increasingly convinced that diversity in languages clothes a common underlying framework. The anthropologist's premise that each culture must be treated as a separate universe, with its own distinctive design, is now in jeopardy.

The anthropologist's problem, in seeking to find a universal structure beneath the diversity of cultures, is partly to search by some more direct route than linguists did. Half a century of describing languages *as if* they were unique has now been superseded; it would be a pity if anthropologists had to follow the same roundabout path. But what kind of structure do we look for? How do we look? Perhaps a universal design of cultures, if there is one, is more structured by genetic programming than older assumptions had allowed us to consider. We have glimpsed the evidence of an innate design for language; in §60, we will speculate about that possibility for other domains of culture.

The patterns of thinking imposed by the brain, applied to the common perceptual features of men's environment and universal elements of human experience, must also limit cultural possibility. Investigations of cultural structure and symbolism have repeatedly brought to light similar modes of thinking in different parts of the world. Most fully explored has been *symbolic opposition*, the dualistic contrast of polarities: LEFT : RIGHT, MOON : SUN, FEMALE : MALE, and so on. We have illustrated the mode of organization in Trobriand culture (Ex. 64). Moreover, as we saw in §57, similar sets of symbolic polarities appear over and over again in different cultures.

These universal patterns imposed by human thinking have been most dramatically and ambitiously explored by the French anthropologist Claude Lévi-Strauss (1962). Lévi-Strauss argues that the logic of thinking is computerlike in that it is digital and binary—that is, based on sets of two-way contrasts, A or not-A, B or not-B, and so on. This relatively simple mode of relational thought is, for primitive man, turned loose on the world of sensory experience: the animals, plants, constellations, individuals, and groups that are his direct evidence about the world. Like the French handyman or *bricoleur* who solves infinitely variable repair problems by rearranging the pieces and materials at hand, primitive man endlessly rearranges and classifies his universe of experience. The precise arrangements are almost infinitely variable; but the *mode* of arrangement, the structure of his designs, is repeated over and over. It is as though the human mind were a snowflake machine which never precisely replicated the same pattern, but which always produced the same *kind* of pattern.

Lévi-Strauss does not argue that there is a "primitive mind," a qualitatively different way of thinking, as had Levy-Bruhl (1923). Modern man lives in a conceptual world whose building materials have been enormously expanded by microscope, telescope, the stuff of science, and the language of mathematics; he has also become a specialist, more like electronics expert than handyman. The mode of thought is the same; the products of thought have been transformed.

The same symbolic polarities—culture versus nature, sacred versus profane, male versus female, right versus left, sun versus moon—run through the domains of a culture. The same formal arrangements of contrast recur again and again within one culture, or from one culture to another. The differences are in the realm of *content*, so that it is possible to show how one design is a replica or a transformation of another (as in an arithmetic equation, if all the signs are changed).

Because the same modes of thinking are applied by primitive man to a world of direct sensory experience that is very much the same in jungle or desert, the same elements and themes and contrasts occur over and over again on different continents: fire, moon, and sun; the contrast between the sexes, between our group and outsiders, between nature and culture; the use of animals and plants to symbolize relations between human groups. Here Turner's emphasis on the use of bodily functions and substances to symbolize social relations and moral principles (Ex. 60) adds a further dimension.

Where American and British anthropologists have usually described "culture" or "social structure" in order to account for the way people in a society actually behave, Lévi-Strauss is seeking to account for the *cultures they build*—and hence is looking for a deeper order of structure less directly relatable to what one can observe and measure. One may legitimately question whether Lévi-Strauss's model of the human mind is partial and prematurely formulated. One may doubt whether the rules of his analytical operation impose enough controls to be sure he *discovers* structure and does not *create* it. But too often he is criticized because the people he describes do not really build their houses in a neat circle, which is largely beside the point.

If we know little yet about the design of cultures, and hence what kind of universal framework we might look for, it is partly because we have never gotten very far in systematically mapping any culture as an ideational system. Proponents of ethnoscience have contended that if we began with systems of folk classification, and applied similar methods to segments like Subanun ceremonies (Ex. 62), our ever-widening circles could ultimately map the whole of a culture. But Bateson's warnings suggest that such an enterprise may never get much farther than it has so far. Lévi-Strauss may well be finding order only in the segments of culture that lie relatively near the "surface." As he and some of his colleagues (such as Simonis, 1968) are beginning to suspect, cultural patterning at deeper levels of the mind may be beyond our analytical reach.

Bateson warns that what we can observe, in consciousness and behavior, is only a partial and distorting reflection of how knowledge is coded. At least until neurophysiology can open to our view the physical circuitry of thinking, knowledge, memory, and choice, an anthropological description of "a culture" will probably be a sketch but not a map—a revealing but incomplete and simplified summation of a people's way of life.

Part Four

THE INDIVIDUAL, CHANGE, AND THE FUTURE

IN LOOKING AT kinship, economics, politics, law, and religion in primitive societies, we have inevitably lost partial sight of the individual: how he is shaped by, and shapes, his culture, how individual differences are socially channeled. In Chapter XVI, we will narrow our focus to the individual.

We have also described "primitive" ways of life as though they were relatively stable and unchanging—as indeed they seemed to be when Europeans first intruded on the scene. That stability was partly an illusion; and in the last century tribal peoples have increasingly been caught up in the swirling tides of change. Chapter XVII deals not only with the impact of the West on traditional societies and the dramatic and often chaotic changes sweeping the non-Western world, but also with the possibilities that anthropology has for guiding the course of change and avoiding disruption.

XVI Culture and
the Individual

A New Guinea tribesman, gravely examining the inkblot patterns on a Rorschach plate proffered to him by an anthropologist, describes what he "sees" in them: a swirl of moving birds, bats, and mythical creatures of the forest where he lives. His fellow villagers had also seen swirling animals and beings in the plates.

The way these tribesmen respond to these plates—not just *what* they see, but the *way* they perceive and report their responses—can be scored by a clinical psychologist, using standardized principles of interpretation. What if he finds in their responses patterns that, if an American produced them, would indicate severe psychological imbalance?

One possibility is that the tribesmen are expressing a personality pattern similar to the American's; but that the kinds of pathological childhood experiences that engendered the personality of the American are standardized in the child-rearing practices of the New Guineans. Hence what is abnormal in America is normal in this New Guinea tribe. Furthermore, it is possible that the tribe's beliefs in dangerous ancestral ghosts, their male cult of mysterious flutes and rites forbidden to women, and the ordeals by which boys are initiated into the cult, are projections of the psychological stresses and conflicts these childhood experiences produce.

Such lines of interpretation build on a series of assumptions—about cultures, about social life, about the depths of the human mind, about the instruments of testing. In the 1940s and 1950s such possibilities were explored by many American anthropologists. "Culture and personality" became a major subfield of the discipline. Spurred by efforts in World War II to delineate the "national character" of enemies and allies, methods for probing personality in other cultures proliferated and were refined.

Yet in recent years, interest in such problems has waned. New conceptions of "culture," new focal points of interest in psychology, and the frustrations and circularities of assaulting such major questions head on, have shifted attention elsewhere. Many anthropologists do not accept the fundamental assumptions of older "culture and personality" studies. What largely remains is a set of narrower but more manageable questions about learning, about psychological abnormality in non-Western societies, about how the genetic diversity and psychological differences within a population are channeled by its culture, about the effects on personality of drastic cultural change. The larger questions and older approaches of "culture and personality" are here set out in §73, treating this as a "school" of anthropological thinking.

Our concern here will be on reconceptualizing the domain of "culture and personality" so as to fit the ideas about culture and process we have been exploring; to examine how cultures are learned; and to glimpse what happens to the individual amid the storms of culture change.

59 · "Culture and Personality" Reconsidered

"A culture," as we have used the concept, is a picture of the ideational world of a people built up as a composite by the anthropologist. He builds that composite by studying the knowledge, beliefs, values, and goals of individuals. He knows that the thought-world of each of them is different from every other's; yet he seeks to discover that knowledge they must broadly share in order to communicate. This focus on what is shared rather than what is distinctive of each individual is useful to an anthropologist trying to make sense of what people are doing. It is a way of summing up what they know and do, what makes their world different from his.

But it creates traps for the unwary. For it leads us too easily to think of "the culture" as something external to and different from the psychological world of the individual tribesman. We forget that his psychological world (as best we could know it) is what we built our composite from in the first place. It is our imaginary composite, not his; and we err if we talk about "it" as shaping his behavior or conflicting with his goals. If a generalized conception of the Trobriand way of life that a Trobriander attributes to other people affects him at all, it is because that conception is *part of*—not external to—his own thought-world.

So let us retrace our steps and start over again. Each individual tribesman—say a Trobriand Islander—lives in a psychological world of knowledge, belief, value, experience, goals, drives, and self-conception which is different in some respects from any other human's; but which is similar enough to those of other Trobrianders that they can converse, grow yams together, make *urigubu* presentations, and conduct *milamila* ceremonial.

The psychological world of a Trobriander, including the dynamics of his unconscious as well as his consciousness, constitute his *personality*. Now note that there are two possible dividing lines, conceptually, between "culture" and "personality" in terms of this psychological world of our individual Trobriander. We could say that "culture" refers to the conceptual systems

Trobrianders share and not to those elements of the Trobriander's thought-world he does not share with his neighbors. But that leads back toward the trap we have just evaded.

Alternatively, we could say that "culture" refers to *some segments* of the thought-world of our Trobriander, but not to the rest. Thus we might want to say that the cultural realm corresponds to what psychologists call "cognition"—knowledge belief, recipes for action—rather than "motivation"—the forces in which man's drives seek expression and are channeled. This kind of separation, deriving from Freudian psychology, underlay much "culture and personality" research. A guiding assumption was that through a society's patterns of child rearing, the early experiences that channel these motivational forces would be broadly common to all members of the group. We might be led to ask, as Malinowski did (1927), whether the matrilineal system of the Trobrianders, where mother's brother is the authority figure and father is indulgent, would produce an Oedipus complex very different from that in Freud's Vienna. Looked at this way, "culture" would be seen not as a force external to the mind of the individual Trobriander but as one element of a process *within* his mind, one side in a continuous contest of opposing forces.

Such a simple model of the human mind will no longer do. For in psychology, in linguistics, in cognitive anthropology, we are beginning to explore the rich complexities of cognition. Through Freud's discoveries, seething forces of unconsciousness invaded and pushed back into superficial levels the rational, the conscious, the conventions of custom. But our probings of cognition, especially through language, are pushing the realm of rational thought back into the deep reaches of the human mind. We have perceived that rules, logical order, formulations of mathematical precision—the epitome of what is "rational"—lie deeply layered in unconsciousness (Bateson, n.d.; Lévi-Strauss, 1962).

The knowledge, beliefs, assumptions, and patterns from which the anthropologist abstracts "culture" pervade these deepest levels of unconsciousness. We are only beginning to map the brain, and the complex workings of the mind. But it is increasingly clear that "personality" and "culture" refer not to two entities that affect one another, or show correlations, but to *two abstractions from the same phenomena*. To ask how "personality" and "culture" are related is a false question; they are the same coin, looked at from two sides.

The notion that people in a society will share a common pattern of motivation or "psychodynamics," standardized through child-rearing experience, has also been increasingly challenged. Unquestionably the forces that move men in a society are shared to some extent. When we go to a tribal people and find that they seem overbearing and arrogant, or hostile and aggressive (recall the Yanomamö in §4), or outgoing and friendly, we are not simply inventing spurious impressions. But does that mean that the motivational depths of these peoples' personalities are culturally standardized and different from ours?

The ways a people respond to an ethnographer, to the tests he gives them, or to one another, are patterned. But these more or less similar patterns reflect, by and large, *something they have learned*. Goals and motives, perceptual patterns, and self-conceptions are acquired in learning contexts that are more or less similar; and they thus constitute part of the cultural learning that equips an individual to act successfully in the situations he will face. The New Guinea tribesmen's common pattern of Rorschach response may reflect less a standardization of the driving inner forces of personality than shared ways of stretching cognitive categories to cope with perceptual ambiguity. It is useless to argue whether these patterns are "culture" or "personality": we have already seen that these are two ways of looking at the same phenomena. But it is equally useless to say that the culture has standardized the personality.

In terms of "psychodynamics" the New Guinea tribesmen are likely to be quite diverse. Here genetic and biochemical factors appear to be much more important in shaping personality than we have been prepared to believe. Human populations apparently contain a reservoir of diversity in such biological templates of personality. Childhood experiences, which are far from standardized in any society, reshape and build on biological templates, and fill them in with the content of cultural learning. This process generates the diverse personalities of a society. We will see shortly how crucial is the sorting out and channeling of such individual diversity into the role system of the society. A Kwaio feast-giver (Ex. 43) makes a conventional speech during his mortuary feast, in which he apologies for his poor resources and inadequate preparations. One man who makes it may be quaking in his bare feet, and meaning what he says; while another may be flushed with pride in being the center of attention, asserting his wealth and "bigness" while overtly apologizing for his poverty. The first, though he may be the oldest son of an important man, with many relatives who would support him, will never become a "big man."

Wallace (1970) has argued that even cognitive patterns, the versions of cultural knowledge individuals learn, need not be standardized. They need only be *congruent*, so they fit together. Any society's members have varying rules and principles, alternative ways of doing things. Wallace has shown neatly how people's expectations can still be borne out, and communication maintained, amid such diversity in cultural codes. It will be suggested in the next chapter that a reservoir of such code diversity within a society is necessary, as is biological diversity, if adaptive change is to be possible.

The relationship between cognition and the realm of motivation and emotion is little understood and relatively uncharted. Here psychologists and anthropologists need further help from neurophysiologists. Pribram

(1967), for instance, has argued that action and emotion are alternative modes for reacting to situational "inputs" to the brain. Both are "cognitive" in the sense that they apply programs or plans that are activated by hierarchies of neural control systems ("servomechanisms"). When neural inputs carry messages about the world to a person's brain, he may respond with *action*— by activating a sequence of rules or plans. Alternatively, he may respond with *emotion* by manipulating the inputs (not the world) and by editing out portions of his mental plans or programs and substituting simpler or earlier versions. The older Freudian notions of the mind as like a hydraulic system, with forces sloshing about under pressure—dammed here, released there— have begun to leak badly. Even the newer ego psychologies of Fromm, Erikson, or Sullivan are being left far behind as we explore those two sides of the same puzzle, the brain and mind. It is clear that no simple idea of cultural code and motivation as two separate sides of the mind or as opposing forces will prove adequate.

We have here, then, a very different perspective on culture and the individual than that which guided the search for "basic personality structure" or "national character" in the 1940s and 1950s. We view the dichotomy between "culture and personality" as the product of a confused view of culture and a far too simple conception of the structure of the mind. The quest for some standard personality type in a society has been guided by an overemphasis on the plasticity of personality and the similarity of early learning experiences in a society, an underemphasis on biological templates of personality and their diversity, and a confusion between culturally patterned behavior and the motivational depths of personality.

In the sections to follow, we will bring this perspective to bear on how cultures are learned in different settings, on how the resources of psychological diversity are socially utilized, and on the effects of drastic cultural change on personality.

60 · Learning a Culture

If anthropologists knew how a child learned his culture, their problems would mainly be solved. For to know this, they would have to understand the nature of an infant—its biological capacities, modes of perception, and predispositions. In short, they would have to know "human nature." They would have to know the design of the brain and whatever program was laid down genetically to be filled in by the content of learning. They would have to know the extent of biological diversity. They would have to know how thinking processes worked and how consciousness and unconsciousness were organized. And they would have to know *what* it is that is learned, in a social setting, that fills in these biological outlines and capacities with the content of cultures.

Scientists know none of these things. Each frontier is still being reconnoitered, and progress on most fronts has been limited. What we can say so far about learning a culture reflects the continuing mystery that is man.

A human infant is, we know, an incredibly complicated pattern of biological systems and capacities, many of which are activated long before birth. But it is also like a seed or bulb that must be implanted in the soil of social experience if it is to grow into a human being.

Men differ from their primate cousins in the degree and duration of their helplessness. Without nurturing over a period of years, a human infant cannot survive. During this long dependence, the child must learn the rich complexity of his way of life. This learning is mediated by the symbolic system he must learn: the child acquires a code of symbols and meanings, which in turn provides a mode of learning, a means of instruction and reinforcement.

The process of learning a culture is called *enculturation*. The alternative term *socialization* is commonly used when stress is placed on an individual learning the groups and roles of his society.

Anthropologists have documented, though often without sufficiently detailed and controlled observation, many variations in the culturally patterned experience of infants and young children in different societies. Even in those respects seemingly directly tied to biological nature, societies may have very different conventions. Many peoples, for example, do not allow a newborn infant to nurse for several days until the mother's breasts have filled with milk (even though the watery colostrum produced at first serves important biological functions). How often and under what circumstances an infant is fed or bathed, how it is held, how and when it is disciplined, the age and circumstances of weaning and toilet training, vary widely and are usually subject to fairly clear cultural conventions. A finer-grained detail and greater comparability of evidence than in earlier studies, have been achieved in the study of child rearing in six societies (in East Africa, Mexico, the Philippines, Okinawa, India, and New England) organized by Beatrice Whiting and her colleagues (Whiting, 1963).

An infant is faced with the challenge of extracting regularities of pattern from the "blooming buzzing confusion"—the noises, visual images, and tactile experiences that are the world "out there." Just how an infant proceeds to build a model of his cultural and social world is little understood because the infant's mind has been a sealed "black box" to the investigator. Yet through modern studies we are acquiring two blurred but crucially important windows into that black box. The first is the progress of developmental neurophysiology, particularly as represented in the work by Eric Lenneberg and his associates on the developmental biology of language learning (1967). The second, which we have already viewed, is transformational linguistics (Chapter IV). Linguists, formalizing grammars as sets of logical rules, have sought to find a universal framework of language. Chomsky and his associates have been able to argue that the child must begin with an innate universal design of language, not a blank slate; and these studies have enabled psycho-linguists to make increasingly educated guesses about the cognitive system of the language learner.

Is there some universal design underlying other domains of culture? It is not the *contents* of cultures that we might expect to be innately specified —they are too variable for that. Thus there can be no innate predisposition to perceive the world as operated by a supreme deity, or several deities, or none. We cannot reasonably expect that human infants are born with a mental pigeonhole for storing "religion" (whatever its form in a society). But it might very well be the case that infants are preprogrammed to learn certain kinds of patterns in specified sequence and to follow certain patterns of logical inference (certain ways of processing "inputs" of evidence about the world so as to arrive at "theories"). One would need to hypothesize only such an innate logic of inference, a predisposition to fill in gaps and follow chains of inference as far as they lead, and a tolerence for only limited degrees of cognitive uncertainty and contradiction, to account for the uni-versality of religion and myth.

The dangers of accounting for shared cultural conventions on the grounds of individual psychology have been repeatedly pointed out; and alternative functional explanations for religions and other institutions have been abundant. There is little direct evidence for hypotheses about innate predispositions. Yet before we reject such possibilities out of hand, it is worth reflecting soberly on recent studies in psycholinguistics. It is also worth reflecting that in an intellectual climate emphasizing the uniqueness of man, the endless plasticity of humans to shaping by their cultures, and the diversity and uniqueness of cultures, we have hardly been prepared to face such possibilities squarely. An emerging intellectual climate that stresses similarities between natural systems of all kinds, biological and social; that assumes that biological and psychocultural are ultimately two sides of the same coin; and that seeks universals rather than insisting on uniqueness and relativism, makes it pos-sible and urgent to ask such questions, whatever the answers turn out to be.

It is clear from modern linguistics, at least, that the human infant must be a theory builder of remarkable capacity. From a limited and imper-fect sample of the possible events in his cultural universe, he must *create a theory* of the rules, programs, and logic of which this sample was an expression. He must continually test and refine elements of his theory. For what social life requires of him is not an enactment of "canned" sequences he has learned and stored. Rather, he must produce sequences *he has never observed* but which are implied by his theory. The situations of social life are ever-changing and often unique. Just as they call for linguistic utterances that the speaker has never heard but which his grammatical theory defines as possible and meaningful, so he must create other behavioral responses that are new to his experience but culturally "grammatical." Whether the human infant could be such a powerful theory builder without considerable biological preprogramming of how to process the "evidence" and how to organize his knowledge seems highly improbable. Given the universality of preprogramming in the animal world, it would be surprising indeed if the human infant had to begin to decipher, entirely from scratch, what kind of world he lived in and what he was supposed to do about it.

Peoples vary in the extent to which cultural routines are taught by verbal instruction rather than observation. Clearly, bodies of specialized knowledge like music, mythology, and mathematics are transmitted largely through language. Yet there are great areas of culture to be learned of which neither adults nor learners are fully conscious and which neither can talk about very well. The codes of gesture, posture, and facial expression, the shared knowledge we use to communicate about moods, contexts, status, and the like, are learned by observation, not instruction. The self-conception that modern personality psychologists increasingly regard as central emerges in large measure from such implicit learning. A person matches and manipulates the private world he has learned but cannot verbalize against a background of the public and ideal virtues, standards, and images espoused by his society.

This usefully can remind us that the stress on early childhood experience in culture and personality research has diverted attention from later learning. What we learn about ourselves, about our way of life, and about our relation to it we do not learn only in infancy. In preadolescence, adolescence, and adulthood crucial learning of cultural patterns and of self-identity is taking place.

Later learning does not simply add new content to the learner's psychological world: it changes the *structure* of that world. The learner often sees himself in relation to the world in new ways—acquiring new "frames" in which to interpret the messages of experience (Bateson, 1955; recall the interpretation of frames of fiction and symbolism in a Bergman film in §16). The importance of initiation rites in cultural learning lies not only in what the initiate is taught about being a man or a woman, and on what mysteries are revealed. By dramatically changing his status, initiation also transforms his *relationship* to the ways of his people, and gives him a new perspective on himself as player in their games of life.

Such a focus on the learning task of the individual can give us a different perspective on child-rearing practices in different societies. It seems reasonably likely (1) that human infants are (among other things) exceedingly complex and intricately programmed learning "devices"; (2) that the bulk of this programming and many of the crucial patterns that are learned are stored deep in unconsciousness; and (3) that man builds, on the higher levels of consciousness, partial and distorted versions of what lies beneath—ideologies, conscious routines of ritual or etiquette, ideal norms, "rules of thumb." If this is so, then a people's child-rearing customs and patterns not only organize the contexts where learning takes place; they also represent that people's ideologies and theories about what children are like and how they learn. Those theories may well have little to do with what and how children actually do learn. It is conceivable that cultural learning takes place not so much through the child-rearing practices of a society as *in spite of them*.

61 · Personality and Role System

Though every normal individual in a society acquires a competence to enact the basic patterns of his culture, we now see that there are considerable variations in temperament and abilities in every generation. This leads to a recurring organizational problem: individuals will be differentially suited to play the various roles that must be filled in a society.

The problem varies in shape and magnitude according to the scale and complexity of the society. Recall that the differentiation of political and economic roles increases markedly as we move from band societies to tribes, to chiefdoms, and to states. Social theorists have characterized this span in terms of a shifting emphasis from *ascribed status* (where roles are fixed by birth) in simpler societies to *achieved status* in more complex societies. But that is too simple for our purposes. Take the political leader, for example, on whom a group's very survival may depend. In band societies the leader (however restricted his powers) is likely to be a man who earned by deeds the respect and loyalty of his fellow band members. The Melanesian "big man" is likewise suited by talent and temperament to enact that role—or he would not be in it. But in a hereditary aristocracy where the oldest son of a king or chief succeeds him, the successor may very well be unsuited in personality and ability to perform the job that is his by right.

Elites manage, by direct or subtle means, to perpetuate themselves. Yet the rigidity of the systems for securing rights across generations restricts the mobility of the genetic hand dealt in each generation. Genetic chance has repeatedly defied the efforts devoted to instilling the values, skills, and knowledge appropriate to a rightful successor's role. A bevy of councilors, ministers, priests, and others have historically buffered kings and other hereditary leaders—so that the succession of an inept or young heir to high office would not be disastrous. The high places that slaves and eunuchs have often occupied in court circles reflect two related advantages: their social mobility to rise to heights of achievement without threatening the formal status of others; and their lack of descendants, so they can found no rival dynasty or faction.

Our focus on uniformity of personality, and on the plasticity rather than the genetic templates of men's nature, has kept this problem in the background. In much older "culture and personality" research (§73), one inferred a society's basic "personality type" by observing culturally standardized ways of behaving, and then "discovered" that this was a culture people with that personality would fit into nicely. How diverse resources of temperament and ability were distributed into social niches was seldom asked. Yet examination of the channels of access and assignment into the role system of a society—how those men become butchers, bakers, candlestick makers, priests, and premiers, who are reasonably suited by personality and abilities to perform these roles—is an important problem on which we need more evidence. At this point we must post a sign, "unexplored territory," and go on.

62 · Personality and Culture Change

In a relatively stable society, a new generation faces the prospect of becoming more or less like previous ones. The cultural code its members learn is closely geared to the situations they will encounter in life.

The era of colonialism has seen primitive peoples overrun by technologically superior forces. Especially in the twentieth century, the disruption of non-Western ways of life has accelerated; and Western peoples themselves have been swept up into the space age. The impact of the West on tribal societies will be a central theme of the next chapter. But here we can usefully look at the psychological consequences of rapid social change and the breakdown of traditional cultural integration.

One side of the psychological stress of drastic change is cognitive. For the categories, ordering principles, and assumptions of one's world may in the space of a few years be turned upside down. The New Guinea tribesman whose inkblot responses were our starting point may in a decade have gone from his tribe's traditional model of the cosmos—populated by ghosts and spirits and controlled by magic—through a series of radical shifts. A Fundamentalist missionary may have persuaded him that in the Book of Genesis and what follows lies the source of the white man's power. Within five more years he is voting for a representative in the House of Assembly, is co-owner of a truck, and has heard about men's landing on a moon that ten years earlier he had regarded as a totemic spirit. How men can cope with such chaotic cognitive shifts without blowing their minds remains a mystery. Sometimes they do not: we will see in §64 the millenial movements that represent a kind of organized and collective mind-blowing under such stress. Even the apparent success of some individuals in mastering two cultures and operating separately in each is achieved at great psychological cost. Americans, faced with a staggering pace of change that humans are ill-equipped to cope with, are not doing that well either.

The problems can usefully be conceptually sorted out. First, cultural codes that once applied neatly to the situations of life may simply not fit new situations. Thus principles of sharing with one's relatives may hopelessly confound any efforts at operating a business. Second, crucial cultural principles that underlay and supported specific beliefs and practices may be pulled out, like the bottom can in a supermarket display. Imagine the impact on the world view and life of a devout Fundamentalist missionary if he decided the Bible was a work of man and not God. Third, an individual may have to live in two cultural worlds or to enact an alien way of life that does not fit his values and ideas. One might imagine what would happen if a Tibetan monk were plunked down in a Madison Avenue advertising agency, and the advertising executive were deposited in the monastery (. . . and that was the end of the monk . . . or perhaps the monastery). Yet peoples all over the world have found themselves caught up in shifts of this magnitude in a twentieth century of runaway change.

Anthropologists used to say with some confidence that a drastic shift in an ideational system would require a generation or two. It was a truism of missionary work that only the children or grandchildren of the first converts could fully acquire a new world view. But humans on all frontiers are being forced either to shift their ideational systems radically and quickly or to live in a thought-world that no longer fits the way their world is. From a society where parents enculturate their children we are moving into a reverse spiral where children must "reculturate" their parents:

> We are going to be fashioning children who are going to be different from any human beings who have ever been—from whom we are going to have to be able to learn things that we could not otherwise know. Although there have been premonitions of it in the past, this is going to be a totally new model of human experience (Mead, 1968: 380).

The "generation gap" of modern Americans partly reflects the cycling continuity ancient in human experience; but it is also a rending of the fabric of social continuity by the first cutting edges of this new mechanism.

As more and more peoples become caught up in Westernization, and the "rewards" of "economic development" become universal aspirations, they react to this challenge in sharply contrasting ways. Some peoples become successful entrepreneurs, technicians, and politicians with an apparent minimum of stress and disorientation. Others cling to traditional ways and values; and when they do change, it may be at great psychological cost or may entail radical cognitive reorganization.

Two comparative explorations of this problem—which clearly has something to do with the fit between the old and the new—will illustrate the lines of recent research.

Example 66: Culture, Personality, and Change in Nigeria

LeVine, in his book Dreams and Deeds *(1966), examines the three major ethnic groups of Nigeria, the Yoruba, Hausa, and Ibo. The Yoruba have long been urbane and Westernized, and have been prominent in the British administration and business world. The Hausa, who are Muslims, remained tightly knit and conservative. The Ibo intruded with great success into the professional and business world fairly recently. LeVine compared the traditional values and social structure of the three peoples, particularly in terms*

*of their congruence with "achievement motivation." The high achievement
motivation of the Ibo, as measured by psychological testing, fits neatly with
inferences about traditional cultural patterns and helps to account for the
Ibo penetration of Nigerian elites that culminated in bitter civil war and
the human tragedy of Biafra.*

Rich evidence on how the traditional culture shapes responses to change
and their psychological consequences comes from the Spindlers' work among
Menomini and Blood Indians (G. D. Spindler, 1955; L. S. Spindler, 1962).

Example 67:   The Menomini and Blood Indians

*The Spindlers used Rorschach tests and their own culture-specific
testing methods to probe the personality of Menomini Indians in Wisconsin.
They divided the Menomini into five categories, ranging from the very
conservative native-oriented to those who had fully adopted white middle-
class culture. They found that Menomini in each category had a distinctive
personality pattern. The native-oriented groups show a psychological pattern
congruent with the restraint and control, and dependence on supernatural
power appropriate to the old Menomini way of life: inward-orientation,
fatalism, lack of overt emotional responsiveness. Those Indians who have
adopted white ways have achieved a reorganization of personality congruent
with the success orientation, competitiveness, and punctuality their jobs
demand of them—though not without costs of anxiety. The transitional group
in the middle of the continuum of change show cognitive disorganization
and its social expression:*

> *Some are striving for an orderly way of life, toward goals recognizable
> in the surrounding non-Indian community; others are withdrawn and mostly
> just vegetate; others go on destructive rampages, during or between drunks
> . . . Like human populations everywhere who have lost their way . . . for
> them neither the goals of the traditional or the new culture are meaningful
> (G. D. Spindler, 1968: 329).*

*The Blood Indians of Canada show marked and significant contrasts.
Like the Menomini, they represent a continuum in their adoption of the
dominant culture and in their standard of living. Yet the bulk have adopted
many white ways without abandoning their identity as Indians. Most still
speak their own language and retain many Indian customs and beliefs.
Beneath the spectrum of differences between modern Blood in socioeconomic
status, the Spindlers found a continuum in underlying culture. Much less
psychological reorganization seems to have occurred than among the Menomini in adaptation to changed ways of life. Apparently traditional Blood
culture and the cognitive and emotional organization it fostered were congruent with the alien culture and new alternatives in a way Menomini
patterns were not. The aggressive, competitive, acquisitive way of life of
the Blood as hunters of the plains apparently fit sufficiently neatly the
modes of life and livelihood whites introduced to the Alberta plains—
especially cattle ranching—that the Blood could adopt new ways without*

fully abandoning old ones, and without a radical shift of psychological integration.

Our understanding of how and why different peoples react in markedly contrasting ways to the impact of the West—and particularly the psychological consequences of radical social change—remains highly inadequate. This reflects both the great gaps in our knowledge of social, cultural, and psychological process and the extreme complexity of the problems. Yet as change accelerates and psychological costs mount, we cannot wait to ask such questions until we acquire the means to answer them fully. We will return to the psychological consequences of change shortly.

XVII *Stability and Change*

IF WE OBSERVE behavior patterns in any community over time, we can see that they change. New events occur, and established behaviors change in observed frequency. Furthermore, the *ideas* of a community's members gradually change. As we know, not every individual has the same mental mapping of the group and its culture; so that change does not simply mean a changing of people's minds collectively, but rather a shift in the *distribution* of ideas within a population.

Anthropologists developed their concepts and theories through study of primitive peoples who, according to popular stereotypes, had retained the same way of life "since time immemorial." And with no written records, no systematic archaeological record of the past, and a seemingly overwhelming force of tradition, these peoples seemed to early anthropologists to be relatively unchanging.

But the same tides that were carrying ethnographers and missionary scholars to far shores were washing over those shores with the seas of change. Old patterns were swept away or carved into different forms, while at the same time native peoples often preserved values and customs remarkably intact in the face of the pressures from the storms of change.

Anthropologists, standing amid these swirling tides, could not ignore them. Trying to reconstruct the shape of things in the old days could not satisfy for long the theoretical and practical challenge of understanding what was happening. Anthropology has become, of necessity, a study of change as well as of stability; and in the process, and through an enriched archaeological record, we have realized how the drifts of change had washed through primitive communities long before white men arrived.

63 · *Anthropological Perspectives on Stability and Change*

The history of anthropological theories of cultural development and change—nineteenth-century evolutionism, diffusionism, and other "schools" of thought—is set out in the next section. We have already touched upon change at many points. In Chapter V, we examined long-term perspectives on the development of culture. In Chapter VII, we looked at how ecological adaptation may shape cultural change and viewed some major modern theoretical positions. At the end of the three chapters on social organization, we looked at theories of how and why change takes place in this realm. In examining economic systems, political processes, and social control, we encountered change as well as stability, the breakdown of traditional rules as well as their enactment.

Anthropologists concerned with cultural dynamics have operated with a kind of split vision. In one direction they have looked at the primitive world before Europeans entered the scene. In the other direction they have viewed the cultural changes set off by the massive intrusion of Western ways of life. To build theoretical models of culture change, however, it has been necessary to view the impact of the West on tribal societies as a special form of a more general phenomenon—*acculturation*, or the prolonged and large-scale contact of peoples whose ways of life are distinct. Acculturation had been going on long before Europeans arrived, as with the surge of Bantu-speaking peoples across the southern half of Africa and the spread of the Mongols into India and China. Here we will set out, first, some modern perspectives on the nature of internal change in a society. Then we will glimpse some guidelines for analyzing the tremendous range of processes and forms generated in acculturation situations. In the sections that follow, we will look in greater detail at that most drastic and critical force of change, the expansion of the West to the farthest corners of the globe; and at the possibilities of applying anthropological knowledge to guide and channel change and lessen its disruptive effects.

Internal Social Change

Looking back at primitive peoples before the white man's massive intrusion on the scene, anthropologists could approach questions of change in terms of two sharply contrasting time scales. In the longer scale of man's time on earth, and even of the last ten thousand years, his ways of life have changed and diversified profoundly. The isolated, diverse tribal peoples of the "ethnographic present"—that hypothetical time line when Europeans first arrived—must thus represent the products of such differentiation and development. Yet these societies seemed in the light of older theory to be relatively unchanging, stable, and self-contained. We might compare two views of biological evolution: in the first, we look at it in terms of the vast spans of geological time, of lines of evolutionary development and the ascendancy of new orders of life; in the second, we focus on the present and see the apparent distinctness and stability of each species. Anthropological theories of development and change, like studies of biological microevolution, have had to relate long-range development, continuity and diversification to the apparent stability and separateness we observe. To relate long-run major changes with apparent short-run stability, anthropologists have looked for mechanisms whereby ongoing minor changes would cumulatively produce major ones (compare the biologist's theories of mutation and natural selection). Older views of cultures in isolation as almost wholly static are clearly inadequate. They admitted an occasional "invention"; but as we have seen in §40, they attributed change and internal complexity to diffusion and even to large-scale "mixing" of different ways of life into a cultural layer cake.

More modern views have recognized that cultures are constantly changing. To the anthropologist studying a people over a short time span, strong "self-correcting mechanisms" make for the appearance of stability and duration: repetitive learning and habit formation, approximations of individual behavior around modes or patterns, the normative grip of premises, values, goals which integrate the way of life, conformity to rules and beliefs. Thus systems are described *as if* they are in equilibrium, though it is theoretically recognized that this ignores continuous minor changes that will cumulatively produce major ones.

Unfortunately, anthropologists' simplifying assumptions about equilibrium, about the uniformity of custom and belief, and about the closed borders of the tribe they happen to be studying, have tended to obscure the *processes* of change we need to understand. It will be useful, in understanding both the relatively isolated society and the one confronted by Western influence, to examine several newer perspectives on stability and change.

One we have already stressed is the distinction between *cultural* and *social* in the conceptualization of change. Culture as an ideational system comprises categories, recipes, and rules for dealing with experience. The social order involves not ideas but people and events. In one of the classic papers of modern social anthropology, Clifford Geertz underlines this contrast between cultural and social orders and illustrates how the gap between them can widen.

Example 68:   A Javanese Funeral

The Javanese town of Modjokuto in many respects still represents the peasant cultural traditions of rural Java, including a religious system that combines elements of Islam, Hinduism, and the older animistic beliefs. Essential here are communal feasts, slametan, *where at important stages in the life cycle members of neighborhood groups gather to make offerings to the spirits and to partake together of the ritual meal. Moslem prayers are part of the proceedings; and Moslem ritual has a particularly central place in the subdued procedure of a funeral, where the living bid leave of the social bonds broken by death.*

But in recent decades, political parties, religious fission, and other discordant elements of modern Indonesian life have torn the harmony of Modjokuto social life. Particularly important has been a split between Masjumi and Permai factions. The Masjumi comprise a national party, militantly Moslem, which presses for a purified form of Islam as the state religion. The Permai party strong in Modjokuto would emphasize the "traditional" Hindu and animistic rites and, being vocally anti-Moslem, would eliminate Islamic prayer and ritual in such affairs as marriage and funerals.

This split precipitated a crisis in Modjokuto when a ten-year-old boy, nephew of a Permai man, died. The Modin, an Islamic religious official responsible for conducting funerals, was summoned. But acting on bureaucratic instructions, he refused to conduct the funeral for the dead boy, claiming that the Permai should—since they object to Islamic funerals—conduct their own.

The result was a stalemate in which the two factions sat immobilized around a dead boy who had to be buried quickly to set his increasingly dangerous spirit at rest. The Permai could come up with no rites of burial themselves, the Masjumi hovered about, and the Modin remained absent. The ritual washing of the corpse, the quiet and orderly procedure culminating in a slametan *reaffirming the unity of the community in the face of death, were still not performed. Finally a Masjumi man friendly with the Permai involved tried to conduct the essential rites. In the midst of all this, the grief the normal funeral rites keep under control burst forth.*

Finally the dead boy's parents arrived from the city. Being less committed religiously, the father authorized the Modin to carry on in the Moslem fashion—though not before the mother had expressed a grief that would normally have remained beneath the surface. By the time the funeral slametan *had been performed, the unity it was intended to affirm had been badly and publicly torn (Geertz, 1957).*

How can we understand the boy's funeral? By seeing as separate, though interdependent, the cultural structure and patterns of social organization we can then perceive how the two had been pulling apart in modern rural Java. The crisis of the funeral reflected "an incongruity between the cultural framework of meaning and the patterning of social interaction." The religious system and skein of ritual procedure appropriate to an older peasant way of life could not sustain and express the changed social relations of an urban setting (Geertz, 1957).

An adequate theory of social and cultural change must view these orders as in a double-sided relationship: changes in the pattern of events, situations, and social arrangements lead to readjustments of the ideational system; yet the ideational system itself is being endlessly tinkered with, leading to shifts in social patterns.

Other new perspectives have come from seeing the "self-contained,

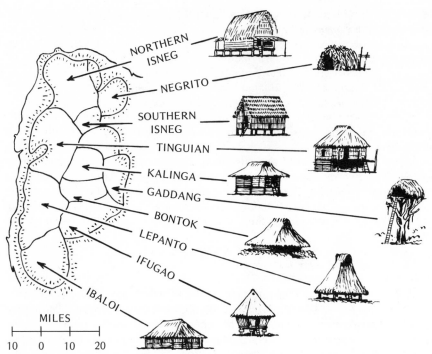

Figure 45. House Styles as Marks of Tribal Distinctiveness. The Negrito and Gaddang houses reflect distinctive modes of subsistence and technology. The rest represent variations on a common pattern, styles that help to mark the distinctiveness of each language group. FMK

homogeneous, stable" primitive tribe in a new light. Let us look first at the boundaries of the tribe, its "self-contained isolation." Peoples speaking different (though often related) languages, living in the same region, symbolically underline the distinctiveness of their ways of life. Thus in Northern Luzon, in the Philippines, the different mountain peoples show visible contrasts in such patterns as dress, hairstyle, and house style. Yet one can now perceive how such marks of cultural distinctiveness, and the style of fieldwork that takes an anthropologist into a single tribe or community, have led him to miss or understimate the ties that link neighboring peoples into wider systems. The *kula* ring of Melanesia, uniting Trobriand Islanders, Dobuans, and many others into a system of trade and ritual exchange, is a dramatic example. Other parts of the primitive world were similarly tied into wider systems by networks of trade, intermarriage, and the flow of ideas.

The openness of societal boundaries, the awareness of what neighboring peoples thought and how they lived, created avenues for social and cultural change that we had been prone to overlook. Older studies of "diffusion," while recognizing that the boundaries of societies were permeable, viewed the spread of elements in overly mechanical fashion and failed to perceive how clusters of peoples were linked into *systems* through which ideas and material goods circulated. Without taking such systems into account, we often cannot make sense of the ritual, mythology, or even kinship and marriage systems of the people under study. Australian Aborigines, devotees of keeping up with the customs of the Joneses in neighboring tribes, are a vivid case in point.

Another insight concerns the uniformity of custom among a particular people. If we imagine a body of custom as something like the rules of a game, or the regulations of a legal code, we are likely to be misled. There would be an unambiguous rule for every situation; and for change in the culture to occur, a rule would have to be changed. If the change comes from inside, it is "innovation"; if it comes from outside, it is "diffusion." But this model distorts both the hierarchical structure of cultural knowledge and the diversity of individuals' versions of that knowledge.

A general ideal principle—such as, in the Trobriands, that things given should be reciprocated or that matrilineal kinsmen should help one another—applies to a great range of concrete situations. Yet how the principle is applied to a particular type of transaction or relationship in a particular situation may be subject to different interpretations. How soon the return should be, whether it is to be in kind or some other equivalence, whether the obligation remains despite the death of one party, whether kinship obligation overrides direct reciprocity in some case—all these may be redefined or reinterpreted without any major change of the principles of reciprocity and kinship. And since actual situations are endlessly variable, what may shift are not even the specific details of "rules," but simply which ones apply in what combinations in what instances.

Furthermore, not every individual has the same mental mapping of "the rules" of social life. Many of these rules are not verbalized, as we have seen, but are implicit. Individuals must learn them by watching and devising theories: "Trobriand culture" is not magically implanted in the heads of Trobriand children (the way the children are implanted by sub-clan ancestors). Each individual learns a partly unique version of his culture. Any society thus contains a *reservoir of diversity* in cultural codes. "The culture" includes sets of alternative and even contradictory principles and rules (recall Geertz's metaphor of the octopus of culture).

Thus change in a culture may involve not a change in "the rules," but a shift in the *distribution of versions of the code* with the society. The anthropologist who has canceled out code diversity to produce a single composite version of "the culture" may, by taking that abstraction too seriously, block his own vision of the changes taking place before his eyes. We can speculate that it is the reservoir of cultural diversity, of alternative ways that events and situations can be defined or responded to, that makes men's ways of life viable and adaptive in the face of shifting environmental pressures. We peculiar, high-powered primates have a remarkable ability both to make adaptive changes and to legitimize them according to our flexible symbolic codes.

The older approaches to changes in a way of life, stressing innovation and borrowing, are dated not because the facts were muddled but because the theoretical framework was inadequate. Diffusion too often was seen as a mechanical transfer, not a highly creative and exploratory reformulation. Whether elements were borrowed, and if so what new meanings they acquired in terms of the categories and values of the borrowing people, scarcely comes through in the older literature. (Kroeber's massive *Anthropology* [1948] remains a major and worthwhile examination of cultural process across the sweep of history, and can be explored with profit by the interested reader).

Innovation, too, in its older treatment, assumes man to be far too passive and tradition bound. The image of a native genius giving an "Aha!" and building a better birdtrap, instead of the kind used by his forefathers for countless generations, will no longer do. Innovation now looks very different, in the light of such new developments as modern linguistic theory. For rule-following is highly creative behavior, in which individuals generate new but "grammatical" responses to situations and events they have never encountered. We are all innovators, just as we are all followers of fashion. Man can no longer be viewed as passive agent in the processes of social life: he is designer and weaver, as well as user, of the fabric of culture.

Acculturation

A different order of social and cultural change comes into play when massive contact between peoples occurs. Such contact, of course, was going on under the nose of the early field anthropologist; but he was slow to recognize it as posing scientific problems and not simply as creating administrative and moral dilemmas and disrupting his data.

Such massive culture change, usually termed *acculturation*, was first legitimized as a central theoretical challenge to anthropology in 1936 by a committee of the Social Science Research Council, consisting of leading theorists Redfield, Linton, and Herskovits. They distinguished acculturation as

> those phenomena which result when groups of individuals having different cultures come into continuous firsthand contact, with subsequent changes in the original culture patterns of either or both groups (Redfield et al., 1936).

Acculturation involves direct and usually prolonged contact, and a cumulative process of culture transfer and reformulation.

Though the practical and theoretical challenge of understanding the impact of Western ways of life on tribal and other non-Western peoples has been paramount, anthropologists have sought to devise a wider framework within which acculturation processes in other times and places can be understood as well.

The same theoretical cutting edges that were useful in separating the tangled phenomena of internal change help to penetrate the greater tangles produced in acculturation. First of all, it is crucial to distinguish again between change in an ideational system—*culture change*—and changes in the material circumstances of life. As Geertz has warned us, they do not change in the same ways, or at the same pace. Recall the effects of money on the Tiv economy (Ex. 41). The Tiv are being caught up in a vast system of interconnected events and things, including money, that is changing what they do, what they have, and what they can choose. These new circumstances of life are very difficult for the Tiv to fit into their conceptual scheme. When a Tiv man bemoans the fact that he now has to "sell" his daughter in marriage, hence to trade down from the most valued exchange category to the least valued—we cannot simply talk about "culture change." The change in Tiv culture is of a different order than the changes in Tiv social life and economic circumstances; and that is part of the problem.

Then we have seen that diversity in cultural codes makes change in an ongoing society hard to understand—especially if we cancel out diversity to produce an idealized description of "the culture." In a society undergoing acculturative change, diversity increases so much that no composite is even possible. Among the modern Tiv one could find government officials with radios and bicycles, conservative elders, young men employed as enterpreneurs, Christian evangelists, and leftist politicians. A single idealized picture of changing "Tiv Culture" clearly will not do—it is changing in all directions for different people. This code diversity has forced many students of change to focus on changes in the patterns of events and the structure of groups, rather than on shifts in ideational systems. In no area of anthropology is the need for an ideational model that builds on code diversity, rather than canceling it out in favor of common denominators, more badly needed.

Finally, the complex internal structure of cultural conceptions, rules, values, and strategies is important in understanding acculturative change. Again and again in acculturative confrontations, peoples change dramatically in some respects and remain remarkably unchanged in other respects. It is possible to summarize and generalize about what elements of a way of life change rapidly and easily, and what elements are relatively impervious to change. F. M. Keesing's *Cultural Anthropology* (1958), on which this book builds, attempted such a formulation. He saw the following areas of a culture as likely to be particularly stable and persistent—"or, if they are disturbed voluntarily or by force, . . . to involve most serious stress and disorganization":

1. Essentials of early constitutional conditioning (fundamental . . . body training habits such as digesting, evacuating, sleeping . . .).
2. Essentials of organic maintenance (materials, techniques, and ideas which a people count vital to their physical survival . . .).

3. Essentials of communication.
4. Essentials of primary group relations or societal security.
5. Essentials for the maintenance of high-prestige status.
6. Essentials of territorial security.
7. Essentials of ideological security (basic intellectual and religious assumptions and interpretations . . .).

He contrasted these to the areas of a culture where change tends to be rapid and achieved with minimal description:

1. Instrumental techniques (means of achieving values and goals . . .).
2. Elements of taste and self-expression.
3. Secondary group relations.
4. Low-status positions.

Though revealing, such a summary must remain relatively general because the organization and integration of cultural knowledge is still largely hidden. To speak metaphorically of what is "deep" or "shallow," as has often been done in the preceding chapters, expresses the general hierarchical mode of organization that seems very likely (though not certain). But until that structure is better explored, we must be cautious about using "deepness" to explain anything. Change in ideational systems entails replacement of content, changes in organization, and changes in basic premises and values; it entails changes in principles and changes in the ways they are applied. Exploring these processes of change is a major challenge to anthropology.

How cultural patterns can persist despite marked outward changes in a people's mode of life is vividly revealed by events of the last century on Tanna Island in the New Hebrides. The Melanesian inhabitants had been decimated in mid-nineteenth century by the brutal "blackbirding" labor trade to Australia, by European attacks, and by introduced diseases. By the early twentieth century, observers reported that the traditional culture had disappeared and that the remnant population was fully Christianized and rapidly adopting European ways. Yet in 1940, the "John Frum" movement, an anti-European cult led by a human manifestation of the ancient spirit of Karaperamun, sprang forth. Old patterns suppressed by the theocratic Presbyterian Church for half a century—polygyny, dancing, kava drinking—suddenly reappeared full-blown. It appears that the cultural structure on which these customs rested had been there all along.

An important dimension of the acculturation process is *congruence* between the two cultural systems involved. Without a better model of cultural structure than we have, it is again hard to be more than metaphorical. But if two ideational systems share certain common premises and values, or can be fitted together, a creative synthesis between them may be possible that otherwise would not. The rapid success of missionaries in some areas and decades of failure in others must reflect not the diligence and zeal of the ideological salesmen, but the salability of their product. Whether Christian belief can be fitted into a people's conceptual world without completely rebuilding it is clearly a crucial variable. Peoples like the Minangkabau of Sumatra and the Tolai of Melanesia have become cultural "middlemen" who far outstrip their neighbors in adapting elements of Western culture and shaping them to their own ends. They doubtless have exploited strategic locations and opportunities; but they have also built on congruences in value and strategy between the new and the old. The difficulty of some hunting and gathering peoples, notably Australian Aborigines (see Ex. 69), to bridge the cultural gap that acculturation demands of them apparently reflects a great gulf in world view and ideology, as well as in technology.

The possibility of creatively synthesizing a traditional model of the world and a new one come out vividly in studies of Mesoamerican Indians. An anthropologist was recently studying a Mayan Indian community that had been converted to Catholicism in the early Spanish conquest period. He joined the Indians after a Christmas Mass in filing past the nativity scene in the church. When he looked into the creche he was jolted to see—Twins!

The modern worship of the Virgin of Guadalupe in Mexico draws heavily on the pre-Spanish worship of an Aztec deity, even to the modes of worship and the sites of churches. South Asia, with its creative syntheses of great religious traditions and local belief systems—such as the deep involvement of rural Sinhalese Buddhists with local cults and beliefs in "goblins"—provides other striking illustrations of cultural synthesis. We are beginning to understand the structure of such ideational systems, through sophisticated modern explorations of belief and ritual action.

Again the reason for distinguishing "culture," as an ideational system, from social and ecological systems is not to examine ideational worlds by themselves. Though for some purposes that may be enough, it does not suffice for understanding change or real people facing real problems and alternatives. The challenge is to see how ideational world, ecosystem, and social process interact in wider systems. Consider the market economy in a Nigerian city. Within the physical setting of a marketplace, transactions interlink Tiv traders with Hausa, Ibo, Yoruba, and members of many other tribal groups, plus Europeans, Arabs, Indians, and others. Each has highly variable versions of different cultural traditions. These cultural patterns shape decision making and value commitments, and they affect the flow of goods into the market system from rural areas (so that large-scale Tiv refusal to sell foodstuffs or grow beniseed on cultural principle might make a slight ripple in the market). But the patterns of decision and the flow of goods and money depend on a wider market *system* very few participants begin to understand. A change in the world market price of cocoa due to events in Asia, Latin America, or the Pacific may have effects in many corners of Nigeria. How such changes in wider systems are conceptually managed by the Tiv is important for understanding events in Tivland. But what we need are better ways of seeing how conceptual systems and event systems interact as larger systems; and how these larger systems are subsystems of subsystems of systems.

Studies of acculturation are beginning to move beyond general type-characterizations of two cultures as "assimilating," "fusing," and so on. The processes we are dealing with are much more complex than that. We badly need more sophisticated ways for studying what changes and what remains the same, for thinking about sameness and differentness, for seeing the interaction between the cultural and the social, for seeing how subsystems form wider systems. If anthropologists try in the less complicated settings of jungle hamlets or peasant villages to analyze how the different facets of life fit together, it is partly in the hope that the vastly complex and fragmented facets of life men struggle to cope with in towns, cities, and world capitals can be understood more clearly, and perhaps placed in new order.

64 · The Impact of the West

For several centuries, non-Western peoples have been shaken, and their social institutions overturned, by the massive force of European domination. Colonialist economic exploitation has been accompanied by a more subtle social and cultural aggression: missionaries, suppression of customs, condescension for the "natives," and their relegation to menial roles as servants of a white aristocracy. In the latter twentieth century, the hatred spawned by his forebears has been turned back on Western man. In a world of new nations, violent hostility to colonialism and what it has come to symbolize, and new power from the East, the ascendancy of the West is in dire jeopardy.

Only in recent years have new perspectives on this cycle and Western man's place in it began to penetrate our smug defenses. The ludicrousness of the notion that Columbus—and not paleo-Indians—"discovered America" is beginning to dawn. Some are beginning to perceive how our history books focus on the smelly and disease-ridden little towns of medieval Europe for a thousand years when the light of learning and civilization burned brightly elsewhere in the great cities of the Arab world, India, and China (and Europe was too unimportant a barbarian peninsula to bother about). Yet the ethnocentrism and Eurocentrism of the days of smug colonialism continue to grip us.

Nor do we, or most of the "underdeveloped nations" of the world, realize the continuing cultural aggression in our exported worship of technology, science, comfort, and hardware. Few African or Asian leaders in quest of a "higher standard of living" reflect that it is our standard, not theirs. Nor do many of them realize that the human costs can be as staggering as the material rewards. When one African leader chides another for not following Roberts' *Rules of Order*, neither is likely to see an element of absurdity.

The cycle of cultural aggression has not yet run its full course. We can begin to examine it by surveying the initial impact of Western ways and domination on primitive man. Here we can only select for illustration a few cases that illustrate important features.

Even among a hunting and gathering people living in an area too marginal for Europeans to intrude in numbers, change can be indirect yet devastating.

Example 69:   Steel Axes for Stone Age Australians

The Yir-Yoront of remote northern Australia, though they had some early and bloody encounters with Europeans, preserved their aboriginal culture largely intact until the 1930s. In 1915 a mission station was established three days away from the heart of their territory, and the first important influences of European civilization began to be felt.

The most important tool for the Yir-Yoront was a polished stone axe. Technologically, it was used for a great many operations crucial in their physical adaptation. But it had an equally central role in the social and symbolic organization. First, stone axes were scarce and owned only by senior men. Women and children had to borrow axes from their immediate male kin to perform their assigned labors. The axe constituted a crucial symbol of masculinity and the male realm, as the only exclusively male item women had to use. All dyadic (two-person) relations among the Yir-Yoront defined one person as senior and the other as junior or subordinate: and the axe helped to express this asymmetry. Second, the axe heads had to be obtained from quarries 400 miles to the south, from which they were traded by networks of trade partners, in exchange for stingray barb spears. At annual ceremonial gatherings, this trade was conducted, providing what was a high point of Yir-Yoront interest. Third, the axes had an important place in the totemic cosmology of the Yir-Yoront. Every element in the traditional way of life had a defined and mythologically validated place in the scheme of things, an association with a patrilineal clan and its ancestors. The axe was, symbolically, the sacred possession of one clan.

The missionaries had set up their station in part to protect the Aborigines from destructive outside influences. They carefully made available only those things they deemed would materially improve the Yir-Yoront standard of living and open the way for a spiritually enriched life. Most importantly these included short-handled steel axes, which the missionaries gave away in quantities and made widely available. The intent was to improve Yir-Yoront technology in a major way, hence freeing time for more important things.

But the result of the steel axes, and other new items, was far more drastic than the missionaries anticipated. The changes were not mainly in the technological realm, where the steel axe did not have the profound advantages the suppliers expected. Lauriston Sharp, who studied the Yir-Yoront, wryly notes that it may have increased their time spent sleeping.

But in other realms, the steel axe had profound and disruptive consequences. Women and young boys acquired axes of their own, as they be-

came plentiful. This led to a "revolutionary confusion" of the rules of sex, age, and subordination. The axe as a symbol of the male realm was destroyed. Trading partnerships and the annual tribal gatherings dwindled in interest and importance, as the need for stone axe heads disappeared. Moreover, the steel axes and other European items—with no defined place in the cosmological scheme that defined the present as a precipitate of the ancestral past—became central points in the breakdown of traditional beliefs and values.

> The steel axe . . . has no distinctive origin myth, nor are mythical ancestors associated with it. Can anyone, sitting in the shade of a ti tree one afternoon, create a myth to resolve this confusion? No one has, and the horrid suspicion arises as to the authenticity of the origin myths, which failed to take into account this vast new universe of the white man. The steel axe . . . is not only replacing the stone axe physically, but is hacking at the supports of the entire cultural system (Sharp, 1952).

> When such supports have fallen, as in most Australian aboriginal groups, the results have often been a devastating apathy in which "native behavior and native sentiments are simply dead."

Encountering many hunting and gathering peoples living in desirable or accessible areas, Europeans rose to the challenge by more or less systematically exterminating them. Thus Tasmanian Aborigines, some American Indian groups, and others around the frontiers of Western expansion were hunted out ("a good Indian is a dead Indian") or killed off by accidentally or intentionally spreading new diseases. Those who survived were relocated in barren areas of no economic interest to the whites (and sometimes not able to support human habitation).

When tribal groups were more isolated or politically organized (or when contact came later, when ideologies of colonial administration were more benevolent), the groups often maintained their identity; the impact of the West hit on a smaller scale and more selectively. There were always missionaries to convince a people that the foundations of their belief system were wicked and deplorable. But once clothed in Mother Hubbards, the childlike savages were allowed to carry on whatever customs did not offend the missionary.

Colonial administrations varied in their treatment of tribal peoples, from ruthless suppression to paternalistic protectionism and sympathy to local custom. Protection against excesses of exploitation has been a theme of the modern colonial period. Thus a British administration in the Trobriand Islands prohibited diving for pearl shell by any outsiders; isolated peoples have sometimes been quarantined as best possible from the spread of Western diseases; and an effort has often been made to respect "local custom" where feasible. Such benevolent (if often condescending) colonial government replaced older and more ruthless styles in many areas in later decades, as ideologies changed and social conscience became focused on the morality of colonialism. The "White Man's Burden" became heavier as the costs of leading a colonial people toward and through self-government came to outweigh the profits flowing back to the colonizing nation. Yet the cynic can find much evidence that even now, when the stakes are sufficiently high, native peoples who stand in the way of dam, uranium, copper, or airfield will be brushed aside as efficiently as ever.

Even where official policy has been relatively enlightened, putting it into practice on a local level has often led to disastrous cross-cultural breakdowns in communication and understanding. The reader who has traced in the preceding pages the labyrinths of custom and belief in the Trobriand Islands can appreciate the confusions a well-meaning government administrator there could fall into. *Urigubu* payments, matrilineal descent, plural marriage, the *kula*, the dogma of procreation—all these could lead an Englishman applying his "common sense" into disastrous misunderstandings. Thus Malinowski writes of the Resident Magistrate who, in land disputes, "adopted a method natural to the European but fatal in a matrilineal community. He would inquire whose father had cut the disputed plot in olden days, a question which, under maternal descent, was beside the point and usually admitted of no answer, since the fathers of both litigants probably belonged to other communities" (1935, I: 103).

Breakdowns in cross-cultural communication were often more spectacular and tragic. A classic case of misunderstanding illustrates a second point as well—how, when the people confronted with colonization were numerous and politically and militarily organized enough, they could put up a dramatic struggle against Western domination (the Zulu and Maori wars are other classic struggles against conquest).

Example 70: The Golden Stool of Ashanti

The most sacred symbol of the great Ashanti Kingdom of West Africa was the Golden Stool. It had been introduced to the Ashanti by a celebrated magician, who had proclaimed that it contained the sunsum *or "soul" of the Ashanti people. He warned that "with it was bound up their power, their honour, their welfare, and that if ever it were captured or destroyed the nation would perish" (E. W. Smith, 1926). The Stool was never sat upon, never allowed to touch the ground; only on great occasions was its sacred power invoked by the Ashanti King.*

In 1910, the British Governor made a series of demands to the leaders of the Ashanti he had summoned to the fort of Kumasi, to which they had come "outwardly submissive, but inwardly boiling over with indignation" (E. W. Smith, 1926: 5). His speech stands out as a gem of colonialist history:

> *Now Kings and Chiefs . . . what must I do to the man, whoever he is, who has failed to give to the Queen [of England], who is the paramount power in this country, the Stool to which she is entitled? Where is the Golden Stool? Why am I not sitting on the Golden Stool at this moment? . . . (Rattray, 1923).*

*The Governor, of course, thought the Golden Stool was an "appurtenance
of the kingly office," and expected that this symbol of his authority should
be given, like the Stone of Scone, to the English monarch.*

*Within a week the Ashanti nation was at war with England. Perhaps
Governor Hodgson suspected his mistake when he and his forces were
subsequently besieged at Kumasi by tens of thousands of Ashanti warriors.*

However oppressive or well-meaning colonial administrations, missionaries, and others have been, they have made one thing uniformly clear
to the colonized peoples: European superiority. "The native" was a creature
apart, removed by his skin color, his cultural backwardness and ignorance,
and the other unfortunate circumstances of his birth, from the grace open
to Europeans. The symbolic relegation of "the native" to a position midway
between animal and Western man was made clear on every side. Some might
after several generations trickle in to the centers of Western learning: Oxford
and Cambridge, Paris, Leiden, Harvard. They learned to be lawyers or
doctors, and perhaps ultimately Prime Ministers. But the stigma of their
birth symbolically remained, even as they were trained to rise above and
reject their traditional ways of life.

We are only now beginning to realize what explosive forces are generated
when ideologies of superiority and inferiority are superimposed on a people,
and their view of themselves and their way of life is shattered. Even if the
material circumstances of their lives have not changed noticeably, a people
no longer live in the same world—a world with themselves in the center.

Whatever course they take—despair, revolt, messianic escapism, resignation, aspiration to the dominant culture—they set in motion forces that are
seething beyond control through the modern world. One of the struggles
of emerging African and Asian and Latin American nations is not simply
to unify culturally diverse peoples but also to forge a new self-identity and
self-respect, to rejoin the broken pieces of self-images shattered by subordination. The quest for symbols of a new identity, the change of valence
from shame to pride, the search for historical roots, the surging new power
and rage, express the emergence of new cultural unities out of the ruins
left by European expansion.

Some social scientists have argued that to interpret social changes
such as millenial movements or nationalist movements in terms of psychological factors (like "self-conception") is inadmissible. One cannot explain
"social facts" by individual psychology. Thus such scholars seek to find
economic or sociological explanations of these movements.

But that misses the point. American Negroes, Latin American peasants,
Africans, and Melanesian tribesmen have not generated sweeping social movements when they have been most exploited, when their economic, social, and
political status was most dismal. The movements have come, by and large,
when things have improved materially; but also, when communication has in-

creased markedly within the subordinate group. And it has been the crystallization of a *collective self-identity* that has opened the way for dramatic movements of change. What is needed is for people to perceive their own way
of life in a new perspective (relative to the dominant group's, or some conception of what is possible)—usually with one or more leaders providing
the ideology and charismatic force. However carefully we probe economic
and sociological factors, dramatic transformations of social life cannot be
anticipated or understood if we overlook the cultural and symbolic elements
in the chemistry of change, and the individuals who act as catalysts.

Dramatic examples of the perception of one's way of life relative to
that of a dominant group come from the "millenial movements" on many
frontiers of Western contact. Most dramatic and intensively studied are
the "Cargo Cults" of New Guinea and neighboring areas of Melanesia. Here
we will examine two of them—one early and clearly oriented toward a
mystical and "irrational" millenium; the second more recent and oriented
toward a much more sophisticated political vision of the millenium.

Example 71: The Vailala Madness

*As of 1919, the Elema of coastal New Guinea had experienced the
waves of European influence: missionary teachings, early experience as
plantation laborers, introduction of the few items of European hardware
the Elema could afford, and pacification.*

*In that year, a movement broke out among the Elema that for a time
set whole villages into collective "head he go round," a psychophysical
state reminiscent of the Dancing Mania of plague-ridden medieval Europe.
People lost control of their limbs, reeled drunkenly, and eventually lost
consciousness. Who formulated the ideology is not clear. Central in it was
a belief that the dead would return, bringing with them a fabulous cargo
of European material goods—knives, cloth, canned goods, axes, and so on.
Sacred bull-roarers and other ritual objects were destroyed in a wave
of iconoclasm, in communities where dramatic rituals and spectacular men's
houses had been focal points of life. The Elema abandoned normal gardening
projects and devoted their efforts to elaborate preparations for the return
of the dead (Williams, 1923).*

*Within a year most overt forms of the movement had subsided. When
Williams, the government anthropologist, returned in 1933, few traces of it
remained, though there were vague traditions that some of the prophecies
had come true.*

Example 72: Maasina Rule in the Solomon Islands

*The Solomon Islands were the scene of major World War II sea and
land battles. A volunteer Melanesian Labor Corps, mainly from Malaita
Island, worked with American troops. From their encounter with staggering
quantities of military hardware and American egalitarian ideologies, a*

Malaitan named Nori and a group of cohorts formulated a new doctrine. The different tribal peoples were to join together, united by a council of nine head chiefs, to negotiate their demands with the returning British administration (which they hoped might be replaced by Americans). Each tribal group was to organize into communal villages, structured in imitation of military units—with roll calls, chiefs to supervise communal labor, and drills with wooden rifles.

Maasina Rule, "The Rule of Brotherhood," was to unite the Solomon Islanders in the social, economic, and political millenium when they would be free and wealthy like the Americans—for which their new way of life was to prepare them. Malaitans refused to work on plantations, and staged large demonstrations in confrontation of the administration. The British jailed the nine head chiefs, but their places were filled again. Supernatural doctrines of the millenium and the imminent return of Americans swept the island; and as prophecies failed to materialize and old conflicts and ecological pressures welled up, the active movement subsided after about seven years of overt social ferment (Worsley, 1957, summarizes published evidence on "Marching Rule").

Another classic millenial movement in the tribal world is the Ghost Dance of western North America, this one particularly interesting because it sought the millenium in a return to the past, not transformation of the past into a new way.

Example 73:   The Ghost Dance

In 1869, a Paiute prophet named Wodziwob had religious visions which foretold the end of the existing world, the ousting of the whites, the return of dead relatives, and the restoration of Indian lands and integrity. These doctrines spread rapidly among Plains tribes whose ways of life had disintegrated under white pressure and the extermination of the buffalo. Though attempts at military resistance generated by cult doctrines were smashed, the cult spread widely and diversified into local versions. Then in 1890 a second Ghost Dance cult inspired by another Paiute prophet, Wovoka, spread eastward across the plains tribes and even to some eastern Woodlands tribes. Again the cult stressed return to traditional ways of life that had broken down. If the patterns of traditional culture were purified and restored, the vanishing buffalo would return, the dead ancestors would come back, and the Indians could drive out the whites with magical protection against the power of bullets (Mooney, 1896).

Interpretations of millenial movements have come not only from anthropologists but from psychologists, historians, sociologists, and students of comparative religion. The movements themselves can be sorted out along various dimensions: whether they reject the past or glorify it, whether the vision of the millenium is mystical or political, and so on.

Many writers have stressed exploitation, economic inequality, and

Figure 46. "Bulletproof" Ghost Shirt. This Arapaho (Plains American Indian) shirt was part of the magical equipment of Ghost Dance adherents, supposedly protecting them against the white man's guns. It is of leather, with both traditional Indian symbols and what appear to be Christian symbols (the cross). (After Mooney.) FMK

relative deprivation, a perceived gap between the desired and possible, between new aspirations and abilities to satisfy them. Anthropologists have been sensitive to cultural factors as well—congruences between new doctrines and old patterns of belief and magical explanation, relations between the role of cult prophet and traditional leader.

Economic and social conditions and cultural background set the stage for a millenial movement. But what is required as well, and has often been ignored by those wary of "psychological explanations," is a change and crystallization of a people's perception of themselves and their way of life. A tribal people in pre-European days simply took their view of the world and their patterns of custom for granted, as the proper way for the world and man to be. The white man's intrusion and dominance led a tribal people to perceive their culture as *a* way of life—not *the* way of life. And it was a way that no longer worked or satisfied new demands. Having come to view their culture as a "thing," they could reject it as having withheld wisdom, wealth, and power from them (as in Cargo Cults). Or they could glorify it as a state of grace from which they had fallen (as in the Ghost Dance). Such a resynthesis, a quest for new integration, requires a *doctrine*—and it is at this point that a prophet entering the scene, combining old and new symbols, can create a cultural "revitalization" (Wallace, 1956).

A world dramatically made small by air travel and worldwide communications, a world dominated by an advanced technology, poses problems of cultural conflict and social integration on a scale unmatched in human history. Since the early empires of Mesopotamia, countless ethnic minorities have been swallowed up in larger states. Their languages and customs were different; and hence the laws and customs of the dominant group could not easily be adopted by, or forced upon, them. How, then, could one reconcile social and political integration with cultural distinctiveness?

The problem is as old as written history. The "solutions"—suppression, assimilation, genocide, indirect rule, separatism—have seldom worked and have seldom been reconcilable with moral codes. In the latter twentieth century, this problem confronts man on a scale, and with a global danger, never faced before.

Throughout the world, peoples emerging from tribalism to "underdeveloped nationhood," and from "underdeveloped" to "developed," are seeking and demanding the material fruits of Western technology. For better or worse, Western "standards of living" are rapidly becoming universal aspirations. But what can this mean in cultural terms? To join into the world economy, and the community of nations, must people abandon their traditional world view, values, and conventions? In many segments of their lives, the question has become academic for formerly tribal peoples. For the impact of the West has broken down economic self-sufficiency, sent the young away from village settings and flocking to cities. Kinship groupings larger than the family have disintegrated or lost their functions. Old religions have been abandoned. Traditional leaders have been bypassed by Western-educated politicians. The old order—were there some compelling reason to preserve it—is gone beyond preservation. New levels of unity are being carved out that bind together formerly diverse tribal peoples.

Are non-Western peoples to lose their cultural distinctiveness? Does a standarization of legal treatment, education, and opportunity in a nation of diverse peoples necessarily mean a cultural uniformity? Must members of a minority group reject what is distinctive of their way of life to achieve equal opportunity? Men are stumbling toward answers, and meanwhile, killing and hating one another.

No modern nation has solved or managed without great costs and grave problems the paradox of reconciling cultural pluralism with political unity and internal order. Some have done better than others. The United States has incorporated fairly successfully large immigrant groups from East and West—with their adaptations ranging from rapid and enthusiastic assimilation to the cultural separatism of a Chinatown. Yet the dilemma of American blacks—to create a new cultural identity and achieve pride and dignity without isolating themselves from the economic and political mainstream—affords no easy answer. For Mexican Americans the dilemma is similar: how to preserve pride and cultural integrity without economic and social rejection.

That is not a singular dilemma. It faces men in Africa, Asia, Latin America, and the Pacific. Do the Kachins of Burma, who through centuries of invasion and political turmoil have preserved their cultural identity, lose it now as part of a modern nation? In the Philippines or India, with scores of local languages and distinct cultural traditions, can representative government and administrative flexibility preserve the integrity of these traditions? And at the same time, can the boundaries of each group be kept open enough that from them can emerge into the mainstream those who aspire to be doctors or politicians or physicists?

In one sense, cultural distinctiveness is an artifact of tribalism—and tribalism and its extension, nationalism, pose grave dangers of mass devastation in a nuclear age. Yet in another sense, the richness of cultural diversity is a crucial human resource. The canceling out of cultural differences and the emergence of a standardized world culture might—while solving some problems of political integration—deprive man of sources of wisdom and vision, and a reservoir of diversity and alternatives, he cannot afford to lose.

Such speculation quickly becomes futile. Yet if the answers are not yet clear, the problem confronts us on all sides. Whatever wisdom cultural anthropology has gleaned in its sweeping study of men's ways of life is wisdom about cultural diversity—its extent, its nature, its roots. And that wisdom, used wisely, can itself be a crucial human resource.

65 · *The Applications of Anthropology*

Can the anthropologist contribute centrally to these problems of cultural diversity, to making social and cultural change less disruptive?

At times anthropologists have had great surges of optimism about what they could tell governments and colonial administrators, or do themselves, to bridge cultural boundaries and make change more smooth or less costly in human terms. At other times the enormity and complexity of the problems and the inadequacies of their knowledge and theories have raised grave doubts and discouragement. The truth of what can and might be accomplished through "applied anthropology" lies somewhere between these poles of optimism and pessimism.

The optimism is generated by the fact that an anthropologist who has lived in a local community, who knows its leaders, its language, its details of custom, can very often see what is going wrong and how it might be set right. Many changes, procedures, laws, or policies that seem sensible enough to the administrator, the missionary, or the doctor, may lead to problems the anthropologist can foresee immediately. What would happen in the Trobriand Islands if a missionary converted the "chiefs" and prohibited plural marriages? What might happen in a society where bridewealth signifies a contract between corporate descent groups and defined rights over the children, if an administrator or missionary outlawed bridewealth payments as "degrading to women"? What might happen among a people who believe in the magical power of substances introduced into the body, or the possibility of sorcery using substances from the body, if a well-meaning doctor gives injections or takes blood samples? I vividly remember watching nervously (and wondering how to avert a massacre or at least be on the winning side) while a member of a visiting medical team took fingernail and hair clippings from Kwaio pagans in the Solomon Islands and put them in cellophane bags; six months earlier a medical missionary had been speared nearby.

Administering, converting, educating, or ministering to the health of a tribal or peasant people involves communication across cultural boundaries, in both directions. Misunderstandings run rampant on both sides, as messages in one cultural code are interpreted in terms of another. The anthropologist, specialist in the nature of cultural codes and conversant with each one, can often serve as "cultural interpreter" or anticipate what messages would be misread and why.

He also can often suggest creative syntheses between the cultural traditions of a people and the changed situations and demands of modern life. A constitution may be possible that recognizes and builds on the authority of traditional leaders rather than bypassing them. A business cooperative might be formed in which the pattern of rights and responsibilities is modeled on traditional corporate or work groups (such as the Trobriand sub-clan or gardening team). Schools might teach the traditions, arts, and skills of a people, instead of European history. Figure 47 illustrates such a synthesis, guided by an anthropologist, of traditional and new elements. Such enterprises can help to foster the pride and cultural identity so crucial to a people as they undergo sweeping changes.

Why, then, the pessimism? Basically, because anthropologists are no better than other social scientists in predicting and anticipating human behavior, in all its manifold complexity. When communication takes place between peoples, we are prone to view this as *two cultures interacting.* But cultures do not interact; warm-blooded individual human beings do, with all their idiosyncracies and unpredictability. An anthropologist might, for

Figure 47. Planned Culture Change: a Community Center in the Palau Islands. An experiment in urban rehabilitation following the destruction of the town of Koror in World War II. Built by the Palauans as a modified form of abai *or traditional community house, with financial aid from the South Pacific Commission, it was planned by anthropologist Homer Barnett. FMK*

example, persuade the government to build a well in the village he studied— and seemingly have anticipated and guarded against cultural misunderstandings. Yet the project might be rejected because political rivalry between two local leaders leads one to condemn the well, or because someone put a curse on it during a quarrel with his wife. Such turns of events are no more predictable in a village setting than they are in a modern nation.

There is another and related problem. When an anthropologist penetrates into another way of life, he does so in layers or stages. After several months of fieldwork, a researcher learns the formal rules and groupings that lie on the surface of a society and its culture. At this stage, he may feel a confidence and understanding that later evaporates into a feeling of ignorance as he penetrates to a deeper level. Such alternating stages of insight and impotence continue as he probes further. Those who have penetrated most deeply into another way of life are more often left with a feeling of how complex it is and how profound and unpredictable are the ramifications of any decision or event than they are with a feeling that all is known, that prediction is possible.

Yet too often attempts at applied anthropology have been made in the flush of superficial understanding. Particularly when administrators need answers, they are not likely to want to wait years. Too often the role of the anthropologist as consultant has taken him into an area just long enough for the formal outlines to come into focus, and not long enough for them to dissolve into a blur again. This premature feeling of confidence has also been fostered by the involvement of partially trained or inexperienced anthropologists. Saving the world by anthropology, as by any other means, looks easier to the idealistic neophyte than to the experienced and battle-scarred campaigner. The partial cultural understanding of Peace Corps volunteers may produce the same overoptimism about the scale of the problems and the effectiveness of the tools we command to solve them. Both sources of premature confidence have contributed to a disillusionment on the part of some governments and anthropologists as to what anthropology can contribute in guiding policy. In the United States administration of Micronesian islands, for instance, the possibilities of applied anthropology were "oversold" in the early stages, and a more sober reassessment has been necessary.

A final problem in applying anthropological knowledge to practical policy is that very often the choice is between a set of dismal alternatives. It is often not a question of which course of action will work best; but rather, which will work less badly than the others. A people whose old order is breaking down, yet who if they opt for Western ways will be condemned by geography and resources to a life of poverty and isolation, have no desirable alternatives. They are the victims of a world that has swept past them; they can neither fully join nor ignore it. In such situations, the satisfactions of applied anthropology are few and the successes are still failures.

The possibilities and difficulties of applying anthropological knowledge to particular problems are set out in a number of books, to which the interested reader might usefully turn: Leighton's *The Governing of Men* (1945); Spicer's *Human Problems in Technological Change* (1952); Mead's *Cultural Patterns and Technological Change* (1953); Barnett's *Anthropology in Administration* (1956); Arensberg and Niehoff's *Introducing Culture Change* (1964); Foster's *Traditional Cultures and the Impact of Technological Change* (1962); and Goodenough's *Cooperation in Change* (1963). Each of them discusses in detail particular cases and problems—and shows (with varying degrees of optimism and pessimism) what has and has not been possible. Spicer's book, for example, describes a series of efforts to introduce technological changes—some of which "worked" and some of which failed dismally. What an applied anthropology might contribute to the problems of our own society, as anthropologists increasingly focus on ourselves rather than remote tribesmen, can be glimpsed if we consider the situation of urban blacks in America.

Social scientists have studied in great detail the problems of black Americans and the roots of hostility and prejudice in both directions. They have looked at the economic plight, psychological state, and sociological condition of urban blacks. But as of the time of writing we understand far less clearly the *culture* of American ghettos. The image urban blacks have of themselves, their condition, and the white majority is rapidly changing and inadequately studied. We know a good deal about how the mother-centered family without a permanently attached father looks to sociologists on the outside; we know much less about how it looks from the inside.

Endless predictions have been made about what would or would not happen if earning power increased markedly in the ghetto, if training for new jobs and access to them were made possible. Yet it is far too often assumed that values and motives in the ghetto are the same as those in white suburbia. The benefits of eliminating exploitative white landlords are explored, but much too little is known by "experts" about the position of such figures in the symbolic system and political process of the ghetto. Black policemen might—for cultural reasons—cause more problems than they eliminate. And the Negro "leadership" visible to white planners and administrators may have little to do with the subtleties of political process within the ghetto community.

"Experts" on urban development and poverty have repeatedly created housing projects that were sterile and inhospitable; and welfare projects that caused alienation and eroded pride. Many of the problems reflect cultural differences: an architect who thinks the apartment he designs is much "nicer" than a tenement may be creating an environment that would turn a bustling and human community into a series of isolated cells. An act intended as friendly concern and humanitarian involvement may be interpreted as condescending charity or alien intrusion. The cultural and symbolic dimensions of black identity and aspirations are emerging as central but remain little understood.

If the anthropologist has a special contribution to make in the study of black or other American minorities, it is because he does not take for granted that his subjects share his code of meanings and premises. He is trained to expect what is different and distinctive—to discover the foundations on which he is to build, not assume them. He knows that ringing doorbells to administer questionnaires, and the "game" of answering them, are elements of white American culture. He is more likely to treat a single family, or a single tenement, or a single street corner (Liebow, 1967) as a microcosm of the whole—not to see how large a sample size he can build up to make his numbers valid. He would seek to penetrate a code from inside, not document it from outside.

Whether a white American anthropologist can gain rapport in such an enterprise raises another question. For there is in these days of increasing sensitivity on all cultural frontiers a strong element of condescension and possible insult in "being studied." Increasingly this feeling pervades the non-Western world as well as American minority groups. Having thrown out the "imperialists," a people emerging onto the world scene may be faced with hordes of visiting social scientists. The anthropologist can hardly be surprised if they come to view this as a new wave of imperialist exploitation and a threat to growing pride.

In the black revolution, there is a quite legitimate feeling that when white America sends its social scientists to the ghettos to "find out what is wrong with them," the same smug assumptions that helped Columbus (and not the Indians) discover America are at work again. What is "wrong" could not be in the hearts and minds of the nice respectable inhabitants of white suburbia: it must be in the ghettos. The anthropology of American suburbia, perhaps most wisely conducted by Trobriand Islanders or Tiv, has scarcely begun. But it is encouraging to note that at the University of Papua–New Guinea, as of 1970, there is a growing body of anthropological literature by Trobrianders and Dobuans concerning themselves and the anthropologists who studied them. With luck we may some day have a Trobriand anthropologist's diary of the rigors of fieldwork among the North American natives.

Anthropology will soon be a less provincial and Western-dominated field. Scholars from India, Japan, Indonesia, Africa, and Latin America are increasingly active. Until anthropology is more broadly represented by scholars from the non-Western world, anthropologists cannot shrug off too casually the doubts some of their colleagues have recently raised: that they too have been in the colonialist ranks, and that academic imperialism can be as insidious as other forms. We also badly need a broadening of perspective such scholars can give. Anthropology has had to rely far too heavily on stretching the premises, logics, and semantic categories of European experience to fit non-Western cultures. We urgently need some stretching of the assumptions and categories of other peoples to fit us and to fit the tribal peoples from whose cultures we have sought to learn about human diversity.

Example 74: A Chinese View of the Zuni

In 1935, a Chinese anthropologist, Li An-Che, spent three months living in a Zuni Indian household. The Zuni were anthropologically well documented by such observers as Stevenson and Bunzel. Yet after his brief immersion in Zuni life, Li was puzzled by the almost stereotyped view of their culture given by American anthropolgists.

Where the Americans had seen in Zuni religion an extreme preoccupation with formal detail, but a lack of emotional commitment, Li was impressed with the reverence and depth of feeling beneath outward formalism. Where Americans had been struck by the lack of competitiveness, and inferred that Zuni were reluctant to assume leadership, Li saw a misplaced application of our own cultural logic: "In the competitive Western world . . . where, if one does not push ahead, one is surely pushed behind" the absence of ambition implies the absence of leadership. "But in another society where mutual give and take is harmoniously assumed among all beings of the world, one might be . . . humble" and still be a leader among men. "Thus leadership is naturally assumed . . . [and] followed by others who do not see in the act of following any degree of humiliation" (Li An-Che, 1937: 68).

Where Americans had been struck by the lack of parental discipline, Li saw a child's behavior as shaped by a united adult front. He indirectly expresses wonderment at the way Americans deal with their children: "To get bodily enjoyment by caressing the baby as a plaything and calling this love is not the pattern in Zuni" (70). Finally, Li was struck in a way American observers had not been with the mirror image relationship between the position of a wife in a patrilineally oriented society like China and the position of a husband among the matrilineal Zuni. He agrees that "It is not correct to say that woman rules man in Zuni, but what is . . . important . . . is that woman is not ruled by man at all" (75).

What Li infers from the very different view of Zuni culture his perspective as a Chinese presented is that observers see some but not all elements in an unfamilar cultural pattern and "are easily led astray by their own background in supplying the missing logic with their own" (70).

Whatever the national origin and credentials of the scholars who bring knowledge of cultural differences to bear on practical problems, they must share in some measure both the optimism and pessimism with which we began. On the one hand, policy laid down in ignorance of cultural differences wreaks havoc needlessly. The decisions that guide communication between peoples could be made much more wisely than they are, if those who perceived how and why could make themselves heard. On the other hand, man is an enormously complicated creature whose modes of thought and action we only partly understand. What experts take to be wisdom may in fact be folly. And in the emerging world of the latter twentieth century, solutions to the central problems of reconciling cultural pluralism with world order still lie beyond the horizon of our vision.

If anthropologists cannot provide simple answers about where man is, and should be going, they can perhaps bring their knowledge of human diversity wisely to bear on a final and crucial problem. In these days of social turmoil, of individual and collective revolution against the patterns of the past, what is the responsibility of the individual toward the codes and conventions of his society? And what are the possibilities that collectively we can reshape them for the better?

Views of man advanced through the centuries by Western thinkers have elevated and lowered him, seen him as debased deity or transformed animal, as perfectible or damned. They have seen men's customary ways of life as expressing their loftiest aspirations or as imprisoning man's true nature, as bringing him to fulfillment or as imposed on him at great cost.

With increased consciousness of man as a microorganism on a tiny speck in the cosmos, with the power to destroy himself and leave that speck barren, these questions haunt us. There is an increasing reverence for man as individual and as species, and a corresponding challenge to those tribal loyalties and conventions that, as a precipitate of men's past, divide them.

Must men then conform? Must they live by standards of cumulated tribal experience they find arbitrary, evil, or absurd? Or can they search individually and collectively for loftier visions of the cosmos and of man, and seek panhuman standards of value, morality, justice, responsibility, and dignity?

As modern thinkers apparently must, the anthropologist has moments of crushing pessimism when man seems in a downward spiral—poisoning and polluting his environment, madly overpopulating his planet, crushing the highest aspirations of the human spirit, and visiting death and destruction in the name of petty principles. But he is also led by visions of what man could be, if he would. His views of human nature, of social life, of cultural order and possibility, fluctuate accordingly.

But somewhere in midswing the anthropologist can bring his evidence to bear on the questions of conformity, individualism, and human nature so central in the vision quests of our time. Let us begin with first principles. The notion that culture is something external to an individual—and which he can reformulate, flout, or do without—is untenable. First of all, human life is basically a process of *communication*. Communication requires a shared code, hence a large measure of conformity between an individual and at least some of his fellows. Being a philosopher-hermit, like returning to a life of self-sufficiency in the woods, is an escape possible to a few because the many maintain a social framework within which it is possible; and collective escapes produce new conformities at the same time they free people, often superficially, from old ones. The picture of rules and conformity that popular writings present is modeled more on the regulations of a swimming pool (no running, no diving) or an army post than on the unconscious rules of a grammar. If the superficial levels of conformity can be manipulated and discarded, the deeper levels constrain and shape the behavior of the most imaginative nonconformist. Moreover, the most avidly proclaimed freedoms from the conventions of society almost always lead the "rugged individualist" to wear the uniform of his particular subculture. Very few people do any really imaginative innovating, like growing a beard on one side of the face and shaving on the other, or painting themselves blue with woad.

But there is another and important side to all this. If man can express his humanity only through culture, if he can communicate only by conforming, that does not mean cultures cannot be reorganized and changed or that Utopias are impossible. The Menomini evidence shows that new ways can be learned and internalized; and the evidence of millenial and other "revitalization" movements shows that world view and social conventions can be radically restructured.

The answers to the dilemma of man, if there are answers, must lie not in a retreat into tribalism (as in quests for a miniature Utopia in the wilderness), but in a transcendence of tribalism. Human values *are* in grave danger in a world of technology and mass society; but dropping out cannot solve problems on a planetary scale, and that is how they must be solved. The challenge, somehow, is to achieve for modern man what the massive intrusion of the West has forced on tribal man—a radical restructuring of world view and experience, and a new integration. Whether that is possible can well be doubted; the challenge is increasingly grave. For our vision of the future, we need not less conformity but conformity to new patterns, collective exploration of new visions. As Margaret Mead pointed out, even our views of Utopia are constricted and drab (1957). Such visions must also be wise and informed. If they are not illuminated by sound understanding of man's biological, social, and cultural nature and the limits of human possibility, they could destroy man, not save him. Here we have no better source of wisdom than the diverse ways of life, the many variations on the theme of being human, that we have glimpsed in these pages.

Part Five

REFERENCE

HERE, IN SECTION I, "Anthropology as a Discipline," we look at the major "schools" and theoretical positions that have shaped the development of anthropology. Many of the names and ideas that have emerged in the preceding chapters will be placed in an intellectual context. At the end, we sketch and speculate about the present and future of anthropology as discipline and profession.

Section II, "Suggestions for Further Reading," lists recommended further readings on each of the numbered sections of the text.

Section III, the Bibliography, lists alphabetically by author the works referred to throughout the text.

Section I

Anthropology as a Discipline

IN THE PRECEDING chapters we have sampled the way anthropologists look at man in comparative perspective. We have taken a theoretical stance, of necessity, on many points where anthropologists are far from in agreement. But at the same time a range of views and approaches has been represented that should make it possible for the interested student to explore further some line of interest—say, in cultural evolution or the "Whorfian hypothesis"—treated here only briefly.

Our focus has been on *problems* and what modern anthropologists have to say about them—not on theoretical "schools" or the scholars who have shaped them. In this section, we will examine the development of anthropology as a discipline, and the major "schools" of anthropological theory. Some of these approaches have been bypassed by increased knowledge and the shifting tides of intellectual fashion. Others continue to have strong influences on present thinking, so the student will be able to trace connections to the modern approaches we have discussed in the preceding chapters.

After reviewing major "schools" of past anthropological thinking, we will speculate about where anthropology is going as a discipline and what opportunities it presents as a profession.

66 · The Historical Background of Anthropology

It is possible to trace the roots of anthropological thinking back to the Greeks or beyond. But that is hardly surprising; and it obscures the recency of professional anthropology and of the idea that the customs of men could be explored by systematic comparative analysis.

For our purposes it is more productive to begin with the age of European discovery and the developments in social thought that roughly coincided with it. Through the voyages of European "discoverers," new peoples different in physique and custom were brought to light progressively in Asia,

Africa, America, and, eventually, the remoter Pacific Islands. At the same time, mythical lands and strange creatures pictured in mythologies and travelers' tales of earlier periods were relegated to limbo. These extensions of knowledge did not fit into the accepted categories of thought about man. The way was opened to fresh speculations and, in due course, to systematic investigation of their place in the human scheme. Comparative studies led in turn to a more conscious examination by Western peoples of their own ways and ideas. Shakespeare's Caliban, Locke's Indian, Defoe's Man Friday, and Rousseau's man of nature were symbols for social and philosophic analysis as well as for literature. Rousseau's interpretations have a particularly modern slant. Lévi-Strauss has recently depicted him as the father of modern anthropology.

By the late eighteenth century an impressive amount of reasonably reliable information had accumulated about the customs of "savage" or "barbaric" peoples (that is, peoples who were more or less different from "civilized" Westerners). The Jesuit missionaries, to cite one instance, left voluminous records dealing with the Indian tribes of eastern and central North America in the seventeenth century; and rich missionary records of Aztec culture provide a wealth of evidence still being tapped today. Western scholars began to systematize such materials, and in doing so were led to compare the different bodies of custom and to speculate on the origin and development of culture and society in general. Much of the pioneering work here was done by social philosophers such as Hobbes, Locke, Voltaire, and Rousseau. Fairly early in the nineteenth century, scientific societies were formed in Europe and the United States for the study of "ethnology." Museum displays were opened and scientific publication series started. Groups or individuals were even brought from overseas countries for display at the royal courts and at public fairs and expositions. Interest in anthropology spread in turn to almost every country in the world, by way of government agencies, scientific societies, museums, and interested scholars and laymen.

Soon after the mid-century, anthropological journals usually had separate sections or book listings for writings in "physical anthropology" (or just "anthropology"); "ethnology" (for those interested in reports on differing customs); "linguistics" (for those interested in language); and "archaeology." The ethnology section was likely to be subdivided in turn into such headings as "religion," "the arts," "economic life," "social organization."

The great age of the earth and of man became recognized and scientifically accepted by the 1840s. Until then, archaeologists had to fit such known sites as the Stonehenge ruin, as well as various crudely shaped stone tools that were coming to light through road building and other excavation, into a timetable that placed creation of the earth in comparatively recent times. A widely accepted dating, worked out by Dr. John Lightfoot of Cambridge University in 1654, placed this event on October 23, 4004 B.C. at 9 A.M. Now geologists and others recognized the vast age of the earth. They also gave it a time clock, including the sequence of glacial periods ("Ice Ages") approximately covering the period of man's early development. A Danish government scientific commission had already (1836) established from shell-mound research a sequence of Stone, Bronze, and Iron Age materials. A drought of 1853–1854 lowered the level in Swiss lakes to reveal the piles and other remains of lake villages of the Neolithic, or New Stone Age. In dealing with tools of the Paleolithic, or Old Stone Age, and with fossilized skeletal materials, anthropologists were daring to go back a million years or more.

Perhaps inevitably, in view of the profound impress of the theory of organic evolution upon the scientific world, later nineteenth-century thinking relating to culture and society was dominated by analogous theories of social or cultural evolution, as we will see in the next section.

Scientific "fieldwork" became increasingly a preoccupation of professional anthropologists. In 1879 the United States government established a "Bureau of American Ethnology," which still exists as one of its official scientific research bodies. This was created from the Geological Survey, primarily to provide technical information on American Indian groups that could be used in assimilating them peacefully into the American milieu. Establishment of this body is one of the landmarks in the development of a professional group of full-time scientists, calling themselves anthropologists, and doing "fieldwork." The anthropological record could no longer rest upon travelers' chance observations, or the asides of officials, missionaries, merchants, and others.

In the early twentieth century, most ethnologists still were attached to museums or scientific societies, or else were in government scientific agencies at home or in overseas territories. Their association with universities tended to be limited to those with museums, such as Oxford and Cambridge in England, Harvard and Pennsylvania in the United States, and corresponding centers in other countries. If the early ethnographers were usually missionaries, explorers, or colonial administrators to whom observations of peoples on the frontiers were a sidelight, the early ethnologists who wrote about their findings were very often gentlemen antiquarians. The late development of anthropology as a profession, and the nature of early ethnology, were shaped by these beginnings as a scholarly pastime of the wealthy.

67 · *Cultural and Social Evolutionism*

As anthropological theory relating to culture first took form, its major goal was to establish if possible grand "laws" such as those that stood as milestones in other sciences: Archimedes' law, Newton's law, Mendel's law of inheritance. Early nineteenth-century thinkers groped particularly after some touchstone idea or sequence that could explain the total panorama of human "progress."

The German scholar Klemm, for example, made a compilation of customs to show how man had passed through successive stages of "savagery" and "tameness" to "freedom." Comte, often called the "father of sociology," had man advancing from the "theological" through the "metaphysical" to the "positive," or scientific. Buckle, in his *History of Civilization in England* (1857–1861), tried to account for man's advancement by way of an interplay of factors such as climate, diet, and physical type. Bastian, a prodigious writer and museum collector, suggested that the similarities in cultures everywhere were based on a common framework of what he called "elementary ideas."

By the 1860s such theorizing became channeled almost wholly into an evolutionary framework. The scholars concerned applied by analogy to culture and society the same overall pattern of thought that Darwin postulated in his *Origin of Species* (1859) for organic evolution. Here seemingly was a grand law that could explain the whole development of custom. It has often been said that in the mid-nineteenth-century atmosphere, when biological evolution was gaining admittance as a critical new "great idea," theory relating to culture and society could hardly have had any other emphasis than an evolutionary one.

Besides the key term *evolution* in such theories, there is a preoccupation with *origins* and *stages*. Elements in modern cultures that appear to persist from the distant past are *survivals*. Though there can be some "degeneration," in which evolutionary "progress" gets setbacks, the trend in cultural or social "organisms" is upward from the "simple" to the complex or "heterogeneous." The great framework of stages is the threefold one of *savagery*, *barbarism*, and *civilization*: the first two are represented not only in the past but also in contemporary "primitive" cultures that have still not evolved beyond one or other of these stages. The viewpoints involved are plausible enough to have wide credence in popular thought and even in some corners of science, other than the social sciences, that have been exposed to anthropological ideas.

The leading theorists of this "school" were practically all armchair scholars who were indefatigable compilers of information on non-Western peoples, but who had little firsthand contact with them in the field. Prior to the 1870s, a number of sporadic ideas had been accumulating along evolutionary lines. A Swiss jurist Bachofen for example, in his *Das Mütterrecht* ("mother-right") published in 1841, suggested that the patrilineal ("father-right") descent system had been preceded by a matrilineal system. Henry Maine, in his *Ancient Law* (1861), pictured the "territorial" tie characteristic of modern political groups as originating with the early Greeks, and all previous societies as aggregated by "blood" or kin ties. McLennan, in *Primitive Marriage* (1865), built up stages in the evolution of marriage and the family, including what he called "bride-capture."

The most notable compiler of the time calling himself an anthropologist was Edward B. Tylor, an English scholar who was an associate of Darwin, Galton, and other leading thinkers of the time, and is often called the "father of ethnology." His outstanding work, *Primitive Culture* (1871), offered the first full-length and careful treatment of the evolutionary point of view, and is a classic of the science. Though Tylor's evolutionary framework has not stood well the test of time, his analyses of social organization, religion, and comparative anthropology remain classics. He is one of the rare early anthropologists whose work stands more solidly and whose insights seem more remarkable and enduring than they did forty years ago.

Another key scholar was the American Lewis Henry Morgan, whose book *Ancient Society* (1877) is a major summation of evolutionary theory. In it he set out an elaborate scheme of cultural evolution, focusing on kinship and social organization. Morgan became fascinated with kinship terminologies among American Indians and solicited kinship terminologies from scholars around the world. His massive and technical analysis of these materials, *Systems of Consanguinity and Affinity in the Human Family* (1870), marks him as the father of kinship studies.

Numerous other evolutionary writers filled up anthropological book-shelves of the time. The most widely known is Sir James Frazer, whose thirteen volumes entitled *The Golden Bough* (published from 1890 on) deal primarily with the origin and nature of religion. This theoretical viewpoint was predominantly an interest of European scholars. Though a few American anthropologists of the time wrote papers with an evolutionary orientation, Morgan alone attempted to work out this line of theory at all fully. American research of the time was concentrated on fieldwork, particularly among Indians, and on hard-headed factual reconstruction of the past.

The evolutionary viewpoint may be appreciated by quoting Tylor (1871):

(By) simply placing (the European) nations at one end of the social series and savage tribes at the other, (and) arranging the rest of mankind between these limits . . . ethnographers are able to set up at least a rough scale of civilisation . . . (representing) a transition from the savage state to our own (I, 26–27).

And again Morgan (1877):

As it is undeniable that portions of the human family have existed in a state of savagery, other portions in a state of barbarism, and still other portions in a state of civilisation, it seems equally so that these three distinct conditions are connected with each other in a . . . necessary sequence of progress. . . . (The) domesticated institutions of the barbarous, and even of the savage, ancestors of mankind are still exemplified in portions of the human family with such completeness that, with the exception of the strictly primitive period, the several stages of this progress are tolerably well preserved (pp. 3, 7).

Morgan's scheme begins with a *Lower Status of Savagery*, an "infancy" of man. *Middle Savagery* starts with fishing and knowledge of the use of fire; *Upper Savagery* with the bow and arrow; *Lower Barbarism* with the invention of pottery; *Middle Barbarism* with the domestication of animals; *Upper Barbarism* with the smelting of iron; and *Civilization* with the alphabet.

This nineteenth-century evolutionary approach is often spoken of, in retrospect, as a kind of "superhistory" or theory of "progress." The "significant cultural system" being studied tends to be always the totality of culture from origins on. This viewpoint took little account of the specific facts relating to ways of life as regional systems or local wholes. Moreover, it used a crude *comparative method* to locate and extract supposed "survivals" in the modern bodies of custom over the world, and then fitted these arbitrarily into "stage" sequences back to origins. Where evidence was vague to nonexistent, evolutionists did not hesitate to make up connecting links: for example, marriage systems supposedly originated from an original stage of "primitive promiscuity." A "pre-economic" man browsing like an animal without organized handling of resources, or a man having initial religious experience through speculations about the dead, or feeling awe before the unknown, or having his magic fail, or making a mistake in language—all these are the creation of evolutionist imagination.

Evolution, as seen by these scholars, was a single or *unilinear* thread throughout cultural history. It was rooted in a vague *psychic unity* by which all human groups were supposed to have the same potential for evolutionary development, though some were further ahead than others because of climate, soil, and other factors. Little was said about the interrelation of groups in terms of the specifics of invention and diffusion, so that an impression is gained of cultures having vague *multiple origins* as a result of each having tendencies to evolve through the cultural and social stages. "Survivals" were the "rudimentary organs of social groups." Thus old folklore themes and "superstitions" might persist even in civilized groups, just as an appendix or an internal tail appeared to be organic survivals with little or no functional importance in the modern human body.

This whole viewpoint has little credibility when set against present-day anthropological and other knowledge of cultural and social origins, development, and dynamics. Such abstract schemes have almost no reality at all to the research worker. He sees societies as working systems having their specific local histories, and non-Western peoples as human beings rather than as repositories of supposed past cultural and social stages. It remained for later schools of thought to define better such terms as "primitive" and "civilized," to refine the concept of "psychic unity," to refashion the concept of evolution, and to make more critical use of "the comparative method."

The first major attack on the basic assumptions of the evolutionists was made by Franz Boas, in an anthropologically famous paper read at a scientific meeting in 1896, with the title "The Limitations of the Comparative Method of Anthropology." He points out that similarities between cultural elements are not necessarily proof of historical connections and common origins. A much more realistic approach for discovering uniformities in cultural process, he says, is to launch scientific inquiry as to the historic origin of specific cultural elements, and as to how they "assert themselves in various cultures." This, he says, calls for

> another method, which in many respects, is much safer (than evolutionist comparison). A detailed study of customs in their relation to the total culture of the tribe practising them, in connection with an investigation of their geographical distribution among neighboring tribes, affords us almost always with a means of determining with considerable accuracy the historical causes that led to the formation of the customs in question and to the psychological processes that were at work in their development. . . . We have in this method a means of reconstructing the history of the growth of ideas with much greater accuracy than the generalizations of the comparative method will permit. (1896; republished 1940: 276).

It was not long before numbers of the European evolutionary scholars were publicly recanting, and attention shifted elsewhere.

During a generation or so, evolutionary viewpoints tended to remain in the background. For nearly all professionals, labels such as "evolution," "stages," "the comparative method," became taboo. Oddly enough, the ideas of Morgan on "ancient society," though so soon relegated to the background by American scholars, have meantime shown great persistence as part of Communist ideology. Engels and others used Morgan's scheme as the basis for their treatment of primitive societies.

In recent years, as the older controversies faded into the background and wider theoretical schemes were once more sought, restatements of the evolutionist position by Leslie White and his students have been widely influential, as we have seen in §28. Evolution, more carefully and cautiously conceived, once more provides a major mode of conceptualizing the sweep of human history and the processes of change.

68 · Historicalism

Boas, in turning anthropological attention toward *specific analysis of culture history*, appears to have been influenced strongly by two scientific traditions accumulating outside the evolutionary viewpoint: one a German "geographic" approach, the other the American "fieldwork" approach. Trained in physics and geography in Germany, he was a product of the first tradition. In the American setting he had as colleagues the factually-oriented staff workers of the Bureau of American Ethnology and the museums. In 1888 he had major responsibilities for handling the anthropological exhibits for the great fair at St. Louis, where the displays illustrated different peoples and their customs.

The historical method, as promoted by Boas and others following him, does not mean just study of the past; it can be applied just as much to observation of the present. The historical viewpoint focuses attention on unique, or specific, objects and events in time and in place. In ethnology it deals with cultural elements as they have actually existed and may exist today, recording their chronological and spatial story. Boas insisted on "the consideration of every phenomenon as the result of historical happenings." As he put it further (1927), in discussing particular cultural systems, each culture represents a "historical growth" shaped by "the social and geographic environment" of a people and by the way a group "develops the cultural material that comes into its possession from the outside or through its own creativeness" (4).

Boas, as teacher and colleague of the major figures in American anthropology in the first half of the century—Kroeber, Lowie, Sapir, Linton, Benedict, Mead, Spier, and Wissler, to name a few—has been much revered as a "father figure." His emphasis on fieldwork, on getting the facts straight, on critical thinking, supplied a badly needed corrective. Yet the position of Boas—whether his influence in retrospect was more negative than positive—has been much debated in recent years. His detractors, principally Leslie White, have argued that he brought theory to a standstill and taught his students to collect facts without asking what they meant or how they fitted together. Despite Boas' years of work on the Kwakiutl Indians, and his "five-foot shelf" of ethnographic reports on them, Murdock has pointed out that there are too many gaps in the Kwakiutl evidence to include them in his sample of world cultures—because this fact gathering was unguided by systematic theory. Boas' proponents point toward his many positive contributions as teacher and scholar, in a wide range of fields, and to his strong influence on thinking outside anthropology.

Boas was central in establishing, especially in American anthropology, a set of premises that might be called *cultural determinism*. These emphasized the plasticity of man—that he could be what his culture made him. Though a culture represented the chance historical confluence of multiple influences and borrowings, it nonetheless was a coherent system that shaped and molded the individual born into it. (Hence Boas violently attacked any form of racial, biological, or geographic determinism.) The premises of cultural determinism further emphasized relativism. One had to take each culture as a separate universe of experience, values, and meanings, and examine it in its own terms. Finally, drawing in part on his work with diverse Indian languages, Boas—and through him his students—emphasized the great *diversity* and *uniqueness* of cultures.

These central premises, followed out by Boas' students, dominated American anthropology for half a century. As a reaction to uncritical comparison, ethnocentrism, and racism they were probably a necessary corrective. As articles of faith or foundations of theory, many anthropologists are finding them limiting and ultimately negative.

Several directions in which they led Boas' students will be retraced in the following sections. However, it is worth first examining the "historicalist" studies of trait distribution that grew out of Boas' emphasis on the particularities of historical connection.

Clark Wissler, a major figure here, proposed a schema or model for the culture area, shown ideally as a circle. It has a *culture center*, which should have the largest frequency of the typical traits, and also a *culture margin*, where the traits tend to thin out and interpenetrate with traits from neighboring culture areas. One of numbers of compilations based on this distributional hypothesis is a study of the Plains Indian "sun dance" by Spier (1921), in which the presence or absence of some 80 traits of this "complex" is plotted for the tribes practicing it. The *age-area* hypothesis, developed in such studies, hypothesizes that older elements will show the widest distribution, and later elements will not have had time to become spread so widely. In the California culture area, to take an example from Kroeber, certain rituals of initiating young people at puberty are widespread, while certain religious "cults" have quite localized distribution. The age-area concept would suggest that the former are older than the latter. Classic studies focused particularly on trait distributions and diffusion among North American Indians.

Such approaches were eventually carried to extremes in studies of "culture element distribution" among Indians of the west coast of America. Fieldworkers carried the isolation and fractionation of "culture traits" to the point of ludicrousness, ending up with lists of as many as 10,000 traits.

The critical if overly atomistic thinking of such historicalist approaches deriving from Boas served to make anthropologists wary of leaping to conclusions about historical connection when some resemblance turned up in art motifs, architecture, religious practice, or words among peoples far removed in time and space. It has become clear that using the standards of "evidence" of a lost continent of Mu or a Kon-Tiki theory, one can "prove" that anyone came from anywhere—as we will shortly see.

In its extreme forms, historicalism produced a unit treatment of culture which gave it, to later eyes, a spuriously objective character. It had an atomistic, rigid, externalized viewpoint which missed much of the rich texture of human action and motivation. It treated the individual much like a passive matrix upon which culture, the active element, was impressed. These offshoots from Boas' work—unlike others we will soon view—gravely underestimated the integration of culture by emphasizing atomistic traits. Nevertheless, there were positive contributions as well as much-needed critical canons of evidence. Historicalism imposed demanding rules for historical reconstruction; tracing (where this was feasible) the actual events of invention and diffusion replaced the loose evolutionary habit of putting bits and pieces of cultural behavior together from all over the world to make a sequence. In classifying traits, scholars began to isolate principles of order, such as patterns and areas. There was a considerable sorting out of the interplay of forces involved in cultural growth and change: the positive factors of habitat, the broad unity of biological-psychological potential, the creative and communicative processes at the cultural and social levels.

The historical method dominated cultural anthropology during the first three decades of the twentieth century. New leads in cultural theory were by then emerging, their exponents including a number of the scholars who were thoroughly steeped in the historical approach and followed the lead of Boas in other directions. But before these leads are explored, a kind of aside in the historical unfolding of theory has to be presented. So-called diffusionistic schools must take the stage briefly.

69 · Diffusionism

The American approach to "diffusion" was an academically restrained one. Scholars in the United States were dealing almost wholly with cultural traditions without written records. Apart from the memories of living informants they had to depend upon archaeological evidence, historically dubious analysis of oral folklore, and even more tricky distributional reconstructions. As a result, studies of actual diffusion sequences were confined almost wholly to regional and local reconstructions: the interrelations of culture areas, the distribution of identifiable customs over larger or smaller segments of the primitive world, and the ever-present problem of New World cultural growth apparently independently of the Old World, as just exemplified.

European scholars, however, were soon using the historical approach in attempts to make a total reconstruction of world cultural history, just as previously they had approached this problem through evolutionism. Schools of thought that emphasize this viewpoint have been called "diffusionistic." Two such schools stand out enough to be discussed here, both having their main popularity in the 1920s: one developed in England, the other in Germany.

The English type of diffusion was highly amateurish, and is referred to here primarily as a warning to the uncritical. Elliott Smith, a very competent student of the human brain, became interested in social anthropology. He and a few associates were impressed by the archaeological findings of Petrie and others in Egypt. As they examined cultural data elsewhere in the world, they came to the conclusion that Egyptians must have traded far and wide for gold, pearls, and other valuables, and at the same time carried their inventions through Asia, and even beyond via the Pacific Islands to Middle America. Without any critical appraisal of the great complexes of behavior involved, they claimed that Egyptian customs, such as the sun cult, kingship, mummification, and megalithic construction, and even earlier elements such as agriculture and improved working of flint, had been carried widely over the world by these "Children of the Sun." Works in this traditions, such as ones by Smith (1915) and Perry (1923), plausible as they may seem, ignore careful standards of comparison. This viewpoint gained no following, even among British anthropologists, outside its small circle, and it has subsequently withered away. It is sometimes called the *heliocentric* ("sun-centered") school.

Far more scholarly, and hence difficult to characterize briefly, has been the German school, though it, too, is now obsolete. This type of diffusionism traces back to the geographic tradition of Ratzel. Its special approach to world culture history was called by its practitioners the *culture historical* method. Graebner (1911), one of its main formulators, indicated its major task to be the tracing, historically and geographically, of combinations of basic elements, called *Kulturkreise*, from which world cultural growth has been woven. A single *Kulturkreis*, variously translated as "culture complex,' 'culture circle,' or 'culture stratum,' is a cluster of meaningfully associated traits that can be isolated and identified in culture history. The earliest *Kulturkreise* were sought through meticulous analysis and comparison of what appear to be the most primitive cultures. For this purpose, said these culture-historicalists, "irrelevant form" is the best criterion of relationship— far more important, for example, than modern spatial distribution.

The outstanding figure among exponents of this school was a Catholic scholar, Father Wilhelm Schmidt, whose base was in Vienna. The English translation of his work, entitled *The Culture Historical Method of Ethnology* (1939), gives the non-German-speaking reader access to its theories. The modern cultural scene is said to result from the complex diffusion of elements from nine main early "culture complexes" (the *Kulturkreise*): three *Primitive* or *Archaic* (with culture elements represented today among [a] Pygmies of Africa and Asia, [b] Arctic primitives, and [c] some of the Australian Aborigine and comparable peoples); three *Primary* (represented in [d] widely spread "higher" food gatherers, [e] pastoral nomads, and [f] gardening groups with certain matrilineal descent rules); and three *Secondary,* all agriculturists, two of which practice other specialized forms of matrilineal descent, the third having patrilineal descent.

Though this looks somewhat like the schemes of cultural evolution, its exponents insisted on the historicity of the method. Critics, however, have pointed out that the "culture circles" were generalized composites, and that no real attempt was made to show how they originated, when and where they existed as entities in the past, and how they supposedly diffused to widely separated areas. Despite the wealth of scholarship that went into their construction, they have a hypothetical character that, for nonadherents (including perhaps all American professional anthropologists), gives a sense of unreality. This approach, sometimes called the "Vienna" or "Anthropos" school (after the anthropological journal *Anthropos*), has been declared inadequate even by its former major European exponents, who are realizing that a much wider range of problems has significance for anthropological attention. Systematic archaeology, modern field evidence, and more sophisticated theories of culture, society, and change have largely bypassed this diffusionist approach.

70 · French Sociology

From the late 1890s until World War I, one of the great efflorescences of modern social thought emerged in France. Its center was Emile Durkheim. Clustered around him were a group of colleagues: his nephew, Marcel Mauss, the historian Henri Hubert, Robert Hertz, and more peripherally Lucien Lévy-Bruhl and Arnold Van Gennep. The course of modern social science might have run quite differently had this group not been shattered by the first world war; yet their influence on British and American anthropological thought is increasing, not waning.

Durkheim's intellectual roots in European thought are too complex to trace here. Yet two influences are particularly important to us. The first is that of the Scottish classicist Robertson Smith, whose studies of *Kinship and Marriage in Early Arabia* (1885) and *Lectures on the Religion of the Semites* (1889) profoundly influenced Durkheim. Particularly in analyzing Semitic sacrifice, Smith argued that those who partook of the sacrificial meal were sharing a sacredness that bound them together symbolically. A second influence was N. D. Fustel de Coulanges, whose *Le Cité Antique* (1864) shook scholars of ancient Greece and Rome by suggesting that central to their social and political organization was a domestic cult of the dead, binding the family and lineage together by shared sacredness and collective rites. Durkheim cast some of his works in an evolutionary framework characteristic of the time. Thus his *Elementary Forms of the Religious Life* sought to find the earliest form of religion, among Australian Aborigines. But the essential and lasting contributions can be sorted out from this evolutionary scheme. Durkheim was centrally concerned with the emergent properties of beliefs, sentiments, and symbols *when they are shared by a group*. Durkheim obviously knew that collective symbolic systems are *composed of* the ideational systems of individuals and can have no existence without them. Yet shared ideational systems (*consciences collectives*) have properties that transcend and cannot be explained in terms of the minds of individuals. To English-speaking readers, especially to the wary American historicalists, this sounded like the worst sort of mysticism, invoking a "group mind" (Goldenweiser, 1924). Yet it was a crucial insight of Durkheim's that could have opened new paths for American anthropology.

Durkheim and his colleagues began to perceive the interplay between social relations and the symbolic systems of ritual and cosmology. Durkheim argued that Australian *totemism*, the treatment of an animal or plant species as sacred, was a projection of the social order. The ritual gatherings of the Aborigines, whereby they left the realm of the profane and mundane and entered the realm of the sacred, in fact symbolized and reinforced the solidarity and collective sentiment of the group. Conceptions of the cosmos represented the social order writ large. This theme was further explored by Durkheim and Mauss in their study of primitive systems of folk classification (1901–1902), where linkages between social groups and conceptualizations of the universe and natural phenomena were traced.

Many of the writings of the French sociologists remain strongly influential, and we have encountered some of them in the preceding chapters: Hertz's study of mortuary rites in Borneo (§56), Mauss's study of gift giving (§47), and Van Gennep's work on rites of passage (§37). Other classic studies in this genre are Hertz's study of symbolic polarities of right- and left-hand, Mauss's analysis of the seasonal shifts in Eskimo social structure and their expression in ritual, and Hubert and Mauss's studies of sacrifice and magic.

What Durkheim and his colleagues had done, for the first time on a large scale, was to demonstrate the rich interconnections between the symbolic systems and social structure of primitive peoples. Because of their intellectual milieu and their reliance on limited library sources (none of them did fieldwork), they looked at this interplay between social organization and the ideational systems of ritual and cosmology primarily from the direction of the social. The cosmos was a projection of the social order; religious belief was a reflection of social action.

This orientation, as we will see, was to influence British anthropology profoundly, especially through the work of Radcliffe-Brown. But on the continent, through the continuing work of Mauss, Granet—the historian of China, the folklorists Dumézil and Propp, and the cosmological studies of Dutch anthropologists, this directionality of influence between social and symbolic systems was balanced and even reversed. It remained for Claude Lévi-Strauss, adding to these insights the models of structural linguistics, to forge a new and important synthesis. In it, as we have seen, he has worked through a theory of kinship and marriage (§34) to a theory of the human mind (§58) and of the realm of myth where it holds purest sway (§57). The *structuralism* of Lévi-Strauss and his followers has become the dominant theme of European anthropology and has profoundly influenced many scholars in England and America.

71 · Functionalism

The theoretical developments now to be traced cannot be properly understood if treated in terms of anthropology alone. As twentieth-century scholarship advanced, the long-standing tendency to treat elements of experience as if they had an objective unit existence began to show major inadequacies. Our Western languages gave difficulty here, for they were filled with unit concepts and contrasts: mind and matter, body and soul, time and space, atoms, chemical elements, behavioral traits. Such a new and necessary point of view as Einstein's relativity theory not only shook the scientific world but also bulged beyond familiar language symbols.

The newer frame of reference, carried partly in fresh concepts, emphasized the interrelations of elements of experience, and the significant combinations of elements comprising whole systems. By the 1920s and 1930s, every field of knowledge from science to philosophy was being strongly affected by these viewpoints. In the philosophy of science, for example, A. N. Whitehead (as in his *Science and the Modern World*, 1926) called the new approach "organismic." Others have called it "holistic," "integrative," "functional" in the sense that all the parts of a system *do* something, that is, have a significant *function* in relation to the whole. In psychology, as many will know, the so-called Gestalt psychology broke in vigorously upon the older types of behaviorism.

Such a viewpoint had been foreshadowed in the work of the American historicalists, from the very nature of cultural materials. Traits were obviously linked into complexes, and cultures patterned into wholes. But the theory of such connections was, on the whole, left implicit. Bringing it out explicitly came to be the task of two British scholars who have given their names to what are now generally called *functional* schools of social anthropology: one a British-naturalized anthropologist of Polish background, Bronislaw Malinowski; the other, Cambridge-educated Alfred Radcliffe-Brown.

It appears significant that each scholar, working independently, brought out in the same year, 1922, his initial field monograph defining a functional approach to the study of culture. Malinowski's *Argonauts of the Western Pacific*, a study of the *kula* in the Trobriand Islands, and Radcliffe-Brown's *The Andaman Islanders*, exploring the meaning of certain group ceremonials among the people of these islands in the Indian Ocean, are both recognized as classics. Each of these scholars, highly individualistic, rarely in personal contact, and more or less rivals for the allegiance of student minds, produced in due course a quite different system of theory. They employed markedly different concepts, and they made sharply contrasting contributions to the development of social anthropology.

Malinowski revolutionized fieldwork through the length and depth of his involvement in the life of the Trobriand Islanders we have encountered so often in the preceding pages. Where earlier fieldworkers had tended to stay on the fringes of native life, working through interpreters and seeing events from the outside, Malinowski penetrated deeply into Trobriand life and gave us incomparably vivid accounts of how it looked and felt from the inside. His study of the *kula* (1922) traced the interconnections of this ceremonial trade into the realms of myth, magic, canoe technology, economic exchange, and sociology. He argued that because of the complex interweaving of different elements of culture, study of any one element would—if followed out—lead into the whole system. This study was followed by a series of important books, characteristically vivid yet too often pompous and polemical. Only in *Coral Gardens and Their Magic* (1935) did he again attain the heights of his first classic on the *kula.*

Up to this time, cultural anthropology had been largely addressing itself to anthropologists. Malinowski, a brilliantly vocal professor at the London School of Economics and Political Science, addressed himself boldly to intellectual circles at large, writing books on topic after topic, mainly using his Trobriand materials for illustration. To the annoyance of colleagues, he not only flailed all other approaches but also claimed to be initiating for the first time a real "science of culture." Every culture, he said (1931), is a working whole, an "integrated" unity, in which every element has a functional contribution to make. The "function" of any "institution" (that is, an organized system of activity) is the part it plays within the interrelated whole in fulfilling human purposes or "needs." In developing this *need* concept he tried out several schemes, but usually he distinguished three types or levels of needs (or "imperatives") that had to be met by all cultures, hence were universal:

Primary or biological needs (or imperatives): procreation, nutrition, defense and protection, and so on.

Derived or instrumental needs (or imperatives), necessary to organized activity: economic organization, law, education.

Integrative or synthetic needs (or imperatives of mental and moral integration): knowledge, magic and religion, art, play.

Unfortunately, Malinowski—energetically attacking real and imagined analytical errors in social science like "conjectural history" and "economic man"—failed to read (or understand?) Durkheim. Repeatedly he sought to explain what is social and shared in terms of the psychological and physical nature of individuals. When he sought to theorize in general terms, he foundered repeatedly on this rock he could have avoided. To his death in 1942, Malinowski was a controversial figure. Retrospectively, his general theories often seem pretentious and shallow (Firth, 1957). He was at his best as observer, raconteur, and analyst of field data. He was also a great teacher. These skills, his virtuosity as a seminar leader and sharp-tongued critic, and his magnetic personality profoundly influenced the leading senior figures in modern British anthropology—among them Raymond Firth, E. E. Evans-Pritchard, Meyer Fortes, Edmund Leach, and Max Gluckman. A standard of field research was set in British anthropology that scholars in other countries have rarely attained.

While Malinowski built his system of thought around the concept of *culture*, Radcliffe-Brown built his around the concept of *society*. The function of a social institution, Radcliffe-Brown wrote, is "the part it plays in the social life as a whole, and therefore the contribution it makes to the maintenance of structural continuity" (1935). Theoretically, Radcliffe-Brown drew heavily on Durkheim. His Andaman Islands study follows closely Durkheim's interpretation of Australian aboriginal religion as maintaining collective sentiment and social solidarity. The function of Andamanese gatherings for feasting, dancing, and ceremonial is to contribute to the *maintenance of the social structure*: that is, of the established interrelations among individuals, hence providing what he called *social integration*. In generalizing this point of view, he frequently used analogies with biological organisms, speaking of a society in terms of its social *morphology* (structure) and *social physiology* (functional "laws"). While he did not deal with individuals and their needs or drives, he did speak of "necessary conditions of existence" to meet the *survival interests* of a society.

Unlike Malinowski, Radcliffe-Brown was not particularly dedicated or successful as a fieldworker. As an analyst in comparative sociology he combined virtuosity with skillful use of powerful theoretical tools. These he had mainly borrowed—from Durkheim, Maine, Fustel de Coulanges, Lowie, and others—but he used them with precision and flourish.

His emphasis was always on the social. Why, he asked, do men have elaborate cults of the dead? Is it because they want to explain such phenomena as shadows, dreams, and reflected images, as Tylor had speculated? Perhaps in part. But it is religious *action*, collective ritual, we should focus on—not belief in an afterlife. Men have ancestral cults and beliefs in an afterlife *primarily* so they can stage collective rites and funerals, and hence ensure social integration in the face of death (Radcliff-Brown, 1952: 155ff.). Note here not only his debt to Durkheim, but also his continuing emphasis on the social as primary, the ideational as secondary.

Radcliffe-Brown revived and elaborated an interest in kinship and marriage systems, and particularly kinship terminologies. Rejecting explanations of social organization based on supposed "survivals" of matrilineal descent and the like, he showed neatly how kinship systems form integrated wholes.

As a general theorist, Radcliffe-Brown, like Malinowski, was disappointing. He was given to misleadingly concrete organic analogies (social structure as like the structure of seashells on the beach), pretentious talk of "social laws" modeled on those in the physical sciences, and (to borrow Murdock's choice phrase) "mere verbalizations reified into causal forces" (1949: 121). Thus the "principle of the equivalence of brothers" was used to "explain" a wide range of kinship phenomena. Yet as a teacher he was profoundly influential. Theoretically he largely shaped the concentration of modern British anthropology on the social rather than the cultural. He inspired the crucial studies of segmentary lineage systems in Africa by Evans-Pritchard (of the Nuer), and Fortes (of the Tallensi), and these in turn pioneered a whole era of research and refinement in the study of social and political structure. While at Chicago, he stimulated an interest in studies of kinship (among students such as Fred Eggan) that has had a major impact on American anthropology.

Ironically, the limitations of the studies inspired by Radcliffe-Brown result from the direction he took into the territory opened up by Durkheim. By taking social relations as primary and ideational systems as secondary— and adding to this an excessively concrete notion of social relationships— he and his students could explore only one side of man. It has been a belated realization of how profoundly ideational systems shape human life and the social order that has generated new excitement on the British scene. Such new perspectives were foreshadowed in the later work of Evans-Pritchard, and have come to the fore in recent work by Edmund Leach, Victor Turner, Mary Douglas, Rodney Needham, and British-trained scholars like T. O. Beidelman and Nur Yalman. The influence of Lévi-Strauss in these developments has been central; the two sides of Durkheim's vision are being joined, in search of a three-dimensional view of man.

Meanwhile "functionalism" as a theoretical concept is still being debated and partitioned. There are several senses of the word "function": (1) *teleological*, where one asks about the goals or ends something serves; (2) *configurational*, where one speaks of the interdependence of a set of elements within a system, and asks what contribution each makes to the whole; and (3) *mathematical*, where one refers to the covariation of a set of variables. Anthropologists have endlessly muddled the three, and then tried to sort out the muddles.

Functional, or "structural-functional," analysis continues to be a central mode of study in social anthropology, though philosophers of science repeatedly underline its inadequacies. By its nature it is static and involuted, "explaining" a system in terms of itself. Theorists emphasizing ecological adaptation or psychological principles have repeatedly sought to break out of this closed circle. Functionalism, moreover, builds on assumptions about a society being self-contained, integrated, and in equilibrium. As we noted in §50, these assumptions that seemed useful for primitive societies fail increasingly to fit the rapidly changing social and political patterns of the latter twentieth century.

72 · Configurationalism

Meanwhile, on the American scene beginning in the 1930s and 1940s, anthropologists took off in a different direction from the work of Boas than did the historicalists discussed in §68.

Alfred Kroeber—a remarkable figure in American anthropology who, over some fifty years, spanned a vast range of problems from historicalist distribution studies to languages, archaeology, social organization, and the rise and fall of civilizations and hemlines—stepped back at times to make perceptive observations about the integration and focal points of cultures.

Another major figure was Edward Sapir, founder of no school or theoretical system as such, but brilliant pioneer of a whole range of anthropological problems. His major early studies were in the field of language, and his book on *Language* (1921) contains many ideas that he applied later to cultural behavior in general. As with the grammar of language, he asserted, behavior has an *unconscious patterning* that ordinarily is not brought to mind. Drawing on his study of the symbolic character of language communication, Sapir emphasized that all cultural behavior is *symbolic*. That is, it is based on "meanings" shared and communicated among individual members of the society. Even to the extent that two individuals might share common understandings—hanging by the same strap on a subway train, exchanging a meaningful wink—they exhibit the essential qualities of cultural behavior.

That culture is a "superorganic, impersonal whole" is a "useful enough methodological principle to begin with," Sapir says (1932). But such a view "becomes a serious deterrent in the long run" to the more dynamic study of the "genesis and development of cultural patterns." The reason is that the latter "cannot realistically be disconnected from those organizations of ideas and feelings which constitute the individual." The so-called culture of a group, as ordinarily treated by the anthropologist, is essentially a systematic list of behavior patterns which "may be illustrated in the actual behavior of all or most of the individuals" concerned. The "true locus," however, of "these processes which, when abstracted in a totality, constitute culture" is not in the "theoretical community of human beings known as society," for the term "society" is "itself a cultural construct." Rather, he says,

> the true locus of culture is in the interactions of specific individuals and, on the subjective side, in the world of meanings which each one of these individuals may unconsciously abstract for himself from his participation in these interactions (1932: 432–435).

From this viewpoint, Sapir reiterates in another paper (1934), the cultures so carefully described in anthropological monographs are not "truly objective entities." They are "abstracted configurations of idea and action patterns," which have "endlessly different meanings for the various individuals" in the group concerned. Here we have a fresh outlook on behavior, culture, society, and personality that was to be profoundly influential.

Another of Boas' students, Ruth Benedict, was following up the ideas implied by Sapir's term "configurations." Throughout her career a member of the anthropology staff at Columbia University, and a poet as well as an anthropologist, she derived from her studies among Southwest Indians a vivid sense of deep contrast between the way of life of the Pueblo peoples and the ways of neighboring peoples such as the Navahos and the hunters and gleaners of prairie and desert. By 1932, in a paper entitled "Configurations of Culture in North America," she crystallized her impressions into a total characterization of these two distinctive cultural types. These were couched in psychological terms—that is, she extended to all the individuals within a culture qualities that psychologists had been attributing to individuals. The Pueblo cultures, she said, were "extrovert"—emphasizing external forms of behavior, ritualistic, conformist, distrusting individualism, avoiding excesses, showing restraint. The neighboring Indian cultures were, by contrast, "introvert"—intensely individualistic, aggressive, valuing violent experience, self-motivated rather than group-motivated. Acknowledging her debt to a somewhat similar duality in the earlier traditions of social philosophy, she borrowed from both Nietzsche and Spengler in naming the first type *Apollonian*, and using Nietzsche's contrasting term *Dionysian*. In this essay, Benedict took to task the "anecdotal" type of anthropological reporting which "made virtue of handling detached objects," and expressed disappointment that functionalists such as Malinowski were failing to "examine cultural wholes."

An initial storm of criticism broke over Benedict's head. She was accused of returning to a philosophical mysticism. Her cultural delineations were called artistic rather than scientific. Her configurations, it was said, were inferred from oversimplification of the cultural materials; the method was subjective, selective. The consistency of a culture was overstressed. Terms valid in individual psychology could not be applied indiscriminately to a culture. In 1934, Benedict's fuller statement of her position in the classic book *Patterns of Culture*, which has an approving introduction by Boas, met these criticisms and gave a less rigid "configurational" interpretation of the Southwestern and some other cultural types, including sketchy comments on patterning in American cultural behavior. A culture, Benedict says, is like an individual in having "a more or less consistent pattern of thought and action." Each culture comes to have its own characteristic "purposes," "emotional and intellectual mainsprings," "configurations," "goals" which pervade the behavior and institutions of the society concerned. Cultures differ not only because one trait is present here and absent there, but "still more because they are oriented as wholes in different directions." Any one society can make use of a "certain segment only" of the great "arc of potential human purposes and motivations," with its many alternatives and contradictions. The significant unit, Benedict insists, is therefore not the trait or the institution but the "cultural configuration."

Efforts to characterize whole cultures, their focal points and integration, have led to a welter of technical terms—themes, premises, values, enthymemes, orientations, ethos, and the like—and a morass of conceptual difficulties. One of the most systematic and perceptive scholars in this difficult field was Clyde Kluckhohn, who combined a humanistic outlook and background in classics with the precise methodological and conceptual standards of philosophy and natural science (the latter through his association with such scientists as L. J. Henderson). We have encountered in §58 Kluckhohn's attempts to distill out the essential principles of Navaho Indian philosophy. Though he sought at various points in his career to create a clearer conceptual order for talking about the unstated and generalized "givens" of a culture, he was still searching at the time of his death in 1960 for some conceptual or methodological key to this rich domain.

Studies of values, bringing together anthropologists and philosophers, became central in American configurational studies of the 1950s. A scholar whose basic training had been in philosophy, David Bidney, was particularly active in raising some of the main issues involved. He coined the special name *meta-anthropology* for studies of the philosophical postulates inherent in cultural systems: the "meta-" indicating "beyond." A focal point in studies of values was the Harvard University Laboratory of Social Relations. Here Ethel Albert, who received her training in philosophy, worked with anthropologists to illumine a concept of basic, or "focal," values (1956). Florence Kluckhohn, a sociologist-anthropologist, as part of a general theory of "value-orientations" (see F. Kluckhohn et al., 1955), suggested that the dominant value profile of a culture can be effectively explored in terms of a number of trichotomies (three-dimensional categories). The view of life of a people may, for example, be oriented primarily toward the past, the present, or the future; toward looking on the universe as basically evil, as neither good nor evil (mixed), or as good; toward seeing man as subjugated to nature, in nature, or over nature. In the first category, for example, traditional Chinese values are strongly oriented toward the past, Hispanic values toward the present, and American values toward the future.

Clyde Kluckhohn subsequently suggested (1956) that key values might be weighted in terms of binary (two-dimensional) contrasts. Here he sought to borrow models from Jakobson's theory of distinctive phonological features in language (§12). Judgments would be made by a specialist in a given culture, or by objective tests on a sampling of the people concerned, as to the prevalent value emphasis: whether, in man's relation to nature, the universe is felt to be predominantly determinate (orderly) or indeterminate (subject to caprice), unitary or pluralistic, evil or good; whether in man-to-man relations the stress is on individual or group, self or other, autonomy or dependence, active or acceptant, discipline or fulfillment (rather like Benedict's Appolonian and Dionysian), physical or mental (sensuous or intellectual), tense or relaxed, now or then; and so on to other possible binary contrasts.

Other important studies included A. I. Hallowell's attempts to characterize the world view and psychological patterning of the Ojibwa Indians, based on years of research (§58); and the project at Chicago, directed by the anthropologist Robert Redfield and the philosopher Milton Singer, which sought to delinate the values and world view of "great" and "little" traditions (§42). From this emerged studies of Chinese, Indian, and Islamic civilizations and Redfield's books generalizing from his studies of Mesoamerican peasantry. *The Primitive World and Its Transformations* (1953); *The Little Community* (1955); and *Peasant Society and Culture* (1956).

Attempts to characterize total-culture configurations have dwindled since 1960—doubtless in part due to the conceptual and methodological morass into which researchers in the field repeatedly became mired. One reason is that two different orders of anthropological questioning were frequently tangled up. The goals of attempts to delinate the configurations of Navaho, or Ojibwa, or Japanese cultures were basically *comparative*. That is, scholars hoped to distill out the essence of cultures so that one could show in what ways Navaho and Trobriand culture were *different*.

We might be able to refine our methods and models so as to infer the major features of Trobriand culture as an ideational system. Trobrianders, after all, manage to learn the "values" and premises that enable them to behave and make decisions in an acceptable Trobriand manner, so the data from which they glean this knowledge must be public and learnable (if not necessarily statable in words). But the Trobriand ideational order contains no information about Navaho Indians, and it is irrelevant in describing Trobriand values how they differ from Navaho ones. Having inferred Trobriand values or premises (which might turn out to be impossible to write down, even in Trobriand), we might well be unable to compare them with anyone else's. Yet the alternative—to try to describe one people's values in terms that contrast them with other people's—precludes our making sense of how Trobriand Islanders make decisions; and hence of relating our "theory" to the only relevant data we (or young Trobrianders) have. That does not rule out a search for universal structures which different cultures modify in different directions.

The rise and decline of configurational studies in American anthropology parallel the rise and decline of a closely related approach that branched off in a similar direction from the influence of Boas—the study of culture and individual personality.

73 · Culture and Personality

Roughly parallel in time to the emergence of total-culture interests, anthropological attention was becoming focused on what study of the individual could contribute to the understanding of culture and society. We have noted the theoretical impact of Sapir's work. Even among conventional historicalists, the individual had received some selective attention. In the course of breaking down naive viewpoints on racial determinism, Boas and others had discussed the nature of psychic capacities in the individual. Standard ethnographic reports usually included an account of the main events of the individual life cycle: for example, birth, naming, initiation to adulthood, and on to death. Furthermore, a number of "life histories" of Indians and others had been accumulating in their ethnographic records, such as Radin's autobiography of the Winnebago Indian "Crashing Thunder" (1926).

The first anthropologist to put the individual in the forefront of theoretical and related fieldwork attention was Margaret Mead. In 1925, when doing research on Samoan culture, she took detailed records on the lives of a number of adolescent girls. One of her resulting publications, *Coming of Age in Samoa* (1928), not only created something of a sensation in child study circles by demonstrating that supposedly universal "adolescent strain and stress" need not occur under some circumstances of child rearing; it also thrust child rearing dramatically into the spotlight as a potential area of action for the understanding of cultural behavior. Mead followed up with a further series of studies in the southwest Pacific that emphasized the relation between child training and what she came to call the "character structure" of adults in a society. Mead's comparative studies of child rearing among Samoans, Balinese, Iatmul tribesmen of New Guinea, and others are well known to laymen as well as to anthropologists.

Mead's work received essentially the same initial criticisms as that of Benedict, with which it became quite closely associated (Mead was Benedict's first graduate student at Columbia). Her generalizations were called subjective, selective as emphasizing major characteristics or model behaviors only, and art rather than science. She has therefore spent much effort on developing methodological controls, including research techniques to be used when, as with studies of peoples "behind the Iron Curtain," direct field checks cannot be made (Mead and Métraux, 1953). Mead's influence outside anthropology has been particularly extensive; she has become better known to the layman, probably, than any anthropologist since Frazer.

From the 1930s on, following up Mead's initial impetus, the anthropological literature on child rearing expanded rapidly. Attempts were made to establish a consistent relation between (a) training methods in a given cultural setting, especially in infancy and early childhood, (b) the types of adult "character" or "personality" favored in that setting, and (c) the institutions and values that are patterned in the culture.

Delineation of a broadly common adult personality, its shaping through child rearing, and its expression in culturally patterned behavior, raised an important challenge—especially since these studies came into focus as the world was plunged into war. Is there a similar common shaping of personality even in a large and complex modern nation? Could German, or French, or Chinese—or American—"national character" be identified and studied? Mead (1943), the Kluckhohns (1948), Gorer (1948), Hsu (1953), Warner (1953), and others have tried delinations of the American "national character." Extensive studies were made during and after World War II, of German, Russian, Japanese, French, Chinese, and other national traditions.

The difficulties of characterizing a complex modern nation are formidable. What, for instance, about the many subcultures of minority groups (the culture of a Chinatown or Polish-American neighborhood or black ghetto) or of upper and lower social strata? The reader critically interested in development of national character studies and their methodological difficulties and shortcomings should consult the critique by Inkeles and Levinson (1954).

Some of these criticisms apply only to the problems of internal diversity and complexity of modern nations; and others to the circularity inherent in studying culture and personality. We must return at this point to examine the theoretically more crucial attempts to study culture and personality in small-scale and relatively homogeneous societies.

While Mead's approach to the individual in culture stressed the subadult, a further important approach was being made by Ralph Linton, another scholar trained in the tradition of American historicalism. In *The Study of Man* (1936), he applied to anthropological materials certain viewpoints then becoming much discussed in sociology on the "status" and "role" of an individual within his society. In any society, he said, no individual learns and transmits the whole cultural tradition. His participation is limited to behavior appropriate to a particular set of statuses he occupies, or roles he plays, in the course of his lifetime. These are defined from infancy by his sex, and perhaps by his order among siblings, his class, and other given status and role specialization, and also build up with his age, his occupation, and similar factors. Some of these statuses are fixed and unchangeable (as he called them, *ascribed*); others are elective and involve choice and effort (hence, *achieved*). Some cultural elements are learned by every individual in the society, that is, they are *cultural universals*; others are *alternatives* with respect to individual participation. The individual, therefore, in the building up of his *personality* draws partly upon these common universals, so that there is a *basic personality* core shared by all, and partly upon *status personality* characteristics associated with his particular roles. Here, for the first time in social anthropology, was an explicit theoretical scheme ticketing neatly, if still very generally, the relation of individual, personality, culture, and society.

Boas retired in 1936, and Linton was given his key academic chair at Columbia University. There Linton became interested in a graduate seminar that Cora DuBois was conducting jointly with a Freudian psychoanalyst, Abram Kardiner. When DuBois went to Indonesia in 1937 to make her well-known study of the Alorese personality and culture (1944), Linton and Kardiner continued the seminar, a collaboration that lasted for some five years. During that time Linton and other anthropologists with field experience acted as informants in presenting to the seminar a detailed description of child rearing, adult behavior, and institutional structures in a series of cultural settings. The way of life was subjected to a kind of prolonged culturo-analysis with strong psychoanalytic overtones supplied by Kardiner. The main findings of this almost laboratorylike dissection process are contained in two works which bear Kardiner's name and strong imprint: *The Individual and His Society* (1939) and *Psychological Frontiers of Society* (1945). Linton presents his own views more directly in a small theoretical book, *The Cultural Background of Personality* (1945).

For each of the societies examined, the group felt itself able to isolate what Kardiner called a *basic personality structure*, that is, the "personality configuration which is shared by the bulk of the society's members as a result of early experiences which they have in common," especially through train-ing in infancy and early childhood. DuBois, after her experience in Alor, suggested that because the degree to which given individuals shared the "basic" behavior varied around certain highest-frequency tendencies, the com-mon core abstracted through scientific analysis could better be called *modal personality*.

To study how early experience shapes adult personality requires a theory of personality-formation and learning. Two bodies of psychological theory profoundly influenced anthropological thinking in this period. The first was Freudian psychoanalytic theory. Though Freud's own forays into anthropology were naive, his theories of man's nature and of personality development were obviously directly relevant to the anthropologist's enterprise; and he, in turn, could hope to separate out, in Freud's theories, what derives from being human from what derives from being Viennese. Freudian theory was carried quite directly into anthropology by Geza Roheim in studies of Australian Aborigines and in modified form by psychoanalysts like Kardiner and psycho-analytically sophisticated anthropologists like LaBarre (1954).

A second major source of psychological theory was the body of learning theory developed at Yale in the 1930s and early 1940s by Clark Hull and his students. "Yale learning theory," worked out mostly in experimental settings with rats and other animals, explored with mathematical precision how reinforcement leads to learning, how goals and drives can be modified, how habits are formed. Anthropologists like Whiting (1941), Murdock (1945), and Gillin (1948) were strongly influenced by the approach to learning, and explored in their research the new elements introduced when the organism that learns is a user of symbols and creature of culture.

Some of the difficulties of culture and personality research, conceptual and methodological, have been encountered in §59. A persistent circularity emerged in these studies. Describing personality in terms of culturally ex-pected behavior patterns, one could obviously demonstrate correlations "be-tween" personality and culture. Thus one could "demonstrate" that this cul-ture was a very appropriate one for people with this personality to enact (be-cause one inferred personality from culturally appropriate behavior patterns in the first place). To break out of this circularity required some way of approaching personality other than through culturally standardized behavior patterns.

The best hope was that the "projective tests" of modern psychology—the Rorschach inkblot plates and the Thematic Apperception Test or TAT (where subjects make up stories about standard drawings)—would work in other cultural settings. Evidently one could persuade primitives to report what they saw in inkblot or TAT plates (sometimes after tasting the corner). But could these responses be scored by the standards worked out in Western psychological and psychiatric practice?

A number of careful research designs, building on the experience of DuBois and Kardiner, were tried. One of the most successful was Gladwin and Sarason's *Truk: Man in Paradise* (1953), where Rorschach tests were scored by a psychologist unfamiliar with the culture and the results compared with cultural and behavioral evidence. Other classics in this field are Anthony Wallace's Rorschach studies of the "modal personality" of the Tuscarora Indians (1952), and the Spindlers' study of the personality of Menomini Indians at three different stages of acculturation (G. D. Spindler, 1955; L. S. Spindler, 1962).

The results of such research are controversial. The responses of non-Western peoples to projective tests often showed remarkable uniformity, raising hopes that in a small-scale, highly integrated, and stable society a basic or modal personality would be fairly standardized (though some deviations were inevitable). But by the early 1960s, the validity of projective tests as cross-cultural windows on personality was being increasingly challenged. Some doubts came from studies of shifting Rorschach responses of the same American subject at different times. Others reflected rising attention to cognition rather than motivation, in psychological and anthropological circles. The possibility that the common Rorschach or TAT response reflected a stretching of cultural categories, and patterning of perception, rather than some standard personality type, had to be squarely faced. Moreover, there were by the early 1960s strong reasons to doubt that even the cognitive categories and rules of any individual (Wallace's "Mazeway" [1970]) are like those of his fellows—not to mention his motivational strivings. Finally, the strong influence of genetic and biochemical forces in shaping personality was beginning to emerge as biochemistry and genetics made great advances.

What had changed was not so much the evidence as ways of conceptualizing culture and psychological structure. Cognitive models of culture and cognitively-oriented theories of the mind turned "personality" and "culture" into a false dichotomy. Before, our questions had seemed straightforward enough; it was our method that had been plagued by circularity. Now the tautologies and circularities were seen to pervade the very questions that had been asked.

Research on this frontier has not ceased, but it has shifted its character. A series of problems that had been united within a single framework remained legitimate individually but ceased to be pieces of one Big Problem. Thus some researchers examine mental illness in cross-cultural perspective. A sample problem, building on the probability that at least some forms of schizophrenia are biochemically generated, is whether the shamans or religious visionaries of some primitive tribes represent the incorporation of schizophrenics into the role system of a society.

The way learning takes place in non-Western settings continues to be an important problem. With the burst of interest in child language learning (and the possibility of an innate language design), it is likely to increase in importance. But the focus is on *process*, not on sweeping correlations between culture and personality as mediated by child-rearing techniques.

The psychological correlates of rapid culture change, where cognitive expectations no longer fit experienced events, pose crucial problems for study. The pace of change has so accelerated that for almost all men the psychological strain of "keeping up" is a major force. For the New Guinea tribesman, listening to House of Assembly debates on his transistor radio and remembering his cannibal boyhood, or for the American watching lunar exploration who vividly remembers reading about the Wright brothers, the psychological challenges of change are awesome and the processes and stresses are still little understood.

74 · The Anthropological Present

Tracing these lines of development in culture and personality research usefully introduces the modern scene. The preceding chapters represent a survey of the present, of what territories anthropologists are mapping and of what is happening on the frontier. But some further drawing together of themes may help to guide the interested reader in understanding what anthropologists are now talking and writing about.

Diversity is a striking feature at any large gathering of anthropologists. Annual meetings of the American Anthropological Association used to be tribal gatherings of a small band of peculiar escapists and adventurers. They now are rather conventional conventions. The diversity of interest and specialization is apparent on all sides. A symposium of papers on "political anthropology" or "economic anthropology," or "kinship" or "ritual," will attract its own following of students, professional specialists and devotees. Most anthropologists have a second kind of bond to a cluster of colleagues who have done fieldwork among neighboring peoples, and they also hold occasional collective rites celebrating their unity (or more often demonstrating their inability to agree about anything beyond the quality of the regional drinking water).

In such a diverse scene, the "chapter title" mode of dividing up the subject matter of anthropology that was rather reluctantly followed in the preceding chapters acquires a rationale it lacks on intellectual grounds: modern anthropologists tend to divide up in the same way, in following their specialized pursuits. But they divide up in other ways as well, in terms of what they write and what they read. Summing up the "schools" and fields of specialization in modern cultural anthropology is exceedingly difficult because there are several crosscutting levels or dimensions on which anthropologists can be grouped together.

First, of course, there are groupings by "chapter" and by area (so that those who study India could be placed together). Second, the scale of the society that scholars concentrate on unifies them in some respects: specialists on hunting and gathering peoples or peasant communities have a core of common concern, no matter how different their approaches are.

Anthropologists also group themselves on the basis of shared commitments about *methods.* Thus specialists in *cross-cultural studies* share certain assumptions about the evidence, the goals, and the methodological canons of their study (§24), even though one of them may see child-rearing techniques as the prime mover and another may look to subsistence technology. An attempt to show men as elements in *ecological systems,* and to trace causal connections between ecological adaptations and social forms, may unite scholars who would argue bitterly about the usefulness of a vast scheme of cultural evolution.

Some specialists in ideational systems would seek to account for their structure as products of the human mind, in the manner of Lévi-Strauss, while minimizing the importance of social forms and processes. Yet one major challenge, as represented in the work of such scholars as Victor Turner and Clifford Geertz, is to show how they fit together. Other explorers of ideational systems, as in "ethnoscience" (§14), see the anthropologist as having a special role to play in *behavioral science.* Cognition, the process of thinking and rule-following, is a major element in human behavior. The linguist is mapping one narrow segment of cognition with great precision; the anthropologist's task is to explore the rest, and map the variable content of cultural codes.

There are vast contrasts between anthropologists in goals and strategies. Compare a scholar who seeks by statistical means to trace the development of uxorilocal residence with his colleague who seeks to explore the structure of the human mind through American Indian myths; or who seeks to find order in the vast sweep of cultural evolution by studying the rise of urban states in Mesoamerica; or who seeks to use the logic of plant classification in an African tribe as a window through which to see cognitive structure; or who studies American Indians or Mexican Americans in urban slums or rural camps to see how they might better achieve their aspirations and develop their pride and cultural identity.

To pull such diverse threads into a few major strands or "schools" would probably be more misleading than helpful. It would also obscure the fact that the parochialism that helped to create the earlier schools, emanating from the few world centers where anthropologists were trained, is rapidly breaking down.

An American graduate student is more likely to be reading Leach or Lévi-Strauss than Kluckhohn or Murdock; and even the British, who have long disdained the goings-on of their American colleagues and have been skeptical of continental theorizing, are becoming more open to ideas from without.

Moreover, the anthropologist who seems to be a narrow specialist, and who might be wedged onto the bed of some theoretical "school," more often than not has some quite different line of research interest as well. The "specialist" on kinship terminologies is quite likely to produce a paper on ecology, art, linguistic history, mythology, or the results of technological change among the people he studies. He is also likely to be—in his teaching if not his writing—a generalist who considers the overall perspective on man that anthropology gives to be more important than the specialized topic he most often writes about. In part, this juxtaposition of narrowness and breadth, of specialization and roving interest, is a product of the anthropologist's encounters with the people he writes about. Fieldwork is, above all, an intense human experience that places him in the midst of real people and their many-sided way of life. A scientist who is not also a humanist can hardly endure such an intense encounter; and the lives of his friends and neighbors refuse to stay within the chapter titles or to focus down to what he, as specialist, may have set out to study.

75 · The Anthropological Future

The future of anthropology as discipline and profession is as misted as the present is muddled. The shifting tides of fashion and the nature of scientific change make it probable that the models and theories that dominate anthropology today will seem in a decade or two to have the same musty aura of poorly asked questions and faltering answers as those we have traced in preceding sections.

Thus "ethnoscience," far from portending the arrival of the anthropological millenium, may well turn out to be another and perhaps minor "school." Given the perspective we have taken on American anthropology—with historicalism, configurationalism, and culture and personality sprouting from the seeds of Boasian cultural determinism—ethnoscience may in fact be a fourth and final offshoot. Central in the assumptions of Boas and his students were (1) the *plasticity* of man, so that he became what his culture made him; (2) *relativism*, where each culture must be viewed in its own terms; and (3) *uniqueness* of each culture. Ethnoscience, building on Boas' early linguistic insights as they were expanded in American descriptive linguistics, exemplifies Boas' preoccupation with details, ethnographic rigor, and description. It reflects his reluctance in comparative theorizing; and its insistence on relativism and uniqueness fits squarely in the Boasian tradition. Ethnoscience may be the last major manifestation of that tradition, however new its garb and however optimistic its vision of the future.

Where, then, is cultural anthropology going? Here each anthropologist would have his own predictions, but at least some broad trends and possibilities can be set out. The gradual disintegration of boundaries between social science disciplines, slow to reach anthropology, is beginning to have an impact. The openness of anthropological frontiers (which seems to have decreased in some respects in the 1960s after some disillusionment in the interdisciplinary ventures of the 1950s) will undoubtedly increase. This will probably lead to greater interest in cybernetics (or, more generally, "general systems theory"), finite mathematics, and other unifying bodies of theory that have profoundly influenced modern thinking about biological and social systems.

Across the social sciences, relativism has been giving way to a search for general principles and universals. We have seen that in linguistics, where the structural uniqueness and hence incomparability of languages had long been assumed, modern transformationalists have sought to find universals of linguistic design in terms of which the particularities of any language can be specified. Similarly we can expect in anthropology increasing efforts to build general theoretical frameworks that link together specific cultures and societies as permutations of more general patterns.

One corollary to the cultural determinism of Boas and his students was the insistence that man is unique in that only he had culture. In recent years, as the postulates of this tradition have been reexamined, this sharp line between culture and nonculture, betwen man and his primate cousins, has become an empirical question, not an article of faith and assumption. We have seen in Chapter III the efflorescence of primate studies and of interest in animal communication that have begun to place human behavior in an adequate evolutionary perspective.

Another assumption deriving from Boas was that man's genetic endowment and biochemistry were so profoundly shaped by the impress of culture (and their investigation so subject to racist misinterpretation) that their influence on behavior was outside the proper domain of study. Anthropologists will inevitably draw on advancing studies of biochemistry and genetic programming as they relate to human behavior.

A major challenge in the years ahead is to map the neurophysiological structure of man's brain and to relate to that structure the processes of thinking, perception, memory, pattern recognition, and emotion. Mapping the correspondences between neurophysiology and the processes of the mind will be extraordinarily difficult and complex. Yet without adequate knowledge of mental processes, forays into the human mind (such as those by transformational linguists, American cognitive anthropologists, and Lévi-Strauss) will be speculative and oversimplified. The anthropologist's role in this multidisciplinary exploration of the brain/mind will be his usual one in the scientific division of labor: to document the range of variability and diversity, and to sort general principles from special cases and particular manifestations.

Dealing with human thought in terms of the "languages" of mathematics and science may limit our view to one side of man at the expense of the other. For if grammatical structure and kinship may yield to formally precise analysis, poetry, metaphor, and music probably will not. We need new formal languages for describing pattern and relationship. And we must face the possibility that the very act of transcribing them *in any formal language* radically transforms and even destroys these patterns. This possibility has begun to trouble profoundly some modern students of the mind. It is a theme as old as the mysticism of East and West—echoed in Zen Buddhism, Hindu mysticism, the work of William Blake, and the Jewish mystical tradition.

This suggests that if anthropology is to perceive man as a whole, not simply as a combination of neat pieces, a rigorous and precise analytical mode of approaching him must alternate with an esthetic grasp for patterns and wholes. An anthropology preoccupied with methodological rigor and formal precision will not live up to its mandate in the sciences or its potentiality for humanistic wisdom. Nor is this need for an alternation between big questions and small ones, wider views and more focused ones, confined to the study of man; we are realizing that it pervades the study of natural systems (Weiss, 1967, 1969; C. S. Smith, 1964, 1968). As Cyril Smith expresses it:

> Understanding can only come from a roving viewpoint and sequential changes of scale of attention. The current precision in science will limit its advance unless a way can be found for relating different but interwoven scales and dimensions. The elimination of the extraneous, in both experiment and theory, has been the veritable basis of all scientific advance since the seventeenth century, and has led us to a point where practically everything above the atom is understood "in principle." Sooner or later . . . science . . . will have exhausted the supply of problems that involve only those aspects of nature that can be freshly studied in simple isolation. The great need now is for concern with systems of greater complexity, for methods of dealing with complicated nature. . . . The artist has long been making meaningful and communicable statements, if not always precise ones, about complex things. If new methods, which will surely owe something to aesthetics, should enable the scientist to move into more complex fields, his area of interest will approach that of the humanist . . . (1964: 532).

This need for new ways to think about and analyze integration and relationship has emerged at several points in the preceding chapters. The anthropologist, like a biologist, can carve out one system at a time—ecological system, economic network, or code for kinship behavior. But he cannot yet show how these systems interrelate to generate patterns and processes that the study of any component system fails to account for.

To understand patterns of events in the Trobriand *kula*, for example, we would need not only to know the cultural code for appropriately exchanging valuables, but other circumstances as well. What happens in the *kula* may depend in part on the increase or decrease of the total number of valuables in the ring (which no Trobriander would know, but an economic analysis might reveal); and a change in rainfall in Dobu or decrease of fish in the Trobriand lagoon might affect the nature of *kula* trade or the timing of voyages. Even people's magic may affect what happens, because Trobrianders will expect it to work, and make their decisions accordingly; and the quarrel To'uluwa had with one of his wives may have *kula* repercussions for miles.

If these things too-complicated-to-account-for seem trivial when we are talking about the Trobriands, they are not trivial when we are trying to understand poverty or political conflict in an emerging African nation or the effects of increased earning power on cultural patterns, economic behavior, and family life in an American ghetto. And with the disappearance and transformation of the primitives whom anthropologists traditionally studied, and with the growing realization of how central cultural differences are in minority problems and rapid social change, more anthropologists will almost certainly be concerned with such problems as scientists as well as citizens. The vanishing of most primitive peoples at a time when the number of field-workers is sharply increasing—if fieldwork remains as central as it has been in the anthropological enterprise—will continue to change the character and the settings where fieldwork takes place.

76 · Anthropology as a Profession

The foregoing comments usefully lead to a very brief, final, examination of anthropology as a future profession. Here one's crystal ball is likely to be shattered by a brick. An earlier generation of anthropologists cloistered in museums has almost passed. The future of anthropology as a profession, at the time of writing in mid-1970, lies in the embattled halls of academia. Whether there will be jobs and research money, whether there will be academic freedom, whether there will be students, whether academic earning power will go up and down like hemlines—that is for some other prophet to say.

But there are some developments on which anthropologists themselves will have more influence. How widely anthropologists move from a university and college base into government, international bodies, or industry will be partly in their hands. So too will be the extent to which anthropology moves as a field into secondary or even primary education. Probably an undergraduate considering anthropology as a profession will have more options in these directions than his predecessors.

Another development in anthropology seems inevitable, given the great increase in the number of anthropologists and of universities awarding advanced degrees; and, at the same time given the rapid transformation of tribal peoples and the rural settings in non-Western societies in which anthropologists have traditionally worked. Fieldwork in non-Western societies will simply not be possible for many aspiring anthropologists. The costs are rising too high, the anthropologists becoming too numerous, the places becoming too few and—perhaps—increasingly inhospitable to "being studied." What will be done about it remains to be seen. Unquestionably, more and more graduate students and professionals will be studying communities and groups in their own society, not in some remote location where a new cultural world will be encountered. They will be hard-pressed to work in ways that are distinctively anthropological, and to avoid simply doing what sociologists have done, but doing it less systematically.

Another possibility is an increased emphasis on advanced research in the library, not the jungle. This need not rule out gaining wisdom and vision—witness Durkheim and Mauss. But it, like anthropological study only of one's own society, erodes that core of experience—fieldwork in another cultural world—around which anthropology has been shaped.

Finally there is a possibility, in anthropology as in other fields, that degrees less demanding than the Ph.D but more useful than the present M.A. will emerge. An M.A. in anthropology now opens few doors, except at a junior college level. Many universities use the M.A. as a stage in the rite of passage at which those not deemed worthy of the final mysteries are sent off with a consolation prize. A more meaningful intermediate degree that depends heavily on library research and emphasizes qualification to teach anthropology might well emerge at many universities.

Whatever the nature of these developments, anthropology offers both a sweeping and humanistic view of man and an extraordinary range of things one can study and places one can study them. If an anthropologist finds himself uninterested in what he is studying, he has only himself to blame. Probably in no other academic field does one get a comparably broad view of man and human possibility; and probably in no other academic field that studies man does one meet him in such rich, vivid, and personal encounters as those of the field anthropologist.

Section II

Suggestions for Further Reading

For each of the numbered sections of the text, I have suggested a brief list of further readings. These will provide a student access to additional technical materials in the field. The suggested readings include key articles, general books (or chapters of general books), and edited compilations of readings in the subfield. The latter give a sampling of the technical literature, often have useful introductions, and contain technical bibliographies.

Depending on the library resources available to the student, additional means of finding technical literature may be available. One of the best sources is the catalogue to the Peabody Museum Library (Harvard University), which is indexed by subject and author and includes detailed cataloging of journal articles as well as books.

Major anthropology journals of possible interest to the student include *American Anthropologist, Ethnology, Man, Southwestern Journal of Anthropology, Current Anthropology, Africa, Journal of the Royal Anthropological Institute* (until 1965), *Oceania, L'Homme, Journal of American Folklore, Journal of the Polynesian Society, Bijdragen Tot de Land, – Taal, – en Volkenkunde, Anthropos,* and *Ethnohistory.*

Some of the numbered sections of the text have been grouped together in the recommended readings below, since the same readings are useful for several sections. The titles listed for each section (or sections) are listed with general or introductory works first, followed by more technical works or collected readings.

Sections 1 and 2

TAX, S., ed. 1964. *Horizons of Anthropology.* Chicago: Aldine Publishing Company.

CLIFTON, J. 1968. Cultural Anthropology: Aspirations and Approaches. In J. CLIFTON, ed., *Introduction to Cultural Anthropology.* Boston: Houghton Mifflin Company.

KLUCKHOHN, C. 1949. *Mirror for Man.* New York: McGraw-Hill, Inc.
STURTEVANT, W. 1968. The Fields of Anthropology. In M. H. FRIED, *Readings in Anthropology,* 2d ed., Vol. 1.
LÉVI-STRAUSS, C. 1966. The Scope of Anthropology. *Current Anthropology* 7:112–123.
KROEBER, A. L. 1952. *The Nature of Culture.* Chicago: University of Chicago Press.

Section 3

KUHN, T. 1962. *The Structure of Scientific Revolutions.* Chicago: University of Chicago Press.
PELTO, P. J. 1970. *Anthropological Research: The Structure of Inquiry.* New York: Harper & Row.
NAROLL, R., and R. COHEN, eds. 1970. *A Handbook of Method in Cultural Anthropology.* Garden City, N.Y.: Natural History Press.
BROWN, R. 1963. *Explanation in Social Science.* Chicago: Aldine Publishing Company.
NAGEL, E. 1968. *The Structure of Science.* New York: Harcourt, Brace & World.
STINCHCOMBE, A. L. 1968. *Constructing Social Theories.* New York: Harcourt, Brace & World.
HEMPEL, C. G. 1965. *Aspects of Scientific Explanation, and Other Essays in the Philosophy of Science.* New York: Free Press.

Section 4

BERREMAN, G. D. 1968. Ethnography: Method and Product. In J. CLIFTON, ed., *Introduction to Cultural Anthropology.* Boston: Houghton Mifflin Company.
———. 1962. *Behind Many Masks: Ethnography and Impression Management in a Himalayan Village.* Ithaca, N.Y.: Soc. for Applied Anth. Monograph No. 4.
PAUL, B. 1963. Interview Techniques and Field Relationships. In A. L. KROEBER, ed., *Anthropology Today.* Chicago: University of Chicago Press.
GOLDE, P., ed. 1970. *Women in the Field.* Chicago: Aldine Publishing Company.
FREILICH, M., ed. 1970. *Marginal Natives: Anthropologists at Work.* New York: Harper & Row.
JONGMANS, D. G., and P. C. GUTKIND, eds. 1967. *Anthropologists in the Field.* Assen: Van Gorcum.
SPINDLER, G. D., ed. 1970. *Being an Anthropologist: Fieldwork in Eleven Cultures.* New York: Holt, Rinehart and Winston.
WILLIAMS, T. R. 1967. *Field Methods in the Study of Culture.* New York: Holt, Rinehart and Winston.
EPSTEIN, A. L., ed. 1967. *The Craft of Social Anthropology.* London: Tavistock.
CASAGRANDE, J. B., ed. 1960. *In the Company of Man.* New York: Harper & Row.
BOWEN, E. S. 1954. *Return to Laughter.* New York: Harcourt, Brace & World.

Section 5

KLUCKHOHN, C., and W. KELLY. 1945. The Concept of Culture. In R. LINTON, ed., *The Science of Man in the World Crisis.* New York: Columbia University Press.
KAY, P. 1965. Ethnography and the Theory of Culture. *Bucknell Review* 19:106–113.
WHITE, L. A. 1959. The Concept of Culture. *American Anthropologist* 61:227–251.
GOODENOUGH, W. H. 1961. Comment on Cultural Evolution. *Daedalus* 90:514–533.

KROEBER, A. L., and C. KLUCKHOHN. 1952. *Culture: A Critical Review of Concepts and Definitions.* Papers of the Peabody Museum of American Archaeology and Ethnology, Harvard University, Vol. 47.

Section 6

GEERTZ, C. 1957. Ritual and Social Change: A Javanese Example. *American Anthropologist* 59:32–54.
SCHNEIDER, D. M. 1968. Introduction to *The American Kinship System.* Englewood Cliffs, N.J.: Prentice-Hall, Inc.
KROEBER, A. L., and T. PARSONS. 1958. The Concepts of Cultural and of Social System. *American Sociological Review* 582–583.

Section 7

HOWELL, F. C. 1967. *Early Man.* New York: Time-Life Books.
PFEIFFER, J. E. 1970. *The Emergence of Man.* New York: Harper & Row.
MONTAGU, M. F. 1968. *Culture: Man's Adaptive Dimension.* New York: Oxford University Press.
CAMPBELL, B. 1966. *Human Evolution: An Introduction to Man's Adaptations.* Chicago: Aldine Publishing Company.
ALLAND, A. 1967. *Evolution and Human Behavior.* Garden City, N.Y.: Natural History Press.
BRACE, C. L., and M. F. A. MONTAGU. 1965. *Man's Evolution.* New York: The Macmillan Company.
CLEGG, E. G. 1969. *The Study of Man: An Introduction to Human Biology.* New York: American Elsevier Publishing Company.

Section 8

DE VORE, I. 1965. *Primate Behavior.* New York: Holt, Rinehart and Winston.
JAY, P., ed. 1968. *Primates: Studies in Adaptation and Variability.* New York: Holt, Rinehart and Winston.
ALTMANN, S. A. 1967. *Social Communication among Primates.* Chicago: University of Chicago Press.
MONTAGU, M. F. 1968. *Culture: Man's Adaptive Dimension.* New York: Oxford University Press.
HOCKETT, C. F., and R. ASCHER. 1964. The Human Revolution. *Current Anthropology* 5:135–168.

Section 9

DOBZHANSKY, T. 1962. *Mankind Evolving.* New Haven, Conn.: Yale University Press.
HAINLINE, L. J. 1965. Culture and Biological Adaptation. *American Anthropologist* 67:1174–1197.
SPUHLER, J. N. 1967. *Genetic Diversity and Human Behavior.* Chicago: Aldine Publishing Company.
MEAD, M., et al., eds. 1968. *Science and the Concept of Race.* New York: Columbia University Press.
BAKER, P. T., and J. WEINER, eds. 1966. *The Biology of Human Adaptability.* Oxford: Clarendon Press.
BARNICOT, N. 1959. Climatic Factors in the Evolution of Human Populations. *Cold Spring Harbor Symposia on Quantitative Biology* 24: 115–129.

Section 10

LANCASTER, J. B. 1968. Primate Communication Systems and Human Language. In P. JAY, ed., *Primates: Studies in Adaptation and Variability*. New York: Holt, Rinehart and Winston.

HOLLOWAY, R. L., JR. 1969. Culture: A Human Domain. *Current Anthropology* 10:395–407.

WHITE, L. A. 1944. The Symbol: The Origin and Basis of Human Behavior. *Etc.: A Review of General Semantics* 1:229–237.

SEBEOK, T., ed. 1968. *Animal Communication*. Bloomington: University of Indiana Press.

LENNEBERG, E. 1967. *Biological Foundations of Language*. New York: John Wiley & Sons.

Sections 11 and 12

LANGACKER, R. W. 1968. *Language and Its Structure: Some Fundamental Linguistic Concepts*. New York: Harcourt, Brace & World.

CHOMSKY, N. 1968. *Language and Mind*. New York: Harcourt, Brace & World.

KEYSER, S. J., and M. HALLE. 1968. What We Do When We Speak. In P. A. KOLERS and M. EDEN, eds., *Recognizing Patterns: Studies in Living and Automatic Systems*. Cambridge, Mass.: MIT Press.

DINNEEN, S.J., F. P. 1967. Noam Chomsky: Transformational Grammar and Linguistic Universals. In F. P. DINNEEN, S.J., *An Introduction to General Linguistics*. New York: Holt, Rinehart and Winston.

LYONS, J. 1970. *Noam Chomsky*. New York: Viking Press.

LYONS, J., ed. 1970. *New Horizons of Linguistics*. London: Penguin.

FODOR, J. A., and J. J. KATZ, eds. 1964. *The Structure of Language: Readings in the Philosophy of Language*. Englewood Cliffs, N.J.: Prentice-Hall, Inc.

Section 13

GREENBERG, J. H. 1963. *Universals of Language*. Cambridge, Mass.: MIT Press.

MC NEILL, D. 1970. *The Acquisition of Language*. New York: Harper & Row.

CHOMSKY, N. 1968. *Language and Mind*. New York: Harcourt, Brace & World.

LANGACKER, R. W. 1968. *Language and Its Structure: Some Fundamental Linguistic Concepts*. New York: Harcourt, Brace & World.

LENNEBERG, E. H. 1969. On Explaining Language. *Science* 164:635–643.

BACH, E., and R. HARMS, eds. 1968. *Universals in Linguistic Theory*. New York: Holt, Rinehart and Winston.

CHOMSKY, N. 1971. *Chomsky: Selected Readings* (J. P. B. ALLEN and P. VAN BUREN, eds.). London: Oxford University Press.

Sections 14 and 15

GREENBERG, J. H. 1968. *Anthropological Linguistics*. New York: Random House.

HYMES, D. H., ed. 1964. *Language in Culture and Society*. New York: Harper & Row.

BURLING, R. 1969. *Man's Many Voices*. New York: Holt, Rinehart and Winston.

TYLER, S., ed. 1969. *Cognitive Anthropology*. New York: Holt, Rinehart and Winston.

GOODENOUGH, W. H. 1957. Cultural Anthropology and Linguistics. In *Report of the Seventh Annual Round Table Meeting on Linguistics and Language Study*. Washington, D.C.: Georgetown University Press.

BURLING, R. 1969. Linguistics and Ethnographic Description. *American Anthropologist* 71:817–827.
WHORF, B. L. 1956. *Language, Thought and Reality*. Cambridge, Mass.: MIT Press.

Section 16

HYMES, D. 1962. The Ethnography of Speaking. In T. GLADWIN and W. STURTEVANT, eds., *Anthropology and Human Behavior*. Washington, D.C.: Anthropological Society of Washington.
———. 1967. The Anthropology of Communication. In F. DANCE, ed., *Human Communication Theory*. New York: Holt, Rinehart and Winston.
BATESON, G. *The Ecology of the Mind*. San Francisco: Chandler Publishing Co. (in press).
SEBEOK, T. A., A. HAYES, and M. C. BATESON, eds. 1964. *Approaches to Semiotics: Transactions of the Indiana University Conference on Paralinguistics and Kinesics*. The Hague: Mouton and Company.
HALLE, E. T. 1959. *The Silent Language*. Garden City, N.Y.: Doubleday & Company.
———. 1966. *The Hidden Dimension*. Garden City, N.Y.: Doubleday & Company.
WATSON, O. M. 1970. *Proxemic Behavior: A Cross-Cultural Study*. The Hague: Mouton and Company.
VON BERTALANFFY, L. 1968. *General Systems Theory*. New York: George Braziller, Inc.
STEINBERG, D. D., and L. JAKOBVITS, eds. *Semantics: An Interdisciplinary Reader in Philosophy, Linguistics, Psychology, and Anthropology*. Urbana: University of Illinois Press (in press).

Section 17

DEETZ, J. 1967. *Invitation to Archaeology*. Garden City, N.Y.: Natural History Press.
HOLE, F., and R. F. HEIZER. 1965. *An Introduction to Prehistoric Archaeology*. New York: Holt, Rinehart and Winston.
BINFORD, L. R. 1962. Archaeology as Anthropology. *American Antiquity* 28:217–225.
CHANG, K. C. 1967. *Rethinking Archaeology*. New York: Random House.
MEIGHAN, C. 1966. *Archaeology: An Introduction*. San Francisco: Chandler Publishing Co.
BINFORD, L. R., and S. BINFORD, eds. 1968. *New Perspectives in Archaeology*. Chicago: Aldine Publishing Company.

Section 18

LEE, R. B., and I. DE VORE, eds. 1968. *Man the Hunter*. Chicago: Aldine Publishing Company.
SERVICE, E. R. 1966. *The Hunters*. Englewood Cliffs, N.J.: Prentice-Hall, Inc.

Section 19

FLANNERY, K. V. 1965. The Ecology of Early Food Production in Mesopotamia. *Science* 147, no. 3663:1247–1256.
MAC NEISH, R. S. 1964. The Origin of New World Civilization. *Scientific American* 211, no. 5:29–37.

BRAIDWOOD, R. J., and G. R. WILLEY, eds. 1962. *Courses toward Urban Life*. Chicago: Aldine Publishing Company.
BRAIDWOOD, R. J. 1960. The Agricultural Revolution. *Scientific American* 203: 131–148.

Section 20

ADAMS, R. N. 1966. *The Evolution of Urban Society*. Chicago: Aldine Publishing Company.
SANDERS, W. T., and B. J. PRICE. 1968. *Mesoamerica: The Evolution of a Civilization*. New York: Random House.

Section 21

LINTON, R. 1955. *The Tree of Culture*. New York: Alfred A. Knopf.

For other general collections on the culture history of particular areas, see library subject catalogues. The extensive literature here is expanding so rapidly that an area-by-area list would quickly be out of date.

Section 22

KLUCKHOHN, C. 1953. Universal Categories of Culture. In A. L. KROEBER, ed., *Anthropology Today*. Chicago: University of Chicago Press.
FRAKE, C. O. 1964. A Structural Description of Subanun "Religious Behavior." In W. GOODENOUGH, ed., *Explorations in Social Anthropology*. New York: McGraw-Hill, Inc.
GOODENOUGH, W. H. 1956. Residence Rules. *Southwestern Journal of Anthropology* 12:22–37.
AL-ISSA, I., and W. DENNIS, eds. 1970. *Cross-Cultural Studies of Behavior*. New York: Holt, Rinehart and Winston.

Section 23

KLUCKHOHN, C. 1962. *Culture and Behavior* (esp. Chaps. 16 and 17). New York: Free Press.
HERSKOVITS, M. 1955. *Cultural Anthropology* (esp. Chap. 19). New York: Alfred A. Knopf.
FIRTH, R. 1951. *Elements of Social Organisation* (esp. Chap. 6). London: C. A. Watts & Co.

Section 24

WHITING, J. W. M. 1968. Methods and Problems in Cross-Cultural Research. In G. LINDZEY and A. ARONSON, eds., *The Handbook of Social Psychology*, 2d ed., Vol. 2. Reading, Mass.: Addison-Wesley.
FORD, C. S., ed. 1967. *Cross-Cultural Approaches*. New Haven, Conn.: HRAF Press.
NAROLL, R., and R. COHEN, eds. 1970. *A Handbook of Method in Cultural Anthropology* (esp. Parts V, VI, and VII). Garden City, N.Y.: Natural History Press.
NAROLL, R. 1962. *Data Quality Control: A New Research Technique*. New York: Free Press.
———. 1968. Some Thoughts on Comparative Method in Cultural Anthropology. In H. M. BLALOCK, ed., *Methodology in Social Research*. New York: McGraw-Hill, Inc.

KÖBBEN, A. F. J. 1967. Why Exceptions? The Logic of Cross-Cultural Analysis. *Current Anthropology* 8:3–34.

EVANS-PRITCHARD, E. E. 1965. The Comparative Method in Social Anthropology. In E. E. EVANS-PRITCHARD, ed., *The Position of Women and Other Essays.* London: Faber & Faber.

MOORE, F. W., ed. 1961. *Readings in Cross-Cultural Methodology.* New Haven, Conn.: HRAF Press.

EGGAN, F. 1954. Social Anthropology and the Method of Controlled Comparison. *American Anthropologist* 56:743–763.

NADEL, S. F. 1952. Witchcraft in Four African Societies: An Essay in Comparison. *American Anthropologist* 54:18–29.

Section 25

VAYDA, A. P., and R. A. RAPPAPORT. 1968. Ecology, Cultural and Noncultural. In J. CLIFTON, ed., *Introduction to Cultural Anthropology.* Boston: Houghton Mifflin Company.

SERVICE, E. R. 1962. *Primitive Social Organization: An Evolutionary Perspective.* New York: Random House.

FRIED, M. 1967. *The Evolution of Political Society.* New York: Random House.

SPIER, R. F. G. 1970. *From the Hand of Man: Primitive and Preindustrial Technologies.* Boston: Houghton Mifflin Company.

BATES, M. 1964. *Man in Nature,* 2d ed. Englewood Cliffs, N.J.: Prentice-Hall, Inc.

DAMAS, D., ed. 1969. *Contribution to Anthropology: Ecological Essays.* Ottawa: Queen's Printer.

VAYDA, A. P., ed. 1969. *Environment and Cultural Behavior: Ecological Studies in Cultural Anthropology.* Garden City, N.Y.: Natural History Press.

Section 26

LEE, R. B., and I. DE VORE, eds. 1968. *Man the Hunter.* Chicago: Aldine Publishing Company.

SERVICE, E. R. 1966. *The Hunters.* Englewood Cliffs, N.J.: Prentice-Hall, Inc.

Section 27

CONKLIN, H. C. 1954. An Ethnoecological Approach to Shifting Agriculture. *Trans. of New York Academy of Sciences* 17, no. 2:133–142.

———. 1961. The Study of Shifting Cultivation. *Current Anthropology* 2:27–64.

RAPPAPORT, R. A. 1968. *Pigs for the Ancestors: Ritual in the Ecology of a New Guinea People.* New Haven, Conn.: Yale University Press.

BENNETT, J. W. 1969. *Northern Plainsmen: Adaptive Strategy and Agrarian Life.* Chicago: Aldine Publishing Company.

BARTH, F. 1968. *Nomads of South Persia.* Oslo: Oslo University Press.

GULLIVER, P. H. 1965. *The Family Herds.* London: Routledge & Kegan Paul.

Section 28

WHITE, L. A. 1959. *The Evolution of Culture.* New York: McGraw-Hill, Inc.

———. 1949. *The Science of Culture.* New York: Grove Press.

STEWARD, J. H. 1955. *Theory of Culture Change.* Urbana: University of Illinois Press.

SAHLINS, M. D., and E. R. SERVICE, eds. 1960. *Evolution and Culture.* Ann Arbor: University of Michigan Press.

Section 29

SCHNEIDER, D. M. 1968. Introduction to *The American Kinship System*. Englewood Cliffs, N.J.: Prentice-Hall, Inc.

GOODENOUGH, W. 1961. Comment on Cultural Evolution. *Daedalus* 90:514–533.

————. 1963. *Cooperation in Change*. New York: Russell Sage Foundation.

Sections 30–32

FOX, R. 1968. *Kinship and Marriage*. Baltimore: Penguin Books.

LÉVI-STRAUSS. 1956. The Family. In H. SHAPIRO, ed., *Man, Culture and Society*. London: Oxford University Press.

MURDOCK, G. P. 1949. *Social Structure*. New York: The Macmillan Company.

FORTES, M. 1959. Primitive Kinship. *Scientific American* June:146–158.

SAHLINS, M. 1968. *Tribesmen*. Englewood Cliffs, N.J.: Prentice-Hall, Inc.

SCHNEIDER, D., and K. GOUGH, eds. 1961. *Matrilineal Kinship*. Berkeley: University of California Press.

LIENHARDT, G. 1964. *Social Anthropology*. London: Oxford University Press.

BEATTIE, J. 1964. *Other Cultures* (Chaps. 7 and 8). New York: Free Press.

BOHANNAN, P., and J. MIDDLETON, eds. 1968. *Kinship and Social Organization*. Garden City, N.Y.: Natural History Press.

FORTES, M. 1953. The Structure of Unilineal Descent Groups. *American Anthropologist* 55:17–44.

Section 33

FOX, R. 1968. *Kinship and Marriage*. Baltimore: Penguin Books.

LEACH, E. R. 1959. Concerning Trobriand Clans and the Kinship Category "Tabu." In J. GOODY, ed., *The Developmental Cycle in Domestic Groups*. Cambridge Papers in Social Anthropology, 1.

LOUNSBURY, F. G. 1964. A Formal Account of the Crow- and Omaha-Type Kinship Technologies. In W. GOODENOUGH, ed., *Explorations in Cultural Anthropology*. New York: McGraw-Hill, Inc.

NEEDHAM, R. 1971. Remarks on the Analysis of Kinship and Marriage. In R. NEEDHAM, ed., *Kinship and Marriage*. ASA Monographs, 11.

SCHEFFLER, H. W. Systems of Kin Classification: A Structural Typology (forthcoming in P. REINING, ed., Centennial Volume for L. H. Morgan). Washington, D.C.: Anthropological Society of Washington.

Sections 34 and 35

LÉVI-STRAUSS, C. 1956. The Family. In H. SHAPIRO, ed., *Man, Culture and Society*. London: Oxford University Press.

FORTES, M., ed. 1962. *Marriage in Tribal Societies*. Cambridge Papers in Social Anthropology, 3.

BOHANNAN, P., and J. MIDDLETON, eds. 1968. *Marriage, Family, and Residence*. Garden City, N.Y.: Natural History Press.

GOODY, J., ed. 1958. *The Developmental Cycle in Domestic Groups*. Cambridge Papers in Social Anthropology, 1.

STEPHENS, W. N. 1963. *The Family in Cross-Cultural Perspective*. New York: Holt, Rinehart and Winston.

SPIRO, M. E. 1954. Is the Family Universal? *American Anthropologist* 56:839–846.

ADAMS, R. N. 1960. An Inquiry into the Nature of the Family. In G. E. DOLE and R. CARNEIRO, eds., *Essays in the Science of Culture*. New York: Thomas Y. Crowell Company.

Section 36

See suggested readings for Sections 30–32 and 34–35.

Section 37

VAN GENNEP, A. 1960. *The Rites of Passage.* London: Routledge & Kegan Paul.
DOUGLAS, M. 1966. *Purity and Danger.* London: Routledge & Kegan Paul.
EISENSTADT, S. N. 1956. *From Generation to Generation: Age Groups and Social Structure.* New York: Free Press.

Section 38

LOWIE, R. H. 1947. *Primitive Society* (Chaps. 10 and 11). New York: Liveright Publishing Corp.
WEDGEWOOD, C. H. 1930. The Nature and Functions of Secret Societies. *Oceania* 1:129–145.
HSU, F. 1963. *Clan, Caste, and Club.* Princeton, N.J.: D. Van Nostrand Company.
TIGER, L. 1969. *Men in Groups.* New York: Random House.
WEBSTER, H. 1968. *Primitive Secret Societies,* 2d ed. New York: Octagon Books.

Section 39

BOHANNAN, P. 1963. *Social Anthropology.* New York: Holt, Rinehart and Winston.
FRIED, M. 1967. *The Evolution of Political Society.* New York: Random House.
DE REUCK, A., and J. KNIGHT, eds. 1967. *Caste and Race: Comparative Approaches.* London: J. and A. Churchill, Ltd.
DUMONT, L. 1970. *Homo Hierarchicus.* Chicago: University of Chicago Press.
PLOTNICOV, L., and A. TUDEN. 1969. *Essays in Comparative Social Stratification.* Pittsburgh: University of Pittsburgh Press.
———— and ————. 1970. *Social Stratification in Africa.* New York: The Macmillan Company.

Section 40

See suggested readings for Section 28. See, also,
MURDOCK, G. P. 1949. *Social Structure.* New York: The Macmillan Company.

Section 41

WOLF, E. R. 1966. *Peasants.* Englewood Cliffs, N.J.: Prentice-Hall, Inc.
REDFIELD, R. 1956. *Peasant Society and Culture.* Chicago: University of Chicago Press.
POTTER, J., M. DIAZ, and G. FOSTER, eds. 1967. *Peasant Society: A Reader.* Boston: Little, Brown and Company.
BOCK, P. K., ed. 1968. *Peasants in the Modern World.* Albuquerque: University of New Mexico Press.
WOLF, E. R. 1970. *Peasant Wars of the Twentieth Century.* New York: Harper & Row.
HUNTER, G. 1969. *Modernizing Peasant Societies: A Comparative Study in Asia and Africa.* London: Oxford University Press.
HOIJER, H., and W. GOLDSCHMIDT, eds. *The Social Anthropology of Latin America: Essays in Honor of Ralph Beals.* Los Angeles: Latin American Center (in press).

Section 42

EISENSTADT, S. N. 1961. Anthropological Studies of Complex Societies. *Current Anthropology* 2:201–210.

BANTON, M., ed. 1966. *The Social Anthropology of Complex Societies.* ASA Monographs, 4. London: Tavistock.

MARRIOTT, M., ed. 1955. *Village India: Studies in the Little Community.* Chicago: University of Chicago Press.

SINGER, M., and B. S. COHN, eds. 1968. *Structure and Change in Indian Society* (Viking Fund Publications in Anthropology, 47). Chicago: Aldine Publishing Company.

Section 43

EDDY, E. M., ed. 1968. *Urban Anthropology: Research Perspectives and Strategies.* Southern Anthropological Society Proceedings, 2. Athens, Ga.: Southern Anthropological Society.

MANGIN, W. P., ed. 1970. *Peasants in Cities: Readings in the Anthropology of Urbanization.* Boston: Houghton Mifflin Company.

SPRADLEY, J. P. 1970. *You Owe Yourself a Drunk: An Ethnography of Urban Nomads.* Boston: Little, Brown and Company.

Sections 44–48

NASH, M. 1966. *Primitive and Peasant Economic Systems.* San Francisco: Chandler Publishing Co.

BELSHAW, C. 1965. *Traditional Exchange and Modern Markets.* Englewood Cliffs, N.J.: Prentice-Hall, Inc.

LE CLAIR, E., and H. SCHNEIDER. 1968. *Economic Anthropology.* New York: Holt, Rinehart and Winston.

DALTON, G., ed. 1967. *Tribal and Peasant Economics.* Garden City, N.Y.: Natural History Press.

FIRTH, R., ed. 1967. *Themes in Economic Anthropology.* ASA Monographs, 6. London: Tavistock.

PANOFF, M., Marcel Mauss' "The Gift" Revisited. *Man,* n.s., 5:60–70.

BOHANNAN, P., and G. DALTON, eds. 1962. *Markets in Africa.* Evanston, Ill.: Northwestern University Press.

Section 49

FRIED, M. 1967. *The Evolution of Political Society.* New York: Random House.

BEATTIE, J. 1964. *Other Cultures* (Chap. 9). New York: Free Press.

COHEN, R., and J. MIDDLETON, eds. 1967. *Comparative Political Systems.* Garden City, N.Y.: Natural History Press.

FORTES, M., and E. EVANS-PRITCHARD, eds. 1940. *African Political Systems.* London: Oxford University Press.

EISENSTADT, S. N. 1963. *Political Systems of Empires.* New York: Free Press.

Section 50

SWARTZ, M., V. TURNER, A. TUDEN, eds. 1966. *Political Anthropology.* Chicago: Aldine Publishing Company.

SWARTZ, M., ed. 1968. *Local Level Politics.* Chicago: Aldine Publishing Company.

BAILEY, F. G. 1969. *Stratagems and Spoils: A Social Anthropology of Politics.* Oxford: Blackwell.

COHEN, A. 1969. Political Anthropology: The Analysis of the Symbolism of Power Relations. *Man*, n.s., 4:215–235.
TURNER, V. 1957. *Schism and Continuity in an African Society*. Manchester: Manchester University Press.

Section 51

FRIED, M., M. HARRIS, and R. MURPHY, eds. 1968. *War: The Anthropology of Armed Conflict and Aggression*. Garden City, N.Y.: Natural History Press.
MONTAGU, M. F., ed. 1968. *Man and Aggression*. London: Oxford University Press.

Sections 52 and 53

HOEBEL, E. A. 1954. *The Law of Primitive Man*. Cambridge, Mass.: Harvard University Press.
POSPISIL, L. 1968. Law and Order. In J. CLIFTON, ed. *Introduction to Cultural Anthropology*. Boston: Houghton Mifflin Company.
NADER, L., ed. 1968. *Law in Culture and Society*. Chicago: Aldine Publishing Company.
POSPISIL, L. 1958. *Kapauku Papuans and Their Law*. New Haven, Conn.: Yale University Publications in Anthropology, 54.
NADER, L., ed. 1965. *The Ethnography of Law*. American Anthropologist Special Publication, Vol. 67, 6, Part 2.

Section 54

LESSA, W., and E. VOGT, eds. 1965. *Reader in Comparative Religion*, 2d ed. New York: Harper & Row.
LESLIE, C., ed. 1960. *Anthropology of Folk Religion*. New York: Random House.
BANTON, M., ed. 1966. *Anthropological Approaches to the Study of Religion*. ASA Monographs, 3. London: Tavistock. (See especially articles by Geertz and Spiro.)
WALLACE, A. F. C. 1967. *Religion: An Anthropological View*. New York: Random House.
EVANS-PRITCHARD, E. E. 1965. *Theories of Primitive Religion*. London: Oxford University Press.

Section 55

MALINOWSKI, B. 1955. *Magic, Science and Religion*. New York: Doubleday & Company.
HORTON, R. The Kalabari World View: An Outline and Interpretation. *Africa* 32:197–220.
WAX, M., and R. WAX. 1963. The Nature of Magic. *Current Anthropology* 4:495–518.
MIDDLETON, J., ed. 1967. *Magic, Witchcraft, and Curing*. Garden City, N.Y.: Natural History Press.
EVANS-PRITCHARD, E. E. 1937. *Witchcraft, Oracles and Magic among the Azande*. Oxford: Clarendon Press.
NADEL, S. F. 1957. Malinowski on Magic and Religion. In R. FIRTH, ed., *Man and Culture*. London: Routledge & Kegan Paul.

Section 56

GOODY, J. 1962. *Death, Property and the Ancestors*. London: Tavistock.
HERTZ, R. 1960. *Death and the Right Hand*. New York: Free Press.

EVANS-PRITCHARD, E. 1953. The Nuer Conception of Spirit in Relation to the Social Order. *American Anthropologist* 55:201–214.

LÉVI-STRAUSS, C. 1963. *Totemism*. Boston: Beacon Press.

MIDDLETON, J. 1960. *Lugbara Religion*. London: Oxford University Press.

DURKHEIM, E. 1957. *The Elementary Forms of the Religious Life*. London: Allen & Unwin.

DURKHEIM, E., and M. MAUSS. 1967. *Primitive Classification*. Chicago: University of Chicago Press.

Section 57

MIDDLETON, J., ed. 1967. *Myth and Cosmos*. Garden City, N.Y.: Natural History Press.

———, ed. 1967. *Gods and Rituals: Readings in Religious Beliefs and Practices*. Garden City, N.Y.: Natural History Press.

TURNER, V. 1967. *The Forest of Symbols*. Ithaca, N.Y.: Cornell University Press.

LEACH, E. R., ed. 1967. *The Structural Study of Myth and Totemism*. London: Tavistock.

DOUGLAS, M. 1966. *Purity and Danger*. London: Routledge & Kegan Paul.

———. 1970. *Natural Symbols: Explorations in Cosmology*. New York: Pantheon.

GEORGES, R. A., ed. 1968. *Studies on Mythology*. Homewood, Ill.: Dorsey Press.

LEACH, E. R. 1970. *Genesis as Myth*. London: Jonathan Cape.

COHEN, P. S. 1969. Theories of Myth. *Man*, n.s., 4:337–353.

Section 58

KLUCKHOHN, C. 1949. The Philosophy of the Navaho Indians. In F. S. C. NORTHROP, ed., *Ideological Differences and World Order*. New Haven, Conn.: Yale University Press.

HALLOWELL, A. I. 1955. *Culture and Experience*. Philadelphia: University of Pennsylvania Press.

GEERTZ, C. 1957. Ethos, World-View and the Analysis of Sacred Symbols. *Antioch Review* 17:421–437.

LÉVI-STRAUSS, C. 1963. *Structural Anthropology*. New York: Basic Books.

———. 1966. *The Savage Mind*. Chicago: University of Chicago Press.

ORTIZ, A. 1969. *The Tewa World*. Chicago: University of Chicago Press.

SIEGEL, J. T. 1969. *The Rope of God*. Berkeley: University of California Press.

FORTES, M., and G. DIETERLEN, eds. 1965. *African Systems of Thought*. London: Oxford University Press.

Section 59

WALLACE, A. F. C. 1970. *Culture and Personality*, 2d ed. New York: Alfred A. Knopf.

———. 1964. The New Culture and Personality. In T. GLADWIN and W. C. STURTEVANT, eds., *Anthropology and Human Behavior*. Washington, D.C.: Anthropological Society of Washington.

NORBECK, E., D. PRICE-WILLIAMS, and W. MC CORD, eds. 1968. *The Study of Personality: An Interdisciplinary Appraisal*. New York: Holt, Rinehart and Winston.

GOODENOUGH, W. H. 1963. *Cooperation in Change*. New York: Russell Sage Foundation.

HONIGMANN, J. J. 1970. *Personality in Culture*. New York: Harper & Row.

Section 60

MC NEILL, D. 1970. *The Acquisition of Language.* New York: Harper & Row.

CHOMSKY, N. 1968. *Language and Mind.* New York: Harcourt, Brace & World.

PRIBRAM, K. H., ed. 1969. *On the Biology of Learning.* New York: Harcourt, Brace & World.

BROWN, R. 1965. *Social Psychology.* New York: Free Press.

WHITING, B. B., ed. 1966. *Six Cultures: Studies of Child Rearing.* New York: John Wiley & Sons.

SHIMAHARA, N. 1970. Enculturation—A Reconsideration. *Current Anthropology* 11:143–154.

MAYER, P., ed. 1970. *Socialization: The Approach from Social Anthropology.* ASA Monographs, 8. London: Tavistock.

Section 61

SMELSER, N. J., and W. T., eds. 1963. *Personality and Social Systems.* New York: John Wiley & Sons.

COHEN, Y. A., ed. 1961. *Social Structure and Personality.* New York: Holt, Rinehart and Winston.

Section 62

SPINDLER, G. D. 1968. Psychocultural Adaptation. In E. NORBECK et al., eds., *The Study of Personality.* New York: Holt, Rinehart and Winston.

WALLACE, A. F. C. 1956. Revitalization Movements. *American Anthropologist* 58: 264–281.

GOODENOUGH, W. H. 1963. *Cooperation in Change.* New York: Russell Sage Foundation.

WALLACE, A. F. C. 1970. *Culture and Personality,* 2d ed. New York: Alfred A. Knopf.

Section 63

KROEBER, A. L. 1948. *Anthropology,* rev. ed. New York: Harcourt, Brace & World.

BARNETT, H. G. 1953. *Innovation: The Basis of Culture Change.* New York: McGraw-Hill.

BOHANNAN, P., and F. PLOG, eds. 1967. *Beyond the Frontier: Social Process and Cultural Change.* Garden City, N.Y.: Natural History Press.

MAIR, L. 1969. *Anthropology and Social Change.* LSE Monograph 38. London: Athlone.

Section 64

WALLACE, A. F. C. 1956. Revitalization Movements. *American Anthropologist* 58: 264–281.

WORSLEY, P. 1968. *The Trumpet Shall Sound,* 2d ed. New York: Schocken Books.

FANON, F. 1963. *The Wretched of the Earth.* New York: Grove Press.

TURNBULL, C. 1962. *The Lonely African.* New York: Simon and Schuster.

STEWARD, J. H., ed. 1967. *Contemporary Change in Traditional Societies* (3 vols.). Urbana: University of Illinois Press.

Section 65

GOODENOUGH, W. H. 1963. *Cooperation in Change.* New York: Russell Sage Foundation.

CLIFTON, J. A., ed. 1970. *Applied Anthropology: Readings in the Uses of the Science of Man.* Boston: Houghton Mifflin Company.

SPICER, E. 1952. *Human Problems in Technological Change: A Casebook.* New York: Russell Sage Foundation.

BARNETT, H. G. 1955. *Anthropology in Administration.* New York: Harper & Row.

FOSTER, G. M. 1969. *Applied Anthropology.* Boston: Little, Brown and Company.

GOLDSCHMIDT, W. 1964. Anthropology and the Modern World. In P. B. HAMMOND, ed., *Cultural and Social Anthropology: Selected Readings.* New York: The Macmillan Company.

BERREMAN, G. 1968. Is Anthropology Alive? In M. H. FRIED, ed., *Readings in Anthropology,* 2d ed., Vol. 2. New York: Thomas Y. Crowell Company.

Sections 66–67 (Part V)

HAYS, H. R. 1958. *From Ape to Angel.* New York: Alfred A. Knopf.

KARDINER, A., and E. PREBLE. 1961. *They Studied Man.* Cleveland: World Publishing Company.

PENNIMAN, T. K. 1952. *A Hundred Years of Anthropology,* 2d ed. London: Gerald Duckworth & Co.

WHITE, L. A. 1966. *The Social Organization of Ethnological Theory.* Houston: Rice University Studies, 52.

LOWIE, R. 1937. *The History of Ethnological Theory.* New York: Holt, Rinehart and Winston.

STOCKING, G. W., JR. 1969. *Race, Culture, and Evolution: Essays in the History of Anthropology.* New York: Free Press.

BREW, J. O., ed. 1968. *One Hundred Years of Anthropology.* Cambridge, Mass.: Harvard University Press.

HARRIS, M. 1968. *The Rise of Ethnological Theory.* New York: Random House.

RESEK, C. 1960. *Lewis Henry Morgan, American Scholar.* Chicago: University of Chicago Press.

HERSKOVITS, M. J. 1953. *Franz Boas: The Science of Man in the Making.* New York: Charles Scribner's Sons.

RILEY, C. L., and W. W. TAYLOR, eds. 1967. *American Historical Anthropology: Essays in Honor of Leslie Spier.* Carbondale, Ill.: Southern Illinois University Press.

BENNETT, J. W. 1944. The Development of Ethnological Theories as Illustrated by Studies of the Plains Indian Sun Dance. *American Anthropologist* 46: 162–181.

LANE, M., ed. 1970. *Structuralism: A Reader.* London: Jonathan Cape.

FIRTH, R., ed. 1957. *Man and Culture: An Evaluation of the Work of Bronislaw Malinowski.* London: Routledge & Kegan Paul.

BENEDICT, R. 1934. *Patterns of Culture.* Boston: Houghton Mifflin Company.

MEAD, M. 1959. *An Anthropologist at Work: Writings of Ruth Benedict.* New York: Atherton Press.

SINGER, M. 1961. A Survey of Culture and Personality Theory and Research. In B. KAPLAN, ed. *Studying Personality Cross-Culturally.* New York: Harper & Row.

LINTON, R. 1945. *The Cultural Background of Personality.* New York: Appleton-Century-Crofts.

BARNOUW, V. 1963. *Culture and Personality.* Homewood, Ill.: Dorsey Press.

GOODENOUGH, W. H. 1970. *Description and Comparison in Cultural Anthropology.* Chicago: Aldine Publishing Company.

EGGAN, F., et al. 1969. *Frontiers of Cultural Anthropology*. Proceedings of the American Philosophical Society. Philadelphia: American Philosophical Society.

TYLER, S. A., ed. 1970. *Concepts and Assumptions in Contemporary Anthropology*. Southern Anthropological Association Proceedings, 3. Athens, Ga.: University of Georgia Press.

LÉVI-STRAUSS, C. 1966. Anthropology: Its Achievements and Future. *Current Anthropology* 7:124–127.

Section III
Bibliography

ABERLE, D. F., U. BRONFENBRENNER, E. HESS, D. MILLER, D. M. SCHNEIDER, and J. SPUHLER. 1963. The Incest Taboo and the Mating Patterns of Animals. *American Anthropologist* 65:253–265.

ABERLE, D. F., A. K. COHEN, A. DAVIS, M. LEVY, and F. X. SUTTON. 1950. The Functional Prerequisites of a Society. *Ethics* 60:100–111.

ADAMS, R. M. 1966. *The Evolution of Urban Society.* Chicago: Aldine Publishing Company.

ALBERT, E. M. 1956. The Classification of Values. *American Anthropologist* 58:221–248.

ALLEE, W. C., et al. 1949. *Principles of Animal Ecology.* Philadelphia: W. B. Saunders Company.

ALLEN, M. R. 1967. *Male Cults and Secret Initiations in Melanesia.* Melbourne: Melbourne University Press.

ALTMANN, S. A. 1967. The Structure of Primate Social Communication. In *Social Communication among Primates*, S. A. ALTMANN, ed. Chicago: University of Chicago Press.

ARDREY, R. 1961. *African Genesis.* New York: Dell Publishing Co., Inc.

———. 1966. *The Territorial Imperative.* New York: Dell Publishing Co., Inc.

ARENSBERG, C. M., and A. H. NIEHOFF. 1964. *Introducing Culture Change.* Chicago: Aldine Publishing Company.

BAKER, P. T., and J. S. WEINER, eds. 1966. *The Biology of Human Adaptability.* Oxford: Clarendon Press.

BANTON, M. 1957. *West African City: A Study of Tribal Life in Freetown.* London: Oxford University Press.

BARNETT, H. G. 1956. *Anthropology in Administration.* New York: Harper & Row.

BARTON, R. F. 1919. *Ifugao Law.* Berkeley: University of California Publications in American Archaeology and Ethnology, 15.

BATESON, G. 1955. A Theory of Play and Fantasy. *Psychiatric Research Reports* 2:39–51. American Psychiatric Association.

———. 1958. *Naven.* 2d ed. Stanford, Calif.: Stanford University Press.

———. 1968. Redundancy and Coding. In *Animal Communication*, T. A. SEBEOK, ed. Bloomington: Indiana University Press.

———. n.d. Style, Grace and Information in Primitive Art. Forthcoming in *The Study of Primitive Art*, R. FIRTH, ed. New York: Oxford University Press.

BEIDELMAN, T. O. 1963. Witchcraft in Ukaguru. In *Witchcraft and Sorcery in East Africa*, J. MIDDLETON and E. WINTER, eds., pp. 57–98. London: Routledge & Kegan Paul Ltd.

BENEDICT, R. 1932. Configurations of Culture in North America. *American Anthropologist* 34:1–27.

———. 1934. *Patterns of Culture*. Boston: Houghton Mifflin Company.

———. 1938. Religion. In *General Anthropology*, F. BOAS, ed. Boston: D. C. Heath and Company.

BERLIN, B., and P. KAY. 1969. *Basic Color Terms: Their Universality and Evolution*. Berkeley: University of California Press.

BEVER, T. G. 1970. The Cognitive Basis for Linguistic Structures. In *Cognition and the Development of Language*, J. R. HAYES, ed. New York: John Wiley & Sons, Inc.

BIRDWHISTELL, R. L. 1966. Communication without Words. In *L'Aventure Humaine*, D. ALEXANDRE, ed. Paris.

BLAKE, R., and R. FRYE (trans.). 1948. Observations on the Manners and Customs of the Northmen Encamped on the Volga (by Ibn Fadhlan). In *A Reader in General Anthropology*, C. S. COON, ed. New York: Holt, Rinehart and Winston, Inc.

BOAS, F. 1896. The Limitations of the Comparative Method of Anthropology. *Science* 4:901–908. (Reprinted 1940 in F. BOAS, *Race, Language and Culture*. New York: The Macmillan Company.)

———. 1927. *Primitive Art*. Oslo: H. Aschehoug and Company.

BOHANNAN, L. 1958. Political Aspects of Tiv Social Organization. In *Tribes without Rulers*, J. MIDDLETON and D. TAIT, eds. London: Routledge & Kegan Paul Ltd.

BOHANNAN, L., and P. BOHANNAN. 1968. *Tiv Economy*. Evanston, Ill.: Northwestern University Press.

BOHANNAN, P. 1954. *Tiv Farm and Settlement*. London: H. M. Stationery Office.

———. 1955. Some Principles of Exchange and Investment among the Tiv. *American Anthropologist* 57:60–70.

———. 1959. The Impact of Money on an African Subsistence Economy. *Journal of Economic History* 19:491–503.

———. 1963. *Social Anthropology*. New York: Holt, Rinehart and Winston.

BROOKFIELD, H. C., and P. BROWN. 1963. *Struggle for Land: Agriculture and Group Territories among the Chimbu of the New Guinea Highlands*. London: Oxford University Press.

CHAGNON, N. A. 1968. *Yanomamö: The Fierce People*. New York: Holt, Rinehart and Winston.

CHOMSKY, N. 1957. *Syntactic Structures*. The Hague: Mouton and Company.

———. 1959. Review of *Verbal Behavior* by B. F. Skinner. *Language* 35:26–58.

———. 1964. *Current Issues in Linguistic Theory*. The Hague: Mouton and Company.

———. 1965. *Aspects of the Theory of Syntax*. Cambridge, Mass.: MIT Press.

———. 1966. Topics in the Theory of Generative Grammar. In *Current Trends in Linguistics*, III, T. SEBEOK, ed. The Hague: Mouton and Company.

———. 1968. *Language and Mind*. New York: Harcourt, Brace & World.

CHOMSKY, N., and M. HALLE. 1968. *The Sound Pattern of English*. New York: Harper & Row.

CODRINGTON, R. H. 1891. *The Melanesians: Studies in Their Anthropology and Folklore*. Oxford: Clarendon Press. (Reprinted 1957 by HRAF Press, New Haven.)

CONKLIN, H. C. 1955. Hanunóo Color Categories. *Southwestern Journal of Anthropology* 11:339–344.

———. 1962. Lexicographic Treatment of Folk Taxonomies. In *Problems in Lexicography*, F. W. HOUSEHOLDER and S. SAPORTA, eds. Bloomington: Indiana University Research Center in Anthropology, Folklore and Linguistics, Pub. 21.

COULT, A. D., and R. W. HABENSTEIN. 1965. *Cross Tabulations of Murdock's World Ethnographic Sample: A Reference Handbook*. Columbia: University of Missouri Press.

DALTON, G. 1961. Economic Theory and Primitive Society. *American Anthropologist* 63:1–25.

———. 1965. Primitive Money. *American Anthropologist* 67:44–65.

DAVENPORT, W. 1969. The Hawaiian Cultural Revolution: Some Political and Economic Considerations. *American Anthropologist* 71:1–20.

DE VORE, I., ed. 1965. *Primate Behavior: Field Studies of Monkeys and Apes*. New York: Holt, Rinehart and Winston.

DIAZ, M. N. 1967. Introduction: Economic Relations in Peasant Society. In *Peasant Society: A Reader*, J. M. POTTER, M. N. DIAZ, and G. M. FOSTER, eds. Boston: Little, Brown and Company.

DOLE, G. E., and R. L. CARNEIRO, eds. 1960. *Essays in the Science of Culture* (in Honor of Leslie A. White). New York: Thomas Y. Crowell Company.

DOUGLAS, M. 1966. *Purity and Danger*. London: Routledge & Kegan Paul Ltd.

DRIVER, H. E. 1961. *Indians of North America*. Chicago: University of Chicago Press.

DRIVER, H. E., and K. F. SCHUESSLER. 1967. Correlational Analysis of Murdock's Ethnographic Sample. *American Anthropologist* 69:332–352.

DRUCKER, P. 1939. Rank, Wealth, and Kinship in Northwest Coast Society. *American Anthropologist* 41:55–65. (Reprinted in HOEBEL, JENNINGS, SMITH, eds., *Readings in Anthropology*. 1955. New York: McGraw-Hill, Inc.)

DUBOIS, C. 1944. *The People of Alor*. Minneapolis: University of Minnesota Press.

DUMONT, L. 1966. *Homo-Hierarchicus: Essai Sur le Système des Castes*. Bibliothèque des Sciences Humaines. Paris: Gallimard.

DURKHEIM, E. 1912. *Les Formes Elémentaires de la Vie Réligieuse: Le Système Totemique en Australie*. Paris: Presses Universitaires.

DURKHEIM, E., and M. MAUSS. 1901–1902. *De Quelques Formes Primitive de Classification*. Contribution a l'Etude des Représentations Collectives. *L'Année Sociologique* 6:1–72. (Translated as *Primitive Classification*. 1963. Chicago: University of Chicago Press.)

EIBL-EIBESFELDT, I. 1968. Ethological Perspectives on Primate Studies. In *Primates: Studies in Adaptation and Variability*, P. JAY, ed. New York: Holt, Rinehart and Winston.

———. 1970. *Ethology: The Biology of Behavior*. New York: Holt, Rinehart and Winston.

EISENSTADT, S. N. 1956. *From Generation to Generation*. New York: The Free Press.

ELWIN, V. 1968. *The Kingdom of the Young*. London: Oxford University Press.

EPSTEIN, A. L. 1968. Power, Politics, and Leadership: Some Central African and Melanesian Contrasts. In *Local Level Politics*, M. J. SWARTZ, ed. Chicago: Aldine Publishing Company.

EVANS-PRITCHARD, E. E. 1940. *The Nuer*. Oxford: Clarendon Press.

———. 1951. *Kinship and Marriage among the Nuer*. Oxford: Clarendon Press.

———. 1956. *Nuer Religion*. Oxford: Clarendon Press.

EVANS-PRITCHARD, E. E., ed. 1954. *The Institutions of Primitive Society*. New York: The Free Press.

FIRTH, R., ed. 1956. *Two Studies of Kinship in London*. London: Athlone Press.

————. 1957. *Man and Culture: An Evaluation of the Work of Bronislaw Malinowski*. London: Routledge & Kegan Paul Ltd.

FISCHER, J. L. 1964. Solutions for the Natchez Paradox. *Ethnology* 3:53–65.

FORD, C. S. 1945. *A Comparative Study of Reproduction*. Yale Publications in Anthropology, 32. New Haven, Conn.: Yale University Press.

FORDE, C. D. 1934. *Habitat, Economy and Society*. New York: E. P. Dutton & Co., Inc. (Rev. ed. 1950.)

————. 1950. Double Descent among the Yakö. In *African Systems of Kinship and Marriage*, A. R. RADCLIFFE-BROWN and C. D. FORDE, eds. London: Oxford University Press.

FORTES, M. 1945. *The Dynamics of Clanship among the Tallensi*. London: Oxford University Press. (For International African Institute.)

————. 1949. *The Web of Kinship among the Tallensi*. London: Oxford University Press. (For International African Institute.)

————. 1959. Introduction. In *The Developmental Cycle in Domestic Groups*, J. GOODY, ed. Cambridge Papers in Social Anthropology, 1. London: Cambridge University Press.

FORTUNE, R. 1932a. *Sorcerers of Dobu*. London: Routledge & Kegan Paul Ltd.

————. 1932b. Incest. In *Encyclopedia of the Social Sciences* 6:620. New York: The Macmillan Company.

FOSTER, G. M. 1961. The Dyadic Contract: A Model for the Social Structure of a Mexican Peasant Village. *American Anthropologist* 63:1173–1192.

————. 1962. *Traditional Cultures and the Impact of Technological Change*. New York: Harper & Row.

————. 1965. Peasant Society and the Image of Limited Good. *American Anthropologist* 67:293–315.

FRAKE, C. O. 1960. The Eastern Subanun of Mindanao. In *Social Structure in Southeast Asia*, G. P. MURDOCK, ed. Viking Fund Publications in Anthropology 29. New York: Wenner-Gren Foundation for Anthropological Research.

————. 1961. The Diagnosis of Disease among the Subanun of Mindanao. *American Anthropologist* 63:113–132.

————. 1962a. Cultural Ecology and Ethnography. *American Anthropologist* 64:53–59.

————. 1962b. The Ethnographic Study of Cognitive Systems. In *Anthropology and Human Behavior*, T. GLADWIN and W. STURTEVANT, eds. Washington, D.C.: Anthropological Society of Washington.

————. 1963. Litigation in Lipay: A Study in Subanun Law. In *Proceedings of the Ninth Pacific Science Congress of the Pacific Science Association* 3:217–222. Bangkok (1957).

————. 1964a. A Structural Description of Subanun "Religious Behavior." In *Explorations in Cultural Anthropology*, W. GOODENOUGH, ed. New York: McGraw-Hill, Inc.

————. 1964b. How to Ask for a Drink in Subanun. In *The Ethnography of Communication*, J. GUMPERZ and D. HYMES, eds. American Anthropologist Special Publication 66, 6, part 2.

FRIED, M., M. HARRIS, and R. MURPHY, eds. 1968. *War: The Anthropology of Armed Conflict and Aggression*. Garden City, N.Y.: Natural History Press.

FUSTEL DE COULANGES, N. D. 1864. *Le Cité Antique*. (Translated as *The Ancient City*, 1956. Garden City, N.Y.: Doubleday & Company, Inc.)

GALLIN, B. 1968. Political Factionalism and Its Impact on Chinese Village Social Organization in Taiwan. In *Local Level Politics*, M. SWARTZ, ed., pp. 377–400. Chicago: Aldine Publishing Company.

GEERTZ, C. 1957. Ritual and Social Change: A Javanese Example. *American Anthropologist* 59:32–54.

———. 1960. *The Religion of Java*. New York: The Free Press.

———. 1962. Studies in Peasant Life: Community and Society. In *Biennial Review of Anthropology, 1961*, B. J. SIEGEL, ed. Stanford, Calif.: Stanford University Press.

———. 1966a. Religion as a Cultural System. In *Anthropological Approaches to the Study of Religion*, M. BANTON, ed. (ASA Monographs, 3.) London: Tavistock.

———. 1966b. *Person, Time, and Conduct in Bali: An Essay in Cultural Analysis*. New Haven, Conn.: Southeast Asia Studies; Cultural Report Studies 14.

GILLIN, J. 1948. *The Ways of Men*. New York: Appleton-Century-Crofts.

GLADWIN, T., and J. B. SARASON. 1953. *Truk: Man in Paradise*. Viking Fund Publications in Anthropology 20. New York: Wenner-Gren Foundation for Anthropological Research.

GLUCKMAN, M. 1940. The Kingdom of the Zulu of Southeast Africa. In *African Political Systems*, M. FORTES and E. E. EVANS-PRITCHARD, eds. London: Oxford University Press.

———. 1955. *Custom and Conflict in Africa*. Oxford: Blackwells.

———. 1963. *Order and Rebellion in Tribal Africa*. London: Cohen and West.

GLUCKMAN, M., J. C. MITCHELL, and J. A. BARNES. 1949. The Village Headman in British Central Africa. *Africa* 19:89–106.

GOLDENWEISER, A. A. 1924. *Early Civilization*. New York: Alfred A. Knopf, Inc.

GOODENOUGH, W. H. 1955. A Problem in Malayo-Polynesian Social Organization. *American Anthropologist* 57:71–83.

———. 1956. Residence Rules. *Southwestern Journal of Anthropology* 12:22–37.

———. 1957. Cultural Anthropology and Linguistics. In *Report of the Seventh Annual Round Table Meeting on Linguistics and Language Study*, P. GARVIN, ed. Washington, D.C.: Georgetown University Monograph Series on Language and Linguistics 9.

———. 1961. Comment on Cultural Evolution. *Daedalus* 90:521–528.

———. 1963. *Cooperation in Change*. New York: Russell Sage Foundation.

GOODY, J. R. 1961. Religion and Ritual: The Definitional Problem. *British Journal of Sociology* 12:142–164.

———. 1962. *Death, Property and the Ancestors*. Stanford, Calif.: Stanford University Press.

GORER, G. 1948. *The American People*. New York: W. W. Norton.

GRAEBNER, F. 1911. *Methode der Ethnologie*. Heidelberg: C. Winter.

GREENBERG, J. H. 1963. Introduction. In *Universals of Language*, J. H. GREENBERG, ed. Cambridge: MIT Press.

———. 1966. Language Universals. In *Current Trends in Linguistics*, T. SEBEOK, ed. Vol. 3. The Hague: Mouton and Company.

GRIAULE, M., and G. DIETERLEN. 1960. The Dogon of the French Sudan. In *African Worlds*, C. D. FORDE, ed. London: Oxford University Press.

GULLIVER, P. H. 1965. *The Family Herds*. London: Routledge & Kegan Paul Ltd.

HALL, E. T. 1959. *The Silent Language*. Garden City, N.Y.: Doubleday & Company, Inc.

———. 1966. *The Hidden Dimension*. Garden City, N.Y.: Doubleday & Company, Inc.

HALL, K. R. L. 1963. Tool-Using Performances as Indicators of Behavioral Adaptability. *Current Anthropology* 4, 5:479–494. (Reprinted in P. C. JAY, ed., *Primates: Studies in Adaptation and Variability*. 1968. New York: Holt, Rinehart and Winston.)

HALLOWELL, A. I. 1955. *Culture and Experience*. Philadelphia: University of Pennsylvania Press.

HERSKOVITS, M. J. 1951. Tender and Tough-Minded Anthropology and the Study of Values in Culture. *Southwestern Journal of Anthropology* 7:22–31.

———. 1955. *Cultural Anthropology*. New York: Alfred A. Knopf, Inc.

HERTZ, R. 1907. Contribution à une Étude sur la Représentation Collective de la Mort. *Année Sociologique* 10:48–137. (Translated in *Death and the Right Hand*, 1960. New York: The Free Press.)

———. 1909. Le Prééminence de la Main Droite: Etude sur la Polarité Religieuse. *Revue Philosophique* 58:553–580. (Translated in *Death and the Right Hand*, 1960. New York: The Free Press.)

HOCKETT, C. F. 1960. The Origin of Speech. *Scientific American* 203 (September): 88–111.

HOEBEL, E. A. 1954. *The Law of Primitive Man: A Study in Comparative Legal Dynamics*. Cambridge, Mass.: Harvard University Press.

HOLLOWAY, R. J., JR. 1969. Culture: A Human Domain. *Current Anthropology* 10:395–407.

HORTON, R. 1960. A Definition of Religion and Its Uses. *Journal of Royal Anthropological Institute* 90.

———. 1962. The Kalabari World View: An Outline and Interpretation. *Africa* 32:197–220.

HSU, F. L. K. 1953. *Americans and Chinese: Two Ways of Life*. New York: Abelard-Schuman, Inc.

HYMES, D. n.d. *On Communicative Competence*. Forthcoming revised version of paper presented at Research Planning Conference on Language Development among Disadvantaged Children. New York: Yeshiva University, 1966.

HYMES, D., ed. 1964. *Language in Culture and Society: A Reader in Linguistics and Anthropology*. New York: Harper & Row.

INKELES, A., and D. J. LEVINSON. 1954. National Character: The Study of Modal Personality and Sociocultural Systems. In *Handbook of Social Psychology*, G. LINDZEY, ed., Vol. 2. Reading, Mass.: Addison-Wesley Publishing Company.

JAY, P. 1968. Primate Field Studies and Human Evolution. In *Primates: Studies in Adaptation and Variability*, P. JAY, ed. New York: Holt, Rinehart and Winston.

JAY, P. C., ed. 1968. *Primates: Studies in Adaptation and Variability*. New York: Holt, Rinehart and Winston.

KARDINER, A. 1939. *The Individual and His Society*. New York: Columbia University Press.

———. 1945. *Psychological Frontiers of Society*. New York: Columbia University Press.

KATZ, J. J., and P. M. POSTAL. 1964. *Integrated Theory of Linguistic Descriptions*. Cambridge, Mass.: MIT Press.

KEESING, F. M. 1958. *Cultural Anthropology: The Science of Custom*. New York: Holt, Rinehart and Winston.

KEESING, R. M. 1970. Shrines, Ancestors, and Cognatic Descent: The Kwaio and Tallensi. *American Anthropologist* 72:755–775.

KEIL, C. 1966. *Urban Blues*. Chicago: University of Chicago Press.

KLUCKHOHN, C. 1942. Myths and Rituals: A General Theory. *Harvard Theological Review* 35:45–79.

———. 1949. The Philosophy of the Navaho Indians. In *Ideological Differences and World Order*, F. S. C. NORTHROP, ed. New Haven, Conn.: Yale University Press.

———. 1953. Universal Categories of Culture. In *Anthropology Today*, A. L. KROEBER, ed. Chicago: University of Chicago Press.

———. 1956. Toward a Comparison of Value-Emphases in Different Cultures. In *The State of the Social Sciences*, L. D. WHITE, ed. Chicago: University of Chicago Press.

KLUCKHOHN, C., and W. H. KELLY. 1945. The Concept of Culture. In *The Science of Man in the World Crisis*, R. LINTON, ed. New York: Columbia University Press.

KLUCKHOHN, C., and F. KLUCKHOHN. 1948. American Culture: Generalized and Class Patterns. In *Conflict of Power in Modern Society*, 1947 Conference on Science, Philosophy, and Religion. New York.

KLUCKHOHN, F., F. STRODTBECK, and J. ROBERTS. 1955. *A Study of Value Orientations*. New York: Harper & Row.

KÖBBEN, A. J. F. 1967. Why Exceptions? The Logic of Cross-Cultural Analysis. *Current Anthropology* 3:19.

KROEBER, A. L. 1923. *Anthropology*. New York: Harcourt, Brace & World.

———. 1948. *Anthropology*. Rev. ed. New York: Harcourt, Brace & World.

KROEBER, A. L., and C. KLUCKHOHN. 1952. *Culture: A Critical Review of Concepts and Definitions*. Peabody Museum Papers 47, 1. Cambridge, Mass.: Harvard University Press.

KUHN, T. 1962. *The Structure of Scientific Revolutions*. Chicago: University of Chicago Press.

LABARRE, W. 1954. *The Human Animal*. Chicago: University of Chicago Press.

LANCASTER, J. B. 1968. Primate Communication Systems and the Emergence of Human Language. In *Primates: Studies in Adaptation and Variability*, P. JAY, ed. New York: Holt, Rinehart and Winston.

LANE, R. B. 1961. A Reconsideration of Malayo-Polynesian Social Organization. *American Anthropologist* 63:711–720.

LEACH, E. R. 1954. *Political Systems of Highland Burma*. Cambridge, Mass.: Harvard University Press.

———. 1958. Magical Hair. *Journal of the Royal Anthropological Institute* 88: 147–164.

———. 1959. Concerning Trobriand Clans and the Kinship Category Tabu. In *The Developmental Cycle of Domestic Groups*, J. GOODY, ed. Cambridge Papers in Social Anthropology 1. London: Cambridge University Press.

———. 1961. *Rethinking Anthropology*. London: University of London Press.

———. 1965. Anthropological Aspects of Language: Animal Categories and Verbal Abuse. In *New Directions in the Study of Language*, E. LENNEBERG, ed. Cambridge, Mass.: MIT Press.

LEACH, E. R., ed. 1960. *Aspects of Caste in South India, Ceylon, and Northwest Pakistan*. Cambridge Papers in Social Anthropology 2. London: Cambridge University Press.

LEE, D. D. 1940. A Primitive System of Values. *Philosophy of Science* 7:355–378.

———. 1949. Being and Value in a Primitive Culture. *Journal of Philosophy* 46, no. 13:401–415.

LEE, R. B. 1968. What Hunters Do for a Living. In *Man the Hunter*, R. B. LEE and I. DE VORE, eds. Chicago: Aldine Publishing Company.

———. 1969. !Kung Bushman Subsistence: An Input-Output Analysis. In *Environment and Cultural Behavior*, A. P. VAYDA, ed. Garden City, N.Y.: Natural History Press. (Revision of a paper originally published in D. DAMAS, ed., *Ecological Essays*. Ottawa: Queens Printer, 1969.)

LEE, R. B., and I. DE VORE. 1968. Problems in the Study of Hunters and Gatherers. In *Man the Hunter*, R. B. LEE and I. DE VORE, eds. Chicago: Aldine Publishing Company.

LEE, R. B., and I. DE VORE, eds. 1968. *Man the Hunter*. Chicago: Aldine Publishing Company.

LEIGHTON, A. H. 1945. *The Governing of Men*. Princeton, N.J.: Princeton University Press.

LENNEBERG, E. H. 1967. *The Biological Foundations of Language*. New York: John Wiley & Sons.

LEVINE, R. A. 1966. *Dreams and Deeds: Achievement Motivation in Nigeria*. Chicago: University of Chicago Press.

LÉVI-STRAUSS, C. 1949. *Les Structures Elémentaires de la Parenté*. Paris: Plon. (Translated as *The Elementary Structures of Kinship*, 1969. Boston: Beacon Press.)

———. 1962. *La Pensée Sauvage*. Paris: Plon. (Translated as *The Savage Mind*, 1966. Chicago: University of Chicago Press.)

———. 1963. *Structural Anthropology*. New York: Basic Books.

———. 1968. The Concept of Primitiveness. In *Man the Hunter*, R. B. LEE and I. DE VORE, eds. Chicago: Aldine Publishing Company.

———. 1969. *The Raw and the Cooked*. New York: Harper & Row. (Translation of *Le Cru et le Cuit*, 1964. Paris: Plon.)

LEVY-BRUHL, L. 1912. *Les Fonctions Mentales dans les Societiés Inférieures*. Paris: F. Alcan. (Translated as *How Natives Think*, 1966. New York: Washington Square Press.)

———. 1923. *Primitive Mentality*. New York: The Macmillan Company.

LEWIS, O. 1961. *The Children of Sanchez*. New York: Random House.

———. 1966. *La Vida*. New York: Random House.

LEWIS, O., and V. BARNOUW. 1956. Caste and Jajmani System in a North Indian Village. *Scientific American* 83, 2:66–81.

LI AN-CHE. 1937. Zuni: Some Observations and Queries. *American Anthropologist* 39:62–76.

LIEBOW, E. 1967. *Tally's Corner*. Boston: Little, Brown & Company.

LINTON, R. 1936. *The Study of Man*. New York: Appleton-Century-Crofts.

———. 1940. Acculturation. In *Acculturation in Seven American Indian Tribes*, R. LINTON, ed. New York: Appleton-Century-Crofts.

LINTON, R., ed. 1945. *The Science of Man in the World Crisis*. New York: Columbia University Press.

LITTLE, K. 1965. *West African Urbanization: A Study of Voluntary Associations in Social Change*. Cambridge: Cambridge University Press.

———. 1967. Voluntary Associations in Urban Life: A Case Study of Differential Adaptations. In *Social Organization: Essays Presented to Raymond Firth*, M. FREEDMAN, ed. Chicago: Aldine Publishing Company.

LIVINGSTONE, F. B. 1958. Anthropological Implications of Sickle-Cell Gene Distribution in West Africa. *American Anthropologist* 60:533–562.

———. 1969. Genetics, Ecology, and the Origins of Incest and Exogamy. *Current Anthropology* 10, 1:45–49.

LORENZ, K. 1966. *On Aggression*. New York: Harcourt, Brace & World.

LOUNSBURY, F. G. 1964. A Formal Account of the Crow- and Omaha-type Kinship Terminologies. In *Explorations in Cultural Anthropology*, W. GOODENOUGH, ed. New York: McGraw-Hill, Inc.

———. 1965. Another View of the Trobriand Kinship Categories. In *Formal Semantic Analysis*, E. A. HAMMEL, ed. American Anthropologist Special Publication 4, 67, part 2. Menasha, Wis.: American Anthropological Association.

MALINOWSKI, B. 1916. Baloma: The Spirits of the Dead in the Trobriand Islands. *Journal of the Royal Anthropological Institute* 46:353–430. (Reprinted in *Magic, Science and Religion*, 1954. Boston: Beacon Press.)

———. 1919. Kula: The Circulating Exchange of Valuables in the Archipelagoes of Eastern New Guinea. *Man* 20:97–105.

———. 1922. *Argonauts of the Western Pacific*. London: Routledge & Kegan Paul Ltd.

———. 1925. Magic, Science and Religion. In *Science, Religion, and Reality*, J. NEEDHAM, ed. London. (Reprinted in *Magic, Science and Religion*, 1954.)

———. 1926. *Myth in Primitive Psychology,*. London. (Reprinted in *Magic, Science and Religion*, 1954).

———. 1927. *Sex and Repression in Savage Society*. London: Routledge & Kegan Paul Ltd.

———. 1929. *The Sexual Life of Savages in Northwestern Melanesia*. London: Routledge & Kegan Paul Ltd.

———. 1931. Culture. In *Encyclopedia of the Social Sciences*. New York: The Macmillan Company.

———. 1935. *Coral Gardens and Their Magic*. 2 vols. London: George Allen & Unwin Ltd.

———. 1944. *A Scientific Theory of Culture and Other Essays*. Chapel Hill: University of North Carolina Press. (Reprinted 1960 by Oxford University Press.)

MARANDA, P., and E. MARANDA. 1970. Le Crâne et l'Uterus: Deux Théoremes Nord-Malaitains. In *Échanges et Communications: Mélanges offerts à Claude Lévi-Strauss*, J. POUILLON and P. MARANDA, eds. The Hague: Mouton and Company.

MARLER, P. 1965. Communication in Monkeys and Apes. In *Primate Behavior: Field Studies of Monkeys and Apes*, I. DE VORE, ed. New York: Holt, Rinehart and Winston.

MARRIOTT, M. 1955. Little Communities in Indigenous Civilization. In M. MARRIOTT, ed. *Village India*. Chicago: University of Chicago Press.

MARRIOTT, M., ed. 1955. *Village India: Studies in the Little Community*. Chicago: University of Chicago Press.

MARSHALL, L. 1960. !Kung Bushmen Bands. *Africa* 30:325–355.

MAUSS, M. 1925. *Essai sur le Don. L'Année Sociologique*, n.s., t. I:30–186. (Translated as *The Gift: Forms and Functions of Exchange in Archaic Society*, 1954. New York: The Free Press.)

MAYBURY-LEWIS, D. H. P. 1967. *Akwe-Shavante Society*. Oxford: Clarendon Press.

MC NEILL, D. 1966. Developmental Psycholinguistics. In *The Genesis of Language*, F. SMITH and G. A. MILLER, eds. Cambridge, Mass.: MIT Press.

———. 1970a. The Development of Language. In *Carmichael's Manual of Child Psychology*, P. A. MUSSEN, ed. New York: John Wiley & Sons.

———. 1970b. *The Acquisition of Language*. New York: Harper & Row.

MEAD, M. 1928. *Coming of Age in Samoa*. New York: William Morrow & Company.

———. 1935. *Sex and Temperament in Three Primitive Societies*. New York: William Morrow & Company.

MEAD, M. 1940. Social Change and Cultural Surrogates. *Journal of Educational Sociology* 14, 2:92–109.

———. 1942. *And Keep Your Powder Dry.* New York: William Morrow & Company.

———. 1957. Toward More Vivid Utopias. *Science* 126:957–961.

———. 1968. Problems and Progress in the Study of Personality. In *The Study of Personality,* E. NORBECK et al., eds. New York: Holt, Rinehart and Winston.

MEAD, M., ed. 1953. *Cultural Patterns and Technological Change.* Paris: UNESCO.

MEAD, M., and R. METRAUX. 1953. *The Study of Culture at a Distance.* Chicago: University of Chicago Press.

MEGGITT, M. J. 1964. Male-Female Relationships in the Highlands of Australian New Guinea. In *New Guinea: The Central Highlands,* J. B. WATSON, ed. American Anthropologist Special Publication 66, part 2.

———. 1965. *The Lineage System of the Mae Enga of the New Guinea Highlands.* Edinburgh: Oliver & Boyd.

MINTZ, S. W. 1959. Internal Market Systems as Mechanisms of Social Articulation. In *Proceedings of the American Ethnological Society,* V. F. RAY, ed. Seattle: University of Washington Press.

———. 1961. Pratik: Haitian Personal Economic Relationships. In *Proceedings of the 1961 Annual Spring Meeting of the American Ethnological Society.* Seattle: University of Washington Press.

MOLTZ, H. 1965. Contemporary Instinct Theory and the Fixed Action Pattern. *Psychology Review* 72:27–47.

MONTAGU, M. F. A. 1968. *The Natural Superiority of Women.* Rev. ed. New York: The Macmillan Company.

MONTAGU, M. F. A., ed. 1968. *Man and Aggression.* New York: Oxford University Press.

MOONEY, J. 1896. *The Ghost Dance Religion.* Bureau of American Ethnology, Annual Report 14. Washington, D.C.: U.S. Government Printing Office.

MORGAN, L. H. 1870. *Systems of Consanguinity and Affinity in the Human Family.* Washington, D.C.: Smithsonian Institution.

———. 1877. *Ancient Society.* New York: Henry Holt and Company.

MORRIS, D. 1967. *The Naked Ape.* New York: McGraw-Hill, Inc.

MURDOCK, G. P. 1945. The Common Denominators of Cultures. In *The Science of Man in the World Crisis,* R. LINTON, ed. New York: Columbia University Press.

———. 1949. *Social Structure.* New York: The Macmillan Company.

———. 1957. World Ethnographic Sample. *American Anthropologist* 59:664–687.

———. 1959. *Africa: Its Peoples and Their Culture History.* New York: McGraw-Hill, Inc.

———. 1968. Patterns of Sibling Terminology. *Ethnology* 7:1–24.

NASH, M. 1961. The Social Context of Economic Choice in a Small Society. *Man* 61, no. 219.

NEEDHAM, R. 1962. *Structure and Sentiment: A Test Case in Social Anthropology.* Chicago: University of Chicago Press.

———. 1971. Remarks on the Analysis of Kinship and Marriage. In *Kinship and Marriage,* R. NEEDHAM, ed. (ASA Monographs, 11.) London: Tavistock.

NETTING, R. M. 1969. Women's Weapons: The Politics of Domesticity among the Kofyar. *American Anthropologist* 71:1037–1045.

PARKINSON, C. N. 1957. *Parkinson's Law.* Boston: Houghton Mifflin Company.

PEACOCK, J. L. 1968. *Rites of Modernization: Symbolic and Social Aspects of Indonesian Proletarian Drama.* Chicago: University of Chicago Press.

PERRY, W. J. 1923. *The Children of the Sun.* London: Methuen & Co., Ltd.

PIKE, K. L. 1967. *Language in Relation to a Unified Theory of the Structure of Human Behavior.* The Hague: Mouton and Company.

PLOTNICOV, L. 1967. *Strangers to the City: Urban Man in Jos, Nigeria.* Pittsburgh: University of Pittsburgh Press.

POLANYI, K. 1957. The Economy as Instituted Process. In *Trade and Market in the Early Empires,* K. POLANYI et al., eds. New York: The Free Press.

———. 1959. Anthropology and Economic Theory. In *Readings in Anthropology,* II, M. H. FRIED, ed. New York: Thomas Y. Crowell Company.

POSPISIL, L. 1963a. *Kapauku Papuan Economy.* New Haven, Conn.: Yale University Press.

———. 1963b. *The Kapauku Papuans of West New Guinea.* New York: Holt, Rinehart and Winston.

———. 1968. Law and Order. In *Introduction to Cultural Anthropology,* J. A. CLIFTON, ed. Boston: Houghton Mifflin Company.

POTTER, J. M., M. N. DIAZ, and G. M. FOSTER, eds. 1967. *Peasant Society: A Reader.* Boston: Little, Brown & Company.

POWELL, H. A. 1960. Competitive Leadership in Trobriand Political Organization. *Journal of the Royal Anthropological Institute* 90:118–145.

———. 1969a. Genealogy, Residence and Kinship in Kiriwina. *Man* 4, 2:177–202.

———. 1969b. Territory, Hierarchy and Kinship in Kiriwina. *Man* 4, 4:580–604.

PRIBRAM, K. H. 1967. The New Neurology and the Biology of Emotion: A Structural Approach. *American Psychologist* 22:830–838.

RADCLIFFE-BROWN, A. R. 1922. *The Andaman Islanders.* Cambridge: Cambridge University Press.

———. 1933. Law: Primitive; Social Sanctions. In *Encyclopedia of the Social Sciences.* New York: The Macmillan Company.

———. 1935. Patrilineal and Matrilineal Succession. *Iowa Law Review* 20, no. 2. (Reprinted in Radcliffe-Brown, 1952.)

———. 1952. *Structure and Function in Primitive Society.* London: Cohen and West.

RADIN, P. 1926. *Crashing Thunder: The Autobiography of a Winnebago Indian.* New York: Appleton-Century-Crofts.

RAPPAPORT, R. 1967. Ritual Regulation of Environmental Relations among a New Guinea People. *Ethnology* 6:17–30.

RASMUSSEN, K. 1922. *Grønlandsagen.* Berlin.

RATTRAY, R. S. 1923. *Ashanti.* Oxford: The Clarendon Press.

RAULET, H. M. 1960. *Social Structure and Ecology in Northwest Melanesia.* Unpublished doctoral dissertation, Columbia University.

REDFIELD, M. P., ed. 1962. *Human Nature and the Study of Society: The Papers of Robert Redfield.* Vol. I. Chicago: University of Chicago Press.

REDFIELD, R. 1953. *The Primitive World and Its Transformations.* Ithaca, N.Y.: Cornell University Press.

———. 1955. *The Little Community.* Chicago: University of Chicago Press.

———. 1956. *Peasant Society and Culture.* Chicago: University of Chicago Press.

REDFIELD, R., R. LINTON, and M. J. HERSKOVITS. 1936. A Memorandum on Acculturation. *American Anthropologist* 38:149–152.

REYNOLDS, P. C. 1968. Evolution of Primate Vocal-Auditory Communications Systems. *American Anthropologist* 70:300–308.

RIVERS, W. H. R. 1906. *The Todas*. New York: The Macmillan Company.
———. 1918. *The History of Melanesian Society*. 2 vols. Cambridge: Cambridge University Press.

ROBBINS, L. 1935. The Subject Matter of Economics. In *An Essay on the Nature and Significance of Economic Science*. London: Macmillan & Co., Ltd.

ROBINSON, M. 1962. Complementary Filiation and Marriage in the Trobriand Islands. In *Marriage in Tribal Societies*, M. FORTES, ed. Cambridge Papers in Social Anthropology 3. London: Cambridge University Press.

RUBIN, J. 1968. *National Bilingualism in Paraguay*. The Hague: Mouton and Company. (Janua Linguarum, Series Practica 60.)

SADE, D. S. 1968. Inhibition of Son-Mother Mating among Free-Ranging Rhesus Monkeys. In *Animal and Human*, J. H. MASSERMAN, ed. *Scientific Proceedings of the American Academy of Psychoanalysis* 7:18–38.

SAHLINS, M. 1958. *Social Stratification in Polynesia*. Seattle: University of Washington Press.
———. 1960. Evolution: Specific and General. In *Evolution and Culture*, M. SAHLINS and E. SERVICE, eds. Ann Arbor: University of Michigan Press.
———. 1961. The Segmentary Lineage: An Organization of Predatory Expansion. *American Anthropologist* 63:322–343.
———. 1963. Poor Man, Rich Man, Big Man, Chief: Political Types in Melanesia and Polynesia. *Comparative Studies in Society and History* 5:285–300.

SAHLINS, M. D., and E. R. SERVICE, eds. 1960. *Evolution and Culture*. Ann Arbor: University of Michigan Press.

SALISBURY, R. 1968. Anthropology and Economics. In *Anthropology and the Neighboring Disciplines*, O. VON MERING and L. KASDAN, eds. Pittsburgh: Pittsburgh University Press.

SANDERS, W. T., and B. J. PRICE. 1968. *Mesoamerica: The Evolution of a Civilization*. New York: Random House.

SAPIR, E. 1921. *Language*. New York: Harcourt, Brace & World.
———. 1929. The Status of Linguistics as a Science. (Reprinted 1949 in *Selected Writings of Edward Sapir*. Berkeley: University of California Press.)
———. 1932. Cultural Anthropology and Psychiatry. *Journal of Abnormal and Social Psychology* 27:229–242.
———. 1934. The Emergence of the Concept of Personality in a Study of Cultures. *Journal of Social Psychology* 5:408–415.
———. 1949. *Selected Writings of Edward Sapir in Language, Culture and Personality*, D. G. MANDELBAUM, ed. Berkeley: University of California Press.

SAUSSURE, F. DE. 1916. *Cours de Linguistique Générale*. Paris: Payot. (Translated as *Course in General Linguistics*, 1959. New York: Philosophical Library.)

SCHALLER, G. B. 1963. *The Mountain Gorilla: Ecology and Behavior*. Chicago: University of Chicago Press.

SCHAPERA, I. 1955. *A Handbook of Tswana Law and Custom*. 2d ed. London: Oxford University Press.

SCHEFFLER, H. W. 1965. *Choiseul Island Social Structure*. Berkeley: University of California Press.

SCHMIDT, W. 1939. *The Culture Historical Method of Ethnology*. New York: Fortuny's, Publishers, Inc.

SCHNEIDER, D. M., and E. K. GOUGH, eds. 1961. *Matrilineal Kinship*. Berkeley: University of California Press.

SCHNEIDER, H. K. 1969. Review of P. and L. Bohannan, *Tiv Economy. American Anthropologist* 71:931–932.

SEBEOK, T. A. 1968. Goals and Limitations of the Study of Animal Communication. In *Animal Communication*, T. A. SEBEOK, ed. Bloomington: Indiana University Press.

SERVICE, E. R. 1962. *Primitive Social Organization: An Evolutionary Perspective.* New York: Random House.

———. 1966. *The Hunters.* Englewood Cliffs, N.J.: Prentice-Hall, Inc.

———. 1968. War and our Contemporary Ancestors. In *War: The Anthropology of Armed Conflict and Aggression*, M. FRIED et. al., eds. Garden City, N.Y.: Doubleday & Company, Inc.

SHARP, R. L. 1952. Steel Axes for Stone-Age Australians. *Human Organization* 11:17–22.

SIDER, K. B. 1967. Affinity and the Role of the Father in the Trobriands. *Southwestern Journal of Anthropology* 23:65–109.

SIMONIS, Y. 1968. *Claude Lévi-Strauss, ou la Passion de l'Inceste: Introduction au Structuralisme.* Paris: Aubier.

SINGER, M., and B. S. COHN, eds. 1968. *Structure and Change in Indian Society.* Viking Fund Publications in Anthropology 47. Chicago: Aldine Publishing Company.

SINGH, J. 1966. *Great Ideas in Information Theory, Language and Cybernetics.* New York: Dover Publications, Inc.

SINHA, S. 1967. Caste in India: Its Essential Pattern of Socio-Cultural Integration. In *Caste and Race: Comparative Approaches*, A. DE REUK and J. KNIGHT, eds. London: J. and A. Churchill, Ltd.

SMITH, C. S. 1964. Structure, Substructure, and Superstructure. *Review of Modern Physics* 36:524–532.

———. 1968. Simplicity and Complexity. *Science and Technology* (May 1968): 60–65.

SMITH, E. W. 1926. *The Golden Stool: Some Aspects of the Conflict of Cultures in Modern Africa.* London: Holborn Publishing House.

SMITH, G. E. 1915. *The Migrations of Early Culture.* Manchester, England: Manchester University Press.

SMITH, W. R. 1885. *Kinship and Marriage in Early Arabia.* Cambridge: Cambridge University Press.

———. 1889. *Lectures on the Religion of the Semites.* New York: D. Appleton & Company.

SMITH, W., and J. M. ROBERTS. 1954. *Zuni Law: A Field of Values.* Peabody Museum Papers 43. Cambridge, Mass.: Harvard University Press.

SORENSEN, A. P., JR. 1967. Multilingualism in the Northern Amazon. *American Anthropologist* 69, 6:670–684.

SPENCER, R. F., J. D. JENNINGS, et al. 1965. *The Native Americans.* New York: Harper & Row.

SPICER, E. H., ed. 1952. *Human Problems in Technological Change: A Casebook.* New York: Russell Sage Foundation.

SPIER, L. 1921. *The Sun Dance of the Plains Indians.* Anthropological Papers 16. New York: American Museum of Natural History.

SPINDLER, G. D. 1955. *Sociocultural and Psychological Processes in Menomini Acculturation.* Berkeley: University of California Publications in Culture and Society 5.

———. 1968. Psychocultural Adaptation. In *The Study of Personality*, E. NORBECK et al., eds. New York: Holt, Rinehart and Winston.

SPINDLER, L. S. 1962. *Menomini Women and Culture Change.* American Anthropological Association, Memoir 91. *American Anthropologist* 64, no. 1, part 2.

SPIRO, M. E. 1966. Religion: Problems of Definition and Explanation. In *Anthropological Approaches to the Study of Religion*, M. BANTON, ed. (ASA Monographs, 3.) London: Tavistock Publications.

STEWARD, J. H. 1955. *Theory of Culture Change*. Urbana: University of Illinois Press.

STEWARD, J. H., ed. 1946–1950. *Handbook of South American Indians*. Bureau of American Ethnology, Bulletin 143 (6 vols.). Washington, D.C.: U.S. Government Printing Office.

SWARTZ, M. 1968. Introduction. In *Local Level Politics*, M. J. SWARTZ, ed. Chicago: Aldine Publishing Company.

SWARTZ, M. J., ed. 1968. *Local Level Politics*. Chicago: Aldine Publishing Company.

SWARTZ, M. J., V. TURNER, and A. TUDEN, eds. 1966. *Political Anthropology*. Chicago: Aldine Publishing Company.

TEXTOR, R. B. 1967. *Cross-Cultural Summary*. New Haven, Conn.: Human Relations Area Files Press.

THURNWALD, R. 1916. *Bánaro Society: Social Organization and Kinship System of a Tribe in the Interior of New Guinea*. American Anthropological Association Memoir 3, no. 2. Lancaster, Pa.: New Era Printing Company.

TIGER, L. 1969. *Men in Groups*. New York: Random House.

TURNBULL, C. M. 1961. *The Forest People: A Study of the Pygmies of the Congo*. New York: Simon and Schuster.

TURNER, T. n.d. *The Fire of the Jaguar*. Chicago: University of Chicago Press. In press.

TURNER, V. 1964. Betwixt and Between: The Liminal Period in Rites de Passage. In *Proceedings of the 1964 Annual Spring Meeting of the American Ethnological Society*, J. HELM, ed. Seattle: University of Washington Press.

———. 1966. Colour Classification in Ndembu Ritual. In *Anthropological Approaches to the Study of Religion*, M. BANTON, ed. (ASA Monographs, 3.) London: Tavistock.

———. 1967. *The Forest of Symbols: Studies in Ndembu Ritual*. Ithaca, N.Y.: Cornell University Press.

———. 1968a. Mukanda: The Politics of a Non-Political Ritual. In *Local Level Politics*, M. J. SWARTZ, ed. Chicago: Aldine Publishing Company.

———. 1968b. *The Drums of Affliction: A Study of Religious Processes among the Ndembu of Zambia*. Oxford: Clarendon Press.

TYLER, S., ed. 1969. *Cognitive Anthropology*. New York: Holt, Rinehart and Winston.

TYLOR, E. B. 1871. *Primitive Culture: Researches into the Development of Mythology, Philosophy, Religion, Art, and Custom*. London: John Murray.

———. 1889. On a Method of Investigating the Development of Institutions; applied to Laws of Marriage and Descent. *Journal of the Royal Anthropological Institute* 18:245–269.

UBEROI, J. P. SINGH. 1962. *Politics of the Kula Ring*. Manchester, England: University of Manchester Press.

VAILLANT, G. C. 1941. *The Aztecs of Mexico*. Garden City, N.Y.: Doubleday & Company, Inc.

VALENTINE, C. A. 1968. *Culture and Poverty: Critique and Counter-Proposals*. Chicago: University of Chicago Press.

VAN GENNEP, A. 1909. *Les Rites de Passage*. Paris: Libraire Critique, Émile Nourry. (Translated as *The Rites of Passage*, 1960. London: Routledge & Kegan Paul.)

VAYDA, A. P. 1961. Expansion and Warfare among Swidden Agriculturalists. *American Anthropologist* 63:346–358.

VOGT, E. Z. 1965. Structural and Conceptual Replication in Zinacantan Culture. *American Anthropologist* 67:342–353.

WALLACE, A. F. C. 1952. *The Modal Personality of the Tuscarora Indians as Revealed by the Rorschach Test*. Bureau of American Ethnology Bulletin 150. Washington, D.C.: U.S. Government Printing Office.

——. 1956. Revitalization Movements. *American Anthropologist* 58:264–281.

——. 1970. *Culture and Personality*. 2d ed. New York: Random House.

WARNER, W. L. 1937. *A Black Civilization*. New York: Harper & Row. (Rev. ed. 1958.)

——. 1953. *American Life: Dream and Reality*. Chicago: University of Chicago Press.

WARNER, W. L., et al. 1949. *Democracy in Jonesville*. New York: Harper & Row.

WASHBURN, S. L., and C. S. LANCASTER. 1968. The Evolution of Hunting. In *Man the Hunter*, R. B. LEE and I. DE VORE, eds. Chicago: Aldine Publishing Company.

WAUCHOPE, R., ed. 1964–1967. *Handbook of Middle American Indians*. 6 vols. Austin: University of Texas Press.

WEISS, P. 1967. One Plus One Does Not Equal Two. In *The Neurosciences: A Study Program*, G. C. QUARTON et al., eds. New York: Rockefeller University Press.

——. 1969. The Living System: Determinism Stratified. In *Beyond Reductionism: New Perspectives in the Life Sciences*, A. KOESTLER and J. R. SMYTHIES, eds. 1970. New York: The Macmillan Company.

WHITE, L. A. 1944. The Symbol: The Origin and Basis of Human Behavior. *Etc: A Review of General Semantics* 1:229–237.

WHITING, B. B., ed. 1963. *Six Cultures: Studies of Child Rearing*. New York: John Wiley & Sons, Inc.

WHITING, J. W. M. 1941. *Becoming a Kwoma*. New Haven, Conn.: Yale University Press.

WHORF, B. L. 1956. *Language, Thought and Reality: Selected Writings of B. L. Whorf*, J. B. CARROLL, ed. Cambridge, Mass., and New York: MIT Press and John Wiley & Sons, Inc.

WILLIAMS, F. E. 1923. *The Vailala Madness and the Destruction of Native Ceremonies in the Gulf Division*. Territory of Papua Anthropological Reports 4. Port Moresby, New Guinea.

WILSON, M. H. 1951. *Good Company: A Study of Nyakyusa Age-Villages*. London: Oxford University Press.

WOLF, E. R. 1957. Closed Corporate Peasant Communities in Mesoamerica and Central Java. *Southwestern Journal of Anthropology* 13:1–18.

——. 1959. *Sons of the Shaking Earth*. Chicago: University of Chicago Press.

——. 1966a. *Peasants*. Englewood Cliffs, N.J.: Prentice-Hall, Inc.

——. 1966b. Kinship, Friendship, and Patron-Client Relations in Complex Societies. In *The Social Anthropology of Complex Societies*, M. BANTON, ed. New York: Frederick A. Praeger, Inc.

WORSLEY, P. 1957. *The Trumpet Shall Sound: A Study of "Cargo" Cults in Melanesia*. London: MacGibbon and Kee. (2d ed. 1968. New York: Schocken Books, Inc.)

YOUNG, F. W. 1965. *Initiation Ceremonies: A Cross-Cultural Study of Status Dramatization*. Indianapolis: The Bobbs-Merrill Company, Inc.

INDEX

Name Index

Subject Index

A

Abnormal behavior (*see* Conformity and Deviance)

Acculturation, 108, 347, 352–355

Achieved status (*see* Status)

Adaptation, biological, 32–35, 46, 48, 50–52, 58
  ecological, 89, 91–92, 131–146, 158–159, 168, 170, 174, 187, 227–232, 248–249, 259, 272

Adolescence, 215, 340, 396

Adoption and fosterage, 157

Adulthood, 217, 340

Affinal kinship (*see* Kinship)

Africa, culture areas, 105–106
  culture history, 105–108
  social structure, 218–219, 223
  urbanization, 243–244

Age, cultural treatment of, 213–219

Age-area hypothesis, 383

Age-grades, 218

Age-sets, 218–219

Aggression, in man, 41, 283–286, 288
  in primates, 39–41

Agnatic descent (*see* Descent groups, patrilineal)

Agriculture, irrigation, 100–101, 105, 109

origins of, Middle East, 95–97

origins of, New World, 98–99

origins of, Southeast Asia, 99

plow, 105, 107, 109

Ainu (Japan), 313

American social organization, 211, 214, 215, 217, 220, 222, 224, 225

Americas, prehistory of, 97–99

Ancestors, 217, 309, 390

Andaman Islanders, 112, 133, 136, 267, 388, 390

Animal behavior, and culture, 37–38, 57–60, 75
  See also Primates

Animal husbandry (*see* Domestication of animals; Pastoralism)

Anthropological linguistics, 7, 75–85
  See also Ethnoscience

Anthropology, distinctiveness of, 4
  as a profession, 405–406
  as a science, 9–10

Applied anthropology, 365–371

Archaeology, 7, 87–89, 97, 376–377

Art, 60, 83, 92–95, 129

Ascribed status (*see* Status)

Ashanti (West Africa), 105–106, 359–360